Fourth
Canadian
Edition

Cultural
Anthropology

WILLIAM A. HAVILAND
University of Vermont

LIAM KILMURRAY
University of Ottawa

SHIRLEY A. FEDORAK
University of Saskatchewan

RICHARD B. LEE
University of Toronto

NELSON / EDUCATION

NELSON EDUCATION

Cultural Anthropology, Fourth Canadian Edition

by William A. Haviland, Liam Kilmurray, Shirley A. Fedorak, and Richard B. Lee

Vice President, Editorial Higher Education:
Anne Williams

Acquisitions Editor:
Maya Castle

Senior Marketing Manager:
Amanda Henry

Senior Developmental Editor:
Linda Sparks

Photo Researcher and Permissions Coordinator:
Daniela Glass

Senior Content Production Manager:
Natalia Denesiuk Harris

Production Service:
MPS Limited, a Macmillan Company

Copy Editor:
Matthew Kudelka

Proofreader:
Susan Fitzgerald

Indexer:
Sonya Dintaman

Senior Production Coordinator:
Ferial Suleman

Design Director:
Ken Phipps

Managing Designer:
Franca Amore

Interior Design:
Lisa Buckley

Interior Design Modifications:
Peter Papayanakis

Cover Design:
Peter Papayanakis

Cover Image:
Salish Path by Susan Point

Compositor:
MPS Limited, a Macmillan Company

Printer:
RRDonnelley

Printed and bound in the United States of America
2 3 4 17 16 15

For more information contact Nelson Education Ltd., 1120 Birchmount Road, Toronto, Ontario, M1K 5G4. Or you can visit our Internet site at http://www.nelson.com

Library and Archives Canada Cataloguing in Publication Data

Cultural anthropology/
William A. Haviland . . . [et al].
—4th Canadian ed.

Includes bibliographical references and index.

ISBN 978-0-17-664880-0

1. Ethnology—Textbooks.
I. Haviland, William A.

GN316.C84 2012 306
C2011-907888-0

ISBN-13: 978-0-17-664880-0
ISBN-10: 0-17-664880-1

Dedicated to
the World's Indigenous Peoples
in Their Quest for Human Rights

Putting the World in Perspective

Although all humans whom we know about are capable of producing accurate sketches of localities and regions with which they are familiar, **cartography** (the craft of mapmaking as we know it today) had its beginnings in 16th-century Europe, and its subsequent development is related to the expansion of Europeans to all parts of the globe. From the beginning there have been two problems with maps: the technical one of how to depict on a flat, two-dimensional surface a three-dimensional spherical object, and the cultural one of whose world view the map will reflect. In fact, the two issues are inseparable, for the particular projection one uses inevitably makes a statement about how one views one's own people and their place in the world. Indeed, maps often *shape* our perception of reality as much as they *reflect* it.

In cartography, a **projection** refers to the system of intersecting lines (of longitude and latitude) by which part or all of the globe is represented on a flat surface. There are more than one hundred different projections in use today, ranging from polar perspectives to interrupted "butterflies" to rectangles to heart shapes. Each projection causes distortion in size, shape, or distance in some way or another. A map that correctly shows the shape of a landmass will of necessity misrepresent the size. A map that is accurate along the equator will be deceptive at the poles.

Perhaps no projection has had more influence on the way we see the world than that of Gerhardus Mercator, who devised his map in 1569 as a navigational aid for mariners. So well suited was Mercator's map for this purpose that it continues to be used for navigational charts today. At the same time, the Mercator Projection became a standard for depicting landmasses, something for which it was never intended. Although an accurate navigational tool, the Mercator Projection greatly exaggerates the size of landmasses in higher latitudes, giving about two thirds of the map's surface to the northern hemisphere. Thus the lands occupied by Europeans and European descendants appear far larger than those of other people. For example, North America (19 million square kilometres) appears almost twice the size of Africa (30 million square kilometres), while Europe is shown as equal in size to South America, which actually has nearly twice the landmass of Europe.

A map developed in 1805 by Karl B. Mollweide was one of the earlier *equal-area projections* of the world. Equal-area projections portray landmasses in correct relative size, but, as a result, distort the shapes of the continents more than other projections. They most often compress

MERCATOR

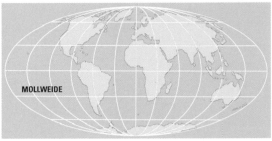

MOLLWEIDE

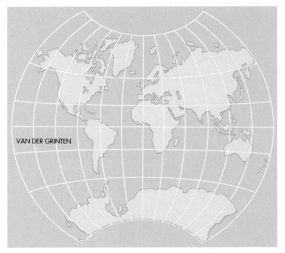

VAN DER GRINTEN

ROBINSON

and warp lands in the higher latitudes and vertically stretch landmasses close to the equator. Other equal-area projections include the Lambert Cylindrical Equal-Area Projection (1772), the Hammer Equal-Area Projection (1892), and the Eckert Equal-Area Projection (1906).

The Van der Grinten Projection (1904) was a compromise aimed at minimizing both the distortions of size in the Mercator and the distortions of shape in equal-area maps such as the Mollweide. Although an improvement, the lands of the northern hemisphere are still emphasized at the expense of the southern. For example, in the Van der Grinten, the Commonwealth of Independent States (the former Soviet Union) and Canada are shown at more than twice their relative size.

The Robinson Projection, which was adopted by the National Geographic Society in 1988 to replace the Van der Grinten, is, to date, one of the best compromises between the distortions of size and those of shape.

Although an improvement over the Van der Grinten, the Robinson Projection still depicts lands in the northern latitudes as proportionally larger at the same time that it depicts lands in the lower latitudes (representing most Third World nations) as proportionally smaller. Like European maps before it, the Robinson Projection places Europe at the centre of the map with the Atlantic Ocean and the Americas to the left, emphasizing the cultural connection between Europe and North America, while neglecting the geographic closeness of northwestern North America to northeastern Asia.

The following pages show four maps, each of which conveys a quite different cultural message. Included among them is the Peters Projection, an equal-area map that has been adopted as the official map of UNESCO (the United Nations Educational, Scientific, and Cultural Organization), and a map made in Japan, showing us how the world looks from the other side.

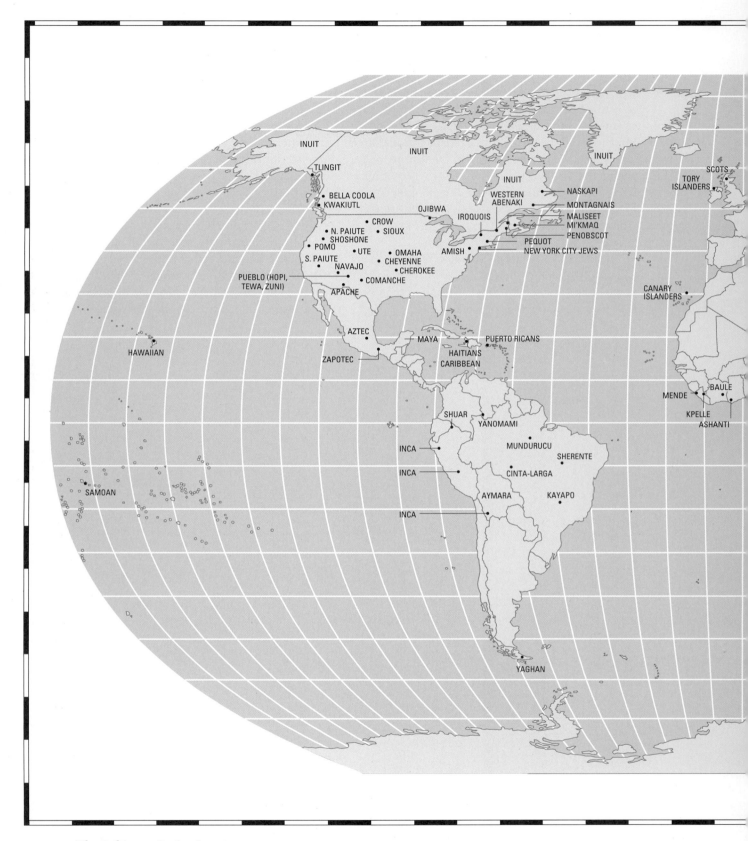

The Robinson Projection

The map above is based on the Robinson Projection, which is used today by the National Geographic Society and Rand McNally. Although the Robinson Projection distorts the relative size of landmasses, it does so much less than most other projections. Still, it places Europe at the centre of the map. This particular view of the world has been used to identify the location of many of the cultures discussed in this text.

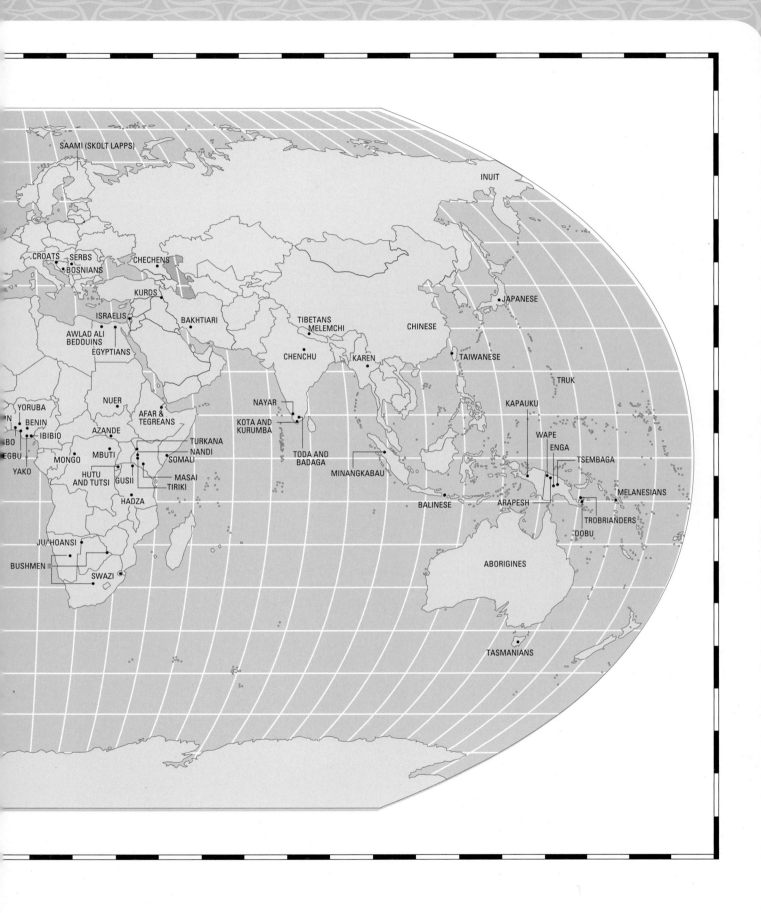

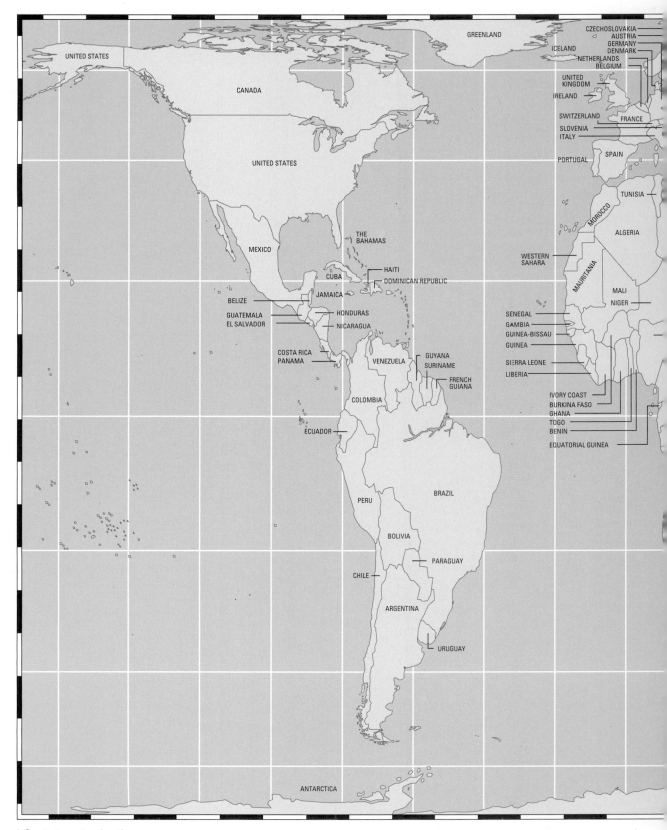

The Peters Projection

The map above is based on the Peters Projection, which has been adopted as the official map of UNESCO. While it distorts the shapes of continents (countries near the equator are vertically elongated by a ratio of 2 to 1), the Peters Projection does show all continents according to their correct relative size. Though Europe is still at the centre, it is not shown as larger and more extensive than the Third World.

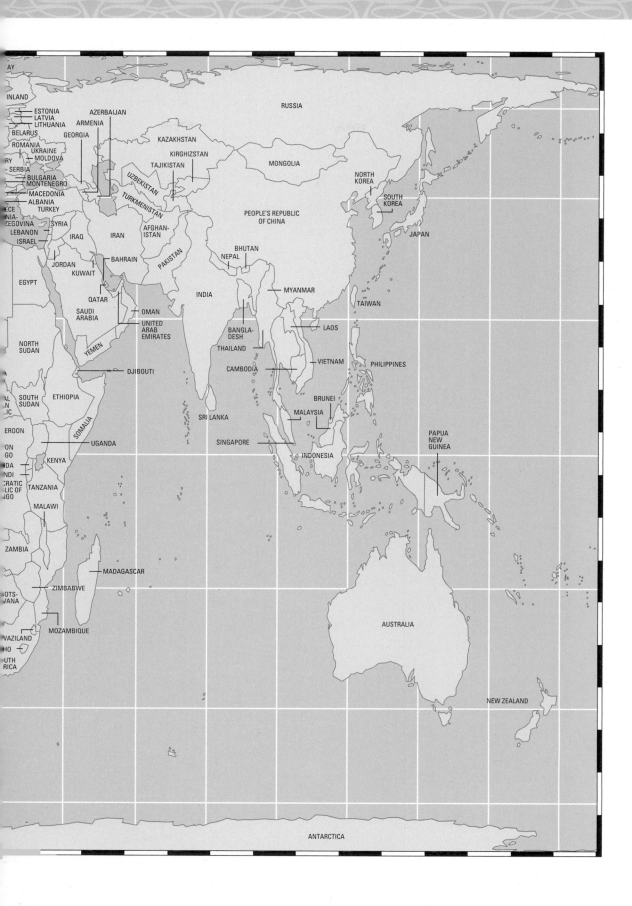

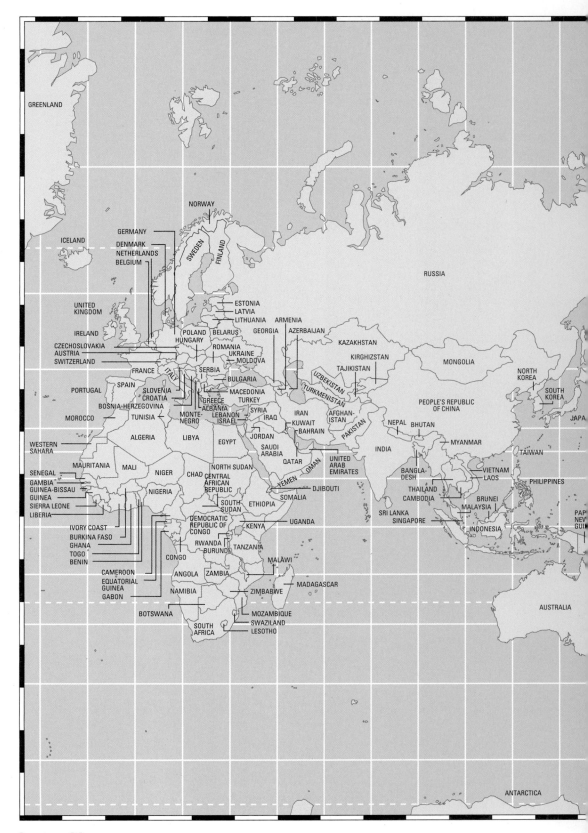

Japanese Map

Not all maps place Europe at the centre of the world, as this Japanese map illustrates. Besides reflecting the importance the Japanese attach to themselves in the world, this map has the virtue of showing the geographic proximity of North America to Asia—a fact easily overlooked when maps place Europe at their centre.

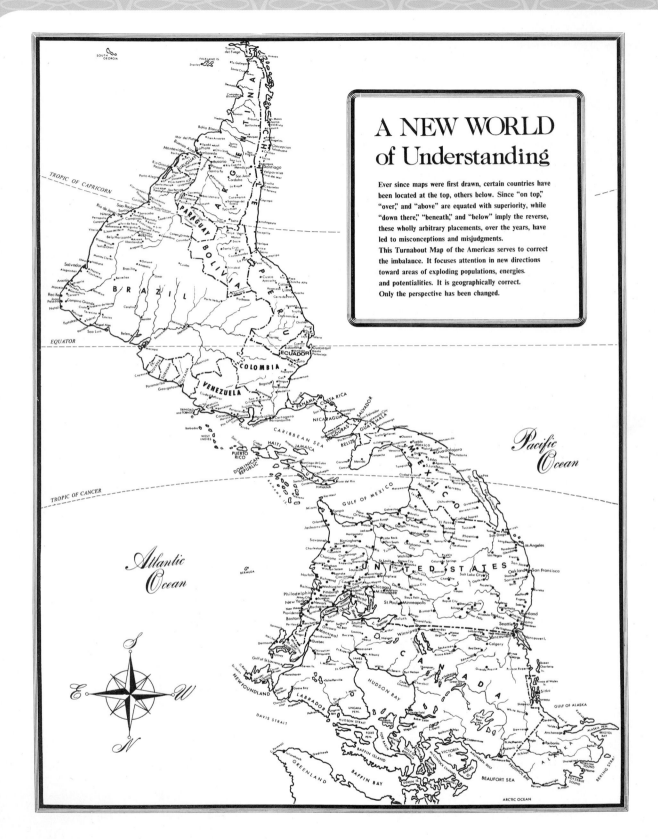

The Turnabout Map

The way maps may reflect (and influence) our thinking is exemplified by the Turnabout Map, which places the South Pole at the top and the North Pole at the bottom. Words and phrases such as "on top," "over," and "above" tend to be equated by some people with superiority. Turning things upside-down may cause us to rethink how North Americans regard themselves in relation to the people of Central America. © 1982 by Jesse Levine Turnabout Map™—Dist. by Laguna Sales, Inc., 7040 Via Valverde, San Jose, CA 95135.

Brief Contents

Contents

CHAPTER 13   The Arts   298

PART V   EXPLORING WORK, CULTURAL CHANGE, AND THE FUTURE OF HUMANITY   324

CHAPTER 14   Anthropology at Work   324

CHAPTER 15   Cultural Change and the Future of Humanity   350

Features Content

Preface

The fourth Canadian edition of Haviland, Kilmurray, Fedorak, and Lee's *Cultural Anthropology* reflects the context, both institutional and national, in which the practice and teaching of anthropology in Canada has developed and continues to develop. To introduce students to the unique history of anthropology in Canada, we have added classic and new Canadian case studies, content about anthropology's long association with museums in Canada, First Nations research, and ethnohistorical case studies. This text has been written specifically for Canadian students, yet we have not included Canadian material gratuitously. We have strived to highlight the contributions that Canadian anthropologists and Canadian institutions have made to the discipline of anthropology, and to do so in an engaging, accessible manner.

Cultural Anthropology has two goals for introductory anthropology courses: to provide an overview of the principles and processes of sociocultural anthropology, and to plant a seed of cultural awareness in Canadian students that will continue to grow and to challenge ethnocentrism long past the end of the semester.

The first and foremost aim of the text is to give students a comprehensive introduction to sociocultural anthropology. Because it draws from the research and ideas of a number of schools of anthropological thought, the text exposes students to a mix of such approaches as evolutionism, historical particularism, diffusionism, functionalism, French structuralism, structural functionalism, and others. The second aim of the text is to open students' eyes to the true complexity and breadth of human behaviour and the human condition. The questioning aspect of sociocultural anthropology is perhaps the most relevant gift we can pass on to our students. *Cultural Anthropology*'s invigorated writing, comprehensive coverage, robust art program, and relevant and engaging ethnographic examples stimulate comprehension of the material. The text continues to discuss early research, key findings, and influential anthropologists, while adding original research on culture change and updating coverage of current controversies. Gender, ethnicity, and stratification concepts and terminologies reflect contemporary thinking, and the narrative has been streamlined using more fully developed, balanced, and global examples. Students will also find interesting such relevant topics as body piercing, body art, and culture shock.

Many Messages, Many Media

The cover image chosen for this edition reflects several key themes in the study of cultural anthropology. The image, *Salish Path* (2010), is by Susan Point, a well-known First Nations Canadian artist from Vancouver, British Columbia. *Salish Path* is based on the artist's *Salish Footprint* granite mosaic, which is embedded in the concrete entrance of the Museum of Anthropology at the University of British Columbia. "The imagery is based on the whorls and lines of a thumb or toe print, transformed using distinctive Salish elements, and incorporating many of the life forms found in the land, sea, and skies surrounding the Museum of Anthropology. The artwork emphasizes the Salish connection to the site—a reminder that the surrounding land is Musqueam traditional territory and a welcome from the Musqueam people to this territory" (Susan Point, www.spiritwrestler.com, accessed November 9, 2011).

Anthropology is arguably among the most naturally "multimedia" of all studies, and we find sociocultural anthropologists working within numerous cultural expressions, ranging from music to oral narrative, ritual dancing, weaving, and spray-paint graffiti. Since anthropology has been an archive of human behaviour, it is important that the discipline show the richness and diversity of humanity through appropriate media. This fourth Canadian edition of *Cultural Anthropology* continues to recognize both students' level of comfort with nonprint media, and the many potential paths to exploring the techniques, processes, and findings of sociocultural anthropology. The art program is an important part of this text's narrative. PowerPoint slides bring the ideas and art of the textbook into the classroom. The CourseMate website to which students gain access with each copy of the text houses video clips, interviews, quizzes, and biographies of Canadian anthropologists. Thus, *Cultural Anthropology* allows instructors to draw upon a broad set of instructional tools to expand their classroom.

ORGANIZATION OF THE BOOK

Part I: "Anthropology and the Study of Culture" introduces students to the development of anthropology, the nature of culture in general, and the beginnings of human culture.

Part II: "Culture and Survival" discusses language and communication, patterns of subsistence and adaptation, and economic systems.

Part III: "The Formation of Groups" examines sex and marriage; family and household; kinship and descent; and grouping by sex, age, common interest, and class.

Part IV: "The Search for Order" explains political organization and the maintenance of order, religion and the supernatural, and the arts.

Part V: "Exploring Work, Cultural Change, and the Future of Humanity" discusses the anthropology of work as well as cultural change and the future of humanity.

WHAT'S NEW IN THE FOURTH CANADIAN EDITION

Dynamic Anthropology

The "Dynamic Anthropology" boxes are new. They address, for the most part, ongoing developments in a wide range of anthropological fields. They aim to supply the student with information regarding current developments in the field of anthropology, whether in Canada or abroad. The goal is not just to situate the reader within the major theme of the chapter itself, but to bring to life the actual current practices of anthropologists. For example, when cultural anthropology is addressed in Chapter 2, the Dynamic Anthropology box takes us to Carleton University, where a new institute for studying the cultures of Africa has been created. Likewise, in Chapter 7, which addresses the topic of marriage, our Dynamic Anthropology box details some of the events in Bountiful, B.C., that have the Supreme Court of British Columbia wrestling with the issue of polygamy. The purpose of these Dynamic Anthropology boxes, then, is to bring to life the standard material that anthropologists examine in order to show today's students the relevance of the area being studied.

The Anthropologist's World

In the other new feature in this text, "The Anthropologist's World," we take a similar approach, but in this case we address a broader range of issues. Some of these are relevant to the chapter in terms of topic; others have been chosen to demonstrate the breadth of anthropological analysis. For example, in the chapter on economics, the standard anthropological constructions and models of economies are extensively covered, but we also take a look at the economics of ancient monuments. In this way, the Anthropologist's World boxes tie in the main theme of the chapter at hand, but also extend the analysis to other realms, whether in the past or in far-off places. These boxes demonstrate the broad applicability of anthropological analysis; they take us on exemplary journeys into the vast array of issues that anthropologists normally address. Such is the case also in Chapter 13, where our new feature box examines the role of museums in anthropology. In this way we connect the chapter on arts to museums, and at the same time link indigenous artists with the collections housed in Canadian museums. As with the new Dynamic Anthropology boxes, the new Anthropologist's World boxes strengthen the material covered in the chapter while also bringing to students the excitement of anthropological analysis by demonstrating the many links that anthropological analysis and theory have with the greater social world around us.

Original Study

The "Original Study" boxes have a similar goal—to introduce to students the contributions of both historical and contemporary anthropologists. These feature boxes tie together the classic works of earlier genres of anthropology; in some cases, they present reappraisals of these former works by more recent researchers. Original Studies such "Aka Pygmies—Best Dads in the World" present up-to-date research on time allocation studies among the Aka people of central Africa, complementing the chapter on family and household. Elsewhere, Chapter 14 presents a firsthand account of forensic anthropologists working on the Pickton Farm murder case. These studies, which reflect important issues in anthropology, strengthen the individual chapters by drawing on current and past exciting research.

Gender Perspectives

The anthropology of gender is an important element of anthropological analysis, one that suffered from neglect for some time. In this new edition we address gender issues in a series of feature boxes titled "Gender Perspectives." Here, contributions from various anthropologists and other scholars address an assortment of issues as they pertain to gender. Beginning in Chapter 1, we examine the concept of gender and discuss the male biases of the past (and present) that have coloured interpretations of cultural phenomena. Topical and hotly debated issues such as female circumcision are analyzed, and the role of women in past and present economic systems is addressed. In addition to these feature boxes, discussions of gender-related issues are interwoven throughout the fourth Canadian edition.

Chapter 1: The Nature of Anthropology

Throughout this chapter, more contemporary references have been added. More Canadian, and specifically Aboriginal Canadian, content has been introduced. An in-depth explanation of the four-field approach has been added. There is an added focus on explaining sociocultural anthropology. Expanded coverage of ethnography is present, with a focus on the early contributions of ethnographers to anthropological theory and practice. The new Dynamic Anthropology box, on the Institute for African Studies, Carleton University, is written by Blair Rutherford, head of that institute. The Anthropologist's World box focuses on a selection of Canadian anthropologists, from Diamond Jenness and the "wreck of the *Karluk*" to the contributions of Regna Darnell. There is also a new Original Study box, "Health and Disease in One Culture: The Ju/'hoansi," by Richard Borshay Lee, Professor Emeritus, University of Toronto.

Chapter 2: The Nature of Culture

This chapter contains expanded coverage of multiculturalism and culture shock. There is increased focus on the symbolic nature of culture and increased coverage of human rights. A new Dynamic Anthropology box focuses on the Institute of Human Origins at Arizona State University and the search for human fossils. The Anthropologist's World box, "New Houses for Apache Indians," discusses architecture, government policy, and the Apache Indians.

Chapter 3: The Beginnings of Human Culture

In this edition, the focus on early primates has been streamlined, and newer dates, theories, and data for the first hominins have been added. There is increased coverage of early paleoanthropologists, such as Eugene Dubois. The coverage of recent DNA data about hominid evolution has been updated and simplified. The Anthropologist's World box profiles the Hadzabe of northern Tanzania, a tribe of hunter-gatherers. The Dynamic Anthropology box focuses on the Canadian Anthropology Society/La Société canadienne d'anthropologie, its conferences, and the range of research topics.

Chapter 4: Language and Communication

This chapter features increased coverage of linguistic constructs such as displacement, as well as expanded discussion of animal communication. There is also more focus on disappearing languages and threatened languages—in particular, Canadian Aboriginal languages. The discussion of the technical (phonological, grammatical, syntactic, etc.) aspects of language has been reduced and simplified. The Dynamic Anthropology feature box explores the World Oral Literature Project—a group of anthropologists and linguists at Cambridge University who are documenting and attempting to salvage the world's threatened languages. The Anthropologist's World box is about Asen Balikci, an innovator in the field of ethnographic film.

Chapter 5: Making a Living

Chapter 5 includes a new discussion of recent developments in ecological anthropology. More Canadian examples have been included: for example, the Ojibwa and Mi'kmaq are addressed in terms of their early adaptations to new social environments. The discussion of foragers has been expanded. There is more information on the emergence of agriculture in the Middle East. The statistics on Canadian farming have been updated. The Dynamic Anthropology box explores the ecological mastery of the Aztec people. The Anthropologist's World box discusses agricultural development.

Chapter 6: Economic Systems

Discussion of women's contributions in ancient and contemporary economic systems has been expanded in this chapter. Also, more is said about craft production among the Canadian Inuit. The discussion of resource depletion includes a new section on the Mi'kmaq. There is a new paragraph on generalized reciprocity. The discussion of trade includes a new section on the Huron. The Dynamic Anthropology box reports on anthropologists' understanding of ancient monuments. The Anthropologist's World box covers ecotourism and its impact on local indigenous culture in Bolivia. The Original Study is new and covers trade and barter in the Trobriand Islands.

Chapter 7: Sex and Marriage

The language in the Human Sexuality section has been updated to reflect present mores. Discussion of Two-Spirits, the Nuer, and ghost marriages has been expanded. There is a new table showing countries where polygyny is practised. The definitions of marriage have been updated. The chapter includes a brief explanation of exogamy. The statistics on Canadian marriage and divorce have been updated. The Dynamic Anthropology box covers polygamy in the community of Bountiful, B.C. The Anthropologist's World box, about combating AIDS in Africa, was written by Suzanne Leclerc-Madlala, an affiliated professor of anthropology at the University of KwaZulu-Natal in Durban, South Africa. The new Original Study discusses honour killings in the Netherlands and was written by filmmaker Clementine van Eck.

Chapter 8: Family and Household

The statistics on Canadian households have been updated. There are additional references to various cultural groups such as the Capela and Efe. The Dynamic Anthropology box explores the implications of global adoption. The Anthropologist's World box on First Nations public health was written by John O'Neil of the University of Manitoba. The new Original Study profiles the Aka Pygmies. Are they the best dads in the world?

Chapter 9: Kinship and Descent

The chapter has a new analytical focus on how anthropologists study descent. There is also a new stress on the role of kinship studies in early anthropology. The Huron Indians are included in the discussion of clans. In the Dynamic Anthropology box, Harald E.L. Prins explores his work as an advocacy anthropologist working with the Aroostook band of Micmac (also spelled Mi'kmaq) in Maine. In the Anthropologist's World box, kinship and descent meet in a riveting tale of forensic anthropological detective work: the case of the 9,300-year-old Cheddar Man fossil. A new Original Study box covers households through the ages.

Chapter 10: Social Stratification and Groupings

This chapter has a new focus, and asks: What is the validity of race as a social category? There is a new discussion of the Native Women's Association. The chapter's content has been updated to reflect current events. Canadian ethnicity statistics have been updated.

The Dynamic Anthropology box discusses gender, racialization, labour, and language in Toronto. The Anthropologist's World box examines Israel's growing Pensioners' Party. A new Original Study explores the concept of race.

Chapter 11: Political Organization and the Maintenance of Order

The Punishment section includes a new discussion of Native healing circles and community healing. The material on bands, chiefdoms, and tribes has been "peopled" with real groups: the Sioux, the builders of Stonehenge, and so on. References to UN-recognized countries and to political leaders have been updated, and Canadian female leaders have been included in the politics and women section. The Dynamic Anthropology box explores the rise of piracy based out of Puntland, an autonomous territory in Somalia. The Anthropologist's World box was written by Rodney Nelson, an Anishinaabeg anthropologist, who examines applied anthropology in the corporate world. The new Original Study discusses social movements from an anthropologist's perspective.

Chapter 12: Religion and the Supernatural

This chapter features updated statistics on Canadian religions and churchgoing. It now includes Clifford Geertz's discussion of religion. Claude Lévi-Strauss has been added to the Mythology section. There is a new discussion of Tenskwatawa, the Shawnee prophet, in the section on priests and priestesses. The section on rites of passage includes a discussion of vision quests. The section on missionism includes information on the tragedy of Canada's residential schools. The Dynamic Anthropology box was written by Edward C. Green, a medical anthropologist at the Harvard School of Public Health. In the Anthropologist's World box, famed Canadian anthropologist Robin Ridington discusses the spiritual practices of the Beaver nation.

Chapter 13: The Arts

This chapter draws on everything from the ancient roots of art to the music of U2. It has a new section on the fascination that art holds for anthropologists and the general public. A section on tattoos and body art includes discussions of Inuit "ink work" and Otzi the Iceman's tattoos. The Dynamic Anthropology box discusses the importance of photography in anthropologists' work.

The Anthropologist's World box considers the work that anthropologists do in museums. There is a new Original Study on Aboriginal art by Simon Brascoupé, an internationally known artist and educator. The new Gender Perspectives box draws on feminist and Marxist scholarship in examining how "manhood" is perceived in a variety of cultures.

Chapter 14: Anthropology at Work

This new chapter examines the multitude of career possibilities available to anthropologists. There are two Dynamic Anthropology boxes: one covers the baby formula controversy; the other, dams. The Anthropologist's World box was written by Neil Ferris and Rhonda Nelson of the University of Western Ontario. It discusses their work cataloguing and classifying some of southwestern Ontario's archaeological heritage. There are two new Original Studies. In the first, Tracy Rogers, the Director of the Forensic Science Program at the University of Toronto in Mississauga, discusses the contributions made by anthropologists in solving the Pickton farm murder case. In the second, Rodney Nelson discusses how the corporate world and applied anthropology intersect with indigenous cultures and traditional knowledge. The new Gender Perspective box examines the role of women in contemporary violence and warfare.

Chapter 15: Cultural Change and the Future of Humanity

This chapter covers recent current events, including the Arab Spring, Darfur, and recent monetary crises in the United States and Europe. Statistics on globalization and culture loss have been updated. The discussion of multiculturalism has been revised, with accounts of recent challenges to it in France and Britain. The discussion of pollution has been updated with new content on the Fukushima nuclear plant in Japan. The Anthropologist's World box was written by Edward J. Hedican, a social anthropologist whose long-term ethnographic interests have focused on Canadian Aboriginal peoples, especially the Ojibwa or Anishenabe peoples living north of Lake Superior.

SPECIAL FEATURES OF THE BOOK

Chapter Openers

Well-designed chapter openers provide previews that summarize the major concepts to be learned in each chapter.

Key Questions

These chapter opening questions mark out the key issues covered in the chapter. The Key Questions also encourage critical reading and provide study points useful when studying for exams.

Maps, Photographs, and Illustrations

Colourful and eye-catching visuals are used to make important anthropological points and to clarify anthropological concepts. These also have proved to be valuable teaching aids.

Even in politically stable countries like Canada, pluralism presents its own challenges. In Canada, the Quebec separatist movement continues to challenge Canadian unity.

The Anthropologist's World

A new feature to this edition, the Anthropologist's World boxes address a broad range of issues. Some are relevant to the chapter topics; others have been chosen to demonstrate the breadth of anthropological analysis.

Dynamic Anthropology

A second new feature to this edition, these boxes address ongoing developments in a wide range of anthropological fields. The Dynamic Anthropology boxes aim to provide students with information about current developments in anthropology, in Canada and abroad.

Original Studies

The Original Studies are excerpts from case studies and other original works by women and men in the field. They illustrate important anthropological concepts and show students how anthropologists study human behaviour, past and present.

Original Study

Health and Disease in One Culture: The Ju/'hoansi

Richard Borshay Lee, University of Toronto

Throughout this text, reference is made to the Ju/'hoansi, one of the best-known examples of a hunting-and-gathering society in anthropology. Medical anthropologists have traced the health of the Ju/'hoansi during the period of great transition from the colonial to the post-colonial period. Health surveys taken in the 1960s when the Ju/'hoansi were still largely living as hunters and gatherers showed them to be relatively healthy. They led active outdoor lives, the men hunting wild game and the women gathering over 100 species of wild plants. It has been estimated that women walked a total of 2,000 kilometres annually, or over 5 kilometres per day, usually carrying loads of 5 to 15 kilograms. Men out hunting could walk and run up to 50 kilometres in a single day.

Analysis of the Ju/'hoansi's varied diet shows it to be well balanced in 1950, close to 40 percent of babies did not survive to maturity. Nevertheless, low net fertility may have been crucial to survival, since a rapidly growing population could not have been sustained. Most remarkable was the absence of symptoms associated with heart disease. Blood pressure did not rise with age, and serum cholesterol levels were among the lowest ever recorded for a human population.

Apart from their healthy diet and lifestyle, what means did the Ju/'hoansi possess for diagnosing and treating illness and trauma? Like all people, the Ju/'hoansi had developed a set of beliefs and practices to face this universal human need. According to the Ju/'hoansi, supernatural forces, primarily the ghosts of ancestors who had passed on to the spirit world, caused sickness and misfortune. For complex motives, these ghosts remained close to the living, hovering around the villages and bringing with them sickness and misfortune.

In response, certain gifted Ju/'hoansi took up the calling of in one place. By the late 1980s this had become largely accomplished, with Ju in semipermanent villages, subsisting on food from an eclectic mix of sources: government food handouts, small-scale farming and herding, receipts from wage labour and handicraft production, and even some foraging. The road into the Dobe area was rebuilt, making the area more accessible to outsiders. Frequent bans on hunting and the ready availability of food handouts led to a sharp decrease in the amount of exercise for adults and loss of a sense of purpose. In the new cash economy, alcohol consumption increased from almost zero in the 1960s to a significant portion of cash expenditures; chronic alcohol abuse had become a health and social problem for the Ju/'hoansi.

A re-examination of the people's overall health status only 20 years after the initial studies revealed dramatic changes. Blood pressure now increased markedly with age, and for the first time there was evidence of hypertension and heart disease. Dental health had deteriorated, with more cavities

Gender Perspectives

Supporting the text's coverage of gender, these features delve into specific gender-related issues.

Gender Perspectives

Women and Economic Development

Laurel Bossen, McGill University

Homa Hoodfar, Vilia Jefremovas, Eva Rathgeber, Ellen Judd, and Laurel Bossen are Canadian anthropologists, educated at or teaching at Canadian universities.

Ester Boserup's pathbreaking work, *Women's Role in Economic Development*, with its demonstration of women's diverse economic roles and its stinging critique of European colonialism and development for undermining women's economic position, was published in 1970. Since then, research on women and economic development in other cultures has grown and anthropologists have contributed greatly to the study of women's work and the gendered impacts of economic, commercial, and technological development (Rathgeber 1994). They have become increasingly

In Egypt, Homa Hoodfar (1997) studied the economic and social roles of poor Muslim women in Cairo, where women's labour force participation is low. Hoodfar found that Islamic marriages aided parents in negotiating financial guarantees for their daughters' marriages. A married woman was not expected to support the household monetarily, but had "an unquestioned right" to economic support from her husband in exchange for housework and childrearing. When wives earned a cash income, men were not authorized to take control of it. Thus, women's conservatism, low labour force participation, and adherence to Islamic traditions had a material basis (102). Yet when some women earned cash incomes, men reduced their household contributions, retaining more for personal consumption. As the goods and services traditionally provided by women became commercialized, "women jealously guarded or tried to salvage what the market had not yet claimed" (272). They ability to claim land rights became problematic as land "moved into firmer male control . . . as coffee merchants and government officials, themselves all males, made their alliances primarily with highland men" (77). Also, the spread of Christian Base Community organizations aiming to "liberate the poor" and render them a political force attracted both women and men, but established a male monopoly of leadership positions (183). Neither the state nor the church fostered organizations that strengthened women's rights.

In Guatemala, my own comparative study of women and the changing division of labour in four contrasting communities (Bossen 1984) showed that increased commercial development did not have a uniform impact, but disproportionately expanded the range of employment options for men. Women were most disadvantaged in the better-paying formal sectors of both the rural and the urban economy. Here, the lono

Glossary

A running glossary is provided in each chapter and compiled at the end of the book to help students master the language of the field.

Glossary

acculturation: Major cultural changes people are forced to make owing to intensive firsthand contact between societies. (p. 355)
Acheulian tradition: A tool tradition associated with *Homo erectus* in Africa and Europe characterized by teardrop-shaped axes and flake tools. Named after the site where it was first defined, St. Acheul, France, it lasted from 1.5 million to about 150 000 years ago. (p. 59)
achieved status: Status an individual earns. (p. 233)
adjudication: Mediation with an unbiased third party making the ultimate decision. (p. 261)
affinal kin: Relatives by marriage. (p. 155)
age grade: An organized category of people based on age; every individual passes through a series of such catego- describe and explain human behaviour. (p. 10)
ascribed status: Status people are born into. (p. 233)
Australopithecus: The earliest well-known hominin, who lived between 1 million and 4.2 million years ago and includes several species. (p. 54)
avunculocal residence: A pattern in which a married couple lives with the husband's mother's brother. (p. 186)
balanced reciprocity: A mode of exchange whereby the giving and the receiving are specific in terms of the value of the goods and the time of their delivery. (p. 132)
band: A small group of related households occupying a particular region who gather periodically but do not yield their sovereignty to the larger collective. (p. 244)
(colonies), administration (military presence), and control of resources, thereby creating a dependency. (p. 5)
common-interest associations: Associations not based on age, kinship, marriage, or territory but that result from the act of joining. (p. 224)
conflict theory of stratification: A theory suggesting that a power struggle takes place between the upper and lower levels of society. (p. 226)
conjugal bond: The bond between a man and a woman who are married. (p. 155)
conjugal family: A family consisting of one (or more) man married to one (or more) woman and their offspring. The female may in fact be male, and the male may in fact be female. (p. 174)
consanguineal kin: Relatives by birth—that is, "blood" relatives. (p. 155)
consanguine family: A family

Chapter Summary

These review sections summarize the chapter's content and are designed to help students master the material.

Chapter Summary

1. What is economic anthropology?
Economic anthropology is a subfield of cultural anthropology. There are a wide variety of economic anthropologists, ranging from those who study prehistoric economies to those who specialize in analyzing contemporary cultures. The economic anthropologist differs from the economist in the way he or she applies anthropological data and theory to understand the broad functioning of economic systems. Beyond money or the market, economic anthropology is interested in the cultural practices that help shape, and are shaped by, the functioning of the total economic system. Therefore, an economic anthropological analysis of hunter-gatherers may focus on the taboos they place on the eating of certain resources, or it may look at the connections between the economy and other cultural realms such as marriage and kinship.

2. How do anthropologists study economic systems?
Anthropologists place the economy in the context of the total culture to understand economic patterns. By understanding the basic trade and exchange systems, anthropologists can understand the economy; however, they go further by addressing the role that other social institutions, such as kinship, marriage, and spirituality, play in the economic realm. Anthropologists attempt to understand the historical factors and the traditional practices that govern the way production and consumption are carried out. One can count all the salmon that the Kwakwaka'wakw catch, but unless practices such as the potlatch are examined, one will not fully understand the economy.

3. How do economies work?
All societies have economies, and they differ only in terms of scale and the values that are attached to each of the component parts of the economic system. Economic anthropologists engage with the cultural subsystems of trade and exchange, consumption and extraction. By doing so, they are able to determine all the elements of how an economy functions.

4. How and why are goods exchanged?
Goods are exchanged so that each society can obtain what it needs or wants but does not have, and trade that which

line. Matrilineal descent is traced through the female line; patrilineal, through the male. The descent system is closely tied to a society's economic base. Patrilineal descent is commonly found where men are the main breadwinners, matrilineal descent where females form the core of social life, but not necessarily are they the main breadwinners. The male members of a patrilineage trace their descent from a common male ancestor. In the matrilineal pattern, descent is traced through the female line. Unlike the patrilineal pattern, which confers authority on men, matrilineal descent does not necessarily confer authority on women, although women usually have more of a say in decision making than they do in patrilineal cultures. The matrilineal system is common in cultures where women perform much of the productive work.

2. What functions do descent groups serve?
Descent groups are often highly structured economic units that provide aid and security to their members. They also may be repositories of religious tradition, with group solidarity enhanced by worship of a common ancestor. In whatever descent system is in operation, marriages between members of different groups represent alliances between the two groups. Descent systems outlive their members, providing ontological security for the clan or lineage.

3. How do descent groups form?
Descent groups develop from extended family groups, usually in response to organizational needs. They emerge usually in food-producing groups, beginning as smaller lineages and often developing into larger groups such as clans. In any culture, rules dictate how kinship relationships are defined. Factors such as sex and generational or genealogical differences help distinguish one kin from another. The Hawaiian system is the simplest system of kinship terminology. All

Questions for Critical Thought

1. How do you identify your relatives? Are you closer to some cousins than to others? Do you have fictive kin who are like family? Do you feel closer to your mother's or your father's side of the family, or both equally? How important to you are your extended kin? How many generations of your kin can you trace?
2. When in your life has the ability to trace your descent been the most important or obvious? When are you made aware of your kin group? In your family are names at birth assigned in reference to ancestors or other kin?
3. How are changes in North American families altering how North Americans view descent? How do these changes contrast with those occurring in other cultures?
4. Do you think that urbanization has affected your kinship networks? If so, in what ways?
5. Identify your kinkeeper. What roles does he or she perform? What would happen to the cohesion of your extended family if you lost this kinkeeper?
6. As an exercise, draw your own kinship chart, using yourself as "ego" at the centre of the chart. How many relatives can you identify?

Internet Resources

The Nature of Kinship

http://www.as.ua.edu/ant/Faculty/murphy/436/kinship.htm

Questions for Critical Thought

The Questions for Critical Thought are designed to encourage students to think critically and apply important concepts to contemporary issues.

its practice (ritual) or on the beliefs that comprise the religion. Religion is found in all cultures. It consists of beliefs and behaviour patterns by which people try to control areas of their world otherwise beyond their control. Religion is organised, social, and transformative. It may be defined as a nonempirical belief and faith in one or multiple gods. Adherents subscribe to articles of faith, such as commandments.

2. What are religion's identifying features?
Religion involves various rituals—prayers, songs, dances, myths, offerings, and sacrifices—that people use in the hope of gaining assistance from supernatural beings and powers. These beings and powers may consist of gods and goddesses, ancestral and other spirits, and impersonal powers. Religion can involve special liturgy and special language, such as Urdu or Latin. Most religions have specialists—priests and priestesses and/or shamans—to guide religious practices and to intervene with the supernatural world.

3. Why is religion a cultural universal?
Religion (including magic and witchcraft) is universal, as is the human need to understand life and death. Religion thus serves a number of important psychological and social purposes. First, it sanctions a wide range of conduct by providing notions of right and wrong. Second, it sets precedents for acceptable behaviour and helps perpetuate an existing social order. Third, religion serves to lift the burden of decision

Internet Resources

Religions of the World

http://www.bbc.co.uk/religion/religions

This site contains descriptions of many religions, past and present, such as Christianity, Mormonism, Taoism, and Islam, as well as world views such as agnosticism and atheism.

The Ute Sun Dance

http://www.crystalinks.com/sundance.html

A description of the Sun Dance in Colorado.

Religion

http://anthro.palomar.edu/religion/default.htm

An introduction to the anthropology of religion, including discussions of common elements, trancing, and magic.

Salem Witch Trials

http://law2.umkc.edu/faculty/projects/ftrials/salem/SALEM.HTM

A riveting account of the trial of Sarah Good for witchcraft. Also provides a link to the Witch Trials Memorial, which

Internet Resources

This section provides Web-based resources for further exploration of the concepts in each chapter.

SUPPLEMENTS TO THE BOOK

Cultural Anthropology comes with a comprehensive supplements program to help instructors create an effective learning environment both inside and outside the classroom, and to aid students in mastering the material.

For the Student  CourseMate

Cultural Anthropology includes CourseMate, which helps you make the grade. CourseMate includes

- an interactive eBook with highlighting, note-taking, and search capabilities
- Test Yourself quizzes
- biographies of anthropologists of note
- note-taking outlines for each chapter
- interactive learning tools, including
  - quizzes
  - flashcards
  - crossword puzzles and concentration games
  - and more!

Using the access card at the front of your book, go to NelsonBrain.com to access CourseMate.

For the Instructor

Enriched NETA Instructor's Manual and NETA Assessment

The Nelson Education Teaching Advantage (NETA) program delivers research-based instructor resources that promote student engagement and higher order thinking.

Instructors today face many challenges. Resources are limited, time is scarce, and a new kind of student has emerged: one who is juggling school with work, has gaps in his or her basic knowledge, and is immersed in technology in a way that has led to a completely new style of learning. In response, Nelson Education has gathered a group of dedicated instructors to advise us on the creation of richer and more flexible ancillaries that respond to the needs of today's teaching environments.

The members of our editorial advisory board have experience across a variety of disciplines and are recognized for their commitment to teaching. They include:

Norman Althouse, Haskayne School of Business, University of Calgary

Brenda Chant-Smith, Department of Psychology, Trent University

Scott Follows, Manning School of Business Administration, Acadia University

Jon Houseman, Department of Biology, University of Ottawa

Glen Loppnow, Department of Chemistry, University of Alberta

Tanya Noel, Department of Biology, York University

Gary Poole, Director, Centre for Teaching and Academic Growth and School of Population and Public Health, University of British Columbia

Dan Pratt, Department of Educational Studies, University of British Columbia

Mercedes Rowinsky-Geurts, Department of Languages and Literatures, Wilfrid Laurier University

David DiBattista, Department of Psychology, Brock University

Roger Fisher, PhD

In consultation with the editorial advisory board, Nelson Education has completely rethought the structure, approaches, and formats of our key textbook ancillaries. We've also increased our investment in editorial support for our ancillary authors. The result is the Nelson Education Teaching Advantage (NETA) and its key components: NETA Engagement, NETA Assessment, and NETA Presentation. Each component includes one or more ancillaries prepared according to our best practices, as well as a document explaining the theory behind the practices.

NETA Engagement presents materials that help instructors deliver engaging content and activities to their classes. Instead of Instructor's Manuals that regurgitate chapter outlines and key terms from the text, NETA Enriched Instructor's Manuals (EIMs) provide genuine assistance to teachers. The EIMs answer questions such as What should students learn?, Why should students care?, and What are some common student misconceptions and stumbling blocks? EIMs not only identify the topics that cause students the most difficulty but also describe techniques and resources to help students master these concepts. Dr. Roger Fisher's *Instructor's Guide to Classroom Engagement (IGCE)* accompanies every EIM. (Information about the NETA EIM prepared for *Cultural Anthropology* is included in the description of the IRCD below.)

NETA Assessment relates to testing materials: not just Nelson's Test Banks and Computerized Test Banks, but also in-text self-tests, Study Guides and Web quizzes, and homework programs like CNOW. Under NETA Assessment, Nelson's authors create multiple-choice questions that reflect research-based best practices for constructing effective questions and that test not just recall but also higher order thinking. Our guidelines were developed by David DiBattista, a 3M National Teaching Fellow whose recent research as a professor of psychology at Brock University has focused on multiple-choice testing. All Test Bank authors receive training at workshops conducted by Prof. DiBattista, as do the copy editors assigned to each Test Bank. A copy of *Multiple Choice Tests: Getting Beyond Remembering,* Prof. DiBattista's guide to writing effective tests, is included with every Nelson Test Bank/ Computerized Test Bank package. (Information about the NETA Test Bank prepared for *Cultural Anthropology,* Fourth Canadian Edition, is included in the description of the IRCD below.)

NETA Presentation has been developed to help instructors make the best use of PowerPoint® in their classrooms. With a clean and uncluttered design developed by Maureen Stone of StoneSoup Consulting, NETA Presentation features slides with improved readability, more multimedia and graphic materials, activities to use in class, and tips for instructors on the Notes page. A copy of *NETA Guidelines for Classroom Presentations* by Maureen Stone is included with each set of PowerPoint slides. (Information about the NETA PowerPoint® prepared for *Cultural Anthropology,* Fourth Canadian Edition, is included in the description of the IRCD below.)

IRCD

Key instructor ancillaries are provided on the Instructor's Resource CD (978-0-17-661597-0), giving instructors the ultimate tool for customizing lectures and presentations. (Downloadable Web versions are also available at www .havilandcultural4e.nelson.com). The IRCD includes

- NETA Engagement: The Enriched Instructor's Manual was written by Terry Webb of the University of Western Ontario. It is organized according to the textbook chapters and addresses eight key educational concerns—for example, the stumbling blocks that student typically face and how to address them. Other features include chapter learning outcomes, lists of key terms in the chapter, and suggested activities for the classroom.
- NETA Assessment: The Test Bank was written by Victor Gulewitsch of the University of Waterloo. It includes more than 1,000 multiple-choice questions

written according to the NETA guidelines for constructing and developing higher order questions. Also included are more than 600 true/false, 200 short-answer, and 200 essay questions. Test Bank files are provided in Word format for easy editing and in PDF format for convenient printing, whatever your system.

The Computerized Test Bank by ExamView® includes all the questions from the Test Bank. The easy-to-use ExamView software is compatible with Microsoft Windows and Mac. Create tests by selecting questions from the question bank, modifying these questions as desired, and adding new questions you write yourself. You can administer quizzes online and export tests to WebCT, Blackboard, and other formats.

- NETA Presentation: Microsoft® PowerPoint® lecture slides for every chapter have been created by Kymberley Schnarr of Georgian College. There are 25 to 30 slides per chapter, many featuring key figures and tables from *Cultural Anthropology,* Fourth Canadian Edition. NETA principles of clear design and engaging content have been incorporated throughout.
- DayOne: Day One—Prof InClass is a PowerPoint presentation that you can customize to orient your students to the class and their text at the beginning of the course.

CourseMate

Nelson Education's CourseMate brings course concepts to life with interactive learning and exam preparation tools that integrate with the printed textbook. Students activate their knowledge through quizzes, games, and flashcards, among many other tools.

CourseMate provides immediate feedback that enables students to connect results to the work they have just produced, increasing their learning effectiveness. It encourages contact between students and faculty: you can choose to monitor your students' level of engagement with CourseMate, correlating their efforts to their outcomes. You can even use CourseMate's quizzes to practise "Just in Time" teaching by tracking results in the Engagement Tracker and customizing your lesson plans to address their learning needs.

Watch student comprehension and engagement soar as your class engages with CourseMate. Ask your Nelson representative for a demo today.

Acknowledgments

In this day and age, no textbook comes to fruition without extensive collaboration. We are deeply thankful for the feedback of reviewers, past and present, whose insights have greatly informed the fourth Canadian edition. Without exception, their suggestions were thoughtful and relevant, and the fourth edition is much better as a result. Although we were not able to address all of their comments, we did our best. Thanks to all reviewers, past and present.

Naomi Adelson, York University

Franca Boag, University of Alberta

Janice Boddy, University of Toronto

Laird Christie, Wilfrid Laurier University

Constance Deroche, University College of Cape Breton

Howard Doughty, Seneca College

Bouglass Drozdow-St. Christian, University of Western Ontario

Christine Elsey, University of the Fraser Valley

Nadia Ferrara, McGill University

Diane French, University of the Fraser Valley

Mathais Guenther, Wilfrid Laurier University

Victor Gulewitsch, University of Waterloo

Chris Holdsworth, University of Calgary

Karen Hutton, University of New Brunswick

Michael Kenny, Simon Fraser University

Doreen Klassen, Sir Wilfred Grenfell College

Harriet Lyons, University of Waterloo

Bruce Miller, University of British Columbia

Laurie Milne, Medicine Hat College

Lisa Mitchell, University of Victoria

Ara Murray, Camosun College

Tim Panas, University of Saskatchewan

Deidre Rose, University of Guelph

David Ryniker, University of British Columbia

David Scheffel, Thompson Rivers University

Josephine Smart, University of Calgary

Angele Smith, University of Northern British Columbia

Patricia Kelly Spurles, Mount Allison University

John Steckley, Humber College

Terry Webb, University of Western Ontario

Marty Zelenietz, Saint Mary's University

FROM THE AUTHOR OF THE FOURTH CANADIAN EDITION

This book is dedicated to my wife, Heather, and to my two sons, Liam óg and Finnegan, without whom I would have been unable to complete this work. Their company has enabled me to remain enthralled to anthropology and to life. I wish to thank, sincerely, Linda Sparks and Maya Castle at Nelson Education for their wonderful support and advice on this project, as well as my copy editor, Matthew Kudelka, and Natalia Denesiuk Harris.

I would also like to thank the following people and institutions for their contributions and for their encouragement and help along the way:

Blair Rutherford, Department of Sociology and Anthropology, Carleton University

Canadian Anthropology Society/La société canadienne d'anthropologie

Institute of Human Origins

World Oral Literature Project, Museum of Archaeology and Anthropology, University of Cambridge

Bonnie McElhinny, Kori Allan, and Lalaie Ameeriar, Department of Anthropology, University of Toronto

Rodney Nelson, Department of Sociology and Anthropology, Carleton University

Robin Ridington

Museum of Anthropology, Vancouver

Simon Brascoupé

Tracy Rogers, Department of Anthropology, University of Toronto

Maurice Lévesque, Department of Sociology and Anthropology, University of Ottawa

Neil Ferris and Rhonda Nelson, Department of Anthropology, University of Western Ontario

Ivy Crescent Book Club

All my former colleagues and students at Cambridge University, Sheffield University, the University of Western Ontario, Carleton University, and the University of Ottawa

Finally, thanks are offered to all the anthropologists who have studied the world's cultures and shared their fascination of humanity with us.

Liam Kilmurray

About the Authors

WILLIAM A. HAVILAND is Professor Emeritus at the University of Vermont, where he founded the Department of Anthropology and taught for thirty-two years. He holds a PhD in anthropology from the University of Pennsylvania.

He has carried out original research in archaeology in Guatemala and Vermont; ethnography in Maine and Vermont; and physical anthropology in Guatemala. This work has been the basis of numerous publications in various national and international books and journals, as well as in media intended for the general public.

Besides his teaching and writing, Dr. Haviland has lectured to numerous professional as well as non-professional audiences in Canada, Mexico, Lesotho, South Africa, and Spain, as well as in the United States. A staunch supporter of indigenous rights, he served as expert witness for the Missisquoi Abenakis of Vermont in an important court case over Aboriginal fishing rights.

Awards received by Dr. Haviland include being named University Scholar by the Graduate School of the University of Vermont in 1990; a Certificate of Appreciation from the Sovereign Republic of the Abenaki Nation of Missisquoi, St. Francis/Sokoki Band, in 1996; and a Lifetime Achievement Award from the Center for Research on Vermont in 2006. Now retired from teaching, he continues his research, writing, and lecturing from the coast of Maine. His most recent book is *At the Place of the Lobsters and Crabs* (2009).

LIAM KILMURRAY completed his graduate work at Cambridge and Sheffield, with a focus on archaeological theory and prehistory. A native of Dublin, Ireland, he became fascinated by ancient history, specifically the Neolithic period of Ireland, and the Atlantic Façade.

Working and travelling abroad, Dr. Kilmurray developed an abiding interest in anthropology. He worked as an archaeologist for over seven years, conducting excavations in Canada and overseas. He has been teaching cultural anthropology at the University of Ottawa for seven years and also teaches anthropology courses at Carleton University. Teaching a wide variety of courses from cultural anthropology to Marxist theory, and being interested in topics such as Neolithic monuments, architecture, and social memory, he continues to be fascinated by the diversity of knowledge that anthropological studies entails. This text, he feels, offers the introductory and advanced reader a detailed coverage of the many exciting fields of anthropology and the wide array of topics that anthropologists study.

Dr. Kilmurray enjoys teaching and hopes that his students gain some flavour of the intricate and rewarding world of anthropology from both his courses and this textbook. In his spare time, he enjoys reading, watching and playing Gaelic football, and, with his wife Heather, driving their two sons to hockey rinks, soccer, or Gaelic football fields.

SHIRLEY FEDORAK was a sessional lecturer in sociocultural anthropology and archaeology at the University of Saskatchewan from 1991 to 2006. During the 1990s, she worked on curriculum projects, including "People in their World: A Study of First Nations Peoples on the Plains," sponsored by the Saskatoon Public School Board. She has also written multimedia courses in anthropology for the University of Saskatchewan. Besides serving as lead author on the first, second, and third editions of Haviland's *Cultural Anthropology,* she co-authored the supplement *Canadian Perspectives on Archaeology and Biological Anthropology* (2002) and the first Canadian edition of *Human Evolution and Prehistory* (2005). Her most recent publications are *Windows on the World: Case Studies in Anthropology* (2006), *Anthropology Matters!* (2007), and *Pop Culture: The Culture of Everyday Life* (2009).

One of her greatest loves is teaching. Her most recent foray into that world was teaching social sciences to senior students at Cairo American College in Egypt. She has learned a great deal from her students over the years, and readily shares her views on the importance and value of an anthropological education in today's rapidly changing world: "Of all the disciplines, cultural anthropology is the one where students actually learn about what it means to be citizens of the world."

RICHARD BORSHAY LEE is Professor Emeritus of Anthropology. He received his BA and MA from the University of Toronto and his PhD from the University of California, Berkeley. He has held academic appointments at Harvard and Rutgers, and more recently visiting positions at Columbia, Australian National, and Kyoto Universities. His research interests include human rights and indigenous peoples, ecology and history, AIDS, the politics of culture, and the anthropology of state societies. Recently, along with his wife, Professor Harriet Rosenberg of York University, he has focused on the critical issues for human health posed by the pharmaceutical industry.

Professor Lee is internationally known for his studies of hunting and gathering societies, particularly the Ju/'hoansi-!Kung San of Botswana and Namibia. His research findings and theories have influenced philosophers, political scientists, psychologists, and biologists. His book *The !Kung San: Men, Women, and Work in a For-* *aging Society*, was listed in *American Scientist* as one of the 100 most important works in science of the 20th century.

Richard Lee has been elected to the U.S. National Academy of Sciences, one of only 20 Canadian scientists in that body and the only anthropologist. He is also a fellow of the Royal Society of Canada and past president of the Canadian Anthropology Society. He holds honorary doctorates from the University of Alaska, Fairbanks, and Guelph University for his research and advocacy on behalf of indigenous peoples.

1 The Nature of Anthropology

Samuel de Champlain (1567–1635) helped establish the French presence in North America. He also did much to develop the fur trade on that continent. His encounters with the Algonquin, Iroquois, and Huron fascinated Europeans. That fascination continues to this day in sociocultural anthropology.

KEY QUESTIONS

1. What Is Anthropology?

Anthropology is the study of humankind in all times and places. Anthropologists seek to produce reliable knowledge about people and their behaviour, about what makes them different and what they all share in common.

2. What Do Anthropologists Do?

Biological anthropologists trace the evolutionary development of humans as biological organisms and investigate biological variations within the species. They also study the physical and behavioural nature of our closest biological relatives: nonhuman primates such as monkeys and apes. *Archaeologists* seek to explain human behaviour by studying material culture. *Linguistic anthropologists* study the way language is used as a resource for practising, developing, and transmitting culture. *Sociocultural anthropologists* are concerned with contemporary human cultures as they have been observed, experienced, and discussed with the people whose cultures they seek to understand.

3. How Do Anthropologists Do What They Do?

Anthropologists, in common with other scientists, are concerned with explaining observed phenomena. Most anthropological investigation involves fieldwork. *Biological anthropologists* and *archaeologists* conduct excavations of sites where evidence of human activity has been found. *Linguistic anthropologists* study how people use language to relate to one another, often living for brief periods with the people whose language they are studying. *Sociocultural anthropologists* immerse themselves in a contemporary culture by living with the people, participating in their daily activities, and observing how they live.

One of the pleasures of travel is the opportunity to live amongst peoples who have not forgotten the old ways, who still feel the past in the wind, touch it in stones polished by rain, taste it in the bitter leaves of plants. Just to know that, in the Amazon, the Jaguar shaman still journey beyond the Milky Way, that the myths of the Inuit elders still resonate with meaning, that the Buddhists in Tibet still pursue the breath of the Dharma is to remember the central revelation of anthropology: the idea that the social world in which we live does not exist in some absolute sense, but rather is simply one model of reality.[1]

For as long as they have lived on earth, people have asked questions about who they are, where they come from, and why they act as they do. For their answers, they have traditionally relied on myth and folklore. Anthropology, over the past two centuries, has emerged as a scientific approach to answering these questions. Simply stated, **anthropology** is the study of humankind in all places and in all times.

Other disciplines, too, are concerned with human beings. Some, such as anatomy and physiology, study humans as biological organisms. The social sciences are concerned with the distinctive forms that human relationships can take, while the humanities examine the great achievements of human cultures. Anthropologists are interested in all of these aspects of humanity; the difference is that they are concerned with everything that has to do with humans. It is this unique, broad perspective that enables anthropologists to deal with that elusive thing called human nature.

Anthropologists have sought to expose the fallacies of racial and cultural superiority, and their devotion to the study of all peoples, regardless of where and when they live, has cast more light on human nature than all the reflections of sages or the studies of laboratory scientists. Anthropology has taken on an added importance in recent years as people everywhere have joined the "global village" and there are more opportunities for cultural understandings and misunderstandings. Globalization is forcing us to deal with issues and face challenges that are no longer "far away." Never have we so desperately needed to understand

anthropology The study of humankind in all times and places.

one another, to accept and appreciate cultural diversity, more than today. Indeed, anthropological knowledge and understanding of the past and the present may even help humankind deal with its future. In the words of Laura Nader (2006, 10): "Anthropology has much to say about human destiny."

THE DEVELOPMENT OF ANTHROPOLOGY

Although works of anthropological significance have a considerable antiquity—two examples are the accounts of other people by Herodotus the Greek and by the Arab Ibn Khaldun, written in the 5th century BC and the 14th century, respectively—anthropology as a distinct field of inquiry is a relatively recent product of Western society.

If people have always been interested in themselves and others, and in their origins, why then did it take such a long time for the discipline of anthropology to appear? In part, the answer to this relates to the limits of human technology. Until recently, people have been restricted in their geographical horizons. Without the means to travel to distant places, observation of distant cultures was a difficult venture if not an impossible one. Extensive travel was usually the exclusive domain of a tiny elite. The study of foreign peoples and cultures was not likely to flourish until adequate modes of transportation and communication could be developed and until a literate audience emerged.

This is not to say that people were unaware of the existence of others in the world who looked and acted differently from themselves. The Old and New Testaments, along with tales, maps, and stories, are full of references to diverse groups of people, among them Jews, Egyptians, Hittites, Babylonians, Ethiopians, and Romans. However, the differences among these peoples pale by comparison with Aboriginal peoples of Australia, the Amazon rainforest, or the Canadian Arctic. With the means to travel to truly faraway places, explorers met and observed, for the first time, radically different people. It was these encounters with hitherto unknown peoples, which developed as Europeans sought to extend their trade and political domination to all parts of the world, that focused attention on human diversity.

Another significant contributor to the slow growth of anthropology was the failure of Europeans to recognize that beneath all the differences, they shared a basic "humanity" with people everywhere. Cultural groups that did not share the fundamental cultural values of Europeans were labelled "savage" or "barbarian." At the root of this cultural arrogance were colonialism, cultural imperialism, and a dominant evolutionary theory within anthropology that viewed Western cultures as the pinnacle of achievement. European **colonialism** reached its zenith in the 17th and 18th centuries, when the Spanish, Portuguese, English, French, and Dutch set up colonies in other lands, including Africa and the Americas, thereby dislocating the indigenous populations living in these places. Other regions, such as India, suffered under the administration of European governments. Although political control and economic gain were the major impetus for colonialism, the European sense of superiority and **cultural imperialism** justified these actions. Cultural imperialism, although often used synonymously with colonialism, really refers to the promotion of one nation's values, beliefs, and behaviour above those of all others. This attitude has resulted in the West inundating other cultural groups with its technology, religion, political organization, economy, and lifestyle.

Not until the late 18th century, as an outgrowth of the Age of Enlightenment, did a significant number of Europeans consider the behaviour of other people relevant to an understanding of themselves. This growing interest in human diversity, coming when efforts to explain reality in terms of natural laws were increasing, cast doubts on the traditional biblical mythology, which no longer adequately "explained" human diversity. The discipline of anthropology, then, arose from early attempts to offer scientific explanations for human diversity.

The Development of Anthropological Thought

A detailed discussion of the theoretical development of anthropology is outside the scope of an introductory text, but some mention of the milestones in the field is necessary. Early anthropological theory introduced the concept of "cultural progress"—that all cultures passed through evolutionary stages until they reached the technologically advanced level of Western societies. This was also the time when the concept of race was put forward, eliciting a contentious debate among scholars that continues to this day. These 19th-century cultural evolutionary theories, proposed by American anthropologists Edward Tylor and Louis Henry Morgan, were challenged by empiricists, who urged anthropologists to base their theories on actual firsthand observation in the field rather than on ethnocentric biases and "armchair anthropology." The most famous of all empiricists was Franz Boas (1858–1942), who argued that every culture is unique, with a unique history, and is neither superior nor inferior to another. Boas rejected racism and promoted cultural relativism (see Chapter 2), that is, the belief that all cultures are equally valid and must be studied on their own terms. Followers of Boas also developed the "Four Field Approach" to anthropology, which is still evident in most anthropology departments.

In the early 20th century, some empiricists turned their attention to the diffusion of customs, material culture, and ideas from one culture to another. They looked at the impact this diffusion may have on similarities between cultural groups. British anthropologists A.R. Radcliffe-Brown and Bronislaw Malinowski turned their attention to the functions of economic, social, religious, and political institutions, all of which are found in every culture. Malinowski argued that anthropologists should consider how the various systems of a culture work to meet the needs of its members; Radcliffe-Brown focused on how culture as a whole functions to maintain itself. Malinowski was one of the first anthropologists to pay close attention to his key informants' point of view—a groundbreaking methodology still employed today.

In the 1950s and 1960s, some anthropologists turned to the study of culture change. Anthropologists such as Leslie White proposed that culture changed in direct response to technological "progress," such as the Industrial Revolution or the introduction of air conditioning and refrigeration. Julian Steward built on the idea of technology as a cultural mover, suggesting that societies evolve to fit a particular ecological niche and that the environment influences the way of life. From a similar standpoint, other anthropologists examined how the environment is exploited using technology to meet basic human needs; they posited that culture change comes about through numerous forces, including population density, trade networks, diffusion, and warfare. However, many anthropologists rejected this materialist approach, with its heavy emphasis on material culture. Claude Lévi-Strauss held that free will and the ability to make choices based on ideas and desires influenced culture. He identified a universal pattern of human thinking in all peoples, while Clifford Geertz took a more particularist approach, studying the uniqueness of each culture and the actions that have meaning for them.

colonialism When one nation dominates another through occupation (colonies), administration (military presence), and control of resources, thereby creating a dependency.

cultural imperialism Promoting one nation's values, beliefs, and behaviour as superior to those of all others. Often associated with the Western world inundating other cultural groups with technology, religion, and ways of living (most often via the media), but also through missionism (see Chapter 12), education, and economic control, thereby strongly influencing how people will live.

The development of anthropological thought has been a long process, with each body of theories building on the strengths and addressing the weaknesses of previous perspectives, and although some of these theories have fallen out of favour, their very presence fuelled debate and theoretical discourse, thereby encouraging further development of anthropological thought. In recent decades, the field of anthropology has continued to expand its body of theory and methodology. For a discussion on other avenues of research, see the section titled "New Directions in Ethnographic Fieldwork" on page 16.

Canadian Anthropology

Canadian anthropology owes its development and continued growth to a number of noteworthy individuals, many of whom are profiled in this book (see the "Anthropologist's World" box for further discussion). Three major influences are evident in the development of Canadian anthropology: museums, academic departments, and applied research. The National Museum of Canada in Ottawa played a major role in the direction of early Canadian anthropology. Anthropologists with the museum, such as Edward Sapir, head of the Anthropology Division of the Geological Survey of the National Museum of Canada (now the Museum of Civilization), Marius Barbeau, David Boyle, and Diamond Jenness, conducted ethnographic, linguistic, and archaeological research into Aboriginal cultures. Besides their academic pursuits, these scholars and others were early advocates for Aboriginal rights to religious and cultural freedom. This tradition of advocacy has remained an integral component of Canadian anthropology to the present day.[2]

In 1925, Thomas F. McIlwraith was appointed lecturer in anthropology at the University of Toronto.[3] Under his guidance, anthropology at the University of Toronto continued to grow in importance until, in 1936, the first Department of Anthropology at a Canadian university was created. After the Second World War, anthropology departments were established at other universities, most notably McGill and UBC. Academic departments became the second stronghold for Canadian anthropology and remain so to this day.

A major source of strength and growth in Canadian anthropology has been applied anthropology. By the 1960s, Canadian anthropologists, such as Harry Hawthorn at UBC, were actively involved in Aboriginal policy issues. Among many applied studies, Hawthorn examined the sociocultural reasons for tensions between local residents and the Doukhobors who had moved to British Columbia from Saskatchewan. As you will see in the following chapters, Canadian applied anthropologists have advocated strongly for First Nations self-government, land claims, health, and community well-being, as well as Quebec nationalism. An example of the latter: French Canadian anthropologists such as Marc-Adélard Tremblay helped shape government policies that have strengthened Quebec's identity and desire for self-determination.

In the latter part of the 20th century, expansion of academic departments continued across the country. Although anthropological and archaeological interest in the Aboriginal peoples of Canada (First Nations, Inuit, and Métis) has remained paramount, Canadian anthropologists have also turned their attention to other issues, such as multiculturalism, ethnicity, immigration, health, and gender.[4] (Indian people in Canada, whether Status or non-Status, refer to themselves as First Nations.) Although anthropology originated in the context of Western society, it has long since gone global. Today it is an exciting international discipline whose practitioners are drawn from all parts of the world. Even cultures that have long been studied by European and North American anthropologists are producing anthropologists who are making their mark on the discipline. For example, Marianne Boelscher Ignace is an Associate Professor of Anthropology at Simon Fraser University's Kamloops Campus and has published a book about Haida social and symbolic discourse. Many Canadian anthropologists, such as Richard B. Lee, David Scheffel, and Bernand Arcand, have conducted international research. By the closing years of the 20th century, Canadian anthropology had matured into a multifaceted, comprehensive, and intrepid discipline, alive with potential and poised to provide valuable insight into Canada's future role in the global community.

A Note About Terminology

Many of the names assigned to Aboriginal peoples, usually by European explorers and colonial governments, were not the terms used by the people to refer to themselves. Often these names had derogatory connotations, such as "Eskimo," which in the Cree language means either "eaters of raw meat" or "he laces snowshoes." Today, concerted efforts are being made to use the names chosen by the people themselves. In Canada we use the terms First Nations, Inuit, and Métis to identify Aboriginal peoples collectively, and their own chosen names to identify distinctive cultural groups (e.g., Kwakwaka'wakw instead of Kwakiutl and Dane-zaa instead of Beaver).

In a text such as this one, where we refer to indigenous peoples around the world, the issue becomes even more complex. In the United States, "Native American" or "Indian" are the preferred terms, although some use the word "Amerindian." In South and Central America,

The Anthropologist's World

Canadian Anthropologists

Throughout this book we will encounter a wide variety of anthropologists, theories, constructs, people, places, and cultures. We will see the tremendous contribution that the science of anthropology has made toward a fuller understanding of humanity in all its manifestations, both past and present. From deciphering Upper Paleolithic cave art to reassembling the bones of *Homo erectus* or studying the kinship structures of contemporary pastoralists, anthropologists have attempted to explain what it means to be human and to understand the roles that culture plays in society.

Canadian anthropologists have made many valuable contributions in these and other areas. Indeed, they have been at the forefront of exciting developments in many different anthropological fields. As with other nations, much of Canadian anthropology is focused on internal phenomena, such as the history of the fur trade, the ethnic breakdown of Canada's provinces, multiculturalism, and the languages of indigenous peoples. However, Canadian anthropologists have also made valuable contributions to the international domain. What follows is a brief analysis, far from exhaustive, of some of the contributions that Canadian anthropologists have made in anthropology. Note that there are many "unsung" Canadian anthropologists, whose work is of great value whether it has garnered international attention or not. We begin by examining the career of the fabled ethnographer Diamond Jenness.

Diamond Jenness (1886–1969)

The famed Canadian anthropologist Diamond Jenness looms large in the early history of Canadian anthropology. Chief of Anthropology at the National Museum of Canada and publisher of important works such as *The People of the Twilight* (1928) and *Indians of Canada* (1932), Jenness made many insightful contributions to our understanding of the Inuit and Indian cultures of Canada. Born in New Zealand and educated at Oxford, Jenness had a knack for languages that he put to good use later in life by learning Inuktitut so as to better communicate with the peoples he studied. His ethnographic career began quite dramatically when, in 1913, he narrowly escaped with his life as the ship he was travelling on was crushed in the Arctic ice. Eleven of his companions eventually perished from cold and hunger, making this one of Canada's worst disasters in the field of scientific inquiry. The ship, the *Karluk*, was undertaking a survey as part of the Canadian Arctic Expedition to the Far North, the purpose of which was to bring geologists, anthropologists, and other scientists to Herschel Island, north of Yukon, where they would construct a base from which to survey the area's people, fauna, flora, mineral deposits, and other significant characteristics. The expedition was also tasked with searching for any new landmasses to the north of Alaska; it was also hoped that the expedition would help assert Canada's sovereignty over the Arctic islands.

After the *Karluk* became trapped in the ice and all hands were evacuated to solid ground, the party split into smaller groups. Jenness went with the expedition's leader (the much criticized Vilhjalmar Stefanson) and two others, and he remained in an Inuit settlement, working and awaiting eventual rescue. Of those who remained behind, four crew members left what became known as Shipwreck Camp and were never heard from again. Four more disappeared looking for a route out of the trapped camp; their bones were finally discovered in 1929. The rest of the *Karluk*'s crew and passengers remained on tiny Wrangel Island awaiting rescue. Three more men died on the island, and the remaining expedition members survived by eating roots and hunting for animals such as walrus, duck, and seal. Eventually, on September 7, 1914, the survivors were rescued from the island—almost eight months after the *Karluk* sank. In total, 11 members of the expedition perished, with 21 surviving, among them Diamond Jenness. After his close encounter with an Arctic death, Jenness undertook studies of the Copper Inuit around Coronation Gulf and of other Arctic Native people. He forever retained a strong admiration and respect for the survival skills of Canada's northern peoples. In 1926 he was made Chief of Anthropology at the National Museum of Canada. From that base, he went on to study many Aboriginal communities in Canada, producing ethnographic analyses that are widely read to this day. The high drama of Diamond Jenness's early career was followed a decade or so later by another remarkable series of events, this time involving an anthropologist from Toronto named Davidson Black.

Davidson Black 1884–1934

Born in Toronto in 1884, Davidson Black grew up fascinated by Native languages, learning Ojibwa as a young man. His other interests included medicine and evolution. He earned a medical degree in 1906 from the University of Toronto, later returning there to study comparative anatomy. After he completed his military service in the Canadian Medical Corps in 1916, the Peking Union Medical College in China offered him the position of Professor of Neurology. He promptly moved to China, where he would later become Director of the Anthropology Department at the University of Peking. From his base in Peking, Black conducted an extensive excavation at Zhoukoudian (Chou-k'ou-tien) Cave, where fossils had recently been unearthed. Among the treasures excavated at Zhoukoudian was a mass of fractured bones—rare remnants of Chinese *Homo erectus*. Black oversaw the laborious work of extracting the precious fossils from the rock matrix in which they were embedded. His work paid off, and several teeth and a skull bone were eventually excavated. This skull was used to designate a new member of the *Homo erectus* family— Peking Man. That discovery would have an important impact on our understanding of the evolution of that species.

CONTINUED

CONTINUED

Most important perhaps was Black's help in casting the irreplaceable fossils. His successor at Zhoukoudian, Franz Weidenreich, used Black's thoroughly cleaned fossils and sketches to make replicas using the "plaster of Paris" technique. These exact copies could be handled, studied, and transported so that the original fossils would not be harmed in any way. This proved to be rather prescient, for the Japanese invasion of mainland China in 1937 forced the evacuation of many laboratories and other institutions. During the evacuation of the original fossils by U.S. Marines, the ship carrying them was sunk, apparently by a Japanese submarine, and the original fossils were lost, never to be seen again. We have the hard work of Davidson Black, who applied novel medical procedures to archaeological preservation, to thank for the survival of the precious casts. The original fossils have been lost, but thanks to the precision of Black's excavations and preservation methods, Peking Man can still be studied. Only late in life did Davidson Black gain recognition for his work. But in 1934, just as it seemed that he would become even more renowned and undertake further important excavations, he passed away while working at his desk. He was only 49.

Marius Barbeau (1883–1969)

Around the time of Black's death, an anthropologist from Quebec named Marius Barbeau was at the height of a long and distinguished anthropological career. Marius Barbeau is considered a pioneer in Canadian anthropology. His contributions to early Canadian ethnography are many, but he is best known as the founder of Canadian folklore studies. Born in Ste-Marie-de-Beauce, he earned a law degree from Laval University and then became the first French Canadian Rhodes scholar at Oxford University, where he earned a degree in anthropology. Returning to Canada in 1911, he accepted a position at the National Museum of Canada (then known as the Geological Survey of Canada). He worked for the museum until his retirement in 1948. Barbeau has been praised by contemporary First Nations for his efforts to record the voices of the people and for his attempts to understand their world

view. He once said, "I'm interested in what they think, in their own happiness, in their dirge songs, in their morality, in their art, in their curing."

In honour of his contributions to Canadian studies, Barbeau received the prestigious Prix David, as well as honorary doctorates from the University of Montreal and Oxford University, and was named a Companion of the Order of Canada. Barbeau's research was quite varied, ranging from West Coast totem poles to Huron—Wyandot culture. During his illustrious career he also collected and recorded more than 400 French Canadian folktales, 7,000 songs, and 2,000 artifacts. He wrote more than 1,000 books and articles and even published a novel, *The Dream of Kamalmouk,* based on his work *The Downfall of Temlaham.* Barbeau's publications highlight the diversity that Canadian anthropologists have at their doorstep. Certain themes are dominant, such as indigenous cultures and languages, both of which are still reflected in the work of more contemporary Canadian anthropologists. Barbeau's work influenced a generation of young Canadian graduate students. His research provided the basis for modern Canadian folklore. His impact on the study of linguistics was also great.

Regna Darnell

Regna Darnell is a renowned Canadian anthropologist and linguist. Her fieldwork among the First Nations peoples of Canada has shed light on the interdependence and dynamics of language and culture. Darnell is a faculty member at the University of Western Ontario, where she also serves as director of the Centre for Research and Teaching of Canadian Native Languages. Her distinguished 30-year career has focused on various aspects of linguistics and culture from a historical, symbolic, and ethnographic perspective. She is fluent in several First Nations languages, including Slavey, Cree, and Mohawk, and versed in their cultures. Among her published works are biographies of Franz Boas and Edward Sapir. She has also written widely on the history of anthropology and has published extensively on First Nations languages and cultures.

The above four figures represent a brief selection from a long list of esteemed Canadian anthropologists, including those who were immigrants to Canada. One might include the groundbreaking ethnographic research into Kalahari hunters by Richard Lee from the University of Toronto, and the research of Robert Ridington into the spiritual practices of the Dane-Zaa. Another is Bruce Trigger, the late anthropologist who, from his base at McGill University in Montreal, became the world's leading expert on the Huron Indians and the fur trade. Then there is the astonishing work of Edward Sapir, who held numerous distinguished positions in Canadian anthropological institutions, and who contributed much to the field of structural linguistics. Canadian anthropologists have had a profound impact in many fields of anthropology. Their work, a sample of which we have discussed here, is part of a unique Canadian anthropology that is distinguished from other national anthropological approaches. This somewhat distinct anthropology stems in part from the presence of vibrant Aboriginal cultures in Canada, as well as from Canada's bilingual and multicultural society. This has resulted in a distinct form of anthropology that places great value on cultural diversity, Aboriginal studies, and linguistics. In the following chapters we will draw upon the research and insights of many Canadian anthropologists so that you will come to understand the important role that Canadians have played, and continue to play, in the field of anthropology.

SOURCES: Julia Harrison and Regna Darnell, Historicizing Canadian Anthropology *(Vancouver: UBC Press, 2007); Peter Harries-Jones, "Canadian Anthropology in an International Context,"* Canadian Review of Sociology and Anthropology *34, no. 3 (1997): 249–58; Jennifer Niven,* The Ice Master: The Doomed 1913 Voyage of the Karluk *(New York: Hyperion, 2000); Canadian Museum of Civilization, 2011, http://www.heritage.nf.ca/exploraion/karluk.html; "Barbeau's Story," http://www.civilization.ca/cmc/exhibitions/tresors/barbeau/mbh1000e.shtml, accessed April 5, 2011; Andrew Nurse, "But How Things Have Changed: Marius Barbeau and the Politics of Amerindian Identity,"* Ethnohistory *48, no. 3 (2001): 433–72; "Meet Regna Darnell," University of Western Ontario, Department of Anthropology 2001, http://publish.uwo.ca/~rdarnell, accessed March 13, 2011.*

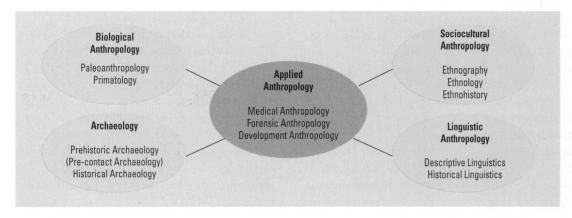

Figure 1.1
The Subfields of Anthropology.

Indian is used. From a Canadian perspective, none of these labels seem appropriate; therefore, the term Aboriginal peoples will be used to refer to all North and South American indigenous groups, unless the legal term Status Indian arises. For other regions of the world, every effort will be made to use the people's preferred name. For example, the Ju/'hoansi of the Kalahari Desert in Africa, a cultural group discussed extensively in this text, used to be called the pejorative "bushmen," later they were called the !Kung, and today we use their own name, Ju/'hoansi (meaning "genuine people"). Yet whichever terms are used, our decisions will not satisfy everyone; indeed, the whole issue of terminology is complicated and highly sensitive, especially since even within Aboriginal groups a consensus regarding appropriate names has not been achieved, and many non-Aboriginal people continue to debate which names should be used. We hope this attempt to use sensitive, culturally appropriate terms is a step in the right direction.

THE DISCIPLINE OF ANTHROPOLOGY

Anthropology is traditionally divided into four fields: biological anthropology, archaeology, linguistic anthropology, and sociocultural anthropology, which together make up the "anthropological perspective." **Biological anthropology** is concerned primarily with humans as biological organisms, while sociocultural anthropology deals with humans as cultural animals. Many Canadian anthropologists received their training at British schools; others were educated at American ones. In the British tradition, the term social anthropology is preferred to cultural anthropology. To accommodate both traditions, we use the term sociocultural anthropology. Archaeology, too, is interested in cultural behaviour, in that it reconstructs the lives of people who lived in the past.

Linguistic anthropology is the study of human languages of the past and present, as a means for people to relate to one another and to develop and communicate ideas about one another and the world. Anthropology's four fields are closely related: we cannot understand what people *do* unless we know what people *are*. And we want to know how biology does and does not influence culture, as well as how culture affects biology. Applied anthropology has become increasingly important and today is often considered a fifth field, one that intersects with the other four (see Figure 1.1 and Chapter 14). Applied anthropologists use their expertise to solve the practical problems of humanity, using the methods and knowledge of anthropology.

Biological Anthropology

Biological anthropology, also known as physical anthropology, is the branch of anthropology that focuses on humans as biological organisms. The subfield of **paleoanthropology** is the study of fossil remains of our ancient ancestors, in order to reconstruct the course of human biological evolution. Whatever distinctions people may claim for themselves, they are mammals—specifically, primates—and as such, they share a common ancestry with other primates, most specifically apes and monkeys. **Primatology** is the study of the biological and social nature of our closest relatives: prosimians, monkeys, and apes. Well-known primatologists Dian Fossey (gorillas),

biological anthropology The study of humans as biological organisms.

paleoanthropology The study of fossil remains with the goal of reconstructing human biological evolution.

primatology The study of nonhuman primates, their biology, adaptation, and social behaviour.

Jane Goodall (chimpanzees), and Canadian primatologists Biruté Galdikas (orangutans) and Linda Fedigan (Japanese macaques and capuchins) have provided us with startling new insights into the complex social behaviour of nonhuman primates. Through the analysis of fossils and observation of living primates, biological anthropologists try to trace the ancestry of the human species in order to understand how, when, and why we became who we are today. **Forensic anthropology** is a relatively new and exciting field within biological anthropology and archaeology with an applied concentration.

Biological anthropologists also study present-day human variation. Although we are all members of a single species, we differ from one another in such visible traits as the colour of our skin and the shape of our noses, and in biochemical factors such as our blood types and our susceptibility to certain diseases. Biological anthropologists apply the techniques of modern molecular biology to learn about human variation and the ways it relates to the different environments people have lived in. Biological anthropologists are also interested in the human condition. For example, a study of the mythologies surrounding menopause in North America and Japan questioned whether menopause is a disease,[5] and medical anthropologists are investigating the buying and selling of body organs, as well as who owns the body.[6]

Archaeology

Archaeology is the study of material remains in order to describe and explain the behaviour of people who have lived before us. The word "archaeology" is derived from two ancient Greek words: *archaios,* meaning "ancient," and *logos,* meaning "word" or "speech." In ancient Greece, archaeology meant a "discussion" or "study" of ancient things. Archaeologists excavate sites where evidence of cultural activity is found. The tools, pottery, and other enduring artifacts that remain are a legacy of the past that reflects certain aspects of human behaviour.[7] For

> **forensic anthropology** A field of applied biological anthropology and archaeology that specializes in the identification of human skeletal remains for legal purposes.
>
> **archaeology** The study of material remains to reconstruct the lives of people who lived in the past.
>
> **prehistoric/pre-contact archaeology** The study of ancient cultures that did not possess writing systems to record their history.
>
> **historic archaeology** The study of past cultures that possessed written records of their history.

example, shallow, restricted concentrations of charcoal that include oxidized earth, bone fragments, and charred plant remains, located near pottery and tools suitable for food preparation are indicative of cooking and associated food processing. From such remains, much can be learned about a people's diet and subsistence activities. In this way, **prehistoric archaeologists** can learn about human behaviour in the distant past, far beyond the mere 5,000 years that historians are limited to by their dependence on written records. In Canada, most anthropologists use the term **"pre-contact"** rather than prehistoric when referring to the ancestors of contemporary First Nations, Inuit, and Métis cultures, to avoid the suggestion that people living in North America before Europeans arrived did not have a history. This, of course, is not true: Aboriginal peoples possess diverse and vibrant cultural histories spanning thousands of years.

Archaeologists are not limited to the study of prehistoric societies; **historic archaeologists** study those cultures with historic documents available in order to supplement the material remains people left behind. In most literate societies, written records are associated with governing elites rather than with people at the "grassroots." Thus, although documents can tell archaeologists a great deal that they would not learn from archaeological evidence alone, it is equally true that archaeological remains can tell historians much about people that is not apparent from written records.

Although archaeologists have concentrated on the human past, some also study material objects in contemporary settings. One example is William Rathje, director of the University of Arizona's Garbage Project (1987–1995), which, by a carefully controlled study of household waste, produced information about contemporary social issues. One aim of this project was to test the validity of interview/survey techniques, on which sociologists, economists, other social scientists, and policy makers rely for their data. The tests clearly show a significant difference between what people say they do and what garbage analysis shows they actually do. In 1973, a questionnaire was administered to determine the rate of alcohol consumption in Tucson, Arizona. In one part of town, 15 percent of respondent households affirmed consumption of beer, but no household reported consumption of more than eight cans a week. Analysis of garbage, however, demonstrated that beer was consumed in more than 80 percent of households and that 50 percent discarded more than eight empty cans a week. Another interesting finding of the Garbage Project was that when beef prices reached an all-time high in 1973, so did the amount of beef wasted by households (not just in Tucson, but in other parts of the United States as well). Although common sense would lead us

Wanuskewin Heritage Park, outside Saskatoon, Saskatchewan, contains virtually every type of archaeological site common to the Northern Plains, spanning some 6,000 years. These sites help archaeologists reconstruct the history of pre-contact Plains peoples in this region.

to suppose just the opposite, high prices and scarcity correlate with more waste rather than less. Such findings suggest that ideas about human behaviour based on conventional interview/survey techniques alone can be seriously in error.

The previous discussion should not lead students to believe that archaeologists are concerned only with material culture; indeed, artifacts are merely a means to interpret and reconstruct human history. Robert McGhee, curator of Arctic archaeology at the Canadian Museum of Civilization, dismisses the value of artifacts as objects; rather, he uses these artifacts to learn about the people who used and then discarded them. Using archaeological evidence, McGhee has highlighted the important role the Arctic has played in human history and how the Inuit have interacted with other cultures, such as Norsemen, Basques, and Asians.

William Rathje, director of the University of Arizona's Garbage Project, holds a newspaper retrieved from deep in a landfill, a vivid demonstration that so-called biodegradables in compacted landfills do not biodegrade as expected.

Linguistic Anthropology

Perhaps the most distinctive feature of humanity is language. Language is what allows us to preserve and transmit our culture from generation to generation. Yet humans are not alone in the ability to symbolically communicate. Studies have shown that the sounds and gestures other animals make—especially apes—may serve functions comparable to those of human language. No other animal, though, has developed a system of symbolic communication as complex as that of humans.

The study of language for language's sake is known as philology; the branch of anthropology that studies human languages is different and is called **linguistic anthropology**. Linguistic anthropologists study the way language is used as a resource for practising, developing, and transmitting culture. They examine how people use language and other means of expression to develop relationships with one another and to maintain social distinctiveness.

Descriptive linguists deal with the description of a language (the way a sentence is formed or a verb is conjugated), and **historical linguists** study the history of languages (the way languages develop and influence

linguistic anthropology The study of how people use language to relate to one another and how they develop and transmit culture.

descriptive linguistics The study of patterns and structure in language.

historical linguistics The study of language origins, language change, and the relationships between languages.

one another with the passage of time). Both approaches yield valuable information, not only about the ways people communicate both verbally and nonverbally, but also about the ways they understand the world around them. The everyday language of North Americans, for example, includes a number of slang words, such as "dough," "loonies," "loot," and "cash," to identify what a person of Papua New Guinea would recognize only as money. Such phenomena help identify items considered important to a culture. Through the study of language in its social setting, known as **sociolinguistics,**[8] anthropologists can understand how people perceive themselves and the world around them (see Chapter 4).

Linguistic anthropologists also make a significant contribution to our understanding of the human past. Horatio Hale was the first ethnographer to discover the linguistic link between Siouan languages and the Tutelos of Ontario.[9] Hale also recorded Iroquoian oral traditions, and in 1883 he published the *Iroquois Book of Rites*. By working out the genealogical relationships among languages and examining the distributions of those languages, linguistic anthropologists may estimate how long the speakers of those languages have lived where they do. Identifying words in related languages that have survived from an ancient ancestral tongue can suggest where and how the speakers of the ancestral language lived.

Applied Anthropology

Applied anthropology is a veritable gold mine of cultural knowledge that, when put to practical use, can help solve or at least alleviate some of the social problems that humans experience. Besides academic settings, applied anthropologists often work within government bureaux, private corporations, and international development agencies. More often than not, they function as mediators between the members of a cultural group and some government or private agency. As mentioned earlier, applied anthropologists have played a prominent role in the development of Canadian anthropology and have provided important background information for First Nations land claims negotiations.

As we shall see in Chapter 14, applied research is extremely important in sociocultural anthropology, but it also affects the other fields of anthropology. Applied

sociolinguistics The study of language in its social setting.

sociocultural anthropology The study of human behaviour in contemporary cultures.

culture bound Theories about the world and reality based on the assumptions and values of one's own culture.

archaeologists work in cultural resource management (CRM), assessing and excavating archaeological sites threatened by human activity, such as dam building. Public archaeologists have worked alongside First Nations groups to develop cultural awareness programs that introduce the public to the value of heritage sites and the history they recount. As noted earlier, forensic anthropology is an excellent example of applied research in biological anthropology. Applied linguistic anthropologists are becoming increasingly involved in language retention among First Nations groups and serve as advisers for bilingual education. Applied medical anthropologists (see Chapter 14) work closely with traditional healers to reconcile traditional medical practices with modern medicine.

Sociocultural Anthropology

While archaeologists have traditionally concentrated on past cultures, the field of **sociocultural anthropology** examines contemporary or recent cultures. And unlike archaeologists, who focus on material objects to learn about human behaviour, sociocultural anthropologists concentrate on the study of human behaviour as it can be seen, experienced, and even discussed with those whose culture is to be understood.

Sociocultural anthropology, which is the dominant form of anthropology in Canada, is closely related to the other social sciences, especially sociology, since both anthropology and sociology attempt to explain people in social contexts. Sociologists, however, mainly study people living in modern North American and European societies, which increases the probability that their theories of human behaviour will be **culture bound**: that is, the type of questions asked, the theories applied, and the interpretations arrived at are based on assumptions that are part of the sociologists' Western upbringing. Since sociocultural anthropologists, too, are products of their own culture, they also are vulnerable to culture-bound theorizing. However, they constantly seek to minimize the problem by drawing together corroborating information from many different cultures before attempting to explain human behaviour. We will return to a discussion of the comparative method later in this chapter.

Sociocultural anthropologists seek to understand the characteristics of diverse cultural groups—how they live their lives—to explain similarities and differences found among human groups. They seek also to understand the interrelatedness of sociocultural systems, the ways in which our economic, religious, and social and political organizations influence one another. Sociocultural anthropologists also study culture change—the ways in which cultures everywhere continue to change as they adapt to new situations. Throughout this book we will be highlighting the value of sociocultural anthropology in solving practical problems; however, the greatest value of sociocultural anthropology in today's global community is to serve as a medium for promoting cultural awareness and appreciation of the world's incredible cultural diversity.

Sociocultural anthropology is both comparative and descriptive. **Ethnography**, for example, involves collecting descriptive material on a specific culture. The information collected provides a descriptive account (or ethnography) of the people. **Ethnology** is the comparative study of patterns witnessed in cultures. Ethnologists attempt to develop generalizations or rules to explain human behaviour. **Ethnohistory** is a method of studying cultures of the recent past using oral histories; archaeological sites; the accounts of explorers, missionaries, and traders; and archival documents such as land titles and birth and death records.[10]

Ethnographic Fieldwork

Today, whenever possible, the anthropologist becomes an ethnographer by living among the people he or she studies. The anthropologist is gathering data not from archival records or second-hand accounts, but by directly observing the culture in operation. This practice is known as **participant observation**—eating a people's food, speaking their language, and personally experiencing their habits and customs. The ethnographer can understand their way of life to a far greater extent than any nonparticipant researcher could ever do. This unique methodology was championed by Franz Boas, who is known as "the father of fieldwork." Boas emphasized the need for collecting empirical data by actually going into the field and living among the people for an extended period of time.

Participant observation may sound straightforward, but it is fraught with difficulties. Indeed, Alice Reich, a cultural anthropologist specializing in gender studies, calls participant observation "a time honoured tradition of making a fool of oneself for a point."[11] Moving into the field involves many challenges, including developing a research proposal, dealing with an ethics and review board, learning the language, overcoming personal and professional insecurities, developing a rapport with community members, and coping with health and safety issues, as well as **culture shock**.[12]

One of the most critical challenges for anthropologists is researcher bias. Anthropologists learn through the lens of their own cultural background, which is laden with cultural baggage and influenced by their gender, age, ethnicity, class, religious teachings, and so on. Cultural baggage (or background) and upbringing can affect a researcher's interpretation of the data: Annette Weiner (1988) found that she had to let go of her preconceived ideas

about work, power, family, and so on, when studying the economic importance of Trobriand women; otherwise, her interpretations would have been culture bound.[13] Bias is a double-edged sword; anthropologists may be limited in the research they can conduct because of their gender. The field experience of Hazel Weidman was difficult because she was a single woman alone in Myanmar.[14] She had difficulty finding a village that would allow her to live with them and conduct her research. Without a doubt, ethnographers in the field for extended periods will find their familiar ways of doing and thinking challenged. The very presence of an ethnographer in the field can change the dynamics and atmosphere of the group, thus calling into question whether the ethnographer is observing the group as they normally live. Ironically, one of the most valuable lessons of fieldwork is experiencing, even for a limited time, what it feels like to be a minority person—to become an object of curiosity and even hostility is an eye-opening experience and a fieldwork rite of passage.

Participant observation does not mean the ethnographer must join in a people's battles in order to study warfare, but by living among a warlike people, the ethnographer should be able to understand the role of warfare in the overall cultural scheme. He or she must be a meticulous observer in order to gather a broad overview of a culture without placing undue emphasis on one of its parts at the expense of another. Only by discovering how all cultural institutions—social, political, economic, religious—relate to one another can ethnographers begin to understand cultural systems. Anthropologists refer to this outlook as the **holistic perspective**, and it is one of the fundamental principles of anthropology. Robert Gordon, an anthropologist from Namibia, speaks of it in

ethnography The collection of descriptive material on a culture.

ethnology The comparative study of cultures to explain human behaviour.

ethnohistory The study of cultures from the recent past using oral histories, archaeological sites, and written accounts left by explorers, missionaries, and traders.

participant observation A method of learning a people's culture through direct observations and participation in their everyday life.

culture shock The difficulty anthropologists have in adapting to a new culture that differs markedly from their own.

holistic perspective A fundamental principle of anthropology, that the various parts of culture must be viewed in the broadest possible context to understand their interconnections and interdependence.

In Cartagena, Colombia, an ethnographer interviews local fishermen.

© Richard Lord

this way: "Whereas the sociologist or the political scientist might examine the beauty of a flower petal by petal, the anthropologist is the person that stands on the top of the mountain and looks at the beauty of the field. In other words, we try and go for the wider perspective."[15]

When participating in unfamiliar cultures, ethnographers enlist the assistance of **key informants/respondents** who are members of the culture the ethnographer is working in, with whom she or he develops close relationships, and who help interpret whatever activities are occurring. As children learn the accepted norms of behaviour from their parents, so do anthropologists in the field need help from their respondents to unravel the "mysteries" of what is, at first, a strange culture.

The importance of fieldwork is conveyed by the experiences of Richard B. Lee, who lived with the Ju/'hoansi of the Kalahari Desert. The following Original Study illustrates the importance of ethnographic research, which in this case was allied with the skills and analyses of medical anthropology to paint a detailed picture of the issues of diet and health facing the Ju/'hoansi.

The popular image of ethnographic fieldwork is that it takes place among far-off, exotic peoples. Indeed, much ethnographic work has occurred in places such as Africa, the Pacific islands, the Australian deserts, and so on. One very good reason for this is that non-Western peoples were ignored too often by other social scientists. Still, anthropologists have recognized from the start that an

key informants/respondents Members of a culture who help the ethnographer interpret what she or he observes. The term "respondents" or "subjects" is lately preferred over "informants," since the latter has negative connotations associated with providing inside information to authorities.

understanding of human behaviour depends on knowledge of *all* cultures, including their own. In the 1950s and 1960s many Canadian anthropologists turned their attention to social issues facing Canadian society. One of the landmark projects during this period was Harry Hawthorn's 1955 report on the impact of providing First Nations peoples with old-age pensions. This study is a historic example of applied anthropology. Hawthorn continued his research, studying social and economic conditions among First Nations peoples of British Columbia. Marius Barbeau actively promoted the folk culture of French Canada—its arts and crafts, literature, and song and dance. In the early 1960s, Marc-Adélard Tremblay, along with Paul Charest and Yvan Breton, conducted a community study of St-Augustin, a Quebec fishing village on the Gulf of St. Lawrence. Along with its ethnographic value, this study is notable for being one of the first to trace the social changes experienced by a traditional community as it became a modern community over the course of 65 years.

This trend toward focusing on contemporary domestic issues continues today. Often, Canadian anthropologists find themselves studying people in Canada that they have studied in other settings. Thus, as people from the Pacific Rim and the Middle East have moved to Canada, or as refugees have arrived from Africa, Central America, and other places, anthropologists have been there not just to study them but also, on occasion, to help them adjust to their new circumstances. Anthropologists are applying the same research techniques that served them so well in the study of non-Western peoples (if occasionally problematically, given the association with colonialism) to the study of such diverse subjects as First Nations self-government and land claims; English–French relations; Asian immigrants; motorcycle gangs; and health-care delivery systems.

∞ *Original Study* ∞

Health and Disease in One Culture: The Ju/'hoansi

Richard Borshay Lee, University of Toronto

Throughout this text, reference is made to the Ju/'hoansi, one of the best-known examples of a hunting-and-gathering society in anthropology. Medical anthropologists have traced the health of the Ju/'hoansi during the period of great transition from the colonial to the postcolonial period. Health surveys taken in the 1960s when the Ju/'hoansi were still largely living as hunters and gatherers showed them to be relatively healthy. They led active outdoor lives, the men hunting wild game and the women gathering over 100 species of wild plants. It has been estimated that women walked a total of 2,000 kilometres annually, or over 5 kilometres per day, usually carrying loads of 5 to 15 kilograms. Men out hunting could walk and run up to 50 kilometres in a single day.

Analysis of the Ju/'hoansi's varied diet shows it to be well balanced in terms of vitamins and minerals, high in proteins, and very low in carbohydrates. No significant shortfalls in nutrition have been recorded, except perhaps for a moderate shortage of overall calories, leading to lower adult weight and stature than among their farming and herding neighbours. Yet the calorie deficit seems to have had no negative effect on their active lifestyle. In fact, recent research in the United States has shown that underconsumption of calories—eating less as you grow older—may be one of the keys to longevity.

Dental examinations reveal an absence of dental caries, but periodontal (gum) disease was fairly common. Fertility was low (on average, there were 4.7 live births per woman), and infant mortality quite high; in retrospective studies of births prior to

1950, close to 40 percent of babies did not survive to maturity. Nevertheless, low net fertility may have been crucial to survival, since a rapidly growing population could not have been sustained. Most remarkable was the absence of symptoms associated with heart disease. Blood pressure did not rise with age, and serum cholesterol levels were among the lowest ever recorded for a human population.

Apart from their healthy diet and lifestyle, what means did the Ju/'hoansi possess for diagnosing and treating illness and trauma? Like all people, the Ju/'hoansi had developed a set of beliefs and practices to face this universal human need. According to the Ju/'hoansi, supernatural forces, primarily the ghosts of ancestors who had passed on to the spirit world, caused sickness and misfortune. For complex motives, these ghosts remained close to the living, hovering around the villages and bringing with them sickness and misfortune.

In response, certain gifted Ju/'hoansi took up the calling of *n/um k'xau*, or "medicine owner," the Ju/'hoan equivalent of shaman. Years of training helped *n/um k'xau* develop the ability to enter trance, diagnose illness, and magically pull sickness from the body and cast it away (see Chapter 12). The Ju/'hoan healers also possessed an extensive pharmacopeia of herbal remedies, which they would administer as infusions or teas or mix with fat and rub into incisions at sites on the body, as a form of subcutaneous injection. Healers rarely if ever charged a fee; their stated goal was to work for the good of the community, although when called to perform by clients from neighbouring tribes, they received a goat or other gift in payment.

With Botswana's achievement of independence in 1966, the government made efforts to entice hunter-gatherers like the Ju/'hoansi to settle

in one place. By the late 1980s this had become largely accomplished, with Ju in semipermanent villages, subsisting on food from an eclectic mix of sources: government food handouts, small-scale farming and herding, receipts from wage labour and handicraft production, and even some foraging. The road into the Dobe area was rebuilt, making the area more accessible to outsiders. Frequent bans on hunting and the ready availability of food handouts led to a sharp decrease in the amount of exercise for adults and loss of a sense of purpose. In the new cash economy, alcohol consumption increased from almost zero in the 1960s to a significant portion of cash expenditures; chronic alcohol abuse had become a health and social problem for the Ju/'hoansi.

A re-examination of the people's overall health status only 20 years after the initial studies revealed dramatic changes. Blood pressure now increased markedly with age, and for the first time there was evidence of hypertension and heart disease. Dental health had deteriorated, with more cavities noted. On the plus side, women (but not men) showed higher skinfold measurements, indicating more stored fat deposits, and children's height for age had increased slightly. People spoke of coping with greater social stress as a result of their sedentary, higher density lifestyle, and they expressed nostalgia for the days before stores and alcohol. These stresses, and the lower quality diet of refined carbohydrates, probably account for the appearance of symptoms associated with diseases of civilization.

As an additional challenge to community health and well-being, HIV/AIDS began to enter the area in the 1990s. However, even though Botswana has the highest HIV-positive rates in the world (38 percent of people aged 15 to 49, in recent UN estimates), the Ju/'hoansi have a 75 to 90 percent lower rate than

CONTINUED

CONTINUED

the national statistics. The combination of isolation, women's empowerment, and common sense about sex and risk probably accounts for the lower rates. But with the opening of the area to tourism and other traffic, there is concern that this picture may change. Tuberculosis also is on the rise and is considered an even bigger health threat than AIDS, although the two often exist as co-infections.

In the first decade of the 21st century, the people of the Dobe area have undergone dramatic changes in diet and lifestyle. In some ways they have benefited from improved access to the outside world by road, two air-

strips, and a radio link. They certainly make good use of the two government clinics in the area, and the seriously ill can be evacuated to hospital by air ambulance. However, perceptive Ju/'hoansi have observed that the very diseases that the clinic is treating them for—including tuberculosis and HIV/AIDS—have themselves been brought in from the outside. In this sense, the gains and losses in health status are equal.

SOURCES: *R.B. Lee,* The Dobe Ju/'hoansi, *3rd ed. (Toronto: Wadsworth/Thomson Learning, 2003); S. Truswell and J.D.L. Hansen, "Medical Research among the !Kung," in* Kalahari Hunter-Gatherers: Studies of the !Kung San and Their

Neighbors, *ed. R.B. Lee and I. DeVore (Cambridge, MA: Harvard University Press, 1976), 166–94; N. Howell,* Demography of the Dobe !Kung, *2nd ed. (Hawthorne: Aldine-DeGruyter, 2000); A.S. Truswell, B.M Kennelly, J.D.L. Hansen, and R.B. Lee, "Blood Pressures of !Kung Bushmen in Northern Botswana," American Heart Journal 84 (1972): 5–12; R. Katz,* Boiling Energy: Community Healing Among the !Kung *(Cambridge, MA: Harvard University Press, 1982); J. Hansen, D. Dunn, R.B. Lee, P. Becker, and T. Jenkins, "Hunter-Gatherer to Pastoral Way of Life: Effects of the Transition on Health, Growth, and Nutritional Status," South African Journal of Science 89 (1994): 559–64.*

Though it has much to offer, the anthropological study of our own culture is not without its own special problems. Sir Edmund Leach, a major figure in British anthropology, put it in the following way:

> Surprising though it may seem, fieldwork in a cultural context of which you already have intimate first-hand experience seems to be much more difficult than fieldwork which is approached from the naive viewpoint of a total stranger. When anthropologists study facets of their own society their vision seems to become distorted by prejudices which derive from private rather than public experience.[16]

This is certainly true of **popular culture**. Anthropologists have been reluctant to consider popular culture worthy of ethnographic research, partly because it is such an intricate part of their own culture that it is often overlooked, and partly because it has been disdained as trivial or lowbrow. Despite this reluctance, more and more anthropologists are recognizing that popular culture has a much greater and more profound impact on society than high culture, and must be studied. As Freccero points out, popular culture can be as complex and worthy of interpretation as great works of art and literature.[17]

Although ethnographers strive to get inside views of other cultures, they do so as outsiders. And the most

successful anthropological studies of their own culture by North Americans have been done by those who also worked in other cultures. In addition to Canadian ethnographers going outside their own culture before trying to study it themselves (so that they may see themselves as others see them), much is to be gained by encouraging anthropologists from Europe, Africa, Asia, and Central and South America to do fieldwork in North America. For example, Yvon Csonka, who is head of the Department of Social and Cultural History at the University of Greenland, has studied the Caribou Inuit of the west coast of Hudson Bay. Her 1995 study supplements the findings of earlier, classic ethnography by Birket-Smith (1929) and Rasmussen (1930).[18] From their outsiders' perspective come insights all too easily overlooked by an insider.

NEW DIRECTIONS IN ETHNOGRAPHIC FIELDWORK

> If ethnography produces cultural interpretations through intense research experiences, how is unruly experience transformed into an authoritative written account? How, precisely, is a garrulous, overdetermined cross-cultural encounter shot through with power relations and personal cross-purposes circumscribed as an adequate version of a more or less discrete "other world" composed by an individual author?[19]

The vitality and worth of any science depends on its ability to evolve and mature as a discipline. Ethnographic fieldwork, in particular participant observation, has

popular culture   The culture of our everyday lives—television, sports, fashion, arts and crafts, fiction, and music.

Dr. Josephine Smart

Anthropologists carry out fieldwork at home as well as abroad. Shown here is anthropologist Dr. Josephine Smart (centre) of the University of Calgary, with her daughter Jasmine Smart and anthropologist Dr. Judith Nagata of York University, outside an Indian restaurant owned and operated by Chinese from Bombay. The visit to this restaurant is related to a broader project on the globalization and localization of Chinese immigrant cuisine in Canada.

been considered the hallmark of anthropological research for more than a century. Indeed, fieldwork was often considered a "rite of passage" for cultural anthropologists. Moreover, remaining scientifically objective, unbiased, and detached from the "study group" has long been the basis of ethnographic research, as well as one of its toughest challenges. In the late 20th century, anthropologists such as J. Clifford, E. Marcus, and M.J. Fischer began asking some difficult questions about ethnographic research. Just how objective can ethnographers be, and do ethnographers have the ability to remain uninfluenced by circumstances, personal biases, and emotions?

Anthropologists are also considering the dynamics of power and authority. Whose voice should be heard in the ethnographic record, the ethnographer's or the informant's? Is there a way to blend the two? And who has the authority to represent the ideology of the study group? [20] Many anthropologists now believe it is impossible for Western ethnographers to completely understand indigenous ideology or point of view; indeed, there are multiple points of view and voices within any cultural group.[21]

Indigenous groups are now representing themselves to the world, and the ethnographer is only one of many voices. Anthropologists like Judith Abwunza acknowledge the value of presenting multiple voices: in studying female power and resistance among Kenyan women, she recorded the women's experiences in their own words. In this way, ethnographers are no longer the only authority responsible for interpreting anthropological data, and the ethnographer's knowledge is not the only knowledge presented. Leslie Main Johnson recognized this potential when she examined indigenous knowledge with the Gitksan people of northern British Columbia. She asked this question: When Gitksan people look at the environment, what do they see?[22]

Anthropologists also are paying closer attention to living histories, through narratives and oral histories. Robin Ridington (see Chapter 12) typifies this new ethnography in his work with the Dane-zaa. Employing a collaborative approach, and recording oral histories and unedited narratives, Ridington set out to tell the story of the Dane-zaa in their own words and using their voices.

As indigenous groups around the world have taken ownership of their history and ideology, ethnographers have begun to work in partnership with these groups. Participatory-action research means that the study groups are involved in the actual research and interpretation of the ethnographic data. A new and exciting approach is the team research model, whereby each ethnographer does research in his or her own area of specialization (e.g., political and legal issues, rituals, demographics, subsistence strategies, and so on). Thus, the field of ethnography is evolving in an attempt to better meet the needs and wishes of the cultural groups under study and to provide a richer and more comprehensive presentation of indigenous world views.

Ethnological Research

Although ethnographic fieldwork is central to sociocultural anthropology, it is not the sole occupation of anthropologists. Largely descriptive in nature, ethnography provides the basic data that the ethnologist may then use to study one particular aspect of a culture by

∞ *Dynamic Anthropology* ∞

The Institute for African Studies, Carleton University

Blair Rutherford

Blair Rutherford is Professor of Anthropology and Director of the Institute of African Studies at Carleton University in Ottawa. His research examines the cultural politics of labour, land, and citizenship in southern Africa.

Blair Rutherford is a sociocultural anthropologist who has carried out his research in southern Africa since the early 1990s. Along with a small group of colleagues and students at Carleton University, he helped establish the Institute of African Studies on that campus. He also had the privilege of being its first director. When it began offering undergraduate programs in 2009, this institute became the only stand-alone current academic unit in Canada that focused on Africa.

Although it provides an interdisciplinary BA degree in African Studies, the institute exemplifies an anthropology that is open to a range of perspectives on the humanities and that seeks to engage a variety of publics in learning. The programs and events offered by the Institute of African Studies provide opportunities for its students and the wider public to learn more about the rich histories and current realities of one of the more poorly understood continents. Like the discipline of anthropology, the institute uses a wide focus, though in its case it is used to examine a geographical region and not humanity writ large. It provides courses and organizes events that examine, among other topics, politics, cinema, international development, literature, histories, economies, languages, social processes, laws, ecologies, refugees, and cultural phenomena with regard to the African continent as a whole or to specific areas or groups, including diasporic ones.

The Institute of African Studies draws on important linkages to experts in the Ottawa-Gatineau region and beyond, including in Africa. It provides experiential learning opportunities for students by offering placement courses among agencies and organizations working on Africa, such as at the many nongovernmental organizations based in Ottawa, at the Africa Bureau of the Department of Foreign Affairs, at other government departments that focus on Africa, and at the many research and community groups in the region. It also enables students to study in Africa, either by going to an African country with one of the more than 40 cross-appointed Carleton professors to have an intensive seminar on a specialized topic, or by going to one of the African universities with which Carleton has a student exchange agreement. Such experiences in an organization working abroad are a form of fieldwork, providing students with insights into the daily practices of African life and the dynamic nature of anthropology.

comparing it with that same aspect in other cultures. Anthropologists constant engage in **cross-cultural comparison**, which, like the holistic approach, is another key characteristic of sociocultural anthropology. The cross-cultural perspective, which can be applied to any current issue, provides anthropology with far richer data than any other social science. Consider the way infants in the United States and Canada are routinely made to sleep apart from their parents, their mothers in particular. To European North Americans, this seems normal, but cross-cultural studies show that "co-sleeping" is the rule in most cultural groups. Only in the past 200 years—generally in Western industrialized societies—has it been considered proper for mother and infant to sleep apart. In fact, it amounts to a cultural

cross-cultural comparison   Comparing one particular aspect of a culture with that same aspect in others.

experiment in childrearing, one that anthropologists have found has some important consequences. For one, sleeping alone increases the length of crying bouts, which may last in excess of three hours a day in the child's second and third months. The benefits of co-sleeping go beyond significant reductions in crying: infants nurse more often and three times as long; they receive more stimuli (important for neurological development); and they are apparently less susceptible to sudden infant death syndrome. The mother benefits as well if frequent nursing delays the return of ovulation after childbirth, and she gets at least as much sleep as mothers do who sleep without their infants (see the Original Study in Chapter 8 on Aka dads).[23]

Such cross-cultural comparisons highlight alternative ways of doing things, so they have much to offer North Americans, large numbers of whom, opinion polls show, continue to doubt the effectiveness of their own ways of doing things. In this sense, we may think of ethnology, and indeed ethnography, as the study of alternative ways of doing things. Also, by making systematic cross-cultural comparisons of cultures, ethnologists may add to the ongoing dialogue regarding the nature of culture.

Ethnohistoric Research

Ethnohistorians study cultures of the recent past, by drawing upon oral histories and written accounts left by explorers, missionaries, and traders, and by analyzing data such as archaeological records and archival materials (e.g., land titles, birth and death records). The ethnohistorical analysis of cultures is a valuable means for understanding culture change. In Canada, ethnohistorians have explored the economic, social, and political changes that First Nations experienced when they joined the colonial fur trade.[24]

Ethnohistoric research is also valuable for assessing the reliability of data used for making cross-cultural comparisons. Anthropologists using HRAF (Human Relations Area Files) have concluded that among foragers, it was the practice for married couples to live in or near the household of the husband's parents (known as patrilocal residence). To be sure, this is what many ethnographers have reported. Most such ethnographies were done among food foragers whose traditional practices had been severely altered by pressures emanating from the expansion of Europeans to all parts of the globe. For example, the Western Abenaki people of northwestern New England are believed to have practised patrilocal residence prior to the invasion of their homeland by English colonists. Ethnohistoric research, however, shows that their participation in the fur trade with Europeans, coupled with increasing involvement in warfare to stave off foreign incursions, led to the increased importance of men's activities and a change from more flexible to patrilocal residence patterns.[25] Other cases of patrilocal residence among food foragers turned out to be similar responses to circumstances associated with the rise of colonialism.

Although a valuable research tool, ethnohistory also has problems and limitations. Early explorers, traders, and missionaries came to Canada with preconceived notions about First Nations peoples; many of the early accounts reflect these biases and suffer from inaccuracies, misinterpretations, and distortions. As an example, ignorance and personal biases are rife in early accounts of practices such as the Sun Dance and potlatch ceremonies. Ethnohistorians must take into consideration the reliability and objectivity of their literary sources, and often rely on several forms of information to validate their findings.

ANTHROPOLOGY AND SCIENCE

The primary concern of all anthropologists, regardless of specialization, is the careful and systematic study of humankind. Anthropology has been called a social or a behavioural science by some, a natural science by others, and one of the humanities by still others. Anthropology displays many of the characteristics of a science; for example, it entails designing hypotheses or tentative explanations for certain observable phenomena, collecting data to test and prove or disprove these hypotheses, and developing a theory to explain the phenomena. Yet the scientific methodology of such a broad discipline can cause difficulties. In order to arrive at useful theories concerning human behaviour, anthropologists must begin with hypotheses that are as objective and as minimally culture-bound as possible. And herein lies a major—some would say insurmountable—problem: as mentioned earlier, it is difficult for someone who has grown up in one culture to develop hypotheses about others that are not culture bound.

Consider the attempts by archaeologists to understand the nature of settlement in the Classic period of Maya civilization. This civilization flourished between AD 250 and 900 in what is now heavily forested northern Guatemala, Belize, and adjacent portions of Mexico and Honduras. Today, this forest, called the Petén jungle, is inhabited by a few people who sustain themselves with swidden farming (i.e., after cutting and burning the natural vegetation, they grow crops for two years or so, before fertility is exhausted and a new field must be cleared). Numerous archaeological sites with large stone temples, palaces, and carved stone monuments have been found in this area, the fantastic site of Mirador being one of the best-known examples. Because of their cultural bias against tropical forests as normal places to live, and against swidden farming as an efficient means of raising food, Western archaeologists asked this question: How could the Maya have maintained large, permanent settlements on the basis of swidden farming? The answer seemed self-evident: they could not; therefore, the great archaeological sites must have been ceremonial centres inhabited by few people, if any. Periodically, a rural peasantry, scattered in small hamlets over the countryside, must have gathered at these centres for rituals or to provide labour for their construction and maintenance.

This view dominated for several decades. Not until 1960 did archaeologists, working at the Mayan site Tikal, begin to ask the simplest and least biased questions they could think of: Did anyone live at this particular site on a permanent basis? If so, how many, and how were they supported? Working intensively for the next decade, with as few preconceived notions as possible, the archaeologists were able to establish that Tikal had been a large settlement inhabited on a permanent basis by tens of thousands of people who were supported by forms of agriculture more productive than swidden agriculture alone. This work at Tikal invalidated the older culture-bound ideas and paved the way for a new understanding of Classic Maya civilization. Indeed, recent research has begun to reexamine the pre-Classic Maya in much the same vein.[26]

Recognizing the potential problems of framing explanations that are not culture bound, anthropologists immerse themselves in the data to the fullest extent possible. By doing so, they become so thoroughly familiar with the minute details that they can, ideally, begin to detect patterns in the data, many of which might otherwise have been overlooked. These patterns allow anthropologists to propose explanations, which may then be subjected to further testing.

As the fieldwork proceeds, ethnographers sort their complex observations into a meaningful whole, sometimes by formulating and testing hypotheses, but often as not by making use of intuition.

Two studies of a village in Peru illustrate the contrast between anthropological and other social science approaches. In the first study, a sociologist conducted a survey and concluded that people in the village worked together on one another's individually owned plots of land. By contrast, an anthropologist who lived in the village for over a year (during which time the sociologist carried out his study) observed the practice only once. Although a belief in exchange relations was important for the people's understanding of themselves, it was not an economic reality.[27]

Another problem in scientific anthropology is the matter of replication. In the other physical and natural sciences, replication of observations and/or experiments is an important means of establishing the reliability of a researcher's conclusions. However, in anthropology, access to a non-Western culture is constrained by the difficulty of getting there and being accepted, by a limited number of ethnographers, by inadequate funding, and by the fact that cultures change, so what is observable at one time may not be at another. Thus, researchers cannot easily see for themselves whether the ethnographer "got it right." For this reason, an ethnographer bears a special responsibility for accurate reporting.

The result of ethnographic fieldwork, if properly carried out, should be a coherent description of a culture, one that provides an explanatory framework for understanding the behaviour of the people who have been studied. And this framework, in turn, is what permits anthropologists to frame broader hypotheses about human behaviour. Plausible though such explanations may be, however, the consideration of a single society is generally insufficient for their testing. As discussed earlier, without some basis for comparison, the hypotheses grounded in a single case may be no more than historical coincidence. Ideally, theories in sociocultural anthropology are generated from cross-cultural comparisons, drawn from the vast data bank of ethnographical information. The researcher examines a sample of societies in order to discover whether explanations of cultural phenomena seem to be universally, or at least broadly, applicable. The sample should be selected at random, thereby increasing the probability that the researcher's conclusions are valid. The researcher, of course, is depending on other ethnographers for accurate data, since it is impossible for any one individual to perform in-depth analyses of a broad sample of human cultures throughout the world. Despite the importance of cross-cultural research for scientific validity, a single case may be enough to cast doubt on, if not refute, a theory that previously had been held valid. The discovery in 1948 that Aborigines living in Australia's Arnhem Land put in an average workday of less than six hours, while living well above a level of bare sufficiency, was enough to call into question the widely accepted notion that food-foraging peoples are so preoccupied with finding food that they lack time for any of life's more pleasurable activities. The observations made in the Arnhem Land study have since been confirmed many times over in various parts of the world.

Development schemes in nonindustrial countries have traditionally favoured projects, such as dam building, that more often than not fail to deliver the expected benefits, owing to the developers' lack of understanding of local peoples' practices and needs.

Gender Perspectives

The Anthropology of Gender

Although gender permeates virtually every aspect of our lives, the term **gender** as opposed to sex is a somewhat elusive concept. Sex refers to the biological and anatomical differences between men and women; humans belong to one of two sexes—male or female. Gender, on the other hand, is a social construct that provides us with guidelines for our social identity, status, and behaviour and that may include more than the feminine and masculine genders, such as the *berdache*, or "Two-Spirits," of some North American Aboriginal cultures, and the *hijra* of India, who are neither man nor woman. The concept of gender was first introduced by feminist anthropologists. **Feminist anthropology** arose to address the gender imbalance or **androcentrism** found in most early ethnographic research.

Gender is learned; through enculturation, we learn the gender roles of our culture. Thus, gender is culturally defined. Anthropologists such as Margaret Mead posited that if gender is culturally defined, then it stands to reason we will find differences in roles and expectations assigned to each gender from one culture to another. Anthropologists examine how gender roles influence and are influenced by such factors as subsistence strategies, marriage practices, political organization, religious beliefs, and kinship, and how these roles affect the status of each gender. Because gender roles differ from culture to culture, levels of status and power relations also vary, leading to what anthropologists call "gender stratification." Feminist anthropologists examine gender inequality or stratification from a cross-cultural perspective.

Studies of gender stratification invariably focus on female inequality. Anthropologists generally agree that some form of gender stratification exists in all present-day societies. Even in so-called egalitarian cultures, such as traditional food-foraging groups, where there is little ranking, slight differences between male and female status are evident. Some anthropologists have gone so far as to suggest a "universal male dominance." Examples of female inequality are readily available: exclusion from leading or participating in religious services, differential value placed on production activities, and lack of control over reproductive decisions.

The study of gender from an anthropological perspective is fairly recent and has been fraught with difficulties and barriers, most notably the anthropologist's inability to see beyond his or her own society's perceptions of gender. To counter this problem, feminist anthropologists work collaboratively with women in their study group, giving the women more voice and opportunities to interpret research from their perspective. Anthropologists from other cultures have brought an added dimension to the field of feminist anthropology; for example, anthropologist Fuambai Ahmadu has offered her insider's perspective on the practice of female circumcision. Feminist anthropologists have also endeavoured to dispel misconceptions regarding the role and status of Islamic women, focusing on the *hijab* (head covering) and *purdah* (seclusion). One of the most significant contributions of feminist anthropology to date is the critical examination of the concepts of human rights, oppression, and exploitation cross-culturally, which has included pointing out that others may not agree with Western interpretations of gender discrimination.

In the following chapters, we will examine many issues of gender, including such controversial subjects as female circumcision and purdah.

SOURCES: F. Ahmadu, "Rites and Wrongs: An Insider/Outsider Reflects on Power and Excision," in Female "Circumcision" in Africa: Culture, Controversy, and Change, *ed. B. Shell-Duncan and Y. Hernlund (London: Lynne Rienner, 2000); J.A. Goulet, "The 'Berdache'/'Two-Spirit': A Comparison of Anthropological and Native Constructions of Gendered Identities among the Northern Athapaskans,"* Journal of the Royal Anthropological Institute *2 (December 1996): 683–701.*

ANTHROPOLOGY AND THE HUMANITIES

Anthropology is the most humanistic of the sciences and the most scientific of the humanities.

—Alfred Kroeber

gender   A set of standards and behaviours attached to individuals, usually but not always based on biological sex.

feminist anthropology   A subfield of anthropology that investigates gender and gender relations and that critically analyzes gender roles, positions, and experiences.

androcentrism   Male-centredness.

Although the sciences and humanities are often thought of as mutually exclusive approaches to learning, they come together in anthropology. That is why anthropological research is funded not only by "hard science" agencies such as the Medical Research Council of Canada, but also by organizations such as the Social Science and Humanities Research Council.

The humanistic side of anthropology is perhaps most immediately evident in its concern with other cultures' languages, values, and achievements in the arts and literature (including oral literature among people without writing systems). Beyond this, anthropologists remain committed to the position that they cannot fully understand another culture by simply observing it; as the term "participant observation" implies, they must experience it as well. Yet anthropologists are not so naive as to believe that they can ever know the culture in the same way as the native does. The humanistic side of anthropology is evident as well in its emphasis on **qualitative research** (detailed description based on observation and interviews) as opposed to **quantitative research** (numerical measurement). This does not mean that anthropologists are unaware of the value of quantification and statistical procedures; they do make use of them for various purposes. However, reducing people and what they do to numbers has a definite dehumanizing effect (it is easier to ignore the concerns of impersonal numbers than those of flesh-and-blood human beings) and ignores important issues that are not susceptible to numeration. For all these reasons, anthropologists tend to place less emphasis on numerical data than do other social scientists.

Given anthropologists' intense encounters with other groups of people, it should come as no surprise that they have amassed as much information about human frailty and nobility—stuff of the humanities—as any other discipline. Small wonder, too, that above all they intend to avoid allowing a "coldly" scientific approach to blind them to the fact that human groups are made up of individuals with a rich assortment of emotions and aspirations that demand respect. Anthropology sometimes has been called the most human of the sciences—a designation anthropologists embrace with considerable pride.

qualitative research   The gathering of data based on interviews, documents, and participant observation to understand human social behaviour.
quantitative research   The gathering of statistical and measurable data.

ANTHROPOLOGY'S CONTRIBUTIONS TO OTHER DISCIPLINES

Students often ask, "Why should we study anthropology?" To answer this question we need to examine the personal, academic, and professional benefits of an education in anthropology. For those of us who have ever wondered why people behave the way they do, believe in what they do, or look the way they do, anthropology can help answer these and many other questions. Anthropologists teach us about the different ways in which people organize their lives and can go a long way toward explaining human behaviour.

Regardless of their field of study, students will benefit academically from an anthropological education. For example, from an economic anthropology course, a student can learn about the myriad ways that people around the world organize their production, exchange, and consumption activities and will come to understand that there are many meanings associated with economic activities. Anthropology also contributes to disciplines outside the social sciences; archaeological and ethnohistorical research has much to offer history and geology, and biological anthropology both benefits from and contributes to the science of biology. Ecological anthropology engages the student in studies of climate change, technology, and social adaptations. Thus, the study of anthropology, however brief, provides a broader, more well-rounded education.

For students majoring in anthropology, there are numerous areas of specialization that prepare them for future careers. For example, urban anthropologists often work in areas of policy, planning, and development in urban settings. Medical anthropologists work alongside other health specialists to identify the beliefs, attitudes, and behaviours that affect health and illness. Anthropologists often find career opportunities in government agencies—for example, in immigration, as policy developers.

Anthropologists are not the only scholars who study people, nor are their findings wholly divorced from those of psychologists, economists, sociologists, or biologists; rather, these disciplines (and many more) contribute to the common goal of understanding humanity, and anthropologists gladly offer their findings for the benefit of other disciplines. Anthropologists do not expect, for example, to know as much about the structure of the human eye as anatomists or as much about the perception of colour as psychologists. Neither would an anthropologist necessarily be familiar with the residential pattern of Asian immigrants to Canada, which would be the realm of the sociologist. As synthesizers, however, they are prepared to understand how these subjects relate to colour-naming behaviour. As a case in point, the Coast Salish languages of southwestern British Columbia do not have separate words to distinguish blue from green, while Russian has a separate word for pale blue and another word for dark blue. Since anthropologists look for broad explanations of human behaviour without limiting themselves to any single social or biological aspect of that behaviour, they can acquire an extensive overview of humans as complex biological and cultural organisms.

Researchers outside the field of anthropology are beginning to recognize the value of one of anthropology's unique methodologies—that of immersion in a culture. Participant observation provides a research model for other disciplines, such as education, geography, and psychology. For example, students of educational psychology gain firsthand experience in counselling by immersing themselves in clinics. Thus, anthropology enhances the research and experience of other disciplines—disciplines that would be diminished if not for the knowledge and research methods of anthropology.

THE QUESTION OF ETHICS

The kinds of research anthropologists carry out and the settings they work in raise a number of important questions concerning ethics. Who will make use of the findings of anthropologists, and for what purposes? In the case of a militant minority, for example, will others use anthropological data to suppress that minority? And what of traditional communities around the world? Who is to decide what changes should, or should not, be introduced for community "betterment"? By whose definition is it betterment—the community's, some remote national government's, or that of an international agency (e.g., the World Bank)? Then consider the problem of privacy. Anthropologists deal with people's private and sensitive matters, including matters that people would not care to have generally known. How do anthropologists write about such matters while protecting the privacy of informants? Not surprisingly, because of these and other questions, anthropologists must carefully consider the ethics of their research.

Anthropologists have obligations to four sets of people: those they study, those who fund the study, student and public bodies, and those in the profession who expect them to publish their findings. Because fieldwork requires a relationship of trust between fieldworker and informants, the first responsibility of any

CP PHOTO/Toronto Sun–Mark O'Neill

Failure to respect the needs of diverse cultural groups can have serious consequences, such as the destruction of this Jewish synagogue.

anthropologist is to his or her informants and their people. Everything possible must be done to protect their physical, social, and psychological welfare and to honour their dignity and privacy. In other words, the primary directive is to *do no harm*. Although early ethnographers often provided the kind of information that colonial administrators needed to control the "natives," they have long since ceased to be comfortable with such work and regard as basic a people's right to their own culture. However, anthropologists realize that they cannot avoid dealing with the moral and political consequences of their findings. As Gregory Starrett states: "It should be clear to anthropologists that anything we say can and will be used in ways outside our control."[28] In the field of corporate anthropology, ethnographers have had to consider the ethics of studying consumers and turning their research over to corporations that plan to entice consumers (especially children) into purchasing more merchandise. To some anthropologists, this must be balanced with more beneficial activities, such as becoming involved in blocking the marketing of harmful products or pointing out environmental hazards caused by corporations.

Anthropologists must often deal with the question of how involved they should become in the community they are studying. They must decide where to draw the line between participation and observation. They are expected to remain objective, yet many anthropologists find it difficult to remain totally dispassionate about the people they are studying. Anthropologists do not set out to transform a culture—to make it over in their own image—yet many anthropologists have encountered situations where they have felt conflicted. This is particularly true when they encounter gender inequalities, where the lives of women are put in peril, or where the protection of children is at issue. At what point can or should anthropologists step outside their position as neutral observers? These are dilemmas that anthropologists often face when in the field.

RELEVANCE OF ANTHROPOLOGY IN CONTEMPORARY LIFE

A question often asked is "What is the relevance of anthropology in contemporary life?" Like all disciplines, anthropology is increasingly called upon to justify its existence and to demonstrate its relevance to contemporary life. Anthropologists attempt to link the exotic nature of anthropological research to the everyday lives of people—to the issues that confront us and challenge our identity and well-being. In Canada, we continue to

grapple with complex issues such as language retention, sovereignty, immigration policies, Aboriginal land claims, defining Canadian culture (or cultures), and Canada's place in the international community. Anthropology can lend its unique perspective to these ongoing challenges.

Just as important is anthropology's role as an educator—providing the general public with the knowledge and understanding of anthropology and its subject matter. Canada is a multicultural society, composed of numerous Aboriginal peoples and immigrants from all corners of the world. As citizens of Canada and the global community, it is important for us to learn to live in peace and harmony, to avoid misunderstandings and condemnations based on ignorance, fear, and an unwillingness to accept different ways of living. Just as Franz Boas exhorted his colleagues to recognize the uniqueness and validity of every culture, contemporary anthropologists must pass along this ideology to the people of their own societies. What anthropology has to contribute to contemporary life, then, is a conceptual framework for promoting understanding, acceptance, and appreciation of the incredible cultural diversity of our global community. In other words, sociocultural anthropology is in an excellent position to promote global cultural awareness. Anthropology is also an examination of our identity—who we are and where we come from. Perhaps, in the end, our satisfaction with our own identities comes from this fundamental understanding. These are nothing less than basic skills for survival in the modern world.

Chapter Summary

1. What is anthropology?
Anthropology is the detailed study of humanity in different times and places. Anthropologists attempt to engender knowledge about diverse peoples and their behaviour, their differences and commonalties. Traditionally, myths and legends provided the answers to these questions. Anthropology offers another approach to answering the questions people ask about themselves. In employing a scientific approach, anthropologists seek to produce a reasonably objective understanding of human diversity and those aspects of life that all humans have in common.

2. What do anthropologists do?
The five major branches of anthropology are biological anthropology, archaeology, linguistic anthropology, applied anthropology, and sociocultural anthropology. Biological anthropology focuses on humans as biological organisms, tracing the evolutionary development of humans and studying biological variation within the species today. Archaeologists

study material objects from past cultures in order to explain human behaviour. Linguistic anthropologists, who study human languages, may deal with descriptions of languages, with histories of languages, or with how languages are used in particular social settings. Applied anthropologists put to practical use the knowledge and expertise of anthropology, whether relating to land claims or human resource managment. Sociocultural anthropologists study contemporary human groups. Ethnographers go into the field to observe and describe human behaviour; ethnologists conduct comparative studies of particular facets of a culture; and ethnohistorians study cultures of the recent past using oral histories and written accounts left by explorers, missionaries, and traders. Each of these subfields faces its own challenges.

3. How do anthropologists do what they do?
A great deal of anthropological investigation involves fieldwork. Physical or biological anthropologists, as well as archaeologists, excavate sites in search of evidence of human activity. Linguistic anthropologists are concerned with understanding how people employ language to relate to one another. Linguistic

anthropologists will often live for brief periods with the people whose language they are studying. Sociocultural anthropologists often immerse themselves in contemporary cultures by living with the group under study, taking part in their routine activities, and observing how they live their lives.

4. What is the "anthropological perspective"?
Anthropologists attempt to answer the questions that people have asked throughout human history, questions such as "Who are we? Where do we come from? Why do we behave as we do?" The multiple fields and subfields of anthropology are put to use in order to gain a thorough knowledge of any phenomenon under study. Combined, these multiple fields, and recourse to both the *longue durée* and a vast data bank of research collected over centuries, result in the anthropological perspective. This holistic approach gives anthropologists a well-rounded knowledge of the people and events they study. As both a science and one of the humanities, anthropology has essential skills to offer the modern world, in which understanding the other people with whom we share this world has become a matter of survival.

Questions for Critical Thought

1. Consider movies you have seen and novels you have read that feature anthropologists as characters. How are they portrayed? How do these characterizations contrast with the discipline as presented in this chapter?

2. Respond to the question, "What good is anthropology, anyway?" How might anthropological knowledge help you understand and interact with people in your chosen career, be it teacher, doctor, police officer, bank teller, or lawyer?

3. If an anthropologist chose your community, college dorm, or organization to study, what information would you willingly share? What information would you be more hesitant to share? How would the anthropologist's presence interfere with your everyday life? Would the gender or age of the anthropologist have any impact on your behaviour? What efforts would you expect on the part of the anthropologist to ensure your privacy?

4. In light of the September 11, 2001, terrorist attacks on New York City and Washington, D.C., many people are unsure of how to deal with the new reality of our Western world. How might anthropology help ease tensions, fears, and misunderstandings that can arise among cultural groups? What future roles do you see for anthropology in our global community?

5. Choose a variety of popular culture (e.g., hip hop). What elements of culture (e.g., values, issues, beliefs, and so on) are reflected in this form of popular culture?

Internet Resources

Anthropology and Ethics
http://research.illinois.edu/ethics/anthropology.asp
This site provides links to anthropology associations, including the Canadian Archaeology Association. In each link the association presents its code of professional ethics and addresses issues such as professional responsibility.

Careers in Anthropology
http://www.aaanet.org/profdev/careers/
Answers questions on what students can do with a degree in anthropology, and provides links to several related pages. This site is a valuable resource for students who are thinking about majoring in anthropology or who will soon graduate with an anthropology degree.

http://www.careerjet.ca/anthropology-jobs.html
This site provides links to career opportunities in anthropological fields.

About Anthropology
http://www.anthropology.about.com/mlibrary.htm
This is an excellent general source for studying anthropology, offering information on a wide range of topics, with links to related sites.

Field School Opportunities
http://www.aaanet.org/profdev/fieldschools/
Provides links to field school opportunities throughout the world.

Forensic Anthropology
http://www.forensicanthro.com/
This site provides a good introduction to the science of forensic anthropology, including the ways that forensic anthropologists determine sex, gender, and age.

Dancing, Language, and Racism— The Passions of Franz Boas
http://wisc.academia.edu/HerbertLewis/Papers/75020/The_Passion_of_Franz_Boas
An extensive description of Franz Boas's life and career, including discussion of his influence on Canadian anthropology.

What Is Anthropology?
http://www.aaanet.org/about/WhatisAnthropology.cfm
A fairly comprehensive explanation of anthropology and its subdisciplines from the American Anthropological Association.

Suggested Readings

For a list of suggested readings, visit the textbook's website at http://www.havilandcultural4e.nelson.com.

Notes

1. W. Davis, *The Wayfinders* (Toronto: Anansi Press, 2009),

2. E.J. Hedigan, *Applied Anthropology in Canada: Understanding Aboriginal Issues* (Toronto: University of Toronto Press, 1995).

3. University of Toronto (2001), *A Brief History of Anthropology at the University of Toronto*, http://www.chass.utoronto.ca/anthropology/history.htm, retrieved June 20, 2001.

4. For a detailed discussion of the development of Canadian anthropology, see A.M. Erwin, *Canadian Perspectives in Cultural Anthropology* (Toronto: Nelson Education, 2000).

5. See M. Lock, *Encounters with Aging—Mythologies of Menopause in Japan and North America* (Berkeley: University of California Press, 1993).

6. See N. Scheper-Hughes, "The Global Traffic in Human Organs," *Current Anthropology* 41, no. 2 (2000): 191–224.

7. Robert L. Kelly and David Hurst Thomas, *Archaeology* (Belmont: Wadsworth, 2010).

8. Florian Coulmas, *Sociolinguistics: The Study of Speakers' Choices* (Cambridge: Cambridge University Press, 2005).

9. H. Hale, "The Tutelo Tribe and Language," *Proceedings of the American Philosophical Society* 21, no. 114 (1993).

10. Shepard Krech, "The State of Ethnohistory," *Annual Review of Anthropology* 20 (1991): 345–75.

11. W. Wickwire, "Women in Ethnography: The Research of James A. Teit," *American Society for Ethnohistory* 40, no. 4 (Fall 1993): 539–67.

12. Giampietro Gobo, *Doing Ethnography* (London: Sage, 2008).

13. A.B. Weiner, *The Trobrianders of Papua New Guinea* (New York: Holt, Rinehart and Winston, 1988).

14. H.H. Weidman, *On Ambivalence and the Field* (1970), Hazel Hitson Weidman Papers, Harvard University.

15. R. Gordon, interview for Coast Telecourses, Inc., Los Angeles, December 1981.

16. E. Leach, *Social Anthropology* (Glasgow: Fontana, 1982), 124.

17. C. Freccero, *Popular Culture: An Introduction* (New York: New York University Press, 1999).

18. R.B. Lee and R. Daly, eds., *The Cambridge Encyclopedia of Hunters and Gatherers* (Cambridge: Cambridge University Press, 1999).

19. James Clifford, *The Predicament of Culture: Twentieth Century Ethnography, Literature, and Art* (Cambridge, MA: Harvard University Press, 1988).

20. Harry F. Wolcott, *Ethnography: A Way of Seeing* (Plymouth: Altamira Press, 2008).

21. G.T. Conaty, "Economic Models and Blackfoot Ideology," *American Ethnologist* 22, no. 2 (May 1995): 403–9.

22. L.M. Johnson, "Indigenous Knowledge as a Basis for Living in Local Environments," in *Ethnographic Essays in Cultural Anthropology: A Problem-Based Approach*, ed. R.B. Morrison and C.R. Wilson (Itasca: F.E. Peacock, 2002).

23. R.G. Barr, "The Crying Game," *Natural History* 47 (October 1997); J.J. McKenna, "Bedtime Story," *Natural History* 50 (October 1997).

24. Bruce Trigger, *Natives and Newcomers: Canada's "Heroic Age" Reconsidered* (Montreal and Kingston: McGill–Queen's University Press, 1985).

25. W.A. Haviland, and M.W. Power, *The Original Vermonters*, rev. and exp. (Hanover: University Press of New England, 1994), 174–75, 215–16, 297–99.

26. Francisco Estrada-Belli, *The First Maya Civilization* (London: Routledge, 2011).

27. R. Chambers, *Rural Development: Putting the Last First* (New York: Longman, 1983), 51.

28. G. Starrett, "Culture Never Dies: Anthropology at Abu Ghraib," in *Talking About People,* ed. W.A. Haviland, R.J. Gordon, and L.A. Vivanco (Toronto: McGraw-Hill, 2006) 24–26.

2 The Nature of Culture

FirstShot/Alamy

The importance of ceremony and ritual for a culture is highlighted in this picture of First Nations people in Vancouver participating in the Salmon Celebration.

KEY QUESTIONS

1. What Is Culture?

Culture, as anthropologists see it, consists of the abstract values, beliefs, and perceptions of the world that lie behind people's behaviour and that are reflected in that behaviour. These elements are shared by members of a cultural group, and when they are acted upon, produce behaviour that is intelligible to other members of that culture. Culture is learned largely through the medium of language, rather than inherited biologically. The parts of a culture such as economy, spirituality, material systems, kinship, and so on, function as an integrated whole.

2. Why Do Cultures Exist?

To survive, a culture must satisfy the basic needs of the society and deal with problems and matters that concern its members. It must provide for its own continuity, and it must furnish an orderly existence. In doing so, a culture must strike a balance between the self-interests of individuals and the needs of society as a whole. Finally, a culture must have the capacity to change and adapt to new circumstances or to altered perceptions of existing circumstances.

3. How Are Cultures Evaluated?

Despite occasional ethnocentric beliefs that other cultures are inferior to one's own, anthropologists believe that all cultures are equally valid and must not be judged according to standards set outside the culture. Yet the right to self-determination and cultural freedom becomes complicated when basic values clash. This has led to controversy over such areas as human rights.

Culture is one of the most important and volatile concepts associated with the human species. Occasionally, people are described as being "uncultured" or of being from a "high culture." This is not the case, as all peoples in all societies have culture. Misunderstood or overly contested, it can lead to genocide. Properly appreciated, understood, and celebrated, culture can reveal humanity at its most beautiful and creative. Students of anthropology are fortunate to find themselves studying a variety of human cultures within different societies, each with its own distinctive system of politics, social organization, economics, and religion. Despite tremendous variation, these cultures have one thing in common: each represents the collective behaviour of people as they cooperate to ensure their collective survival and well-being. For this to work, some degree of predictable behaviour is required of each individual within the culture, for group living and cooperation are impossible unless individuals know how others are likely to behave in any given situation. For the human species, it is culture that sets the limits of behaviour and that guides people along predictable paths.

THE CONCEPT OF CULTURE

In 1871, British anthropologist Sir Edward Burnett Tylor defined culture as "that complex whole which includes knowledge, belief, art, law, morals, custom and any other capabilities and habits acquired by man as a member of society." Since Tylor's time, definitions of culture have proliferated. In the early 1950s, North American anthropologists A.L. Kroeber and Clyde Kluckhohn collected more than one hundred definitions of culture from the literature. Recent definitions tend to distinguish between actual behaviour on the one hand and the abstract values, beliefs, and perceptions of the world that lie behind that behaviour on the other. Culture, then, is

culture The shared ideals, values, and beliefs that people use to interpret experience and to generate behaviour and that are reflected by their behaviour.

not only observable behaviour but also the shared ideals, values, and beliefs that people use to interpret experience and generate behaviour and that are reflected in their behaviour. Newer definitions in anthropology are complimented by the fact that anthropology is no longer the domain solely of white, Western males; today the field includes anthropologists from all walks of life.

Culture enables people to adapt to a wide range of environments and circumstances. By manipulating their environment through cultural means—technology and social relations, for example—people have been able to move into the Arctic and the Sahara and have even occupied orbiting space stations. This does not mean that humans do everything in response to their environment or their own biological natures; rather, their beliefs and attitudes and the consequences of their behaviour all affect the way humans organize their world.

Culture provides the means for producing and distributing goods and services considered necessary for life. Such necessities include biological continuity (through the reproduction of a culture's members), teaching children appropriate behaviour (so that they will become functioning adults), maintaining order among the members of a culture, maintaining appropriate relations with those outside the culture, and encouraging members of the culture to find meaning in their lives. Also, a culture must be able to change if it is to remain functional. Through culture, then, the human species has secured not just its survival but its expansion as well.

CHARACTERISTICS OF CULTURE

Although each culture is unique, anthropologists note that all cultures display remarkable similarities as they go about fulfilling their members' needs. Through the comparative study of many cultures, anthropologists have arrived at an understanding of the basic characteristics shared by all cultures. An in-depth study of these characteristics helps us see the importance and the function of culture.

Culture Is Shared

As stated earlier, **culture** is a set of shared ideals, values, and standards of behaviour; it is the common denominator that makes the actions of individuals intelligible to other members of the same culture. They share a cultural identity, separate from other cultures. Because they share a common culture, people can predict how others are most likely to behave in a given circumstance and can react accordingly. When people move to another culture, they leave their familiar world behind and enter a new one that operates under a different set of rules. The ability to predict other people's behaviour is lessened, which creates uncertainty. The confusion, hostility, and anxiety that many people experience when living in an unfamiliar culture is known as culture shock, a term first coined by Kalervo Oberg in the 1950s.[1] Since then, psychologists and other researchers have studied the stress caused by adjusting to a foreign environment.

Anthropologists in the field may too experience bouts of culture shock until they become familiar with the customs and language and learn the appropriate behaviour in the culture under study. The extent of culture shock can be affected by the degree of differences between the field anthropologist and the "host"' culture and also by the personality of the anthropologist. In the mid-1990s, when anthropologist William C. Young moved to Sudan to study the Rashaayda Bedouin, he entered a vastly different world: instead of cars, he rode on a camel; instead of cities with houses, he lived in a goat-hair tent in the middle of a desert; and the close-knit, highly structured society of the Rashaayda made him feel uncomfortable.[2] Anthropologists, because of the nature of their research, tend to be highly motivated to learn the new culture as quickly as possible. Young, it should be noted, came from the "dominant" white culture of the West. As Young made friends with the Rashaayda and learned their way of life, his culture shock diminished. Reverse culture shock strikes when anthropologists or others returning to their native culture must readjust to their home culture. Young left the Rashaayda Bedouin after two years; when he returned home to the United States, he found it difficult to adjust to using utensils for eating, to the excessive use of water for cleaning floors or watering lawns, to the immodest dress code of most women, and to city landscapes of towering buildings and speeding vehicles.

Culture shock affects people immigrating to a country like Canada. Most immigrants attempt to fit into their new society, adopting many of its social and cultural features while preserving some aspects of their traditional culture. For example, Chinese Canadians possess a cultural identity that is neither Chinese nor Canadian, but Chinese Canadian. Despite their willingness to assimilate, culture shock is an inevitable reality for new immigrants when they find themselves in an environment where people believe, think, and act differently. This "otherness" makes people uncomfortable and insecure, and they may find themselves constantly questioning the way of life in their new country as well as in their "old" country. Nor will they become comfortable until they learn their new culture. For further discussion of the difficulties of immigrating to a new culture, see the Gender Perspectives box on page 38.

From a Canadian perspective, culture differs from society. A **society** is a group of people who live in the same geographical region, speak the same language, and are interdependent to a certain extent. A society often contains more than one cultural group—for example, in Canada there are First Nations peoples, Inuit, Métis, and English- and French-speaking Canadians, as well as immigrants from around the world. The way people in a society depend on one another is reflected in their economic systems and their family relationships. Members of a society are held together by a sense of common identity, and this identity may even be grounded in a *diversity* of identities, such as is witnessed in the **multiculturalism** of Canada, which, despite its problems and a disjuncture between theory and practice, appears to functional fairly well as a model for society. The relationships that hold a society together are known as its **social structure**.

> **society** A group of people who live in the same region, speak the same language, and are interdependent.
>
> **multiculturalism** Descriptor for a society, community, etc., made up of, involving, or relating to several distinct racial or religious cultures. Contrast with biculturalism or monoculturalism.
>
> **social structure** The relationships of groups within a society that hold it together.

In human cultures, gender roles are absorbed both consciously and unconsciously through children's play.

Original Study

The Importance of Trobriand Women

Annette B. Weiner

Walking into a village at the beginning of fieldwork is entering a world without cultural guideposts. The task of learning values that others live by is never easy. The rigors of fieldwork involve listening and watching, learning a new language of speech and actions, and most of all, letting go of one's own cultural assumptions in order to understand the meanings others give to work, power, death, family, and friends. As my fieldwork in the Trobriand Islands of Papua New Guinea was no exception, I wrestled doggedly with each of these problems. Doing research in the Trobriand Islands created one additional obstacle. I was working in the footsteps of a celebrated anthropological ancestor, Bronislaw Kasper Malinowski. . . .

In 1971, before my first trip to the Trobriands, I thought I understood many things about Trobriand customs and beliefs from having read Malinowski's exhaustive writings. Once there, however, I found that I had much more to discover about what I thought I already knew. For many months I worked with these discordant realities, always conscious of Malinowski's shadow, his words, his explanations. Although I found significant differences in areas of importance, I gradually came to understand how he reached certain conclusions. The answers we both received from informants were not so dissimilar, and I could actually trace how Malinowski had analyzed what his informants told him in a way that made sense and was scientifically significant—given what anthropologists generally then recognized about such societies. Sixty years separate our fieldwork, and any comparison of our studies illustrates not so much Malinowski's mistaken interpretations but the developments in anthropological knowledge and inquiry from his time to mine.

Although Malinowski and I were in the Trobriands at vastly different historical moments and there also are many areas in which our analyses differ, a large part of what we learned in the field was similar. From the vantage point that time gives to me, I can illustrate how our differences, even those that are major, came to be. Taken together, our two studies profoundly exemplify the scientific basis that underlies the collection of ethnographic data. Like all such data,

© Dr. William E. Mitchell

In the Trobriand Islands, women's wealth consists of skirts and banana leaves, large quantities of which must be given away on the death of a relative.

however, whether researched in a laboratory or a village, the more we learn about a subject, the more we can refine and revise earlier assumptions. This is the way all sciences create their own historical developments. Therefore, the lack of agreement between Malinowski's ethnography and mine must not be taken as an adversarial attack against an opponent. Nor should it be read as an example of the writing of ethnography as "fiction" or "partial truths." Each of our differences can be traced historically within the discipline of anthropology.

My most significant point of departure from Malinowski's analyses was the attention I gave to women's productive work. In my original research plans, women were not the central focus of study, but on the first day I took up residence in a village I was taken by them to watch a distribution of their own wealth—bundles of banana leaves and banana fiber skirts—which they exchanged with other women in commemoration of someone who had recently died. Watching that event forced me to take women's economic roles more seriously than I would have from reading Malinowski's studies. Although Malinowski noted the high status of Trobriand women, he attributed their importance to the fact that Trobrianders reckon descent through women, thereby giving them genealogical significance in a matrilineal society. Yet he never considered that this significance was underwritten by women's own wealth because he did not systematically investigate the women's productive activities. Although in his field notes he mentions Trobriand women making these seemingly useless banana bundles to be exchanged at a death, his published work only deals with men's wealth.

My taking seriously the importance of women's wealth not only brought

women as the neglected half of society clearly into the ethnographic picture but also forced me to revise many of Malinowski's assumptions about Trobriand men. For example, Trobriand kinship as described by Malinowski has always been a subject of debate among anthropologists. For Malinowski, the basic relationships within a Trobriand family were guided by the matrilineal principle of "mother-right" and "father-love." A father was called "stranger" and had little authority over his own children. A woman's brother was the commanding figure and exercised control over his sister's sons because they were members of his matrilineage rather than their father's matrilineage.

According to Malinowski, this matrilineal drama was played out biologically by the Trobrianders' belief that a man has no role as genitor. A man's wife is thought to become pregnant when an ancestral spirit enters her body and causes conception. Even after a child is born, Malinowski reported, it is the women's brother who presents a harvest of yams to his sister so that her child will be fed with food from its own matrilineage, rather than its father's matrilineage. In this way, Malinowski conceptualized matrilineality as an institution in which the father of a child, as a member of a different matrilineage, was excluded not only from participating in procreation but also from giving any objects of lasting value to his children, thus provisioning them only with love.

In my study of Trobriand women and men, a different configuration of matrilineal descent emerged. A Trobriand father is not a "stranger" in Malinowski's definition, nor is he a powerless figure as the third party to the relationship between a woman and her brother. The father is one of the most important persons in his child's life, and remains so

even after his child grows up and marries. Even a father's procreative importance is incorporated into his child's growth and development. A Trobriand man gives his child many opportunities to gain things from his matrilineage, thereby adding to the available resources that he or she can draw upon. At the same time, this giving creates obligations on the part of a man's children toward him that last even beyond his death. Therefore, the roles that men and their children play in each other's lives are worked out through extensive cycles of exchanges, which define the strength of their relationships to each other and eventually benefit the other members of both their matrilineages. Central to these exchanges are women and their wealth.

That Malinowski never gave equal time to the women's side of things, given the deep significance of their role in societal and political life, is not surprising. Only recently have anthropologists begun to understand the importance of taking women's work seriously. In some cultures, such as the Middle East or among Australian aborigines, it is extremely difficult for ethnographers to cross the culturally bounded ritual worlds that separate women from men. In the past, however, both women and men ethnographers generally analyzed the societies they studied from a male perspective. The "women's point of view" was largely ignored in the study of gender roles, since anthropologists generally perceived women as living in the shadows of men—occupying the private rather than the public sectors of society, rearing children rather than engaging in economic or political pursuits.

SOURCE: A. W einer, The Trobrianders of Papua New Guinea, *1st ed. (1988). Reprinted with permission of Wadsworth, an imprint of Thomson Learning.*

Although a culture is shared by its members, it is not entirely uniform. No member has the exact same version of his or her culture as another. Cultural variation beyond the individual is seen in the differences between the roles of men and women. These differences stem from the fact that male and female anatomy and physiology differ in obvious ways—women give birth, men do not. Every culture gives meaning to these differences by designating

expected behavioural patterns of gender. Every culture specifies how the genders should relate to each other and to the world at large. As with culture, we learn these gender roles from birth. Since each culture teaches gender roles in its own way, tremendous variation exists from one culture to another even as variation occurs *within* each culture. Given their own inherent gender bias, it is often difficult for anthropologists to interpret another culture's gender roles. Annette Weiner found that her interpretation of Trobriand gender roles for women differed considerably from that of Bronislaw Malinowski, as shown in the Original Study above, "The Importance of Trobriand Women."

The process of aging is influenced by culture. The meaning of growing old, and even how members of a culture define "old," can differ markedly, and the status and power that elderly people possess may depend on their roles and experiences in earlier life. Other examples of cultural variation involve ethnicity, occupation, social

 subculture   A cultural subgroup differentiated by status, ethnic background, residence, religion, or other factors that functionally unify the group and act collectively on each member.

class, sexual orientation, geographical distribution (e.g., eastern Canada–western Canada, rural–urban), physical or mental challenges, and special interests (such as snowboarding). Even in small groups that may appear culturally uniform, there will be many differences. Take, for example, the Muslim community of Montreal. They are all Muslims, but they come from many different countries, both Arab and non-Arab, and thus they exhibit cultural and linguistic diversity, as well as a wide range of socioeconomic statuses. When there are such groups within a society, each functioning according to its own standards of behaviour while at the same time sharing some common standards, we speak of **subcultures**. (The word "subculture," it should be noted, carries no connotation of lesser status relative to the word "culture.")

The Anthropologist's World

New Houses for Apache Indians

George S. Esber

George S. Esber teaches at Miami University and held prior teaching positions at the University of Arizona, Oberlin College, Alliance College, and Earlham College. In other applied anthropological work, he completed research projects for the National Park Service and has completed several community-driven research efforts for the Tijua Tribe of Ysleta del Sur Pueblo.

The United States, in common with other industrialized countries of the world, contains a number of more or less separate subcultures. Those who live by the standards of one particular subculture have their closest relationships with one another, receiving constant reassurance that their perceptions of the world are the only correct ones and coming to take it for granted that the whole culture is as they see it. As a consequence, members of one subculture frequently have trouble understanding the needs and aspirations of other such groups. For this reason anthropologists, with their special understanding of cultural differences, are frequently employed as go-betweens in

situations requiring interaction between peoples of differing cultural traditions.

As an example, while I was still a graduate student in anthropology, one of my professors asked me to work with architects and a community of Tonto Apache Indians to research housing needs for a new Apache community. Although the architects knew about cross-cultural differences in the use of space, they had no idea how to get relevant information from the Indian people. For their part, the Apaches had no explicit awareness of their needs, for these were based on unconscious patterns of behavior. For that matter, few people are consciously aware of the space needs for their own social patterns of behavior.

My task was to persuade the architects to hold back on their planning long enough for me to gather, through participant observation and a review of written records, the data from which Apache housing needs could be abstracted. At the same time, I had to overcome Apache anxieties over an outsider coming into their midst to learn about matters as personal as their daily lives as they are acted out, in and around their homes. With these hurdles overcome, I was able to identify and successfully communicate to the architects those features of Apache life having importance for home and community design. At the same time, discussions of my findings with the

Apaches enhanced their own awareness of their unique needs.

As a result of my work, the Apaches moved into houses that had been designed with their participation, for their specific needs. Among my findings was the realization that the Apaches preferred to ease into social interactions rather than to shake hands and begin interacting immediately, as is more typical of the Anglo pattern. Apache etiquette requires that people be in full view of one another so each can assess the behavior of others from a distance prior to engaging in social interaction with them. This requires a large, open living space. At the same time, hosts feel compelled to offer food to guests as a prelude to further social interaction. Thus, cooking and dining areas cannot be separated from living space. Nor is standard middle-class Anglo kitchen equipment suitable, since the need for handling large quantities among extended families requires large pots and pans, which in turn calls for extra-large sinks and cupboards. Built with such ideas in mind, the new houses accommodated long-standing native traditions.

Adapted from G.S. Esber, (1987). "Designing Apache Houses with Apaches," in *Anthropological Praxis: Translating Knowledge into Action*, ed. R.M. Wulff and S.J. Fiske (Boulder: Westview, 1987), 2007 update by Esber.

Hutterites are an example of an ethnic subculture found in Canada and the United States. Hutterites are one of four surviving groups (the others being the Amish, the Mennonites, and the Brethren) descended from 16th-century Anabaptists from Austria and Moravia. They fled Europe to escape religious persecution. Today more than 35,000 Hutterites live in 400 communities spread across Montana, Washington, the Dakotas, Minnesota, Manitoba, Saskatchewan, Alberta, and British Columbia.[3] The Hutterites branched into three groups named after their leaders: Schmiedeleut, Dariusleut, and Lehrerleut.

The Hutterites are a pacifist, agrarian people, and their lives revolve around deep religious beliefs. They value simplicity, hard work, and a close-knit communal lifestyle, mingling as little as possible with non-Hutterites. They dress in a distinctive modest garb, and even today they own little personal property. The colonists live a communal lifestyle, eating in a common dining hall and sharing laundry facilities, although each family has its own private apartment. Unlike the Amish or the Mennonites, Hutterites do not shun modern conveniences such as tractors, combines, appliances, and even computers.

Hutterite children attend school within their communities, where they are taught by Hutterite teachers who are committed to Hutterite values. In recent years, more emphasis has been placed on higher education, with some children completing grade twelve, some taking vocational training, and still others attending university, especially teacher-training programs.

Hutterite colonies are stratified based on gender and age. Men hold positions of authority in the colony; women cannot sit on the council or vote in colony matters, although they can express their opinions to their husbands. Young people are highly valued in Hutterite colonies but do not have any official say in the running of the colony until they are baptized in their early twenties.

The different lifestyles of Hutterites relative to mainstream Canadian society—such as choosing to live in self-sufficient, closed communities—has caused occasional misunderstandings with their neighbours. Most informed people, however, recognize that Hutterites do contribute to Canadian society. It is often thought that Hutterites do not use modern technology, but this is not the case. They purchase and use farm equipment; visit dentists, doctors, and optometrists; use banks in nearby urban centres; buy household appliances and goods; sell turkeys, chickens, hogs, and cattle to markets; and offer services such as equipment repair in nearby communities. In today's multicultural Canadian society, Hutterites are accepted and respected for their successful agricultural enterprise. For the most part, the Hutterite subculture lives in peace, isolated from yet part of Canadian society.

The experience of the Hutterites offers one example of a subculture fitting into the larger society. Different as they are, they actually practise many of the values that citizens of Canada respect in the abstract: thrift, hard work, independence, and a close family life. The degree of tolerance accorded to them is also due in part to the fact that Hutterites descend from white-skinned Europeans. Canadian Aboriginal groups were treated very differently by Europeans, who came to North America as conquerors and who defined Aboriginal values as "savage." Europeans and their descendants in what is now Canada generally accepted the notion that Aboriginal cultures would gradually assimilate into Euro-Canadian culture. But despite assimilation programs, such as residential schools, just the opposite has happened: First Nations, Métis, and Inuit cultures continue to flourish as distinct entities even as they take their place in Canadian society.

The Acadians of New Brunswick and Nova Scotia are another example of a subculture that has sought a new life in Canada (or to renew their life in Canada). Despite serious political and economic challenges, they have managed to retain their language, customs, and beliefs for centuries. The Acadians are descendants of approximately 100 French families who settled on the banks of the Bay of Fundy in the 17th century.[4] They were fishers and farmers with a strong sense of community and independence, living peaceful, prosperous lives and raising large families (i.e., relative to today's smaller families).

In 1755 the British government demanded that the Acadians sign an oath of allegiance to the Crown. Those who refused (about 8,000 people) were deported to New England, the American colonies, and Europe. This expulsion had a dramatic impact on the Acadians' sense of security and community; it also had a lasting effect on their economic well-being. Even though the Acadians were allowed to return to Canada in 1764, they found their fertile lands in the hands of new settlers. The Acadians were forced into small settlements scattered along the remote coastal regions, which had the effect of breaking up their tight-knit communities.

In the 21st century, economic problems are the greatest threat to Acadian solidarity and cultural integrity. The land they farm is poor, their fishing grounds are nearly depleted, and the region has little economic or industrial development. Each year more young Acadians are forced to leave their communities in search of employment in other parts of Canada. Consequently, the Acadian subculture and way of life are once more in jeopardy, this time from economic rather than political causes.

Implicit in the discussion thus far is the fact that subcultures may develop in different ways. The Hutterite subculture emerged as the product of how they have communicated and interacted in pursuit of their common goals within the wider society, whereas the

Acadians, although still quite distinct, have undergone some assimilation owing to economic realities that have forced many to leave their communities. Meanwhile, Aboriginal subcultures are the result of once independent cultures having been forcibly brought under the control of the Canadian federal government.[5] Although all Aboriginal cultures have undergone change as a result, they have remained different enough from Canadian immigrant subcultures to be considered distinct cultures as opposed to subcultures. In this sense, *culture* and *subculture* represent opposite ends of a continuum, with no clear dividing line in the "grey area" between.

Sometimes a subculture appears to operate outside mainstream society, as in the case of Goth, "Gamer," or hip-hop subcultures. Young people, wearing unique clothing and hairstyles and various body piercings, join punk subcultures partly because they feel alienated from mainstream adolescent culture and yearn to be part of a meaningful group outside the norm. Punk subcultures tend to be male dominated; however, Dr. Lauraine Leblanc of McGill University refutes the male-centred view that females are passive participants in punk subcultures. Rather, she suggests that by joining punk groups, females are resisting the gender norms of mainstream society. Punk subcultures offer young women a place in the world where they do not have to conform to typical gender roles and take on a "normal" gender identity, and where they can assert their independence and individuality.[6]

This examination of culture and subculture reveals the pluralistic nature of Canadian society. Canada is a cultural mosaic of many ethnic subcultures, as are most societies today (see Figure 2.1). For well over a century, people have been coming to Canada from virtually every corner of the world.[7] These people have brought their ideals, beliefs, languages, and cultural customs and traditions to their new home. And although these home cultures have changed over time, today's Canadian identity owes much to these intrepid immigrants. **Pluralistic societies**, such as Canada, contain several distinct cultures and subcultures. Although we define subculture as any group of people with a set of standards and behaviour distinct from the larger society, we are usually referring to ethnic subcultures when we say that Canada is a pluralistic society. Ethnic subcultures possess an ethnic identity or **ethnicity** that

pluralistic societies Societies that contain several distinct cultures and subcultures.

ethnicity A group of people who take their identity from a common place of origin, history, and sense of belonging.

ethnic boundary markers Those indicators or characteristics, such as dress and language, that identify individuals as belonging to a particular ethnic group.

Figure 2.1

Shown here are a few of the ethnic groups of the Russian Federation. Contrary to popular belief, the ethnic conflicts that have broken out since the collapse of the Soviet Union stem not from the supposedly conflictive nature of ethnicity but from Stalin's policy of emphasizing ethnicity while preventing its expression and forcibly removing populations from their homelands to new localities.

is based on a shared sense of identity drawing on cultural traits passed down through generations. These cultural traits, or **ethnic boundary markers**—which include history, beliefs, values, traditions, language, dress, and food—set ethnic subcultures apart from other groups. Religion is one marker that distinguishes ethnic subcultures; for example, the Sikhs of India identify with their religious beliefs, which are separate from those of other Indians. Place of origin and history can also provide groups with a distinctive identity. Ukrainian Canadians' identity originates in several regions of the Ukraine (e.g., Karpatu) from which their ancestors immigrated to Canada. On the other hand, the diasporic Roma (Gypsies of Europe) do not possess an actual homeland; they take their ethnic identity from their lifestyle and history.[8] The Roma have been living in different nations for centuries, such as Romania, France, Greece, Hungary, and Bulgaria. Language is one of the most powerful boundary markers, as seen in the Québécois and the Acadians of Canada, although the Acadians separate their culture from that of the Québécois and base their ethnic identity on a distinctive history and heritage. A sense of historical continuity also gives diasporic Jews their identity, even if they no longer attend synagogue, speak Yiddish or Hebrew, or follow Jewish customs. Nova Scotia blacks settled in small communities such as Africville, on the outskirts of Halifax, in the 1800s. Their strong sense of community sustained them even in the face of systemic racism, and when Halifax officials forcefully relocated them, their memories of their community bonds continued to give them a sense of identity. Indeed the history of some of the immigrant groups to Canada has not been without hardships. Chinese immigrants were forced to pay a "head tax," and many Japanese immigrants were interred in camps during the Second World War. Recent apologies from the federal government notwithstanding, the memories of these hardships inflicted by the Canadian government have lingered on.

Distinctive clothing and food, such as the Sikh turban (*dastar*), Scottish kilts, Ukrainian perogies, and Mexican tacos, are all symbols easily associated with particular ethnic subcultures. However, identification of ethnic subcultures is not always so clear-cut. For example, Serbs and Croats speak the same language, Serbo-Croatian, yet they are distinct ethnic subcultures; and the Samals of the Philippines, Moors of Sri Lanka, and Pashtun of Afghanistan are all Muslim, yet they are distinct ethnic subcultures.

The importance of ethnicity may also vary. In some ethnic subcultures, such as the Palestinians, ethnicity and ethnic identity are of paramount importance, while in others it may no longer seem so relevant. A lack of emphasis on ethnicity is most evident in countries like Canada, where some descendants of 19th- and 20th-century immigrants may seldom consider their ancestry. Although not that common, new ethnic groups may also arise, as occurred when French voyageurs and Scottish settlers married First Nations women in Canada, sometimes Cree, during the fur trade era and their offspring became the Métis. Métis means "mixed," and they are considered one of the three Aboriginal groups in Canada, along with the Inuit and First Nations. The National Historic Site of Batoche, near Saskatoon, celebrates the Métis culture; interpretive displays at that site describe Métis cultural aspects such as their clothing (the famous sashes and HBC blankets), their food (bannock), and their language (Michif). The Métis are testament to the fact that cultural diversity and emerging subcultures existed in Canada long before the decades of modern immigration.

The pluralistic nature of Canadian society is not without its problems. Members of one cultural group may have difficulty understanding the needs and concerns of another. The separatist movement in Quebec is a case in point. French Canadians have always feared losing their language and culture and becoming assimilated into English Canada. These fears have created a strong Quebec nationalism and a vocal movement to achieve independence from the rest of Canada. French Canadian alienation has led to two Quebec referendums on the question of separation from Canada—one in 1980 and the most recent in 1995, when separatism was narrowly defeated. Despite repeated attempts on both sides to develop a symbiotic relationship, the future of Quebec in Canada remains unclear.

However, most subcultures in Canadian society have found ways to adapt to the pluralistic nature of Canada. Today, most subcultures have embraced Canadian society and willingly contribute to Canada's well-being with their beliefs in social tolerance and harmony.

The Canadian government has endeavoured to accommodate the needs of subcultures as much as possible in order to build peaceful relations among subcultures. However, the degree of cultural accommodation is always in question and at times has caused generated tensions between groups. The recent attempt to adopt *sharia* law when dealing with some family disputes in Ontario is a case in point.[9] *Sharia* law is generally sensationalized and misunderstood by non-Muslims; as a result, the proposal to adopt it was met with outrage and fear by many Canadians, including Canadian Muslims. *Sharia* law is interpreted in different ways and deals with a wide variety of issues such as secular law, criminal law, and daily behaviour. Many women feared that *sharia* law would threaten the equality of Muslim women and that Muslim women would be discriminated against in divorce or child custody cases. In the face of these objections, the Ontario government backed away from religious-based arbitration for all religions in Ontario.[10]

CP Photo/Paul Chiasson

Even in politically stable countries like Canada, pluralism presents its own challenges. In Canada, the Quebec separatist movement continues to challenge Canadian unity.

Gender Perspectives

Gender Inequities in the Canadian Immigrant Experience

Canada's multicultural image draws thousands of new immigrants to the country every year. But is immigrating to Canada always a positive experience? According to Giles (2002), Canada's immigration policy is deeply gendered. She found that Portuguese immigrant women experience gender inequities, beginning with the qualification process, which is based on work skills. Given the generally low education levels and skills training among women in developing countries, this policy ensures that many immigrant women will be defined as familial dependants (financially dependent on their husbands), which in turn places them in a subordinate position compared to men, even if they find employment to help support their families.

Once in Canada, both male and female immigrants face daunting challenges as they begin adjusting to a new and strange environment, one in which their traditional cultural system may no longer fit. Many immigrant men and women experience difficulty in finding employment in their field, regardless of their professional status in their home country. Although they are promised economic prosperity and career opportunities before immigrating to Canada, many immigrants once here find that employers are reluctant to hire them for reasons as far ranging as poor English or French language skills, inadequate training or qualifications, or lack of Canadian experience. Language fluency presents a major challenge for immigrant women, who may be more housebound than their husbands or who may experience difficulty finding child care in order to take language courses.

In a qualitative study of immigrant experiences among Pakistani women, Khan and Watson (2005) found that joblessness and underemployment were the main reasons for stress in their families, and that the women expressed grief over the "loss of prosperity, the good life, and professional status" they enjoyed in their home countries (308). Accounts of doctors and engineers whose professional credentials have not been accepted in Canada and who have been forced to take low-paying, dead-end jobs to support their families are all too common. Indeed, Statistics Canada reported that in 2004, low-income rates were 3.2 times higher in immigrant families (Jiménez 2007) than in the general population.

Gender relationships and power structures may become strained in immigrant families. Immigrants from a patriarchal society, in which women are subordinate, may experience difficulties with the changing dynamics within families. Giles (2002) found that some women continued to accept their subordinate position, while others struggled against it; this likely caused added friction within the family. These occurrences were particularly true of second-generation Portuguese women, who challenged the traditional gender roles of their mothers yet still felt a compelling responsibility toward their families. Some Pakistani women in Khan and Watson's (2005) study reported deteriorating spousal relationships, mainly because of their dire financial situation.

Generational clashes are also a very real possibility in immigrant families. In this form of culture shock, parents wish to hold on to their traditional family values, including modest dress codes, supervised dating, and marriage rules for their children. Portuguese mothers and daughters clash over gender relations, with the mothers intent on maintaining traditional gender roles, while the daughters, who have become immersed in Canadian culture, challenge these restrictions. Pakistani mothers also worry that their children will pick up immoral sexual behaviour from other Canadians or become disrespectful to their elders. Some Canadian students of East Indian descent reach a compromise with their traditional parents over dating: the parents choose a prospective partner for their daughter to date, but the young woman can refuse to marry the man if she does not like him.

Readers should not construe that immigrants are helpless victims. Although their first few years in Canada may be challenging, once they apply coping strategies to help them adjust to their new home, they become comfortable in Canadian society. Pakistani women reported turning to their religion and reading the Quran to find strength. This is a common strategy, as a religious community can provide a place for immigrants to meet and broaden their social and ethnic networks. Acquiring language skills, an education, and employable skills are also valuable coping strategies.

SOURCES: W. Giles, Portuguese Women in Toronto: Gender, Immigration, and Nationalism (Toronto: University of Toronto Press, 2002); S. Khan and J.C. Watson, "The Canadian Immigration Experiences of Pakistani Women: Dreams Confront Reality," *Counselling Psychology Quarterly* 18, no. 4 (2005): 307–17; N. Jiménez, (2007, January 31). *"Immigrants Battle Chronic Low Income,"* CTVglobemedia.com.

Culture Is Learned

All culture is learned rather than biologically inherited. This has prompted anthropologist Ralph Linton to refer to it as humanity's "social heredity." People learn their culture as they grow up. Since culture first emerged early in our species' history, it has been taught and learned. Whether this is seen in early hominid infants watching an elder make stone tools millions of years ago, or teenagers learning the skill of hunting by studying the cave paintings in France 30,000 years ago, we have watched, learned, copied, and improved on our cultural skills. The process whereby culture is transmitted from one generation to the next is called **enculturation**.

Through enculturation we learn the socially appropriate ways to satisfy our biologically determined needs. Most animals eat and drink whenever the urge arises. Humans, however, do most of their eating and drinking at certain culturally prescribed times and feel hungry as those times approach. These eating times vary from culture to culture, as does what is eaten and how it is eaten. Food is used to do more than merely satisfy nutritional requirements. When used to celebrate rituals and religious activities, food "establishes relationships of give and take, of cooperation, of sharing, of an emotional bond that is universal."[11] Besides food and sleep, humans require shelter, safety, and sexual gratification. We must distinguish between the needs themselves, which are not learned, and the learned ways they are satisfied. Thus, a Canadian's idea of a comfortable way to sleep may vary greatly from that of a Japanese person.

Besides satisfying biological needs, enculturation teaches us how to "fit in" and be accepted by other members of our cultural group. Every society, Canada included, possesses multiple enculturative forces. Take, for example, a young child entering school. From the very first day of kindergarten, a child begins learning how to act and behave appropriately—at least in an educational environment. Other enculturative forces include family, peers, religious organizations, and the media (it should be noted that not all enculturative forces are positive all of the time—learning to smoke, for example). The enculturation process is never complete. Old patterns of behaviour are altered to meet the changing needs of society, and new patterns are developed. Although the older generation typically passes on knowledge to the younger generation, older people can also learn from the young, especially during times of rapid change.

To return to our earlier discussion of culture shock, once an individual living in a foreign country learns the customs, beliefs, and norms of the culture, he or she will no longer experience culture shock. However, we should recognize that this is an ongoing process that requires patience, persistence, and a great deal of time.

Culture Is Based On Symbols

Culture is symbolic in nature. Language, signs, dress, and behaviour are all cultural and all based on the use of symbols. When anthropologist Leslie White observed that human behaviour originates in the use of symbols, he was expressing a view widely shared by anthropologists. For example, a Christian cross, an Islamic crescent, a Jewish Star of David, or any object of worship may bring to mind centuries of struggle and persecution or may symbolize a philosophy or creed.

The most important symbolic aspect of culture is language—the ability to name and pronounce ideas and things. Language makes it possible for people to learn from cumulative shared experience and to transmit culture from one generation to the next. Without it, we could not inform others about events they were not a party to; express ideas, hopes, and dreams; or teach appropriate behaviour. We will consider the important relationship between language and culture in greater detail in Chapter 4.

Culture Is Integrated

For comparison and analysis, anthropologists normally break a culture down into many seemingly discrete parts, even though such distinctions are arbitrary. While

Courtesy of Shirley Fedorak

This *inukshuk* is a symbol of presence, left by Inuit people as they travelled their lands. They served a variety of functions; for example, they were used as landmarks or to locate food caches.

enculturation The process that transmits a society's culture from one generation to the next.

examining one specific aspect of a culture, because many aspects are linked, the anthropologist must examine other aspects as well. The tendency for all aspects of a culture to function as an interrelated whole is called **integration**.

The integration of the economic, political, and social aspects of a culture can be illustrated by the Kapauku Papuans, a mountain people of western New Guinea studied in 1955 by American anthropologist Leopold Pospisil.[12] The Kapauku economy relied on plant cultivation, along with pig breeding, hunting, and fishing. Although plant cultivation provided most of the people's food, men achieved political power and positions of legal authority through the complex business of pig breeding.

Kapauku pig breeding relied on sweet potatoes grown in garden plots by the women, who also cared for the pigs. Thus, to raise many pigs, a man needed many women in the household. Multiple wives (polygyny) was not just permitted—it was highly desired by the Kapauku. For each wife, however, a man paid a bride price. Furthermore, wives had to be compensated for their care of pigs. Put simply, it took pigs, by which wealth was measured, to get wives, which were necessary to raise pigs in the first place. Needless to say, this required considerable entrepreneurship. It was this entrepreneurial ability that produced leaders in Kapauku society.

The interrelatedness of the various parts of Kapauku culture was even more complex than this. For example, one condition conducive to polygyny was a surplus of adult women. In the Kapauku case, warfare was endemic and regarded as a necessary evil. By the rules of Kapauku warfare, men were killed but not women. This system created the kind of imbalance of sexes that facilitated polygyny. Also, polygyny works best if wives come to live in their husband's village rather than the other way around, and this was the case among the Kapauku. Thus, the men of a village were "blood" relatives of one another, creating a patrilineal (descent reckoned through men) emphasis in Kapauku culture.

This historical example by no means exhausts the interrelationships found in Kapauku culture. For example, both patrilineality and endemic warfare promoted male dominance, so it is not surprising to find that positions of leadership in Kapauku society were held exclusively by men, who appropriated the products of women's labour in order to play their political "games." Despite assertions to the contrary, male dominance is not characteristic of all human

societies. Rather, as with the Kapauku, it arises only in particular circumstances that, if changed, would alter the way men and women relate to each other.

From what has been said so far, we might suppose that the various parts of a culture must operate in perfect harmony at all times.

While a degree of harmony is necessary in any properly functioning culture, we should not assume that *complete* harmony is required. Because no two individuals experience the enculturation process in precisely the same way, no two individuals perceive their culture in the same way, and this creates potential for change. There is usually an element of consistency in culture. So long as the parts are reasonably consistent, a culture will operate reasonably well. If, however, that strain toward consistency breaks down, a situation of cultural crisis ensues.

POPULAR CULTURE

As you have seen, culture is shared, learned, symbolic, and integrated. One element of culture that has until recently suffered from anthropological neglect, yet epitomizes this statement, is popular culture.[13] Popular culture is the culture of our everyday lives—the music, dance, legends, food, games, and folk art—that every cultural group enjoys and that gives meaning to their lives. The artifacts or symbols of popular culture—the vampire movies, car hood automobilia, sports clothing, patchwork quilts, banana skirts, children's dolls, and so on—all hold meaning and provide messages about a people and their way of life.

Like all culture, popular culture is dynamic; each generation learns, modifies, and makes popular culture its own. Rock 'n' roll is an example of the durability, yet adaptability, of popular culture. Rock 'n' roll music has been amazingly popular for more than four decades, yet within the genre, there is considerable variety in styles, from country rock to heavy metal, from glam rock to punk rock. Each type of rock 'n' roll has its own fans, who may take a shared identity from their particular brand of rock 'n' roll, even to the point of forming **microcultures**, such as the new wave hip-hop movement. Forms of popular culture may also disappear if they are

integration   The tendency for all aspects of a culture to function as an interrelated whole.

microculture   A group of people who share common interests and or experiences, from which they take their identity.

no longer valued by consumers. This happened to North American drive-in restaurants with their roller-skating carhops; although very popular gathering places for young people in the 1950s and 1960s, they were rejected in the 1970s as young people turned to shopping malls for their meeting places. Yet elements of popular culture that fade away may re-emerge years later and become popular once again, two examples being retro furniture and the dreaded bell-bottom pants. Since culture is integrated, to study popular culture would be impossible without also examining related institutions of culture. For example, Islamic Ramadan contains many elements of popular culture, just as Christian Christmas does, but we cannot ignore the underlying religious and ritual significance.

Popular culture is linked to class—those of the elite upper classes will have access to Shakespearean plays and symphonies, while hip-hop music, bars, and other forms of popular culture are more accessible to the far more numerous lower classes. Obviously, popular culture can be used to demarcate social boundaries. Popular culture is also a powerful influence on our ideas and values; it can generate political commentary, mirror changing social values and societal practices, and even influence the way we view the world around us. This becomes evident from a historical perspective if we examine the impact of the punk rock movement of the 1970s. Punks rejected mainstream society and advocated an anarchic social "order" that, although short-lived, provided powerful influences on many elements of Western mainstream society—such as its music (Sex Pistols, Green Day), appearance (leather clothing), and social behaviour (antisocial views, mindaltering drugs)—influences that persist to this day.

Popular culture also symbolizes the struggle to maintain a distinctive social and/or cultural identity. Ojibwa artists who create dream catchers—a craft that has been handed down through the generations—are expressing and preserving their cultural identity. Quilt making is an age-old folk art that possesses substantial cultural meaning and remains an integral part of the history and heritage of groups such as the Canadian Doukhobors, a group of Christians who came to Canada in the late 19th century from Russia and who believe in a literal reading of the Bible.

It has often been asked whether mass media popular culture has a negative effect on consumers. Critics have voiced concern about too much violence, explicit sex, escapism, and hyperconsumerism. On the other hand, audiences today are more highly educated, more aware of the world around them, and more willing to become involved in the global community than any generation before them. Indeed, popular culture can promote tolerance of other entertainments and perpetuate a form of cultural pluralism.[14]

Global communication systems and mass media have facilitated the diffusion of popular culture. There are worries that diffusion of Western popular culture to

Alexander Nicholson/Sandy Nicholson/Getty

Sports, as a major component of popular culture, play an important role in daily life. Ice hockey is considered Canada's national sport. In this image, Canadian ice hockey players contemplate their next move.

other countries may result in a homogenization of popular culture and the loss of many of its traditional forms. Will this happen? Some, such as Combs, believe that we are already seeing the formation of a "common language" that is uniting young people the world over, people who dress similarly, idolize the same rock groups, read the same popular fiction, and watch the same movies.[15] On the other hand, a resurgence of traditional popular culture is just as likely. Diffusion of popular culture is a reciprocal process; traditional popular culture, often in the form of music or fashion, has also diffused to Western popular culture.

As mentioned earlier, anthropologists have been reluctant to consider popular culture as a serious research topic. Yet popular culture permeates virtually every aspect of our lives, and therefore is a powerful force in human cultures.

CULTURE AND CHANGE

All cultures change over time, although not always as rapidly or as dramatically as many are doing today. Missionism, colonialism, and other forces have sent waves of culture change through most cultures. In North American culture, clothing fashions change frequently. In the past few decades

Dynamic Anthropology

Canadian Anthropology Society/La Société canadienne d'anthropologie

Liam Kilmurray

Culture, in all its manifestations, is the stock and trade of anthropology. In Canada, one of the prominent institutions that promotes cultural research is the Canadian Anthropology Society/ La Société canadienne d'anthropologie (CASCA). CASCA was founded in 1974 at Laval University and underwent a series of name changes and incorporations until 1988. Some of the goals of CASCA are to ensure continuing financial support for anthropological research; "to commit to excellence in Canadian anthropology graduate programmes and in the teaching of undergraduate anthropology; and to provide a platform to anthropologists practicing the discipline outside of academia."

CASCA publishes a journal called *Anthropologica* and a bulletin called *Culture*, both of which report on Canadian anthropological research as well as cultural developments around the world. Contributors come from both academic and professional (applied) anthropology. Since 2005, CASCA has held annual conferences, sometimes outside Canada—for example, in 2005 it was held at Mérida in the Yucatan. The 2010 conference was held at Concordia University in Montreal as part of the 2010 Congress. That anthropology conference was titled "Anthropological Connections" and focused on how modern technologies such as the Internet might harness and facilitate anthropological research. The Concordia conference drew together a large number of Canadian and international anthropologists, professors, graduate and undergraduate students, and interested members of the public.

The importance of CASCA to Canadian anthropological research into culture is evident in the diversity of the attendees and in the topics addressed at its conferences, where well-known Canadian and international anthropologists present new ideas and research into cultural fields. Also, students wishing to present their research or simply listen to debates and presentations have been present at many of the sessions.

At one such session, chaired by this author (Kilmurray), topics ranged from the interpretation of 5,000-year-old European monuments, to the oral traditions of contemporary Cree goose hunters in northern Ontario, to media coverage of breast cancer among Canadian women. Such a broad range of cultural issues made this a fascinating gathering devoted to the study, understanding, promotion, and preservation of the anthropological study of culture in Canada. CASCA is only one of the organizations in Canada devoted to the study of culture. There exist a wide array of similar organizations, some regional in scale, others provincial or national. What they share is a commitment to learning and understanding the fascinating world of culture.

For students wishing to get involved with CASCA or to learn more about it, the website is http://www.cas-sca.ca.

it has become culturally permissible for men and women alike to bare more of their bodies, and not just while swimming but on the street as well. Along with this change has come greater permissiveness about the body in photographs and movies, as the sexual attitudes and practices of North Americans have become less restrictive. These changes are interrelated, reflecting an underlying change in attitudes toward cultural rules regarding sexuality.

Although cultures must be able to adapt, cultural change can bring unexpected and often disastrous results. A case in point is the droughts that periodically afflict so many people living in Africa just south of the Sahara Desert. Native to this region are some 14 million pastoral nomadic people whose lives are centred on cattle and other livestock, which they herd from place to place as required for pasturage and water. For thousands of years these people went about their business, efficiently using vast areas of arid lands in ways that had allowed them to survive severe drought many times in the past. Unfortunately for them, their nomadic lifestyle, which makes it difficult to impose controls on

them and takes them across international boundaries at will, makes them a source of annoyance to some governments of the postcolonial states of the region. Seeing nomads as a challenge to their authority, these governments have tried hard to convert them into sedentary villagers. Overgrazing has resulted from this loss of mobility, a problem compounded by governmental efforts to involve the pastoralists in a market economy by encouraging them to raise many more animals than required for their own needs in order to have a surplus to sell. The resultant devastation, where previously no significant overgrazing or erosion had occurred, now makes droughts far more disastrous than they would otherwise be and places the former nomads, very existence in jeopardy.[16]

Historically, First Nations peoples of Canada have undergone dramatic changes in their lifestyles, largely as a result of European (English, French, and Spanish) colonial expansion into North America. Many First Nations groups were encouraged to give up their traditional subsistence strategies and enter the commercial fur trade. When the fur trade collapsed, they were

Although pastoral nomads are often blamed for causing the sort of environmental degradation evident here, the fault is not theirs. Rather, it lies with the governments of countries that restrict their movements, thereby causing overgrazing.

Sean Sprague/Sprague Photo

faced with economic ruin. At the same time, bison populations were declining dramatically, and European settlers were coveting First Nations' traditional hunting territories. All of these factors left many First Nations peoples destitute. The government's response was to relocate (sometimes forcefully) First Nations peoples onto resource-poor reserves and compel them to take up European-style agriculture. Government officials, aided by European missionary services, removed (again forcefully) First Nations children from their homes and settled them in residential schools to be "civilized." These measures led to the disruption of First Nations cultures. Today, however, First Nations peoples are reclaiming their heritage and demanding that their needs be recognized. They are regaining control of their lives through land claims settlements, social healing, and self-government. Thus a future culture change is envisioned, whereby First Nations become more self-sufficient and recover from enforced colonial culture change.

CULTURE, SOCIETY, AND THE INDIVIDUAL

Ultimately, culture and society are no more than a union of individuals, all of whom have their own special needs and interests. If a society is to survive, it must succeed in balancing the self-interests of its members, often from many cultural backgrounds, against the demands of the society as a whole. To accomplish this, a society offers rewards for adherence to its standards.

To ensure the survival of the group, each person must learn to overcome certain immediate satisfactions. Yet the needs of the individual cannot be suppressed too far, lest stress levels become too much to bear. Hence, a delicate balance always exists between personal interests and the demands the group makes on each individual.

Take the matter of sex, which is important in any culture, for it helps strengthen cooperative bonds between men and women and ensures the perpetuation of the culture itself. Yet sex can be disruptive to social living; if it is not clearly spelled out who has sexual access to whom, over-competition for sexual privileges can destroy the cooperative bonds that human survival depends on. Uncontrolled sexual activity, too, can result in reproductive rates that cause a society's population to outstrip its resources. Hence, as it shapes sexual behaviour, every culture must balance the needs of the whole against the need for sufficient individual gratification, lest frustration build until it causes disruption. Of course, cultures vary widely in the ways they resolve this dilemma. Resolutions range all the way from the restrictive approach of British and Canadian society in the late 19th and early 20th centuries, which specified no sex out of wedlock, to practices among the Canela of eastern Brazil that

Stephen Homer/First Light

In Canada, First Nations peoples have exhibited symptoms of stress brought on by frustration and a sense of hopelessness when their needs are not met by society. Yet Aboriginal peoples of Canada have shown remarkable resilience. Shown here is a woman fishing from a canoe.

guarantee that, sooner or later, everyone in a given village will have had sex with just about everyone of the opposite sex. Permissive though the latter situation may seem to Westerners, strict rules specify how the system operates.[17]

It is not just in sex that cultures must strike a balance between the needs of individuals and those of society. When the needs of society take precedence, people can experience excessive stress. Symptomatic of this stress are increased levels of mental illness and behaviour regarded as antisocial: violence, crime, abuse of alcohol and other drugs, suicide, and alienation. If not corrected, the situation can result in cultural breakdown. But just as problems develop if the needs of society take precedence over those of individuals, so do they develop if the balance is upset in the other direction.

EVALUATION OF CULTURE

The question often arises: Which culture is best? In the 19th century, Europeans (and European North Americans), in the throes of colonialism, had few doubts about the answer—they saw their civilization as the peak of human development. At the same time, though, anthropologists were intrigued to discover that all cultures they encountered saw themselves as the best of all possible worlds. Commonly, this point of view was reflected in peoples' names for their societies, which, roughly translated, usually meant "we human beings," as opposed to outsiders, who were called, essentially, "you subhumans." For example, the name Inuit means "the people." Anthropologists now know that many cultures regard themselves as the best, a view reflecting a phenomenon known as **ethnocentrism**. Hence, the 19th-century Europeans and Euro-Canadians were merely displaying their own ethnocentrism. Ethnocentrism is a deeply engrained attitude found in most cultures; to believe that our culture is functioning at optimum efficiency and that we are living a good life is a natural feeling. Problems arise when ethnocentrism is taken to extremes; then it becomes harmful. The Nazi program of extermination can be said to have stemmed from ethnocentric thinking, as could the idea that Aboriginal peoples were inferior. Ethnocentrism can prevent us from questioning our customs, traditions, and even our beliefs, and perhaps developing new ways of doing things. Ethnocentrism can also hinder understanding and appreciating other cultures and other ways of living. In its extreme form, ethnocentrism can lead to prejudice and

racism—ethnic conflict common throughout the world, in part as a result of extreme ethnocentrism.

Anthropologists have been engaged actively in the fight against ethnocentrism ever since they started to study non-Western peoples and discovered they were just as human as anyone else. As a consequence, anthropologists began to examine each culture on its own terms, asking whether or not the culture satisfied its people's needs and expectations, and acknowledging that the way "others" see the world is as just as valid. If a cultural group practised human sacrifice, for example, anthropologists investigated the circumstances that made the taking of human life acceptable according to the culture's values. The idea that one must suspend judgment on other peoples' practices in order to understand them in their own cultural terms is known as **cultural relativism**. Cultural relativism refutes ethnocentrism and, like holism and cross-cultural comparison, has become common in anthropological fieldwork. The anthropologists' mission is not to transform a culture, nor to judge it, although they will form their own opinions; rather, it is to determine the reasons for certain behaviour. Only through such an approach can anthropologists gain an undistorted view of another people's ways, as well as insights into the practices of their own culture.

Take, for example, the 16th-century Aztec practice of sacrificing humans for ritual purposes. Few (if any) North Americans today would condone such practices, but by suspending judgment we can get beneath the surface and understand how it functioned so as to reassure the populace that the Aztec state was healthy and that the sun would remain in the heavens. Beyond this, we might understand how the death penalty functions in the same way in countries such as the United States and China today. Numerous studies by a variety of social scientists have shown clearly that the death penalty does not deter violent crime, any more than Aztec sacrifice really provided sustenance for the sun. In fact, cross-cultural studies show that homicide rates mostly decline after abolition of the death penalty.[18] For the Aztec, sacrifice was a "symbolic representation of hierarchical relations and tribute obligations, death as a sacrificial offering was a fitting punishment for insubordination and the refusal to pay tribute."[19] As anthropologists Anthony Parades and Elizabeth D. Purdum point out, it "reassures many that society is not out of control after all, that the majesty of the law reigns and that God is indeed in his heaven."[20]

Cultural relativism is an important approach in anthropology, but one that is not without controversy. Many anthropologists question the distance and objectiveness they must maintain to be culturally relative. Furthermore, they grapple with issues of human rights versus anthropological professionalism and how to reconcile one's own deep beliefs with the professional "distance" that anthropology sometimes requires. Human rights advocates argue

ethnocentrism The practice of judging other cultures from the perspective of one's own culture.

cultural relativism The thesis that one must suspend judgment on other peoples' practices to understand them in their own cultural terms.

that cultural freedom does not give *carte blanche* to practices such as ethnic cleansing, political torture, or gender inequalities. If a practice is potentially harmful to members of the culture, they feel it should be stopped. Anthropologists struggle to reconcile their own sense of human rights and morality with their responsibilities as objective scientists.

Human rights is a difficult concept to define clearly, since it appears to mean different things to different people and tends to be misused in order to serve various agendas. One definition is found in the UN's Preamble to the Universal Declaration of Human Rights (1948): "Recognition of the inherent dignity and of the equal and inalienable rights of all members of the human family is the foundation of freedom, justice and peace in the world." So the question becomes, "What is a violation of human rights?" For example, is requiring women to follow *purdah* and wear the *hijab* an *expression* or a *violation* of human rights? Is placing elderly North Americans in seniors' residences a form of elder abuse or a protection of their human rights and dignity? These are difficult questions, and the answers will vary from one culture to another, and indeed, within any given culture. Anthropologists are not required to provide the answers, although they will certainly express their opinions if asked; they must, however, serve as a conduit for voices from within a culture that may otherwise go unheard. Although it is extremely difficult, anthropologists must attempt to strike a balance between cultural relativism and human rights.[21]

Anthropological cultural relativism is an important counter to ethnocentrism, because if we refuse to recognize that there are other world views and other ways of living that are just as valid as our own, then we face the danger of cultural imperialism. As we saw in Chapter 1, cultural imperialism is the promotion of one culture's values, customs, and beliefs over all others, which ultimately results in the destruction or significant alteration of another culture. Cultural imperialism is very evident in the West: we often use our economic, political, and military power to force other nations to adopt our values, beliefs, and customs and leave behind their traditional lifeways.

While anthropologists avoid the "anything goes" position of cultural relativism, they also must avoid the pitfall of judging the practices of other cultures in terms of ethnocentric criteria. A still useful formula for measuring the success of a culture was devised more than 40 years ago by anthropologist Walter Goldschmidt.[22] In his view, the important question to ask is this: How well does a given culture satisfy the physical and psychological needs of those whose behaviour it guides? Specific indicators are found in the nutritional and physical and mental health of its population; the incidence of violence, crime, and delinquency; the demographic structure; the stability and tranquillity of domestic life; relations with neighbouring groups; and the group's relationship to its resource base. The culture

One sign that a culture possesses structural problems and has malcontent within it relates to the occurrence of crime and punishment. According to the International Centre for Prison Studies at Kings College London, in December 2008 the United States had the highest number of prison inmates per capita in the world. American inmate populations were 2.29 million; the same year, in China, there were 1.57 million sentenced prisoners with a further 850,000 held in "administrative detention"; if these had been included, the overall Chinese total would have been over 2.4 million that year, and the world total over 10.65 million. In Russia there were 890,000 inmates (see Roy Walmsley, *World Prison Population List* (8th ed.), http://www.kcl.ac.uk/depsta/law/research/icps/downloads/wppl-8th_41.pdf).

of a people who experience high rates of malnutrition, violence, crime, delinquency, suicide, emotional disorders and despair, and environmental degradation may be said to be operating less successfully. In a well-working culture, people "can be proud, jealous, and fascinating and live a very satisfactory life without feeling 'angst,' 'alienation,' 'anomie,' 'depression,' or any of the other pervasive ills of our own sometimes inhuman and civilized way of living."[23]

A culture is essentially a system to ensure the continued well-being of a group of people; therefore, it may be termed successful as long as it secures the survival of a society in a way that its members recognize as reasonably fulfilling. What complicates matters is that any society is made up of groups with different interests, which raises the possibility that some people's interests may be served better than others. Therefore, a culture that is quite fulfilling for one group within a society may be less so for another. For this reason, anthropologists always must ask this: Whose needs, and whose survival, are best served by the culture in question? The anthropological approach can provide a reasonably objective judgment regarding how well a culture is working.

human rights A set of guidelines for the equal treatment of all people, regardless of gender, age, or ethnicity.

Chapter Summary

1. What is culture?

As anthropologists see it, culture consists of the abstract values, beliefs, and perceptions of the world that lie behind people's behaviour and that are reflected in that behaviour. These elements are shared by members of a cultural group, and when they are acted upon, they produce behaviour that is intelligible to other members of that culture. Culture is learned largely through the medium of language rather than inherited biologically. The parts of a culture such as economy, spirituality, kinship, and so on, function as an integrated whole.

2. Why do cultures exist?

While distinct cultures differ in numerous ways, anthropologists have noted that cultures display remarkable similarities in that they fulfill the needs of their members. To survive, a culture must satisfy the basic needs of its members and deal with problems and matters that concern these members. It must provide for its own continuity, and it must furnish an orderly existence. In doing so, a culture must strike a balance between the self-interests of individuals and the needs of society as a whole. Also, a culture must have the capacity to change and adapt to new circumstances or to altered perceptions of existing circumstances.

3. How are cultures evaluated?

Cultures are not uniform. All is not uniform within any culture; one reason is that some differences exist between male and female roles in any human society. Anthropologists use the term "gender" to refer to the elaborations or meanings that cultures assign to the biological differences between men and women. Age variation is also universal, and in some cultures other subcultural variations also occur as well. Individual members of a society learn the accepted norms of social behaviour through the process of enculturation; without enculturation people suffer culture shock, such as that experienced by new immigrants. Culture shock is defined as the trauma one experiences when moving into a culture different from ones' home culture. The loss of familiar symbols and the experience of being a complete outsider can result in culture shock. The extent of culture shock can be affected by the degree of differences between the field anthropologist (the ethnographer) and the "host" culture. Ethnocentrism is the belief that our own culture is superior to all others. To avoid making ethnocentric judgments, anthropologists adopt the practice of cultural relativism, which requires examination of each culture in its own terms and according to its own standards. Anthropologists respect all cultures because they firmly believe that all cultures are equally valid and must not be judged according to a set of standards from outside the culture. The possession of a culture, any culture, is a deep expression of the history and the ability of a group to survive and flourish.

Questions for Critical Thought

1. Have you ever had an experience that made you aware of profound cultural differences between yourself and someone else? How did you react (e.g., discomfort, stress, fear)? How did any other parties react? How did you attempt to overcome the cultural differences?

2. How would you respond to this question: "Which culture is best?"

3. To what extent have you ever felt yourself a member of a distinct subculture? Have you ever experienced negative feedback from other people because of your subcultural identity?

4. Write about your experiences with culture shock (perhaps as a first-year university student moving to an urban centre or while backpacking through Europe). How did this experience challenge your assumptions about the world around you? How did you feel, emotionally and physically? At what point did you make the adjustment to the new cultural environment—or did you? When you returned home, was there a period of readjustment to your own culture?

5. Enculturative forces within any society are not always positive. Can you identify any enculturative forces in Canadian society that may be perceived as negative (at least some of the time)?

6. If you immigrated to another country, would you attempt to adopt local behaviour as your own, or would you try to maintain your own traditions and identity? Which of your behaviours would you most likely try to preserve, and which would be most difficult to give up? What would be the basis for your choices?

Internet Resources

Hutterites

http://www.hutterites.org

A comprehensive history and description of Hutterite communities in North America.

Canadian Museum of Civilization

http://www.civilization.ca

This extensive site provides significant information on Canadian history, including diverse topics such as postage stamps, glass-making, religion and ritual, Inuit and folk art, social movements, and cultural traditions found within and outside Canada. An excellent resource for students from many disciplines.

Body Ritual among the Nacirema

http://www.msu.edu/~jdowell/miner.html

Read the classic article "Body Ritual among the Nacirema" for an enlightening and delightful introduction to the many pitfalls of anthropological research.

What Is Culture?

http://anthro.palomar.edu/culture/Default.htm

An education site that explores the nature of culture, including its basic characteristics and the methods used by anthropologists to learn about culture.

Popular Culture

http://www.ucalgary.ca/applied_history/tutor/popculture

An extensive site that introduces the concept of popular culture and discusses popular sports and leisure, popular literature, popular art and music, and new media.

Anthropology and You

http://anthropology.utoronto.ca/about/research/social-cultural

A detailed and inclusive website from University of Toronto that provides links to Internet resources for social and cultural anthropology.

Suggested Readings

For a list of suggested readings, visit this textbook's website at **http://www.havilandcultural4e.nelson.com.**

Notes

1. K. Oberg, "Culture Shock: Adjustments to New Cultural Environments," *Practicing Anthropology* 7 (1960): 177–82.

2. W.C. Young, *The Rashaayda Bedouin: Arab Pastoralists of Eastern Sudan* (Toronto: Harcourt Brace, 1996).

3. "Together They Stay a World Apart," *Smithsonian Magazine* 29, no. 8 (1998).

4. The Francophone Connection, *The Acadians of Nova Scotia*, http://www.francophonie.gc.ca, accessed August 13, 2003.

5. James Frideres and Rene R. Gadacz, *Aboriginal Peoples in Canada* (Toronto: Pearson Education, 2010).

6. P. Rains, "Review of *Pretty in Punk: Girls' Resistance in a Boys' Subculture* by L. Leblanc," *Canadian Review of Sociology and Anthropology* 37, no. 2 (2000): 113.

7. The first trickle of European immigrants arrived in Canada four centuries ago.

8. G.A. De Vos, "Concepts of Ethnic Identity," in *Ethnic Identity: Creation, Conflict, and Accommodation,* 3rd ed., ed. L. Ramanucci-Ross and G.A. De Vos (Walnut Creek: Altamira Press, 1995), 15–47.

9. *Sharia* law follows the teachings of the Quran and is used to settle Muslim family disputes, such as divorce and child custody.

10. L. Keith, "McGuinty Rejects Ontario's Use of Shariah Law and All Religious Arbitrations," *Canadian Press,* September 11, 2005, http://www.nosharia.com, retrieved October 21, 2006.

11. J. Caroulis, "Food for Thought," *Pennsylvania Gazette* 95, no. 3 (1996): 16.

12. L. Pospisil, *The Kapauku Papuans of west New Guinea* (New York: Holt, Rinehart and Winston, [1978]1963).

13. Johannes Fabian, *Moments of Freedom: Anthropology and Popular Culture* (Charlottesville: University of Virginia Press, 1998); David Howes, ed., "Law and Popular Culture," *Canadian Journal of Law and Society,* Special Issue 10, no. 2 (1995); Marcel Danesi, "Youth Culture," in *International Encyclopedia of the Social Sciences,* 2nd ed., vol. 9, ed. W.A. Darity (Detroit: Macmillan Reference, 2008), 167–68.

14. A. Ross, *No Respect: Intellectuals and Popular Culture* (New York: Routledge, 1989).

15. J. Combs, *Polpop: Politics and Popular Culture in America* (Bowling Green: Bowling Green University Popular Press, 1984).

16. Mark Q. Sutton and E.N. Anderson, *Introduction to Cultural Ecology* (Walnut Creek: Altamira, 2004).

17. W.H. Crocker and J. Crocker, *The Canela: Bonding Through Kinship, Ritual, and Sex* (Fort Worth: Harcourt Brace, 1994), 143–71.

18. C.J. Ember and M. Ember, "What Have We Learned from Cross-Cultural Research?" *General Anthropology* 2, no. 2 (1996): 5.

19. John Ingham, "Human Sacrifice at Tenochtitlan," *Comparative Studies in Society and History* 26, no. 3 (1984): 379–400 at 394.

20. J.A. Parades, and E.D. Purdum, "Bye, Bye Ted ..." *Anthropology Today* 6, no. 2 (1990): 9.

21. E. Messer, "Anthropology and Human Rights," *Annual Review of Anthropology* 22 (1993): 221–49.

22. S. Fedorak, *Anthropology Matters!* (Peterborough: Broadview, 2007).

23. J.H. Bodley, *Victims of Progress,* 3rd ed. (Mountain View: Mayfield, 1990), 138.

3 The Beginnings of Human Culture

Liam Kilmurray

Human culture has a deep history, one that is accessible by investigating the artistic creations and other remnants of ancient human activities. Although primate evolutionary history lies outside the realm of cultural anthropology, it nevertheless colours our interpretations of human cultures. The long history of primate evolution provides us with fascinating insights into the struggles and successes of our own species. By studying the behaviour and biology of other primates, we can learn what makes us distinct from them as well as from other animals.

KEY QUESTIONS

1. To What Group of Animals Do Humans Belong?

Humans are classified by biologists as belonging to the Primate Order, a group that also includes lemurs, lorises, tarsiers, monkeys, and apes. By studying the anatomy and behaviour of monkeys and apes—the primates most closely related to us—we draw closer to understanding how and why humans developed as they did.

2. When and How Did Human Culture Evolve?

Human culture appears to have really developed when some early hominins began making stone tools to butcher animals for their meat. Actually, the earliest stone tools and evidence of significant meat eating date to between 2.5 and 2 million years ago, along with the appearance of the genus *Homo*, whose brain was significantly enlarged over that of any other early hominin. From then on, the increasing importance of culture in human survival favoured the evolution of a better brain, which in turn made possible improvement in culture as the vehicle that humans used to secure their survival. By about 200,000 years ago, the human brain had reached its modern size. However, culture has continued to evolve and change down to the present.

3. When and How Did Humans Evolve?

Present evidence suggests that humans evolved from small, ape-like primates that lived between 15 and 8 million years ago. By 4.4 million years ago, human ancestors had become fully adapted for moving about on the open savannah on their hind legs in the distinctive human manner. Otherwise, the behaviour of these early hominins probably was comparable to that of modern-day chimpanzees.

4. What Were the Significant Developments in the Upper Paleolithic?

By the beginning of the Upper Paleolithic period (40,000 to 10,000 years ago), humans had evolved complex cultural systems. Technology, art, and language were developing much more rapidly than before. The explosion of art, witnessed at famous sites such as Chauvet and Lascaux in France, signals the cognitive complexity now possessed by humans. New technologies, such as the burin and the atlatl, were invented, and raw materials such as bone and antler provided a medium for creating new tools and personal ornaments. Upper Paleolithic populations, with their increased intelligence and complex cultural developments, spread throughout Eurasia and to many formerly uninhabited islands in the Pacific and elsewhere, reaching Australia some 50,000 or 60,000 years ago. The achievements of the Upper Paleolithic were significant and coincided with the disappearance of the Neanderthals. By around 17,000 years ago—possibly earlier—humans had also crossed into the Americas.

What thoughts went through the mind of the australopithecine as she walked through the savannah of Hadar, Ethiopia, some 4 million years ago? What did *Homo habilis* dream of at night under the African sky? Did *Homo erectus* or early *Homo sapiens* laugh at the antics of their infants as they learned how to fashion cutting tools? While paleoanthropologists might not be able to answer these questions, they form part of the fascination that drives them to dig in the African sun for decades just to expose the tiniest fragments from antiquity.[1]

The early forerunners of humanity, like all other creatures, depended a great deal on physical attributes for survival. Although learned behaviour was certainly important to them, much of what they did was still dictated by their biological natures. In the course of evolution, however, humans came to rely increasingly on learned behaviour as an extremely effective way to adapt to their environment. They learned to manufacture and use tools; they organized into social units more proficient at foraging for food than their ancestors had been; and at some point they learned to use symbols in order to preserve their traditions and knowledge. In other words, humans became increasingly committed to culture as a vehicle for solving the problems they confronted.

This cultural ability has made humans unique among the creatures on this planet. Humans do not merely adapt to the environment; they attempt to mould and manipulate it to suit the needs and desires they themselves define. If they succeed in avoiding self-destruction through misuse of their technology (and it is by no means certain they will), their medical technology eventually may enable them to control genetic inheritance and thus the future course of their biological evolution. Space technology may enable them to propagate their species in extraterrestrial environments. And computer technology enables them to correlate and organize an ever-increasing amount of knowledge as they themselves attempt to keep pace with the changes they have wrought.

Humans have gotten where they are today in an extraordinarily short period; human culture, as we know it, came into existence a mere 2.5 million years ago. By looking backwards to see where we came from and how we became the way we are today, we gain insight into how human culture arose and how it increasingly took on the job of solving the problems of human existence. In the process, we gain a fuller understanding of culture itself.

Primate Order The group of mammals that includes lemurs, lorises, tarsiers, monkeys, apes, and humans.

natural selection The evolutionary mechanism by which individuals with characteristics best suited to a particular environment survive and reproduce with greater frequency than those without them.

HUMANS AND THE OTHER PRIMATES

Biologists classify humans as belonging to the **Primate Order,** a group of mammals that includes lemurs, lorises, tarsiers, monkeys, and apes. We might properly question the value of studying primates other than humans, when humans and their distinctive cultural capacities are what concern us. Humans, however, did not start out as humans. Their roots, like those of the other living primates, lie in ancient times and in less specialized biological creatures; their development was influenced by the same evolutionary processes. By studying the environment of those times, the anatomical features that evolved in the context of that environment, and the rudimentary cultural adaptations of those primates we are related to, we may draw closer to understanding how and why humans developed as they did.

Primate evolution is intricately connected to trees. The first primates originated at a time when a new, mild climate favoured the spread of dense tropical and subtropical forests over much of the earth, including North and South America, Southeast Asia, the Middle East, and most of Africa. Forestation set the stage for evolutionary development from a relatively inconspicuous ground existence to tree living.

Evolution Through Adaptation

The term *adaptation* refers to a process that organisms undergo to achieve a beneficial adjustment to an available environment; it also refers to the results of that process—the characteristics of organisms that fit them to the particular set of environmental conditions they generally are found in. **Natural selection** favours not just the survival of well-adapted individuals but also the propagation of their genetic traits. The well-adapted individuals produce the greater percentage of offspring for the next generation. Although some individuals less suited to the environment may survive, they often do not reproduce; they may be incapable of attracting mates, they may be sterile, or they may produce offspring that do not survive birth.

By chance, the ancestral primates possessed certain characteristics that allowed them to adapt to life in the forests. Their relatively small size allowed them to use the small branches of trees; larger and heavier competitors and predators could not follow. The move to the small branches also opened up an abundant new food supply. The primates could gather leaves, flowers, fruits, insects, birds' eggs, and even nesting birds, rather than having to wait for them to fall to the ground.

The tree-dwelling primates, however, were obliged to develop both flexible behaviour and virtually automatic mechanisms for moving through the trees, for if they were no longer limited to roaming on the ground, they also no longer had the certainty of a substantial surface directly beneath their feet. Initial forays into the trees must have included many errors in judgment and coordination, leading to falls that injured or killed those who were poorly adapted to arboreal life. Natural selection favoured those who judged depth correctly and who gripped the branches tightly. Early primates who took to the trees had the potential for successful adaptation to another way of life merely by possessing characteristics adaptive to one way of life that, purely by chance, also were suitable for a different way of life. In other words, as ground dwellers they happened to possess features potentially useful to tree dwellers. Nevertheless, the transition to life in the trees required important physical adjustments.

Anatomical Adaptation

From the study of both ancient and modern primates, anthropologists have worked out a list of characteristics common to them all.

Modern lemurs, endemic to the island of Madagascar, represent highly evolved variants of an early primate model. In them, primate characteristics are not as prominent as they are in monkeys, apes, and humans.

Mark Phillips/Photo Researchers

Primate Dentition

The diet available to arboreal primates—shoots, leaves, insects, and soft fruits—required relatively unspecialized teeth. The mammals ancestral to the primates possessed three incisors, one canine, four premolars, and three molars on each side of the jaw, top and bottom totalling 44 teeth. The incisors were used for gripping and cutting, the canines for tearing and shredding, and the molars and premolars for grinding and chewing.

With fewer, smaller teeth doing more work, the canines of most of the primates grew longer, enabling them to rip open tough husks of fruit and other foods. Over the millennia, the first and second premolars disappeared altogether; the third and fourth premolars grew larger and added a second pointed projection, or cusp, thus becoming bicuspid.

Sense Organs

Arboreal adaptations also involved changes in sensory apparatus. The sense of smell declined, while that of sight became highly developed. Travelling through trees demands judgments concerning depth, direction, distance, and movement through vines or branches. Tarsiers, monkeys, apes, and humans developed stereoscopic colour vision—that is, the ability to see the world in the three dimensions of height, width, and depth. This requires two eyes set next to each other on the same plane so that the visual fields of the two eyes overlap. This led to increased brain size in the visual area and more complex nerve systems.

An effective feeling and grasping mechanism helped prevent primates from falling and tumbling while speeding through the trees. The early mammals from which primates evolved possessed tiny hairs that gave them extremely sensitive tactile capacities. These hairs were replaced by sensitive pads backed up by nails on the tips of the fingers and toes.

The Primate Brain

The most outstanding characteristic of primate evolution has been the great increase in brain size. The cerebral hemispheres—the areas of conscious thought—have grown dramatically. In monkeys, apes, and humans they completely cover the cerebellum, which coordinates the muscles and maintains body equilibrium.

An animal living in the trees is constantly acting and reacting to the environment. Messages from the hands, feet, eyes, and ears, as well as from the sensors of balance, movement, heat, touch, and pain, are simultaneously relayed to the cortex. An enlarged cortex not only made the primates more efficient in the daily struggle for survival but also prepared the way for heightened cerebration, or thought—an ability that would play a decisive role in humanity's emergence.

The Primate Skeleton

The skeleton of vertebrates protects and supports soft tissue and organs. The opening of the skull through which the spinal cord passes and connects to the brain is an important clue to evolutionary relationships. A downward shift, from head to heel, enables the backbone to join the skull at the centre of its base, which is a more advantageous arrangement for upright posture. The head thus is balanced on the vertebral column instead of projecting forward from it.

Below the primate skull and neck is the clavicle, which acts as a strut, placing the arms at the side of the body, thus permitting them to swing sideways and outward from the trunk. Apes and humans can move their arms with great freedom, enabling them to swing and hang vertically from tree branches.

The hands and feet have five extremely flexible digits, with sensitive pads backed up by flat nails. These provide an excellent grasping device when moving from branch to branch. The thumb and great toe are opposable to varying degrees so that food can be handled easily, branches grasped, and objects manipulated.

The retention of the primitive primate hand proved a valuable asset to later primates, for it enabled our ancestors to manufacture and use tools and thus alter the course of their evolution.

Adaptation Through Behaviour

Social behaviour, too, plays an important role in adaptation. The range of behaviours that living primates show is great. Chimpanzees and the other great apes have adapted to environments somewhat similar to those our own ancestors faced millions of years ago. Although we must realize that no living primate represents a precise analogue for the behaviour of our ancient ancestors, Jane Goodall's pioneering study of wild chimpanzees in Tanzania provided startling new insights into chimpanzee behaviour.

Language Research Center

This bonobo (pygmy chimpanzee) figured out by himself how to make stone tools like those our own ancestors made 2.5 million years ago.

Chimpanzee Behaviour

Like all primates, chimpanzees are social animals.[2] The largest wild organizational unit is composed of 50 or more individuals. Rarely, though, do they gather all at once; usually they are found ranging singly or in small subgroups consisting of adult males together, females with their young, or males and females together with young. In their travels, subgroups may join forces and forage together, but these will break up again into smaller units. When they do, members are often exchanged so new subunits are composed that are different from those that initially came together.

To avoid friction, chimpanzees practise certain affiliative behaviours. Groups possess dominance hierarchies; they also perform grooming and use a variety of body postures and signals to appease and reassure members of the group.

Among chimps, the mother–infant bond is especially strong for the first five years, with a close association commonly continuing after this period.

Chimpanzees show a remarkable dependence on learned cultural behaviour. This behaviour is to some extent

Ableimages/Getty

Grooming is an important affiliative behaviour witnessed in primates. In this image, a mother grooms her daughters, hair.

Dynamic Anthropology

Institute of Human Origins

Liam Kilmurray

The Institute of Human Origins (IHO) at Arizona State University was founded in 1981 at Berkeley, California, by founding director Donald C. Johanson. The IHO conducts, interprets, and publicizes scientific research on humans. Its unique approach brings together scientists from diverse disciplines to develop integrated bio-behavioural investigations of human evolution. Through research, education, and the sponsorship of scholarly interaction, the IHO advances scientific understanding of our origins and its contemporary relevance. Combining interdisciplinary expertise with targeted funding, the IHO fosters the pursuit of integrated answers to the most important questions about the course, cause, and timing of events in human evolution.

In conjunction with various international research centres and universities, the IHO also runs several field schools in **paleoanthropology**. The skills taught and applied in these field schools include how to recognize and find fossils as well as how to clean, date, and analyze them. Other skills taught include GPS

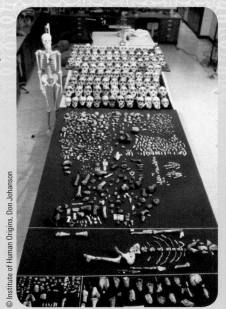

© Institute of Human Origins, Don Johanson

mapping, ecological and paleoecological analysis, and a broad range of excavation skills and techniques. For example, the Hadar Paleoanthropology Field School, scheduled for the fall of 2011, provides advanced undergraduate and graduate students the opportunity to view original fossils of *Australopithecus afarensis* and famous *Homo* material at the National Museum of Ethiopia.

The IHO is involved in a number of fascinating research projects that continue to shed light on the ancient past and the evolution of the human species. Among these projects is the Hadar Project in Ethiopia, which addresses the early evolution and ecological variation of *Australopithecus* (3.0–3.4 my) as well as the origin of *Homo* and stone-tool making (2.3 my). Elsewhere, the IHO's Hominin Sites and Paleolakes Drilling Project collects drill cores from paleolake sediments adjacent to fossil and artifact sites to assemble high-resolution paleoclimatic records for between 4 and 1 million years ago, linking records of evolutionary and local-to-global environmental change.

The newsletter of IHO, *Human Origins*, is available free to anyone who asks to be placed on its mailing list (send the request to iho@asu.edu). This newsletter contains updates and analysis on recent excavations as well as publications in the field of paleoanthropology. Institutions such as the IHO strive to fully understand the evolution of our species, providing anthropologists with the information needed to create our family tree. As Don Johanson, who helped discover the famous *Australopithecus* "Lucy," puts it: "There is a desire amongst people to know about origins of all sorts of things ... most importantly, origins of themselves."

different from one chimpanzee group to another. Young chimpanzees learn to use tools, even to modify them. They select objects with a future use in mind. Tool use and problem-solving skills are found in chimpanzees, bonobos, and orangutans. Chimpanzees have been observed using grass stalks, twigs they have stripped of leaves, and sticks up to a metre long to "fish" for termites. By stripping the leaves they are actually making tools, not simply using them. They then insert the stick into a termite nest, wait a few minutes, pull the stick out, and eat the insects clinging to it.

They use leaves as sponges, as wipers, and as vessels for drinking water; they also crack open nuts with hammer stones. This may reflect one of the preliminary adaptations that, in the past, led to human cultural behaviour.

The more we learn about chimpanzees, the more we become aware of a degree of intelligence and capacity for conceptual thought hitherto unsuspected for any nonhuman primate. By studying living and fossil primates we come closer to an understanding of human origins.

HUMAN ANCESTORS

Genetic, biochemical, and anatomical data confirm that chimpanzees and gorillas are our closest living relatives, more closely related to us than to orangutans. Genetically, humans and chimpanzees are at least 98 percent identical, so it is estimated that our evolutionary lines must have separated from a common ancestral stock somewhere between 5.5 and 8 million years ago. The fossil record tells us that humans were going their separate evolutionary way by at least 4.4 million years ago.

paleoanthropology The study of extinct members of the genus *Homo sapiens*

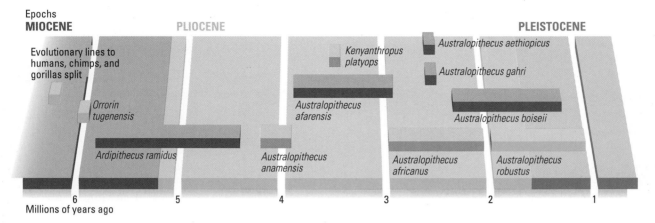

Figure 3.1

The earliest hominin fossils and the scientific names by which they have been known, arranged according to when they lived. *A. aethiopicus, A. boisei,* and *A. robustus* are all robust australopithecines; *A. afarensis, A. africanus,* and *A. anamensis* are gracile australopithecines. Recently, *Sahelanthropus tchadenisis* was added to the record (7 million to 6.5 million years ago). Whether all the different species' names are warranted is hotly debated.

The best evidence is that our ancestry lies among a group of apelike animals living in Africa that were forced by climatic changes down onto the ground to get from one stand of trees to another as well as to supplement food that was becoming increasingly scarce in the trees. Since they did not have arms as long as those of modern apes nor as massive upper bodies, they tended to move on their hind legs when on the ground, with their bodies in an upright position. Advantages of this kind of bipedal locomotion.[3] were that the arms and hands were free to quickly gather food, to transport it to safe places for consumption, and to wield objects effectively in threat displays as protection against ground-dwelling predators. Additionally, our ancestors could transport offspring more effectively than merely allowing the latter to hang on by themselves. Finally, erect posture on the ground minimized the body area exposed to the hot sun, thereby helping avoid overheating.

The First Hominins

The first undoubted **hominins,** known today as Ardipithecines, inhabited East Africa 5.8 to 4.4 million years ago. Two species of them are known to us today:

> **hominid** Any member of a family (Hominidae) of two-legged primates, including all forms of humans, extinct and living.
>
> **hominin** A tribe of hominoid primates, the hominini, to which all human species, including those that are extinct, are assigned.
>
> ***Australopithecus*** The earliest well-known hominin, who lived between 1 million and 4.2 million years ago and includes several species.

A. kadaba (5.8–5.2 million years ago) and *A. ramidus* (4.4 million years ago). *A. kadaba* was more primitive. *A. ramidis* is better known to us today: around 110 specimens have been unearthed to date.[4] Using paleoanthropological skills, we can learn much from these fragments. The **hominid** known as *Ardipithecus* lived in Ethiopia some 4.4 million years ago, and although much smaller than a modern chimpanzee, it is more chimpanzee-like in its features than any other hominin. Unlike chimpanzees, it walked upright, on two feet in a fully human manner—that is, bipedally. However, it did retain a grasping foot, which would have helped it remain efficient at tree climbing.

Two potential hominins are older than 6 million years. The first, *Sahelanthropus tchadenisis,* found in northern Chad, is dated 7 to 6 million years ago. It had a small braincase like an ape, small canines, and a human-like face. A recent three-dimensional digital reconstruction of its cranium, which corrects for the distortion caused by fracturing and deformation over time, confirms that it was more closely related to the hominin line rather than the great apes and that it was probably bipedal.[5] For now, it is the only known candidate that could be ancestral to all hominins. The second hominin, *Orrorin tugenensis,* is about 6 million years ago. Its status as a direct human ancestor is debated, for its molars are similar to those of *Australopithecus* but its status as a biped is unknown.

Descendants of *Ardipithecus* are assigned to one or another species of the genus ***Australopithecus*** (see Figure 3.1). Opinions vary on just how many species existed; for the sake of simplicity, we refer to them simply as australopithecines. The earliest australopithecine fossils date to around 4.2 million years ago;[6] the most recent ones are only about 1 million years ago. They have been

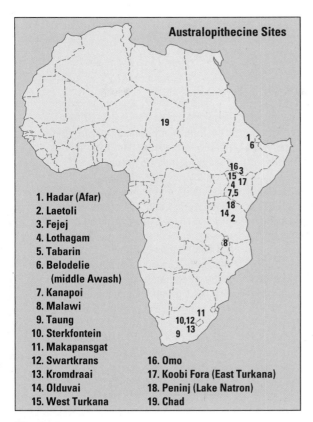

Australopithecine Sites

1. Hadar (Afar)
2. Laetoli
3. Fejej
4. Lothagam
5. Tabarin
6. Belodelie
   (middle Awash)
7. Kanapoi
8. Malawi
9. Taung
10. Sterkfontein
11. Makapansgat
12. Swartkrans
13. Kromdraai
14. Olduvai
15. West Turkana
16. Omo
17. Koobi Fora (East Turkana)
18. Peninj (Lake Natron)
19. Chad

Figure 3.2

Australopithecus fossils have been found in South Africa, Malawi, Tanzania, Kenya, Ethiopia, and Chad.

found along the length of eastern Africa from Ethiopia to South Africa and westward into Chad (see Figure 3.2).

Australopithecines were not as large as early hominins but were muscular for their size. In structure and size, their teeth were more like those of modern people than those of apes. The condition of australopithecine molars indicates that they chewed their food in hominin

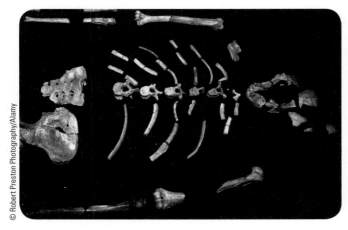

Sufficient parts of the skeleton of "Lucy," a hominin that lived between 2.6 million and 3.3 million years ago, survived to permit this reconstruction. Her hip and leg bones reveal that she moved around in a fully human manner.

fashion, with a grinding motion, rather than with a simple up-and-down movement of the jaws.

The australopithecines retained other apelike features; otherwise, their jaws were very similar to those of early *Homo*. Their brain/body ratio, which permits a rough estimate of intelligence, suggests that their intelligence was comparable to that of modern chimpanzees or gorillas. Moreover, the outside appearance of the brain was more apelike than human, suggesting that cerebral organization toward a human condition had not yet occurred.

Australopithecine fossils tell us that by 4 million years ago, this hominin was walking erect. Hominins acquired this erect bipedal posture long before they acquired their highly developed brain. With dispersed resources, such as in the savannah environment, a biped could not run as fast as a quadruped but could travel long distances in search of food much more efficiently, carrying food and infants to safe places. Also, it was exposed to less direct heat from the sun than when in a quadrupedal position.

While bipedal skills had increased, tree climbing remained important. Trees continued to serve as refuges from dangerous predators and as locations where food could still be found. The hominins of 4 million years ago were sexually dimorphic (literally, "two body sizes"), with males almost twice the size of females—a pattern witnessed in orangutans today. This dimorphism, which is believed to have resulted from both natural and sexual selection, can be seen to this day in the slight difference in body size between modern human males and females.

With the advent of cooler, drier weather 2.6 to 2.3 million years ago, hominins began to utilize a major new food source: flesh. Changing climate and altered environmental conditions were soon to bring about a major evolutionary leap.

Homo habilis

Homo habilis (Latin: "handy man") is known from a number of fossilized remains dated 2.5 to 1.5 million years ago, mainly in South and East Africa. Similar to the earlier australopithecines in body, yet possessed of a larger brain and smaller teeth, *Homo habilis* was an intermediate species that would eventually lead to *Homo erectus*. With a more complex cerebral hemisphere, which is associated with speech, *Homo habilis*, whether able to fully speak or not, displayed an advance in information processing capacity over the australopithecines. The enlargement of the brain and reduction in tooth size set the "habilines"

Homo habilis The earliest species of the genus *Homo*

Gender Perspectives

Gender Bias in Primatology?

A popular but controversial view holds that, until female primatologists began to study primates, the female primates were undervalued and misunderstood. The early-20th-century primatologist S. Zuckerman, who was a male, saw aggression, violence, and a well-defined hierarchy in baboons confined in the London Zoo. To what extent were his interpretations related to who he was as an individual and to his choice of a zoo as his study site? How the role of the observer may affect observations and interpretations is an important question. For example, male scholars had apparently constructed theories about male dominance hierarchies through their filter of masculinity. Biruté Galdikas, Jane Goodall, and Dian Fossey—all three prominent primatologists in the public eye—reinforce another view, which is that women are disproportionately drawn to and qualified to conduct primatology. In fact, there are probably as many male primatologists as there are female ones. Also, many of them have studied with the same professors, and some of the earliest studies of monkeys by male scholars paid close attention to female roles.*

The idea that male and female scientists approach issues differently isn't new. Naomi Quinn is a prominent feminist anthropologist who holds that academia in general is a male world and that men produce male-biased theory and treat women as inherently inferior. In her view, a feminist approach considers cooperation, empathy, and holism, whereas a masculine approach does not. Linda Fedigan, though, raises questions about the issue of gender and research, the answers to which are not all that clear. What is gender, and why is it relevant? Why would we want to know whether the gender or sex of a researcher affects his or her research? We need to come to terms with such questions in order to understand whether the gender of a researcher affects research.

Linguists use "gender" to describe gendered words. Psychologists have transformed the concept to one that is related to the sexes but not primarily biological. Today, gender is considered to be the cultural construction of masculinity and femininity as well as third genders and androgynous identities and roles. Shirley Strum, a baboon researcher, believes that being a female has had no impact on her work. Her approach is based on many years of studying baboons. Japanese primatologists, as a group (mainly men), appear to have approaches that fit the stereotype of Western female scholars. There is no agreement on how to evaluate gender and its effects in science, let alone primatology. Some support the idea that men and women do science differently; others do not.

*S.C. Strum, e-mail exchanges, in *Primate Encounters: Models of Science, Gender, and Society*, ed. S.C. Strum and L. Fedigan (Chicago: University of Chicago Press, 2000).

apart. The combined changes visible in them indicate that "handy man" was heading in a more human direction. Increased meat consumption was important in this regard: the human brain consumes 20 to 25 percent of an adult's energy, more than twice what is found in nonhuman primates.[7] Meat is more energy-dense than plant food and would have been important for the evolving brain.

Homo habilis procured its meat not by hunting but by scavenging, or even by stealing it from other predators. Teeth like those of australopithecines are poorly suited for meat eating. Even chimpanzees, whose canine teeth are far larger and sharper, often have trouble tearing through the skin of other animals. In the absence of teeth like those of carnivorous animals, what hominins need for efficient use of meat are sharp tools for butchering. The earliest tools of this sort, found in Ethiopia, are

dated to 2.5 million years ago. The only tools used before this time were probably heavy sticks to dig up roots or ward off animals, unshaped stones to use as missiles for defence or to crack open nuts, and perhaps simple carrying devices made of knotted plant fibres.

The earliest *identifiable* tools consist of implements made by striking flakes from the surface of a stone core, leaving either a uni- or bi-faced tool. These *choppers*—flakes with sharp edges—and hammer stones were used for cutting meat and for cracking bones to extract marrow. These, together with the cores they were struck from, are known today as **Oldowan tools**. Their appearance marks the beginning of the **Paleolithic**, or Old Stone Age. It is significant that the earliest *Homo habilis* fossils to exhibit the trend towards modern human features appeared by 2.4 million years ago, soon after the earliest evidence of stone-tool making and increased meat consumption.

Tools, Meat, and Brains

The significance of stone-tool making and meat eating for future human evolution was enormous. These two developments provided a secure source of high-quality

Oldowan tools The earliest identifiable stone tools, which first appeared 2.5 million years ago.

Paleolithic The Old Stone Age, characterized by chipped stone tools.

protein; they also made possible the development of a larger brain. Animals that live on plant foods must eat large quantities of vegetation, which takes up much of their time. Meat eaters, by contrast, have no need to eat so much or so often. Consequently, meat-eating hominins may have had more leisure time available to explore and manipulate their environment.

Homo habilis got meat by scavenging from carcasses of dead animals rather than by hunting live ones. We know this because the marks of stone tools on the bones of butchered animals commonly overlie marks made by the teeth of carnivores. Clearly, *Homo habilis* did not get to the prey first. Because carcasses are usually widely scattered, the only way these early hominins could have obtained a reasonably steady supply of meat would have been to range over vast areas in search of dead animals.[8] Bipedal locomotion allowed them to do just that, without tiring, in an energy-efficient way. Thus bipedalism, which arose for reasons having nothing to do with scavenging, made it possible for our ancestors to take up a new mode of life on the savannah.

Several lines of evidence suggest it was probably males rather than females who scavenged for food. As already noted, somewhat different foraging patterns by the earlier australopithecines appear to have predisposed the males more than the females in this direction. Furthermore, without contraceptive devices and formulas for bottle-feeding infants, females in their prime, when not pregnant, must have had infants to nurse. This would not have restricted their local mobility, any more than it does a female ape or monkey, but it would have made it harder for them than for males to range over the vast distances (on the order of 83 square kilometres) necessary to search out carcasses. We should not assume that *Homo habilis* had meat on a daily basis; the point here is that a reasonably steady supply would have required that substantial amounts of time and energy be devoted to the search for carcasses. It is possible that increased consumption of meat by *Homo habilis* promoted the sharing of food between the sexes, although not necessarily between mated males and females—it could just as well have been between brothers and sisters or mothers and sons. On the other hand, the potential of females to be constantly receptive sexually may have promoted sharing between a male and one or more sex partners, for among most monkeys and apes, males attempt to monopolize females when the latter are at the height of sexual receptivity. As discussed in Chapter 7, the human female's ability, alone among the primates, to respond sexually at any time probably was an incidental byproduct of bipedal locomotion; hence, it should have been characteristic of the earliest hominins.

For this new pattern of sharing to work, the females, no less than the males, had to "sharpen their wits." They continued to gather the same kinds of foods as their ancestors had been eating all along, but instead of consuming all this food themselves as they gathered it (as other primates do), they had to gather enough to share with the males, from whom they got a portion of the meat. This required future planning to decide where food would be found in sufficient quantities. Habilines also had to figure out ways to transport food to some previously agreed upon location for division, all the while taking precautions to prevent either spoilage or loss to animals such as rats, mice, and other predators. These altered female activities would have played a key role in the development of larger and better organized brains.

Finally, tool making played a role in the evolution of the human brain. First of all, it put a premium on hands' dexterity and precision (as opposed to mere power). This in turn put a premium on improved organization of the nervous system. Second, the stones used to make the tools were procured at some distance from where the tools were actually used to process parts of carcasses. This long-distance travel and repeated journeying accelerated the development of the habilines' memory.

In sum, a combination of factors, all of them somehow associated with the addition of more meat to the human diet, imposed strong selective pressures for better brains in *Homo habilis,* for females as well as males. From this point on, the archaeological record reveals increasing brain size relative to body size and increasing cultural development, each presumably reinforcing the other.

Homo habilis was a key though rather short-lived species in the evolution of *Homo sapiens*. The next species on this evolutionary trajectory, evolving directly from *Homo habilis,* is today called **Homo erectus**.

Homo erectus, Homo ergaster, and Homo georgicus

Homo erectus was discovered in 1891 by Eugene Dubois on the island of Java and was given the name Java Man. His skull cap was originally dated to around 500,000 years ago. Recent research has suggested that the Java fossils date in fact to somewhere around 1.6 million years ago.[9] *H. erectus*, however, had like others before her first

Homo erectus The species of *Homo* immediately postdating *Homo habilis.* The species generally refers to the Asian species, but some scholars contend that the African and European specimens are also this species.

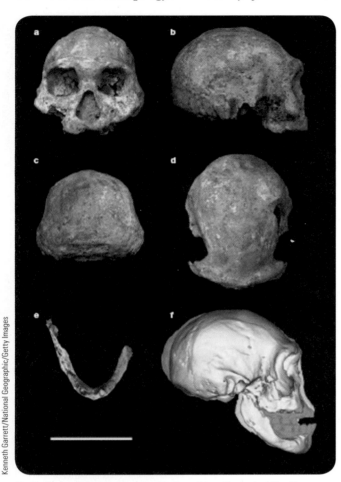

Kenneth Garrett/National Geographic/Getty Images

Skull of a toothless *Homo* (classified as either *Homo habilis*, *Homo erectus*, or *Homo georgicus*) from Dmanisi, Republic of Georgia. Bottom row, right, are comparative computer-tomography–based lateral views of an adult skull (coloured), a juvenile skull (light grey), and a cranium with articulated mandible (dark grey).

evolved in Africa before migrating to Asia. If there is one view that dominates discussions of human origins, it is that early humans migrated out of Africa after developing certain physical and cultural abilities. From the habiline fossils found in South Africa, Tanzania, Kenya, and Ethiopia, it is clear that they were widespread in eastern Africa, whereas the remains of *Homo erectus* have been found not only in Africa and Southeast Asia but also well into China and Europe. Grasslands dominated Asia and provided a narrow range of plant foods

Homo ergaster An alternative (and the original) classification of the African species of *Homo* that is also called *Homo erectus*.

Homo georgicus A species of *Homo* dating to 1.8 million years ago in the Republic of Georgia. There is some question about whether it is actually *Homo habilis* or *Homo erectus*.

for early humans. Meat, however, would have been readily available. The new commitment to a carnivorous diet would have provided the means to survive outside Africa.[10] In turn, the larger brains that were being fed by this diet would have enabled successful cultural innovations such as fire, clothing, and even language; all of these would have helped early humans succeed at more northern latitudes such as in Europe and northern Asia. The earliest *Homo* fossils outside Africa contradict this long-standing view. At the Dmanisi site in the Republic of Georgia, dating to about 1.8 million years ago, is perhaps the best collection of *Homo* fossils ever found from any single site.

These fossils are difficult to assign to a particular species because they share characteristics with both earlier and later fossils. They may be *Homo habilis*, **Homo ergaster**, or a new species, dubbed **Homo georgicus**. However they are classified—and in paleoanthropology things are likely to change with time—their brain size is small, within the range of *Homo habilis*. The tools at the site are of the Oldowan technology, so they did not yet have the hallmarks of the larger brained and more culturally developed *Homo erectus* or *Homo heidelbergensis*, which lived in Europe after 1 million years ago. An even more astounding discovery is that one of the individuals lost most of its teeth long before death.[11] This individual may have eaten soft foods such as bone marrow, brain tissue, or soft plant foods. The same individual would also appear to have needed more group care than witnessed among other primates. Dmanisi is challenging established views of the evolutionary sequence of early *Homo*.

In East and Southeast Asia, the immediate descendants of *Homo habilis* are classified as *Homo erectus*. The oldest date to about 2 million years ago. Many specialists prefer to classify the African representatives as *Homo ergaster*, reserving *Homo erectus* for the Asian specimens. Some scholars posit that these fossils are a single species; others, representing today's majority view, maintain that the differences between the Asian and African specimens are significant enough to classify them as different species. These fossils indicate that these *Homo* species had a body much like our own, although with heavier musculature and a smaller birth canal. Differences in body size between the sexes were considerably reduced, relative to early *Homo habilis*. The brain size of *H. erectus/ H. ergaster* was significantly larger than that of *Homo habilis* and well within the lower range of modern brain size. The dentition was fully human, although relatively large by modern standards.

As one might expect, given its larger brain, *Homo erectus* and *Homo ergaster* outstripped their predecessors in cultural development. In Africa the Oldowan chopper was transformed into the more sophisticated hand axe—the

Volker Stegen/Nordstar/Science Photo Library

Shown here is a fossilized skeleton of an early human *(Homo ergaster)*.

teardrop-shaped hand axe that characterizes the **Acheulian tradition**. That tradition lasted from about 1.5 million years ago to 150,000 years ago. In parts of Europe, chopper tools continued to be made, but later, in both Africa and Europe, the hand axe was further refined and developed.

During this time, tool kits also began to diversify, indicating the increased efficiency of *Homo erectus* and *Homo ergaster* at adapting to diverse environments. At first, the hand axes—shaped by regular blows that gave them a larger and finer cutting edge than chopper tools—were probably all-purpose implements, useful in food processing, hide scraping, and defence. But these hominins then developed cleavers (like hand axes but without points), which could be used for killing as well as butchering; several different types of scrapers for processing hides for bedding and clothing; and flake tools to cut meat and process vegetables. Adaptation to the specific regions that *Homo erectus* and *Homo ergaster* inhabited is also indicated by different assortments of tools found in these regions.

The improved technological efficiency of *Homo erectus* and *Homo ergaster* is also evident in the selection of raw materials. Instead of making a few large tools out of large pieces of stone, these hominins placed a new emphasis on smaller tools that were more economical with raw materials. Moreover, new techniques were developed to produce thinner, straighter, and sharper tools. A hard

wooden baton for flaking produced shallow flake scars, rather than the crushed edge found on the older tools. By first preparing a flat platform on a core, from which flakes could be struck off, these hominins could make even sharper and thinner implements. The toolmaker also could shape the core so that flake points 7.5 to 8.5 centimetres long could be struck off ready for use.

By 700,000 years ago—as attested by an identifiable hearth in a rock shelter in Thailand—*Homo erectus* had learned how to use fire.[12] This enabled the dispersal of early humans into regions where winter temperatures regularly went below 10°C, as they must have in China and most of Europe. There is evidence that *Homo* had moved as far north as Dmanisi, Georgia, by 1.8 million years ago, suggesting that fire was being used quite early in human history.

Besides keeping them warm—something that many people take for granted today—the use of fire enabled *Homo erectus* and *Homo ergaster* to cook food. This was a major breakthough in human cultural adaptation, for it altered the forces of natural selection, which had till then favoured individuals with heavy jaws and large, sharp teeth (uncooked food is tougher and needs more chewing). The way was thus paved for a reduction in tooth size and in supportive facial architecture. Cooking, however, did more than this: it made it possible to detoxify otherwise poisonous plants; it altered digestion-inhibiting substances so that important vitamins, minerals, and proteins could be absorbed in the gut instead of being passed through unused; and it rendered digestible complex and high-energy carbohydrates, such as starch. Cooking, then, substantially increased and made more secure the basic resources available to humans.

Like technological developments, then, fire gave people more control over their environment. It may have been used—if not by *Homo erectus* and *Homo ergaster*, then by subsequent hominins—to frighten away cave-dwelling predators, thus allowing humans to use caves; it then could be used to provide warmth and light in these cold and dark habitations. For ancient humans, the ability to control fire enabled the conquest of the night. Advanced technology, the control of fire, and cooking imply at least rudimentary linguistic ability (see Chapter 4 for more on language origins).

As *Homo erectus* and *Homo ergaster* became technologically more proficient, hunting began to replace scavenging as the principle means for procuring meat as

Acheulian tradition A tool tradition mainly associated with *Homo ergaster* in Africa and Europe, characterized by teardrop-shaped axes and flake tools. Named after the site where it was first defined, St-Acheul, France, it lasted from 1.5 million to about 150,000 years ago.

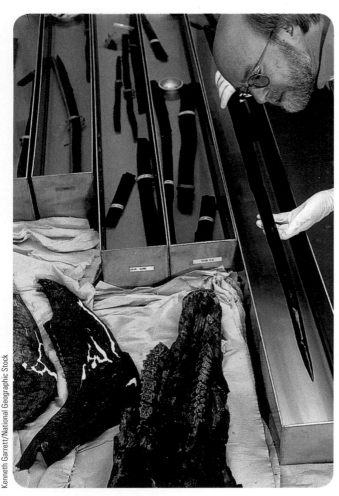

Kenneth Garrett/National Geographic Stock

Shown here are wooden spears made by *Homo erectus* 400,000 years ago. Found in a bog in northern Germany, they are anything but crude, testifying to the sophisticated tool-making and hunting skills developed by then.

well as other essential animal products such as animal hides and sinew. That these hominins were hunters by 400,000 years ago is attested by the recovery of sophisticated spears of this age that had been preserved in a bog in northern Germany. The complexity of hunting techniques by this time suggests, however, more than just greater technological capability; it also reflects an increased organizational ability. For example, excavations in Spain at Ambrona and Torralba indicate that group hunting techniques were being used by this time to drive a variety of large animals (including elephants) into a swamp so that they could be killed easily.[13]

With *Homo erectus* and *Homo ergaster*, then, we find a clearer manifestation than ever before of interplay

Homo heidelbergensis The species of *Homo* from about 500,000 or as much as 800,000 years ago to the appearance of Neanderthals. An alternative to the term "archaic *Homo sapiens*."

Homo sapiens The modern human species.

among cultural, physical, and environmental factors. Social organization and technology developed along with an increase in brain size and complexity. Cultural adaptations such as cooking and more complex tool kits facilitated dental reduction; dental reduction in turn encouraged an even heavier reliance on tool development and facilitated language development. Evidence from tools and fossils indicates that just as *Homo erectus* and *Homo ergaster* were able to live in areas previously uninhabited by hominins (Europe and Asia), *Homo sapiens*—our next subject—were the next major step in the evolutionary trajectory that began to gather steam some 8 million years ago. As they evolved, they spread to areas previously uninhabited by any other hominins.

The Beginnings of *Homo sapiens*

At various famous archaeological sites in Europe and Africa, a number of hominin fossils have been found that date between 800,000 and 120,000 years ago. Fossils from sites such as Steinheim, Germany, and Swanscombe, England, have been attributed *Homo sapiens* but have a mixture of characteristics of earlier and later forms. For example, skulls from Ethiopia, Steinheim, and Swanscombe have rather large brains for *Homo erectus* or *Homo ergaster*. Their overall appearance, however, is different from that of modern human skulls: they are large and robust, and they have more prominent brow ridges, larger faces, and bigger teeth. One skull from Morocco, which had a rather small brain for *Homo sapiens*, looks surprisingly modern from the back. Finally, various jaws from Morocco and France seem to combine features of *Homo erectus* or *Homo ergaster* with those of the European Neanderthals.

Some anthropologists lump these fossils into a group called archaic *Homo sapiens* because of their apparent similarity to modern humans. Others, increasingly becoming the majority, interpret the variations as representing different species. They assign the earlier Middle Pleistocene fossils, particularly those from Europe and Africa, to **Homo heidelbergensis**. This hominin is the best candidate for the common ancestor to both the Neanderthals *(Homo neanderthalensis)* and **Homo sapiens**.

Archaic *Homo sapiens*

The abundance of human fossils more recent than 200,000 years ago is in marked contrast to the scarcity of more ancient ones. The younger fossils are assignable to *Homo sapiens* or *Homo neanderthalensis*. By about 30,000 years ago, *Homo sapiens* had supplanted *Homo neanderthalensis* everywhere. Recently, 12 faceless skulls, or calvaria, found near the Solo River on the island of Java have been cited as an exception. Recently redated to between

53,000 and 27,000 years ago, they retain features of earlier Javanese *Homo erectus*, leading some anthropologists to regard them as the same species. Earlier researchers, however, had labelled them "neanderthaloid,"[14] the implication being that they were not yet modern *Homo sapiens*. Like the Neanderthals, their brain size falls within the modern range, while the outside of the skull retains a somewhat "primitive" look. Because the Solo River skulls fit within the normal range of variation for *Homo heidelbergensis*, they probably are members of that species or a type of archaic *Homo sapiens*.

No representatives of Middle Pleistocene *Homo* are better known than the Neanderthals, whose fossils are confined to Europe and the Middle East, dating from 125,000 to 30,000 years ago, though recent evidence suggests they may have survived in Moravia, in the Czech Republic, until around 26,000 years ago.[15] Regardless, these extremely muscular people, while having brains of modern size, possessed faces distinctively different from those of modern humans. Neanderthals were "prognathic"—that is, like a dog, they had a midfacial projection of their noses and teeth that formed a kind of prow. Over the eyes were prominent brow ridges, while on the back of the skull a bony mass called an occipital bun provided for the attachment of powerful neck muscles. They are so distinctive that they are classified as a separate species, *Homo neanderthalensis*.

Living in other parts of the world were variants of *Homo* that lacked the extreme midfacial projection and massive muscle attachments on the back of the skull characteristic of the Neanderthals. The Solo River skulls from Java are a prime example. In them, features of *Homo erectus* are combined with those of archaic as well as more modern *Homo sapiens*. The fossils look like robust versions of some more recent Southeast Asian populations or, if one looks backward, somewhat less primitive versions of the *Homo erectus* populations that preceded them in this region. Fossils from various parts of Africa, the most famous being a skull from Kabwe in Zambia, show a similar combination of ancient and modern traits. Finally, equivalent remains have been found at several localities in China.

Adaptations to the environment by archaic *Homo sapiens* (such as the Neanderthals) were, of course, both physical and cultural, but the capacity for cultural adaptation was much greater than it had been. The Neanderthals' extensive use of fire, for example, was essential to survival in the Arctic-like climate of Europe at this time. They lived in small bands or single-family units, both in the open and in caves, and undoubtedly communicated by speech (see Chapter 4). Importantly, there is evidence of deliberate burials, which seems to indicate complex ritual behaviour. Moreover, the remains of an amputee discovered at Shanidar Cave in Iraq reveal that the Neanderthals possessed compassion. Similarly, an arthritic man unearthed in France implies that Neanderthals took care of their disabled—an unprecedented example of social concern.

Archaic *Homo* roved and scoured the land for game perhaps much more than their predecessors. Hunting techniques improved along with social organization and weapon- and tool-making technology. The tool-making tradition of all but the latest Neanderthals (whose technology was comparable to that of anatomically modern *Homo sapiens*)[16] is called **Mousterian** after a site (Le Moustier) in France. Mousterian tools, dating from 100,000 to 40,000 years ago, characterize this period in Europe, North Africa, and southwestern Asia.

Mousterian tools are generally lighter and smaller than those of earlier traditions. Whereas previously only two or three flakes could be obtained from the entire core, Neanderthal toolmakers obtained many smaller flakes, which they skillfully retouched and sharpened. Their tool kits also contained a greater variety of types than before: hand axes, flakes, scrapers, borers, notched flakes for shaving wood, and many types of points that could be attached to wooden shafts to make spears.

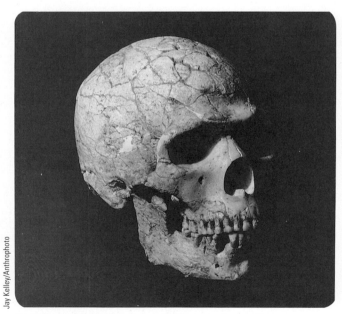

Jay Kelley/Anthrophoto

Skull of transition between archaic *Homo sapiens* or *Homo heidelbergensis* and modern *Homo sapiens*.

Neanderthal *Homo neanderthalensis*, the representative group of the genus *Homo* living in Europe and the Middle East from about 125,000 years ago to about 30,000 years ago.

Mousterian A tool-making tradition of the Neanderthals and their contemporaries of Europe, southwestern Asia, and North Africa.

This variety of tools facilitated more effective use of food resources and enhanced the quality of clothing and shelter.

For early *Homo sapiens* and for Neanderthals, improved cultural adaptation was no doubt related to the fact that their brain had achieved modern size (and in the case of the Neanderthals, exceeded it). This made possible not only sophisticated technology but also conceptual thought of considerable complexity. Evidence of this is provided by the ceremonial burial of the dead, as well as by objects that demonstrate symbolic significance. Among the latter are nonutilitarian items, such as pendants, as well as carved and engraved markings on objects that would have required some form of advanced linguistic communication. Other examples include the oldest known flute (made of bone) and the common use of red ochre (a red pigment).[17]

One of the great debates in anthropology today is whether the Neanderthals played a role in the evolution of modern *Homo sapiens*. The "multiregional hypothesis" interprets the fossil evidence as indicating that local populations in eastern and southern Asia, as well as in Africa, made the transition from *Homo erectus/Homo ergaster* to modern *Homo sapiens*. In contrast, a comparison of molecular data from modern human populations living in diverse geographic regions has led some anthropologists to argue that all modern people are derived from a single population of *Homo sapiens* that evolved in Africa. These modern people eventually replaced the Neanderthals, who left no descendants. This "Eve hypothesis" has been criticized on several grounds. One is that it conflicts with the archaeological evidence for continuity between older and more recent populations not just in Africa but in China, Southeast Asia, and parts of the Middle East, even if not in Western Europe. There is scant evidence for any major transitions in fossil evidence, or indeed in technological evidence. There is also a lack of archaeological evidence suggesting a migration to Asia by people possessing a different technology. Finally, it has been said that these molecular data analyses have serious problems.[18] Even a recent analysis of DNA (deoxyribonucleic acid) extracted from a Neanderthal skeleton, which relegates these hominins to a side branch of human evolution, is open to a different interpretation.[19] Thus the debate surrounding the "replacement model" can not be considered closed. At the same time, new life has been breathed into the Eve hypothesis with two recent reports of skulls from Ethiopia that provide good evidence for near-modern humans

that are significantly older than the Neanderthals. Human skulls discovered near Herto, Ethiopia, including one of a child dating to 160,000 years ago, are classified as *Homo sapiens idaltu*.[20] The child's skull shows evidence of long-term handling, suggesting that ancestors were venerated. The second report is a redating of the context in which two skulls, Omo I and II from Kibish, Ethiopia, were found in 1967.[21] Once thought to be about 130,000 years ago, the skulls are now dated to about 195,000 years ago, making them even older than the Herto fossils. Thus evidence for modern *Homo sapiens* evolving in Africa earlier than the Neanderthals and then living outside the Neanderthals' distribution is now relatively clear.[22]

Anatomically Modern Peoples and the Upper Paleolithic

Although populations of archaic and anatomically modern *Homo sapiens* managed to coexist for a time, by about 30,000 years ago peoples whose physical appearance was similar to our own had the world to themselves (with the possible exception of *Homo floresiensis;* see page 67). As is usual in human populations, these **Upper Paleolithic peoples** reveal considerable physical variability, but generally speaking, they all had characteristically modern-looking faces.

At this point in the long tale of human evolution, culture had become a more potent force than biology. By the time of archaic *Homo sapiens*, new technological developments had contributed to the increasing complexity of the brain, and this complexity now enabled people to create a still more sophisticated technology. Similarly, it seems that conceptual thought had developed beyond that of archaic *Homo sapiens,* as had symbolic behaviour. Thereafter, intelligence would provide the key to humanity's increased reliance on cultural rather than physical adaptation.

In Upper Paleolithic times (roughly 40,000 to 10,000 years ago), human intelligence enabled people to manufacture more complex tools and to develop more efficient means of social organization and cooperation. All of this made them far more proficient at hunting and fishing as well as at gathering. Cultural adaptation also became highly specific and regional, which increased human chances for survival in a variety of environmental conditions. This versatility also permitted human habitation of new areas, most notably Australia (roughly 60, or between 50 and 60 years ago) and the Americas (by 12,500 years ago at the very latest).

This degree of specialization required improved manufacturing techniques. The blade method of manufacture (see Figure 3.3), invented by archaic *Homo sapiens*

Upper Paleolithic peoples The first people of modern appearance, who lived in the last part (Upper Paleolithic) of the Old Stone Age.

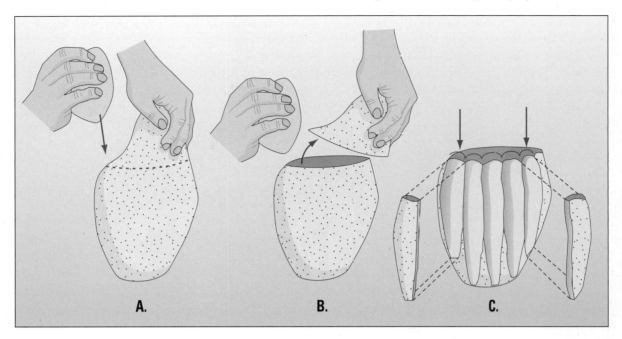

Figure 3.3

During the Upper Paleolithic, a new technique was used to manufacture blades. The stone was broken to create a striking platform, and then vertical blades were flaked off the sides to form sharp-edged tools.

and later used widely in Europe and western Asia, required less raw material than before and resulted in smaller and lighter tools with a better ratio between weight of flint and length of cutting edge. The pressure-flaking technique—in which a bone, antler, or wooden tool was used to press off small flakes from a flint core—gave the toolmaker greater control over the tool's shape than was possible by simply striking it directly with another stone or piece of antler.

The burin—a stone tool with chisel-like edges—although invented earlier by Mousterian toolmakers, came into common use in the Upper Paleolithic. The burin was an excellent means of carving bone and antler, both of which were used for tools such as fishhooks and harpoons. The atlatl—a piece of wood with a groove for holding and throwing a spear—also appeared at this time. With the atlatl, hunters were able to increase the force behind their spear throws. Later in time, the bow and arrow went even beyond this. The bowstring increased the force on the arrow, enabling it to travel farther and with greater effectiveness than a spear thrown with an atlatl.

One important aspect of Upper Paleolithic culture is its art. Setting aside some tantalizing early dates suggested for Australian Aborigines' rock art, as far as we know, humans had not produced artwork of this calibre before; therefore, the level of artistic proficiency is certainly amazing. In some regions, tools and weapons were decorated with engravings of animal figures;

pendants were made of bone and ivory, as were female figurines; and sculptures were made of clay. More spectacular—and, significantly, quite unlike anything the earlier Neanderthals created—are the cave paintings in Spain and France and the paintings and engravings on the walls of rock shelters in southern Africa. Made with mineral oxide pigments, these skillfully executed paintings depict humans and animals that coexisted with Upper Paleolithic peoples. Because the southern African rock art tradition lasted a full 27,000 years into historic times, we have learned that it depicts visions of the artists when in trance. Along with the animals, the art includes a variety of geometric motifs of a sort the human nervous system generates spontaneously when in trance. Australian rock art, some of it older than European cave art, is also associated with trancing and includes similar motifs. Since the same geometric designs occur in the cave art of Europe, it seems that it, too, depicted images seen in altered states of consciousness. Just as the rock art of southern Africa and Australia is related to what we would label religious experiences, so was the Stone Age art of Europe.

Peopling the New World

The peopling of the Americas represents the last radiation of *Homo sapiens*. Genetic and linguistic evidence indicates that the process of peopling the New World was anything but simple. Aboriginal peoples of the Americas have the most diverse languages of any continent. At least

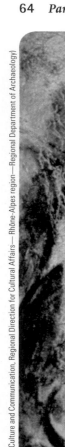

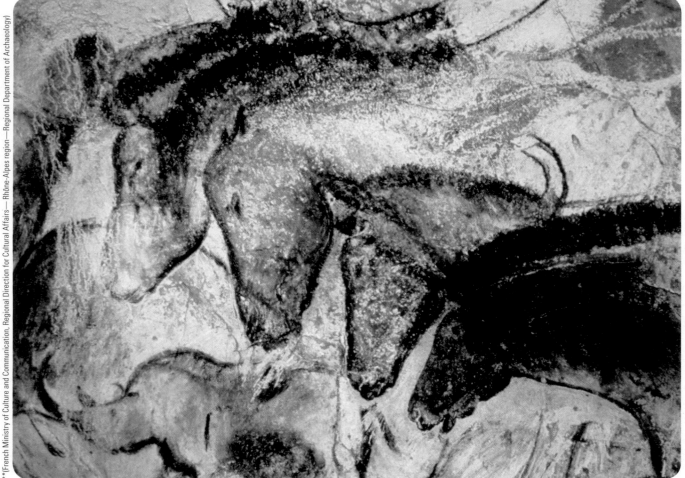

The intellectual capabilities of Upper Paleolithic peoples, whose skeletons differ in no significant ways from our own, are reflected in the efficiency with which some of them hunted game far larger and more powerful than themselves, as well as in the sophistication of their art. Paleolithic paintings of animals like the one shown here attest not only to the artists' technical skills but also to their knowledge of animal anatomy.

five distinct genetic groupings have been found among pre-contact and later Aboriginal peoples. There may have been many migrations or there may have been a single one, lasting millennia. We are far from a clear answer. Archaeologists agree, however, that the Aboriginal peoples of the Americas have their roots in Siberian northeast Asia.[23]

Upper Paleolithic cultures were so well adapted to their environment that Siberia presented few obstacles to these skilled modern humans. They were widespread in the region by 18,000 to 14,000 years ago, specifically in the Yakutia region. Just how early they arrived is unknown, but firm evidence suggests they were there by around 15,000 years ago. By 11,200 years ago, a Paleoindian tradition known as Clovis, unique to the New World, was centred in the southeastern United States, although the tradition is found over a much larger area. The origin of Clovis is debated, but because it is not found in the Old World or Alaska and Yukon, many archaeologists feel that it developed from an as yet undefined earlier

tradition. Clovis was followed by what is known as the Folsom tradition. Folsom projectile points are smaller compared to those of Clovis—a development that seems linked to the disappearance of large game by the end of the Folsom tradition. Linguistic diversification in the Americas would have needed far more than 11,000 years, according to language specialists. Evidence for people in the New World before 11,200 years ago is slowly growing.

Three times during the last glacial period, sea levels were low enough to make Siberia, Alaska, and Yukon one contiguous land mass known as Beringia. Here, Upper Paleolithic people lived as they did elsewhere in Asia, following and hunting animals in their seasonal rounds and moving to collect plants when they were in season for food, teas, medicines, and other purposes. In 1976, at the Bluefish Caves in Yukon, bones and small tools were discovered that indicated human presence there between 15,000 and 12,000 years ago. Canadian archaeologist Jacques Cinq-Mars excavated the site between 1978 and 1979.[24]

The Anthropologist's World

The Hadzabe

Liam Kilmurray

To most people, the crouched hunters, dressed in animal skins and silent and keen as their weapons, appeared to be hunting a leopard. To the anthropologists who have studied the Hadzabe, it was not the leopard that was the prey, but the mythical giant !esengego, the man-eating giant that forms part of the rich body of folklore associated with the Hadzabe. The Hadzabe people (Hadza is singular) inhabit the Eyasi Basin in northern Tanzania, which is dominated by the southern end of the East Rift Valley System. It is warm and dry (mean annual temperatures between 25 and 30°C), with an annual rainfall ranging from 300 to 600 mm, most of it falling during the wet season (March to April). The vegetation is a mixture of savannah grasslands, woodlands, and deciduous bushlands.

However, for anthropologists and interested laypeople, the Hadzabe occupy a totally different place, one located in the prehistorical imagination, that of the world of hunter-gatherers (or foragers). Anthropologists study the Hadzabe for several reasons: they are a fascinating example of modern hunter-gatherers and they are a source of inference as to how early humans may have lived. For good and bad, the Hadzabe are cited as an example of the mode of production that all humans practised for millions of years before the advent of agriculture some 10,000 years ago. The introduction of cereals and animal domestication pushed hunters and foragers to the margins, socially, politically, and physically. Whether from land appropriation or development, the incursions of pastoralists or farmers, or political decisions that further marginalize them, their way of life is fast disappearing.

It would appear that the Hadzabe and their ancestors have occupied this area for at least thousands of years. Mabulla states that many anthropologists consider the Hadzabe a "relic

© PhotoStock-Israel/Alamy

population descending from proto-Bushmen peoples who inhabited eastern, central and southern Africa in the MSA about 100,000 years ago" (2007, 28). Exact population size is difficult to determine, but given their mobility and their occasional avoidance of authorities, a good estimate appears to be around 1,000.

Around one-quarter of the Hadzabe maintain themselves following the ancient lifestyle. They hunt and gather or pursue food for around six hours a day. Their primary food sources are honey, fruit, and wild game when available. Using their wooden bows, men and boys hunt for impala, zebra, eland, giraffe, lion, and leopard. Sometimes they hunt scavengers like jackals, hyenas, and vultures. They tend no crops or livestock, have no permanent shelters, and are mobile and egalitarian. This "immediate return system" (the anthropological term) makes the Hadzabe a source of fascination for a variety of anthropologists, such as ethno-archaeologists, ethnographers, and economic anthropologists.

The Hadzabe manufacture their huts by weaving branches into round structures, usually six feet in height. They dress themselves in animal skins or traded cloth and warm themselves at fires made by rubbing sticks together.

They move camp with the seasonal schedules of plants and animals or when someone falls ill or dies. The Hadzabe possess an egalitarian structure, with no hierarchical divisions. Their technology is both simple and elaborate, made up of stone tools and wooden spears, which are often tipped with poison. The Hadzabe speak an ancient "click" language known as Hadzane, which is unrelated to any neighbouring languages.

Over the past 30 years many non-hunter-forager groups have entered their lands, placing great stress on resources, overexploiting the landscape, and creating friction between the Hadzabe and the newcomers and government authorities. Tree cutting has altered the growth patterns of grasses, and ever-increasing herds of domestic animals are degrading the environment and reducing the water resources. In the face of all this, the ability of the Hadzabe to support themselves in their traditional lifestyle is threatened. In recent decades, roughly 70 percent of the Hadzabe have partly abandoned the hunting lifestyle and are now employed at least part-time by farming groups as field hands or guards (Marlowe 2002). Land rights are essential to the well-being and future of the Hadzabe, and their fight for them is being aided by

CONTINUED

CONTINUED

CUSO (Canadian University Student Organization).

For almost four decades the Tanzanian government has sought to convert the Hadzabe from hunter-gatherers into settled farmers, usually with very little success. The government's reasons for trying are complex—it wants to "civilize" the Hadzabe, but it also wants to appropriate their land for other uses. Despite incursions and attempts to settle them, a large number of the Hadzabe maintain a proud and independent foraging lifestyle. Their population may dwindle, but their commitment to their ancient customs lingers on. What is happening to the Hadzabe today serves as an example of what has been happening to the rest of the world's "last" hunter-gatherers. Perhaps the Hadzabe will be the very last reminder of our most distant past.

SOURCES: Audax Z.P. Mabulla, "Hunting and Foraging in the Eyasi Basin, Northern Tanzania: Past, Present, and Future Prospects," African Archaeological Review 24 (2007): 15–33; Andrew Madsen, "The Hadzabe of Tanzania: Land and Human Rights for a Hunter-Gatherer Community," Copenhagen, IWGIA Document no. 98 (2000); F. Marlowe, "Why the Hadza Are Still Hunter-Gatherers," in Ethnicity, Hunter Gatherers, and "Other": Association or Assimilation in Africa, ed. S. Kent (Washington: Smithsonian Institution Press, 2002), 247–75.

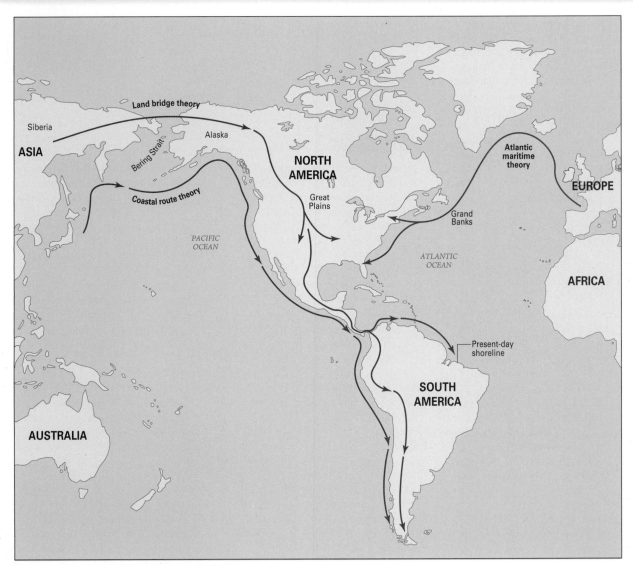

This map shows possible routes taken by Paleolithic people into the New World.

These easternmost Siberians were blocked from land access to the southern Americas by two continental glaciers. Even if the two glaciers occasionally separated during mild episodes, the corridor between them would have been inhospitable.

Nevertheless, people eventually spread as far as southern South America, where the Monte Verde site was occupied by 12,500 years ago. By 11,000 years ago, non-Clovis peoples at the Quebrada Jaguay site in coastal Peru were exploiting maritime resources. For people to

Skull of *Homo floresiensis* from Flores Island.

have reached Monte Verde so early, they would have had to circumvent the glacier barrier covering Canada. The most likely way was in boats, hopping down the west coast of the Americas from landfall to landfall. Evidence for this will be difficult to find because the ancient shoreline is now submerged. Sites such as Debert in Nova Scotia, dating to 10,600 years ago, show that as the glaciers retreated, people moved quickly from the south to form the ancestral First Nations of Canada.

Homo floresiensis

In 2004, palaeoanthropologists made a controversial discovery that suggested a shocking conclusion: *Homo sapiens* was not the only member of the genus surviving after 25,000 years ago. Routine archaeological investigation of the Liang Bua site on Flores Island in Indonesia brought to light at least two adult hominins, one represented by a mandible, the other by a cranium, mandible, and numerous postcranial bones. These hominins stood about a metre tall and had a cranial capacity of about 380 cubic centimetres.[25] Subsequent research has found bones of at least seven more individuals. The remains date to about 18,000 years ago. Other archaeological evidence, such as stone tools, suggests that this hominin lived here from at least 95,000 to 12,000 years ago. When anthropologists analyzed the cranium in

particular, they found that it was quite distinct from that of *Australopithecus* (who also had a small brain) in having a relatively vertical face and smaller teeth. The morphology of the skull, human-like bipedalism, and teeth similar to those of modern humans all argued for this hominin being a unique member of the genus *Homo*, so it was called *Homo floresiensis*. Modern humans did not appear on the island until about 10,000 years ago.

The stone tools of *H. floresiensis* are made of elongate flakes struck from cores as well as flakes from cobbles. A few have been retouched and shaped so that they have pointed projections. They also made fire and hunted. This behaviour is unlike that of *Australopithecus*, which also had a small brain, so the Flores discovery seems to contradict assumptions about brain size and early human culture. The same kinds of tools have been recovered from sites on the island dating to 840,000 years ago, indicating that the Flores hominin population extended well back, to the time that *Homo erectus* was in Southeast Asia.[26] One explanation for this unusual population is that an early *Homo* was living on the island when sea levels rose, completely isolating it from its ancestral population. The population later evolved into a unique, small species of *Homo*. Size reduction is an evolutionary trend that has been found in other species isolated on islands.

Not everyone agrees that the recent Flores Island discovery represents a new species of *Homo*. T. Jacob and colleagues have examined the bones and propose that they belong to modern humans who suffered abnormal growth and development, resulting in anatomical anomalies.[27] They collected data from the modern population living on the island and found that the chin and molar features thought not to be not present in modern populations are, in fact, present on the island. Among 140 features they examined, not one lies outside the range of modern humans. The short stature and small brain of the Flores remains are certainly unusual. Jacob's team proposes an explanation for these features. The evidence to them is consistent with individuals suffering from microcephaly, a disorder caused by genetic abnormalities and environmental factors that influence prenatal and postnatal development. They also argue that early populations on the island were never completely isolated and that the hypothesis of only one migration to the island cannot be justified. They also argue that an estimated population of between 5,800 and 7,300 individuals would have been all the island could have supported by hunting and gathering, and that was too small a breeding population to survive for the 40 generations they would have been isolated. Isolation on an island need not be the only reason for stature reduction, considering that African pygmies are not particularly isolated. The two distinct views of just who the Flores people are will be debated for some time. This debate indicates just how difficult it can be to interpret the early human record.

With people moving into the New World at the end of the Upper Paleolithic, we have reached a logical place to end our examination of the beginnings of human culture. This closure should not be taken to mean that human evolution stopped at the end of the Paleolithic.

Since then, the human species has continued to change biologically, even though it remains the same species now as then. Culture, too, has continued to change, and revolutionary developments, such as the development of food production and, later, state-level societies, came after the Paleolithic. These developments will be touched on in subsequent chapters, especially Chapters 5 and 15.

Chapter Summary

1.   To what group of animals do humans belong?
The archaeological study of primates helps anthropologists understand the physical and cultural evolution of our earliest ancestors. Current research into chimpanzee groups reveals that, like all monkeys and apes, chimpanzees live in structured social groups and express their sociability through communication by visual and vocal signals. They also exhibit learning, but unlike most other primates, they can make and use tools.

2.   When and how did human culture evolve?
The emergence and elaboration of culture sets humans apart from all other animals. The first indications of cultural complexity are evidenced in advances in tool technology, as early hominins began to butcher animals and skin their hides. This begins with *Homo habilis* but would have had its roots in the earliest hominins, which used sticks and rocks to fend off predators and to smash open nuts and bones.

3.   When and how did humans evolve?
The human species evolved from ancient hominins dated roughly to 7 million years ago. Although the earliest sequence is only dimly known, there is broad agreement that the australopithecines represented the real beginnings of the evolutionary sequence that would lead to the genus *Homo*. These early (4 million years ago) bipedal creatures led to the emergence of *Homo habilis* some 2.5 million years ago. *Homo habilis* was the first toolmaker, with an enlarged brain over that of the australopithecines. Following rapidly (in paleoanthropological terms) on the heels of the habilines was *Homo erectus*, who emerged some 2 to 1.9 million years ago. *H. erectus* had an even larger brain than the habilines, used fire, and created a more elaborate tool technology. *Homo erectus* was also the first hominid to leave Africa and head for Asia and parts of Europe.

4.   What were the significant developments in the Upper Paleolithic?
During the Upper Paleolithic (40,000 to 10,000 years ago), anatomically modern humans began the process of rapid cultural evolution. This culminated in increased artistic ability, the manufacture of very elaborate tool types, and the eventual displacement of the last remaining non-sapiens, the Neanderthals. With their advanced technologies and increased intelligence, *Homo sapiens* reached parts of the globe that were hitherto unoccupied, including Australia.

By the end of this period, the Americas were inhabited and *Homo sapiens* were the only surviving member of the genus *Homo*.

Questions for Critical Thought

1. How does primatology help us understand human origins?

2. Should the genetic similarity of humans and chimpanzees lead to legislation to stop chimpanzee use in biomedical research? Why or why not? What about other, less closely related primates? Supposing they possess a degree of self-awareness comparable to that of humans, what are the ethics of holding chimpanzees captive and carrying out laboratory research on them?

3. Why are the "invention" of human culture and tool use connected? What other activities, such as language or living in groups, could have affected the early evolution of human culture? What other kinds of tools might our human ancestors have developed that we might be unlikely to find now? Why wouldn't we find them today? What might such tools have told us about these peoples?

4. What methodological limitations hamper our understanding of early human culture? What aspects of the earliest human culture are so far invisible or difficult to ascertain?

5. What is the evidence, for and against, that Neanderthals became extinct in the early part of the Upper Paleolithic?

6. The last major human migration into a pristine continent brought people to the New World from Asia. What factors may have been responsible for this event?

Internet Resources

Canadian Physical Anthropology

http://capa.fenali.net

Provides information relevant to the discipline of physical anthropology, particularly as it is practised in Canada.

Jane Goodall Institute

http://www.janegoodall.ca/prog-africa-sanctuaries.php

This site addresses the current situation in the Congo Basin, where wildlife is being threatened by new incursions onto the land. For anyone who is interested in wildlife protection, the environment, and cultural practices, this is a good site to visit.

Biographies of Primatologists

http://pin.primate.wisc.edu/edu/careers/bio.html

This site lists many well-known primatologists and provides a biography of each, including the "greats" such as Dian Fossey (of *Gorillas in the Mist* fame), Jane Goodall, Biruté Galdikas, and Mary Leakey, as well as several primate biographies, such as one of Booee the chimpanzee.

Early Human Phylogeny

http://www.mnh.si.edu/anthro/humanorigins/ha/a_tree.html

A good site for students to examine the complexity of deciphering our ancient family tree; presents new fossil evidence that further obscures the links among early humans.

Paleoanthropology Society

http://www.paleoanthro.org

Home page of the Paleoanthropolgy Society; includes links to journals, conferences, publications, and ongoing excavations.

Geological Time Scale

http://www.zoomdinosaurs.com/subjects/geologictime.html

This Enchanted Learning Software site offers students a superior geological time scale and an excellent discussion of plate tectonics and continental drift. Each epoch has further links to describe the nature of the earth and its inhabitants at that time. This is a highly recommended site for anthropology, biology, and geology students and instructors alike.

Homo habilis

http://www.archaeologyinfo.com/homohabilis.htm

This site provides details of *Homo habilis* and outlines the complications in its definition. Links are provided to specific fossils.

Earliest Modern Humans

http://iho.asu.edu

This site details ongoing and past excavations undertaken by the Institute for Human Origins. It contains many links and documents relevant to paleoanthropology and human evolution.

Oldest Human Remains

http://www.talkorigins.org/faqs/homs/herto.html

This site details the background to the oldest modern human remains so far discovered (in Ethiopia).

Neanderthals

http://www.digitaljournal.com/article/291135

This Web page offers the research presented on April 17, 2010, at the annual meeting of the American Association of Physical Anthropologists in Albuquerque, New Mexico, regarding the "disappearance" of the Neanderthals. Evidence is reviewed which suggests that extinct species such as the Neanderthals interbred with the ancestors of modern humans.

Neanderthal DNA

http://www.nature.com/news/2010/100420/full/news.2010.194.html

This site contains interesting information regarding the possible interbreeding between Neanderthal and human populations.

http://news.nationalgeographic.com/news/2006/11/061115-neanderthal-dna.html

This National Geographic Society news story outlines the recent research on Neanderthal DNA. The site has links to other stories about human DNA.

Early Modern Human Culture

http://anthro.palomar.edu/homo2/mod_homo_3.htm

http://anthro.palomar.edu/homo2/mod_homo_5.htm

Detailed discussion of early modern human cultures, beginning around 100,000 years ago until approximately 17,000 years ago. Focuses on Cro-Magnons and their artwork.

The *Homo floresiensis* Brain

http://anthropology.net/2010/01/28/reduced-brain-size-of-homo-floresiensis-hints-at-her-likely-ancestors

This site examines the evolutionary implications for the brain size of *Homo floresensis*.

http://www.pbs.org/wgbh/nova/sciencenow/3209/01-endocast.html

Detailed comparison of the brain of *Homo floresiensis* with that of a chimpanzee and a modern human.

Suggested Readings

For a list of suggested readings, visit this textbook's website at **www.havilandcultural4e.nelson.com.**

Notes

1. Richard G. Delisle, *Debating Humankind's Place in Nature: 1860–2000, the Nature of Paleoanthropology.* (Upper Saddle River, NJ: Pearson-Prentice Hall, 2007.

2. J. Goodall, *The Chimpanzees of Gombe: Patterns of Behavior.* (Cambridge, MA: Belknap Press, 1986).

3. John H. Langdon, *The Human Strategy: An Evolutionary Perspective on Human Anatomy* (Oxford: Oxford University Press 2005), 116–26.

4. Anne Keenleyside and Richard Lazenby, *A Human Voyage: Exploring Biological Anthropology* (Toronto: Nelson Education, 2011).

5. C.P.E. Zollikofer, M.S. Ponce de Leon, D.E. Lieberman, F. Guy, D. Pilbeam, A. Likius, H.T. Mackaye, P. Vignaud, and M. Brunet, "Virtual Cranial Reconstruction of *Sahelanthropus tchadensis*," *Nature* 434 (2005): 755–59.

6. M. Wolpoff (1996). "*Australopithecus*: A New Look at an Old Ancestor," *General Anthropology* 3, no. 1 (1996): 2.

7. W.R. Leonard, "Food for Thought," *Scientific American* 13, no. 2 (2003): 62–71.

8. R. Lewin, "Four Legs Bad, Two Legs Good," *Science* 235 (1987): 969.

9. C.C. Swisher III, G.H. Curtis, T. Jacob, A.G. Getty, A. Suprijo, and Widiasmoro, "Age of the Earliest Known Hominids in Java, Indonesia," *Science* 263 (1994): 1118-21.

10. R. Dennell and W. Roebroeks, "An Asian Perspective on Early Human Dispersal from Africa," *Nature* 438 (2005): 1099–104.

11. D. Lordkipanidze, A. Vekua, R. Ferring, G.P. Rightmire, J. Agusti, G. Kiladze, A. Mouskhelishvili, M. Nioradze, M.S. Ponce de León, M. Tappen, and C.P.E. Zollikofer, "The Earliest Toothless Hominin Skull," *Nature* 434 (2005): 717–18.

12. G. Pope, "Bamboo and Human Evolution," *Natural History* 98 (October 1988): 56.

13. L.G. Freeman, "Ambrona and Torralba: New Evidence and Interpretation," Paper presented at the 91st Annual Meeting, American Anthropological Association, Chicago, 1992.

14. W.E.L. Clark, *The Fossil Evidence for Human Evolution* (Chicago: University of Chicago Press, 1955), 76–79.

15. E.M. Wild, M. Teschler-Nicola, W. Kutschera, P. Steier, E. Trinkaus, and W. Wanek, "Direct Dating of Early Upper Palaeolithic Human Remains from Mladeč," *Nature* 435 (2005): 332–35.

16. P. Mellars, "Major Issues in the Emergence of Modern Humans," *Current Anthropology* 30 (1989): 356–57.

17. R.G. Bednarik, "Concept-Mediated Marking in the Lower Paleolithic," *Current Anthropology* 36 (1995): 606. See also P.C. Rice, "Paleoanthropology 1996—Part II," *General Anthropology* 3, no. 2 (1997): 10.

18. A. Cooper, H.N. Poinar, S. Pääbo, J. Radovčić, A. Debénath, M. Caparros, C. Barroso-Ruiz, J. Bertranpetit, C. Nielsen-March, R.E.M. Hedges, and B. Sykes, "Neanderthal Genetics," *Science* 277 (1997): 1021–24.

19. Ibid.

20. T.D. White, B. Asfaw, D. DeGusta, H. Gilbert, G.D. Richards, G. Suwa, and F. Clark Howell, "Pleistocene *Homo sapiens* from Middle Awash, Ethiopia," *Nature* 423 (2003): 742–47.

21. I. McDougall, F.H. Brown, and C.J. Fleagle, "Stratigraphic Placement and Age of Modern Humans from Kibish, Ethiopia," *Nature* 433 (2005): 733–36.

22. H.M. McHenry, "Human Evolution," in *Evolution: The First Four Billion Years*, ed. Michael Ruse and Joseph Travis (Cambridge, MA: Belknap, 2009).

23. E. James Dixon, "Peopling of the Americas," *Athena Review* 3, no. 2 (2002).

24. J. Cinq-Mars and R.E. Morlan, "Bluefish Caves and Old Crow Basin: A New Rapport," in *Ice Age Peoples of North America,* ed. Robson Bonnichsen and Karen L. Turnmire (Corvallis: Oregon State University Press for the Center for the Study of the First Americans, 1999), 200–12.

25. P. Brown, T. Sutikna, M.J. Morwood, R.P. Soejono, Jatmiko, E.W. Saptomo, and R.A. Due, "A New Small-Bodied Hominin from the Late Pleistocene of Flores, Indonesia," *Nature* 431 (2004): 1055–61.

26. A. Brumm, F. Aziz, G.D. van den Bergh, M.J. Morwood, M.W. Moore, I. Kurniawan, D.R. Hobbs, and R. Fullagar, "Early Stone Technology on Flores and Its Implications *Homo floresiensis*," *Nature* 441 (2006): 624–28.

27. T. Jacob, E. Indriati, R.P. Soejono, K. Hsu, D.W. Frayer, R.B. Eckhardt, A.J. Kuperavage, A. Thorne, and M. Henneberg, "Pygmoid Australomelanesian *Homo sapiens* Skeletal Remains from Liang Bua, Flores: Population Affinities and Pathological Abnormalities," *Proceedings of the National Academy of Sciences* 103 (2006): 13421–26.

4 Language and Communication

The richness of human culture is made possible by language, one of our most distinctive characteristics. Shown here is a young girl using American Sign Language, a distinctive form of language for hearing-impaired individuals.

KEY QUESTIONS

1. What Is Language?

Language is a system of sounds or gestures that, when put together following certain rules, results in meanings intelligible to all speakers. Although humans rely primarily on language to communicate with one another, it is not their only means of communication. Language is embedded in a gesture-call system that consists of paralanguage (extralinguistic noises that accompany language) and kinesics (body motions that convey messages). We also convey messages through the use of space and touch.

2. How Is Language Related to Culture?

Languages are spoken by people who are members of distinctive cultures. Social variables, such as the history, class, gender, and status of the speaker, influence language use. Moreover, people communicate that which is meaningful to them, and what is or is not meaningful is defined by their particular culture. Our language use affects our culture and is affected by it. Language retention in today's world is of particular concern to Aboriginal cultures.

3. How Did Language Begin?

Many explanations have been proposed regarding how language originated. Human language may have begun as a rudimentarily structured system of gestures. A key factor in its elaboration may have been the need for our ancient ancestors to plan ahead. Since speech, like gestures, is a product of muscular movements, it is possible that spoken language emerged as the muscles of the mouth and vocal tract were favoured so that people could use their hands for other things while they talked; this allowed them to communicate with others without having to be in full view.

Many Gaelic folk tales begin with the phrase *fado fado fado,* which means "Long, long ago …" Much like "Once upon a time, in a distant land, …" this phrase sets the tone for a coming tale and situates the listener, or reader, in space and time. Linguists call this **displacement:** the ability to describe actions and objects that occurred in another time and place. It was this ability that helped ancient humans communicate, strategize, and analyze the world around them, setting them apart from the animal world. This linguistic competency also set humans on the path toward cultural complexity, borne on the back of linguistic efficiency. It enabled early human groups to communicate much more "deeply" than contemporary hominid populations; it also ensured that human culture could be communicated efficiently across time and space.

Animal communication is complex. In this image, two prairie dogs kiss.

Language is not just a system; it is a completely symbolic system. There is no necessary connection between a sound (word) and the concept signified; different languages have different words for the same concepts. This means that the relation is arbitrary and symbolic; each word represents a concept.[1]

Anthropologists understand that culture is learned and that its transmission from one person to another, and from one generation to the next, depends on an effective communication system that is far more complex than that of any other animal. Thus, a basic requirement for any culture is a means of communication between individuals. All cultures accomplish this communication through some form of language, which is perhaps the most distinctive of all human characteristics.

Barring some ailment, all humans have the ability to speak and spend a considerable part of each day doing so. Indeed, **language** permeates everything we do, and everything we do is reflected in our language. Our ability to speak, be it through sounds or through gestures (sign languages, such as American Sign Language, or ASL, are fully developed languages in their own right), is based on bio-

displacement The ability to refer to objects and events removed in time and space.

language A system of communication using sounds or gestures put together in meaningful ways according to a set of rules.

symbols Sounds or gestures that stand for meanings among a group of people.

signal A sound or gesture that has a natural or self-evident meaning.

logical factors. We are "programmed" to speak, although only in a general way. Beyond the cries of babies, which are not learned but which do communicate, humans must learn how to speak. We are taught to speak a particular language, and all children from anywhere in the world readily learns whatever languages are spoken around them. Language is a system for communicating in **symbols**. A "symbol," in our definition, is any sound or gesture to which cultural tradition has assigned meaning; by contrast, a symbol that has a natural or self-evident meaning is what language specialists call a **signal**. A smile is a signal of happiness, and laughing is a signal of some kind of emotional or physical state. The *word* "laughing," however, is a symbol—that is, a group of sounds to which we have learned to assign the meaning of a particular action and which we can use to communicate meaning whether or not anyone around us is actually laughing.

Currently, language experts are unsure whether animals—such as dolphins or chimpanzees—possess the ability to use symbols as well as signals, even though these animals and many others have been found to communicate in remarkable ways. Several apes have been taught ASL. As an example, Chanteh the orangutan has learned 150 different signs, developing the communication skills of a two- to three-year-old child. Even prairie dogs use many different calls for communication, and these are not mere indexes for some degree of arousal or fear; rather, they are acts of meaningful communication.

What can nonhuman communication tell us about the evolution of language? To answer that question, we will need to develop a better understanding of animal communication than we now have. What *is* clear today is that animal communication cannot be dismissed as a set of simple reflexes or fixed action patterns, even though debate continues over just how human and animal communication relate to each other.[2] The fact is that human culture, as we know it, ultimately depends on a system for communicating that is far more complex than that of any other animal. Human cultures are so rich in content that they require communication systems that not only give precise labels to various classes of phenomena but also permit people to think and talk about their own and others' experiences in the past and future as well as the present. The central and most highly developed human system of communication is language. Knowledge of the workings of language, then, is essential to a full understanding of culture.

THE NATURE OF LANGUAGE

Any human language—French, English, Chinese, Hadzane, Algonquin—is a means of transmitting information and sharing cultural and individual experiences with others. Language is also a system that enables us to translate our concerns, beliefs, and perceptions into symbols that others can understand and interpret. In spoken language, this is done by taking a few sounds—most languages use about 50—and developing rules for putting them together in meaningful ways. There are roughly 6,000 living languages, which display astonishing variety and complexity. All languages, though, whether living or dead, are organized in the same basic manner.

The roots of **linguistics**, the modern scientific study of language, extend deep into history, to the works of ancient grammarians in India more than 2,000 years ago. In the age of exploration and discovery, the scientific study of language was given impetus by the accumulation of facts—that is, by the collection of sounds, words, and sentences from all the different languages encountered

For linguist Megan Biesele studying the Ju/'hoansi language in the field, the tape recorder has become an indispensable tool.

by explorers, invaders, and missionaries in exotic lands. In the 21st century, researchers are still collecting data and have made considerable progress in understanding the underlying logic of languages, testing and working from new and improved theories. Linguistic anthropology has many areas of inquiry, including this one: how people use language, both verbal and nonverbal, to develop social relationships with one another and to create, maintain, and reproduce social distinctions.

The Sound and Shape of Language

To understand a spoken language, you need a trained ear and a thorough understanding of how speech sounds are produced. Linguistic anthropologists undergo special training in **phonetics**, which is the systematic study of the production, transmission, and reception of speech sounds.

Phonology

The exciting task of analyzing and describing a language requires that the researcher compile an inventory of all its sounds and develop an accurate way of writing them down. This is exactly what the Jesuit priest Jean de Brébeuf did when living among the Algonquin and Huron Indians in Canada during the 17th century. What missionaries and ethnographers have learned is that some sounds of other languages may be similar to the researcher's own; others (such as the "clicks" in San languages) may be sounds the researcher has never consciously produced. Once a researcher knows all the possible sounds in a language, he or she can study the patterns these sounds take as they are used to form words. From here, the person can discover the underlying rules that explain which combinations of sounds are permissible in the language and which are not.

The next step is to isolate the **phonemes**, or the smallest classes of sound that make a difference in meaning. The linguist tries to find two short words that appear to be exactly alike except for one sound, such as *bit* and *pit* in English. If the substitution of *b* for *p* in this minimal pair makes a difference in meaning (which it does in English), then those two sounds are distinct phonemes of the language and will require two different symbols to record. If, however, the linguist finds two different pronunciations,

linguistics The modern scientific study of all aspects of language.

phonetics The study of the production, transmission, and reception of speech sounds.

phonemes In linguistics, the smallest classes of sound that make a difference in meaning.

as when *butter* is pronounced "budder," and then finds that their meaning is the same for a native speaker, the sounds represented are variants of the same phoneme. For greater accuracy and to avoid confusion with the various sounds of the researcher's language, the symbols of a phonetic alphabet—such the one developed by Edward Sapir for the American Anthropological Association—are used to distinguish the sounds of most languages in a way that is comprehensible to anyone who knows the system.

Morphology

Studying an inventory of sounds is a lengthy task, as the linguist must work out all the combinations of sounds that seem to have meaning. These are called **morphemes**, and they are the smallest units that have meaning in any language. *Cat* and *dog* are, of course, morphemes, or meaningful combinations of phonemes, in English. By pointing to two of either of these animals, the linguist then elicits *cats* and *dogs*. This indicates that another unit, –s, carries a meaning and can be added to the original morpheme to mean "plural." A morpheme that, like –s, cannot occur in the language unattached is called a **bound morpheme**; because *dog* and *cat* can occur unattached to anything, they are called **free morphemes**. Because the sound represented in writing –s is actually different in the two words (*s* in *cats* and *z* in *dogs*), the sounds *s* and *z* are two varieties of the same morpheme (even though they may be two different phonemes) occurring in different contexts but with no difference in meaning.

Grammar and Syntax

The next step is to put morphemes together to form phrases or sentences. Linguists use a method called **frame substitution**. The linguist identifies strings such

---

morphemes In linguistics, the smallest units of sound that carry meaning.

bound morpheme A morpheme that can occur in a language only in combination with other morphemes, as –s in English does to signify the plural.

free morphemes Morphemes that can occur unattached in a language; for example, *dog* and *cat* are free morphemes in English.

frame substitution A method used to identify the syntactic units of language. For example, a category called nouns may be established as anything that will fit the substitution frame "I see a ..."

syntax In linguistics, the rules or principles of phrase and sentence making.

grammar The entire formal structure of a language, consisting of all observations about the morphemes and syntax.

form classes The parts of speech or categories of words that work the same way in a given sentence.

---

as *my cat*, *your cat*, *I see your cat*, and *she sees my cat*. This begins to establish the rules of phrase and sentence making, the **syntax** of the language.

A language may make extensive use of utterances that are not found in the linguist's language and that the linguist may not even think of asking for. Furthermore, some speakers may pretend they cannot say (or may truly not be able to say) certain words their culture considers impolite, taboo, or inappropriate for mention to outsiders. This makes the true translation of another's language an exceptionally difficult task.

The **grammar** of a language consists of all observations about its morphemes and syntax. For example, a linguist may establish a category called *nouns*, defined as anything that will fit the substitution frame "I see a ..." The researcher makes the frame, tries out a number of words in it, and has a native speaker indicate "yes" or "no" for whether the words work. In English, the words *house* and *cat* will fit this frame and can be said to belong to the same **form class**, but the word *think* will not. Another possible substitution frame for nouns might be "The _____ died," in which the word *cat* will fit, but not the word *house*. In this way the linguist can identify subclasses of English nouns: in this case, "animate" or "inanimate" subclasses. The same procedure can be followed for all the words of the language, using as many different frames as necessary, until a lexicon, or dictionary, can be created that accurately describes the possible uses of all the words in the language.

THE GESTURE-CALL SYSTEM

Efficient though languages are at naming and talking about things, all are deficient to some degree in communicating certain kinds of information that people need to know in order to understand what is being said. That is why human language is always embedded in a *gesture-call system* (also known as nonverbal communication). The various sounds and gestures of this system serve to "key" speech, thus providing listeners with the appropriate frame for interpreting what a speaker is saying. Through that frame, we learn information such as the age and gender of the speaker, as well as his or her individual identity if it is someone we already know. The frame also conveys subtle messages about emotions and intentions. Is the speaker happy, sad, enthusiastic, tired, or in some other emotional state? Very little of this information is conveyed by spoken language alone. In English, for example, at least 90 percent of emotional information is transmitted not by the words spoken but rather by body language and tone of voice. No language communicates people's emotions and intentions as effectively as the gesture-call system.

Kinesics

The gestural component of the gesture-call system consists of postures, facial expressions, and bodily motions that convey messages. For example, humans are *capable* of producing 250,000 facial expressions, though we use far fewer in daily life.[3] The method for notating and analyzing this body language is known as **kinesics**. Kinesic messages may be communicated directly, such as with gestures. In North America, for example, scratching our scalp, biting our lip, or knitting our brows are ways of conveying doubt. Posture is another form of nonverbal communication and can provide clues about the social status, level of education, and mental acuity of the speakers, as well as their emotional state and interest in the conversation. More complex examples are the gender signals that North American men and women send. Although some regional and class variation occurs, women when standing generally bring their legs together, at times even crossing them. Men, by contrast, hold their legs apart, with the upper legs at a 10 or 15 degree angle.

Kinesic messages often complement spoken messages. An example is nodding the head while affirming something verbally; another is smiling to indicate appreciation and enjoyment. Still other examples are punching the palm of the hand for emphasis, raising the head and brows when asking a question, and using the hands to illustrate the subject being talked about. Such gestures are rather like bound morphemes: they have meaning but do not stand alone, except in particular situations, such as a nodded response to a question.

Cross-cultural research has shown many similarities in such basic facial expressions as smiling, laughing, crying, and showing anger. The smirks, frowns, and so forth that we have inherited from our primate ancestors require little learning. Great similarity, too, exists around the world in the routine for greeting over a distance. Europeans, Balinese, Papuans, Samoans, Ju/'hoansi, and at least some South American Aboriginals all smile and nod, and if the individuals are especially friendly, they will raise their eyebrows with a rapid movement, keeping them raised for a fraction of a second. By doing so, they are signalling a readiness for contact. The Japanese, however, do not raise the eyebrows, regarding it as indecent, which shows that important differences, as well as similarities, occur cross-culturally. This point can be further demonstrated by gestural expressions for "yes" and "no." In North America, we nod our heads for "yes" or shake them for "no." The people of Sri Lanka, also, will nod to answer "yes" to a factual question, but if they are asked to do something, a slow sideways movement of the head means "yes." In Greece, the nodded head means "yes," but "no" is indicated by jerking the head back so as to lift the face, often with the eyes closed and the eyebrows lifted. Known as **conventional gestures**, body movements and gestures such as these are a result of lengthy social developments, which vary cross-culturally and have to be learned.

Touch

Touch is an interesting form of body language. Through touch we express all sorts of messages—greetings, friendship, love, sympathy, and even anger. For example, North American businesspeople shake hands when they meet; men who are old friends may slap each other on the back; women may embrace and kiss each other on the cheek. We hug family members or close friends as a sign of love and affection; while in sports such as basketball, one player may grab another in a show of force. All of these actions are transmitting messages. As with

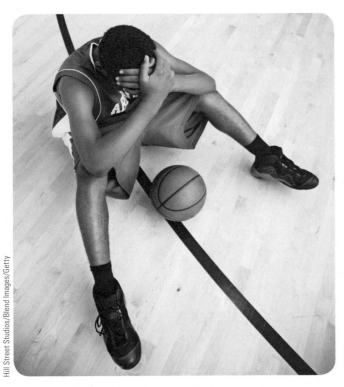

Hill Street Studios/Blend Images/Getty

This basketball player's body language clearly communicates the message of disappointment and defeat.

kinesics A system of notating and analyzing postures, facial expressions, and body motions that convey messages.

conventional gestures Body movements that have to be learned and can vary cross-culturally.

touch A form of body language involving physical contact.

There is a great deal of similarity around the world in such basic expressions as smiling, laughing, crying, and anger, evident in the expressions of these children from Asia and the Canadian Arctic.

all forms of nonverbal communication, the use of touch to convey messages varies from one culture to another. Some non-Western cultures, such as people from the Middle East, are much more touch-oriented than many North Americans.

Proxemics

The use of space, like that of touch, is culturally defined. The way we arrange the space around us and the messages conveyed by this arrangement may vary significantly from one culture to another. Canadians tend to avoid invading someone's "personal space," viewing this as a breach of good manners. In other regions of the world, however, the orderly lineup for a bus is uncommon. In many parts of Europe, purchasing a ticket for a bus sometimes involves a disorderly rush. There, people crowd together, sometimes pushing and shoving toward the ticket window. Personal space appears irrelevant in such a situation. Even within a single culture,

proxemics The study of how people use physical space in interpersonal interaction and the role that cultural paradigms play in defining what is proximate and what is overproximate.

paralanguage The extralinguistic noises that accompany language, such as crying or laughing.

gender and degree of intimacy may influence how much personal space individuals maintain. Friends will likely stand closer to each other than students and their professor; men and women tend to maintain more space than men do with other men or women do with other women. Some anthropologists study the human body, how it is perceived, how it is treated, and how it relates to spatial understandings.[4] The study of the cultural use of space, which can reveal much about cultural understandings of the body, is known as **proxemics**.

Paralanguage

Another important component of the gesture-call system, **paralanguage**, consists of cries, laughs, groans, and other sounds that are not part of language but always accompany it. The importance of paralanguage is suggested by this remark: "It's not so much what was said as how it was said." Recent studies have shown that subliminal messages communicated by seemingly minor differences in phraseology, tempo, length of answers, and the like are far more important in courtroom proceedings than even the most perceptive trial lawyer may realize. Among other things, how a witness gives testimony alters how jurors receive that testimony and bears on the witness's credibility where inconsistencies exist in testimony.[5]

Different physical stances communicate various messages. In this photo the player in the background applauds the decision of the referee, who has authoritatively shown the yellow card to the player on the ground, whose body posture communicates resignation, submission, and dejection.

Voice Qualities

It is not always easy for the linguist to distinguish between the sounds of language and paralinguistic noises. That said, two different kinds of the latter have been identified. The first has to do with **voice qualities**, which operate as the background characteristics of a speaker's voice. These involve pitch range (from low to high pitched); lip control (from closed to open); glottis control (sharp to smooth transitions in pitch); articulation control (forceful or relaxed speech); rhythm control (smooth or jerky setting off of portions of vocal activity); resonance (from resonant to thin); and tempo (an increase or decrease from the norm).

Voice qualities are capable of communicating much about the speaker's state. An obvious example is slurred speech, which may indicate that the speaker is intoxicated or ill. Or if someone says rather languidly, coupled with a restricted pitch range, that he or she is delighted with something, it probably indicates that the person is not delighted at all. The same words said more rapidly, with increasing pitch, might indicate that the speaker is genuinely excited about the matter.

Vocalizations

The second kind of paralinguistic noises consists of **vocalizations**. These are identifiable noises that are turned on and off at perceivable and relatively short intervals. They are, nonetheless, separate from language sounds. One category of vocalizations is **vocal characterizers:** the sounds of laughing or crying, yelling or whispering, yawning or belching, and the like. Speakers "talk" through vocal characterizers, which generally indicate their attitude. If a person yawns while speaking to someone, for example, this may indicate boredom. *Breaking*, an intermittent tensing and relaxing of the vocal musculature that produces a tremulousness while speaking, may indicate great emotion on the part of the speaker.

Another category of vocalizations consists of **vocal qualifiers**. These are of briefer duration than vocal characterizers, limited generally to the space of a single intonation (rather than over whole phrases). They modify utterances in terms of intensity (loud versus soft), pitch (high versus low), and extent (drawl versus clipping). Vocal qualifiers indicate the speaker's attitude in specific phrases, such as stressing the "out" in "Get out!" The third category consists of **vocal segregates**. Sometimes called *"oh oh* expressions," these are somewhat like the actual sounds of language but do not appear in the kinds of sequences that can be called words. For example, *shh, uh-uh,* or *uh-huh*. Unlike paralinguistic sounds such as sobs, giggles, and screams, *oh oh* expressions are conventional, learned, and far more variable from culture to culture.

LINGUISTIC CHANGE

Of the various approaches to linguistics, *synchronic linguistics* is concerned with registering and explaining all the features of a particular language at a given time in its history. This approach concentrates, for example, on the way modern French or Spanish functions now, without any reference to historical reasons for its development. Yet languages, like the rest of culture, have histories.

A second approach, called *historical linguistics*, examines the relationships between earlier and later

voice qualities In paralanguage, the background characteristics of a speaker's voice.

vocalizations Identifiable paralinguistic noises turned on and off at perceivable and relatively short intervals.

vocal characterizers In paralanguage, sound productions such as laughing or crying that humans "speak" through.

vocal qualifiers In paralanguage, sound productions of brief duration that modify utterances in terms of intensity.

vocal segregates In paralanguage, sound productions that are similar to the sounds of language but do not appear in sequences that can be properly called words.

© Richard Wareham Fotografie / Alamy

Figure 4.1
The Indo-European languages.

forms of the same language, looks for antecedents in older languages for developments in modern ones, and seeks evidence for relationships between languages. Historical linguists, for example, attempt to identify and explain the development of different dialects of the Cree language by investigating both natural change in the original language and the influence of contacts with other groups. No conflicts exist between historical and synchronic linguists; the two approaches are recognized as interdependent. Even a modern language is constantly changing; consider, for example, the changed meaning of the word *gay* in English, which today is used to refer to homosexual persons. Its meaning in the title of the 1942 play *Our Hearts Were Young and Gay* illustrates the word's changing usage. Such changes occur according to principles that can be established only historically.

language family A group of languages ultimately descended from a single ancestral language.
linguistic divergence The development of different languages from a single ancestral language.

Historical linguists have achieved considerable success working out the genealogical relationships among different languages. These relationships are reflected in classification schemes. For example, English is one of a number of languages classified as member of the Indo-European **language family** (see Figure 4.1). This family has 11 subgroups, which reflect the long period (8,000 years or so) of **linguistic divergence** from an ancient unified language (referred to as Proto-Indo-European) into separate "daughter" languages. English is only one of a number of languages in the Germanic subgroup (see Figure 4.2); all are more closely related to one another than to the languages of other subgroups of the Indo-European family. The same is true of French, which is one of the Romance subgroups, along with Italian, Spanish, Romanian, and so on (Figures 4.1 and 4.2). So, in spite of the differences among them, the languages of one subgroup share certain features when compared to other subgroups. As an illustration, the word for *father* in the Germanic languages always starts with an *f* or closely related *v* sound (Dutch *vader*, German *Vater*, Gothic *Fadar*). Among the Romance

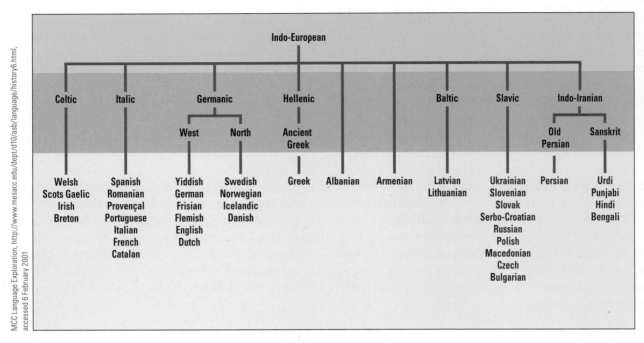

MCC Language Exploration, http://www.mesacc.edu/dept/d10/asb/language/history6.html, accessed 6 February 2001

Figure 4.2

This simplified diagram shows the relationships of languages in the same subgroup. The root was Proto-Indo-European, a language spoken by a people who spread westward over Europe, bringing with them both their customs and their language.

languages, by contrast, the comparable word always starts with a *p* (French *père*, Spanish and Italian *padre*), and all are derived from the Latin *pater*. The original Indo-European word for *father* was *p'ter*, so in this case, the Romance languages have retained the earlier pronunciation, whereas the Germanic languages have diverged.

Historical linguists have successfully described the changes that have occurred as languages have diverged from more ancient parent languages. They also have developed a means of estimating when certain migrations, invasions, and contacts of peoples took place, on the basis of linguistic similarities and differences. The concept of linguistic divergence is used to make an educated guess concerning when one group of speakers of a language separated from another group. Anthropologists use the methods and knowledge of historical linguistics as a supplement to archaeological investigations of the early histories of nonliterate peoples. For instance, the study of shifts in language forms has helped us determine how Austronesian language groups developed over the past 9,000 years as they expanded from their early homeland in Southeast Asia to Madagascar in the west and Polynesia in the east. A more complicated technique, known as **glottochronology**, was developed by Swadesh and Lees in the early 1950s to try to date the divergence of related languages, such as Latin and Greek, from an earlier common language. This technique is based on the assumption that changes in a language's **core vocabulary**—pronouns, lower numerals, and names for body parts and natural objects—change at a more

or less constant rate. By applying a logarithmic formula to two related core vocabularies, linguists should be able to determine how many years the languages have been separated. Although not as precise as this might suggest, glottochronology may be used in conjunction with archaeological data to provide a useful way to estimate when languages may have separated. As Lord Colin Refrew, the famous British prehistorian writes:

> One other recent development in the field of historical linguistics is of great potential relevance to the historical understanding of particular languages and language groups. This is the approach known as glottochronology. The basic idea is a very simple one. It begins with the general observation that the greater the time-depth which separates the members of a language family from the point of separation from their common ancestor, the greater the degree of differentiation between them.[6]

One force for linguistic change is borrowing from another language; but if borrowing were the sole force for change, linguistic differences would become less pronounced over time. Another force is novelty. Humans tend to admire the person who comes up with a new and clever

glottochronology In linguistics, a method of dating divergence in branches of language families.

core vocabulary In language, pronouns, lower numerals, and names for body parts, natural objects, and basic actions.

idiom, a new and useful word, or a particularly stylish pronunciation, so long as these do not seriously interfere with communication. Indeed, in linguistic matters, complexity tends to be admired, while simplicity seems dull. Hence, about as fast as a language is simplified, purged of needlessly complex constructions or phrases, new ones arise.

Group membership also plays a role in linguistic change. Part of this change is functional: professions, sects, and other groups in a society often need special vocabularies to communicate effectively about their interests. Beyond this, special vocabularies may serve as labelling devices; those who use such vocabularies are set off as a group from those who do not. Here, we have the paradox of language acting to prevent communication, in this case between members of different groups (e.g., parents and youth). Such linguistic barriers serve to create a strong sense of group identity. This is certainly evident in instant messaging (IM) language. IM language is a form of online communication that is becoming increasingly popular with Internet users, particularly teenagers. It is composed of short, concise sentences or fragments of sentences, as well as acronyms, abbreviations, and emoticons. IM language is another way for young people to express their small-group identity, along with dress, speech codes, hairstyles, and music.[7] At least in its early stages, it provided a "secret code" that teens could use to communicate with one another without their parents or other adults understanding.

One concern regarding IM language is whether it is having an adverse effect on Standard English, so that teenagers are losing their ability to communicate formally, especially in written form. A group of University of Toronto researchers refuted this suggestion; they found that IM language mirrored typical speech patterns.[8] Although the study group used popular abbreviations, such as "lol" (laugh out loud), "ttyl" (talk to you later), and "brb" (be right back), and various emoticons, they also used formal language they had learned in English classes. On the other hand, Naomi Baron, a professor of linguistics at American University, predicts that spelling and grammatical conventions will become even more casual with the use of abbreviations.[9] IM language is no longer the sole domain of teenagers; indeed, it appears to be finding its way into the general populace, which negates its exclusivity. It is also finding its way into professional groups. Corporate IM language is generating new words, abbreviations, and slang that fit the work situation, such as "e-dundancy" or "multi-asking" to refer to a person e-mailing and having an IM conversation at the same time.[10]

IM language is the newest manifestation of group membership affecting language change, but there are others. When a military officer speaks of "incontinent ordinance" and "collateral damage," a physician of "exsanguination," a dentist of the "oral cavity," or an anthropologist of "the structural implications of matrilateral cross-cousin marriage," they are all expressing, in part at least, their membership in a profession and their command of its language. For these "insiders," professional terminology reinforces their sense of belonging to a select in-group; to "outsiders," it often seems an unneeded and pretentious use of "bafflegab," given that

Instant communication has become embedded in our daily routines, and going online is part of our everyday lives.

perfectly adequate and simple words would do just as well. Whether needed or not, professional terminology does serve to differentiate language and to set the speech of one group apart from that of others.

Pronunciation differences between groups may be regarded in the same light as vocabulary differences. In a class-structured society, for example, members of the upper class may try to keep their pronunciation distinct from that of the lower classes. An example of a different sort involves coastal communities in Maine. In the past, people in these communities developed a regional dialect with a pronunciation style quite distinct from that of "inlanders." More recently, as outsiders have moved into these coastal communities, the traditional coastal style has come to identify those who adhere to traditional coastal values, as opposed to those who do not. In English Canada, accents tend to be fairly uniform from coast to coast.[11] Variation does exist, of course; for example, recent immigrants to Canada speak English or French with an accent, but by the second generation these accents tend to disappear. Exceptions to this homogeneity, somewhat similar to the Maine example, are evident in the Atlantic provinces, rural Ontario, and Newfoundland. Newfoundlanders' sounds and vocabulary differ from those of mainland Canadians, although as the generations pass, these linguistic differences are diminishing. However, the Newfoundland accent is derived mainly from Irish and southwestern English immigrants in the nineteenth century, so it may well take a long time for it to vanish, if it ever does.

One other far-reaching force for linguistic change is **linguistic nationalism**, which refers to an attempt by an entire country to proclaim its distinctiveness by purging its vocabulary of "foreign" terms. This phenomenon is encountered in former colonial countries in Africa and Asia. But it is by no means limited to those countries, as evidenced by periodic attempts by French Canadians to purge their language of Anglicisms such as *le weekend*. In an effort to protect the French language, which it perceived to be endangered, Quebec's government passed the French Language Charter, Bill 101, in 1976.[12] Bill 101, which declared French the sole language of Quebec, soon became an emblem of linguistic nationalism for French Canadians. Among other things, this bill requires that all public signs be in French, that immigrant children attend French schools, and that businesses over a certain size be able to conduct their business in French. The nature of Quebec's struggle for language equality and official bilingualism is explored in this chapter in Monica Heller's Original Study, "Speak Bilingue?" Also in the category of linguistic nationalism are revivals of languages, long out of common use, by ethnic minorities and sometimes even entire countries. In the latter group is the successful revival of Hebrew as Israel's first language, although not without a bitter campaign against its competitor, Yiddish.

Language Retention

Any examination of language change would be incomplete without a discussion of language retention. Indeed, linguistic diversity is seriously threatened around the world (see the Dynamic Anthropology box on page 89).[13] Of the 6,500 extant languages in the world today, nearly half are spoken by fewer than 2,500 people. Linguist Michael Krauss, a founder of the Alaskan Native Language Center, estimates that at present, only 600 of the world's languages are safe from extinction, meaning that children are still learning them at home and in school.

Language loss is not a new phenomenon; at the dawn of the 15th century, around 15,000 languages were spoken. Since then, wars, genocides, legal bans, and European expansion and assimilation agendas have led to the disappearance of more than half of these languages. The process continues: most of the 250 indigenous languages in Australia are nearing extinction (of the 50 Aboriginal languages in Queensland, most have fewer than 20 speakers); most South American languages were wiped out following the Spanish conquest; in Africa, 54 languages are dead and another 116 are near extinction; and in Asia, half the native languages are spoken by fewer than 10,000 speakers.

According to the Constitution Act of 1982, Canada's Aboriginal peoples are divided into three distinct political groups: Indian, Inuit, and Métis. The term "First Nations" was adopted by the Assembly of First Nations in the early 1970s. It was preferred over the term "Indian," and its use has become widespread. First Nations peoples have 10 language families: Algonquian, Athapaskan, Haida, Kutenai, Salishan, Siouan, Tlingit, Tsimshian, Iroquoian, and Wakashan. Inuit peoples of the Arctic speak Inuktitut, which belongs to the Aleut-Eskimo language family. Michif, an example of a mixed or contact language, is unique to Canada's Métis, most of whom are descendants of Cree or Ojibwa women and French Canadian fur trappers. In Michif, Plains Cree words and grammar are used for its verbs, while French words and grammar are used for its nouns. Interestingly, Michif is not mutually intelligible with Cree or French.[14]

linguistic nationalism The attempt by ethnic minorities, and even countries, to proclaim independence by purging their languages of foreign terms or reviving unused languages.

Original Study

Speak Bilingue?

Monica Heller,
University of Toronto

In many parts of Canada, someone who speaks only English can understandably arrive at the conclusion that French–English bilingualism is a matter of zones—French in some places, English in others—and that without too much effort, the twain do not have to meet except perhaps in the virtual worlds of channel hopping or product labelling. In some parts of Canada, even people who speak only French could live an almost monolingual life, if it were not for the fact that English does in the end dominate and touches almost everybody one way or another. But language borders are as fictive as national borders, as messy, and as complicated. Scratch the surface and you find many people who are themselves bilingual and many others who, while monolingual, nonetheless find their lives affected by the fact that the relationship between speakers of French and speakers of English is one of the structuring principles of the organization of Canadian society.

Sometimes this is pure fun. Bilinguals tell the wildest jokes (unfortunately, they are the only ones who understand them). One of my favourites was reported to me by a kindergarten teacher. One of the five-year-olds in her class came up to her to ask: *Qu'est-ce que «je m'en fiche» veut dire?* ("What does 'je m'en fiche' [I don't care] mean?"). Being a teacher who believes in self-directed learning rather than the transmission model, she instructed him to find out for himself. A while later, he came back and announced that he had found the answer: *Ca veut dire «je m'en poissonne»!* Seeing her puzzled look (she had learned English relatively late in life), he spelled it out for her: "*Fiche*, fish, *poisson* ..." and fell on the floor laughing. Now not everyone in Canada can do this; those who do, use it to great effect, and not just to amuse themselves and one another. Such performances also serve (albeit largely unconsciously) as markers of the special place that bilinguals occupy astride the language border, and may help them deal with some of the tensions that can arise there.

Which brings me to the part that is perhaps not so amusing: French–English bilingualism can also be a domain of competition and conflict. First, there are many people, of many different language backgrounds, and themselves frequently bilingual or multilingual, who sincerely believe that being monolingual is the best way for individuals or societies or both. Often this perspective is connected to a sense that realism dictates recognizing the language of power (in this case, English) for what it is, and making sure that everyone has equal access to it. It can also be connected to a commitment to achieving equity through identity—that is, giving everyone a fair chance by making sure everyone is fundamentally the same. But it can also be connected to the fear that dominant groups often feel about the ways in which difference can threaten their power.

Then there are the questions that apply to those who in principle agree that speaking both French and English is a good thing. How to explain why parents in Calgary line up all night to enroll their children in French immersion? Or why francophones in Quebec argue about when to introduce English in school? What about fights in francophone-minority communities over whether to have bilingual or French-only programs, and how much French students and parents should speak in order for students to be admitted to their schools? Or the tensions in the federal civil service between anglophones who feel they have made a commitment to learning French, only to find that their francophone workmates won't speak to them in French, and francophones who don't understand why they should act as unpaid language teachers on the job when they themselves learned English before they were in the job market? Why would a 17-year-old francophone in Toronto, talking about English speakers in French immersion, say, *«Les anglo-phones nous ont tout pris, maintenant ils veulent nous prendre notre langue»* ("The anglophones have taken everything from us, now they want to take our language")?

Clearly, for many people in Canada, French–English bilingualism is an important resource, one they believe gives them a head start in life, whether in education, in the job market, or simply in terms of enriching life experiences. The problem is that this resource is not equally distributed; some people get access to it from birth, in their families or neighbourhoods, while others must rely on schools or the media. But a more fundamental problem has to do with who will count as the best, or the real, bilinguals. And for many francophones it is frustrating to see the one advantage that came from being in a minority position being eroded by anglophone access to the same advantage. In other words, underlying many of these tensions is a competition between anglophones and francophones, understood as distinct social groups, over access to the resource of bilingualism, in the service of gaining or maintaining a position in Canadian society in which life conditions will be good.

But we must also note competition within these groups. Among anglophones, as mentioned earlier, not everyone agrees that it is important to speak French. Even among those who do strive for some form of bilingualism, there is disagreement about what the nature and extent of that bilingualism should be. Among francophones, it may be difficult to find people who deny the importance of English, but there are struggles over how to articulate the relationship between the two—that is, over how to become and to be bilingual.

Two competing views of bilingualism dominate the debate, for both groups. One is a view that is usually held by schools and other agencies or individuals who accord themselves, or are accorded, the authority to pronounce on such matters. This view (which can be seen to originate in 19th-century European ideas about the links among unified nations, states, cultures, and languages) holds that the best—indeed perhaps the only—real bilingualism is a kind of double monolingualism. Such speakers can act as though they were both monolingual speakers of English and monolingual speakers of French.

But as any bilingual will tell you, keeping your languages separate is not such an easy task, and besides, doing so cuts out all those hysterically funny bilingual jokes that keep popping unbidden into your brain. Instead, many bilinguals (more often those who learned their languages outside school, or who are far from the realms of power and prestige in Canadian society and therefore mainly working-class francophones) mix their languages. Most of them accept others' judgment of this practice as low-status; people will say they know they "don't sound too intelligent" when they talk like that, or that their French is "bad." Nonetheless, the practice persists, in a form of minority resistance and ethnoclass solidarity, the importance of which should not be underestimated. Middle-class anglophones who mix their languages, on the other hand, often confer upon the practice a mark of prestige; in any case, they also know that they can turn in a perfectly good monolingual performance, at least in English, when they need to. For them, French is not imposed, and they are in a position to define the value of their own performances. These two competing views of bilingualism are mainly about class relations and about the ways in which language and ethnicity crosscut them.

At the same time, relations across ethnoclasses are a daily occurrence in some parts of Canada. These relations have to be conducted on an ongoing basis, and many people feel they add a pleasurable intensity to life. One hears this comment often enough in Montreal, probably the place in Canada where you find the most discussion about these matters. But what is also common in Montreal is a strategy, which emerged at least 25 years ago, that allows everyday life to go on in a city where it is usually impossible to know what kind of person you are speaking to, and even less what their language politics are likely to be. *Bonjour*, hello? May I help you, *puis-je vous aider*? Bilingual talk in service encounters is increasingly routine and helps people in business make sure that the customer is always right.

Now this has just been about English and French. Let's throw Inuktitut and Cree into this mix, and Italian and Bengali. The relevance of the French–English binary categorization may go the way of the overwhelming 19th- and early 20th-century relevance of religious distinctions between Catholics and Protestants. More and more Canadians not only speak French and English but also have some knowledge of, or feel some authentic tie to, many other languages. One nation, one language, one identity: that constellation is increasingly not only impossible for many, but also not particularly interesting. People can stake claims to many identities and do not always link language to all or any of them.

Through the lens of bilingualism we can see the changes in Canadian society, what matters to whom, and why. We may not all share the same vision of our country, we may not all want to go about our lives the same way, but we ignore one another at our peril. Speak *bilingue*?

Aboriginal language conservation among First Nations, Métis, and Inuit peoples is a matter of great concern and has taken on a sense of urgency as each year fewer Aboriginal people speak their mother tongue.

In Canada's 2006 Census, the Aboriginal population is listed as 1,172,790 people, with 250,000 native speakers (21 percent). Of those who speak an Aboriginal language, just over half (51.9 percent) do so in the home. Some Native languages are flourishing, such as Cree, Inuktitut, and Ojibwe, but others are in serious decline, such as Mohawk and Tlingit. Of concern is the number of children speaking their native language. Statistics indicate that 19 percent of Aboriginal children speak an Aboriginal language; but for those living off-reserve, this figure is reduced to 6 percent for those with registered Indian status and 1 percent for those without registered Indian status.[15]

To offset the rapid disappearance of Aboriginal languages in Canada, Aboriginal language training programs are being established.

Since language retention is an important component of cultural identity, the Aboriginal peoples of Canada are fearful—and rightfully so—that 19th-century assimilation policies may come to pass in the 21st century. Attempts to revitalize Aboriginal languages are hampered by the sheer size of Canada and by the fact that Aboriginal linguistic enclaves are scattered throughout the country, surrounded by English- or French-speaking people. Yet ongoing efforts to develop Aboriginal language curriculum materials and educational programs, alongside a national policy on Aboriginal languages, are meeting with some success. A resurgence of interest in their mother tongue by young Aboriginal people offers some hope.

States often use language suppression to assert their dominance over minorities within their borders. The suppression of Scots Gaelic and Basque are two examples. In early-20th-century Canada, First Nations children were taken from their parents and placed in residential schools, where the use of Aboriginal languages was absolutely forbidden and punished with physical abuse and humiliation. In the mid-20th century, the Canadian federal government began to reverse its assimilation policies. However, it was not until the 1970s that First Nations children attending band-operated schools could receive instruction in their traditional Aboriginal language. And although the 1982 Canadian Charter of Rights and Freedoms offers vague reference to Aboriginal languages, the Assembly of First Nations (AFN) is still seeking official status for their languages in the form of constitutional recognition and legislative protections.[16]

Even Europe is not immune from language loss, despite the dominance of its languages (e.g., English, French, and Spanish) around the world. Manx, once spoken on the Isle of Man, became extinct in 1974 when its last speaker died, and when Turkish farmer Tefvik Esenc died in 1992, Ubykh, a Caucasus language with the highest number of consonants ever recorded, died with him. The loss of so many languages is a form of cultural impoverishment; we are losing not only linguistic diversity but also the links to our past. As we have already seen, language provides clues to human history, to the migrations and contacts of people in the past. Just as with

℘ *The Anthropologist's World* ℘

Visual Anthropology and Ethnographic Film: Asen Balikci

Anthropologists have long recognized the research and educational value of visual media, in particular, ethnographic films. Franz Boas and Margaret Mead readily adopted this medium to ethnographically record the lives of little-known indigenous peoples around the world. Historically, ethnographic films were used to visually present detailed and objective records of cultures, but more recently ethnographic films have been used to tell the story of a group of people, in some cases a story that otherwise would be lost. Outstanding series, such as *The Disappearing World*, bring the lives of exotic peoples to the attention of Western viewers. This form of media, then, becomes a vehicle for culture.

One of the most influential early ethnographic filmmakers was Asen Balikci, Professor of Anthropology at the University of Montreal until his retirement in 1994. Following several years (1957–65) of fieldwork in the Canadian Arctic, where he studied the Pelly Bay Netsilingmiut (Netsilik) Inuit, Balikci returned to make a series of films on the traditional lives of the Netsilik Inuit before Europeans arrived in Canada. The series was made possible through grants from the U.S. National Science Foundation and the Ford Foundation, and in association with the National Film Board of Canada (see http://www.nfb.ca for Balikci films, and others, streamed free).

The films were originally designed to eliminate the ethnocentrism prevalent in U.S. history and social sciences courses through a comparative study of world cultures. The Inuit were chosen as the first study group because North Americans had particularly simplistic and naive ideas about the Inuit. In charge of film content, Asen Balikci set out to change this perception by showing the Inuit in their traditional life as highly organized hunters who had adapted with great ingenuity to a harsh environment. Balikci chose to reconstruct the annual migration cycle of the Netsilik from traditional times, before contact with Europeans and the acquisition of rifles for hunting. Balikci studied Netsilik subsistence strategies, settlement patterns, technology, and organization, providing detail in the film about how they caught salmon and hunted seals and caribou.

Spending 13 gruelling months in the field, overcoming the elements and other hardships and accidents, Balikci and the crew shot close to 600 rolls of film and ended up with 10 hours' worth of an integrated series of films, known as the Netsilik Eskimo series. As a result of budget constraints and the failure of the public, educators, and politicians to grasp the educational value of such media, the series was removed from American grade five curricula. The American public seemed unable to deal with a realistic picture of how the Inuit really lived; rather, they preferred dramatizations and romanticized views of happy-go-lucky, primitive sport hunters. This type of "whitewashing" of the facts, ignoring realities such as tuberculosis epidemics, high infant mortality rates, and hunger, is evident in many of the ethno-documentaries available on television today.

Balikci believes that visual anthropology, although still in its infancy and often misused and neglected, has much to offer in our search for understanding human cultures. Visual anthropology also provides opportunities for people who in the past were the subject of ethnographic films to use media to present their world view, as a form of ethnic self-assertion. Regardless of other uses, ethnographic film in an academic setting is a valuable teaching tool, as it can show in one scene what could never be adequately described in a thousand words.

SOURCE: A. Balikci, "Anthropology, Film, and the Arctic Peoples: The First Forman Lecture," Anthropology Today 5, no. 2 (1989): 4–10. Copyright © Blackwell Publishing 2006. See also Zacharias Kunuk's Atanarjuat: The Fast Runner (2001) and The Journals of Knud Rasmussen (2006).

the ongoing loss of biodiversity, the disappearance of languages and their vocabularies deprives us of a great deal of the human experience, both past and present. When any language is lost, a unique way of viewing the world is also lost.

In many human societies, it is not unusual for people to be fluent in several languages, but to become so it is important to begin learning these languages as children. In Canada, this recognition led to the establishment of French immersion programs across the country. Rather than spending a few minutes each day learning French, these students are immersed in the French language for most of their instructional day. Parents and students alike have enthusiastically embraced French immersion programs, with more than 300,464 students enrolled in 2007–08.[17] Multicultural language schools that attempt to conserve other heritage languages, such as Italian, Mandarin, Greek, and Ukrainian, also have become increasingly popular in Canada. However, not everyone agrees that linguistic diversity has benefits. In the United States, proponents of an "English only" national policy argue that multilingualism is divisive, as an example often citing French separatism in Canada. What they do *not* cite are examples such as Nepal and Rwanda; in both those countries, speaking a single language has not prevented violence between factions. Nor do they mention countries like Finland, where three official languages are spoken, or Switzerland, where four exist without people being at one another's throats. The fact is, where linguistic diversity is divisive, it is often because of official policies that favour monolingualism.

LANGUAGE IN ITS CULTURAL SETTING

As the preceding discussion suggests, language is not simply a matter of combining sounds according to certain rules to come up with meaningful utterances. It is important to remember that languages are spoken by people, who are members of distinctive cultures. Social variables such as class, ethnicity, and status and outside influences such as the media all affect language use. Moreover, people choose words and sentences to communicate meaning, and what is meaningful in one culture may not be in another. In other words, our use of language affects and is affected by the rest of our culture.

Questions about how language relates to other aspects of culture are the domain of **ethnolinguistics**, a blending of ethnology and descriptive linguistics that has become almost a separate field of inquiry. Ethnolinguists study how languages classify the world; thus they are concerned with all aspects of the structure and use of

language that have anything to do with society, culture, and human behaviour.

Language and Thought

An important ethnolinguistic concern of the 1930s and 1940s was whether language might actually determine other aspects of culture. Do we see and react differently to the colours blue and green, with different cultural symbolism for each colour, only because our language has different names for these two neighbouring parts of the unbroken colour spectrum? When anthropologists noticed that some cultures, such as the Coast Salish of southwestern British Columbia, lump together blue and green with one name, they began to wonder. American linguists Edward Sapir and Benjamin Lee Whorf, drawing on experience with the Hopi language, developed a full-fledged theory known as the **Sapir-Whorf hypothesis**. Whorf proposed that a language is not simply an encoding process for voicing ideas and needs; rather, it is a shaping force—one that, by providing habitual grooves of expression that predispose people to see the world in a certain way, guides their thinking and behaviour. Some later formulations of Whorf's theory about which came first, thinking and behaviour or language, have since been criticized as both logically unsound and not amenable to any experimentation or proof. Critics have labelled the hypothesis an example of linguistic determinism; in other words, it reads too much into the culture based on its language. The hypothesis's primary value is that it draws attention to the relationship between language and the rest of culture. For example, it leads us to ask just how strong the connection is between Aboriginal language retention and cultural survival.

Linguists have found that although language is generally flexible and adaptable, once a terminology is established, it tends to perpetuate itself and to reflect and reveal the social structure and a group's common perceptions and concerns. For example, English is richly endowed with words having to do with computers—their technology, software, and function. Computer metaphors abound, as when we speak of "downloading" information, going "online," and opening "windows" using an "icon" or "button." We search for informative

ethnolinguistics The study of the relationship between language and culture.

Sapir-Whorf hypothesis The hypothesis, proposed by linguist B.L. Whorf, that states that language, by providing habitual grooves of expression, predisposes people to see the world in a certain way and thus guides their thinking and behaviour.

So important are cattle to the Nuer of southern Sudan that they have more than 400 words to describe them.

Klaus D. Francke/Peter Arnold Inc.

"sites," update our "address book," and cannot survive without our "mouse." An observer from an entirely different culture could understand a great deal about the importance of computer technology in our lives simply from our language (though only the shape of the computer mouse might reveal anything of value to them!). Similarly, anthropologists have noted that the language of the Nuer, a nomadic people of southern Sudan, is rich in words and expressions having to do with cattle. The Nuer have more than 400 words for describing cattle, and Nuer boys actually take their names from them. The Inuit have many words for snow, and the Irish have plenty of words to describe different types of rain. Thus, by studying the language, we can determine the importance and prevalence of certain resources and phenomena and their relationships to local groups.

But language does not prevent its speakers from thinking in new ways. If this new way of thinking leads to important changes in common perceptions and concerns, then language can be expected to change accordingly. Politically correct language—or more preferably, sensitive language—reflects new ways of thinking through language use. We can demonstrate respect and sensitivity for cultural groups by using their choice of a name, rather than a name given by some colonial power—for example, Inuit instead of Eskimo, Pikani instead of

Piegan, Siksika instead of Blackfoot, First Nations instead of Indian, and Ju/'hoansi instead of Bushmen or !Kung. We can also use expressions that consider the feelings of people, such as the hearing or visually challenged, and gender-inclusive terms such as humankind.

Social Dialects

In our previous discussion of linguistic change, phonological and vocabulary differences among groups were noted as important forces for linguistic change. Varying forms of a language similar enough to be mutually intelligible are known as **dialects.** Dialects are a concern of **sociolinguistics**. Sociolinguists are also concerned with the effects that society has on languages and on how "speech communities" emerge and are sustained. For example, the emergence of international call centres has been the source of recent research in which the goal is to examine how multinational companies "mould" speakers from different countries with different languages and dialects into a common "speech community" through which a standardized tone and pattern of discourse is sought.[18] Sociolinguistic analysis focuses much of its attention on dialects. Technically, all dialects are languages—they have nothing partial or sublinguistic about them. Also, the point where two dialects become distinctly different languages is roughly where speakers of one are almost totally unable to communicate with speakers of the other. Boundaries may be psychological, geographic, social, or economic and are not always very clear. Regional dialects often have a transitional territory, or perhaps a buffer zone, where features of both are

dialects Varying forms of a language that reflect particular regions or social classes and that are similar enough to be mutually intelligible.

sociolinguistics The study of the structure and use of language as it relates to its social setting.

found and understood, as between regions in China. Of the many languages spoken in China, some are offshoots or dialects of Mandarin, while others, like Cantonese and Tibetan, are totally different, originating in other language families, reflecting the ethnic diversity and historic movements of Chinese people. From a fairly young age, all schoolchildren are taught standard Beijing Mandarin, and the language of government and nonlocal business is Mandarin. However, owing to China's enormous size and diverse geography, there are numerous differences in the way people speak Mandarin. These variations are based partly on the linguistic patterns of local languages influencing the way certain sounds are made. The "shr" sound of a Beijing resident turns into a "si" sound for a resident of Guangzhou (Canton). People who speak standard Mandarin will be understood anywhere they travel in China, but they will have some difficulty understanding people in regions where the common dialect is Sichuanese or Shanghaiese.

A classic example of the kind of dialect that may set one group apart from others within a single society is one spoken by many inner-city African Americans. Technically known as African American Vernacular English, it often has been referred to as Black English or (more recently) as Ebonics.

A widespread perception among upper- and middle-class Euro-North Americans and African Americans alike is that this dialect is somehow substandard or defective, which it is not. A basic principle of linguistics is that the selection of a prestige dialect—in this case, what we may call Standard English as opposed to Ebonics—is determined by extralinguistic forces and is not dependent

 Dynamic Anthropology

World Oral Literature Project: Voices of Vanishing Worlds?

The World Oral Literature Project is an urgent global initiative to document and make accessible endangered oral literatures before they disappear. It is based at Cambridge, England.

From the Department of Archaeology and Anthropology at Cambridge University, England, comes a fascinating new project titled the World Oral Literature Project. The project is an urgent global initiative to document and make accessible endangered oral literatures before they disappear without record. The project was established in 2009 with the goal of supporting local communities and committed fieldworkers engaged in the collection and preservation of all forms of oral literature, by providing funding for original research, a digital repository for contemporary and heritage recordings, and a website through which to host open-access recordings.

For many communities around the world, the transmission of oral literature from one generation to the next lies at the heart of their cultural practice. "Oral literature" is a broad term that may include performances of ritual texts, curative chants, epic poems, musical genres, folk tales, creation tales, songs, myths, spells, legends, proverbs, riddles, tongue twisters, word games, recitations, life histories, or historical narratives. Most simply, oral literature refers to any form of verbal art that is transmitted orally or delivered by word of mouth.

These creative works are an invaluable part of a community's heritage; they are increasingly threatened when their mother tongue becomes endangered and can be lost when the language dies out. Of the world's 6,500 or so living languages, around half will cease to be used as spoken vernaculars by the end of this century. Many of the languages that once dominated parts of Canada will likely be gone. Some of the Aboriginal languages that were the first human sounds to echo across North American landscapes, and the first tongues to greet Europeans, will disappear in just a few decades. Oral traditions are usually not translated when a community switches to speaking a more dominant language. Many of these endangered languages and associated oral traditions are unwritten and undocumented, meaning that there will be no trace of them once the language becomes extinct.

While our European epics and classics are exhaustively researched and taught as literature in schools and universities, oral narratives have rarely had that chance and have been disparaged because they are not widely thought to be 'literature' by conventional Western definitions. Yet oral literature must be seen for what it is: complex, beautiful, and sophisticated, often on a par with the writings of our great authors and worthy itself of being documented, archived, and, most important, saved. While this project highlights the ongoing disappearance of many of the world's languages, it also offers some degree of hope. The World Oral Literature Project has committed itself to helping local communities, anthropologists, and linguists collect, protect, and even revitalize these voices of vanishing worlds by providing fieldwork grants and a safe digital repository and by publishing the products of critical research. The World Oral Literature Project also demonstrates the role of anthropologists and linguists in preserving and developing the diversity of languages around the world.

SOURCE: World Oral Literature Project, Museum of Archaeology and Anthropology, University of Cambridge.

on indirect virtues of the dialects themselves. In fact, African American Vernacular English is a highly structured mode of speech, capable of expressing anything its speakers care to express, often in extremely creative ways (as in "rapping"). Many of its distinctive features stem from the retention of sound patterns, grammatical devices, and even words of the West African languages spoken by the ancestors of today's African Americans. Compared with the richness of Ebonics, the Standard English dialect lacks certain sounds; contains some unnecessary sounds that others may serve for just as well; doubles and drawls some of its vowel sounds in unusual sequences that are difficult to imitate; lacks a method of forming an important aspect (the habitual); requires more ways than necessary to indicate tense, plurality, and gender; and does not mark negatives so as to make a strong negative statement.

Because their dialect differs so much from Standard English and has been stigmatized so often, speakers of African American Vernacular English often find themselves at a disadvantage outside the community of speakers. In many schools, African American children have often been judged by teachers as deficient in verbal skills and even have been diagnosed—quite wrongly—as "learning impaired." One great challenge for American schools is to find ways to teach these children how to use Standard English in situations where it would be to their advantage to do so, without belittling them for speaking the community dialect or affecting their ability to do so.

In parts of Scotland, Scots English is recognized in the schools as a valid and valued way of speaking, and it is used in teaching Standard English. As a consequence, individuals become skilled at switching back and forth between the two dialects, depending on the situation. Without being conscious of it, we all do something similar when we switch from formal to informal speech, depending on where we are and with whom we are speaking. The process of changing from one level of

Gender Perspectives

Gender in Language

The relationship between men and women has been handled in different ways, and here language can be revealing. In Japanese, for example, men and women vary their word choices depending on whom they are speaking with and the perceived status and respect of the listener. In English, words spoken by or about women imply, sometimes subtly and sometimes not, a lesser status. For example, behaviour described as "forceful" for a man might be described as "pushy" for a woman. Or, while a man "passes out" (falling directly to the ground), a woman "faints" (as if giving way to weakness). While a man is "a fighter," a woman is "spunky" or "feisty," words suggestive of lesser power. In numerous ways the traditional inequality of men and women in North American society receives linguistic expression.

Sexist language perpetuates stereotypes of women and their place in society. Take the word *housewife*. The word suggests that domestic chores are the exclusive burden of females; it gives females the idea that they were born to keep house, and it teaches males they should expect laundry, cooking, and housecleaning services from the women in their life. Another favourite is *mankind*. In this case, the word *man* or *mankind* contrives to keep women invisible by representing everyone, yet not women. The generic pronoun *he* serves the same purpose. Advocates of gender-neutral language have promoted forms such as *person* and *people* and *he or she* to replace *man*, *he*, and *his*. The title *Ms.*, to replace *Miss* and *Mrs.*, is an attempt by women to gain an identity of their own, regardless of their marital status. Recent word suggestions, such as *herstory* for history and *sportsoneship* for sportsmanship, are attempts to rewrite the English language to be more gender inclusive, yet they have met with derision and obstinacy. Negative stereotypes about men are also perpetuated using language: women are "sensitive"; men are "wimpy." We also reflect gender bias by using derogatory terms to describe men and women in a homosexual context, such as "girlie" for a gentle man, "butch" for a strong woman.

Language reflects the values and beliefs of a culture. It can also reflect changes in those values and beliefs. In Western society we hold dear the ideal of marriage and the family. Value-laden terms such as *old maid* and *spinster* show our inherent disapproval of women who do not fulfill these traditional roles, while terms such as *bachelor* for an unmarried man suggest an entirely different status. Yet as men and women became more equal in the workforce and in the home, these terms have given way to new words, such as the more gender-neutral *singles*.

The English language reflects a long-standing ideology of male dominance in Western societies. On the surface, we resolutely endorse gender equality; but when we use language that demeans women or men and essentially trivializes their existence, we are continuing to perpetuate stereotypes and reinforce gender bias in our society. The issue of gender bias in language is not a feminist issue; it is a *societal* issue.

SOURCES: C. Miller and K. Swift, "One Small Step for Genkind," in The Gender Reader, 2nd ed., ed. G.A. Ashton-Jonesand M.G. Olson (Needham Heights: Allyn and Bacon, 2000), 289–300; A.P. Nilsen, "Sexism in English: A 1990s Update," in ibid., 301–12.

language to another as the situation demands, whether from one language to another or from one dialect of a language to another, is known as **code switching**, and it has been the subject of a number of sociolinguistic studies.

Pidgin and Creole Languages

Code switching is also evident in pidgin and creole languages. **Pidgin** languages arise out of the necessity to communicate when people speaking different languages come into close and prolonged contact. A pidgin language combines, in a simplified form, the syntax, vocabulary, and grammar (e.g., prepositions omitted) of several languages. Pidgin formation is most often linked to trade and colonialism, to areas where several cultures and languages meet.

After generations of use, pidgin languages may transform themselves into **creole** languages, which possess more complex grammars and are sometimes considered the mother tongue of the speakers. A creole develops among children who are taught a pidgin as their first language. French Creole is spoken today in several regions of the Caribbean. It is a mixture of 17th-century French vocabulary, Western African syntax, and elements from American Aboriginal, Anglo-Saxon, and Hispanic languages.[19] In Haiti, 8 million people (some 80 percent of the population) speak French Creole as their mother tongue. According to Milan Kundera, French Creole was born during "the shaping of a violent civilizational process mixing elements from Europe, Africa, America, and later Asia. Creole is the bitter-sweet result of the colonial era."[20] French Creole is relatively poor in vocabulary (e.g., it is difficult to express abstract concepts), but when spoken is rich with images and humour that give the language a colour and deepness. It is through oral literature that Creole comes into its own. The true nature of French Creole is found in its songs; in it stories, which mix European and African legends; in its fairy tales and animal stories (such as Brer Rabbit and Uncle Remus); and in its jokes, riddles, and humorous images.

THE ORIGINS OF LANGUAGE

In attempting to understand the conditions that gave rise to spoken language, anthropologists examine the fossil record, the emergence of complex tools, and the communicative abilities of primates. The advantages of spoken over gestural language for a species increasingly dependent on tool use for survival are obvious. To talk with their hands, people must stop whatever else they are doing with them; speech does not interfere with that. Other benefits include the ability to talk in the dark, past

opaque objects, or among speakers whose attention is diverted.

Attempts to teach nonhuman primates to speak like humans have not succeeded. In one famous experiment in communication that went on for seven years, the chimpanzee Viki learned to voice only a few words, such as *up*, *mama*, and *papa*. When researchers changed tactics and taught chimps and gorillas to use Ameslan (ASL), they met with much greater success. Psychologists Allen and Beatrice Gardner began teaching ASL, used by the hearing impaired, to their young chimpanzee Washoe, the first of several who have since learned to sign. With vocabularies of more than 400 signs, chimps have shown they can transfer each sign from its original referent to other appropriate objects and even pictures of objects. Their vocabularies include verbs, adjectives, and words such as *sorry* and *please*. Furthermore, they can string signs together properly to produce original sentences, even inflecting their signs to indicate people and places. More impressive still, Washoe has been observed spontaneously teaching her adopted offspring Loulis how to sign by deliberately manipulating his hand. For five years, humans refrained from signing when in sight of Loulis while he learned no fewer than 50 signs. Today, Loulis and Washoe live with three other signing chimpanzees, all of whom have shown via remote videotaping that they use signs to communicate among themselves when no humans are present. Such research has been very valuable to anthropologists studying language development.

Gorillas and orangutans also have been taught ASL, with results that replicate those obtained with chimps. As a consequence, there is now a growing consensus that all of the great apes can develop language skills at least to the level of a two- to three-year-old human.[21] Not only are the comprehension skills similar, but so is acquisition order: *what* and *where*, *what to do* and *to whom*, as well as *how* questions are acquired in that order by both apes and humans. Like humans, apes are capable of referring to events removed in time and space, a phenomenon, as we saw, known as displacement and one of the distinctive features of human language.

code switching The process of changing from one level of language to another.

pidgin A language that combines and simplifies elements (vocabulary, syntax, and grammar) of two or more languages.

creole A more complex pidgin language that has become the mother tongue of a significant population.

Experiments with teaching non-human primates, especially gorillas and chimpanzees, have met with some success using American Sign Language.

The realization of language's central importance to human culture leads inevitably to speculation about how language might have begun. The origin of human language has long been a popular subject, but with so little concrete evidence, most early explanations amounted to little more than speculation. The result was a reaction against such speculation, exemplified by the ban that the Société de Linguistique de Paris imposed in 1866 against papers on linguistic origins. Today researchers have more evidence to work with—better knowledge of primate brains, new studies of primate communication, more information on the development of linguistic competence in children, more human fossils that can be used to tentatively reconstruct ancient brains and vocal tracts, and a better understanding of early hominine ways of life. Researchers still cannot prove how and when human language developed, as frustrating for many anthropologists as this fact is. As the paleoanthropologist John H. Langdon puts it, "Unfortunately, the capacity for language, depending as it does on neuronal circuitry and soft tissue anatomy, is very difficult to identify in the fossil record. Therefore we are very uncertain when and why language evolved."[22]

Exactly when the changeover was made to spoken language remains unknown, although all would agree that spoken languages are at least as old as anatomically modern *Homo sapiens* and possibly as old as 200,000 years. Based on inferential evidence, such as the manufacture of material artifacts with symbolic associations, recent anthropological literature posits a minimum date of around 75,000 years ago for the emergence of complex language.[23] What's more, no anatomical evidence exists to support arguments that the Neanderthals and other representatives of archaic *Homo sapiens* were incapable of speech. Perhaps its emergence began with *Homo erectus*, the first human ancestors to live in regions with cold climates. The ability to plan ahead for changes in seasonal conditions was crucial for survival and would not have been possible without a grammatically structured language, be it gestural or vocal. We do know that having the use of fire, *Homo erectus* would not have had to cease all activity when darkness fell. Extrapolating from this, what do we do when sitting around a campfire—talk! We also know that the vocal tract and brain of *Homo erectus* were intermediate between that of *Homo sapiens* and the earlier *Australopithecus*. It may be that the changeover from gestural to spoken language was a driving force in these evolutionary changes. Such change would likely have been gradual, but even slight changes would have had a profound impact on human evolution.

The ability to communicate, whether in written form, gestures, song, or speech is definitive of humanity, as Regna Darnell, the renowned Canadian linguist from the Department of Anthropology at the University of Western Ontario in London, Ontario, observes: "Language is the hallmark of our species. It is upon language that human culture itself depends."

Chapter Summary

1. What is language?

Language makes communication of infinite meanings possible by employing sounds or gestures that, when combined according to certain rules, result in meanings intelligible to all speakers. Linguistics is the modern scientific study of all aspects of language. *Phonetics* focuses on the production, transmission, and reception of speech sounds, or phonemes. *Phonology* studies the sound patterns of language to extract the rules that govern the ways sounds are combined. *Morphology* is concerned with the smallest units of meaningful combinations of sounds—morphemes—in a language. *Syntax* refers to the principles with which phrases and sentences are built. The entire formal structure of a language, consisting of all observations about its morphemes and syntax, constitutes its *grammar.*

2. How is language related to culture?

Language is a key component of culture. Components of culture, such as history, class, and gender, all affect language use. The languages, and the words, that people use reveal much about their cultural world. Language has a strong impact *on* culture and is also influenced *by* culture. In the modern world, the retention of language has become a key concern for linguistic anthropologists, as many languages are threatened with extinction.

3. How did language begin?

One theory of language origins is that our human ancestors, their hands having been freed by their bipedalism, began using gestures as a tool to communicate and implement intentions within a social setting. When *Homo erectus* moved out of the tropics, they needed to be able to plan for the future in order to survive seasons of cold temperatures; probably, this in turn required structured sentences to communicate information about events removed in time and space. By the time archaic *Homo sapiens* appeared, the developed ability to finely control movements of the mouth and throat had probably given rise to spoken language.

Questions for Critical Thought

1. Do you use IM language when chatting online? Do you think IM language has or will have an impact on standard written language? If so, in what ways? If not, why not?

2. How does your vocabulary reflect your interests? your opinions? the groups and culture you belong to? How does your language change in the classroom? when you are shopping or are with your family? Is your vocabulary larger or smaller than five years ago? 15 years ago? Do you use any specialized vocabulary, for example, because of a job, hobby, or a special interest in sports or music?

3. Do you know of any new languages? If so, how did they originate? What is new about them—vocabulary? grammar? syntax? How might they differ from an "older" language such as English? Can languages die? Are Latin and Sanskrit dead?

4. Do you try to use politically correct or sensitive language? Why or why not? How can your choice of words reflect your attitude toward others? How can your choice of words affect others? Explain.

5. What impression does an individual convey when he or she slouches around, avoiding eye contact? What impression does an individual convey when he or she purposefully strides into a room, head up, smiling in greeting? Do you judge people by these nonverbal messages? Explain.

6. What examples of gender bias or sexual orientation bias in your language can you identify? What does the use of these words tell you about attitudes regarding gender and sexual orientation in our society? What does it tell you about the people who use these terms?

7. Try invading someone's personal space in a social setting. Note how this person responds to your behaviour. Carry on a conversation with someone without using any body language or paralanguage. How difficult was it for you to communicate, and how much of your message was lost?

Internet Resources

What Is Language?

http://anthro.palomar.edu/language/language_2.htm

A general introduction to the concept of language, including dialects and pidgins.

Canadian Bilingualism

http://canadaonline.about.com/cs/bilingualism

This site provides two good links to discussions of Canadian bilingualism issues.

http://www.pch.gc.ca/pgm/lo-ol/annual_reports-eng.cfm

A link to the Canadian Heritage Official Languages Annual Reports.

Aboriginal Language Initiative

http://firstnationhelp.com/ali

This site looks at First Peoples heritage, language, and culture and provides a discussion of attempts to revitalize Aboriginal languages. Offers links to other information on First Nations culture.

Origins of Language

http://www.putlearningfirst.comlanguage/01origin/01origin .html

A site that addresses the nature of language and provides a time line of the origin of language.

Primate Use of Language

http://www.pigeon.psy.tufts.edu/psych26/language.htm

This extensive site discusses recent research on primates' ability to acquire language. Several projects are described.

World Languages

http://www.oralliterature.org

The website of the World Oral Literature Project. This project seeks to document and classify the world's languages, under the heading oral literatures, before they disappear without record.

Tonal Language

http://www.mnsu.edu/emuseum/cultural/language/tonal.html

An introductory look at tonal languages—the use of pitch to signal different meaning.

Suggested Readings

For a list of suggested readings, visit this textbook's website: **http://www.havilandcultural4e.nelson.com.**

Notes

1. C. Delaney, with D. Kaspin, *Investigating Culture* (Malden: Wiley-Blackwell, 2011), 118.

2. D.F. Armstrong, W.C. Stokoe, and S.E. Wilcox, "Signs of the Origin of Syntax," *Current Anthropology* 35 (1994): 349–68.

3. Christine L. Lisetti and Diane J. Schiano, "Automatic Facial Expression Interpretation: Where Human-Computer Interaction, Artificial Intelligence, and Cognitive Science Intersect," *Pragmatics and Cognition,* Special Issue on Facial Information Processing: A Multidisciplinary Perspective, 8, no. 1 (2000): 185–235.

4. Delaney, *Investigating Culture.*

5. W.M. O'Barr and J.M. Conley, "When a Juror Watches a Lawyer," in *Talking About People,* 2nd ed., ed. W.A. Haviland and R.J. Gordon (Mountain View: Mayfield, 1993), 42–4.

6. Colin Renfrew, *Archaeology and Language: The Puzzle of Indo-European Origins* (London: Random House, 1987), 113–14.

7. O'Barr and Conley, "When a Juror Watches a Lawyer."

8. N. Wright, "IM language Is Not Spoiling English, Say Canadian Researchers," 2006, http://www.earthtimes.org/articles/show/7898.html, accessed February 8, 2007.

9. N. Baron, "Viewpoint: Instant Messaging and the Future of Language," *Communications of the ACM* 48, no. 7 (July 2005): 29–31.

10. A. Storer, "Mobile Computing News: ConfucisIM and IMuttering: The new language of IM," 2005, http://searchmobilecomputing.techtarget.com/originalContent/0,289142,sid40 _gci1086276,00.html, accessed February 8, 2007.

11. J.K. Chambers, "English: Canadian Varieties," in *Language in Canada,* ed. J. Edwards (Cambridge: Cambridge University Press, 1998).

12. F. Genesee, "French Immersion in Canada" in *Language in Canada,* ed. J. Edwards (Cambridge: Cambridge University Press, 1998). See also Larrivee, *Linguistic Conflict and Language Laws: Understanding the Quebec Question* (New York: Palgrave Macmillan, 2003).

13. P. Sampet, "Last Words," *World Watch* 14, no. 3 (2001).

14. University of Calgary, "Aboriginal Languages," 2003, http://64.26.129.156/misc/nfnlsip.pdf, accessed January 16, 2007.

15. Statistics Canada, "Aboriginal Languages," 2004, http://www.statcan.ca/english/freepub/89-589-XIE/language.htm, accessed January 16, 2007.

16. L. Drapeau, "Aboriginal Languages: Current Status," in *Language in Canada,* ed. J. Edwards (Cambridge: Cambridge University Press, 1998).

17. *Official Languages: Annual Report 2007–2008,* vol. 1, *Official Language Support Programs,* cat. no. CH10-2008-1 (Ottawa: Canadian Heritage, 2008), 31.

18. A.K. Hultgren, "'Building Rapport' with Customers Across the World: The Global Diffusion of a Call Centre Speech Style," *Journal of Sociolinguistics* 15, no. 1 (2011): 36–64.

19. Multimania, "French Creole: A Language and a Culture" (n.d.), http://www.multimania.com/fdl/e-kreyol.htm, accessed June 21, 2001.

20. Ibid.

21. H.L.W. Miles, "Language and the Orangutan: The Old 'Person' of the Forest," in *The Great Ape Project,* ed. P. Cavalieri and P. Singer (New York: St. Martin's Press, 1993), 46.

22. J.H. Langdon, *The Human Strategy* (Oxford: Oxford University Press, 2005).

23. C. Heshilwood, F. d'Errico, M. Vanhaeren, F. Niekerk, and Z. Jacobs, "Middle Stone Age Shell Beads from South Africa," *Science* 304, no. 5669: 404; S. Mithen, *The Singing Neanderthals: The Origins of Music, Language, Mind, and Body* (London: Weidenfeld and Nicholson, 2005).

5 Making a Living

The basic business of a culture is securing the survival of those who live by its rules, by providing the necessities of life—food, water, shelter, hygiene, and protection from the elements. At this Bolivian market, Indian women display their wares and await customers. The study of subsistence is a fundamental aspect of anthropological study.

KEY QUESTIONS

1. What Is Adaptation?

Adaptation refers to the interaction between changes an organism makes in its environment and changes the environment makes in the organism. This kind of two-way adjustment is necessary for the survival of all life forms, including humans. Social adaptation is also a crucial facet of all human cultures, as social structures and political structures must be functionally suited to how the social formation has adapted to its environment. The degree to which the environment influences social behaviour is a much debated question in anthropology.

2. How Do Humans Adapt?

Humans adapt through the medium of culture as they develop ways of doing things compatible with the resources they have available to them and within the limitations of the environment in which they live. Humans have used various strategies to fulfill their needs; these adaptations are known as patterns of subsistence. These adaptations may be remarkably stable for long periods of time.

3. How Does Human Adaptation Differ From That of Other Animals?

Because humans possess culture and language, as well as the ability to symbolize, their adaptation and their very survival are best studied on several levels:

- the ecological adaptation, involving the provision of food and shelter and the maintenance of health as the basis of all human life;
- the social adaptation, which concerns sociability between individuals and groups, the maintenance of order, and reproduction, both biological and social, involving not only sexuality but the creation of affective ties between and among parents and offspring; and
- the psychological adaptation, which relates to how humans through language and symbolic action create and maintain meaning and coherence in their lives.

4. What Sorts of Adaptations Have Humans Achieved Through the Ages?

Foraging is the oldest and most widespread type of human adaptation. To it we owe such important elements of social organization as the sexual division of labour, food sharing, and the *domus*, a home base as the centre of daily activity. The domestication of plants and animals developed in some parts of the world between 9,000 and 11,000 years ago. Horticulture— the cultivation of domestic plants with using simple hand tools— made possible a more stationary way of life. In a pastoralist economy, which can be nomadic or seminomadic, the reliance on raising herds of domestic animals continued, but new modes of interaction with other peoples developed. Approximately 6,000 years ago, intensive agriculture produced sufficient food to support urban populations in certain places. Mechanized agriculture today is a technologically complex form of intensive agriculture associated with corporate farming and the loss of smaller farms, genetically modified foods, and environmental damage.

A culture exists to satisfy human wants and needs, but how a culture does this is highly variable. Certain needs are inescapable. First, we all must eat and drink, that is, we must ingest water, calories, and certain nutrients, and so some sort of an economic organization is required.[1]

All living beings, humans included, must satisfy certain basic needs in order to stay alive. Among these needs are food, water, and shelter. Humans may "not live by bread alone," but nobody can live for long without any bread at all, and no creature can survive for long if its relations with its environment are random and chaotic. Living beings must have regular access to a food supply, water, and a reliable means of obtaining and using these. People have an overwhelming advantage over other creatures: we have culture. If our meat supply dwindles, we can turn to a vegetable, such as the soybean, and process it to taste like meat. When our tools fail, we replace them or invent better ones. Even when our stomachs are incapable of digesting food, we can predigest food by boiling or puréeing. We are, however, subject to the same needs and pressures as all living creatures, and it is important to understand human behaviour from this point of view. The crucial concept that underlies such a perspective is *adaptation*—that is, the way humans adjust to their environments to fulfill their needs.

Throughout human history, people have adopted various strategies to secure their basic needs, such as food; these adaptations are known as **patterns of subsistence** (or the *subsistence round*). Anthropologists have identified five patterns of subsistence: foraging (hunting and gathering), pastoralism, horticulture, intensive agriculture, and mechanized agriculture (industrialism). It would be misleading to suggest that all people have followed one of these five subsistence strategies; there is a great deal of diversity in the ways people adapt to one environment or another. The Aka of South Central Africa and the historic Blackfoot of western Canada are good examples of this diversity: both are considered foragers, yet each developed a distinctly different way of making a living. We will examine the foraging practices

of these two groups later in this chapter. Even within the same cultural groups, there can be variations in subsistence strategies from region to region. Moreover, any one group may practise more than one subsistence strategy, although one form is usually dominant.

Beyond issues of resource supply and technology, however, people must also adapt socially. Communities must possess laws, rights, and regulations. How resources are harvested and allocated is important, and societies have evolved coping mechanisms that anthropologists refer to as the relations of production. These relations, and the social adaptations they require of people, such as agreement and consent, are essential adaptations if society is to function properly.

Since culture is integrated, the subsistence patterns that groups follow will influence all other aspects of their culture, from community size and permanence of settlements to marriage customs and kinship. As an example, hunter-gatherers such as the Assiniboine lived in small nomadic bands in order to follow the vast herds of bison that roamed the Canadian prairies before the Europeans arrived.

In this chapter we will briefly survey the subsistence patterns practised by humans, as well as the social behaviours that affect and are affected by these patterns. Our discussion will emphasize foraging practices, in part because this subsistence pattern continues today in various parts of the globe, and in part because it provides us with a fascinating introduction to this simple fact: all peoples of the world are descended from foragers.

ADAPTATION

The adaptation process establishes a moving balance between the needs of a population and the potential of its environment. The Tsembaga highlanders of New Guinea, who support themselves chiefly through **horticulture**—the cultivation of crops using simple hand tools—illustrate this process well.[2] Although they also raise pigs, these are eaten only under conditions of illness, injury, warfare, or celebration. At such times, the

patterns of subsistence Food-procuring strategies. Sometimes called the subsistence round.

horticulture Normally small-scale cultivation of crops using hand tools such as digging sticks or hoes.

pigs are sacrificed to ancestral spirits and their flesh is ritually consumed by the people involved in the crisis. This guarantees a supply of high-quality protein when it is most needed.

In precolonial times, the Tsembaga (also referred to as the Maring) and their neighbours were bound together in a unique cycle of pig sacrifices, which served to mark the end of hostilities between groups. Frequent hostilities were set off by a number of ecological pressures in which pigs played a significant role: since very few pigs normally were slaughtered and their food requirements were great, they could very quickly eat a local group out of house and home. The need to expand food production to support the high-prestige but hungry pigs put a strain on the land, which was best suited for farming. Therefore, when one group had driven another off its land, hostilities ended, and the new residents celebrated their victory with a pig festival. Many pigs were slaughtered, and the pork was widely shared among allied groups. Even without hostilities, festivals were held whenever the pig population became unmanageable—every five to ten years, depending on the groups' success at farming. Thus the cycle of fighting and feasting maintained balance among humans, land, and animals.

The term "adaptation" also refers to the functional response of organisms or populations to their environment. Humans have a strong impact on their environment, causing a range of changes through a process known as **anthropogenesis**. Humans have adapted to a range of environments, including anthropogenic ones. The spread of the gene for sickle-cell anemia is a case in point. Long ago, in the tropics of central Africa, a genetic mutation appeared in human populations, one that produced red blood cells that take on a sickle shape under conditions of low oxygen pressure. Because those who receive a gene for this trait from each parent usually develop severe anemia and die in childhood, natural selection operated against the spread of this gene in the local gene pool. Then slash-and-burn horticulture was introduced into this region, creating a change in the natural environment by removal—through cutting (slashing) and burning—of the natural vegetative cover. This form of anthropogenesis was conducive to the spread of mosquitoes that carry the parasite causing falciparum malaria. When transmitted to humans, the parasites live in the red blood cells and cause a disease that is always debilitating and very often fatal. Individuals who received the gene for the sickle-cell trait from only one parent, however (receiving one "normal" gene from the other), turned out to have a natural defence against the parasite, and therefore against malaria. The gene's presence caused only some of the cells to take on a sickle shape; when those cells circulated through the spleen, which routinely screens out all damaged or worn

red blood cells, the infected cells and the parasites along with them were destroyed. Since these individuals did not succumb to malaria, they were favoured by selection, and the sickling trait became more and more common in the population. Having some sickled cells offered a protection against malaria, but having too many resulted in disease and death. This is a harsh example of evolutionary change. The case of the sickle cell is what biological anthropologists refer to as biocultural evolution. Thus, while people changed their environment, their environment also changed them. Nor is this an isolated example; analogous forms of hereditary anemias that protect against malaria followed the spread of farming from southwest Asia and southeast Asia as well.

Although environments do not determine culture, they do present certain possibilities and limitations. Consider the example of a group of lakeside people who survive on a diet of fish. The fish in turn live off smaller organisms, which in turn consume green plants; plants liberate minerals from water and mud and, with the energy from sunlight, transform these minerals into proteins and carbohydrates. Dead plant and animal matter is decomposed by bacteria, returning chemicals to the soil and water. Some energy escapes from this system in the form of heat. Evaporation and rainfall constantly recirculate the water. People add chemicals to the system in the form of their wastes, and, if they are judicious, they may help regulate the balance of animals and plants.

Some anthropologists have borrowed the ecologists' concept of **ecosystem**. An ecosystem is composed of both the physical environment and the organisms living in it. The system is bound by the activities of the organisms, as well as by physical processes such as erosion and evaporation.

Human ecologists (also known as cultural or social ecologists) generally are concerned with detailed microstudies of particular human ecosystems; they emphasize that all aspects of human culture must be considered, not just the most obvious technological ones. Ecological anthropology is quite similar to human ecology, but it focuses more on how cultures interact with their environment.[3] The Tsembaga's attitude toward pigs and their cycle of sacrifices both have important economic functions; at least, that is how outsiders may see it, even if the

anthropogenesis The process whereby ecosystems are influenced or altered by humans. Examples include human impact on the environment through pollution, farming, or construction.

ecosystem A system, or a functioning whole, composed of both the physical environment and the organisms living within it.

The Great Plains of western North America supported a variety of adaptations. Before the arrival of the Europeans, the Blackfoot were nomadic bison hunters. Farther south on the upper Missouri River, the Hidatsa were semi-sedentary farmers. The Crow and Sioux farmed in the forest margins of Minnesota and Manitoba.

The arrival of the horse in North America caused profound changes. The first horses were strays from Spanish soldiers in Mexico or had been taken during raids against the Spanish by Southwestern tribes. Once horses became common, the peoples of the Plains underwent a dramatic transformation, becoming mounted hunters, and largely abandoned their agricultural past.

SOURCES: *Hidatsa Village*, George Catlin/Smithsonian American Art Museum/Art Resource, NY (left); *Cree Indians Travelling*, *Plains Cree, North Saskatchewan*, Paul Kane, 1848–1856, oil on canvas/With permission of the Royal Ontario Museum (right)

Tsembaga do not. The Tsembaga, instead, are motivated by their belief in the powers and needs of their ancestral spirits. Although the pigs are consumed by the living, they are sacrificed for ancestors. Human ecosystems often must be interpreted in cultural terms.

Adaptation also must be understood from a historical point of view. The Ojibwa, who once lived on the northern shores of Lakes Huron and Superior, provide a good example.[4] In their original home, they lived in small family units for most of the year, hunting moose, deer, bear, and beaver and gathering plant foods. During the fall months, they fished, mainly for sturgeon, while in the spring they tapped maple trees for syrup, and in the summer they harvested wild rice along the edges of the lakes. This type of subsistence enabled the Ojibwa to live a fairly sedentary life with abundant food resources.[5]

After the arrival of Europeans, the Ojibwa were one of the first groups to actively engage in the lucrative fur trade, and by the last few decades of the 18th century, many Ojibwa had obtained horses. This enabled them to become more mobile and expand their range westward, into eastern Saskatchewan and Manitoba, in search of

Groups such as the Cree and the Ojibwa did not begin life on the Great Plains. However, once they migrated westward they quickly adapted to local conditions and became successful hunters of bison.

Saying that a society is stable is not saying that it is unchanging. These northwest coastal Kwakwaka'wakw (Kwakiutl) are descendants of people who maintained a stable way of life for thousands of years, even though they often incorporated new elements into their culture. Even today, hundreds of years after the Kwakwaka'wakw's first contact with Europeans, many traditional values and practices endure.

new trapping lands.[6] Here, they readily adopted the Plains nomadic lifestyle, becoming bison hunters and accepting Plains rituals such as the Sun Dance into their culture. The Plains Ojibwa, also known as Saulteaux, did not completely abandon their woodlands heritage. They tended to live on the edge of the Plains, preferring the parkland environment. They returned to the forests to collect maple sugar each spring, and they continued to fish, although most other nomadic hunters of the Plains scorned such food. The Plains Ojibwa also retained their Midewiwin (Grand Medicine Society) curing rituals and soon became famous throughout the Plains for their conjuring powers and love charms. Cultural borrowing was not entirely in one direction; the Ojibwa introduced their Woodlands floral designs to the Plains groups. In moving from one environment to another, and in evolving from one way of life to another, the Ojibwa were able to capitalize on their existing cultural capabilities to flourish in their new environment while retaining valued elements of their own culture.

THE FORAGING WAY OF LIFE

The pygmies have been in the forest for many thousands of years. It is their world, and in return for their affection and trust it supplies them with all their needs. They do not have to cut the forest down to build plantations, for they know how to hunt the game of the region and gather the wild fruits that grow in abundance there, though hidden to outsiders. . . . They know the tiny sounds that tell where the bees have hidden their honey; they recognize the kind of weather that brings a multitude of different kinds of mushrooms springing to the surface; and they know what kind of wood and leaves often disguise this food. . . . They know the secret language that is denied all outsiders and without which life in the forest is an impossibility.[7]

Thus Colin Turnbull somewhat romantically described the Mbuti foragers of the Ituri rainforest in 1961. Today, perhaps a quarter of a million people—less than 0.00005 percent of the world's population of over 7 billion—support themselves chiefly through hunting, fishing, and gathering wild plant foods. Yet before the domestication of plants and animals, which began a mere 10,000 years ago, all people supported themselves through some combination of wild plant collection, hunting, and fishing. Of all the people who have ever lived, 90 percent have been foragers, and it was as foragers that we became truly human, acquiring the basic habits of dealing with one another and with the world around us that still guide the behaviour of individuals, communities, and nations today. Thus, if we want to know who we are and how we came to be, if we want to understand the relationship between environment and culture, and if we want to comprehend the institutions of the food-producing societies that have arisen since the development of farming and animal husbandry, we should turn first to the oldest and most universal of fully human lifestyles—the foraging adaptation. The beginnings of foraging were examined in Chapter 3.

Ten thousand years ago the world was sparsely populated and foragers could pick and choose their environments. Most of these areas have long since been appropriated by agricultural and (more recently) industrial societies. Today, foragers are found only in the world's marginal areas—the Arctic tundra, deserts, and inaccessible forests.

Some have assumed that a foraging life was difficult and that people had to struggle just to stay alive. Famously, the philosophers T. Hobbes and C. B. Macpherson described prehistoric life in this way: "No arts; no letters; no society; and which is worst of all, continual fear, and danger of violent death: and the life of man, solitary, poor, nasty, brutish and short." Behind this view lies the Western notion of progress, which, although widely accepted as a fact of nature, is actually nothing more than a culturally conditioned bias. This bias predisposes us to see what is new as generally preferable to what is old and to read human history as a more or less steady climb up an evolutionary ladder of progress. Thus, many assume that because foraging is much older than industrial society and requires less technology, it must be inferior to modern adaptations. Hence, foraging societies are referred to as "primitive," "backward," or "undeveloped"—terms that economists, politicians, and other members of industrial or would-be industrial societies use to express their own sense of superiority. Actually, though, foraging societies were and are highly developed, but in ways quite different from those of industrial societies.

Detailed studies have revealed that foragers' diets were well balanced and ample and that they were far less likely than farmers to experience severe famine. Even today, foragers who live on marginal lands lead less arduous lives than we think. The Ju/'hoansi of southern Africa's Kalahari Desert—scarcely what we would call a "lush" environment—obtain in an average work week of about 20 hours a diet that surpasses internationally recommended levels of nutrients. Add the time spent making and repairing equipment, and their total work week rises to just over 23 hours, while the equivalent of Western housework adds another 19. The grand total, just over 42 hours (44.5 for men, 40.1 for women), is still less than the time spent in North America today on the job (currently 41 hours for manufacturing jobs, just under 44 hours for white-collar jobs), on maintenance tasks, and on housework.[8] Their lives are rich in human warmth and aesthetic experience, displaying a balance of work, love, ritual, and play that many of us might envy. Small wonder, then, that some anthropologists have gone so far as to label foragers "the original affluent society." And the Ju/'hoansi are not exceptional among foragers today. We can only wonder about the level of affluence achieved by their ancient counterparts who lived in lusher environments.

All modern foragers have had some degree of interaction with neighbours whose ways of life differ radically from their own. The Ju/'hoansi, for example, have interacted periodically for 2,000 years with Bantu farmers, who keep cattle and sheep. Likewise, the foraging Mbuti of the Congo's Ituri rainforest live in a complex patron–client relationship with their neighbours, Bantu- and Sudanic-speaking peoples who are agriculturalists. They exchange meat and other forest products for farm produce and manufactured goods. During part of the year, they live in their patron's village and are incorporated into his kin group, even to the point of allowing him to initiate their sons.[9]

Some modern foragers, such as the Mbuti, have continued to maintain traditional ways while adapting to neighbours and traders; various other groups, though, have turned to this way of life after giving up other modes of subsistence. Some, such as the Cheyenne of the Great Plains, were once farmers; others, such as some of the San of southern Africa, have at times been either farmers or pastoral nomads. Nor are such transformations always of the past. In the 1980s, when a world economic recession led to the abandonment of many sheep stations in the Australian Outback, a number of Aboriginal people returned to foraging, thereby emancipating themselves from dependency on the government welfare state.

An important point that emerges from the preceding discussion is this: people in the world today who subsist by hunting, fishing, and gathering wild plants are not following an ancient way of life because they do not know any better; they are doing it either because they have been forced by circumstances into a situation

Foraging has by no means disappeared, even in industrial societies such as Canada and the United States. Some people forage occasionally for pleasure, as William A. Haviland and his brother-in-law are shown doing in the photo at the left—gathering wild mussels. Some, such as commercial fishers, like the Kwakwaka'wakw of British Columbia, forage full time.

where foraging is the best means of survival or because they simply prefer to live this way. In many cases, they find so much satisfaction in living the way they do that, like the Hadza of northern Tanzania, they go to great lengths to avoid adopting other ways of life.[10] The fact is that foraging constitutes a rational response to particular ecological, economic, and sociopolitical realities. Moreover, for at least 2,000 years, a need has existed for at least some specialist "commercial" hunter-gatherers to supply the wild forest commodities that have helped feed east–west trade since ancient times.[11]

Characteristics of Foragers

Mobility and Technology

Foragers are by definition people who do not farm or practise animal husbandry. Therefore, they must live where food sources are available, and this necessitates frequent movement. This mobility is not aimless wandering but is done within a fixed territory. Some groups—such as the Ju/'hoansi, who depend on the reliable and highly drought-resistant mongongo nut—may keep to fairly fixed annual routes and cover only a restricted territory. Others have to cover a wider territory. For example, the Great Plains Blackfoot followed a route that was determined by the seasonal movements of the bison herds. The mobility of foraging groups may also depend on the availability of water, as among the Hadza and other groups.

Hunting styles and equipment also may play a role in determining population size and movement. The Mbuti pygmies of the Ituri forest sometimes hunt with nets. This requires the cooperation of 7 to 30 families; consequently, their camps are relatively large. But the camps of Mbuti who hunt with bow and arrow number from 3 to 6 families. If there were too many archers in the same

locale, each would have to travel a great distance each day to keep out of the others' way. So only in midsummer do the Mbuti archers gather at larger camps, for spiritual ceremonies, to make matrimonial arrangements, and for social exchange. At this time the bowmen turn to communal hunts. Without nets they are less effective than their neighbours; only when the net hunters are widely dispersed in the pursuit of honey (and not competing for meat) can the archers come together and still hunt.

All over the world, foraging peoples followed an annual cycle of congregation in one season and dispersion in another. Canadian First Nations social groups illustrated this important seasonal pattern. The Mi'kmaq of the Maritimes, for example, traditionally dispersed in the winter to scattered camps composed of a few related families. They hunted seal, beaver, moose, and caribou, and in the spring remained in villages on the coast. During the summer, when resources were more plentiful, especially fish, they formed bands of several hundred people, usually at the mouth of a river, which facilitated access to other locations by birchbark canoe.[12] The Cree, who traditionally inhabited subarctic lands, lived in small social groups, constantly on the move searching for scarce resources. The Montagnais and Naskapi (Innu) of eastern Quebec and Labrador also congregated and dispersed depending on the season. They lived in winter hunting camps composed of several related nuclear families; in the summer these small groups emerged from the woods and gathered in large groups of up to 300 on the shores of lakes to fish. But in some cases the seasons were reversed. The First Nations groups of coastal British Columbia and southeastern Alaska dispersed in the summer months to fishing sites and congregated in large semipermanent winter settlements to carry out important ceremonials.[13] Regular dispersal and aggregation are hallmarks of the forager way of life; these groups survive by following ripening schedules.

Camp Organization

Another characteristic of the foraging adaptation is the small size of local groups, which usually include fewer than 100 people. Although no completely satisfactory explanation of group size has yet been offered, it seems certain that both ecological and social factors are involved. Among those suggested are the **carrying capacity** of the land, or the number of people the available resources can support at a given level of food-getting techniques, and the **density of social relations**, or roughly the number and intensity of interactions among camp members. More people means a higher social density, which in turn means more opportunities for interacting but also for conflict. Population size may also depend on a group's understanding of the environment, on spiritual components, and on cultural preferences.

Among the Ju/'hoansi, exhaustion of local food resources, conflict within the group, or the desire to visit friends or relatives living elsewhere may cause people to leave one group for another. As Richard Lee notes, "Ju love to go visiting, and the practice acts as a safety valve when tempers get frayed. In fact, the Ju usually move, not when their food is exhausted, but rather when only their patience is exhausted."[14] The ratio of children to adults may also contribute to fluctuating membership. If a camp has so many children as to create a burden for the working adults, some young families may be encouraged to join others where fewer children live. Conversely, groups with few children may actively recruit families with young children in order to ensure the group's survival. Redistribution of people, then, is an important mechanism for regulating social density, as well as for ensuring that the size and composition of local groups are suited to local variations in resources.

Band membership among the Blackfoot was also fluid. Because of limited resources, the people broke into smaller groups in early November to winter in protected areas away from the harsh winds and deep snow.[15] In the spring, they left their camps and followed the bison as they began drifting away from their winter habitat. The scattered bands reassembled in the summer for communal hunts and to celebrate the Sun Dance. In the fall, they killed large numbers of bison cows, preserving most of the meat for the long winter months. Thus, Blackfoot movements depended on the seasonal availability of food resources as well as on weather conditions.

carrying capacity The number of people the available resources can support at a given technological level.

density of social relations Roughly the number and intensity of interactions among the members of a camp or other residential unit.

Gallo Images/Getty

The foraging lifestyle does not allow for many offspring. Frequent nursing of children suppresses ovulation, reducing the likelihood of pregnancies. Among the Pygmy people of the Congo, women generally give birth to one child every three or four years.

Foragers must also make *long-term* adjustments to resources. Most foraging populations seem to stabilize at numbers well below the carrying capacity of their land. In fact, the home ranges of most foragers could support from three to five times as many people as they typically do. In the long run, it may be more adaptive for a group to keep its numbers low, rather than to expand indefinitely and risk destruction by a sudden and unexpected natural reduction in vital resources such as water. The population density of foraging groups rarely exceeds one person per 2.5 square kilometres—a very low density—even though their resources could usually support greater numbers.

How foraging peoples regulate population size relates to how they care for their children. Infants are nursed several times an hour for as many as four or five years. The constant stimulation of the mothers' nipples suppresses the hormones that promote ovulation, making conception unlikely, especially if their work keeps them physically active and they do not have large stores of body fat to draw on for energy.[16] Because they nurse for several years, women give birth only at widely spaced intervals, and the total number of offspring remains low.

Division of Labour

The division of labour, which is a crucial component of social organization and cooperation, has been observed in all human societies and is probably as old as human culture. The hunting and butchering of large game and the processing of hard or tough raw materials are almost universally masculine occupations. Women's work, by contrast, usually consists of gathering and processing a variety of vegetal foods, as well as other domestic chores. Historically, this pattern appears to have its origins in an earlier era, when hominid males, who were twice the size of females, obtained meat by scavenging it from the carcasses of dead animals, butchered it with stone tools, and shared it with females. The latter, for their part, gathered wild plant foods, probably using digging sticks and carrying devices made of soft, perishable materials. The hunting of live animals gradually replaced scavenging as a source of meat, and the biological differences between the sexes were reduced; however, the essence of the original division of labour persisted. This persistence is not novel; in many cases, past practices linger on long after their functional utility has passed.

Among foragers today, the work of women is no less arduous than that of men. Ju/'hoansi women, for example, may walk as many as 10 kilometres a day two or three times a week to gather food, carrying not only their children but also, on the return home, anywhere from 7 to 15 kilograms of food. Still, they do not have to travel quite so far afield as do men on the hunt, nor is their work usually quite so dangerous. Their tasks require less rapid mobility, do not need complete and undivided attention, and are readily resumed after interruption. All of this is compatible with the biological differences that remain between the sexes. Certainly, women who are pregnant or who have infants to nurse cannot travel long distances in pursuit of game, as men can. Besides having to range widely, the successful hunter must be able to produce high bursts of energy. Although it is certain that some women can run faster than some men, on average men can run faster than women, even when the latter are not pregnant or encumbered with infants. Because human females must be able to give birth to infants with relatively large heads, their pelvic structure differs from that of human males to a greater degree than among most other species of mammals. Generally, women have less bone mass than men, and their pelvic structure is wider. This difference provides men with an advantage in running efficiency.

On the Canadian Northern Plains, men and women tended to work together as a team—the men hunted bison and other animals, such as antelope, and the women gathered berries, tubers, and other plant foods found close to camp. Among the Sioux, a man would sometimes wear a wolf or other animal-skin robe and sneak up on a bison to kill it. Blackfoot men used several resourceful techniques for hunting bison. For example, they would lure the animals between drive lanes of stone or brush and down a hillside into a pound (a heavy corral) built of logs and branches, or they would drive the bison over a steep cliff. (This "buffalo jump" technique has ancient roots on the plains: the Head-Smashed-In Buffalo Jump in Alberta has been dated to around 3000 BC.) The men would then cut the carcasses into five or six manageable pieces each and haul them to a nearby processing area, where they would butcher and process the meat. Besides gathering plant foods (such as wild turnips, nuts, and many varieties of berries), Blackfoot women were responsible for the everyday functioning of the camp: food preparation, child care, and sewing. They also excelled at the complex task of tanning hides; indeed, they gained status within their

Foragers like the Korowai have a division of labour in which women gather and prepare food and the men hunt, whereas in pastoral groups such as the Kurds, women are responsible for tending the herds and carrying out such chores as milking the ewes.

community from their skill as tanners. The hides were used to make clothing, moccasins, and tipi covers. Blackfoot women were also gifted artists, painting designs on their tipis and clothing and decorating their clothing and moccasins with quillwork and beads.

The men and women worked together after a successful hunt, stripping hides off the carcasses, extracting marrow from the long bones, and collecting sinews for later use. Some of the meat was roasted or boiled and then eaten immediately; the rest was dried and then pounded into powder and mixed with melted bison fat and wild-cherry berries to make pemmican.[17] The vast majority of the animal was used, with very little wasted. Interestingly, the Blackfoot hardly ever ate fish, a food they found distasteful.

After the horse arrived on the Plains in the mid-18th century, hunting bison became easier and more efficient, and pedestrian hunters became mounted or equestrian hunters.[18] The white settlers moving west saw the autonomy of the mounted Aboriginals as a threat and by the 1880s had systematically slaughtered the bison herds, depriving the Aboriginal people of their means of subsistence. This slaughter accompanied environmental changes (drought, cold) that also contributed to the decline of the bison.

The nature of women's work in foraging societies is such that women can do it while taking care of children. They also can do it in company with other women, which helps alleviate the monotony of the work. In the past, the cultural gender biases of European and North American anthropologists caused them to underestimate the contributions that the food-gathering activities of women made to the survival of their group. We now know that modern foragers may obtain 60 to 70 percent of their diet from plant foods and from the fish and shellfish that women also sometimes provide. (The exceptions tend to be foragers living in the Far North, where plant foods are not available for much of the year.)

Women in foraging societies may spend some time each day gathering plant food; men do not spend all or even the greater part of their time hunting. The amount of energy expended in hunting, especially in hot climates, is often greater than the energy return from the kill. Too much time spent searching out game actually may be counterproductive. Energy itself is derived

---

 Gender Perspectives

Gender Autonomy in Foraging Groups

Although some researchers have argued that men in traditional foraging groups dominate and control women through such practices as arranging marriages and excluding women from decision making, the ethnographic literature suggests otherwise.

Foraging groups exhibit a great deal of variability in their marriage practices. For example, not all groups arrange marriages for their young people, and even in those that do, both parents have a say in choosing a prospective spouse; in fact, women often possess a great deal of influence over these decisions. A Ju/'hoansi first marriage, when the youths tend to be fairly young, is arranged, but for subsequent marriages both men and women may choose their own partners. If a marriage is an unhappy one, the woman can return home, ending the marriage. In most cultural systems, a young groom is wise to get on the good side of his future mother-in-law; otherwise, the marriage might not take place. When an Ojibwa man met a woman he wished to marry, he had to prove to her family, especially the mother, that he was a good hunter and provider. Thus, even though marriage arranging has been viewed as wife exchange organized by the men, in reality women exert a great deal of control through such practices as mother-in-law relationships, divorce rights, and choosing their own partners.

In subsistence activities, hunter-gatherers leave decision making regarding men's work to the men and women's work to the women, thus allowing the experts in each area to make the decisions. As for group decisions, both age and gender play a significant role. For example, older men and women in the Evenki culture of eastern Eurasia coordinate activities within the community. Even among the Netsilik Inuit, where most food resources come from hunting and the men make decisions about when and where to move, the women strongly influence their husbands' decisions and maintain autonomy and high status within their own domains. Women are also valued for their skill in making warm winter clothing and boots. If they didn't have those skills, the men would perish when out hunting. Young Inuit men defer to older men, and young women defer to older women, and while males rule the household, they are careful not to interfere with women's work and to always defer to their elderly grandmothers.

In many foraging groups the men consistently seek wisdom and approval from the women; consensus and discussion between both genders were and still are typical decision-making practices in foraging groups.

SOURCES: K.L. Endicott, "Gender Relations in Hunter-Gatherer Societies," in The Cambridge Encyclopedia of Hunters and Gatherers, *ed. R.B. Lee and R. Daly (Cambridge: Cambridge University Press, 1999); J.W. Friesen,* Rediscovering the First Nations of Canada *(Calgary: Detselig, 1997); A.D. McMillan,* Native Peoples and Cultures of Canada: An Anthropological Overview *(Vancouver: Douglas and McIntyre, 1988).*

primarily from plant carbohydrates, and it is usually the female gatherer who provides the bulk of the calories. A certain amount of meat in the diet, though, guarantees high-quality protein that is less easily obtained from plant sources, for meat contains exactly the right balance of all the amino acids (the building blocks of protein) that the human body requires. No single plant food does this, and in order to get by without meat, people must hit on exactly the right combination of plants to provide the essential amino acids in the correct proportions.

Food Sharing

One of the defining characteristics of foragers is the sharing of food between adults—a practice also seen among nonhuman primates, but quite rare. The functional utility of sharing is evident, with women supplying one kind of food and men another. Among many foraging groups, women have control over the food they collect and can share it with whomever they choose. Men, by contrast, are constrained by rules that specify how much meat is to be distributed and to whom. Thus, a hunter has little effective control over the meat he brings into camp. For the individual hunter, meat sharing is really a way of storing it for the future; his generosity, obligatory though it might be, gives him a claim on the future kills of other hunters. As a cultural trait, food sharing has the obvious survival value of distributing needed resources.

A final distinctive feature of the foraging economy is the importance of the camp as the centre of daily activity and as the place where food sharing takes place. Historically, foraging people have lived in camps of some permanence, ranging from the dry-season camps of the Ju/'hoansi, which serve for the entire winter, to the wet-season camps of the Hadza, which are oriented to berry picking and honey collecting and which serve for a few weeks at most. Moreover, human camps are more than sleeping areas; they are places of congregation, where eating, socializing, and food sharing occur.

Egalitarian Society

An important characteristic of the foraging society is its egalitarianism. Foragers are usually highly mobile and, lacking animal or mechanical transportation, they must be able to travel without many encumbrances, especially on food-procuring expeditions. The material goods of foragers must be limited to the barest essentials, which include implements for hunting, gathering, fishing, building, and making tools; cooking utensils; traps; and nets. The average weight of an individual's personal belongings among the Ju/'hoansi, for example, is just under 11 kilograms. They have little chance, or need, to accumulate luxuries or surplus goods, and the fact that no one owns significantly more than others helps limit status differences. Age and gender are usually the only sources of significant status differences.

It is important to realize that status differences by themselves do not imply any necessary inequality—a point that all too often has been misunderstood, especially where relations between men and women are concerned. In traditional foraging societies, there is no basis for male dominance. To be sure, women may be excluded from some male rituals, but the reverse is also true—an example is the *elima* ceremony of the Mbuti, which marks the coming of age of women. Moreover, the fruits of women's labour are not controlled by men but by the women themselves. Nor do women sacrifice their autonomy, even in societies in which male hunting rather than female gathering brings in the bulk of the food. Such was the case among the Montagnais and Naskapi (Innu) people of Labrador. The hunt was overwhelmingly important in their society. For their part, women manufactured clothing and other necessities but provided much less of the food than is common among foragers. Until recently, women as well as men could be shamans. Nevertheless, while women were excluded from ritual feasts having to do with hunting, men were excluded from ritual feasts held by women. Thus each sex carried out its own activities, with neither interfering in the activities of the other. Early missionaries to the Montagnais and Naskapi as well as to other North American First Nations groups lamented that men had no inclination to make their wives obey them. Such were the complaints of the Jesuit missions to the Huron in early 17th-century Canada, who worked long and hard to convince the First Nations men that civilization required men to impose their authority on women.

Foragers make no attempt to accumulate surplus foodstuffs, which in agrarian societies are often an important source of status. This does not mean, however, that they live on the edge of starvation. Their environment is their storehouse, and except in the coldest climates (where a surplus must be stored to see people through the lean season), or in times of acute ecological disaster, some food is always to be found in a group's territory. Because food resources are typically distributed equally within the group, no one achieves the wealth or status that hoarding might bring. In such a society, wealth is a sign of deviance rather than a desirable characteristic. This is the opposite of the logic of a capitalist economy.

The forager's concept of territory also contributes to social equality. Most local groups use home ranges where access to resources is open to all members: what is available to one is available to all. If a Mbuti hunter discovers a honey tree, he has first use rights; but when he has taken his share, others have a turn. In the unlikely possibility that he does

The forager pattern of generalized exchange, or sharing without any expectation of a direct return, also serves the end of balancing resource distribution with social equality. Refusing to share—hoarding—would be morally wrong. By sharing whatever is at hand, foragers achieve social levelling and ensure their right to share in others' windfalls.

There is remarkable diversity within foraging groups, both in the past and in the present. Their propensity to readily adopt new technologies and practices as their circumstances change underscores the flexibility of human economic systems. The same can be said for food-producing societies.

THE FOOD-PRODUCING WAY OF LIFE

The transition from food forager to food producer that began between 9,000 and 11,000 years ago in several parts of the world (Figure 5.1) has been termed the Neolithic Revolution. By changing the way they provided for their subsistence, people changed the very nature of human society.

Just why this change occurred is one of the most debated issues in anthropology. Since food production by and large requires more work than foraging, is more monotonous, promotes larger, more complex communities in which diseases easily mutate and spread, and

not take advantage of his discovery, others will. No one owns the tree; the system is first come, first served.

Although most foragers own little property, an interesting exception developed on the Great Plains after 1730, when the Blackfoot acquired horses. This significantly altered the fairly egalitarian nature of their culture. Horses soon became the most valuable possession of the Blackfoot hunters; marriages and alliances were made with the exchange of horses. With horse ownership (a form of property) came social distinctions and the beginnings of a class system.

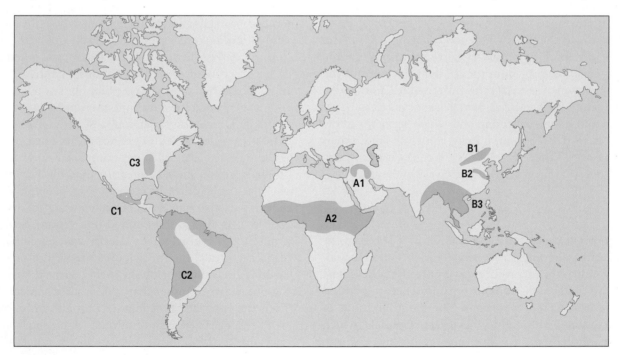

Figure 5.1

Early plant and animal domestication occurred in such widely scattered places as southwest Asia (A1), central Africa (A2), north China (B1), south-central China (B2), South and Southeast Asia (B3), Mesoamerica (C1), South America (C2), and eastern North America (C3).

Paul Conklin/Photoedit

While it supports larger and more sedentary populations than foraging, farming generally requires longer and more monotonous work.

Ernest Smith/Rochester Museum and Science Center

Although we tend to think of people as either foragers or food producers, there are numerous examples of people like the Iroquois, shown here, who rely on a mix of wild and domesticated resources. The Iroquois were swidden farmers, growing corn, squash, sunflowers, tobacco, and beans, but they also hunted, fished, and gathered wild plant foods.

is generally associated with intensive competition for resources such as land, it is unlikely that people planned to become food producers at the very beginning of the **Neolithic Age**. It appears that food production first arose as an unintended byproduct of existing food management practices. Whether by accident or design, whether by diffusion or invention, people started to tend wild stands of grasses more regularly. Some argue that this was a result of climate change; that is, the arid conditions of the Near East made hunting a less attractive prospect and caused people to rely more on domesticated crops and (later on) domesticated animals. These new food management practices promoted the development of new varieties of particular plants and animals, which came to take on increasing importance for people's subsistence. Food production probably did not provide much more food at the beginning, but it helped even out the seasonal fluctuations in wild resources and brought a heretofore unknown predictability to life.

The Settled Life of Farmers

Whatever the causes, one of the most significant correlates of this new way of life was the development of permanent settlements where families of farmers lived together, staying near their gardens. The practice of food production lent itself to a different kind of social organization; the production of crop and animal products was sufficient to yield a surplus and to provide food for all members of the community. This enabled some people to devote their time to inventing and manufacturing the equipment needed for a new, sedentary way of life. Soon after, there emerged harvesting and digging tools, pottery for storage and cooking, clothing made of woven textiles, and housing made of stone, wood, or sun-dried bricks.

The Neolithic transition brought with it a change in the division of labour. Hunting steadily decreased; men cleared fields, manufactured tools and crafts, and controlled trade. Women planted and tended the crops and animals, prepared food, looked after the house, and played the central role in child care. The transition also brought important changes in social structure. At first, social relations were egalitarian and hardly different from those that prevailed among foragers. As settlements expanded and populations grew, however, and large numbers of people began to share the same important resources, such as land and water, society became more elaborately structured. Multifamily kinship groups such as lineages, which people belong to by virtue of descent from a common ancestor but which do not commonly play a large part in the social order of foragers, were probably the organizing units. As will be discussed in Chapter 9, lineages provide a convenient way to handle the distinctive problems of land use and ownership that arise in food-producing societies.

Human groups adapted to this new way of life in a number of ways. Some became horticultural—small communities of gardeners working with simple hand tools and using neither irrigation nor the plough. Horticulturists usually cultivate several varieties of crops together in small gardens they have cleared by hand. Because these gardeners

Neolithic Age New Stone Age. In the Middle East, this period is dated between 8300 and 4500 BC. The Neolithic Age signalled the introduction of domesticated plants and animals, ceramics, and polished tone tools—all related to a change in the subsistence strategy from foraging to horticulture and agriculture. The name, derived from Greek, translates as "new stone age" (*neo* = "new," *lithos* = "stone").

This swidden plot in Chiapas, Mexico, shows what such gardens look like after slash has been burned but before the crops have begun to grow. Although it looks destructive, if properly carried out, swidden farming is an ecologically sound way of growing crops in the tropics.

DDB Stock Photography

typically use a given garden plot for only a few years before abandoning it in favour of a new one, horticulture may be said to constitute an extensive form of agriculture.

One of the most widespread forms of horticulture, especially in the tropical forests of Mesoamerica, South America, and Southeast Asia, is slash and burn, or **swidden farming**. In slash-and-burn horticulture, the natural vegetation is manually cut down, allowed to dry, and then burned. Crops are quickly planted in the ash, which fertilizes the nutrient-poor soil. After one to three years, the plot is abandoned and the natural vegetation is allowed to grow back. Use of fire to clear vast tracts of Amazonian or Indonesian forest for cattle raising and other development schemes has led many people to view slash-and-burn farming in a negative light. In fact, it is an ancient and ecologically sophisticated and sustainable way of raising food when carried out under the right conditions: low population densities and adequate amounts of land. Only when pursued in the absence of these conditions does the practice lead to environmental degradation and destruction. Properly carried out, swidden farming mimics the diversity of the natural ecosystem; moreover, growing several crops together in the same field makes them less vulnerable to pests and plant diseases than growing single crops. The system is ecologically sound; it is also far more energy-efficient than farming as carried out in countries such as Canada and the United States, which requires eight or more energy units of input for every unit of food produced. By contrast, for every unit

of energy expended, slash-and-burn farming produces between 10 and 20 units. Slash-and-burn agriculture also reduces the risk of major forest fires, because the old, dry wood is burned under controlled conditions.

Technologically more complex than horticulture is **intensive agriculture**. Intensive agricultural practices usually result in far more alteration of the landscape and the ecology than those of horticulturalists. Intensive agriculturalists use irrigation, fertilizers, and equipment such as wooden or metal ploughs, which are pulled by harnessed draft animals. Intensive agriculturalists can grow enough food to provide not just for their own needs but for those of various full-time specialists as well. This surplus may be sold for cash or may be taken from the farmers through taxes or rent paid to landowners. These landowners and other specialists typically reside in substantial towns or cities, where political power is centralized in the hands of a social elite. The distinction between horticulturalists and intensive agriculturalists is not always easy to draw. For example, the Hopi of the American Southwest traditionally employed irrigation in their farming while using simple hand tools. Moreover, they produced for their own immediate needs and lived in towns without centralized political government.

As food producers, humans have developed several major crop complexes: two adapted to seasonal uplands, two to tropical wetlands. In the dry uplands of southwestern Asia, for example, their agricultural activities follow the rhythm of the changing seasons; they cultivate wheat, barley, flax, rye, and millet. In the tropical wetlands of Southeast Asia, rice and tubers such as yams and taro are cultivated. In the Americas, people have adapted to environments similar to those of the Old World but have cultivated different plants. Maize, beans, squash, and potatoes are typically grown in drier areas, whereas manioc is grown extensively in the tropical wetlands.

swidden farming An extensive form of horticulture in which the natural vegetation is cut, the slash is subsequently burned, and crops are planted among the ashes.

intensive agriculture Large-scale cultivators employing fertilizers, irrigation, equipment, and draft animals.

Pastoralism

The smell of dung; the feel of grass on bare or sandaled feet; the sounds of cows, sheep, horses, and singing; a vast, open, arid landscape under an endless sky. These are some of the sensations of the pastoralist life—sensations that in many places are vanishing as the world Westernizes or globalizes and as pastoralists come under pressure from agriculturalists and governments bent on their "domestication."

The history of pastoralism stretches far into the past, when these communities began to travel with their herds and flocks from region to region, seeking new pastureland. They began a symbiotic relationship with their herds and flocks. The seasonal movements and the demands of herding created a particular social identity. Pastoralism was a unique adaptation, for those who practised it were not part of the settled world; they lived apart from horticulturalists and agriculturalists, yet they also interacted with and in some ways depended on these settled peoples for trade. Mobility marked the pastoralist regime as something different. The constant movement echoed a forager past, but their transience was, in the end, based on the domestication of animals.

Pastoralism is a form of agriculture with roots going back to at least 5000 BC in the Middle East. The oldest evidence of the domestication of sheep dates back some 10,000 years, to a site called Zawi Chemi Shanidar in Iraq. The age profile of the bones is suggestive of early herding practices.[19]

As a subsistence strategy, pastoralism is based on animal husbandry, the domestication of the herd, and seasonal movements in search of pasture. Anthropologists generally define a culture as pastoralist if approximately 60 percent of its nutritional needs come from its herds. Pastoralists trade for those food resources that are not provided by the herd, such as vegetables and fruits. There are limitations to the pastoralist economy, in that a commitment to mobility reduces the contribution of domesticated crops and plants in the diet. In the absence of horticultural components in the overall adaptive strategy, extensive trading networks between pastoralists and agriculturalists and hunter-foragers are important.

Pastoral production is found on roughly 25 percent of the earth's surface and produces around 10 percent of the meat eaten by the world's population.[20] Pastoralists exist in areas of the world that are considered marginal by others, such as arid land, scrubland, desert, and snow-covered mountains. The animals that are central to the pastoralist mode of production are herbivores such as horses, cows, sheep, goats, camels, and reindeer—animals that usually live in herds and feed on grasses and other plant foods. The herd basically converts grasses and plants that humans can't eat into meat that humans *can* eat, and provides other resources. From the animals the pastoralist is able to produce not only food (meat, milk, butter), but also clothing, shelter, fuel, and even companionship.

Social Structures

Many different social structures are encountered among pastoralists, but some generalizations can be made here. In general terms, the family is the basic unit of production, there is little overlap between male and female tasks, and usually, the men tend the herd while the women process its products. The children often help with the herding, driving the animals to water holes and even singing them to sleep at night. Pastoralist societies, whether in Mongolia or Africa, place the highest value on mobility. Some are nomadic, such as the Saami/Lapp populations of northern Scandinavia, but most are seminomadic, meaning that some community members remain in "permanent" villages while others move the herds to different pasturing areas. With seminomadic pastoralism, we witness what is termed transhumance. For example, sheep are moved between the cool highland valleys in the summer and warmer lowland valleys in the winter. Seminomadic pastoralists will migrate between the two locations, at each of which there will be a regular encampment or a stable settlement. Whether transhumance is being practised or not, and whether the herd is camels, goats, or horses, pastoralists show a strong commitment to social equality.

Populations

Establishing population figures for the world's pastoralists is difficult, given their mobility and the fact that many exist outside the "state" they reside in. The most authoritative study puts the world population of pastoralists at around 25 million, with 17.3 million in Africa, 3.5 million in the Middle East and South Asia, and more than 2 million in Central Asia.[21] There are smaller concentrations of pastoralists in Scandinavia and in the United States. Well-known groups such as the Maasai have long been a source of fascination for anthropologists. The Maasai are cattle pastoralists, and cattle permeate every aspect of their lives. They give names to their cattle and write poems about them. Among the Maasai, cows are very rarely killed; instead they are accumulated as a sign of wealth and traded or sold to settle debts.

pastoralism A subsistence strategy that relies on domesticated herd animals and usually requires seasonal movement to pastures.

The Maasai are one of the best known pastoralist groups, but there are many others, such as the Navajo of the United States and the Dhangars of India, both of whom practise sheep pastoralism. There are also llama breeders in the Andes, and in North America, Mongolia, and other parts of Central Asia, horse pastoralism is practised. The domestication of horse herds was much more common in prehistory. Today, horse pastoralism is really a form of modern ranching and is integrated with the broader agricultural system; this links it more to farming than to pastoralism, though horse ranching and pastoralism share certain characteristics.

Camels: Modern Pastoralist Examples

Most people do not associate camels with a pastoralist economy, because they are normally used as baggage carriers in desert areas. In fact, though, camels are a fairly large component of world pastoralism. Camel pastoralism is practised in broad areas of North Africa and the Middle East and in parts of India as well. In semi-arid and arid nations such as Ethiopia, Kenya, and Djibouti, camel pastoralism is crucial for the survival of some of the world's poorest peoples. A further challenge for those who would adapt to these marginal environments is the seasonal concentration of water, which forces these pastoralists to manage their time, resources, and knowledge systems very carefully. In these conditions, the camel is an important adaptation. There are, it is estimated, some 17 million camels worldwide, 15 million of which are of the one-humped variety (and 12 million of which are found in the "Arab" world). As the Bedouin have demonstrated for millennia, the camel is a crucial resource in desert environments. Camels can lose 40 percent of their body weight yet still function efficiently, making them essential to adaptation in these areas.

The Bedouin peoples are renowned for their camel herds and long-distance trading. But since the 1960s, under pressure from governments and industrial and agricultural projects, more and more Bedouin have given up the pastoralist life and settled in towns and cities. There are other places where camel pastoralism is not only still practised but is actually increasing. In Iran, 90 percent of which is arid or semi-arid, many areas are inhabited largely by nomadic pastoralists. It is estimated that about 1 million Iranians are pastoralists; among the many different pastoralist groups in that country are the Qashqai and the Bakhtiari of the Zagros Mountains. The pastoral life of the Bakhtiari revolves around two seasonal migrations. In the fall, before the harsh winter comes to the mountains, the nomads load their tents and other belongings on donkeys and drive their flocks down to the warm plains that border Iraq; grazing land there is excellent and well watered in

the winter. In the spring, when the low-lying pastures dry up, the Bakhtiari return to the mountain valleys, where a new crop of grass is sprouting. For this trek, they split into five groups, each containing about 5,000 individuals and 50,000 animals. The persistence of the pastoralist economy in Iran demonstrates both the historical continuity of the pastoralist way of life and the contemporary viability and sustainability of this mode of production.

Changes and the Future

In some parts of the world, pastoralism is on the rise. After the breakup of the Soviet Union, the Kyrgyz people turned more and more toward pastoralism, to such an extent that there are now some 4 million pastoralists in Kyrgyzstan alone. However, pastoralist groups face many social problems. In general, pastoralists are among the most marginalized people in the world. They have short life spans, and they must contend with ill health, a lack of education, and a lack of access to water and sanitation. In many places, their economy is under threat from the encroachment of farming land, the ambivalence or hostility of governments, and extremes of weather.[22] Lately, concerns about the environmental impact of pastoralism have been raised. Pastoralists have been blamed for the historic depletion of fertile lands—for example, for creating the desert conditions of North Africa. It is true that overgrazing reduces biotic diversity and contributes to desertification. Burning for pasture reduces forest coverage, resulting in less diversity and soil erosion. Yet against this there is another argument to be made—namely, that the migrations of herds and flocks contribute to biodiversity, as predators and other creatures follow the herds.[23] Also, there are plenty of examples of stable pastoralist communities. Having said that, even careful range and livestock management will do some damage to rangelands. So the long-term impact of pastoralism must be carefully weighed against biodiversity and other ecological values.

The future of pastoralism, this unique and creative adaption to marginal ecological conditions, is both bright and dark. The winter of 2010 was so cold in Mongolia that between 1 and 3 million livestock deaths were reported, threatening the way of life for some 2.5 million pastoralists. In places such as Kyrgyzstan where pastoralism has increased, this has been due to the collapse of other forms of economy. In other places, such as Africa and Iran, there are political opponents who would deny pasture grounds to pastoralists and have them settle in towns and villages. Droughts, wars, overpopulation, and competition from agriculturalists all threaten the existence of pastoralism. Yet it has proved resilient: it is a flexible adaptation, it is practised on marginal lands, and its ecological impact is in fact less than that of some other practices. The Maasai still sing songs about their cattle, believing they were placed on earth to herd cattle, and the Borana still sing songs to their cows. Perhaps one day these pastoralist peoples will begin to settle into agricultural or industrial communities, but for now they persist, reminding us of the adaptive flexibility of humanity and of our ancient past.

Intensive Agriculture and Nonindustrial Cities

Many of the settled agricultural communities of the Neolithic grew into large urban centres. Their production of a food surplus released some people to work in other areas, whether as scribes, ritual specialists, soldiers, or craftsmen. These craft specialists, who included carpenters, blacksmiths, sculptors, basket makers, and stonecutters, contributed to the vibrant, diversified life of the city.

Unlike horticulturalists and pastoralists, the growing populations of large urban centres needed not only to domesticate plants and animals, but also to domesticate themselves. That is, they needed to construct social relations that went beyond the immediate kinship structures of foragers and small horticultural communities. Urbanization brings with it a new social order: marked inequality develops as societies become stratified and people are ranked according to their gender, the work they do, or the family into which they are born. As social institutions cease to operate in simple, face-to-face groups of relatives, friends, and acquaintances, they become more formal and bureaucratic and develop specialized political institutions, and social adaptation becomes necessary.

Large centres such as Ur, Mohanjo-Daro, and Thebes marked the first major urbanization of the human species. This urbanization led to several other innovations. Trade intensified and expanded, The wheel, the sail, and writing were all invented, and metallurgy and other crafts were developed. In many early cities, monumental buildings, such as royal palaces and temples, were built by thousands of men, some of them slaves taken in war; these feats of engineering continue to amaze architects and engineers. The inhabitants of these buildings— the ruling class composed of nobles and priests—formed a central government that dictated social and religious rules; in turn, the merchants, soldiers, artisans, farmers, and other citizens carried out the rules.

Aztec City Life

> Then Montezuma took Cortes by the hand and told him to look at his great city . . . and we saw that huge and cursed temple . . . the 3 causeways which led into Mexico . . . and we saw oratories and fortresses all gleaming white, and it was a wonderful thing to behold.[24]

The Aztec empire, which flourished in Mexico in the 16th century, was a good example of a highly developed urban society among non-Western peoples.[25] It was just one in a long line of ceremonial cities with plazas and pyramids that were so characteristic of Mesoamerican cultures. The Aztec peoples built upon the knowledge of the Toltec who came before them and were heavily influenced by Tiotihuacan, the plaza complex located just north of present-day Mexico City. The architectural signature of Tiotihuacan is reflected in the capital of the Aztec empire. Tenochtitlán (modern-day Mexico City) was located in the fertile Valley of Mexico, 2,133 metres above sea level. Its population, along with that of its sister city, Tlatelolco, was about 200,000 in 1519, when Hernán Cortes first saw it. That made it five times more populous than. London was at the time. The Aztec metropolis had been built on an island in the middle of a lake that has since dried up. Two aqueducts brought in fresh water from springs on the mainland. A 16-kilometre dike rimmed the eastern end of the city to

The famous Temple of the Sun at Tiotihuacan, constructed in the first century, influenced both the Maya and the Aztec peoples.

Dynamic Anthropology

The Chinampas of the Aztec

Liam Kilmurray

In the late 15th and early 16th centuries, the Aztec people went from being just one among a number of groups crowding around the shores of Lake Texcoco to becoming the dominant power in the region, eventually carving out a huge empire. This empire was to be short-lived, collapsing after the arrival of the Spanish and the subsequent conquest of the Aztecs and other groups.

What was the basis of this rapid and successful expansion of the Aztec people? There have been two major explanations. The first touches on the military skill of the Aztec and the initially mercenary role their warriors played. The second points to the subsequent importation of large amounts of foodstuffs in the form of tribute from conquered peoples. However, even all this tribute could not have sustained such a vast and growing population in the urban centres around Lake Texcoco, specifically in the Aztec capital, Tenochtitlán, which had been built on an island in the lake. This lake was the site of a fascinating horticultural practice in this region: the *chinampas*.

Chinampas are sometimes referred to as floating gardens, though technically they do not float, but instead are raised fields in water. (There *are* floating gardens, both ancient and contemporary, but these are usually made from interwoven reeds forming a mat on which flowers are grown. These are towed from place to place, and thus the name "floating garden.")

The actual *chinampas*, though, were a remarkable form of irrigation agriculture that integrated the production of maize, flowers, beans, chilis, squash, amaranth, and tomatoes. These structures were constructed by dredging soil from the lake bed and adding this soil to small islands or creating small islands in the lake from scratch. Lake Texcoco was a freshwater lake, so the plots of land were watered directly from the lake itself. As more soil was dredged and added to the island, the production of maize and flowers increased. These two crops were especially important for the Aztec, one for food, the other for decorating clothes and houses and for use in the many ceremonies and rituals that were so characteristic of Aztec society.

Around the boundary of the *chinampas*, willow trees were planted. As Sutton and Anderson illustrate, these trees had several functions; they provided shade for the crops and the farmers, they helped anchor the soil by spreading a root matrix below, and they attracted birds that rested in their branches. Over time, the *chinampas* expanded until some of them supported houses. Most of them, however, remained fairly small, perhaps the size of an ice hockey rink on average. More and more artificial islands were constructed in Lake Texcoco and other smaller lakes. As the number and productivity of *chinampas* in Lake Texcoco increased, they supplied food to the population of a growing city around the lake and on the islands themselves. The city would become known as Tenochtitlán, the capital of the Aztecs, where the palace of the living god Moctezuma was located and where human sacrifice was a common sight.

Ecologically speaking, the *chinampas* were an integrated system. The farmers would plant corn seeds in smaller beds away from the main corn beds and would wait to see which ones germinated, so that as one corn yield was being harvested another could be transplanted from the smaller beds. This had the added advantage that only those corn seeds that had germinated would be selected for planting, thus saving time and effort on dead seeds. Another important component of this integrated horticultural system involved the canals that formed in the gaps between the numerous small islands. These canals were attractive to fowl, which were hunted avidly and which supplemented the Aztec diet. They also provided easy irrigation for the plants, and were used to transport the crops once they were harvested. Many species of fish were drawn to the canals, and these too became part of the productive integrated system of *chinampas*. Finally, the canals stored heat throughout the day and warmed the land overnight.

The *chinampas*, with their constantly germinating plants, allowed for year-round production of crops. It is estimated that in an area known as the Chalco zone, some 10,000 hectares supported some 100,000 people in 1519. Tenochtitlán eventually became a major metropolis. The city became synonymous with the Aztec people themselves, set in the centre of the lake as it was, its famous causeways linking it to the mainland. *Chinampas* agriculture helped Tenochtitlán grow, and as an agricultural practice it was a wonderful adaptation to a local environment—one that demonstrated the creativity of Mesoamerican cultures.

SOURCES: R.E.W. Adams, Prehistoric MesoAmerica *(Norman: University of Oklahoma Press, 1991), 377; M.Q. Sutton and E.N. Anderson,* Introduction to Cultural Ecology *(Mayfield: Altamira, 2004); F.F. Berdan,* The Aztecs of Central Mexico *(New York: Holt, Rinehart and Winston, 1982).*

prevent nearby salty waters from entering the lake around Tenochtitlán.

As in the early cities of southwest Asia, the foundation of Aztec society was intensive agriculture. Corn was the principal crop. Each family was allotted a plot of land by its lineage, where it cultivated any of a number of crops, including beans, squash, gourds, peppers, tomatoes, cotton, and tobacco. Unlike in Old World societies, only a few animals were domesticated; these included dogs and turkeys (both for eating).

Aztec agricultural success resulted in a growing population and the diversification of labour. Skilled artisans,

The Anthropologist's World

Agricultural Development and the Anthropologist

High in the Andes Mountains of South America lies the vast intermontane plain known as the Bolivian Altiplano. On this plain, not far from where the modern countries of Bolivia, Chile, and Peru meet, is Lake Titicaca, the world's highest navigable body of water. A kilometre or so from this lake's southern end stands the elaborate, monumental architecture of Tiwanaku, one of the most impressive archaeological sites in the region. Some 500 years ago, the region constituted the southern quarter of the Inca Empire. Today, it is a bleak and barren landscape where some 20,000 Aymara struggle for survival.

We now know that Tiwanaku was a major city, inhabited during its Classic Period (AD 375 to 725) by 20,000 to 40,000 people. Another 200,000 lived in the surrounding Titicaca Basin, all under the political control of Tiwanaku, a true imperial city that controlled a vast empire for centuries, at a time when the Incas were a relatively insignificant people living in the mountains north of Tiwanaku. Its political control stretched well beyond the Altiplano into northern Chile and southern Peru, where administrative centres, satellite cities, and even colonies were established.

To support the huge population of the Altiplano, Tiwanaku carried out massive land reclamation, constructing an extensive system of raised and ridged fields where hardy crops could be grown intensively. Because the builders did not have the wheel, their construction achievements must be even more appreciated. These fields have been studied by anthropologist Alan Kolata of the University of Chicago. Raised to a height of 1 to 1.5 metres with cobblestones, clay, gravel, and topsoil, these fields were carefully layered to prevent crop-killing salt from leaching into the ground. Between the fields ran canals that filled with groundwater. These 1.5-metre-wide trenches were oriented to soak up the maximum amount of solar heat during the day, thus acting as a kind of solar sump. Altiplano agriculture is so difficult today partly because of periodic frost; as much as 90 percent of a harvest can be lost as a result of it. In Tiwanaku times, however, the heat stored in the canals radiated over the fields' surfaces, raising the ambient temperatures as much as 2°C or 3°C, which is more than enough to prevent frost. In addition, the canals functioned as fertilizer factories. Organic sediments that settled in the canals could be scooped out at the end of each growing season and dumped on the fields, thereby renewing their fertility.

Having figured out how the system worked, in 1988 Kolata began to put his knowledge to work in the service of the Aymara farmers living in the region today. In selected communities, Kolata has secured the cooperation of local farmers by guaranteeing a harvest even if their experimental fields fail. Planting onions, beets, and potatoes, they have increased their yields significantly. They get up to twice as many potatoes per plant, for instance, and the potatoes are bigger and of better quality. Moreover, the farmers do not have to use scarce funds for fertilizer, since the canal muck is free, and they are not causing pollution by using chemical fertilizers.

By reintroducing an ancient technology that was lost after the Tiwanaku empire disintegrated some 1,000 years ago, Kolata is improving the quality of life for countless Aymara, reversing the poor harvests that have driven many men from the Altiplano into the valleys to the south and east, where coca is grown to be turned into cocaine. Given the technique's success, Kolata has predicted that the ancient raised-field technology will be widely used not only in Bolivia but also in many other parts of South and Central America where it is suitable.

SOURCE: Straughan, B, "The Secrets of Ancient Tiwanaku Are Benefiting Today's Bolivia," in Talking About People, 2nd ed, ed. W.A. Haviland and R.J. Gordon (Mountain View, CA: Mayfield, 1996), 76–78.

such as sculptors, silversmiths, stone workers, potters, weavers, feather workers, and painters, made good livings by pursuing their crafts exclusively. Since religion was central to the Aztec social order, these craftspeople were engaged continuously in the manufacture of religious artifacts, clothing, and decorations for buildings and temples. Other nonagricultural specialists included some of the warriors, travelling merchants (*pochteca*), priests, and the government bureaucracy of nobles.

As specialization increased, both among individuals and among the empire's cities, markets became extremely important economic and social institutions. Besides the daily markets in each city, larger markets were held in the various cities at different times of the year. Buyers and sellers travelled to these from the far reaches of the empire. The market at Tlatelolco was so vast that the Spanish compared it to those of Rome and Constantinople. At the Aztec markets, barter was the primary means of exchange. At times, however, cacao beans, gold dust, crescent-shaped knives, and copper were used as currency. In addition to its economic function, the market served social functions: people went there not only to buy or sell but also to meet other people and to hear the latest news. The other major economic institution—trade or tribute networks between the Aztec capital and other cities—brought into Tenochtitlán foods such as chocolate, vanilla beans, and pineapples, as well as luxury items such as feathers and precious stones.

Shown here is an artist's impression of the city of Tenochtitlán, with the temple plaza at the centre and the causeways leading out to the mainland.

© Gianni Dagli Orti/CORBIS

The Aztec social order was stratified into four main classes: nobles, commoners, serfs, and slaves. The nobles, among whom gender inequality was most marked, operated outside the lineage system on the basis of the land and serfs the ruler allotted to them (both acquired through conquest). The commoners were divided into lineages, on which they depended for land. Within each of these lineages, or *calpulli*, those more closely related to the lineage founder possessed higher status than those whose kinship was more distant. The third class in Aztec society consisted of serfs bound to the land and of porters employed by merchants as carriers. The lowest class were the slaves. Some voluntarily had sold themselves into bondage; some entered bondage because of gambling debts; others were captives taken in war.

The Aztecs were governed by a semidivine king, whom a council of nobles, priests, and leaders chose from among candidates of royal lineage. The king was an absolute monarch, though his counsellors advised him on affairs of state. Government officials oversaw various sites and functions, such as the tax system, the courts of justice, the government storehouses, and, importantly, military training.

The typical Aztec city was rectangular and reflected how land was divided among lineages. In the centre was a large plaza, where the temple was located as well as the house of the city's ruler. At Tenochtitlán (total area: about 52 square kilometres), a huge temple called the Templo Mayor and two lavish palaces stood in the central plaza called the Sacred Precinct. Surrounding this area were other ceremonial buildings associated with each lineage.

As in a modern city, housing in Tenochtitlán ranged from squalid to magnificent. On the outskirts, on some *chinampas*, were the farmers' huts, made from wooden posts, thatched straw, and wattle plastered with mud. In the city proper were the houses of the middle class— graceful, multiroomed, one- and two-storey buildings of mortared stone, each surrounding a flower-filled patio and resting on a stone platform for protection against floods. It is estimated that Tenochtitlán had about 60,000 houses. The focal points of the city were the *teocallis*, or pyramidal temples, where religious ceremonies, including human sacrifices, were held.

The palace of the emperor Moctezuma boasted numerous rooms for attendants and concubines, a menagerie, hanging gardens, two zoos, and a swimming pool. Since Tenochtitlán sat in the middle of a lake, it was unfortified. It was connected to the mainland by three causeways. Communication among different parts of the city was easy; people could travel by land or by water. Canals bordered by footpaths ran throughout the city. The Spaniards reported that thousands of canoes plied these canals, carrying passengers and cargo; they were so impressed by this communication network that they called Tenochtitlán the Venice of the New World.

Ancient cultures such as the Aztec achieved spectacular results in the fields of architecture, astronomy,

Shirley Fedorak

Complex machinery, such as the combines shown here on a Saskatchewan farm, lightens workloads and enables agriculturalists to open up larger farms.

Shirley Fedorak

Family-run grain farms, such as the one shown here, are fast becoming a thing of the past as young people seek employment in urban centres rather than brave the uncertainties of farming.

arts, and technology. Most of these achievements were based upon intensive agricultural practices.

MECHANIZED AGRICULTURE

Mechanized agriculture, or *industrial agriculture,* relies on complex technological and production practices rather than on human power. This versatile form of agriculture exhibits characteristics and faces challenges not as evident in intensive agriculture.[26] Farm mechanization has resulted in larger farms that use more machinery and less human labour and in the intensive use of fertilizers, insecticides, and other chemicals to maximize yields. The use of chemicals and complex machinery has downsides: both are expensive and consume large amounts of energy, and environmental damage—such as water pollution from pesticide runoff—is inevitable. Plant hybrids and genetically enhanced seeds have increased production. However, in recent years there has been growing concern over possible health risks associated with genetically altered foods.

The Canadian Family Farm

More than a century ago, immigrants from other countries began arriving on the Canadian prairies, bringing with them agricultural expertise and the strong resolve to build a better life for their families. Canadian farming practices have changed drastically since that time: farms have grown in size, and agriculture has become increasingly dependent on machinery, fertilizers, and irrigation. With the advent of corporate farming, there is a growing threat to the family farm, which has long been the essence of Canadian agriculture. Independent,

family-owned and -operated enterprises are disappearing more and more rapidly.

The division of labour on Canadian family farms tends to be gender specific. The men operate the farm equipment, ready the fields for seeding, care for livestock, and take off the harvest, while the women manage the household chores, prepare meals, and tend gardens. If the need arises, however, women often help with "male duties," feeding livestock, driving grain trucks, and picking up machine parts in town. Children, too, begin helping on the farm at an early age; they operate farm equipment well before they reach adulthood, care for younger children, plant and weed gardens, and generally contribute to the farm's upkeep.

Family farms were thriving until the mid-1970s. But in the years since, Canadian farmers have faced seemingly insurmountable obstacles: low commodity prices, European and American subsidies, rising expenses and increasing debt, fears of environmental contamination and ecological disturbance, and government unwillingness to provide meaningful assistance. These problems are wreaking havoc on Canadian agriculture and threatening to destroy the family farm and depopulate rural Canada. Statistics tell the story: in 1976 Canada had 338,552 farms; by 1986 this number had fallen to 293,089; by 2001, to only 246,923. As of 2006, only 229,373 viable farms remained in Canada.[27] If the family farm disappears, it will be an incalculable loss for Canadian society.

mechanized agriculture Large-scale agriculture dependent on complex technology and biotechnology rather than human power to increase production.

Chapter Summary

1.   What is adaptation?

Adaptation is both a physical process and a social process. The manner in which different groups and societies adapt to their environment is referred to as their subsistence round, or their mode of production. Human groups have adapted to a wide variety of environments and practise an equally wide variety of ways to make a living. Foraging, which includes hunting, gathering, and fishing, is one of the oldest adaptations of humanity and requires a set of social structures that are compatible to mobile societies. Horticulture is almost as old as foraging and was the first adaptive strategy of humans; it relied on the domestication of plants. This adaptive strategy required settling down and building villages, which in turn required social adaptation. Other modes of adaptation are agriculture, which includes the domestication of plants and animals, and pastoralism, which is the movement of domesticated herds and flocks on a seasonal basis in search of pasture lands.

2.   How do humans adapt?

The adaptive strategy a human group chooses has a profound impact on its social adaptation, the enactment of rules and norms, and the form of social order. These cultural patterns in turn affect the laws, customs, and traditions of human societies, helping structure marriage, kinship, and legal systems. Throughout human history, the ways in which humans have adapted have demonstrated remarkable continuity.

3.   How does human adaptation differ from that of other animals?

Humans differ from animals in that they adapt to their environments not only physically but also culturally. The latter includes the use of language and technology. The advent of large urban centres with complex social structures required that human groups develop a hierarchy of order. This often resulted in the development of kingship, egalitarian rule, or chiefdoms displaying a mix of both. Society as created by human adaptations can contain many different occupations and even different ethnicities. Human groups respond by creating internal order and structures based on symbols, language, and laws.

4.   What sorts of adaptations have humans achieved through the ages?

As this chapter has demonstrated, humans have gone from being scavengers, to hunters, to collectors, to producers. Each mode of production has its own intricacies and peculiarities, but all serve the same goal of sustaining the physical and social needs of human groups. With the emergence of agriculture some 10,000 years ago, the human species began a process of adaptation that saw increasing degrees of specialization, until it reached the advanced and intensive agriculture we are familiar with today.

Questions for Critical Thought

1. Is change always adaptive? What are examples of nonadaptive change in North American culture?

2. The Incas of South America did not have or widely use the wheel or the concept of zero. Does this mean that Incan culture was nonadaptive?

3. Is cultural change or increasing technical complexity the same as progress? Why or why not? Do you believe in human "progress"? If so, in what sense do we progress?

4. Can large-scale, technologically advanced societies and small-scale societies coexist? Under what circumstances could they coexist?

5. If global warming causes dramatic climate changes, how might we adapt? For example, if the temperatures increase and the moisture levels decrease, what adaptations will agriculturalists have to make? Will we be able to adapt?

6. If the Canadian family farm disappears, how will this affect the economic and social life of all Canadians?

7. In North America, our reliance (some would say overreliance) on technology makes us vulnerable if that technology fails us. As a case in point, the August 2003 blackout in eastern North America affected 50 million people. Have we become too reliant on advanced technology? What would happen if this technology failed us (e.g., what would happen if we no longer had access to gasoline for our vehicles)? Are there ways for us to avoid or reduce the impact of technology failures?

8. Since culture is an integrated system, to what degree do the subsistence patterns that groups follow influence other aspects of their culture, from community size and permanence of settlements to marriage customs and kinship?

Internet Resources

Horticulture—The Swidden Ecosystem

http://www.nusantara.com/heritage/swid/index.html

A small site with pictures displaying the six stages of swidden horticulture.

Chinampas—Aztec Farming

http://www.plu.edu/~mayac

A succinct, descriptive website that chronicles the stages of *chinampas* agriculture.

Nonviolent Societies

http://www.peacefulsocieties.org

This site documents current examples of foraging and non-foraging societies that are able to live their lives successfully, largely without violence.

Hunter-Gatherers

http://www.heritage.nf.ca/aboriginal/beothuk.html

A comprehensive site that covers many aspects of the now-extinct Beothuk people's culture.

http://www.cambridge.org/9780521571098

This site briefly describes the *Cambridge Encyclopedia of Hunters and Gatherers* (2004), a comprehensive source on all aspects of hunter-gatherer life, with 50 case studies and special essays on social life, gender, music, and art, as well as on hunter-gatherers' political position in the modern world.

Ju/'hoansi and San People

http://www.kalaharipeoples.org

The Kalahari Peoples Fund (KPF) of Austin, Texas, provides aid, assistance, and advocacy for San and other peoples of semi-arid southern Africa. Founded in 1973 by anthropologists, the KPF projects have included community-based resource management, mother-tongue curricula, and research on land rights and community development.

Blackfoot People

http://www.blackfeetnation.com

The official site of the Blackfeet Nation.

http://whc.unesco.org/en/list/158

UNESCO website regarding the Head-Smashed-In Buffalo Jump site.

Canadian Agriculture

http://www.agr.gc.ca

An extensive government-sponsored site with information on many aspects of Canadian agriculture, such as marketing, policies, imports and exports, and the past, present, and future of agriculture in Canada.

Suggested Readings

For a list of suggested readings, visit the textbook's website at **www.havilandcultural4e.nelson.com**.

Notes

1. Mark Q. Sutton and E.N. Anderson, *Introduction to Cultural Ecology* (Toronto: Altamira, 2004), 96.

2. R.A. Rappaport, "Ritual Regulation of Environmental Relations Among a New Guinea People," in *Environment and Cultural Behavior,* ed. A.P. Vayda (Garden City: Natural History Press, 1969), 181–201.

3. Conrad P. Kottak, "The New Ecological Anthropology," *American Anthropologist,* New Series, 101, no. 1 (March 1999): 23–35.

4. A.D. McMillan, *Native Peoples and Cultures of Canada: An Anthropological Overview* (Vancouver: Douglas and McIntyre, 1988), 140–41.

5. John W. Friesen, *Rediscovering the First Nations of Canada* (Calgary: Detselig, 1997), 85.

6. Friesen, *Rediscovering the First Nations of Canada,* 121.

7. Colin M. Turnbull, *The Forest People* (Toronto: Touchstone, 1961), 14.

8. E. Cashdan, "Hunters and Gatherers: Economic Behavior in Bands," in *Economic Anthropology,* ed. S. Plattner (Stanford: Stanford University Press, 1989), 23–24.

9. Turnbull, *The Forest People,* 14.

10. K. Hawkes, J.F. O'Connell, and N.G. Burton Jones, "Hadza Women's Time Allocation, Offspring Provisioning, and the Evolution of Long Postmenopausal Life Spans," *Current Anthropology* 38 (1997): 552.

11. D. Stiles, "The Hunter-Gatherer 'Revisionist' Debate," *Anthropology Today* 8, no 2 (1992): 15.

12. Bruce R. Morrison and Roderick C. Wilson, eds., *Native Peoples: The Canadian Experience* (Toronto: Oxford University Press, 2004).

13. McMillan, *Native Peoples and Cultures of Canada: An Anthropological Overview,* 128–37.

14. R. Lee, *The Dobe Ju/'hoansi,* (Fort Worth: Wadsworth-Thomson, 2003), 65.

15. J.C. Ewers, *The Horse in Blackfoot Indian Culture* (Washington: Smithsonian Institute Press, 1985).

16. M.F. Small, "Making Connections," *American Scientist* 85 (1997): 503.

17. K.E. Kidd, "Blackfoot Ethnography," Archaeological Survey of Alberta, No. 8 ([1937]1986).

18. McMillan, *Native Peoples and Cultures of Canada: An Anthropological Overview,* 128–37.

19. Chris Scarre, *The Human Past* (London: Thames and Hudson, 2005), 211–12.

20. Roger Blench, *Pastoralists in the New Millennium* (London: Overseas Development Institute, 2001).

21. S. Sandford, *Management of Pastoral Development in the Third World* (London: John Wiley, 1983).

22. "Harsh Weather Leaves Millions of Livestock Dead in Mongolia," *The Economist* (2010),

http://www.economist.com/blogs/banyan/2010/03/harsh_winter_and_uncertain_future_mongolias_pastoralists.

23. Jonathan Davies, "Turning the Tide: Enabling Sustainable Development for Africa's Mobile Pastoralists," *Natural Resources Forum* 32 (2008): 175–184.

24. Bernard Díaz del Castillo, 1519 (1632/1963), *Historia verdadera de la conquista de la Nueva España* [The Conquest of New Spain Penguin Classics], trans. J.M. Cohen (Harmondsworth: Penguin Books, 1973).

25. Most of the following information is taken from F.F. Berdan, *The Aztecs of Central Mexico* (New York: Holt, Rinehart and Winston, 1982).

26. Barlett, P.F. (1989). "Industrial Agriculture," In *Economic Anthropology,* ed. S. Plattner (Stanford: Stanford University Press, 1989).

27. Statistics Canada, 2006 Census of Agriculture, http://www.agrifood.info/connections/2007/Statistics_Canada_(2).pdf.

6 Economic Systems

The fundamental characteristic of the market in non–Western societies is that it always involves a marketplace, where actual goods are exchanged. In this photo, people transport the goods they have produced to a floating market in Thailand. These goods will be sold or exchanged for goods that they do not produce themselves.

KEY QUESTIONS

1. What Is Economic Anthropology?

Economic anthropology is a subfield of cultural anthropology that studies the economic practices of past and present societies. Besides strictly analyzing economics, though, anthropologists examine the intricate relationships between economic structures and the social structures of societies. Past economic logic was often very different from today, and it is partly by comparing non-Western systems that anthropologists can reveal the current economic logic of Western capitalism. Economic anthropology reveals how the economy is connected with human kinship, marriage, and residential systems. It also examines a fascinating variety of indigenous economic systems.

2. How Do Anthropologists Study Economic Systems?

Anthropologists study how goods are produced, distributed, and consumed in the context of the total culture. Although they have borrowed theories and concepts from economists, most anthropologists feel that the principles derived from studies of Western market economies have limited applicability to economic systems in which people do not produce and exchange goods for profit.

3. How Do Economies Work?

Every human culture has a division of labour by age and sex, with some additional craft specialization. Land and other valuable resources usually are controlled by groups of relatives, such as bands or lineages, or by private ownership. Production takes place in the quantity and at the time required, and most goods are consumed by the group that produces them. Levelling mechanisms ensure that no one accumulates significantly more goods than anyone else.

4. How and Why Are Goods Exchanged?

People exchange goods through reciprocity, redistribution, and market exchange. *Reciprocity* involves the exchange of goods and services of roughly equivalent value and is often undertaken for ritual purposes or to gain prestige. *Redistribution* requires some sort of centralized authority and/or religious elite to collect and then reallocate resources in the form of either goods or services. *Market exchange* in nonindustrial societies means going to a specific place for direct exchange of goods. *Consumption*, meaning the food and beverages we intake and the resources we use, is the third component of any economic system.

Every group of people, each distinct culture, and all societies operate within an **economic system** that regulates the production, distribution, and consumption of goods. Whether in desert environments populated by mobile Bedouin, or in the crowded prehistoric towns of Lower Egypt, economic systems operate to ensure the survival of human groups and their cultures. As noted earlier, subsistence patterns are an important part of any economy. Yet economic *systems* encompass far more than we have covered so far. This chapter will examine the systems of exchange, redistribution, and consumption.

ECONOMIC ANTHROPOLOGY

Studying the economies of nonliterate peoples is where we are most likely to fall prey to interpreting anthropological data in terms of our own technologies, our own conceptions of work and property, and our own determinations of what is rational. For example, different cultures place different values on production and consumption. Leisure time in the Amazon does not mean the same thing as a long weekend in British Columbia. As the French anthropologist Maurice Bloch once commented about the Balinese, "time is not money everywhere."[1] Some cultures work fewer hours than others and produce fewer material items than others. To Western observers, such people are apt to appear lazy: "instead of disciplined workers, they are reluctant and untrained laborers."[2] If the people happen to be hunters and gatherers, even the hard work is likely to be misinterpreted. In Western culture, hunting is defined as a "sport"; hence, the men in food-foraging groups often are perceived as spending virtually all their time in "recreational pursuits," while the women are seen as working themselves to the bone. This perception was evident when Europeans encountered First Nations hunter-gatherers, who appeared somewhat lazy and casual about acquiring resources. These early explorers did not realize that traditional hunting-and-gathering First Nations cultures were present-oriented, survival-centred societies.[3] When they required meat, they hunted to fill their current needs, and when they required plant foods, they gathered what they needed.

Conventional economists have come to appreciate this quite different way of approaching the fundamental economics of everyday life. John Gowdy has used the abundant evidence from studies of foraging peoples to urge on his fellow economists a reappraisal of the fundamental assumptions of scarcity and limited means on

which modern economics is based.[4] People such as the Mi'kmaq were not given to storing food in anticipation of the future, except for foods such as dried fish to sustain them for short periods. On the other hand, First Nations groups on Canada's Pacific coast preserved and stored large quantities of berries, shellfish, and fish, using such techniques as sun- and wind-drying and smoking. The foods were often packed in carved, red cedar bentwood boxes to be consumed or distributed during the winter season, when they devoted much of their time to ceremonial life.

To understand how the schedule of wants or demands of a given society is balanced against the supply of goods and services available, it is necessary to introduce a noneconomic variable—the anthropological variable of culture. In any given economic system, economic processes cannot be interpreted without culturally defining the demands and understanding the conventions that dictate how and when these demands are satisfied. The fact is that the economic sphere of behaviour is not separate from the social, religious, and political spheres and thus not free to follow its own purely economic logic. Certainly, economic behaviour and institutions can be analyzed in purely economic terms, but to do so would mean to ignore crucial noneconomic considerations.

As a case in point, we may look briefly at yam production among the Trobriand Islanders, who inhabit a group of coral atolls to the north of New Guinea's eastern end.[5] Trobriand men spend a great deal of their time and energy raising yams, not for themselves or their own households but for their sisters and married daughters. The purpose of this yam production is not to provision the households they are given to, because most of what people eat they grow for themselves, in gardens where they plant taro, sweet potatoes, tapioca, greens, beans, and squash, as well as breadfruit and banana trees. The reason a man gives yams to a woman is to show his support for her husband and to enhance his own influence.

Once the woman receives the yams, they are loaded into her husband's yam house, symbolizing that he is a man of power and influence in his community. Some of these yams he may use to purchase a variety of things, including arm shells, shell necklaces and earrings, pigs, chickens, and locally produced goods such as wooden bowls, floor mats, lime pots, and even magic spells. Some he must use to discharge obligations, presenting yams to the relatives of his daughter's husband when she marries or making required contributions following the death of a member of his lineage. Finally, any man who aspires to high status and power must show his worth by organizing a yam competition, during which he gives away huge quantities of yams to invited guests. As anthropologist Annette Weiner explains, "A yam house, then, is like a bank account; when full, a man is wealthy and powerful.

economic system The production, distribution, and consumption of goods.

 *Dynamic Anthropology*

The Economics of Ancient Monuments

Liam Kilmurray

Economic anthropologists not only document contemporary communities but also look to the distant past. For some anthropologists, the illumination of ancient practices is an end in itself; for others, understanding past economies and the role that monuments played in them is equally important. Ancient monuments are closely associated with economic change—that is, with the advent of agriculture.

The Medicine Wheels of the Canadian Prairies, the stepped ziggurats of the Sumerians, the pyramids of the Egyptians, and the colossal temples of the Maya were all collective architectural projects associated with ritual, an economic surplus, and the emergence of social complexity. As agriculture spread westwards from the Middle East, several millennia after its introduction around 10,000 years ago, the societies that adopted it slowly abandoned hunting and foraging, and most began to construct large-scale monuments.

Between 4500 and 2000 BC, in the part of the world known as the Atlantic façade—the coastal areas of Western Europe, including Spain, France, Holland, Denmark, Britain, and Ireland—a particular type of monument came to dominate. These are the megaliths, such as Stonehenge, Newgrange, and the astonishing stone rows of Carnac in France.

Types of Monuments

There are more than 100,000 megalithic monuments of various types along the Atlantic façade. They range from simple dolmens to complex passage graves. The latter consist of two rows of orthostats (upright stones), which, when covered with capstones, form a corridor. This stone corridor leads to an inner tomb, often containing a corbelled arch, an ingenuous invention in the absence of the true arch. The bones of the dead were often located in recesses within these end tombs. Many passage graves are associated with a circle of standing stones, Calanais being a prime example. The stone circle is a major monument type in itself, whether or not it is associated with another monument. Stonehenge is an example of such a standing stone circle set within a henge

that contained the cremated remains of thousands of people.

There are many other types of megalithic monuments, including the dolmen, the wedge tomb, and the court tomb. There are also, built roughly at the same time, thousands of nonmegalithic monuments such as the Dorset cursus, which are built of soil, and Silbury Hill, Europe's largest man-made structure. There are many types of Neolithic monuments, but they all share one central component. As Bradley notes for the Neolithic period in Western Europe, during the fourth and third millennia BC, "of all the developments that can be identified during this period, only one was shared with the communities of the Neolithic: the mobilisation of human labour for building public monuments."

An Economic Interpretation?

These megalithic monuments pose specific questions for economists of prehistory. Just as the foraging and hunting groups of these areas began to abandon their ancient lifestyles and adopt agriculture or horticulture, monuments became their defining characteristic. Why did people without stone tools, with very little power from animals (if any), and with limited numbers of people, invest such vast amounts of time, effort, and labour to erect monuments that, on the face of it, did not appear to have any economic functions? Also, the people of the Atlantic façade had fairly short life spans, with most people dying in their mid-thirties. This made the construction of these monuments all the more remarkable, raising the prospect that it was mainly teenagers or people in their early twenties who built monuments such as Stonehenge.

The changes generated by the introduction of agriculture were monumental. It affected every aspect of a way of life that had persisted for many millions of years. The economic changes brought on by agriculture led to changes in mobility, kinship, religion, relationships, and other social arenas. Change

Megalithic monuments are common along the Atlantic façade of Western Europe and the Mediterranean. Built of stone, before the age of metals, many—such as the one at Calanais, Outer Hebrides, Scotland—have survived the ravages of time (ca. 3000 BC)].

Liam Kilmurray

CONTINUED

CONTINUED

was monumental also in the sense that many communities laboured for decades, even centuries, to construct lasting testaments of their communities in the form of monumental architecture. The process of change was slow, and some monuments may actually have preceded the changes in economic practices that farming caused. We do know that within a century after agriculture was introduced, the communities of the entire Atlantic façade were primarily agricultural. What, then, was the relationship between these monuments and farming? And what can prehistorians who are interested in ancient economies learn from the monuments of the Atlantic façade?

Technology and Labour

The sheer scale of the megaliths speaks of an output of human labour unparalleled anywhere during this time period. Many monuments, such as Carnac, Stonehenge, Newgrange, and Calanais, involved tremendous amounts of power. The individual rocks themselves are often of epic proportions, as are the mounds that often cover them.

At Newgrange, the passage grave and mound contains some 180,000 tons of material: rock, stone, and soil. The Sarsen stones that make up the trilithons at Stonehenge weigh over 20 tons each. The famous Stonehenge bluestones (actually, they are speckled dolomite) were transported some 250 miles from a site in Wales. More than 50 of them, weighing around 4 tons each, were floated up rivers and streams, dragged across downs, and pulled up hillsides to reach Stonehenge. It has been estimated that some 30 million work hours went into the construction of this wonderful monument. The Carnac rows in France contain some 3,000 large stones. Many more monuments have been built in high locations with minimal technology. Clearly, then, the monuments were important enough to warrant such efforts. They would have eaten up much of the economic surplus

Liam Kilmurray

Stonehenge, southern England, was begun around 3000 BC. The final stage of the monument, which stands today, was completed approximately 3,500 years ago (1500 BC).

of small communities. The remnants of daily life are not as well known as monuments or burials. The archaeologist Geoffrey Bibby once wrote that "if settlements were lacking, graves were abundant, and nothing in the life of the prehistoric European was so well illuminated as his leaving of it."

Our contemporary understandings of effort, scale, surplus, economy, and "time on the job" cannot be made to "fit" the logic of monumental constructions. The key lies in interpreting just what the monuments were for. In this regard, there is no singular answer. The many different types of monuments served multiple purposes: some were for burial, some were astronomically significant, others had no burials and no significant alignments, and others may hint at territorial marking. Many are simply not understood in terms of function. Whatever the actual explanations or functions of any given monument, what they have in common is the process of altering the earth, of marking the land, and of creating permanent testaments to the community, its past, and its future. The effort of constructing and

maintaining a monument may have been connected to the economy in terms of keeping a workforce together for those times of the year when the agricultural regime required large numbers of people to sow and harvest.

The economic costs of the monuments were astonishing; the input of materials and labour were enormous. The persistence of monuments reveals to us the determination, the abilities, and the economic success of Neolithic communities. Economists of prehistory remain fascinated by the monumental scale of the past. Monuments such as Calanais and Stonehenge stand today as reminders of a distant time when communities banded together in common cause to build monuments that were meant to last the ages.

SOURCES: R. Bradley, The Significance of Monuments *(London: Routledge, 1998), 161;* L. Kilmurray, *"The Re-Generation of the Neolithic: Social Memory, Monuments, and Generations,"* British Archaeological Reports, *August 2009;* G. Bibby, The Testimony of the Spade *(London: Knopf, 1956), 241.*

Until yams are cooked or they rot, they may circulate as limited currency. That is why, once harvested, the usage of yams for daily food is avoided as much as possible."[6]

By giving yams to his sister or daughter, a man not only expresses his support for the woman's husband but also makes the latter indebted to him. Although the recipient rewards the gardener and his helpers by throwing a feast of cooked yams, taro, and ample pieces of pork, this in no way pays off the debt. Nor does the gift of a stone axe blade (another valuable in the Trobriand

© Dr. William E. Mitchell

Trobriand Island men devote a great deal of time and energy to raising yams, not for themselves but to give to others. These yams, which have been raised by men related through marriage to a chief, are about to be loaded into the chief's yam house.

system), which may reward an especially good harvest. The debt can be repaid only in women's wealth, which consists of bundles of banana leaves and skirts made of the same material dyed red.

Like people the world over, the Trobriand Islanders assign meanings to objects that make the objects worth far more than their cost in labour or materials. Yams, for example, establish long-term relationships that lead to other advantages, such as access to land, protection, assistance, and other kinds of wealth. Thus, yam exchanges are as much social and political transactions as they are economic ones. Banana leaf bundles and skirts, for their part, are symbolic of the political state of lineages and of their immortality. In their distribution, which is related to rituals associated with death, we see how men in Trobriand society are ultimately dependent on women and their valuables. So important are these matters to the Trobrianders that even in the face of Western money, education, religion, and law, these people remain as committed today as in the past to

yam cultivation and the production of women's wealth. Viewed in terms of Western economics, these activities appear to make little sense, but viewed in terms of Trobriand values and concerns (using cultural relativism), they make a great deal of sense.

In any examination of world economic systems, it is also important to point out that, unlike in the past, contemporary small-scale cultures do not operate in isolation; today each group of people is connected to a larger economic system—namely, the market economy—and a political organization—the state. Small-scale economic systems often coexist within this larger economic sphere, although at times they may also come into conflict. It is also notable that many markets, especially in the developing world, operate as a form of black market outside the national economic system.

RESOURCES

In every culture, customs and rules govern the kinds of work done, who does the work, who controls the resources and tools, and how the work is accomplished. Raw materials, labour, and technology are the productive resources a social group uses to produce desired goods and services. The rules surrounding the use of these resources are embedded in the culture and determine the way the economy operates.

Patterns of Labour

Every human culture has a division of labour based on sex and age categories. Dividing by sex increases the chances that learning necessary skills will be more efficient, since only half the adult skills need be learned by any individual. Dividing labour by age provides sufficient time for developing those skills.

Sexual Division of Labour

Whether men or women do a particular job varies from group to group, but some types of work are likely to be set apart as the responsibility of either one sex or the other. Tasks most often regarded as "women's work" tend to be carried-out near home. The tasks most often regarded as "men's work" tend to require strength, rapid bursts of energy, frequent travel away from home, and higher levels of risk and danger. However, many exceptions occur, as in cultures where women regularly carry burdensome loads or put in long hours of hard work cultivating crops in the fields. As mentioned in Chapter 5, on Canadian family farms, women often work alongside the men, driving grain trucks and combines or picking up spare parts in town. They do this work on top of their regular household duties—seasonal gardening and preserving (canning, freezing, pickling), the cooking of hearty meals, and the demanding work of raising children. Before the advent of sophisticated farm machinery, their duties were even more physically challenging. In the 19th-century kingdom of Dahomey, in West Africa, thousands of women served as warriors for the Dahomean king; in the eyes of some observers, they were better fighters than their male counterparts. During the Second World War, Soviet women fought on the front lines, and in the Cuban revolution there were women commanders. In modern guerrilla uprisings, women often fight. Clearly, the sexual division of labour cannot be explained simply as a consequence of male strength, male expendability, or female reproductive biology.

Instead of looking for biological imperatives to explain the sexual division of labour, a more productive strategy is to examine the kinds of work men and women do in the context of specific cultures to see how the work relates to cultural practices and historical factors. Researchers find three configurations, one featuring flexibility and sexual integration, another involving rigid segregation by sex, and a third combining elements of the other two.[7] The flexible/integrated pattern is exemplified by people such as the Mbuti and is seen most often among foragers and subsistence farmers. In such cultures, both sexes perform up to 35 percent of activities with approximately equal participation, while tasks deemed appropriate for one sex may be performed by the other without loss of face. Boys and girls grow up in much the same way, learn to value cooperation over competition, and learn to interact with one another on a relatively equal basis.

Sexually segregated cultures rigidly define almost all work as either masculine or feminine, so men and women rarely engage in joint efforts of any kind. Task differentiation was highly developed amongst many Inuit groups.[8] In such cultures, it is inconceivable that someone would do something considered the work of the opposite sex. This pattern is often found in pastoral nomadic, intensive agricultural, and industrial societies, where men's work keeps them outside the home for much of the time. Thus, boys and girls alike are raised primarily by women, who encourage compliance in their charges. At some point, however, boys undergo a role reversal to become men. To do this they must prove their masculinity through assertions of male superiority, and hence authority over women.

In the third, or dual sex, configuration, men and women carry out their work separately, but the relationship between them is one of balance rather than inequality. Although competition is a prevailing ethic, each sex manages its own affairs, and the interests of both men and women are represented at all levels. Thus, as in sexually

Often, work that is considered inappropriate for men (or for women) in one culture is performed by them in another. Here, a laundryman works in Bangalore, India, and women work on construction.

AFP/Getty Images

The age division of labour has come sharply to the fore in the coping strategies of those affected by the AIDS crisis in Africa. With women and men dying from the disease in the prime of life, many grandmothers have stepped in to raise their children's children. Nevertheless, the economic situation of African families has been severely strained.

integrated cultures, neither sex exerts dominance over the other. The dual sex orientation was common among First Nations peoples, whose economies were based on subsistence farming, as well as among several West African kingdoms, including the Dahomeans.

Age Division of Labour

Dividing labour according to age is also typical of human cultures. Among the Ju/'hoansi, children are not expected to contribute to subsistence until they reach their late teens. The Ju/'hoansi equivalent of "retirement" comes somewhere around the age of 60. Elderly people are not expected to contribute much food. However, older men and women alike play an essential role in spiritual matters; freed from food taboos and other restrictions that apply to younger adults, they may handle ritual substances considered dangerous to those still involved with hunting or having children. By virtue of their old age, they also remember things that happened far in the past. Thus they are repositories of accumulated wisdom and social memory and can suggest solutions to problems younger adults have never before had to face. Thus they are far from being unproductive members of society.

In some foraging cultures, women do continue to make a significant contribution to provisioning in their older years. Among the Hadzabe of Tanzania, their contribution is critical to their daughters, whose foraging abilities are significantly impaired when they have new infants to nurse. Lactation is energetically expensive, while holding, carrying, and nursing an infant interferes with the mother's foraging efficiency. Those most affected are a woman's weaned children, who are not yet old enough

to forage effectively for themselves. The problem is overcome, however, by the foraging efforts of grandmothers, whose time spent foraging is greatest when their infant grandchildren are youngest and their weaned grandchildren receive the least food from their mothers.[9] The role of grandmothers has become particularly critical in many parts of contemporary Africa, where the AIDS epidemic claims its primary victims among women and men in the childbearing years. In taking over the raising of a generation of AIDS orphans, grandmothers are playing a critical role in sustaining families through the crisis.

In many nonindustrial cultures, children may make a greater contribution to the economy in terms of work and responsibility than is common in modern North America. In Maya communities in southern Mexico and Guatemala, young children look after their younger brothers and sisters and help with housework. Girls begin to make a substantial contribution to household work by age 7 or 8 and by age 11 are constantly busy grinding corn, making tortillas, fetching wood and water, sweeping the house, and so on. Boys are given small tasks, such as bringing in the chickens or playing with a baby; by age 12, they are carrying toasted tortillas to the men working in the fields and returning with loads of corn.[10]

Similar situations are not unknown in industrial societies. In Naples, Italy, children play a significant role in the economy. At a young age, girls begin to take on responsibilities for housework, freeing their mothers and older sisters to earn money for the household. Nor is it long before girls are apprenticed to neighbours and kin, who teach them skills that enable them, by age 14, to enter a small factory or workshop. The wages earned are

Mark Richards/Photoedit

This Thai girl exemplifies the use of child labour in many parts of the world, often by large corporations. Even in Western countries, child labour plays a major economic role.

typically turned over to the girls' mothers. Boys, too, are apprenticed at an early age, although they may achieve more freedom from adult control by becoming involved in various street activities not available to girls.[11] On North American grain farms, young boys are expected to work alongside their fathers as soon as they are able; the school calendar is set around this tradition.

The use of child labour has become a matter of increasing concern as large corporations rely on the manufacture of goods in the world's poorer countries. Although reliable figures are hard to come by, there are likely some 15 million indentured child labourers in South Asia alone, including some as young as four years old. Each year, Western countries import millions of dollars' worth of products children manufacture, ranging from rugs and carpets to clothing and soccer balls.[12]

The issue of child labour, however, is not as simple as Western crusaders sometimes imply. Discussions concerning child labour laws often ignore the harsh realities of life in many countries. When officials or charitable groups, usually funded through Western agencies, remove a child from a "job," they are often taking away a family's main source of income. In addition, these agen-cies fail to consider whether there is an infrastructure in place to help families survive if child labour is banned. In other words, what will happen to the child who used to earn a wage—will he or she end up on the streets begging? And what about the family whose only source of income came from their child "lucky" enough to work in a carpet factory? Anthropological input can thus often be a double-edged sword.

Cooperation

Human beings can claim a long and once universal heritage of cooperative work, dating back to foraging times. Cooperative work groups may still be found in nonindustrial as well as industrial societies. Often, if the effort involves the whole community, a festive spirit permeates the work. Jomo Kenyatta, the anthropologist who later became a respected statesman and the "father" of an independent Kenya, described the time of enjoyment after a day's labour in his country: "If a stranger happens to pass by, he will have no idea that these people who are singing and dancing have completed their day's work. This is why most Europeans have erred by not realizing that the African in his own environment does not count hours or work by the movement of the clock, but works with good spirit and enthusiasm to complete the tasks before him."[13]

Among the Ju/'hoansi, women's work is often highly social. About three times a week, they go out to gather wild plant foods away from the camp. They usually go out in groups, talking loudly all the while. This not only turns what might otherwise seem a monotonous task into a social occasion, but it also causes large animals—potential sources of danger—to move elsewhere.

In most human societies, the basic cooperative unit is the household. It is a unit of both production and consumption; only in industrial societies have these two activities been separated. The Maya farmer, unlike his North American counterpart (but like subsistence farmers everywhere), is running not so much a commercial enterprise as a household. He is motivated by a desire to provide for the welfare of his own family, and each family, as an economic unit, works as a group for its own good. Cooperative work may be undertaken outside the household for other reasons, although not always voluntarily. It may be part of fulfilling duties to in-laws, or it may be performed for political officials or priests by command or as a means of binding a community together, such as with neighbourhood barn raisings and quilting bees (common in rural Canada in the early 20th century) and community harvesting, which is still practised today. Thus, institutions of family, community, religion, and the state all may act as organizing elements that define the nature and condition of each worker's cooperative obligations.

Craft Specialization

In nonindustrial societies, each person in the society has knowledge and competence in all aspects of work appropriate to his or her age and sex. In modern industrial societies, by contrast, many more specialized tasks are performed and no individual can begin to learn them all. Yet even in nonindustrial societies, some specialization of craft occurs. This is often minimal in foraging societies, but even here the arrow points of one man may be in some demand because of his particular skill at making them. Contemporary First Nations groups are enjoying a resurgence of their traditional crafts, such as beading and quillwork. These crafts provide extra income for specialists as well as an opportunity to pass traditional skills on to the next generation. Contemporary Inuit peoples in Canada, for example, have their own organizations devoted to the preservation, teaching, and passing on of artistic skills (http://www.inuitart.org).

Among people who produce their own food, specialization is more likely to occur. In the Trobriand Islands,

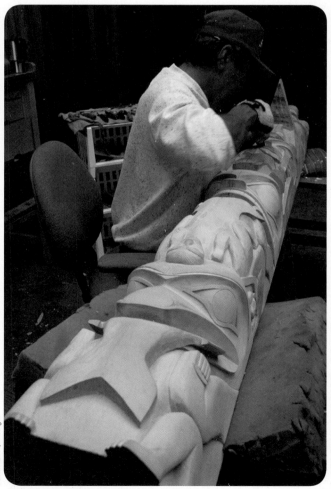

David Nunuk/Firstlight

Craft specialization provides additional income for First Nations and Inuit craftspeople. Shown here is Haida carver Wilfred Stevens of Haida Gwaii, British Columbia.

when a man wanted stone to make axe blades, he had to travel some distance to an island where the kind of stone was quarried; clay pots, however, were made by people living on yet another island.

One example of specialization is afforded by the Afar people of Ethiopia's Danakil Depression. Afar men are salt miners. This salt is mined from the crust of an extensive salt plain in the north part of the depression, and to get it is a risky and difficult business. The heat is extreme during the day, with shade temperatures close to 60°C not unusual. Shade is not found on the salt plain, however, unless a shelter of salt blocks is built. Nor is there food or water for man or beast. To add to the difficulty, until recently the Muslim Afars and the Christian Tegreans, highlanders who also mine salt, were mortal enemies.

Successful mining, then, requires specialized skills in planning and organization, as well as physical strength and the will to work under the most trying conditions.[14]

Control of Land

All cultures have regulations that determine the way land resources are allocated. Foragers determine who can hunt game and gather plants and where these activities take place. Cree elders determine traplines for band members. Horticulturists decide how their farmland is to be acquired, worked, and passed on. Pastoralists require a system that determines rights to watering places and grazing land, as well as the right of access to land they move their herds over. Intensive agriculturalists must have some means of determining title to land and access to water supplies for irrigation. In industrialized Western societies, a system of private ownership of land and rights to natural resources generally prevails.

In nonindustrial societies, land is often controlled by kinship groups such as the lineage or band, rather than by individuals. Among the Ju/'hoansi, each band of anywhere from 10 to 30 people lives on roughly 650 square kilometres of land, which they consider their territory. These territories are defined not in terms of boundaries but in terms of water holes located within them. The land is "owned" by those who have lived the longest in the band, usually a group of brothers and sisters or cousins. Their ownership, however, is more symbolic than real. They cannot sell (or buy) land, but outsiders must ask their permission to enter the territory. To refuse such permission, though, would be unthinkable.

The practice of defining territories on the basis of core features, be they water holes, distinctive landscape features where ancestral spirits are thought to dwell (as among Australian Aborigines), watercourses (as among First Nations of northeastern North America), or other features, is typical of foragers. Territorial boundaries are left vaguely defined at best. The adaptive value of this is clear: The size of band territories, as well as the size of the bands, can be adjusted to keep in balance with availability of resources.

Agriculture raises the stakes for landownership, bringing with it more secure forms of tenure. Among some West African farmers, a feudal system of land ownership prevails: All land is said to belong to the head chief. He allocates it to various subchiefs, who in turn distribute it to lineages. Lineage leaders then assign individual plots to each farmer. Just as in medieval Europe, these African people owe allegiance to the subchiefs and the principal chief. The people who work the land must pay taxes and fight for the chief when necessary. Yet these people do not really own the land; rather, it is a form of lease. No user can give away, sell, or otherwise dispose of a plot of land without approval from the elder of the lineage. When an individual no longer uses the allocated land, it reverts to the lineage head, who reallocates it to some other member of the lineage. The important operative principle here is that the system extends the individual's right to use land for an indefinite period, but the land is not "owned" outright. This system maintains the integrity of valuable farmland, preventing its loss through subdivision and conversion to other uses.

Technology

All societies have some means of creating and allocating the tools and other artifacts used for producing goods and for passing them on to succeeding generations. The number and kinds of tools a group uses—which, together with knowledge about how to make and use them, constitute its **technology**—are related to the lifestyles of its members. Foragers and pastoral nomads are apt to have fewer and simpler tools than more sedentary farmers, in part because a great number of complex tools would decrease their mobility.

Foragers make and use a variety of tools, and many are ingenious in their effectiveness. Some of these they make for their individual use, but codes of generosity are such that a person may not refuse giving or loaning what is requested. For example, a Ju/'hoan who gives his arrow to another hunter has a right to a share in any animals the hunter kills with it. Game is considered to "belong" to the man whose arrow killed it, even when he is not present on the hunt.

Among horticulturists, the axe, machete, and digging stick or hoe are the primary tools. Since these are relatively easy to produce, every person can make them. Although the maker has first rights to their use,

technology Tools and other material equipment, together with the knowledge of how to make and use them.

when that person is not using them, any family member may ask to use them and usually is granted permission. Refusal would cause people to treat the tool owner with scorn for this lack of concern for others.

With the rise and spread of capitalism, outright ownership of complex tools has become firmly entrenched. Individual ownership is more absolute, as are the conditions under which persons may borrow and use such equipment. It is relatively easy to replace a knife lost by a relative during palm cultivation but much more difficult to replace an iron plough or a power-driven threshing machine. Rights to the ownership of complex tools are more rigidly applied; capital purchases are normally enabled with bank loans, and failure to repay can result in the bank repossessing the article.

Resource Depletion

The way people organize their productive activities is important to all cultures, but what happens when resources become depleted or disappear altogether? What are the social and economic implications for people who depend on those resources? The ecological crisis facing fisheries around the world and threatening the economic future of people who make their living by fishing is a case in point. Historically, the Grand Banks off Newfoundland and the eastern Newfoundland–Labrador continental shelves were among the richest fishing grounds in the world, cod being the most commercially important species. However, in the 30-year period following the Second World War, the cod stocks declined by 99 percent.[15] In 1992 the Canadian government placed a temporary moratorium on northern cod, followed in 1995 by the indefinite closure of commercial fishing around Newfoundland.[16] As a result, Newfoundland's main economic activity all but disappeared. Fish plants closed down, fishing companies sold their boats, and fishers found themselves unemployed (at a rate of 63.6 percent) and forced to rely on government compensation to survive. Some Newfoundlanders, especially younger people, have left the region in search of employment. Others have remained in their home communities, surviving through informal occupations such as gardening, making and selling preserves and crafts to tourists, gathering and preserving wild berries, and hunting rabbits, moose, and seabirds. With so much out-migration, the long-term viability of local communities is in question.

The loss of this industry is significant not just to Newfoundland and Labrador but to Canada as well. Fishing has been a part of Canada for thousands of years; First Nations peoples on the West Coast, such as the Kwakwaka'wakw, relied on salmon for food, trade, and ceremonial purposes. The Kwakwaka'wakw continue to be fishers today. The

adding to the overexploitation of the fish stocks. Although the government was aware of all these problems, fisheries management and conservation remained sporadic and fraught with controversy; experts could not predict whether fish stocks would recover or even explain why those stocks had collapsed, nor have government regulations been able to control overexploitation.[18] Environmental problems such as ocean pollution and ozone depletion have placed added pressure on fish stocks. By the early 1990s, fish had become smaller, there were fewer of them, the "mother fish" that ensure the survival of a species had disappeared, and groundfish stocks had collapsed, resulting in the cod moratorium. Despite a reportedly large increase in cod populations off Newfoundland's underwater plateau in 2010, as reported by the Northwest Atlantic Fisheries Organization, cod stocks are still low. The World Wildlife Fund of Canada fears that they will decline further.[19]

For a great many years, marine and freshwater fisheries shaped the cultural, social, and economic lives of maritime Canada. The 1995 cod moratorium in Newfoundland was socially disruptive and continues to have a profound effect on individuals and local communities. An entire way of life, one deeply embedded in the ecology and economy of fisheries, is in danger of disappearing.

DISTRIBUTION AND EXCHANGE

In cultures without money as a medium of exchange, the rewards for labour are usually direct. The workers in a family group consume what they harvest, they eat what the hunter or gatherer brings home, and they use the tools they themselves make. But even where no formal exchange medium exists, some distribution of goods occurs. Karl Polanyi, a world-famous economist who spent the latter part of his life in Canada, made an enduring contribution to economic anthropology with his argument that all forms of human exchange can be classified into one of three modes: reciprocity, redistribution, and market exchange.[20]

Reciprocity

Reciprocity refers to a transaction between two parties whereby goods and services of roughly equivalent value are exchanged. Reciprocal transactions are those in which a gift or service is rendered in expectation of

Resource depletion has cost many jobs in eastern Canada. In this image, the centrality of cod to Newfoundland fishing communities is captured, as is the continuing sense of humour of the locals.

Mi'kmaq of the Maritimes have long fished the Atlantic waters off Canada. They continue to do so, despite a turbulent history of clashes with non-Mi'kmaq people. Early European immigrants to eastern Canada readily adopted the fishing industry and maintained the tradition for another 500 years. Migratory fishing, or **marine transhumance**, gave way to small-boat family operations in the 1800s.[17] In the mid-20th century, commercial fleets under foreign flags with high-tech equipment collected large fish harvests and thus began marginalizing small fishers. As fish stocks dwindled, competition between fishers increased. Aboriginal fishers such as the Mi'kmaq, with their treaty rights to fish, clashed with non-Aboriginal fishers, who had to contend with government-controlled quotas. One incident, which captured international headlines, occurred at Burnt Church, New Brunswick, where in Mi'kmaq lobster fishers clashed with non-native fishers and police. The result was damaged and sunken boats, riots, and massive arrests. Foreign fishers also encroached on the fishing grounds off the coast of Newfoundland,

marine transhumance Seasonal migration of people from one marine resource to the next.

reciprocity The exchange of goods and services of approximately equal value between two parties.

NA/2750-20/Glenbow Archive

In the Canadian Arctic, Inuit hunters shared their kill, to ensure that no families suffered hardship owing to a hunter's bad luck.

a gift or service in return. Reciprocity might be best compared in North American society to giving a dinner party. Friendship and warmth is mixed to a degree with the sense of social obligation and expectation of return: that, sooner or later, the individual will be invited to similar parties by some, although perhaps not all, of the guests. There are different forms of reciprocity. **Generalized reciprocity** is practised by hunter-gatherers as they divide resources such as meat. A hunter who makes a kill is socially obliged to share the meat, in the expectation that when another hunter succeeds, he too will share the resources. Generalized reciprocity contains what anthropologists also call "delayed" reciprocity, in that the gift giving is a way of storing up "credit" for the future.

Balanced reciprocity differs in that it is not part of a long-term process. The giving and receiving, as well as the time involved, are more specific; a person has a direct obligation to reciprocate promptly in equal value if the social relationship is to continue. Examples of balanced reciprocity in North American society include practices such as trading baseball cards or buying drinks when one's turn comes at a gathering of friends or associates. Examples from a non-Western culture include those that anthropologist Robert Lowie related in his classic account of the Crow.[21] A woman skilled in the tanning of buffalo hides might offer her services to a neighbour who needed a new cover for her tipi. It took an expert to design a tipi cover, which required from 14 to 20 skins.

> **generalized reciprocity** A mode of exchange in which the value of the gift is not calculated, nor is the time of repayment specified.
>
> **balanced reciprocity** A mode of exchange whereby the giving and the receiving are specific in terms of the value of the goods and the time of their delivery.
>
> **negative reciprocity** A form of exchange whereby the giver tries to get the better of the exchange.

The designer might need as many as 20 collaborators, whom she instructed on the sewing together of the skins and whom the tipi owner might remunerate with a feast. The designer herself would be given some kind of property by the tipi owner.

Giving, receiving, and sharing constitute a form of social security or insurance. A family contributes to others when they have the means and can count on receiving from others in time of need. A levelling mechanism is at work in the process of generalized or balanced reciprocity, one that promotes an egalitarian distribution of wealth over the long run.

Negative reciprocity is a third form of reciprocity exchange, in which the giver tries to get the better end of the deal. The parties involved have opposing interests, usually are members of different communities, and are not closely related. The ultimate form of negative reciprocity is to take something by force. Less extreme forms involve guile and deception or, at the least, hard bargaining. In North America, an example would be the stereotype of the car salesperson who claims a car was "driven by a little old lady to church" when in fact it was not and is likely to develop problems soon after it leaves the sales lot. Among the Navajo, according to anthropologist Clyde Kluckhohn, "to deceive when trading with foreign peoples is morally accepted."[22]

Barter and Trade

Exchanges that occur within a group usually take the form of generalized or balanced reciprocity. When they occur between two groups, the potential for hostility and competition exists. Therefore, such exchanges may well take the form of negative reciprocity, unless some sort of arrangement has been made to ensure at least an approach to balance. Barter is usually a form of negative reciprocity, involving the exchange of scarce items from one group for desirable goods from another group. Relative value is calculated, and despite an outward show of indifference, sharp trading takes place.

An arrangement that combined elements of balanced reciprocity as well as barter existed between the Algonquin and the Huron. During the 17th century, the Huron acted as middlemen in the growing trade between Indians and the French. The symbiotic relationship that developed between the Huron and French traders benefited both groups. The Huron, as agriculturalists, traded their surplus corn to the Algonquin hunters for furs. The Huron then exchanged the furs with the French for European trade items. As intermediaries, they made large profits bartering for robes and pelts, trading goods they had acquired from Europeans to the Algonquin and other First Nations groups.

The Assiniboine, who lived around Lake Winnipeg and Lake of the Woods, also acted as intermediaries

✦ *Original Study* ✦

The Kula Ring

Although we tend to think of trade as something undertaken for purely practical purposes, in order to gain access to desired goods and services, not all trade is motivated by economic considerations. A classic case of this is the Kula ring, an interisland trading system involving the Trobriand and their neighbours whereby prestige items are ceremoniously exchanged. Malinowski first described the Kula in 1920, but it is still going strong today. Men periodically set sail in their canoes to exchange shell valuables with their Kula partners, who live on distant islands. The valuables are red shell necklaces, which always circulate in trade in a clockwise direction, and ornate white arm shells, which move in the opposite direction (see Figure 6.1). These objects are ranked according to their size, their colour, how finely polished they are, and their particular histories. Such is the fame of some that when they appear in a village, they create a sensation. No one man holds these valuables for very long—at most, perhaps ten years. Holding on to an

arm shell or necklace too long risks disrupting the "path" it must follow as it is passed from one partner to another. Until the next voyage is made, the shell or necklace is possessed by the new owner, whose ownership adds to the biography of the object itself.

Although men on Kula voyages may use the opportunity to trade for other goods, this is not the reason for such voyages, nor is the Kula even necessary for trade to occur. In fact, overseas trade is regularly undertaken without the exchange of shell valuables. Instead, Trobriand men seek to create history through their Kula exchanges. By circulating armbands and necklaces that accumulate the histories of their travels and the names of those who have possessed them, men proclaim their individual fame and talent, in the process gaining considerable influence for themselves. Although the idea is to match the size and value of one shell for another, men draw on all their negotiating skills, material resources, and magical expertise—involving incantations, spells, and rituals—to gain access to the strongest partners and the most valuable shells. Thus, an element of negative reciprocity arises when a man diverts shells from their proper "paths" or entices others to compete for whatever necklaces and armbands he may have to offer. Yet when all is said and done, success is limited, for although a man may keep a shell for five or ten years, sooner or later it must be passed on to others. The Kula ring works because it establishes reciprocal relationships among trading partners. It also continues the tradition of voyages among the islands, thereby

These photos show Kula valuables and a canoe used for Kula voyages.

cementing partnerships and ensuring alliances.

The Kula is a highly elaborate complex of ceremony, political relationships, economic exchange, religion, and social integration. To see it only in its economic aspects is to misunderstand it completely. The Kula demonstrates once more how inseparable economic matters are from the rest of culture and shows that economics is not a realm unto itself.

SOURCES: A.B. Weiner, The Trobrianders of Papua New Guinea (New York: Holt, Rinehart and Winston, 1988), 139–57; A. Appadurai, ed., The Social Life of Things (Cambridge: Cambridge University Press, 1986).

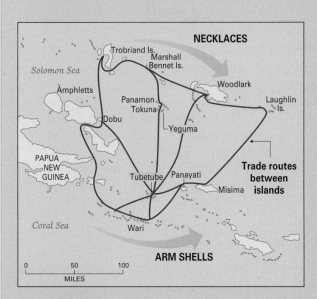

Figure 6.1

The ceremonial trading of necklaces and arm shells in the Kula ring encourages trade throughout Melanesia.

Trade is an important element in most human societies. Trade between nations is an essential part of international relations. In this picture the Group of 20 meet in Toronto, Canada, in 2010.

between the European fur companies and various First Nations groups. When the fur trade moved farther west, so did the Assiniboine, who gave up their woodland traditions and adopted the Plains lifestyle, becoming warriors and bison hunters. The arrival of guns and horses on the Prairies enhanced the Assiniboine trading role, and by the mid-18th century they were highly regarded as traders, hunters, and guides.

Silent trade is a specialized form of barter with no verbal communication. In fact, it may involve no actual face-to-face contact at all. Such cases have often characterized dealings between foraging peoples and their food-producing neighbours, as the former have supplied for the past 2,000 or so years various commodities in demand by the world economy. The process goes something like this:

> The forest people creep through the lianas to the trading place, and leave a neat pile of jungle products, such as wax, camphor, monkeys' gall bladders, birds' nests for Chinese soup. They creep back a certain distance, and wait in a safe place. The partners to the exchange, who are usually agriculturalists . . . lay down beside it

silent trade A form of barter with no verbal communication.

what they consider its equivalent in metal cutting tools, cheap cloth, bananas, and the like. They too discreetly retire. The shy folk then reappear, inspect the two piles, and if they are satisfied, take the second one away. Then the opposite group comes back and takes pile number one, and the exchange is completed.[23]

The reasons for silent trade can only be postulated, but in some situations trade may be silent for lack of a common language. More often it may serve to control situations of distrust so as to keep relations peaceful. In a very real sense, good relations are maintained by limiting face-to-face relations. Another possibility, which does not exclude the others, is that it makes exchange possible where problems of status might make verbal communication unthinkable. In any event, it provides for the exchange of goods between groups in spite of potential barriers.

Redistribution

In cultures with a sufficient surplus to support some sort of centralized authority, income flows into the public coffers in the form of gifts, taxes, and the spoils of war; then it is distributed again. Economic systems can operate on a small to a very large scale. Trobriand chiefs with their redistributions of harvested yams are an example of the former; the Inca empire, which stretched along the Andes Mountains from Ecuador to Chile, demonstrated redistribution on a large scale.

The administration of the Inca empire in Peru was one of the most efficient the world has ever known, in terms of both tax collection and methods of control.[24] A census was kept of the population and its resources. Tributes in goods and services were levied. Each craft specialist had to produce a specific quota of goods from materials supplied by overseers. Forced labour was used for agricultural or mining work. Forced labour was also used in public works, such as building roads, bridges, aqueducts, and food storehouses. An emergent bureaucratic class kept careful accounts of income and expenditures. This government bureaucracy ensured that production was maintained and that commodities were distributed.

Through the activities of the centralized authority, **redistribution** took place. The ruling class lived in great luxury, but goods were redistributed to the common people when necessary. In redistribution systems, the exchange is not between individuals or between groups; rather, products are funnelled into one source and parcelled out again as directed by a central administration. In large-scale systems, commonly, it involves an element of coercion. In North America, taxes are a form of redistribution. People pay taxes to the government: some of these support the government itself; the rest are redistributed either as cash, through social programs and business subsidies, or as services, such as health care, education, food and drug inspection, and highway construction. With the growth of the federal deficit in the past few decades, wealth in Canada is being redistributed more and more from middle-income taxpayers to wealthy holders of government securities. For redistribution to be possible, a society must have a centralized political organization, as well as an economic surplus beyond people's immediate needs.

Distribution of Wealth

In cultures where people devote most of their time to subsistence activities, gradations of wealth are small and are kept that way through **levelling mechanisms** that compel people to divest themselves of wealth. This prevents them from accumulating more than others. Systems of reciprocity distribute in a fairly equitable fashion what little wealth exists.

In cultures where a substantial surplus is produced, display for social prestige—what economist Thorstein Veblen called **conspicuous consumption**[25]—is a strong motivating force for the distribution of wealth. It has, of course, long been recognized that conspicuous consumption plays a prominent role in Western societies as individuals compete with one another for prestige.

Indeed, many North Americans spend their lives trying to impress others, and this requires a display of items that symbolize a prestigious position in life.

A form of conspicuous consumption also occurs in some nonindustrial societies. One example, more aptly termed "conspicuous generosity," is the **potlatch**, practised by First Nations groups on the Northwest Coast of North America, including the Nuu-chah-nulth (Nootka), Coast Salish, Kwakwaka'wakw (Kwakiutl), Bella Coola, Haida, Tsimshian, and Tlingit.[26] The potlatch is a special celebration in which the people of a community—perhaps even more than one community—come together to enjoy elaborate feasts, ceremonial dancing and singing, speeches, and gift giving. Northwest Coast peoples place great emphasis on inherited rank and privileges.[27] The potlatch serves as an opportunity for the conferring of titles and for chiefs to enhance their status with public displays of generosity. The potlatch also showcases the host's status by demonstrating his wealth, and it serves as an occasion to announce and display ceremonial and inherited privileges, or to transfer these privileges to an heir.[28]

An important component of the potlatch is the gift giving; in fact, in the Chinook language, the word "potlatch" means gift. Each guest, from the youngest child to the highest ranking elder, receives a gift; the value of the gifts is based on the guest's rank. In this way the gift giving validates the status not only of the host but also of his guests. In former times, favourite gifts included Hudson's Bay blankets; household goods such as kettles, dishes, sewing machines, and furniture; food, especially flour; and canoes. Elders and other honoured guests might also receive some cash along with their other gifts. Today, gifts are more likely to be money; crafts, such as embroidered or crocheted doilies; housewares; clothing; and dry goods.

The potlatch was an opportunity for the host to gain status from his generosity, but it served other purposes as well. The spiritual component of the potlatch publicly

redistribution A form of exchange in which goods flow into a central place where they are sorted, counted, and reallocated.

levelling mechanism A societal obligation compelling people to redistribute goods so that no one accumulates more wealth than anyone else.

conspicuous consumption A term Thorstein Veblen coined to describe the display of wealth for social prestige.

potlatch A special celebration in which the people of a community come together to enjoy elaborate feasts, ceremonial dancing, and gift giving. The potlatch serves as an opportunity for chiefs to enhance their status with public displays of generosity.

Chief Fred Smith dispensing goods at a Kwakwaka'wakw potlatch, Hee-Ghums, British Columbia, Canada.

announced and validated symbolic property, such as a new name. Masked dancers representing supernatural forces announced these privileges through naming and ceremonial dances. The Kwakwaka'wakw, for example, traditionally held potlatches to mark critical stages in life: the birth or adoption of a child, the onset of puberty or marriage, the death of a loved one. The host, often a chief, might use the potlatch as an opportunity to name a newborn child. A potlatch might be held to save face in the event of a misfortune such as the birth of a malformed child. Contemporary potlatches are held for much the same reasons, including baby showers, namings, weddings, anniversaries, special birthdays, graduations, and memorials for the dead.[29] Regardless of the reason, the hosts invited people to witness their generosity—the more extravagant the potlatch, the more status for the host. Reciprocity was expected; guests at a potlatch would be honour-bound to hold their own potlatch in the near future, keeping the circle of gift and counter-gift unbroken.

Anthropologists have interpreted the potlatch in various ways. Some view it as competitive, especially in the past; the giving away of food and other possessions laboriously accumulated over months or years inevitably caused financial hardship for the hosts. This competitiveness may have been the case among some groups, such as the Kwakwaka'wakw; but in other First Nations groups, such as the Nuu-chah-nulth and Salish, it certainly was not. Other anthropologists recognize the social importance of the potlatch, in which gift giving and the sharing of food seem to be forms of communication, establishing bonds and support networks among the people of the

community and even among members of more than one community. Also, the potlatch ceremony may have been used to ensure that other communities received adequate resources, especially during times of feast and famine. Groups, such as the Kwakwaka'wakw from British Columbia, enjoying an abundance of resources would be obliged to hold a potlatch to redistribute goods throughout the region. In this way the potlatch served not only as a form of economic redistribution, but also as a levelling mechanism, preventing any one group or individual from becoming too wealthy or powerful.

First Nations coastal groups continue to hold potlatches today, but potlatches reached their peak during the 18th and 19th centuries. Europeans, especially missionaries, and their paternalistic governments viewed these ceremonies as wasteful in the extreme and as an obstacle to eliminating heathen practices and converting Aboriginal people to Christianity. Recognizing the importance of the potlatch as a cultural practice that fostered social cohesion and identity, the Canadian government banned potlatches in 1884. This intervention failed to consider that the potlatch accomplished many important social, economic, and political goals for the Northwest Coast peoples, and during the years potlatching remained illegal (1884–1951), many groups secretly continued the practice.

Unlike conspicuous consumption in Western societies, the emphasis in the potlatching system was not on displaying or hoarding goods, which would make them unavailable to others, but rather on *giving away* goods. In fact, today, the gift-giving part of the ceremony is called the "give-away." The potlatch developed economic, social,

The Toronto Stock Exchange, where people are buying and selling shares in companies, even though no goods are physically present.

and political relationships among people, and it continues to do so. It is a way to publicly recognize inheritance rights and individual status. As a form of economic redistribution, the potlatch is a unique and appealing way to distribute goods throughout the region.

Market Exchange

To an economist, **market exchange** has to do with the buying and selling of goods and services, with prices set by the powers of supply and demand. Loyalties and values are not supposed to play a role, but they often do. *Where the buying and selling take place is largely irrelevant, so we must distinguish between market* exchange *and the* marketplace. Although some modern market transactions do occur in a specific identifiable location—much of the

market exchange The buying and selling of goods and services, with prices set by the powers of supply and demand.

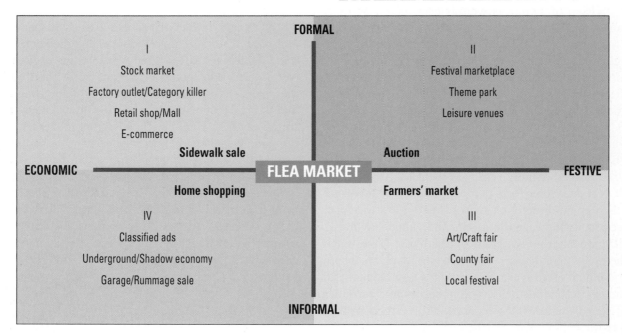

Figure 6.2

Marketplace structure and function may range from formal to informal and from economic to festive, as this diagram suggests.

Even in Western societies, the market is an important focus of social as well as economic activity, as typified by this farmers' market in St. Albert, Alberta.

Ancient Lydian money: the world's first coins. Lydia was located in Anatolia, which is now Turkey.

trade in cotton, for example, happens in the New Orleans Cotton Exchange—it is also quite possible for North Americans to buy or sell goods without ever being on the same side of the continent as the other party. When people talk about a market in today's world, the particular place where something is sold is often not important at all.

Until well into the 20th century, market exchange typically was carried out in specific places, as it still is in much of the non-Western world. In peasant or agrarian societies, marketplaces overseen by a centralized political authority provide the opportunity for farmers to exchange some of their livestock and produce for needed crafts and factory-made items. Thus, some sort of complex division of labour as well as centralized political organization is necessary to the existence of markets. In the marketplace, land, labour, and occupations are not bought and sold as they are through the Western market economy. In other words, what happens in these marketplaces has little to do with the price of land, the amount paid for labour, or the cost of services. The market is local, specific, and contained. Prices are likely to be set on the basis of face-to-face bargaining (buy low and sell high is the order of the day), rather than by faceless "market forces" wholly removed from the transaction itself. Nor does some form of money need to be involved; goods may be directly exchanged through some form of reciprocity between the specific individuals involved.

In non-Western societies, marketplaces have much of the excitement of a fair. They are vibrant places where an individual's senses are assaulted by a host of colourful sights, sounds, and smells. The noneconomic activities may even overshadow the economic. Social relationships are as important there as they are anywhere else. As anthropologist Stuart Plattner observes, the marketplace is where friendships are made, love affairs begun, and

marriages arranged.[30] Dancers and musicians may perform, and the end of the day may be marked by drinking, dancing, and fighting. At the market, too, people gather to hear news. In ancient Mexico, Aztec people were required by law to go to the market at specific intervals to keep informed about current events. Government officials held court and settled judicial disputes at the market. Thus, the market is a gathering place where people renew friendships, see relatives, gossip, and keep up with the world while procuring needed goods they cannot produce for themselves. The "market peace"—that is, rules for banning conflict in the marketplace—allowed warring parties to trade in peace before resuming hostilities after returning home.[31]

Although marketplaces can exist without money exchange of any sort, no one doubts that money facilitates trade. **Money** may be defined as something used to make payments for other goods and services as well as to measure their value. Its critical attributes are durability, portability, divisibility, recognizability, and fungibility (ability to substitute any item of money for any other monetary item of the same value, as when four quarters are substituted for a dollar). The wide range of things that have been used as money in various societies includes salt, shells, stones, beads, feathers, fur, bones, teeth, and (of course) metals, from iron to gold and silver. The ancient Spartan leader Lycurgus, however, banned money made from gold and silver, ordering that it be made of iron instead. As a form of currency, though, iron was too heavy, with little intrinsic value, so it hampered trade.

money Anything used to make payments for goods or labour as well as to measure their value; may be special-purpose or multipurpose.

Chinese Canadian Contributions to the Canadian Economy

For more than a century, Canada has been a preferred destination for immigrants seeking a better life. Some have come for the stable economic and social environment, others for Canada's multiculturalism and embrace of ethnic diversity. Many people choose to immigrate to Canada because of its economic opportunities. Chinese are one of the oldest groups to have made Canada their home. The first of them came to Canada some 130 years ago, mainly to help build the Canadian Pacific Railway. Many thousands more have followed, with the largest wave in the years immediately before and after 1997, when Britain returned control of Hong Kong to China. By 2001, 1.1 million Chinese had made Canada their home.[32] They brought with them finances, skills, and an infectious entrepreneurial spirit that has revitalized cities like Vancouver and Toronto.

Chinese Canadians have contributed enormously to the Canadian economy. They have opened up small businesses, creating vibrant Chinese commercial districts. They send their children to school and have fuelled the real estate market in large centres like Vancouver. Those who have come to Canada looking for investment and entrepreneurial opportunities have brought significant capital with them. Indeed, the economic contributions of the Hong Kong Chinese have helped sustain Canadian cities during recessionary times. Many Asian organizations contribute significantly to Canadian charities; for example, the Tzu Chi Buddhist foundation gave a Vancouver hospital $6 million.[33]

Along with their economic contributions, Chinese Canadians have contributed to the cultural growth and diversity of Canada, introducing traditions such as dragon boat races and Chinese New Year celebrations, which boost local economies by drawing in visitors. Chinatowns and Chinese shopping centres have helped create a cosmopolitan atmosphere in many of Canada's larger cities. These places also offer employment to many Chinese people, including refugees, who may not possess the education, skills, or necessary Canadian qualifications to find other employment.

Chinese immigrants, in particular immigrants from Hong Kong, make up the majority of the 3 million or so Asian people who have come to Canada. However, many other Asian groups are part of the multicultural mosaic. Japanese began coming to Canada in the 1890s to work as merchants and fishers, and today there are around 90,000 Japanese Canadians. Since the 1970s, Koreans (138,000 in Canada), Vietnamese (170,000), and many other Asian groups have chosen Canada for their new home and have added to the Canadian economy. Clearly, Asian immigration to Canada has resulted in a tremendous expansion of the Canadian economy.[34]

CONSUMPTION

The third component of any economic system, after production and distribution, is **consumption**. Anthropologists view consumption from two perspectives. First, it is the food, beverages, goods, and services we consume as well as the accompanying rituals and customs. Second, it is the resources we use or exploit in our everyday lives. Consumption meets our basic needs for food, liquids, and protection from the elements (energy, clothing, and shelter); it also fulfills our wants and desires—that is, it includes the resources we exploit to create our tools, weapons, vehicles, art and entertainment, and numerous other materials that enrich our lives. The needs and wants of people differ from one culture to another, but we all desire to make our lives more comfortable.

Consumption in industrial societies has grown dramatically in recent years. This was demonstrated by the 2003 blackout in eastern North America, which was at least partially due to the insatiable demand of North Americans for power to fuel their technological society. This is only one example of Western overconsumption of limited world resources. The consumption demands of small-scale cultures, such as foragers, are much less; their needs are few and are easily fulfilled without overexploitation of the ecosystem. In societies that have adopted new forms of production (e.g., nomadic pastoralists forced to settle in one place and become agriculturalists), people often have difficulty fulfilling their consumption needs and wants. Access to modern communication systems (e.g., television and computer networks) has increased consumer demand in developing countries, such as China, and this has placed additional strain on already overstretched resources. Chapter 11 will address the social inequality of access to resources.

In Chapter 5 we examined the use of resources in productive activities, and earlier in this chapter we discussed the distribution and exchange of goods. These are the usual themes that occupy sociocultural anthropologists,

consumption The ingestion of food and the exploitation of available resources.

but consumption extends beyond these, to the actual *consuming* of food and the meanings associated with this consumption. One fascinating aspect of consumption is the rules of behaviour that govern how we consume food.

Food Taboos

Because of the cultural significance of eating, many taboos have developed regarding what people can and cannot eat. For example, there was a time when Hawaiian women were not allowed to touch pork, coconuts, or certain kinds of fish; hence, the men cooked the food.[35] Also, Hawaiian women could not eat with the men, and women's food was not cooked in the same oven as men's food. Similarly, Muslims and Jews prohibit eating pork, citing religious doctrine regarding cleanliness. In the Hindu religion, higher caste members are not allowed to eat sacred cows. Fasting is also a part of food taboos—for example, Muslims, during the month of Ramadan, do not eat between dawn and sunset. A classic example of a gender-determined taboo is alcohol. Until some 40 years ago, many beer parlours on the Canadian Prairies had separate entrances for men and women, and others simply would not allow women on the premises unless men escorted them.

Food as Ritual and Social Interaction

Food is commonly used in rituals, such as for sacrifices at religious shrines. Anthropologists have found that the connections between humans and the divine often depend on ritual transactions of food. In Hindu pilgrimage towns, sacred food is first offered to the deity and then consumed by the pilgrims.[36] Blessings of food figure prominently in the Ukrainian culture. At Easter, ritual foods, such as *babka* and *paska* (egg-rich Easter breads), hard-boiled eggs, and baked cheese are placed in a basket covered with a sacred cloth and taken to church to be blessed before eating.

Food also seems to play a powerful role in the formation and maintenance of social groups; people come together at social gatherings such as weddings, bar and bat mitzvahs, and funerals to share food and enhance kinship networks and social relations. Gift giving often involves food, for example, during potlaches (see earlier in this chapter). Similarly, Ukrainian ritual foods serve to solidify ethnic identity. Ukrainians gather together on holy days and joyously consume their ritual foods, thus celebrating their ethnicity. Ritual foods can also symbolize status; for example, cooks renowned for their ability to produce perfect *babka* or *paska* are held in high esteem in their communities.

In a pluralistic society like Canada, the study of food systems as social constructs takes on an added dimension; ethnic food systems are clearly evident, and so is the diffusion of those systems throughout Canadian society. Ukrainian food is an excellent example: hardly anyone in Canada is unaware of the culinary delights of *perogies* (a Canadianized version of *verenyky*), which are sold at markets and restaurants across Canada and around the world. Thus, consumption plays an integral role in any culture's economic system.

ECONOMICS, CULTURE, AND THE WORLD OF BUSINESS

At the start of this chapter, we noted that we are perhaps most likely to fall prey to our ethnocentric biases when we study the economies of nonliterate peoples. The misunderstandings that result from our failure to overcome these biases are of major importance to us in the modern world in at least two ways. First, they encourage development schemes for countries that by Western economic standards are "underdeveloped" (a comfortably ethnocentric term)—schemes that all too often result in poverty, poor health, discontent, and a host of other ills. In northeastern Brazil, for example, large-scale plantations to grow sisal for export to the United States overwhelmed smaller farms where peasants grew food to feed themselves. This forced those peasants into the ranks of the unemployed. Because the farmers were unable to earn enough money to feed themselves, malnutrition rates rose dramatically. Similarly, development projects in Africa, designed to change local patterns of hydrology, vegetation, and settlement—and even programs aimed at reducing certain diseases—often have led directly to increased disease rates.[37] Fortunately, awareness is growing among development officials that future projects are unlikely to succeed without the expertise that anthropologically trained people can bring to bear.

Second, achieving an understanding of the economic systems of other peoples that is not bound by the hopes and expectations of our own culture also has become important for today's corporations. Two examples: A cosmetics manufacturer based in New York City was about to release an ad in Italy featuring a model holding some flowers, when it learned that the flowers were the kind traditionally given at Italian funerals. Along the same lines, the Chevrolet Nova did not sell well in Spanish-speaking countries because in Spanish, "No Va" means "No Go." Anthropologists Edward and Mildred Hall describe yet another case of the same sort:

> José Ybarra and Sir Edmund Jones are at the same party and it is important for them to establish a cordial relationship for business reasons. Each is trying to be warm and friendly, yet they

John Moss/Photo Researchers

In Africa, much of the farming is the job of women. Failure to accept this fact is responsible for the failure of many development schemes, since outside experts design projects that usually assume that the men are the farmers.

will part with mutual distrust and their business transaction will probably fall through. José, in Latin fashion, moved closer and closer to Sir Edmund as they spoke, and this movement was miscommunicated as pushiness to Sir Edmund, who kept backing away from this intimacy, and this was miscommunicated to José as coldness.[38]

When the developing nations in Africa, Asia, and South and Central America are involved, the chances for cross-cultural misunderstandings increase dramatically. The executives of major corporations depend on these countries for raw materials, are increasingly inclined to manufacture their products in these countries, and see their best potential for market expansion as lying outside North America and Europe. That is why business recruiters on postsecondary campuses in North America are on the lookout for job candidates with the kind of understanding of the world that anthropology provides.

The Global Economy

The cross-cultural misunderstandings examined above take on a new sense of urgency when we realize that the market economy has changed dramatically in recent years as globalization has swept the world. **Globalization** means that every country is becoming part of one large, interdependent system of commerce, communication, and power.[39] Markets around the world have been opened to free trade, resulting in stiff competition between states for lucrative markets, skilled labour, and limited resources. A close-to-home example of globalization is

the North American Free Trade Agreement (NAFTA). The basic goal of this agreement—and of similar ones, such as the European Economic Union (EEU)—is to remove barriers such as tariffs that restrict the movement of goods and services across political boundaries.

Several forces are driving globalization, and although the term was not coined until 1989, these forces were at work much earlier. Technology is one of the most influential of these drivers.[40] Rapid and relatively inexpensive transportation has now reached all corners of the world, and electronic communication systems now provide almost unlimited opportunities for international commerce. The global marketplace has changed the way we do business and the way we perceive the world around us. Globalization has manifested itself in consumption, such as with entertainment culture, which has seen worldwide consumer demand for all things Western, including clothes, movies, and technology. It has also changed the way we set up our work environments. People are no longer tied to a physical office and instead can work from home using electronic equipment. Nor are they required to meet face to face with business associates—e-mail, Skype, and the Internet provide fast and efficient ways of communicating, although they also can lead to increased isolation. One aspect of globalization that interests anthropologists is the domestic and transnational migration of labour forces.[41] For example, they consider how labour migrations affect workers' ethnic, cultural, and national identities.

globalization The process of opening up world markets using modern technology.

Although touted as the means to eliminate the world's economic inequalities, globalization has caused many problems. Detractors contend that globalization has benefited rich and powerful Westerners while doing little to help anyone outside this elite—in many cases, they say, it has caused a great deal of harm. Multinational corporations are increasingly moving their operations to developing countries to take advantage of cheaper labour costs, and this has jeopardized the economic well-being of North American workers. Activists protest the exploitation of developing countries, both the human toll and the damage to environments where few protective controls are in place.

Despite the promises, prosperity for developing countries has not been achieved; indeed, the gap between the have and have-not nations continues to grow. This widening gap in wealth, both between individuals and between nations, has generated a burgeoning worldwide anti-globalization movement, one that has placed the darker side of globalization under increasing scrutiny and that has won some key victories at world trade conferences in Seattle, Quebec City, Cancun, and Toronto. The concerted efforts of citizens will be necessary to counter those policies that mainly benefit the corporate elite. Jonathan Schell has characterized the growing global citizenry opposing globalization as "the other superpower."[42] The work on women and development in the Gender Perspectives box exemplifies this exciting new trend.

 Gender Perspectives

Women and Economic Development

Laurel Bossen,
McGill University

Homa Hoodfar, Vilia Jefremovas, Eva Rathgeber, Ellen Judd, and Laurel Bossen are Canadian anthropologists, educated at or teaching at Canadian universities.

Ester Boserup's pathbreaking work, *Women's Role in Economic Development*, with its demonstration of women's diverse economic roles and its stinging critique of European colonialism and development for undermining women's economic position, was published in 1970. Since then, research on women and economic development in other cultures has grown and anthropologists have contributed greatly to the study of women's work and the gendered impacts of economic, commercial, and technological development (Rathgeber 1994). They have become increasingly attuned to changing gendered divisions of labour; to women's access to income, property, and markets beyond the household; and to the diverse ways in which households, local cultures, governments, and planned development interventions affect women's ability to participate in and benefit from economic change. There is no universal pattern to these changes: different cultures and states face specific gender challenges as their economies develop.

In Egypt, Homa Hoodfar (1997) studied the economic and social roles of poor Muslim women in Cairo, where women's labour force participation is low. Hoodfar found that Islamic marriages aided parents in negotiating financial guarantees for their daughters' marriages. A married woman was not expected to support the household monetarily, but had "an unquestioned right" to economic support from her husband in exchange for housework and childrearing. When wives earned a cash income, men were not authorized to take control of it. Thus, women's conservatism, low labour force participation, and adherence to Islamic traditions had a material basis (102). Yet when some women earned cash incomes, men reduced their household contributions, retaining more for personal consumption. As the goods and services traditionally provided by women became commercialized, "women jealously guarded or tried to salvage what the market had not yet claimed" (272). They invested time and energy in subsistence housework and in careful shopping that minimized the use of cash and that maximized the use of state-subsidized goods and services. These resourceful consumer strategies were a response to changing market conditions but did not translate into increased power for women.

Gloria Rudolf's 1999 study of small farmers in Panama found that as the economy became more commercialized, gender inequality increased. Women's ability to claim land rights became problematic as land "moved into firmer male control . . . as coffee merchants and government officials, themselves all males, made their alliances primarily with highland men" (77). Also, the spread of Christian Base Community organizations aiming to "liberate the poor" and render them a political force attracted both women and men, but established a male monopoly of leadership positions (183). Neither the state nor the church fostered organizations that strengthened women's rights.

In Guatemala, my own comparative study of women and the changing division of labour in four contrasting communities (Bossen 1984) showed that increased commercial development did not have a uniform impact, but disproportionately expanded the range of employment options for men. Women were most disadvantaged in the better-paying formal sectors of both the rural and the urban economy. Here, the long history of Hispanic conquest, military governments, and civil war also promoted male dominance within both indigenous Maya and Hispanic populations.

Rejecting universal theories which claim that capitalist development or commercialization inevitably undermines women's role in the economy, Vilia Jefremovas (2000) emphasized the importance of local gender ideology and of viewing gender as a negotiated process. Among the Sagada Igorots of

North Luzon in the Philippines, local ideology resisted gender stratification. Despite commercialization, land inheritance has remained bilateral. Men and women share most subsistence and domestic tasks, and cash cropping has not had a negative impact on women (133). In this area, women have been important traders since pre-colonial times (134), and still play significant roles in trade, moneylending, and money management.

In China, socialist revolutionary policies of collective landownership designed to eliminate rural inequality were in force for almost three decades (1950s to 1980s). Despite the theory that if women participated equally in farming they would gain equality with men, gender inequality persisted in lower pay as well as in family, kinship, and village organization. Ellen Judd (1994) noted that in the reform period beginning in the 1980s, gender equality dropped out of official discourse. Although state policies favouring decollectivization, rural industry, and market revival appeared to be gender-neutral, the

continuity of an unofficial, customary, and deeply embedded system of male dominance remained central to Chinese society and the state. Ironically, the widespread "feminization" of farming in rural China over the past two decades is not a sign of women's growing economic influence. Because land plots are very small and cannot be enlarged (village land has been contracted to households but cannot be sold to other farmers), the returns to farming are low and men are leaving farms for more lucrative non-agricultural work (Bossen 2002).

Anthropological studies of women and economic development in different societies and cultures indicate that gender is intimately related to production, reproduction, and consumption. State policies, religion, and local history and customs have different and complex effects on gender. Women's opportunities to contribute to and benefit from economic development and commercialization are continuously renegotiated in response to changing market opportunities interacting with state and local configurations of gender and power.

SOURCES: E. Boserup, Women's Role in Economic Development *(New York: St. Martin's Press, 1970); L. Bossen,* The Redivision of Labor: Women and Economic Choice in Four Guatemalan Communities *(Albany: SUNY Press, 1984); and* Chinese Women and Rural Development *(Lanham: Rowman and Littlefield, 2002); H. Hoodfar,* Between Marriage and the Market: Intimate Politics and Survival in Cairo *(Berkeley: University of California Press, 1997); V. Jefremovas, "Women Are Good with Money: The Impact of Cash Cropping on Class Relations and Gender Ideology in Northern Luzon, the Philippines," in* Women Farmers and Commercial Ventures: Increasing Food Security in Developing Countries, *ed. Spring (Boulder: Lynne Rienner, 2000); E. Judd,* Gender and Power in Rural North China *(Stanford: Stanford University Press, 1994); E. Rathgeber, "WID, WAD, GAD. Tendances de la recherche et de la pratique dans le champ du développement," in* Women, Feminism, and Development/Femmes, féminisme et développement, *ed. H. Dagenais and D. Piché (Montreal and Kingston: McGill-Queen's University Press for the Canadian Research Institute for the Advancement of Women, 1994), 77–95; G. Rudolf,* Panama's Poor: Agents, Victims, and Historymakers *(Gainesville: University Press of Florida, 1999).*

❧ *The Anthropologist's World* ❧

Global Ecotourism and Local Indigenous Culture in Bolivia

Amanda Stronza

We travelled in a small fleet of motorized canoes. As the sun dipped behind the trees one steamy afternoon in April 2002, we turned the last few bends of the Tuichi River and arrived at our destination, the Chalalán Ecolodge of northern Bolivia. Our group included eighteen indigenous leaders from various parts of the Amazon rainforest, a handful of regional tour operators, conservationists, environmental journalists, and me—an applied anthropologist studying the effects of ecotourism on local livelihoods, cultural traditions, and resource use. We had been navigating for nine hours through lowland rainforest to visit one of the first indigenous, community-run ecotourism lodges in the world.

As we wended our way, combing the riverbanks for caimans, capybaras, tapirs,

and jaguars, our conversations meandered too. Mostly, the indigenous leaders shared stories of how ecotourism had affected their own forests and communities. They spoke of tourists who brought both opportunities and conflicts, and of their own efforts to balance conservation and development. They compared notes on wildlife in their regions, the kinds of visitors they had attracted, the profits they'd earned, the new skills they had gained, and the challenges they were facing as they sought to protect their lands and cultural traditions while also engaging with the global tourism industry.

Having studied ecotourism in the Amazon since 1993, I felt honoured to be on board participating in these discussions. With support from the Critical Ecosystem Partnership Fund, I had the opportunity that year—the

CONTINUED

CONTINUED

International Year of Ecotourism—to assemble leaders from three indigenous ecotourism projects in South America. All three were partnerships between local communities and private tour companies or nongovernmental organizations. For example, the lodge we were visiting, Chalalán, had come about through a partnership between the Quechua-Tacana community of San José de Uchupiamonas, Bolivia, and two global organizations, Conservation International and the InterAmerican Development Bank. Much of the $1,450,000 invested in Chalalán had gone toward preparing community members to assume full ownership and management of the lodge within five years. After a successful transfer in 2001, the lodge now belonged to San José's 600-member Quechua-Tacana community.

The indigenous leaders who had gathered for this trip had keen, firsthand knowledge about the costs and benefits that ecotourism can bring. They were former hunters, now leading tourists as birding and wildlife guides; small farmers and artisans making traditional handicrafts to sell to visitors; river-savvy fishermen supplementing their incomes

by driving tour boats; and local leaders whose intimate knowledge of their communities helped them manage their own tour companies. Among them was Chalalán's general manager, Guido Mamani, who recounted the benefits that Chalalán had brought to the Tacana of San José. "Ten years ago," he recalled, "people were leaving San José because there were few ways to make a living. Today they are returning because of pride in the success of Chalalán. Now they see opportunity here." As a result of their renewed pride in their mix of Quechua and Tacana histories, the community has begun hosting tourists for cultural tours in San José. "We want to give tourists presentations about the community and our customs," Mamani explained, "including our legends, dances, traditional music, the coca leaves, the traditional meals. We want to show our culture through special walks focusing on medicinal and other useful plants."

Mamani and the other indigenous ecotourism leaders characterized the success of their lodges in three ways: economic, social, and environmental. Chalalán, for example, counted its economic success in terms

of employment and new income. It directly employs 18 to 24 people at a time, and additional families supply farm produce and native fruits to the lodge. With artisans selling handicrafts to tourists, the community has gained regional fame for its carved wooden masks. The social benefits of Chalalán include new resources for education, health care, and communication. With its profits from tourism, the community has built a school, a clinic, and a potable water system. It has also purchased an antenna, solar panels, and a satellite dish to connect with the world from the remote forests along the Tuichi River.

Beyond these sorts of material improvements, ecotourism has catalyzed symbolic changes for the people of San José. "We have new solidarity in our cultural traditions," one woman noted, "and now we want to show who we are to the outside world." These experiences of Chalalán and similar projects suggest that ecotourism may be more than just a conservation and development idea—it may also be a source of pride, empowerment, and strengthened cultural identity among indigenous peoples.

Chapter Summary

1.   What is economic anthropology?

Economic anthropology is a subfield of cultural anthropology. There are a wide variety of economic anthropologists, ranging from those who study prehistoric economies to those who specialize in analyzing contemporary cultures. The economic anthropologist differs from the economist in the way he or she applies anthropological data and theory to understand the broad functioning of economic systems. Beyond money or the market, economic anthropology is interested in the cultural practices that help shape, and are shaped by, the functioning of the total economic system. Therefore, an economic anthropological analysis of hunter-gatherers may focus on the taboos they place on the eating of certain resources, or it may look at the connections between the economy and other cultural realms such as marriage and kinship.

2.   How do anthropologists study economic systems?

Anthropologists place the economy in the context of the total culture to understand economic patterns. By under-

standing the basic trade and exchange systems, anthropologists can understand the economy; however, they go further by addressing the role that other social institutions, such as kinship, marriage, and spirituality, play in the economic realm. Anthropologists attempt to understand the historical factors and the traditional practices that govern the way production and consumption are carried out. One can count all the salmon that the Kwakwaka'wakw catch, but unless practices such as the potlatch are examined, one will not fully understand the economy.

3.   How do economies work?

All societies have economies, and they differ only in terms of scale and the values that are attached to each of the component parts of the economic system. Economic anthropologists engage with the cultural subsystems of trade and exchange, consumption and extraction. By doing so, they are able to determine all the elements of how an economy functions.

4.   How and why are goods exchanged?

Goods are exchanged so that each society can obtain what it needs or wants but does not have, and trade that which it has most of. A variety of systems are involved in this exchange process, and different cultural practices are witnessed. The exchange of goods varies through space and time, and the value placed on the goods, and the rituals and practices that attend these exchanges, reveal a great deal about specific cultures. The complexity of the social formation affects the types of production as well as the exchange system. Hunter-gathers practise various forms of reciprocity, while early horticulturalists developed centralized distribution. Sedentary communities have the largest economic surplus and the most complex market mechanisms, and they practise a form of centralized redistribution in which taxes are distributed in the form of services and subsidies.

Questions for Critical Thought

1. In terms of the three-part scheme of generalized, balanced, and negative reciprocity, how would you characterize each of the following economic transactions found in your community?
   a. A yard sale.
   b. A pot luck supper.
   c. A routine family meal.
   d. Volunteering at a homeless shelter.

2. Identify levelling mechanisms in your community, province, and country. How do these levelling mechanisms serve to redistribute goods and services to the community?

3. Do we judge people by their table manners? Can you identify some practices (e.g., belching) that are considered good manners in one culture but not in another?

4. What would happen to our economy if we experienced agricultural exhaustion (i.e., if the soil could no long support crops of any kind)? Are there alternative economies we could turn to? What social impact would an ecological disaster of this magnitude have on us?

5. Take a look around your community. How are you and the members of your community economically enriched by the presence of people from diverse ethnic backgrounds? Socially enriched?

Internet Resources

Inuit Art Foundation

http://www.inuitart.org

This site provides detailed information on Inuit art, including journals, shops, educational programs, and the history of Inuit art and artists.

Gifting and Feasting in the Northwest Coast Potlatch

http://www.peabody.harvard.edu/potlatch/default.html

This site provides several links that explain what a potlatch is, describe the feasting and gifting, and feature contemporary potlatches. Photos and illustrations are included in each link.

Economic Anthropology

http://www.questia.com/library/sociology-and-anthropology/economic-anthropology.jsp

This site covers a broad range of topics in economic anthropology and introduces the reader to some of the classic works in the field by Raymond Firth, Marshall Sahlins, and Mary Douglas.

Gender Inequality and Economics

http://www.unfpa.org/swp/2000/english/ch05.html

An impressive site addressing many issues relevant to students of anthropology. Consists of major topics such as "The Cost of Economic Invisibility," "The Costs of Denying Health Care," "Maternal Mortality and Morbidity," "The Economic Cost of HIV/AIDS," "Gender-Based Violence," and "Education: Costs of the Gender Gap."

Energy, Environment, and Sustainable Development

http://ec.europa.eu/environment/eussd/

A large site with links that examine the environment, energy, and globalization from a European perspective. Numerous links to sites on topics such as quality of water, climate change, marine ecosystems, the city of tomorrow and cultural heritage, and renewable resources.

The Anthropology of Business

http://www.biblio.liuc.it/liucpap/pdf/42.pdf

A comprehensive and balanced overview of the applications of anthropology to the world of business.

Suggested Readings

For a list of suggested readings, visit the textbook's website at http://www.havilandcultural4e.nelson.com.

Documentaries

Is the Crown at War with Us? (NFB: Alanis Obomsawin, 96m).

This documentary addresses the events at Burnt Church, New Brunswick, involving Mi'kmaq fishers, non-native fishers, and the Canadian government. A National Film Board of Canada production,

http://www.nfb.ca/film/is_the_Crown_at_war_with_us.

Notes

1. Maurice Bloch, *How We Think They Think: Anthropological Approaches to Cognition, Memory, Literacy* (Boulder: Westview, 1998).

2. Ibid., 609.

3. J.W. Friesen, *Rediscovering the First Nations of Canada* (Calgary: Detselig, 1997).

4. John Ed. Gowdy, *Limited Wants, Unlimited Means: A Hunter-Gatherer Reader in Economics and the Environment* (Washington: Island Press, 1998).

5. A.B. Weiner, *The Trobrianders of Papua New Guinea* (New York: Holt, Rinehart and Winston, 1988).

6. Ibid., 86.

7. P.R. Sanday, *Female Power and Male Dominance: On the Origins of Sexual Inequality* (Cambridge: Cambridge University Press, 1981), 79–80. Cf. Sanday, *Woman at the Center: Life in a Modern Matriarchy* (Ithaca: Cornell University Press, 2004).

8. Robert McGhee, *The Last Imaginary Place: A Human History of the Arctic World* (New York: Oxford University Press, 2005).

9. K. Hawkes, J.F. O'Connell, and N.G. Blurton Jones "Hadza Women's Time Allocation, Offspring, Provisioning, and the Evolution of Long Postmenopausal Life Spans, *Current Anthropology* 38 (1997): 551–77. See also J.C. Berbesque and F.W. Marlowe, "Sex Differences in Food Preferences of Hadza Hunter Gatherers," *Evolutionary Psychology* 7, no. 4 (2009): 601–16.

10. E.Z. Vogt, *The Zinacantecos of Mexico: A Modern Maya Way of Life*, 2nd ed. (Fort Worth: Holt, Rinehart and Winston, 1990), 83–87.

11. V. Goddard, "Child Labor in Naples," in *Talking About People*, ed. W.A. Haviland and R.J. Gordon (Mountain View: Mayfield., 1993), 105–9.

12. "It's the Law: Child Labor Protection," *Peace and Justice News* 11 (November–December 1997).

13. M. Herskovits, *Economic Anthropology: A Study in Comparative Economics*, 2nd ed. (New York: Knopf, 1952), 103.

14. H.M. Mesghinua, "Salt Mining in Enderta," *Journal of Ethiopian Studies* 4, no. 2 (1966); K. O'Mahoney, "The Salt Trade," *Journal of Ethiopian Studies* 8, no. 2 (1970).

15. M.G. Villagaria, R.L. Haedrich, and J. Fischer, "Groundfish Assemblages of Eastern Canada Examined over Two Decades," in *Fishing Places, Fishing People: Traditions and Issues in Canadian Small-Scale Fisheries*, ed. D. Newell and R.E. Ommer (Toronto: University of Toronto Press, 1999).

16. P.R. Sinclair, H. Squires, and L. Downton, "A Future Without Fish? Constructing Social Life on Newfoundland's Bonavista Peninsula After the Cod Moratorium," in *Fishing Places, Fishing People: Traditions and Issues in Canadian Small-Scale Fisheries*, ed. D. Newell and R.E. Ommer (Toronto: University of Toronto Press, 1999).

17. R.E. Ommer, "Rosie's Cove: Settlement Morphology, History, Economy, and Culture in a Newfoundland Outport," in *Fishing Places, Fishing People: Traditions and Issues in Canadian Small-Scale Fisheries*, ed. D. Newell and R.E. Ommer (Toronto: University of Toronto Press, 1999).

18. D. Newell and R.E. Ommer, "Introduction: Traditions and Issues," in *Fishing Places, Fishing People: Traditions and Issues in Canadian Small-Scale Fisheries*, ed. D. Newell and R.E. Ommer (Toronto: University of Toronto Press, 1999).

19. CBC News, "Grand Banks Cod Stocks Grow 69% Since 2007," September 16, 2010, http://www.cbc.ca/technology/story/2010/09/16/cod-grand-banks-wwf-nafo.html.

20. K. Polanyi, "The Economy as Instituted Process," in *Economic Anthropology: Readings in Theory and Analysis*, ed. E.E. LeClair, Jr., and H.K. Schneider (New York: Holt, Rinehart and Winston, 1968), 127–38.

21. R. Lowie, R. (1956). *Crow Indians* (New York: Holt, Rinehart and Winston [1935]1956), 75.

22. C. Kluckhohn, quoted in M. Sahlins, *Stone Age Economics* (Chicago: Aldine, 1972), 200.

23. C.S. Coon, *A Reader in General Anthropology* (New York: Holt, Rinehart and Winston, 1948), 594.

24. M.A. Malpass, *Daily Life in the Inca Empire* (London: Greenwood Press, 1996).

25. T. Veblen, *Theory of the Leisure Class: An Economic Study in the Evolution of Institutions* (New York: Macmillan, 1899).

26. M. Seguin, "Understanding Tsimshian 'Potlatch,'" in *Native Peoples: The Canadian Experience*, ed. R. Bruce Morrison and C. Roderick Wilson (Toronto: McClelland and Stewart, 1986), 473–500.

27. A.D. McMillan, *Native Peoples and Cultures of Canada: An Anthropological Overview* (Vancouver: Douglas and McIntyre, 1988).

28. Peabody Museum of Archaeology and Ethnology (1999), "Gifting and Feasting in the NWC Potlatch: What Is a Potlatch?" http://140.247.102.177/potlatch/page2.html, accessed June 25, 2001.

29. Ibid.

30. S. Plattner, "Markets and Market Places," In *Economic Anthropology*, ed. S. Plattner (Stanford: Stanford University Press, 1989), 171.

31. P. Bohannon and G. Dalton, eds., *Markets in Africa* (Garden City: Doubleday, 1968).

32. Statistics Canada, "2006 Census," http://www.statscan.ca.

33. J. McLellan, "Buddhism in the Multicultural Context of Toronto, Canada: Local Communities, Global Networks," http://alcor.concordia.ca/~csaa1/porter/lectures/JanetMcLellan.html, accessed August 17, 2003.

34. G. Tian, *Chinese-Canadians, Canadian-Chinese Coping and Adapting in North America* (Queenston: Edwin Mellen Press, 1999).

35. E. Berry, "Foreword," in *Eating and Cooking Around the World: Fingers Before Forks* (New York: John Day, 1963).

36. R.S. Khare and M.S.A. Rao, "Introduction," in *Aspects in South Asian Food Systems: Food, Society, and Culture*, ed. R.S. Khare and M.S.A. Rao (Durham: Carolina Academic Press, 1986).

37. J.H. Bodley, *Victims of Progress*, 3rd ed. (Mountain View: Mayfield, 1990), 141.

38. E.T. Hall, and M.R. Hall, "The Sounds of Silence," in *Anthropology 86/87*, ed. E. Angeloni (Guilford: Dushkin, 1986), 65.

39. R.B. Morrison and C.R. Wilson, *Ethnographic Essays in Cultural Anthropology: A Problem-Based Approach* (Itasca: F.E. Peacock, 2002).

40. R.F.M. Lubbers, "The Globalization of Economy and Society" (1999), http://globus.lubpdfs/globaliz/thegloba/doc, accessed August 20, 2003.

41. Ibid. http://www.angelfire.com/ia/infovault/globalize. html.

42. J. Schell, *The Fate of the Earth and The Abolition*, Stanford Nuclear Age Series (Stanford: Stanford University Press, 2000).

7 Sex and Marriage

A traditional wedding in India. In all cultures, marriage establishes a continuing sexual relationship between individuals, backed by legal, economic, and social forces. Thus, unlike mating (which is biological), marriage is distinctly cultural. In India, marriages reflect rituals, customs, and elaborate celebrations.

Blaffer-Hrdy/Anthro-Photo File

KEY QUESTIONS

1. How Is Human Sexuality Viewed and Controlled?

Anthropologists have encountered difficulties in the study of human sexuality, partly because of its sensitive nature, and partly because the topic has remained a professional taboo until recently. However, new studies of human sexuality show a remarkable diversity in sexual identity, meaning, practices, and acceptance. The control of sexual behaviour also varies significantly.

2. What Is Marriage?

Marriages recognize intimate relations between spouses, and they create culturally recognized and legally enforceable relations regarding children and in-law kin. Although most marriages tend to involve one spouse, many cultures permit, and even regard as desirable, marriage of an individual to multiple spouses. New forms of marriage are emerging, such as common-law marriage and same-sex marriage. Marriage is a cultural construct, then, backed by social, legal, and economic forces.

3. Why Is Marriage Universal?

A complex issue universal to all human groups is the need to control sexual relations so that competition over sexual access does not disrupt society. The specific form marriage takes is related to who has rights to offspring, as well as how property is divided.

4. What Cultural Institutions Are Linked to, and Affected by, Marriage?

Throughout this chapter we will see that in most cultures, the structure of marriage is related to other social areas, such as kinship, economy, ritual and religion. The specific form marriage takes is related to who has rights to offspring, as well as how property is distributed.

Among the Trobriand Islanders, whose yam exchanges and Kula voyages we examined in Chapter 6, children who have reached age seven or eight begin playing erotic games with one another and imitating adult seductive attitudes. Within another four or five years they begin to pursue sexual partners in earnest, changing partners often, sometimes experimenting sexually first with one and then another. By the time they are in their mid-teens, meetings between lovers take up most of the night, and affairs between them are likely to last for several months. Ultimately, lovers begin to meet the same partner again and again, rejecting the advances of others. When the couple is ready, they appear together one morning outside the young man's family house as a way of announcing their intention to be married.

For young Trobrianders, attracting sexual partners is an important business, and they spend a great deal of time making themselves look as attractive and seductive as possible, using paints, dyes, costumes, and hairstyles. Youthful conversations are loaded with sexual innuendos, and magical spells as well as small gifts are used to entice a prospective sex partner to the beach at night or to the house (where boys sleep apart from their parents). Because girls, too, sleep apart from their parents, youths and adolescents have considerable freedom to arrange their love affairs. Boys and girls play this game as equals, with neither sex having an advantage over the other.

As anthropologist Annette Weiner points out, all of this sexual activity is not a frivolous, adolescent pastime. Attracting lovers

> is the first step toward entering the adult world of strategies, where the line between influencing others while not allowing others to gain control of oneself must be carefully learned. … Sexual liaisons give adolescents the time and occasion to experiment with all the possibilities and problems that adults face in creating relationships with those who are not relatives. Individual wills may clash, and the achievement of one's desire takes patience, hard work, and determination. The adolescent world of lovemaking has its own dangers and disillusionments. Young people, to the degree they are capable, must learn to be both careful and fearless.[1]

The Trobriand attitude toward adolescent sexuality seems to stand in marked contrast to that of contemporary North American society. Theoretically, North Americans will not have sexual relations outside of wedlock, although a considerable discrepancy between theory and practice exists. Nonetheless, premarital sexual activity in North American society is not conducted with the openness and approval that characterizes the Trobriand situation. As a consequence, before marriage, many North Americans have unresolved issues regarding their sexuality.

HUMAN SEXUALITY

Human sexuality is a topic of considerable, albeit fairly recent, interest to anthropologists. Bronislaw Malinowski (1929) and Margaret Mead (1935) were two of the earliest anthropologists to study humans as sexual beings. However, since this pioneering work, anthropologists have paid very little attention to human sexuality. Indeed, there was no anthropology of sexuality before the late 1970s; it was a taboo subject in the field, touched on only by accident or while dealing with another subject. One

To attract lovers, young Trobriand Islanders must look as attractive and seductive as possible. The young men shown here have decorated themselves with Johnson's Baby Powder.

Dr. William E. Mitchell

difficulty that anthropologists have encountered is how private people are about their sexual lives. Most people are uncomfortable talking about their sex lives and their feelings concerning sexuality. This is especially the case if their sexuality sits outside the "norms" of a culture—for example, if they are gay or lesbian or if they are sexually active teenagers. Anthropologists may also find it difficult to broach the subject because of their own discomfort, or because of gender barriers (e.g., females refusing to discuss their sexuality with a male stranger). Fortunately, both "virtual" (Internet) research and cross-cultural studies of human sexuality have become more common since the 1980s.

Anthropologists are finding a great deal of cultural variation in the ways sexuality is viewed, practised, and controlled. Jeffrey Weeks contends that diversification of sexual practices, subcultures, and identities is characteristic of our history.[2] To define human sexuality would require as many definitions as experiences. A woman in a lesbian relationship likely views sexuality differently from a woman in a heterosexual relationship, and a man in a small-scale society in Africa likely sees human sexuality in a different light than someone in an industrial society. Why? Because although human sexuality is rooted in our biological nature, it is also a cultural construct. Put another way, our sexuality has been formed at least partly by our cultural environment and, it follows, will differ from that of someone in another culture. To illustrate this point, the Mukkuvar people of southern India see female sexuality as a kind of social prosperity inseparable from fertility, whereas many societies rooted in Christianity place a high value on chastity. Much like the Trobriand Islanders, the Ju/'hoansi view sexuality among their adolescents (both heterosexual and homosexual) as natural, although they too have rules that govern this behaviour. Thus, human sexual relations are dealt with in all cultures, but in different ways.

Homosexuality

Homosexuality is common worldwide, yet anthropologists continue to grapple with a cross-cultural understanding of the many meanings attached to it.[3] Only recently have many accepted that homosexuality is not a disease but simply another sexual preference. Even the terminology is confusing: lesbian, gay, queer, transgender, transsexual, bisexual, homogender, and so on. In Western cultures, homosexuality is usually defined as the desire to have sexual relations with someone of the same sex. However, this is a rather narrow definition, for it treats homosexuality as solely a matter of sexual attraction, while ignoring **sexual orientation** and sexual identity. For example, among the Navajo, homosexuality

is based on gender and gender roles and is a social construct, whereas sexual orientation refers to the biological and psychological makeup of an individual. Our **sexual identity** comes from the identity we own based on our sexual preference.[4]

Homosexuality is an interesting example of culture change in action—not so much the behavioural aspects of culture, but certainly the ideas and attitudes that invoke behaviour. In the mid- to late 1880s, scholars and theologians conceded that what had once been considered sinful behaviour was really a perversity or abnormal behaviour. Still later, it became classified as a disease. It was around this time that the term "homosexuality" was first coined, and that the sexual identity which came with the term was recognized. This is when sexuality first became politicized, which eventually led to sexual identity movements, such as Free Love in the 1960s, and later to gay and lesbian social movements.[5] These movements have generated further changes in attitudes regarding homosexuality and, indeed, toward sexual identity itself.

In many cultures, both in the past and in the present, homosexual behaviour is viewed as natural and is even expected. In ancient Greece and Rome, homosexuality was considered socially acceptable behaviour, as it is today in Papua New Guinea, where young men undergo initiation rites that include an element of homosexuality. After initiation, they are expected to partake in homosexual behaviour for a number of years before they marry and begin a heterosexual relationship. The Etero of New Guinea actually prefer homosexual relations, believing that sex between males and females weakens the male and should occur only for reproductive reasons.[6]

Several groundbreaking anthropological studies have dramatically increased our understanding of human sexuality and homosexuality. Gilbert Herdt investigated sexual rituals of the Sambia in Papua New Guinea in the mid-1970s.[7] Although missionaries, colonialists, and the winds of culture change storming over Melanesia have since battered these customs, the research that Herdt and others such as Knauft[8] have conducted has significantly increased our understanding of human sexuality. One question Herdt considered was whether Sambia male initiation rituals were homosexual in nature. In these

homosexuality Sexual attraction to (or sexual relations with) persons of the same sex.

sexual orientation The biological and psychological makeup of an individual.

sexual identity The identity a person takes based on his or her sexual preference.

rituals, older boys orally inseminated younger boys. Semen was believed to give the boys strength and warrior prowess and to help them grow into masculine, adult males. The Sambia called this ritual a secret marriage. Although Herdt initially labelled this practice "ritualized homosexuality," he later changed his mind, for two reasons. First, this same-sex behaviour lasted only until the male married a woman and produced children, and temporary same-sex relations do not fit the definition of homosexuality as a lifestyle. Second, the Sambia did not recognize any type of same-sex partnership for life; in their eyes, this ritual was an initiation rite within a secret male cult that had a purpose and meaning. Today, Herdt refers to these rituals as "boy-insemination" and defines them as outside homosexuality.

Different approaches to sexuality are evidenced in alternative genders, or transgenders. That is, the sexual identities of some biological men and women are ambiguous, fitting into neither the female nor the male gender. This has been identified in many cultures, both historically and in contemporary times. The Two-Spirit, or *berdache*, of North America has been recorded in at least 113 historical Aboriginal groups ranging from the Zuni and Cheyenne to the Ingalik of Alaska and the Mojave of California.[9] Two-Spirits, who could be men or women, had a dream or vision that explained and legitimized their choice to become another gender; in this way, they represented a third and fourth gender.[10] Two-Spirits formed sexual and emotional relationships with a member of their own sex and fulfilled important social, religious, and economic roles. For example, female Two-Spirits might become hunters, warriors, or chiefs, and they enjoyed a special status in their community. Male Two-Spirits did not have to enter battle or become warriors, which, given the history of many of these cultures, evidenced a tremendous degree of tolerance.

One of the most extensively studied examples of institutionalized same-sex relations is the 19th-century Chinese sisterhood in the province of Guangdong. Chinese sisterhood movements involved thousands of women, who entered into sexual relations with other women and who vowed before their goddess Guan Yin never to marry a man.[11] These sisterhoods, which had names such as the Golden Orchid Association, served as support networks, whose members lived in cooperative houses. Following the victory of the Red Army in 1949, the sisterhoods were banned and many of the women fled to other countries. Most early studies of these sisterhoods avoided their lesbian nature, preferring to examine other issues, such as employment. Fortunately, this gap in research is changing. In this same vein, Gloria Wekker paid particular attention to sexual identity when she investigated the *mati* of Paramaribo, Suriname. These Creole women engage in sexual relations with men and with women, either simultaneously or consecutively. Ethnographic studies such as Wekker's have raised some interesting questions regarding homosexual behaviour and homosexual identity.[12]

CONTROL OF SEXUAL RELATIONS

Humans engage in sexual relations when it suits them and when it is deemed appropriate by the standards of their culture. Many of the controls or restrictions placed on sexual activity involve adolescents. By their early teens, males and females are biologically able to participate in sexual activity, yet every culture has its own rules regarding when sex is permitted. Thus, among the Trobriand Islanders and the Huron, sexual discovery and experimentation among adolescents is accepted. In these cultures, young people usually marry soon after they have reached biological maturity. Among the Maasai, little girls engage in sexual play with older warriors until they reach the age of sexual maturity (at menarche). To avoid pregnancy outside marriage, the young females are circumcised and are married to much older men. Conversely, many cultures strictly control sexual behaviour, especially among adolescent females. In the Middle East, the virginity of young girls is highly prized. To this end, the behaviour of females is controlled to varying degrees,[13] and they are protected from unwanted advances.

Control over gay and lesbian sexuality varies from culture to culture. "Permissive" cultures tend to view same-sex relationships with more tolerance than "restrictive" cultures, but even in such cultures, gay relationships between men are more accepted than lesbianism. A 1951 study by Clellans Ford and Frank A. Beach of male homosexuality in 76 cultures around the world found that 64 percent recognized male homosexual activity as normal and socially acceptable.[14] Yet as Christianity exerted its influence worldwide, rejection of homosexuality became more common. The trend is once again changing, and homosexuality is becoming more acceptable in Western societies, although gays and lesbians still have to fight for social, economic, and political recognition.

In recent years, Western social scientists have noticed two major trends: more people are entering into sexual relationships outside marriage, and women are gaining greater control over their sexual lives. Regardless of these changes, just as a culture dictates what, when, and how people should eat, so does it tell them when, where, how, and with whom they can have sex.

∞ *The Anthropologist's World* ∞

Fighting HIV/AIDS in Africa: Traditional Healers on the Front Line

Suzanne Leclerc-Madlala

Map of South Arfica

An affiliated professor of anthropology at the University of KwaZulu-Natal, Durban, South Africa, Dr. Leclerc-Madlala is currently a senior fellow in the Bureau for Global Health, Office on HIV/AIDS, US Agency for International Development in Washington, DC. Her work involves advancing the understanding of

sociocultural perspectives relevant to HIV, gender, and sexuality, particularly in the sub-Saharan context, and working on the U.S. government's response to the global HIV/AIDS epidemic.

In the 1980s, as a North American anthropology graduate student at George Washington University, I met and married a Zulu-speaking student from South Africa. It was the height of apartheid, and on moving to that country I was classified as "honorary black" and forced to live in a segregated township with my husband. The AIDS epidemic was in its infancy, but it was clear from the start that an anthropological understanding of how people perceive and engage with this disease would be crucial for developing interventions. I wanted to learn all that I could to make a difference, and this culminated in earning a PhD from the University of Natal on the cultural construction of AIDS among the Zulu. The HIV/AIDS pandemic in Africa became my professional passion.

Faced with overwhelming global health care needs, the World Health Organization passed a series of resolutions in the 1970s promoting

collaboration between traditional and modern medicine. Such moves held a special relevance for Africa, where traditional healers typically outnumber practitioners of modern medicine by a ratio of 100 to 1 or more. Given Africa's disproportionate burden of disease, supporting partnership efforts with traditional healers makes sense. But what sounds sensible today was once considered absurd, even heretical. For centuries, Westerners generally viewed traditional healing as a whole lot of primitive mumbo jumbo practised by witch doctors with demonic powers who perpetuated superstition. Yet its practice survived. Today, as the African continent grapples with an HIV/AIDS epidemic of crisis proportions, millions of sick people who are either too poor or too distant to access modern health care are proving that traditional healers are an invaluable resource in the fight against AIDS.

Of the world's estimated 40 million people currently infected by HIV, 70 percent live in sub-Saharan Africa, and the vast majority of children left orphaned by AIDS are African. From the 1980s onward, as Africa became synonymous with the rapid spread of HIV/AIDS, a number of prevention programs have involved traditional healers. My initial research in South Africa's KwaZulu-Natal province—where it is estimated that 36 percent of the population is HIV infected—revealed that traditional Zulu healers were being consulted regularly for the treatment of sexually transmitted diseases (STDs). I found that such diseases, along with HIV/AIDS, were usually attributed to transgressions of taboos related to birth, pregnancy, marriage, and death. Moreover, these diseases were often understood within a framework of pollution and contagion; and like most serious illnesses, they were ultimately believed to have their causal roots in witchcraft.

In the course of my research, I investigated a pioneer program in STD and HIV education for traditional healers in the

Medical anthropologist Suzanne Leclerc-Madlala visits with traditional healer Koloko in KwaZulu-Natal, South Africa. This Zulu traditional healer proudly displays her official AIDS training certificate.

CONTINUED

CONTINUED

province. The program aimed to provide basic biomedical knowledge about the various modes of disease transmission, the means available for prevention, the diagnosing of symptoms, the keeping of records, and the making of patient referrals to local clinics and hospitals.

Interviews with the healers showed that many maintained a deep suspicion of modern medicine. They perceived AIDS education as a one-way street intended to press them into formal health structures and convince them of the superiority of modern medicine. Yet today, few of the 6,000-plus KwaZulu-Natal healers who have been trained in AIDS education say they would opt for less collaboration; most want to have more.

Treatments by Zulu healers for HIV/AIDS often take the form of infusions of bitter herbs to "cleanse" the body, strengthen the blood, and remove misfortune and "pollution." Some treatments provide effective relief from common ailments associated with AIDS such as itchy skin rashes, oral thrush, persistent diarrhea, and general debility. Indigenous plants such as *unwele (Sutherlandia frutescens)* and African potato *(Hypoxis hemerocallidea)* are well-known traditional medicines that have proven immuno-boosting properties. Both have recently become available in modern pharmacies packaged in tablet form. With modern anti-retroviral treatments still well beyond the reach of most South Africans, indigenous medicines that can delay or alleviate some of the suffering caused by AIDS are proving to be valuable and popular treatments.

Knowledge about potentially infectious bodily fluids has led healers to change some of their practices. Where porcupine quills were once used to give a type of indigenous injection, patients are now advised to bring their own sewing needles to consultations. Patients provide their own individual razor blades for making incisions on their skin, where previously healers reused the same razor on many clients. Some healers claim they have given up the practice of biting clients' skin to remove foreign objects from the body. It is not uncommon today, especially in urban centres like Durban, to find healers proudly displaying AIDS training certificates in their inner-city "surgeries," where they don white jackets and wear protective latex gloves.

Politics and controversy have dogged South Africa's official response to HIV/AIDS. But back home in the wattle-and-daub, animal-skin–draped herbariums and divining huts of traditional healers, the politics of AIDS holds little relevance. Here the sick and dying are coming in droves to be treated by healers who have been part and parcel of community life (and death) since time immemorial. In many cases, traditional healers have transformed their homes into hospices for AIDS patients. Because of the strong stigma that still plagues the disease, those with AIDS symptoms are often abandoned or sometimes chased away from their homes by family members. They seek refuge with healers, who provide them with comfort in their final days. Healers' homes are also becoming orphanages as healers respond to what has been called the "third wave" of AIDS destruction: the growing legions of orphaned children.

The practice of traditional healing in Africa is adapting to the changing face of health and illness in the context of HIV/AIDS. Those who are suffering go to traditional healers not only in search of relief for physical symptoms, but also to learn about the ultimate cause of their disease—something other than the immediate cause of a sexually transmitted "germ" or "virus." They go to find answers to the "why me and not him" questions, the "why now" and "why this." As with most traditional healing systems worldwide, healing among the Zulu and most all African ethnic groups cannot be separated from the spiritual concerns of the individual and the cosmological beliefs of the community at large. Traditional healers help restore a sense of balance between the individual and the community, on one hand, and between the individual and the cosmos, or ancestors, on the other. They provide health care that is personalized, culturally appropriate, holistic, and tailored to meet the needs and expectations of the patient. In many ways it is a far more satisfactory form of healing than that offered by modern medicine.

Traditional healing in Africa is flourishing in the era of AIDS, and understanding why this is so requires a shift in the conceptual framework by which we understand, explain, and interpret health. Anthropological methods and the comparative and holistic perspective can facilitate, like no other discipline, the type of understanding that is urgently needed to address the AIDS crisis.

Adapted from S. Leclerc-Madlala, (2002). "Bodies and Politics: Healing Rituals in the Democratic South Africa," in Les cahiers de 'l'IFAS 2, ed. V. Faure (Johannesburg: French Institute).

Rules of Sexual Access

Cultures develop rules regarding acceptable sexual behaviour that serve to control sexual relations to some extent. Regardless of sexual behaviour, there is a worldwide expectation of marriage for the purpose of creating

marriage The social institution under which a man and woman, or partners of the same gender, live as husband and wife by legal commitments and establish a claim to sexual access to each other.

a base for economic, religious, and social activities, and to produce and raise children.[15] This applies to Canada and the United States, where all sexual activity outside of wedlock is considered taboo and where individuals are expected to establish a family through marriage. We may define **marriage** as a relationship between spouses who are recognized by society as having a continuing right to sexual access to each other. Actually, only about 5 percent of known societies prohibit all sexual involvement outside marriage, and even North American society has become less restrictive. Among other peoples, as we have seen, practices are quite diverse. For example, the Nayar of southern India have a traditional marriage system that is quite different from North American practices.[16]

The Nayar were a landowning warrior caste from southwest India. Their estates were held by corporations of sorts, which were comprised of kinsmen related in the female line. These kinsmen all lived together in a large household, called a *taravad*, with the eldest male serving as manager.

Three Nayar transactions are of interest here. The first, known as the *tali-tying* ceremony, occurred shortly before a girl experienced her first menstrual cycle. It involved a ceremony that joined the girl with a young man in a temporary union. This union, which may or may not have involved sexual relations, lasted for a few days and was then dissolved. This transaction established the girl's eligibility for sexual activity with men her household approved of, and she officially became an adult.

The second transaction occurred when a woman entered into a continuing sexual liaison with an approved man. This was a formal relationship, which required the man to present her with gifts three times each year until the relationship ended. In return, the man could spend the nights with her. In spite of continuing sexual privileges, however, the man had no obligation to support his sex partner economically, nor was her home regarded as his home. In fact, she might have such an arrangement with more than one man at the same time. Regardless of how many men were involved with one woman, this second Nayar transaction, known as the *sambandham*, clearly specified who had sexual rights to whom so as to avoid conflict, a danger to small-scale societies.

The previous definition of marriage is universal, presumably because the issues it deals with are universal. As the Nayar case demonstrates, however, marriage need not have anything to do with starting a new family or even establishing a cooperative economic relationship between people of the opposite gender.

Without effective birth control devices, the usual outcome of sexual activity between individuals of opposite sex is that, sooner or later, the woman becomes pregnant. When this happened among the Nayar, some man would have to formally acknowledge paternity—the third transaction. He did this by making gifts to the woman and the midwife. Although he might continue to take much interest in the child, he had no further obligations, for the child's education and support were the responsibility of the child's mother's brothers, with whom the child and its mother lived. This transaction established the child's legitimacy. In 21st-century Canadian society, the child of a single mother is seldom spoken of as "illegitimate," and even if it is, his or her citizenship and inheritance rights are not denied. Nor

does legitimacy require the father to be married to the mother. Among the Pueblo peoples (such as the Hopi) of the American Southwest, fatherhood is irrelevant to the child's legitimacy. Legitimacy comes automatically from the mother, whether she is married or not.

The Nayar marriage system faded away in the late 19th century, owing to insidious economic, religious, and political influences. When the British gained control of the region, they dissolved the warrior caste. The men returned to their estates and became increasingly involved in the market economy, which brought to an end the corporate nature of their landholdings. Moral criticism from the British colonialists also played a part in the breakdown of the Nayar traditional marriage ceremonies. Legislation that prohibited polygyny and that changed inheritance laws further eroded the practice in the 20th century. Today, the Nayar follow a monogamous marriage system.

Before we leave the Nayar, we should note that nothing in this culture is comparable to the North American family. The group that forms the household does not include **affinal kin**, or individuals joined in a **conjugal bond** established by marriage. Among the Nayar, the household is composed wholly of what we often call "blood" relatives, technically known as **consanguineal kin**. Sexual relations are with those who are not consanguineal kin and thus live in other households. This brings us to another supposed human universal, the incest taboo.

The Incest Taboo

The universality of the **incest taboo** has long fascinated anthropologists. This taboo prohibits sexual relations at least between parents and their offspring and usually between siblings as well. Incest taboos have become something of a challenge for anthropologists to explain, both regarding their supposed universality and why incest is regarded as such loathsome behaviour.

The simplest and least satisfactory explanation is based on "human nature"—that is, on an instinctive horror of incest. It has been documented that human beings raised together have less sexual attraction for one another, but this "familiarity breeds contempt"

affinal kin Relatives by marriage.
conjugal bond The bond between a man and a woman who are married.
consanguineal kin Relatives by birth—that is, "blood" relatives.
incest taboo The prohibition of sexual relations between specified individuals, usually parent–child and intersibling relations at a minimum.

Gender Perspectives

Female Circumcision

No other cultural practice has raised the ire of social activists as much as **female circumcision**. Human rights and feminist groups, medical practitioners, religious and political organizations, and many others have raised their voices against this ancient custom. Yet many anthropologists believe we must look beyond the "shock" value and listen to the people who value female circumcision. Only then will we understand the cultural meanings behind female circumcision, and only then can we offer an informed opinion, one that is not rooted in cultural imperialism.

The origin of female circumcision remains unclear, although it dates back at least 3,000 years. The practice is widespread in Africa and is found in some areas of the Arabian Peninsula as well as Indonesia and Malaysia. The World Health Organization (WHO) conservatively estimates that 130 million women worldwide have undergone some form of female circumcision. Until the early 1900s, clitoridectomies were also practised in Western Europe and the United States to cure everything from masturbation to frigidity, and today immigrants have reintroduced female circumcision to the West.

Female circumcision involves the cutting, removal, or altering of part or all of a female's external genitalia, often without anaesthetic and sterilized tools. The least invasive procedure, known as sunna circumcision, involves removing the clitoral prepuce (hood). In a clitoridectomy, part or all of the clitoris and labia minora are removed. The most invasive procedure, pharaonic circumcision, involves the complete removal of external genitalia, as well as infibulation—stitching the cut tissue to leave a small opening for urine and menstrual flow. Government-trained midwives or an older relative such as the woman's aunt perform the procedure. In some cultures, babies as young as a few weeks are circumcised; in others, women may not be circumcised until just before marriage, at around age 15.

Besides excruciating pain and terror, the young women may experience physical problems following the procedure, including infection, hemorrhage, septicemia, shock, and even death. Infibulation can cause urine and menstrual retention, bladder and bowel incontinence, and urinary tract and pelvic inflammations. When an infibulated woman is married, she must be cut open before intercourse and then restitched following childbirth. This repeated cutting and stitching causes a buildup of scar tissue and complications during childbirth. These health risks are used by outsiders as justification for ending the procedure, although much of the information on complications dates back to British colonial medical practitioners in the 1930s and 1940s. These "facts" are often not supported by the experiences of the women. Nor can outsiders fully comprehend the significance of female circumcision. For example, the lack of anaesthetic during the procedure horrifies Westerners; however, the ability to bear pain with courage is an important part of these initiation rites, bringing honour to the young woman and her family.

Many reasons for continuing this practice have been offered—tradition being one. When asked, many adherents will explain that it is the custom and always has been. A woman's status may be closely linked to her role as a mother and wife, and men will marry only circumcised females. Indeed, Jomo Kenyatta, the first president of Kenya (1964–78) unequivocally stated, "No proper Kikuyu would dream of marrying a girl who has not been circumcised." Controlling women's sexual behaviour is another reason. Losing her clitoris reduces a woman's sexual pleasure, and presumably her desire. Infibulation means that a woman is "sewn up" and cannot be unfaithful, which ensures virginity before marriage and fidelity after marriage. Religious beliefs are also cited as an underlying reason. Many Sudanese believe that Islam commands pharaonic circumcision. Although Islamic scholars strongly refute this interpretation, the

belief that the Prophet Mohammed commanded the practice persists.

For people unfamiliar with the cultural significance of female circumcision, it is difficult to understand why anyone, especially mothers, would allow this procedure to be performed on their daughters. It is important to understand that female circumcision is not an act of cruelty; these parents care about their daughter's well-being as much as any parents do. The most contentious issue is global advocacy for human rights—a vague term often used or misused to satisfy various agendas. Opponents assert that forcing young women to undergo this unnecessary ritual is against their human rights. Yet forcibly ending this practice, and taking away a woman's right to be circumcised and enjoy her new-found status, could also be construed as a violation of her rights. The word "choice," bandied around by feminists and social activists, is also at issue. Do the parents and the young woman really have a choice? A community's societal expectations are powerful forces, and this holds true in all societies. Men are often blamed for perpetuating female circumcision, yet the procedure is controlled and maintained by women, and rather than oppressing them, female circumcision may actually empower women. Finally, to suggest that women who continue to practise female circumcision are submissive or "brainwashed" into continuing the practice is an insult to the intelligence and strength of all women.

Efforts to abolish female circumcision have met limited success, especially in rural areas. WHO and UNICEF have pressured governments to ban female circumcision, and a few African governments have complied. Others have attempted to modify the procedure or provide more sanitary conditions, with little effect. The 1995 International Conference on the Status of Women, held in Beijing, China, declared female genital mutilation[1] a violation of human rights, and Canada and the United States have granted women political asylum based on the likelihood they or their children would face the procedure if forced to return to their homeland. However, some African feminist scholars take exception to the West's insensitive condemnation of this practice—what Morsy (1991) calls "rescue and civilizational" missions that are really attacks on their culture.

Even anthropologists have difficulty reaching a consensus on this issue. Mary Daly calls female circumcision "a manifestation of planetary patriarchy" and accuses anthropologists of ignoring or minimizing this ritual under the guise of cultural relativism. On the other hand, Janice Boddy points out that female circumcision downplays the sexuality of women and emphasizes their role as future mothers of men. Thus female circumcision is an important component of gender identity. Anthropologist Fuambai Ahmadu has firsthand experience with this procedure; she was circumcised during initiation into a secret women's society in Sierra Leone. From her perspective, protecting the rights of "a minority of women who oppose the practice is a legitimate and noble cause. . . . Mounting an international campaign to coerce 80 million African women to give up their tradition is unjustified."[2]

Female circumcision presents an ethical dilemma for anthropologists. Should they ignore the fundamental principle of anthropology—cultural relativism—and work toward the abolishment of female circumcision? Or should they remain neutral, acting only as observers? It seems clear that genuine, lasting change must come from within the societies that practise female circumcision, in the form of social movements led by women, and only after the socioeconomic problems faced by these women are addressed. Outside interference will do little to eradicate this practice, and excessive pressure from foreign agencies will only create a backlash and force the practice underground.

1. The politics of words is evident here; the term "female genital mutilation" is used to symbolize Western disapproval.
2. B. Shell-Duncan and Y. Hernlund, "Female 'Circumcision' in Africa: Dimensions of the Practice and Debates," in *Female "Circumcision" in Africa: Culture, Controversy, and Change*, ed. B. Shell-Duncan and Y. Hernlund (London: Lynne Rienner, 2000), 2.

SOURCES: *F. Ahmadu, "Rites and Wrongs: An Insider/Outsider Reflects on Power and Excision," in* Female "Circumcision" in Africa: Culture, Controversy, and Change, *ed. B. Shell-Duncan and Y. Hernlund (London: Lynne Rienner, 2000), 283–312; J. Boddy*, Wombs and Alien Spirits *(Madison: University of Wisconsin Press, 1989); M. Daly, "African Genital Mutilation: The Unspeakable Atrocities," in* The Gender Reader, *ed. E. Ashton-Jones, G.A. Olson, and M.G. Perry (Needham Heights: Allyn and Bacon, 2000), 462–85; J. Kenyatta*, Facing Mount Kenya *(New York: Vintage Books, 1965); L. Leonard, "Adopting Female 'Circumcision' in Southern Chad: The Experience of Myab," in* Female "Circumcision" in Africa, *167–92; S.A. Morsy, "Safeguarding Women's Bodies: The White Man's Burden Medicalized,"* Medical Anthropology Quarterly *5, no. 1 (1991): 19–23; Shell-Duncan and Hernlund, "Female 'Circumcision' in Africa: Dimensions of the Practice and Debates," in* Female "Circumcision" in Africa, *1–40.*

argument, or **instinct explanation**, may substitute the result for the cause. The incest taboo ensures that children and their parents, who are constantly in intimate contact, avoid regarding one another as sexual objects. However, if an instinctive horror of incest exists, how do we account for violations of the incest taboo, such as occur in Canadian society? (One in three Canadian females and one in six males suffer sexual abuse before age 18; 80 percent of the abusers are fathers, step- or foster fathers, or another relative.)[17]

Various **psychoanalytical explanations** of the incest taboo have also been advanced. Sigmund Freud tried to account for it in his psychoanalytic theory of the unconscious. According to him, the son desires the mother, which creates a rivalry with the father. Freud called this the Oedipus complex. The son must suppress these feelings or earn the wrath of the father, who is far more powerful than he. Similarly, the attraction of the daughter to the father (the Electra complex) places her in rivalry with her mother. Thus incest avoidance would help, at least to some degree, to maintain family harmony. Freud also suggested that incest taboos prevent social stagnation by ensuring that individuals participate in social units beyond their direct family. Some psychologists have argued that young children can be emotionally scarred by sexual experiences, which they may interpret as violent and frightening acts of aggression. The incest taboo thus protects children against sexual advances by older members of the family.

Early students of genetics argued that the incest taboo precluded the harmful effects of inbreeding—the **genetic explanation**. Yet it is also true that inbreeding can *increase* desired characteristics. Furthermore, undesirable effects show up sooner with inbreeding, so whatever genes are responsible for these negative effects

female circumcision The removal of all or part of a female's genitalia for religious, traditional, or socioeconomic reasons.

instinct explanation Sometimes known as "familiarity breeds contempt," this explanation suggests that long-term association with family members discourages sexual interest.

psychoanalytical explanation Incest taboos are an attempt by offspring to repress their sexual feelings toward their parents of the opposite gender.

genetic explanation Inbreeding is forbidden because cultural groups recognize the potential for impaired offspring.

are quickly eliminated from the population. However, a preference for a genetically different mate does tend to maintain a higher level of genetic diversity within a population, and in evolution this generally works to a species' advantage. Without genetic diversity, a species cannot adapt biologically to a changing environment when and if this becomes necessary.

Bronislaw Malinowski suggested that if incest were practised within families, this would cause tension, competition, and conflict, resulting in an unhealthy environment for children. This **social explanation** or "peace in the family" hypothesis contends that tensions would likely interfere with normal family interactions and functions and could prove disastrous among groups such as foragers, who rely on cooperation to survive.

A truly convincing explanation of the incest taboo has yet to be advanced. It should be noted that for millions of years our ancestors, living in small groups, practiced exogamy, that is, marriage outside the group, in order to establish alliances and, perhaps, in recognition of the possible harmful effects of interbreeding among close relatives. Certainly, there are persistent hints that it may be a cultural elaboration of an underlying biological tendency toward avoidance of inbreeding. Studies of animal behaviour have shown such a tendency to be common among relatively large, long-lived, slow-to-mature, and intelligent species. Humans qualify for membership in this group on all counts. Children raised together on an Israeli kibbutz, although not required or even encouraged to do so, almost invariably marry outside their group. In this case, however, appearances may be deceiving. There is hardly a kibbutz without a report of heterosexual relationships between adolescents who have grown up together since infancy.[18] As for marriage, most Israeli youths leave the kibbutz in their late teens to serve in the armed forces. Thus, they are away from the kibbutz precisely when they are most ready to consider marriage. Consequently, those most available as potential spouses often are from other parts of the country.

An even greater challenge to the "biological avoidance" theory, however, is raised by detailed census records made in Roman Egypt that conclusively demonstrate that brother–sister marriages were not just common—they were *preferred* by ordinary members

Ted Speigel/Corbis Canada

Although children raised together on an Israeli kibbutz rarely marry each other, it may not be because of any instinctive desire to avoid mating with people who are close. Rather, they marry outside their group because service in the military takes them out of their kibbutz, where they meet new people, precisely when they are most likely to begin thinking about marriage.

of the farming class. Moreover, anthropologist Nancy Thornhill found that, in a sample of 129 societies, only 57 had specific rules against parent–child or sibling incest (so much for the universality of the incest taboo). Twice that number, 114, had explicit rules to control activity with cousins, in-laws, or both.[19]

If indeed a biological basis for inbreeding avoidance exists among humans, it is clearly far from completely effective. So we are left with questions such as these: Why do some societies have an explicit taboo while others do not? And why do some societies not only condone certain kinds of incest but even favour them?

Endogamy and Exogamy

Closely related to prohibitions against incest are rules against **endogamy**, or marriage within a particular group of individuals (e.g., cousins and in-laws). If the group is defined as an individual's immediate family alone, then cultures generally prohibit or at least discourage endogamy, and they practise or at least encourage

social explanation Sometimes known as the "peace in the family" theory, this explanation suggests that competition over mates would interfere with normal family functions, such as acquiring adequate food resources.

endogamy Marriage within a particular group or category of individuals.

exogamy—marriage outside the group. Yet a society that practises exogamy at one level may practise endogamy at another. Among the Trobriand Islanders, for example, each individual has to marry outside his or her own clan and lineage (exogamy). However, since eligible sex partners are found within their own community, village endogamy, although not obligatory, is commonly practised. This is true of the Chipewyan in northern Canada; their young people are most likely to choose a mate within the community.[20] Considerable variation exists among societies regarding which relatives are or are not covered by exogamy rules. In Europe, the Catholic Church prohibits marriages to first cousins, and some American states still prohibit first-cousin marriages. In Canada, first cousins are allowed to marry, but marriages between uncles and nieces and aunts and nephews are prohibited.[21] Yet in many other societies, first cousins are preferred spouses.

In the 19th century, Sir Edward Tylor theorized that alternatives to inbreeding were either "marrying out or being killed out," now known as the **cooperation explanation** of incest taboos.[22] Our ancestors, he suggested, discovered that intermarriage had the advantage of creating bonds of friendship. Claude Lévi-Strauss elaborated on this premise. He saw exogamy as the basis of a distinction between early hominine life in isolated endogamous groups and the life of *Homo sapiens* in a supportive society. Alliances with other groups, established and strengthened by marriage ties, made possible a sharing of culture. Anthropologist Yehudi Cohen suggests that exogamy was an important means of promoting trade between groups, thereby ensuring access to needed goods and resources not otherwise available. Noting that incest taboos necessitating exogamy are generally most widely extended in the least complex of cultures but do not extend beyond parents and siblings in industrialized societies, he argues that as formal governments and other institutions have come to control trade, the need for extended taboos has been removed.

Exogamy also helps explain some exceptions to the incest taboo, such as obligatory brother-and-sister marriage within the royal families of ancient Egypt, the Inca empire, and Hawaii. Members of these royal families were considered semidivine, and their very sacredness kept them from marrying mere mortals. The brother and sister married so as not to share their godliness, thereby maintaining the "purity" of the royal line—and maintaining, as well, control of royal property. In Roman Egypt, where property was inherited by women as well as by men and where the relationship between land and people was particularly tight, brother–sister marriages among the farming class acted to prevent fragmentation of a family's holdings.

Common Law Marriages

In Canada, common law marriages or partnerships are legally recognized after a couple has been living together for one year. Common law partnerships are defined as "the relationship between two persons who are cohabiting in a conjugal relationship, having so cohabited for a period of at least one year."[23] These couples enjoy all the rights and responsibilities of husbands and wives, including pension plans, old age security, tax breaks, and so on. The number of Canadians entering into common law relationships continues to increase: close to 1.2 million couples were living in common law relationships in 2001, up 20 percent from 1995.[24] Quebec leads the provinces in common law relationships. According to the 2006 census, common law families were increasing at a rate five times faster than that of married-couple families.[25]

Same-Sex Marriages

Although marriage is usually defined in terms of a continuing sexual relationship between a man and woman, the cultural nature of gender is such that the "man" may in fact be a female or the "woman" a male. Thus, marriages between individuals of the same sex may be regarded as proper and normal. In some cases, these marriages provide a way to deal with problems for which opposite-sex marriage offers no satisfactory solution. This is true for the woman–woman marriage practice sanctioned in many cultures and in nations such as Canada, the Netherlands, Spain, Sweden, and Portugal, although it never involves more than a small minority of women.

The Nandi of western Kenya are a pastoral people who also do considerable farming.[26] Most property as well as the primary means of production—livestock and land—are exclusively in the hands of men and may be transmitted only to male heirs. Since polygyny (men have more than one spouse at a time) is the preferred form of marriage, a man's property is normally divided equally among his wives for their sons to inherit. Each wife has her own house, where she lives with her children, but all are under the authority of the woman's husband. In such situations, the position of a woman who bears no sons is difficult; not only does she not help perpetuate her husband's male line—a major concern among the Nandi—but she has no one to inherit the proper share of her husband's property.

exogamy Marriage outside the group.

cooperation explanation Forcing people outside their familial unit.

To get around these problems, a woman of advanced age who bore no sons may become a female husband by marrying a young woman. The purpose of this arrangement is for the wife to provide the male heirs that her female husband could not. To accomplish this, the woman's wife enters into a sexual relationship with a man other than her female husband's male husband; usually it is one of his male relatives. No other obligations exist between this woman and her male sex partner, and her female husband is recognized as the social and legal father of any children born under these conditions.

The individuals who are parties to woman–woman marriages enjoy several advantages. By assuming a male identity, a barren or sonless woman raises her status considerably and even achieves near equality with men. A woman who marries a female husband is usually one who is unable to make a good marriage, often because she has lost face as a consequence of premarital pregnancy. By marrying a female husband, she too raises her status and also secures legitimacy for her children. Moreover, a female husband is usually less harsh and demanding, spends more time with her, and allows her a greater say in decision making than a male husband does. Her one prohibition is engaging in sexual activity with her marriage partner; in fact, female husbands are expected to abandon sexual activity altogether, even with their male husband, to whom they remain married even though the women now have their own wives.

This type of same-sex marriage among the Nandi is an example of a socially sanctioned practice. The same cannot be said for same-sex couples in North America, where the struggle for equality for same-sex couples has been a long and difficult road. On June 10, 2003, Ontario's Court of Appeal ruled that the current definition of marriage, as between a man and a woman, was unconstitutional. The court redefined marriage as a union between two people, opening the door for gays and lesbians to legally marry in Ontario, followed by seven other provinces and one territory (British Columbia, Saskatchewan, Manitoba, Quebec, Nova Scotia, New Brunswick, Newfoundland, and Yukon). Despite angry protests from conservative and religious quarters, Jean Chrétien and his federal government quickly announced that they accepted Ontario's repudiation of the current definition of marriage. On June 28, 2005, the Canadian parliament passed Bill C-38 legitimizing same-sex marriages, becoming the fourth country to do so. Bill C-38 also changed the definition of marriage in Canada as between two people rather than a man and a woman.

In other parts of the world as well, the movement is gaining strength. In 1989, Denmark recognized same-sex partnerships, essentially sanctioning gay marriages. In 1996, Norway, Sweden, and Iceland passed similar legislation, followed by Finland in 2002. In April 2001, the Netherlands passed a law allowing same-sex couples to marry, giving them the same rights to adoption as heterosexual couples. Belgium followed in 2003, and in 2005 Spain granted gay couples the right to marry and adopt children. Israel recognizes same-sex marriages performed outside their country, though the practice is not legal within the country. Germany allows same-sex couples to register as life partners, France and New Zealand allow civil contracts, Australia and Luxembourg recognize same-sex partnerships, and Britain passed legislation in 2005 giving registered same-sex couples the same rights as married couples. Even in the United States, Vermont and Massachusetts have passed legislation that provides same-sex couples with the legal rights, benefits, and responsibilities of heterosexual couples; Hawaii allows adults who cannot legally marry to register as domestic partners; and California has legalized civil unions between same-sex couples.[27]

Since June 28, 2005, same-sex couples in Canada have been able to legally marry.

In Canada, as in most Western countries, monogamy is the only legally recognized form of marriage.

Those who are opposed to same-sex marriage often argue that marriage has always been between one man and one woman and that only heterosexual relations are normal. Yet as we have seen, neither assertion is true. Anthropologists have documented same-sex marriages in many human groups, where they are regarded as acceptable under appropriate circumstances. As for homosexual behaviour, it is quite common in the animal world (including among humans).[28] The only difference between humans and other animals is that humans culturally specify when, where, how, and with whom sex is appropriate.

FORMS OF MARRIAGE

Monogamy, where an individual has one spouse, is the form of marriage that North Americans are most familiar with. It is also the most common, but for economic rather than social and moral reasons. A man must be fairly wealthy to afford **polygyny**, or marriage to more than one wife. Among the Kapauku of western New Guinea, the ideal was to have as many wives as possible, and a woman actually urged her husband to spend money on acquiring additional wives.[29] She even had the legal right to divorce him if she could prove he had money for bride-prices but refused to remarry. As we saw in Chapter 2, wives were

desirable because they worked in the fields and cared for pigs, by which wealth was measured. But not all men were wealthy enough to afford bride-prices for multiple wives.

Among the Nuer pastoralists of Africa, other forms of "marriage" were practised, called "women unions." These "marriages" were more of an economic union than a "proper" marriage. In these unions, an older woman would take a younger woman as a wife. The younger woman brought wealth with her in the form of cattle. The younger woman's children would be raised by the older woman, whom they called "female father." This form of marriage was economically expedient, in that Nuer men were often away for lengthy periods of time whether with their cattle or engaged in trade or warfare. Interestingly, the Nuer also practised what is called the ghost marriage, where a man would stand in for his deceased brother. This form of marriage ensured the continuance of the family and household, with the dead husband's brother fulfilling the role of the deceased. A male child born from this union would take the name of the deceased husband.

Although monogamy may still be the most common form of marriage around the world, polygyny is permitted in most of the world's cultures. Even in North America, thousands of people in the Rocky Mountains live in polygynous households. In spite of its illegality, regional law enforcement officials have adopted a "live and let live" attitude toward polygyny. Nor are those involved in such marriages uneducated. One woman—a lawyer and one of nine co-wives—expresses her attitude as follows:

> I see it as the ideal way for a woman to have a career and children. In our family, the women can help each other care for the children. Women in monogamous relationships don't have that luxury. As I see it, if this lifestyle didn't already exist, it would have to be invented to accommodate career women.[30]

Polygyny was especially common in cultures that supported themselves by growing crops and where women did the bulk of the farm work (see Table 7.1). Under these conditions, women were valued both as workers and as childbearers. Because the labour of wives in polygynous households generated wealth and little support was required from husbands, the wives had a strong bargaining position within the household. Often, they had considerable freedom of movement and some economic independence from the sale of crops. Commonly,

monogamy Marriage in which an individual has one spouse.

polygyny The marriage custom in which a man has two or more wives simultaneously; a form of polygamy.

Jeremy & Sinead van Olst

Dynamic Anthropology

Bountiful Polygyny

Liam Kilmurray

The real issue here is not an ancient patriarchal practice that treats women as chattels and sexual collectables, but whether the B.C. Supreme Court will uphold the sections of the Charter of Rights and Freedoms that guarantee women equality with men. That is the crux of the matter, no more, no less. Polygamy comes to us from the dark ages; the practice harms women and children and reduces women to second-class citizenship. It is more than past time that it was dumped into the garbage can of history, where it should have been discarded decades ago. It's 2010 AD, not 2010 BC.

Thus opines one resident of British Columbia, quoted in the *Globe and Mail*, who sees polygamy, at least in Canada, as an unwanted and harmful form of marriage. This letter was written in response to a series of media reports regarding the polygamous community of Bountiful, British Columbia. In North America, there has been an increasing debate surrounding the issue of polygamy, along with an explosion in media coverage of the topic. Documentaries from National Geographic keep the issue topical, as do TV shows such as *Big Love* and *Sister Wives*, which address the issue of polygamy. In Utah, Texas, and Arizona, U.S.-based polygamous groups have many ties to those in Canada, specifically in BC.

The Supreme Court of British Columbia case concerns whether Section 293 of the Criminal Code makes polygamous marriages unconstitutional (they are illegal under the law). Supporters of polygamous marriage contend that banning the practice violates the individual's right to freedom of religion under the Canadian Charter of Rights and Freedoms. Polygamy is illegal in Canada, but previous cases brought against BC communities have foundered owing to legal technicalities, the status of the law, and the reluctance of authorities to prosecute those who enter into polygamous marriages. The Supreme Court of Canada will eventually hear the final appeal in this case.

Anthropologists and sociologists have been following this case carefully,

© Associated press

and some have been called as expert witnesses. They note that the acceptance of polygamy by many of the world's cultures stands in contrast to its rejection by many Western countries. Polygamy is legal in many countries—for example, in Kenya, Tibet, South Africa, and Sudan. Anthropologists have noted that in places such as Tibet, where polyandry (multiple husbands) is practised, and in Islamic nations, where polygyny (multiple wives) is legal, these practices are linked to social and economic factors. In such places, there is a shortage of either males or females, or there is a large economic imbalance in the earnings of either sex. Thus polygamy is considered appropriate, even desirable, in many places.

Those who oppose polygamy (in the case of Bountiful, BC, it is polygyny) contend that allowing some communities or individuals to practice polygyny could lead to the trafficking of underaged girls and the forcing of these girls to marry much older men. They also argue that these communities discriminate against older boys and men, who are forced to leave the community since only a select few elder men have access to spouses.

This issue often generates considerable passions on both sides. For some groups, such as Mormons, Muslims, and some forms of Judaism, polygamy is a component of religious practice. This makes the practice of polygamy in immigrant nations such as the United States and Canada especially problematic. Indeed, one of the arguments against allowing polygamy in Canada is that it will encourage the practice among those immigrant and resident Canadians whose cultural or religious backgrounds accept multiple spouses. In Canada, Crown lawyer Craig Jones has said that failure to ban or prosecute polygamy will lead to "an influx of polygamous families who are presently barred from the country."

Polygamy is a source of interest to anthropologists. Yet what was once studied ethnographically, typically in distant lands, has now come closer to home. The reaction of contemporary North Americans to polygamy is of considerable interest. Anthropologists will carefully follow this case in Bountiful, BC, because it is often when cultural or religious practices are challenged that we learn most about them.

SOURCES: *Letter to the Editor*, Globe and Mail, *November 23, 2010, A24;* "Uphold Polygamy Law, B.C. Court Urged," Globe and Mail, *November 23, 2010, A18;* "Polygamy on Trial," Globe and Mail, *November 22, 2010.*

TABLE 7.1	SELECT LIST OF COUNTRIES THAT PERMIT POLYGYNY (MULTIPLE WIVES)						
Afghanistan	Cameroon	Egypt	Iraq	Mali	Pakistan	Singapore	Togo
Algeria	Chad	Gabon	Jordan	Mauritania	Palestine	Somalia	UAE
Bahrain	C.A.R.	Gambia	Kuwait	Morocco	Qatar	Sri Lanka	Yemen
Bangladesh	Comoros	India	Lebanon	Myanmar	S. Arabia	Sudan	Zambia
Brunei	Congo	Indonesia	Libya	Niger	Senegal	Syria	
Burkina Faso	Djibouti	Iran	Malaysia	Oman	S. Leone	Tanzania	

each wife within the household lived with her children in her own dwelling, apart from her co-wives and husband, who occupied other houses within a larger household compound. Because of this residential autonomy, fathers were usually remote from their sons, who grew up among women. Some argue that this setting was conducive to the development of aggressiveness in adult males, who had to prove their masculinity. As a consequence, a high value was often placed on military glory, and one reason for going to war was to capture women, who then became a warrior's co-wives. This wealth-increasing pattern in polygamy was found in its fullest elaboration in sub-Saharan Africa, although it was known elsewhere as well. Moreover, it is still intact in the world today, because its wealth-generating properties at the household level make it an economically productive system.[31]

In cultures practising wealth-generating polygyny, most men and women enter into polygynous marriages. This practice is made possible by a female-biased sex ratio and/or by a mean age at marriage for females significantly below that for males (this creates a cohort of women looking for husbands larger than the cohort of men looking for wives). By contrast, in cultures where men are more heavily involved in productive work, generally only a small minority of marriages are polygynous. In these circumstances, women are more dependent on men for support, so they are valued as childbearers more than for the work they do. This is commonly the case in pastoral nomadic societies, such as the Borana of eastern Africa, where men are the primary owners and tenders of livestock. This makes women especially vulnerable if they prove incapable of bearing children, which is one reason why a man may seek another wife. However, where men do most of the productive work, they must work exceptionally hard to support more than one wife, and few actually do so. Usually, it is the exceptional hunter, a male shaman ("medicine man") in a food-foraging culture, or a particularly wealthy man in an agricultural or pastoral society who is most apt to practise polygyny. When he does, it is usually of the *sororal* type, with the co-wives being sisters. Having already lived together before marriage, the sisters continue to do so with their husband instead of occupying separate dwellings of their own.

Polygyny was also evident among First Nations groups of Canada, particularly on the northern Plains, where, in the 17th century, the expansion of the fur trade and an influx of horses led to a new economic order that required changes in traditional marriage patterns. Equestrian hunters, such as the Blackfoot or Lakota, were able to kill many bison in a short period of time. However, the hides had to be tanned quite quickly or they lost their value and could not be sold. This was too much work for any one woman. Thus hunters took more than one wife.

> The more wives a man had, the more women's labour he controlled. His wives provided him with additional children whose labour he also managed. Sons helped in hunting and raiding, and daughters aided their mothers in tanning hides.[32]

To this end, polygyny on the Plains was viewed as a feature of economic production rather than a social construct.

Although monogamy and polygyny are the most common forms of marriage in the world today, other forms do occur, however rarely. **Polyandry**, the marriage of one woman to two or more men simultaneously, is known in only a few societies, partly (perhaps) because men's life expectancy is shorter than women's, and partly (again perhaps) because male infant mortality is high. Thus, a surplus of men in a society does not occur. Where sex ratios are balanced, many women are likely to remain unmarried. Another reason for polyandry's rarity is that it limits a man's descendants more than any other pattern. Fewer than a dozen societies are known to have favoured this form of marriage, including the Eastern Inuit of Baffin Island, the Quebec-Labrador peninsula, and coastal Greenland; the Marquesan Islanders of Polynesia; and Tibetans. In Tibet, where inheritance goes through the male line and arable land is limited, the marriage of brothers to a single woman averted the danger of constantly subdividing farmlands among all the sons of any one landholder. Unlike monogamy, it also restrained

polyandry The marriage of one woman to two or more men simultaneously.

Shown here is a polyandrous family, a woman with her two husbands and their child.

population growth, avoiding increased pressures on resources. Polyandry also provided the household with an adequate pool of male labour. For tripartite economies of farming, herding, and trading, trifraternal polyandry was highly valued, as it allowed the three brothers who were co-husbands to pursue all three options at once.[33]

Group marriage, in which several men and women have sexual access to one another, also occurs rarely. Even in recent communal groups, among young people seeking alternatives to traditional marriage, group marriage seems a transitory phenomenon, despite the publicity it garners.

The Levirate and the Sororate

If a husband died, leaving a wife and children, it was often the custom that the wife married one of the dead man's brothers. This custom, called the **levirate**, provided security for the widow and her children and was also a way for the husband's family to maintain their rights over her sexuality and her future children. Thus, it acted to preserve relationships previously established. When a man married the sister of his dead wife, it was

> **group marriage** Marriage in which several men and women have sexual access to one another.
>
> **levirate** The marriage custom whereby a widow marries a brother of her dead husband.
>
> **sororate** The marriage custom whereby a widower marries his dead wife's sister.
>
> **serial monogamy** A marriage form in which a man or a woman marries or lives with a series of partners in succession.

called the **sororate**. In traditional societies that practised the levirate and sororate, the relationship between the two families was maintained even after a spouse's death. In such cultures, an adequate supply of brothers and sisters was generally ensured by the structure of the kinship system, such that individuals that North Americans call "cousins" were classified as brothers and sisters.

Serial Monogamy

A form of marriage increasingly common in North America today is **serial monogamy**, whereby the man or the woman marries or lives with a series of partners in succession. In 2006, there were 1,629,490 divorced Canadians—about 5 percent of the population.[34] Upon dissolution of a marriage, the children more often than not remain with the mother. This pattern is an outgrowth of one that sociologists and anthropologists first described among people living in the West Indies and among low-income urban African Americans. Early in life, women begin to bear children by men who are not married to them. To support her children, a woman must look for work outside the household, but to do so she must seek help from other kin, most commonly her mother. As a consequence, households are often headed by women (about 32 percent are so headed in the West Indies). After a number of years, however, an unmarried woman usually does marry a man, who may or may not be the father of some or all of her children. Under poverty conditions—where this pattern has been most common—women are driven to seek this male support, owing to the difficulties of supporting themselves and their children while fulfilling their domestic obligations. This pattern is also evident among urban First Nations women in Western Canada.

With the increasing need for women to seek work outside the home, and rising divorce rates, serial monogamy is becoming more common among middle-class people. In most divorce cases, it is the woman who assumes responsibility for any children. By the 2006 Canadian census, there were some 1.4 million single-parent families, and 26 percent of families with children were headed by a single parent; also, roughly four out of five of the children in single-parent families lived with a female parent.[35] Often isolated from kin or other assistance, women in single-parent households (which now outnumber nuclear family households) commonly find it difficult to cope. Within a year after divorce, the standard of living for women drops dramatically, whereas that of men improves. To be sure, fathers of children are usually expected to provide child support, but the failure of fathers to live up to their obligations is far from rare. One solution for unmarried women has been to marry again to get the assistance of another adult.

Choice of Spouse

The Western egalitarian ideal that an individual should be free to marry whomever he or she chooses is an unusual arrangement, certainly not one that is universally embraced. However desirable such an ideal may be in the abstract, it is fraught with difficulties and likely contributes to the instability of marital relationships in modern North American society. Part of the problem is the emphasis placed on the importance of youth, beauty, and romantic love. Female youth and beauty are perhaps most glaringly exploited by the women's fashion, cosmetics, and salon industries, but movies, television, and the music industry do not lag far behind. By no means are all North Americans taken in by this, but it does influence marriage decisions, which tend to be based on trivial and transient characteristics. In contrast, in most other parts of the world, marriage and the establishment of a family are considered far too important to be left to the whims of young people. The marriage of two individuals, who are expected to spend their entire lives together and to raise their children together, is incidental to the more serious matter of making allies of two families through the marriage bond. Marriage involves a transfer of rights between families, including rights to property and rights over the children, as well as sexual rights. Thus, marriages tend to be arranged for the economic and political advantage of the family unit.

Arranged marriages are not commonplace in North American society, but they do occur. Well into the 20th century, young Canadian women, especially in rural regions, found themselves "matched" to a male neighbour in need of someone to keep house and help with farm work. Among ethnic minorities, such as East

Marriage is a means of creating alliances between groups of people. Since such alliances have important economic and political implications, the decision cannot be left in the hands of two young and inexperienced people. Shown here is an East Indian bride, whose marriage has been arranged between her parents and those of the groom.

Indians, arranged marriages may help preserve traditional values that people fear might otherwise be lost. Families of wealth and power may "arrange" marriages by segregating their children in private schools and carefully steering them toward "proper" marriages.

Cousin Marriage

In some cultures, preferred marriages are those in which a man marries his father's brother's daughter. This is known as **patrilateral parallel-cousin marriage**. Although not obligatory, such marriages were favoured historically among some Arab groups, the ancient Israelites, and in ancient Greece and traditional China. All of these societies were hierarchical; that is, some people had more property than others, and although male dominance and descent

patrilateral parallel-cousin marriage Marriage of the children of two brothers.

❦ *Original Study* ❦

Honour Killings in the Netherlands

Clementine van Eck

When I first told my anthropology professors that I wanted to write my dissertation on honour killing among Turkish immigrants in the Netherlands, they told me no way. It was the mid-1990s, and everyone seemed to feel that writing negative things about struggling immigrants was discriminatory. Better to choose a subject that would help them deal with the challenges of settling in Dutch society, such as the problems they experienced as foreigners in school or at work. But I was quite determined to investigate this issue and finally found a professor who shared my interest—Dr. Anton Blok. He himself specialized in the Italian Mafia, and so was quite used to violence of the cultural sort.

Before getting into some of the details of my research, I need to set the stage. Until the 1960s, the Netherlands was a relatively homogeneous society (despite its colonial past). The major differences among its people were not ethnic but religious—namely, their distinct ties to Catholicism or Protestantism (of various kinds). The country's population makeup began to change dramatically after the economic boom of the 1960s created a need for cheap labour, which led to an influx of migrants from poorer Mediterranean countries.

These newcomers came not as immigrants but as "guest labourers" (*gastarbeiders*), who were expected to return to their countries of origin, which included Italy, Yugoslavia, Turkey, and Morocco. While many did go back home, many others did not. In contrast to most of the guest workers from southern European nations, those from Turkey and Morocco are mainly Muslim. And unlike southern European workers, who stayed on as immigrants and assimilated successfully into Dutch society, many of the Muslim newcomers formed isolated, diasporic communities.

Over the past three decades, these communities have expanded and are now concentrated in certain areas of various cities. Today, the Turkish population in the Netherlands is about 350,000. Most of them have become Dutch citizens, but they maintain some key cultural features of their "honour-and-shame" traditions. And this is what is at stake when we are dealing with the problem of honour killing.

Anthropologists have identified honour-and-shame traditions in many parts of the world, especially in remote, traditional herding and farming societies, where the power of the political state is either absent or ineffective. People in such areas, my professor, Dr. Blok, explained,

> cannot depend on stable centres of political control for the protection of life and patrimony. In the absence of effective state control, they have to rely on their own forces—on various forms of self-help. These conditions ... put a premium on self-assertive qualities in men, involving the readiness and capacity to use physical force in order to guarantee the immunity of life and property, including women as the most precious and vulnerable part of the patrimony of men. The extremes of this sense of honour are reached when even merely glancing at a woman is felt as an affront, an incursion into a male domain, touching off a violent response.

Beyond serving as a means of social control in isolated areas, honour-and-shame traditions may be used in situations where state mechanisms are alien to a certain group of people, as among some Turkish and Moroccan migrants in the Netherlands. Focusing on the latter, I tried to make sense of certain cultural practices that often baffle indigenous Dutch citizens, who are accustomed to a highly organized bureaucratic state where personal security and justice are managed effectively by social workers, police, courts, and so on. Most of all, I wanted to understand honour killings.

Honour killings are murders in the form of a ritual and are carried out to purify tarnished honour—specifically, honour having to do with something that Turks refer to as *namus*. Both men and women possess *namus*. For women and girls, *namus* means chastity, while for men it means having chaste family members. A man is therefore dependent for his *namus* on the conduct of the womenfolk in his family. This means in effect that women and girls must not have illicit contact with a member of the opposite sex and must avoid becoming the subject of gossip, since gossip alone can impugn *namus*. The victim of an honour killing can be the girl or woman who tarnished her honour or the man who did this to her (usually her boyfriend). The girl or woman is killed by her family members; the man is killed by the family of the girl/woman whose honour he has violated.

As I was wrapping up my PhD in 2000, Dutch society still didn't seem quite ready to acknowledge the phenomenon of honour killing. That year a Kurdish boy whose parents were born in Turkey tried to shoot the boyfriend of his sister. Because the attempt took place in a high school and resulted in injury to several students and a teacher, authorities focused on the issue of school safety rather than on the cultural reasons behind the murder attempt.

A shift in government and public awareness of honour killing took place in 2004. That year, three Muslim Turkish women were killed by their former husbands on the street. Coming in quick succession, one after the other, these murders did not escape the attention of government officials or the media. Finally, honour killing was on the national agenda. In November of that year, I was appointed cultural anthropologist at the Dutch police force in The Hague and began working with law enforcers on honour killing cases there (and soon in other areas of the country).

On November 2, 2004, the day I gave an opening speech about honour killings to colleagues at my new job, a radical Muslim migrant from Morocco shot the famous Dutch author and film director Theo van Gogh, who was well known for his critical and often mocking views on Islam. Although his murder was not an honour killing, it had key elements of that cleansing ritual: it happened in a public place (on the street) in front of many people, the victim had to die (injury would not suffice), the killer used many shots (or knife thrusts), the killing was planned (it was not the product of a sudden outburst), and the killer had no remorse.

Let me tell you about a recent and quite typical case. On a Friday evening, the local police in an eastern Dutch community called in the help of our police team. A 17-year-old Turkish girl had run away to the family home of her Dutch boyfriend, also 17. Her father, who had discovered that this boy had a police record, telephoned his parents and asked them to send his daughter home. The parents tried to calm him down and told him his daughter was safe at their house. But as he saw it, she was in the most unsafe place in the world, for she was with the boy she loved. This could only mean that her virginity was in jeopardy and therefore the *namus* of the whole family.

My colleagues and I concluded that the girl had to be taken out of her boyfriend's home that same night: the father knew the place, he didn't want the boy as a son-in-law, and he believed his daughter not mature enough to make a decision about something as important as marriage. ("Just having a boyfriend" was not allowed. You either marry or you don't have a boyfriend, at least not an obvious one.) Because of my research, I was well aware of similar situations that had ended in honour killings. To leave the girl where she was would invite disaster.

After we persuaded the prosecutor that intervention was necessary, the girl was taken from her boyfriend's house and brought to a guarded shelter to prevent her from fleeing back to him the next day. This is anthropology in action. You cannot always just wait and see what will happen (although I admit that as a scholar this is very tempting); you have to take responsibility and take action if you're convinced that a human life is at stake.

When I took up the study of cultural anthropology, I did so simply because it intrigued me. I never imagined that what I learned might become really useful. So, what I would like to say to anthropology students is this: Never give up on an interesting subject. One day it might just matter that you have become an expert in that area. At this moment I am analyzing all kinds of threatening cases and drawing up genealogies of the families involved—all in the effort to deepen our understanding of and help prevent honour killings.

SOURCES: A. Blok, The Mafia of a Sicilian Village, 1860–1960 (New York: Harper and Row, 1974); "Rams and Billy-Goats: A Key to the Mediterranean Code of Honour," Man, New Series, 16, no. 3 (1981): 427–40; C. Van Eck, Purified by Blood: Honour Killings Amongst Turks in the Netherlands (Amsterdam: Amsterdam University Press, 2003).

were emphasized, property of interest to men was inherited by daughters as well as sons. Thus, when a man married his father's brother's daughter, property was retained within the male line of descent. In these cultures, generally speaking, the greater the property, the more this form of parallel-cousin marriage was apt to occur. This form of marriage is also common among royal families.

Matrilateral cross-cousin marriage—that is, marriage of a man to his mother's brother's daughter or of a woman to her father's sister's son (a cross cousin is the child of a mother's brother or a father's sister)—was a preferred form of marriage in a number of societies, ranging from food foragers (Australian Aborigines and the Haida of Haida Gwaii) to intensive agriculturists (such as among various peoples of southern India). Among food-foraging peoples, who inherit relatively little property, such marriages help establish and maintain ties of solidarity between social groups. The young men of the Tlingit, living on the northwest coast of British Columbia and southwestern Alaska, traditionally preferred **patrilateral cross-cousin marriage**. Marriage to a close relative kept wealth within the family and enabled individuals to marry someone of equal rank.[36] In agricultural communities, however, the transmission of property is an important determinant. For instance, cultures that trace descent exclusively in the female line usually pass property and important rights from a man to his sister's son. Under cross-cousin marriage, the sister's son is also the man's daughter's husband.

Marriage Exchanges

In the Trobriand Islands, when a young couple decided to get married, they sat in public on the veranda of the young man's adolescent retreat, where all might see them. There they remained until the bride's mother brought the couple cooked yams, which they then ate together, making their marriage official. This was followed a day later by the presentation of three long skirts to the bride by the husband's sister, a symbol that the sexual freedom of adolescence was now over. This was followed by a large presentation of uncooked yams by the bride's father and her mother's brother, who represented both her father's and her own lineages.

matrilateral cross-cousin marriage Marriage of a woman to her father's sister's son or of a man to his mother's brother's daughter (her cross-cousin on the paternal side, his cross-cousin on the maternal side).

patrilateral cross-cousin marriage Marriage of a man to his father's sister's daughter.

In many African societies, bride-price takes the form of cattle, which are paid by the groom's family to the bride's family.

In many societies, when a woman marries she receives a dowry, normally a share of the family inheritance. In Somalia, a large ornate silver chest pendant is a valuable wedding dowry.

Meanwhile, the groom's father and mother's brother—representing his father's and his own lineages—collected important gifts such as stone axe blades, clay pots, money, and the occasional Kula shell to present to the young wife's maternal kin and father. After the first year of the marriage, during which the bride's mother continued to provide the couple's meals of cooked yams, each of the young husband's relatives who had provided valuables for the bride's relatives received yams from her maternal relatives and father. All of this gift giving served to bind the four parties together so that people respected and honoured the marriage and created obligations for the woman's kin to take care of her husband in the future.

As seen among the Trobriand Islanders, marriages in many groups are formalized by some sort of economic exchange. **Bride-price**, sometimes called bride wealth, is a common form of exchange. This involves payments of money or other valuables to a bride's parents or other close kin. This usually happens in patrilocal groups (see Chapter 8), where the bride becomes a member of the household in

bride-price Compensation the groom or his family pays to the bride's family on marriage.

bride service A designated period after marriage when the groom works for the bride's family.

dowry Payment of a woman's inheritance at the time of her marriage, either to her or to her husband.

which her husband grew up; this household will benefit from her labour as well as from the offspring she produces. Thus, her family must be compensated for their loss.

Bride-price is not a simple "buying and selling" of women. The bride's parents may use the money to buy jewellery or household furnishings for her or to finance a costly and elaborate wedding celebration, an important social act. The bride-price also contributes to the stability of the marriage, because it usually must be refunded if the couple separates. Other forms of compensation are an exchange of women between families—"my son will marry your daughter if your son will marry my daughter"—or **bride service**, a period of time during which the groom works for the bride's family.

In a number of cultures—more or less restricted to the western, southern, and eastern margins of Eurasia, where the economy is based on intensive agriculture—women often bring a **dowry** with them at marriage. This practice occurs in Canada in the form of the custom that the bride's family pays the wedding expenses. In effect, a dowry is a woman's share of parental property that, instead of passing to her on her parents' death, is distributed to her at the time of her marriage. This does not mean she retains control of this property after marriage. In a number of European countries, for example, a woman's property falls exclusively under her husband's control. Having benefited by what she has brought to the marriage, however, he is obligated to look out for her future well-being, even after his death. Thus, one of the functions of dowry is to ensure a woman's support in widowhood (or after divorce)—an important consideration in a society where men carry out the bulk of productive work and women are valued for their reproductive potential rather than for the work they do. In such societies, women incapable of bearing children are especially vulnerable, but the dowry they bring with them at marriage helps protect them against poverty and/ or desertion. The property a woman brings with her at marriage demonstrates that the man is marrying a woman whose standing is on a par with his own. It also permits women, with the aid of their parents and kin, to compete through dowries for desirable (that is, wealthy) husbands.

Marriage itself is an important form of economic exchange, in essence creating affinal alliances between two kin groups. The bride-price and dowry just discussed symbolize these affinal ties, as well as the responsibilities that come with them. Thus, marriage alliances enhance each kin group's chance of survival and create a cooperative support network between large kin groups.

DIVORCE

Like marriage, divorce in non-Western cultures is a matter of great concern to the couple's families. Since marriage is more often an economic than a religious matter, divorce arrangements can be made for a variety of reasons and with varying degrees of difficulty.

Among the Gusii of Kenya, sterility or impotence were grounds for a divorce. Among the Chenchu of Hyderabad and certain First Nations of northern Canada, divorce was discouraged after children were born, and couples usually were urged by their families to settle their differences. By contrast, in the southwestern United States, a Hopi woman might divorce her husband at any time merely by placing his belongings outside the door to indicate that he was no longer welcome. Divorce was fairly common among the Yahgan, who lived at the southernmost tip of South America, and was seen as justified if the husband was considered cruel or failed as a provider.

Divorce in these societies seems familiar and even sensible, and in one way or another, the children are taken care of. An adult unmarried woman is almost unheard of in most non-Western cultures; a divorced woman soon remarries. Economic considerations are often the strongest motivation to marry. On the island of New Guinea, among some of its many cultures, a man does not marry because of sexual needs, which he can readily satisfy out of wedlock, but because he needs a woman to make pots and cook his meals, to fabricate nets, and to weed his plantings. Similarly, a man without a wife among the Australian Aborigines is in an unsatisfactory position, since he has no one to supply him with food or firewood.

Although divorce rates may be deemed high in some non-Western cultures, they have become so high in the West as to cause many North Americans to worry about the future of marriage and the family in the contemporary world. Undoubtedly, the causes of divorce in North America are many and varied. Among them are the trivial and transient characteristics we have already mentioned that marriages may all too easily be based upon. Beyond this, a North American marriage is supposed to involve an enduring, supportive, and intimate bond between a woman and a man, full of affection and love. In this relationship, people are supposed to find escape from the pressures of the competitive workaday world, as well as from the legal and social constraints that so affect their behaviour outside the family. Yet in a society where people are brought up to seek individual gratification, where this often is seen to come through competition at someone else's expense, and where women traditionally have been expected to be submissive to men, it should not come as a surprise to find that the reality of marriage in North America does not always live up to the ideal.

Harsh treatment and neglect of spouses—usually of wives by husbands—in North America is neither new nor rare; furthermore, people are more tolerant of violence directed against spouses and children than they are of violence against outsiders. As anthropologists Collier, Rosaldo, and Yanagisako have observed,

> a smaller percentage of homicides involving family members are prosecuted than those involving strangers. We are faced with the irony that in our society the place where nurturance and noncontingent [unconditional] affection are supposed to be located is simultaneously the place where violence is most tolerated.[37]

However, what has happened in recent years is that people have become less inclined toward moral censure of those—women especially—who seek escape from unsatisfactory marriages. No longer are people as willing to "stick it out at all costs" no matter how intolerable the situation may be. Thus, divorce is increasingly exercised as a sensible reaction to marriages that do not work. Such different approaches to marriage and divorce are of great interest to anthropologists, demonstrating the cultural diversity of the world and how the institution of marriage is linked to other aspects of the social structure.

Chapter Summary

1.   How is human sexuality viewed and controlled?

Due to the sensitive nature of the topic, only in recent years have anthropologists really studied human sexuality. They document the immense cultural variations in how human sexuality is perceived, practised, and controlled and in the meanings associated with those variations. For example, the near universality of the incest taboo, which forbids sexual relations between parents and their children, and usually between siblings, has long interested anthropologists.

2.   What is marriage?

Marriage is the relationship between two or more people who are recognized as having continuing claims of sexual access to each other. Monogamy, or the taking of a single spouse, is the dominant form of marriage, but many cultures practise marriages in which more than one spouse is involved. Throughout the world, past and present, different forms of marriage are found. The levirate is a system in which the wife of a deceased man may marry one of the brothers of the dead man. Other forms exist, such as the ghost marriage, the cross-cousin marriage, and the sororate, where a man marries the sister of his deceased wife. All these forms of marriage are linked to underlying economic practices. In the past few decades, newer forms of marriage have emerged, such as same-sex marriages and common law marriages. Recognized marriages are backed by social, legal, and economic forces.

3.   Why is marriage universal?

Marriages are universal because they are linked to certain basic social institutions that cater to universal human needs. Two important factors are the need to divide property efficiently and to create inheritance rules. Most marriage forms are underpinned by two human desires: to regulate sexual relations and to maintain a coherent base for socializing children.

4.   What cultural institutions are linked to, and affected by, marriage?

Marriage is not a stand-alone institution; it is linked to many other social institutions. The types, practices, and rules of marriage are linked to the spheres of economics, kinship, descent, and religion. Just as these social structures differ throughout the world, so do the forms of marriage and their relationships to other institutions.

Questions for Critical Thought

1. Why do the forms and rules surrounding marriage vary so greatly across cultures? Does this variation weaken or reinforce the anthropological understanding of marriage? Explain how.

2. Assuming that marriage is a cross-cultural institution, why don't all humans marry? Why is marriage prohibited for certain categories of people, such as Roman Catholic and Eastern Orthodox priests and nuns?

3. How might an anthropologist sensitively approach the study of human sexuality within a cultural group?

4. Should anthropologists involve themselves actively in the struggle to end female circumcision? If no, why not? If yes, what role(s) should they play? How do they reconcile their responsibilities as professional anthropologists with their responsibilities as human beings?

5. In what ways can an understanding of a specific form of marriage inform anthropologists about other social practices in a given society? For example, anthropologists can link cross-cousin marriages in Africa to economics, in that this type of marriage is geared toward keeping wealth from leaving the group or lineage. What other examples might be studied?

Internet Resources

Female Circumcision

http://www.ucl.ac.uk/network-for-student-activism/w/ Female_genital_cutting:_A_woman%E2%80%99s_right_ to_choose

A website devoted to exploring female circumcision and the view from anthropology.

http://www.religioustolerance.org/fem_cirm.htm

A discussion of the ongoing debate among Muslims regarding female circumcision.

The Fight for Gay Rights: Canada Timeline

http://archives.cbc.ca/IDD-1-69-599/life_society/ gay_lesbian/

A historical examination of the struggle for gay rights in Canada.

Canada's Youth Diversity Initiative

http://JersVision.org

Award-winning activist and University of Ottawa alumnus Jeremy Dais's organization works to address bullying and discrimination, and helps youth promote diversity.

The Kibbutz

http://www.mfa.gov.il/mfa/go.asp?mfah0gal0

An overview of the kibbutz system, some history, the way the system works, and demographic statistics.

http://i-cias.com/e.o/kibbutz.htm

http://

A Brief Look at The History and Organization of the Kibbutz, as Well as Maps, Charts, and a Photo.

Suggested Readings

For a list of suggested readings, visit the textbook's website at **http://www.havilandcultural4e.nelson.com**.

Notes

1. A.B. Weiner, *The Trobrianders of Papua New Guinea* (New York: Holt, Rinehart and Winston, 1988), 71.

2. R.W. Connell, "Making Gendered People: Bodies, Identities, Sexualities," in *Revisioning Gender,* ed. M.M. Ferree, J. Locker, and B. Hess (Thousand Oaks: Sage, 1999).

3. G. Wekker, "What's Identity Got to Do with It? Rethinking Identity in Light of the Mati Work in Suriname," in *Female Desires: Same-Sex Relations and Transgender Practices Across Cultures,* ed. E. Blackwood and S.E. Wieringa (New York: Columbia University Press, 1999).

4. G. Herdt, *The Sambia: Ritual, Sexuality, and Change in Papua New Guinea,* 2nd ed. (Belmont: Thomson Wadsworth, 2006).

5. S. Staggenborg, *Social Movements* (Toronto: Oxford University Press, 2008).

6. R. Kelly, "Witchcraft and Sexual Relations," in *Man and Woman in the New Guinea Highlands,* ed. P. Brown and G. Buchbender, Special Publication No. 8 (Washington: American Anthropological Association, 1976).

7. Herdt, *The Sambia.*

8. B. Knauft, "Violence and Sociality in Human Evolution," *Current Anthropology* 32 (1991): 391–409.

9. N. Bonvillain, *Women and Men: Cultural Constructs of Gender* (Upper Saddle River: Prentice Hall, 1998).

10. S. Lang, "Lesbians, Men-Women and Two-Spirits: Homosexuality and Gender in Native American Cultures," in *Female Desires: Same-Sex Relations and Transgender Practices Across Cultures,* ed. E. Blackwood and S.E. Wieringa (New York: Columbia University Press, 1999).

11. E. Blackwood and S.E. Wieringa, "Sapphic Shadows: Challenging the Silence in the Study of Sexuality," in *Female Desires: Same-Sex Relations and Transgender Practices Across Cultures*, ed. E. Blackwood and S.E. Wieringa (New York: Columbia University Press, 1999).

12. Wekker, "What's Identity Got to Do with It?"

13. Despite some recent progressive developments, the degree of control or seclusion experienced by young women in Arab countries varies enormously, from the restrictive system in Saudi Arabia to the much more secular environments of Syria and Egypt.

14. R. Weitz, "What Price Independence? Social Relations to Lesbians, Spinsters, Widows, and Nuns," in *The Gender Reader,* ed. E. Ashton-Jones, G.A. Olson, and M.G. Perry (Needham Heights: Allyn and Bacon, 2000).

15. G. Herdt, *Same Sex, Different Cultures: Perspectives on Gay and Lesbian Lives* (Boulder: Westview Press, 1997).

16. Haviland's interpretation of the Nayar follows W.H. Goodenough, *Description and Comparison in Cultural Anthropology* (Chicago: Aldine, 1970), 6–11. It should be noted that this marriage custom has not been practised by the Nayar for many years.

17. University of Victoria Sexual Assault Centre. (1999, July 13.) Childhood Sexual Abuse Statistics. Retrieved February 13, 2007, from http://www.safekidbc.ca/statistics.htm.

18. G.C. Leavitt, "Sociobiological Explanations of Incest Avoidance: A Critical Review of Evidential Claims," *American Anthropologist* 92 (1990): 973.

19. N. Thornhill, quoted in *Talking About People,* ed. W.A. Haviland and R.J. Gordon (Mountain View: Mayfield, 1939), 127.

20. W.H. Oswalt and S. Neely, *This Land Was Theirs: A Study of North American Indians,* 5th ed. (Mountain View: Mayfield, 1996).

21. Brian Schwimmer, University of Manitoba, "Exogamy and Incest Prohibitions," November 1989, http://umanitoba.ca/faculties/arts/anthropology/tutor/marriage/incest.html, accessed April 12, 2001.

22. Quoted in R.M. Keesing *Cultural Anthropology: A Contemporary Perspective* (New York: Holt, Rinehart and Winston, 1976), 286.

23. Bill C-23, Section 3(3), http://www.parl.gc.ca/Content/LOP/LegislativeSummaries/40/3/c23b-e.pdf, accessed March 3, 2001.

24. M. Jacobs, "Living Together Replacing 'I Do' for Many," *Edmonton Sun,* July 17, 2002.

25. Statistics Canada (2006), "Family Portrait: Continuity and Change in Canadian Families and Households in 2006," http://www12.statcan.ca/english/census06/analysis/famhouse/cenfam1.cfm, accessed September 12, 2007.

26. The following is based on R.S. Obler, "Is the Female Husband a Man? Woman/Woman Marriage Among the Nandi of Kenya," *Ethnology* 19 (1980): 69–88.

27. This information has been compiled from K. Lahey and A. Alderson *Same-Sex Marriage: The Personal and the Political* (Toronto: Insomniac Press, 2004); and Demian, "Marriage Traditions in Various Times and Cultures," 2005, http://www.buddybuddy.com/mar-trad.html, accessed June 31, 2005. Readers should note that the number of countries allowing same-sex marriages/unions is changing daily, so that the above list is by no means comprehensive.

28. R.C. Kirkpatrick, "The Evolution of Human Homosexual Behavior," *Current Anthropology* 41 (2000): 384.

29. L. Pospisil, *The Kapauku Papuans of West New Guinea* (New York: Holt, Rinehart and Winston, 1963).

30. D. Johnson, "Polygamists Emerge from Secrecy, Seeking Not Just Peace but Respect," in *Talking About People,* ed. W.A. Haviland and R.J. Gordon, 2nd ed. (Mountain View: Mayfield, 1996), 129–31.

31. D.R. White, "Rethinking Polygyny: Co-wives, Codes, and Cultural Systems," *Current Anthropology* 29 (1988): 529–72.

32. A.D. McMillan, *Native Peoples and Cultures of Canada: An Anthropological Overview* (Vancouver: Douglas and McIntyre, 1988), 140–41.

33. N.E. Levine and J.B. Silk, "Why Polyandry Fails," *Current Anthropology* 38 (1997): 375–98.

34. Statistics Canada, 2006 Census, http://www12.statcan.ca/census-recensement/2006/rt-td/index-eng.cfm, accessed 3August 3, 2011.

35. Ibid.

36. Oswalt and Neely, *This Land Was Theirs,* 258.

37. J. Collier, M.Z. Rosaldo, and S. Yanagisako, "Is There a Family? New Anthropological Views," in *Rethinking the Family: Some Feminist Problems,* ed. B. Thorne and M. Yalom (New York: Longman, 1982), 36.

8 Family and Household

Tripod/Getty Images

One of the basic functions of the family is raising children.

KEY QUESTIONS

1. What Is the Family?

The human family is a group composed of a married or common law couple with or without children, or a lone parent with dependent children. The family can take many forms, from a married or common law couple (including same-sex couples) with children, as in North American society, to a large group composed of several brothers and sisters with the sisters' children, as in southwest India among the Nayar. The specific form that families take is related to particular social, historical, and ecological circumstances.

2. What Is the Difference Between Family and Household?

Households are task-oriented residential units within which economic production, consumption, inheritance, childrearing, and shelter are organized and implemented. In the vast majority of human cultures, households consist of families, even though some household members may not be relatives of the family.

3. What Are Some of the Problems of Family and Household Organization?

Although families exist to solve the problems people must deal with, the different forms that families may take are all accompanied by their own characteristic problems. Where families are small and relatively independent, as they are in North American society, individuals are isolated from the aid and support of kin and must fend for themselves in many situations. By contrast, families that include several adults in the same large household must find ways to control tensions that invariably exist among their members.

Family, *falu, familia,* familiar: these words and their derivatives have come to stand for an essential human cultural artifice. "Family"—from the 14th-century Latin, designating the members (or servants) of a household—has long been regarded as a core social institution. Today, in many parts of the world, that institution is undergoing fundamental changes. Widespread anthropological interest in the family is reflected in renewed discussion of so-called traditional family values—a euphemism for two-parent, opposite-sex, legal marriages in which the woman stays home to raise children. Yet the increasing prevalence of blended, single-parent, common law, and same-sex families is challenging the concept of a typical or traditional family.

THE FAMILY DEFINED

Our understanding of what constitutes a **family** is ever changing. This dynamism makes it difficult to develop a functional definition of family. If we were to define family in terms familiar to most Canadians—as requiring a father, a mother, and children—then we would have to say that people like the Nayar of southern India (see Chapter 7) did not have families. A typical definition of a family is a group composed of a woman and her dependent children and at least one adult male joined through marriage or blood relationship.[1] Yet if a woman is raising her children alone, is this not a family? And if two males are joined in a same-sex common law relationship or marriage and they have children, how do we account for them according to this the definition? Another possible definition of family is "a kinship group providing the nurturant socialization of their children (natural or adopted)."[2] Although more cross-culturally acceptable, this deliberately vague definition proves less than satisfactory when we attempt to define a "family" without children, or a lone parent of any marital status living with one or more children.[3] Throughout this chapter we will aim to illustrate the difficulties with developing an inclusive definition of family that is not **culture-bound.**

In traditional times, the Nayar marriage system maintained a **consanguine** (or "blood") **family** consisting of a woman, dependent offspring, and the woman's brothers. In such societies, men and women marry but do not live together as members of one household. Rather, they spend their lives in the households they grew up in, with the men "commuting" for sexual activity with their wives. Economic cooperation between men and women occurs between sisters and brothers rather than husbands and wives.

By contrast, families formed on the basis of marital or common law ties between husband and wife are called conjugal families. Minimally, a **conjugal family** consists of a married or common law couple (which may be a same-sex couple) with their dependent children, otherwise known as the **nuclear family**. Other forms of conjugal families include a **polygynous family** with

family A married or common law couple with or without children, or a lone parent with dependent children. May sometimes include non-kin members.

culture-bound The interpretation of other practices and beliefs from the standpoint of one's own culture. A culture-bound interpretation can be biased and unwilling to accept the validity of alternative phenomena.

consanguine family A family unit consisting of a woman, her dependent offspring, and the woman's brothers.

conjugal family A family consisting of two or more married or common law people, including same-sex people, with their dependent children.

nuclear family A married or common-law couple and their dependent children.

polygynous family A family consisting of a man and his multiple wives, along with their dependent children.

Roberto Condé/agefotostock/Firstlight

The nuclear family, consisting of a married or common law couple and their dependent offspring, is held up as the ideal in Canada.

multiple wives of a single husband and their dependent children, and a **polyandrous family**, which includes the multiple husbands of a single wife and their dependent children. Both may be thought of as aggregates of nuclear families having one spouse in common.

Historical and cross-cultural studies of the family reveal as many family patterns as the human imagination can invent. The one considered most typical in North America, the nuclear family, is in fact no more normal or natural than any other and cannot be used as the standard for measuring other forms. Neither universal nor even common among human societies, the independent nuclear family emerged only recently in human history. Its roots go back to a series of regulations that the Roman Catholic Church imposed in the 4th century that prohibited close marriages, discouraged adoption, and condemned polygyny, concubinage, divorce, and remarriage (all of which previously had been perfectly acceptable, as the Old Testament of the Bible, among other sources, makes clear). This prohibition strengthened the conjugal tie between one man and one woman at the expense of consanguineal ties; it also ensured that large numbers of people would be left with no male heirs. It is a biological fact that 20 percent of all couples will have only daughters and that another 20 percent will have no children at all. By eliminating polygyny, concubinage, divorce, and remarriage and by discouraging adoption, the Church removed the means for people to overcome these odds and to make sure they would have male heirs. The result was to facilitate the transfer of property from families to the Roman Catholic Church, which rapidly became the largest landowner in most European countries, a position it retained until recently. By embedding itself in the very fabric of domestic life, heirship, and marriage, the Church gained tremendous control over society, enriching itself in the process.[4]

With the industrialization of Europe and North America, the nuclear family became further isolated from other kin. One reason is that industrial economies require a mobile labour force: people must be prepared to move where the jobs are, which they do most easily without excess kin in tow. The family also came to be seen as a kind of refuge from a public world, which people saw as threatening to their sense of privacy and self-determination.[5] It was supposed that within the family, relationships were enduring and noncontingent, entailing love and affection, based on cooperation and governed by feelings and morality.

Although families are still considered the foundation of Canadian life, the composition of families has changed over the past few decades. Statistics Canada identifies three family structures in Canadian society: lone-parent families (15.9 percent), common law families (15.5 percent), and married couples or nuclear families (68.6 percent). As an example of evolving Canadian family structures, by 2006, 12 percent of all Canadian couples with children were stepfamilies, and common law families had become the fastest growing family structure in Canadian society.[6] In addition, around 16 percent of the roughly 16,000 female same-sex couples in Canada were living with children, and around 3 percent of male same-sex couples were living with children.[7]

The family as it has emerged in Europe and North America, then, is the product of particular historical and social circumstances. Where these circumstances have differed, so have family forms. Thus, how men and women in other cultures live together must be studied, not as bizarre and exotic forms of human behaviour but as logical outcomes of people's experiences living in particular times, places, and social situations.

Our discussion has emphasized North American perceptions of the family, but it is important to note that the family in one form or another is a universal feature of human social organization. The family as an institution serves the same functions cross-culturally: that of nurturing children and creating a cooperative economic unit, the household. Many North Americans think of families as standing in opposition to the rest of society, but in truth they are affected by, and in turn affect, the values and structure of the society in which they are embedded. Anthropologists have also found that the concept of family is not as clear as originally believed. The following Original Study examines fatherhood among the Aka pygmies of central Africa.

polyandrous family A family consisting of a woman and her multiple husbands, along with their dependent children.

✖ *Original Study* ✖

Aka Pygmies—Best Dads in the World

Liam Kilmurray

Aka fathers do more infant care-giving than fathers in any other known society.

Hewlett (1991, 167)

As marriage and fatherhood undergo profound changes in much of the world, the first extensive study of father–infant relations in non-Western groups is revealing. The Aka pygmies are a hunter-gatherer people of the western Central African Republic and northwestern Congo (RPC) who call themselves *BiAka* but are also known as *Babenzele.** Time allocation studies of the Aka reveal the extent to which Aka fathers physically interact with infants (generally defined as birth to one year old). These studies suggest that Aka fathers spend more time than any other known human culture with their children. Indeed, Aka fatherhood is renowned throughout Africa, and the anthropological world, as something quite extraordinary and compelling.

As a pygmy people, the Aka fall into a category much researched by anthropologists and sociologists. Pygmies have long been a source of fascination and study by outsiders. Knowledge of the existence of pygmies stretches back into the distant past. During the Sixth Dynasty in Egypt, some 4,000 years ago, the Egyptians referred to the "pygmy" peoples of central Africa as "dwellers in the land of trees" (Turnbull 1965, 149). The ancient Greeks also commented on the existence of pygmies; Homer referred to them as the "Pygmaean race." After infrequent references to them in later Roman records, the pygmies "disappeared" from world history for over

1,000 years, for they lived deep in the forests of central and southern Africa. Although pygmies are found in other parts of the world, such as Australia, Thailand, Malaysia, Indonesia, the Philippines, Papua New Guinea, and Brazil, it is the pygmy peoples of Africa that have been most widely studied.

General interest in the pygmies gathered steam in the 19th century, as explorers and early ethnographers encountered the "elusive bush men." In the 20th century, as a decline in Africa's pygmy population set in,

© FatherWorld/afrol News

they were the source of much media interest. The film *The Gods Must Be Crazy* drew international attention to the plight of Africa's pygmies. During the apartheid era in South Africa and a series of wars in Namibia, the pygmies were recruited by various factions for their tracking abilities, which astonished seasoned soldiers of, for example, the South African Army. Modern anthropological interest in the pygmies is reflected in several major publications and studies. Turnbull's sympathetic portrayal of the Mbuti of the Ituri Forest stands out as a work of clarity and vivid description, though arguably it is ethnographically defective. Turnbull brought much attention to the lives of the Mbuti pygmies, and an increase in scholastic inquiry soon followed. Major studies of the

Kalahari bushmen and the Baka or Bongo followed. What has emerged is an understanding of the sheer variety of pygmies, both within Africa and without.

Anthropologists employ a rough barometer to determine what constitutes a pygmy. They are generally described as less than 4 feet 11 inches tall, as spending at least four months of the year in the tropical forest hunting and gathering, and as having a strong identity with and preference for forest life. Pygmy groups maintain complex social and economic relations with neighbouring farming populations, from which they receive part-time employment and with whom they trade. Often this involves the exchange of forest products such as meat and honey for village products such as carbohydrates and vegetables. All pygmies practise important ritual activities associated with hunting. Most of these characteristics are applicable to the Aka pygmies.

Genetic analysis indicates that the Aka, much like the related Efé and Hadzabe, are among the oldest existing modern humans. Their DNA is one of the least "transmuted," meaning that they, as a population, are among the most ancient of human groups. Indeed, pygmies have often been held up as representative of the first human groups to evolve from archaic *Homo sapiens*. The study of the pygmy way of life, then, becomes a study not just of one cultural grouping, but of human origins.

The Aka inhabit the rainforest of central Africa, an ecologically diverse area of semideciduous and evergreen forest, parcels of open savannah, and river valleys with marsh forest. There are two seasons: a long rainy season and a shorter, slightly drier season. The Aka hunt a variety of game and gather any wild resources they can. Wild game includes the duiker, whose skins they traded in colonial times, and which still provide much of the meat and fur requirements for today's Aka. Other animals hunted include antelope, rats, civets, squirrels, wild pigs, gorillas, chimpanzees, and birds and monkeys. Monkeys are difficult to capture, and the mangabey, quenon, and colobus are preferred if they can be caught. Aka people also gather mushrooms, caterpillars, and fruits. For carbohydrates, they trade meat and furs to neighbouring farming peoples such as the Ngandu. During the dry season, some Aka work on nearby coffee plantations or in lumber operations. They return to the forest and the hunt when they have made enough money, or simply when they wish to return—or as they say, "when the forest calls them." The Aka have hunted elephants for centuries, perhaps even longer. In the 19th century, they kept the elephant meat but traded the ivory to outsiders such as European collectors and colonists, using the Ngandu as middlemen. Some elephants are still hunted today. For much of the first half of the 20th century, the Aka tapped rubber trees and deposited the hardened sap with the Ngandu, who, again acting as middlemen, traded it to outsiders, paying the Aka mainly in produce. In the 1950s, the Aka hunted—many think they overhunted—the duiker, a medium-sized antelope, for its meat and valuable skins.

The basic social unit of the Aka is the camp. Families, clans, and bands are of less importance to them, except on special occasions. Most camps are comprised of 20 to 35 individuals— usually three or four related males and their families. Camps grow in size during the dry season and relocate seasonally or when circumstances dictate.

There are around 30,000 Aka today. They are still mainly hunter-gatherers, who trade with horticultural groups for crops and other products that the forest does not provide them. The Aka are renowned for their musical abilities, which have been the subject of much ethnographic research (see Kisliuk 2000). Their musical instruments include cylindrical single-skin drums, water drums, and the arched harp. Aka musical performances, which include dances and polyphonic singing, are popular around the world. Like all hunter-gatherers, the Aka spend less time hunting than most Westerners spend at work. For 25 hours or so per week, they divide their time between hunting and gathering. Generally speaking, the men hunt singly with spears, though they will travel in small groups. They hunt in the forest from early morning to late afternoon, taking advantage of foraging opportunities along the way. Meat is not always caught, and when it is, it is a source of pride, celebration, and sharing, one of the dominant aspects of the hunter-gatherer way of life.

Women's work mainly involves childrearing, gathering, and camp maintenance. They prepare food as well as forage for it. Women will sometimes work in the fields of the Ngandu. Men and women will hunt together, in family groups, when a net hunt is undertaken. In this type of hunt, forest animals are driven and chased into waiting nets. Usually, the women attend to the nets while the men drive the game into them.

The Aka employ a range of weapons and tools in order to survive and indeed flourish. They hunt with nets, spears, and bows, employing microlithic spears and arrow heads. They also use small metal axes and digging sticks, and a variety of baskets. But perhaps the mightiest weapon in the Aka armoury is their knowledge of the forest and its animals and plants. Their understanding of these is unsurpassed and enables them to survive in a highly challenging environment.

The Aka, like all forest peoples, have developed complex rituals and beliefs. Colin Turnbull, enthralled, described them as "a people who had found in the forest something that made their life more than just worth living ... a wonderful thing of joy and happiness and free of care" (1962, 27). The Aka perceive the forest as a living thing. The entity they mention most often is Djengi, a powerful but mostly benevolent forest spirit. Communication with Djengi takes place through a traditional healer (*tuma*), who has the ability to translate the supernatural language. The Aka believe that deceased family members do not completely leave earth after death. Instead, the spirits of their ancestors (*edjo*) remain behind, visiting family members and sometimes asking for things. Most Aka believe in witchcraft, mainly to explain the unexpected deaths of adults.

Quite unique about the Aka is how fathers tend to their children. Research into fathers and infant caregiving reveals that Swedish men undertake some 45 per cent of child care, the highest in Europe. Worldwide, men perform around 25 to 30 percent of child care duties. It is Aka men, though, who top the list at some 47 percent. Aka fathers also sleep with their children—a custom that many North Americans do not practise. While studying the Aka over two decades, the American anthropologist Barry Hewlett compiled statistics on parental caregiving, specifically along the following parameters: holding, proximity, availability, and nearest neighbour. Hewlett recorded the times and duration that each parent, and others, held or were proximate to infants. Noteworthy here was the net hunt, which the family— wife, husband, and children—undertake together. Deep in the forest there are many dangers, which include swamps, snakes, and aggressive animals. When infants are present in this type of hunt, they must be carried back and forth to the hunting ground and then held frequently throughout the hunt. This care is usually provided by the male, given that he is stronger and is holding the weapons. The women then chase the game that is being hunted,

CONTINUED

CONTINUED

driving them into nets or catching them themselves.

Hewlett did more than examine parent–infant holding patterns. He also observed the daily routine of Aka adults, and found that Aka spent around 56 percent of the day hunting, 27 percent foraging, and some 17 percent working in neighbours' villages. From these figures and ethnographic analysis, he concluded, 'Aka infancy is indulgent: Infants are held almost constantly, they have skin to skin contact most of the day as Aka seldom wear shirts or blouses, and they are nursed on demand and attended to immediately if they fuss or cry. Aka parents interact with or stimulate their infants throughout the day. They talk to, play with, show affection to, and transmit subsistence skills to their infants during the day" (Hewlett 1991, 32; cf. Hewlett and Lamb 2005, 49).

The amount of time that Aka dads spend with their infants is of more than passing interest. Aka parenting practices reveal a great deal about Aka society and offer valuable lessons for today's rapidly changing societies. As Aka infants mature, their personalities are affected by exposure to both parents. Child psychologists, anthropologists, and sociologists of all shades agree that an infant's proximity to the father *and* mother leads to positive emotional development. In later life, it is argued, close parenting results in emotional and social well-being and a sense of self-assuredness, as well as strong feelings of autonomy.

The amazing devotion of Aka dads has been attributed to several factors. First is the net hunt, already mentioned. Second is the relationship between husband and wife, which is long-lasting and mutually reinforcing. The near absence of violence (including warfare) among the Aka is another factor for understanding Aka parenting. The egalitarian nature of Aka society is yet another. It is noteworthy that striking a child is considered grounds for divorce among the Aka (though not among other pygmy groups, such as the Mbuti).

Today's globalized world has crashed into the central African rainforests that are home to many pygmy groups, including the Baka and Aka in the north, the Bongo of Gabon, and the Efé of central Africa. Those forests are under threat from warfare, the hunting of endangered species, the expanding timber industry, and encroaching agriculture. Many pygmies are surviving the destruction of their habitat by staying longer and longer in the villages of neighbouring non-pygmies, working from time to time in the fields. Others, ironically, have found work in the lumber industry, helping fell the very forests that gave birth to them. The Aka are surviving (though for how much longer is anyone's guess), but they are considered close to if not on the list of endangered human cultures. Their importance cannot be understated: the Aka "extend our potential of human understanding" (Hewlett 1991, 171). They live on today as a reminder of past ways of living and as a testament to an alternative society in which parenting is not so one-sided and whose fathers are, quite simply, the best in the world.

* The term "pygmy" is sometimes considered pejorative, and many groups prefer to be called by their actual names.

SOURCES: *S. Bahuchet, "Spatial Mobility and Access to Resources Among the African Pygmies," 1991, http://hal.archives-ouvertes.fr/hal-00261573/en; R.J. Gordon,* The Bushman Myth *(Boulder: Westview Press, 1992); B.S. Hewlett,* Intimate Fathers *(Ann Arbor: University of Michigan Press, 1991); B.S. Hewlett and M.E. Lamb, eds.,* Hunter-Gatherer Childhoods *(New Brunswick, New Jersey: Transaction Publishers, 2005); M. Kisliuk, "Seize the Dance!" BaAka Musical Life and the Ethnography of Performance *(Oxford: Oxford University Press, 2000); C. Turnbull, "The Mbuti Pygmies: An Ethnographic Survey,"* Anthropological Papers of the American Museum of Natural History 50, *pt. 3 (1965); Turnbull,* The Forest People *(New York: Touchstone, 1962); Turnbull,* The Mbuti Pygmies: Change and Adaptation *(New York: Holt, Rinehart, and Winston, 1983). See also these Web pages:* Medical News Today, *http://www.medicalnewstoday.com/articles/26042.php; and Guardian.co.uk, http://www.guardian.co.uk/society/2005/jun/15/childrensservices.familyandrelationships.*

FUNCTIONS OF THE FAMILY

Among humans, reliance on group living for survival is a basic characteristic. We have inherited this from our primate ancestors, although we have developed it in our own distinctively human ways.

Nurturance of Children

The sexual division of labour among humans has developed beyond that of other primates. Until the emergence of synthetic infant formulas, human females were often occupied much of their adult lives with childrearing. Human infants need active "mothering" since they are helpless at birth and the period of infant dependency is quite long. Studies have shown that human infants need more than just food and physical care if they are to develop normally. But among humans, unlike other primates, the infant's biological mother does not have to provide all this "mothering." Not only other women but also men may provide the child with much of the attention it needs. In many cultures, children are handled and caressed as much by men as by women, and in some cultures men are more nurturing to children than are women. Changing trends in the Canadian workforce—most notably women working outside the home—have resulted in men becoming more involved in childrearing. Although it is not yet common, some men are choosing to stay at home and care for their young children, enabling their wives to pursue careers.

Through enculturation, children begin learning their culture soon after birth. Parents, and especially mothers, are the first people responsible for enculturating children. In North America, a family ideally includes a mother and father (or stepmother/father) and the child's siblings, although this is not always the case. In other cultures the father may seldom have contact with his children in their early years; indeed, in some cultures men do not even live with the mothers of their children. In such cases, brothers of the child's mother play important roles in raising their nieces and nephews. Grandparents, other wives of the father, brothers of the father, and sisters of the mother, not to mention their children, are also important in the enculturation process. The Capela of Amazonian Brazil, and other South American cultures, believe that a man who has intercourse with a pregnant woman shares the fatherhood.[8] Normally there is only one accepted father, but there will be multiple social fathers. In some societies—Canada is a good example—professional nannies, teachers, and day care workers are brought into the enculturation process to provide formal care and instruction.

Children learn much of what they need to know through observation and participation. Jean Briggs studied the unique childrearing practices of the Inuit of Baffin Island. The adults used emotionally powerful questions about moral and social dilemmas to informally socialize their children. Questions such as "Why don't you kill your little brother?" encouraged a child to admit to jealousy but also love for the little brother.[9] These types of dilemmas encouraged Inuit children to think about how they should treat other people.

Canadian men are increasingly involved in childrearing, enabling their wives to pursue careers.

The development of self-awareness is part of the enculturation process. North American children tend to lag behind children in other cultures in self-awareness, possibly because close human contact and active stimulation of infants is curtailed in North America. North American children do not normally sleep with their parents; rather, they are placed in a room by themselves with little stimulation. In more traditional cultures, such as the Ju/'hoansi, infants routinely sleep with their parents, or at least their mothers. When awake, they are carried most of the time, with frequent nursing. Among the Ju/'hoansi, infants are nursed four or five times an hour, for one or two minutes at a time. Overall, a 15-week-old Ju/'hoansi infant is in close contact with its mother about 70 percent of the time, compared with 20 percent for home-reared infants in mainstream Canadian society. Among the Efé pygmies of Africa, there is multiple caregiving and different mothers of newborns take turns breast-feeding a baby. Inuit babies and small children receive a great deal of love and attention from their mothers and other members of their families. Mothers tend to nurse their infants on demand, holding and cuddling them most of the time. In fact, Inuit infants are seldom left alone when awake. Adult Inuit rarely become angry with their children or scold them, feeling that to do so is a sign of immaturity.

This near-constant stimulation of infants in traditional cultures is important. Recent studies show that stimulation plays a key role in the "hardwiring" of the brain; stimulation is necessary for the development of the neural circuitry. Nor should the role of frequent nursing be overlooked, since the longer a child is breast-fed, the higher it will score on cognitive tests and the lower its risk of having attention deficit disorder (hyperactivity). Furthermore, breast-fed children have fewer allergies, fewer ear infections, and less diarrhea, and are at less risk of sudden infant death syndrome.[10]

Economic Cooperation

The economic activities of women generally have complemented those of men, even though individuals may perform tasks normally assigned to the opposite sex as the occasion dictates. Thus, men and women could share the results of their labours on a regular basis.

An effective way to facilitate economic cooperation between the sexes while at the same time providing for a close bond between mother and child is by establishing residential groups that include adults of both sexes. The differing nature of male and female roles, as these are defined within a culture, requires

Gender Perspectives

The Motherhood Mandate

In her essay "The Motherhood Mandate," Susan Basow suggests that all "normal" women want to become mothers and that each woman experiences a deep-rooted "maternal instinct" pushing her toward this goal. Women who cannot have children are pitied, and those who choose not to have children are considered lazy, selfish, and cold-hearted—unnatural women.

From an early age, little girls are socialized into becoming "good" mothers—playing house with the requisite baby dolls, toy ovens, and ironing boards. And when they are older, their first job is likely as a babysitter, now with "living dolls." Thus, their gender identity is firmly entrenched. The media, a powerful socialization tool, inundate girls and young women with images of motherhood as the perfect life choice. Idolized role models (such as movie stars and models) enthusiastically endorse the joys of motherhood, the suggestion always being that a mother can still maintain an exciting career, a lovely home, and a perfect size-five body.

The motherhood mandate, which remains a powerful force in many secular and religious ideologies, romanticizes motherhood as the only way a woman can be "fulfilled." But this ignores the realities of motherhood—the endless chores, the isolation, and the exhaustion involved in being a mother 24/7. It also ignores the heavy responsibility placed on a mother's shoulders to raise a bright, well-adjusted, happy child, and the blame that is placed on her if this does not happen.

Once North American women become mothers, they quickly realize the true nature of motherhood. Out of desperation, and perhaps guilt, some adopt the media image of a supermom. The supermom can do all things and be all things to all people. Supermoms are portrayed as women with boundless energy and enthusiasm, enviable time management skills, and an innate ability to nurture; they are women who have it all—career, marriage, children, community volunteer work, not to mention a sparkling clean floor. In essence, Western supermoms are a product of both the traditional and the modern world—they are "blended" mothers, still attempting to maintain the traditional values of motherhood emanating from the 1950s, while also buying into the image of a "modern" woman, one who can juggle the multiple roles of wife, mother, and career.

Casting aside the motherhood mandate and the supermom image is a difficult decision for most modern women. The desire to be a good mother, coupled with years of socialization into these roles, seems to force women to maintain this impression of motherhood. This is unfortunate, because until women themselves accept the realities and limitations of motherhood, modern Western society will continue to undervalue the role of motherhood, while still setting unrealistic expectations for mothers.

SOURCES: E.D. Nelson and B.W. Robinson, eds., Gender in Canada *(Toronto: Prentice Hall Allyn and Bacon, 1999);* S.A. Basow, "The Motherhood Mandate," *in same.*

Zev Radovan/PhotoEdit

One alternative to the family as a childrearing unit is the Israeli kibbutz. Here, the children of a kibbutz engage in a supervised session of creative play.

a child to have an adult of the same sex available to serve as a proper model for the appropriate adult role. The presence of adult men and women in the same residential group provides for this.

Well suited though the family may be for these tasks, we should not suppose it is the only unit capable of providing such conditions. In fact, other arrangements are possible, such as the Israeli kibbutz, where paired teams of male and female specialists raise groups of children. In many traditional food-foraging groups, all adult members of a community shared in the responsibilities of child care. Thus, when parents went hunting or collecting plants and herbs, they left their children behind, secure in the knowledge that they would be looked after by whatever adults remained in the camp. Yet another arrangement may be seen among the Mundurucu, a horticultural people of South America's Amazon forest. Their children lived in houses with their mothers, apart from all men until age 13, whereupon the boys left their mothers' houses to live with the village men.

FAMILY AND HOUSEHOLD

Although it is often stated that some form of family is present in all human cultures, the Mundurucu case just cited demonstrates this is not so. In Mundurucu villages, the men all lived together in one house with all boys over age 13; women lived with others of their sex as well as younger boys in two or three houses grouped around the men's house. As among the Nayar, married men and women were members of separate households, meeting periodically for sexual activity.

The **household**, defined as the basic residential unit for economic production, consumption, inheritance, childrearing, and shelter is universally present. Among the Mundurucu, the men's house constituted one household, and the women's houses constituted others.

Most households constitute families, although other sorts of households may be present as well. Often, a household consists of a family along with more distant relatives. Co-residents may be unrelated, such as the service personnel in an elaborate royal household, apprentices in the household of craft specialists, or low-status clients in the households of rich and powerful patrons. In such cases, people may think in terms of households rather than families, but the households are built around the latter. Thus, in the vast majority of human cultures the family is the basic core of the household.

FORM OF THE FAMILY

As suggested earlier, the family may take any number of forms in response to particular social, historical, and ecological circumstances. A distinction must be made between conjugal families, which are formed on the basis of marital ties, and consanguineal families, which are not. As defined earlier, consanguineal families consist of related women, their brothers, and the women's offspring. Such families are not common; the classic case is the Nayar household group. The Tory Islanders, a Roman Catholic, Gaelic-speaking fisherfolk living off the coast of Ireland, do not marry until they are in their late 20s or early 30s and thus experience tremendous resistance to breaking up existing household arrangements. Because the community numbers only a few hundred people, husbands and wives are within easy commuting distance of each other.

The Nuclear Family

The form of conjugal family most familiar to North Americans is the independent nuclear family, which in spite of its steady decline is still widely regarded as the "standard" in Canada and the United States. In these countries, unlike the Tory Islands, it is not considered desirable for young people to live with their parents beyond a certain age, nor is it considered the responsibility of a couple to take their aged parents into their home when the parents can no longer care for themselves. Retirement communities and nursing homes provide these services. However, decades of government cutbacks have created a shortage of good nursing homes at the same time as Canadian seniors are living longer. This has forced more and more middle-aged adults to care for their elderly parents or find private care.

The nuclear family is also likely to be prominent in cultural groups such as the Inuit, who live in a harsh northern environment. In traditional times, nuclear families exploited the vast Arctic wilderness for food. The men hunted and fished and built shelters while the women cooked, cared for the children, and sewed and repaired clothing. The wife and her children could not survive without the husband, and life for a man was unimaginable without a wife.

> **household** The basic residential unit where economic production, consumption, inheritance, childrearing, and shelter are organized and implemented; may or may not be synonymous with family.

∞ *Dynamic Anthropology* ∞

Transnational Child Exchange?

Settling into her seat for the flight to Boston, Kathryn cradled the sleepy head of her newly adopted son, Mesay. As the plane lifted away from African soil and presented a sweeping view of Ethiopia's capital, tears slid down her cheeks. Were the tears for Ethiopia's loss of a boy, a boy's loss of Ethiopia, or her profound joy for the gift of adoption?

Child exchange is a universal phenomenon, taking place across the world and throughout human history. Just as marriage and kinship mean different things in different cultures, so does child exchange, referred to in the English language as "adoption." In some cultures, adoption is quite rare, while in others, such as in Polynesian communities in the Pacific Islands, it is very common. For instance, in a small village in Tahiti it was found that over 25 percent of children were raised by adoptive parents.

A cross-cultural understanding of adoption is vital now that child exchange has become part of the global flow, especially from poor countries in Africa, Latin America, Southeast Asia, and eastern Europe, to affluent countries in North America and western Europe. The global exchange of children initially involved war orphans after the Second World War. In recent decades, extreme poverty has become a major factor, as mothers confronting serious deprivation may feel forced to abandon, give away, or sometimes sell their children. Whether brokered by government or nongovernmental agencies, by for-profit or not-for-profit enterprises, global child exchange has become a big business—legal and illegal, moral and amoral, happifying and horrifying. This is especially true in poor countries, where most workers earn less than a dollar a day and a foreign adoption nets $12,000 to $35,000 in broker fees.

Since the early 1970s, about 500,000 foreign children have been adopted into families in the United States alone. A nearly equal number have ended up in other wealthy countries. The global flow to the United States peaked in 2004 when nearly 23,000 arrived—most from China (30 percent), Russia (25 percent), Guatemala (14 percent), and Korea (7 percent), with 5,500 flown in from other poor countries such as India, the Philippines, Ukraine, and Vietnam. Statistics vary (and shift) according to adoption rules. Some countries have shut the door on foreign adoptions owing to accusations of "exporting" or even "selling" children. Others restrict or prohibit it for religious reasons. Sudan, for example, forbids foreign adoption of Muslim children and automatically classifies religiously unidentified orphans as Muslim.

A country that does not discriminate on the basis of religion is its neighbor, Ethiopia, which has gained popularity as an infant-provider country. One of six U.S. agencies officially approved to do foreign adoptions from Ethiopia is Wide Horizons for Children in Waltham, Massachusetts, which has placed many Ethiopian children with American families. Among them is Mesay, now settled into his new life with Kathryn, her husband, and their four other children, including a sister about his age, adopted from China as an infant.

Certain parallels can be drawn between the nuclear family in industrial societies and families living under especially harsh environmental conditions. In both cases, the family is an independent unit that must be prepared to fend for itself; this creates a strong dependence on one another. Minimal help is available from outside in the event of emergencies or catastrophes. In the event of the mother's or father's death, life becomes precarious for their children. Yet this form of family is well adapted to a life that requires a high degree of geographic mobility. For the Inuit, this mobility permitted them to hunt for food; for most North Americans, the hunt for jobs and improved social status requires a mobile form of family unit.

When Inuit families were hunting or foraging individually, it was regarded as a matter of temporary expediency; when food sources were abundant or more labourers were necessary, larger social groups would come together. For example, the Netsilik Inuit of the Arctic coast west of Hudson Bay congregated to watch the breathing holes during the winter sealing hunts, and the Labrador and Mackenzie Delta Inuit came together in large numbers during whaling season. Even during these times of congregation, the basic family unit remained the nuclear family, and each family was free to go elsewhere as it pleased.[11] Thus families cooperated with one another on a daily basis, sharing food and other resources, looking out for the children, and sometimes even eating together.

The sense of shared responsibility for one another's children and for the general welfare in Inuit multifamily groups contrasts with other families in North America, which are more "on their own." Canadian parents receive some help from local and federal governments, in the form of child tax credits, universal medicare, and an extensive social welfare program. However, this assistance is mainly economic rather

flocks are kept, and carry out other part-time economic pursuits considered necessary for existence. At the turn of the 20th century, Canadian immigrants—such as Ukrainians—maintained extended family structures to provide enough labour for work on their farms. As Canada became more urbanized, these extended families gave way to nuclear families.

Changing labour patterns also can affect family dynamics. Traditionally, a Chinese daughter-in-law cared for her husband's elderly parents. This custom is not nearly as evident in Chinese Canadian families, partly because the daughter-in-law may work outside the home, and partly because many Chinese Canadian seniors now prefer to live apart from their adult children. However, extended families in Canada have not totally disappeared; in 2001, 13 percent of men and 12 percent of women over 65 lived with one or more of their children.[12]

Extended families living together in single households were often an important social unit among the Iroquois First Nations of southern Quebec and Ontario. The Huron and Iroquois lived in extended families in villages of bark-covered longhouses, each housing several families. This extended family structure developed in response to a horticultural economy, with a mix of agriculture, wild plant gathering, fishing, and some hunting. After marriage a woman brought her husband into the home of her mother and sisters. The women worked together, planting crops of beans, corn, and squash and gathering wild plants, while their husbands cleared the lands, hunted, and fished.[13]

than emotional or physical. To be sure, families can and often do help one another out, but they are under no obligation to do so. In fact, once children reach the age of majority (18), parents have no further legal obligation to them, nor do the children to their parents. When families do have difficulty fulfilling their functions—as is increasingly the case—even if it is through no fault of their own, less support is available to them from the community at large than in other cultures, including that of the Inuit.

The Extended Family

In North America, nuclear families have not always had the degree of independence they came to have with the rise of industrialism. In an earlier, more agrarian era, the small nuclear family commonly was part of a larger **extended family.** This kind of family, part conjugal and part consanguine, might include grandparents, mother and father, brothers and sisters, perhaps an uncle and aunt, and a stray cousin or two. All these people lived and worked together. Because members of the younger generation brought their spouses (husbands or wives) to live in the family, extended families, like consanguine families, had continuity through time. As older members died off, new members were born into the family.

Extended families are most likely to be found in cultures with an economy based on subsistence farming. Such families are important, for they provide the large labour force necessary to till the soil, tend whatever

Extended-family living arrangements are common throughout the world. Shown here is an Iroquois longhouse where several families would have lived and worked together.

extended family A collection of nuclear families, related by ties of blood, that live together in one household.

The 1960s saw a number of attempts by young people in Canada and the United States to reinvent a form of extended family. These families (often called "communes") were groups of unrelated nuclear families that held property in common and lived together. It is further noteworthy that the lifestyle of these families often emphasized the kinds of cooperative ties found in rural North American extended families of old, which provided a labour pool for the many tasks required for economic survival. In some of these communes the members reverted to traditional gender roles; the women took care of the childrearing and household chores, while the men took care of tasks outside of the household.

Same-Sex Families

Of the many forms a family can take, perhaps the most controversial is the gay or lesbian family. Same-sex families face social stigma and discrimination predicated on flawed assumptions about gay and lesbian people and their ability to be good parents. Many same-sex couples live in fear of losing custody of their children. In Western societies, gay and lesbian couples with children have lobbied for the right to be recognized as legitimate family units.[14]

Opponents of same-sex families express concern regarding the impact that gay and lesbian parents may have on their children's sexual, psychological, and social development. Yet fears that children raised in a same-sex family will be emotionally or physically harmed have proven groundless. In fact, there is no evidence that children in gay and lesbian families differ from other children in academic, social, or psychological health, nor are their sexual orientation and gender development affected. Much of the ignorance concerning same-sex families could be eliminated if we sought to understand them in their own right.

Same-sex families can be divided into two main categories: stepfamilies and co-parent families. In stepfamilies, children were conceived in previous heterosexual relationships, and the parent in the same-sex relationship (usually the woman) has retained custody after the breakup of the heterosexual relationship. Co-parent families exist when one or both lesbian mothers conceive a child through donor insemination, or when men have children through adoption, fostering, or surrogacy. The most prevalent same-sex families are lesbian stepfamilies. Like opposite-sex families, same-sex families exhibit a great deal of diversity based on ethnicity, age, perceived gender roles, community, and so on.

RESIDENCE PATTERNS

Where some form of conjugal or extended family is the norm, family exogamy requires that either the husband or wife, if not both, move to a new household upon marriage. A newly married couple may adopt one of five common patterns of residence, the primary determinants of which are ecological circumstances. One option is **patrilocal residence;** as described for the Maya, a woman goes to live with her husband in the household he grew up in. Favouring this arrangement are cultures with a predominant role for men in subsistence, especially if they own property that can be accumulated, if polygyny is customary, if warfare is prominent enough to make cooperation among men especially important, and if there exists an elaborate political organization in which men wield authority. These conditions are most often found together in cultures that rely on animal husbandry and/or intensive agriculture for their subsistence. Where patrilocal residence is customary, the bride often must move to a different band or community. In such cases, her parents' family is not only losing the services of a useful family member, but is losing her potential offspring as well. Hence, some kind of compensation to her family, most commonly bride-price, is usual.

Matrilocal residence, in which the man leaves the family he grew up with to live with his wife in her parents' household, results if ecological circumstances make the women's role predominant in subsistence. It is found most often in horticultural societies, where political organization is relatively uncentralized and where cooperation among women is important. The Iroquois provide one example: In traditional times it was the women who did the farming, who controlled access to land, and who "owned" the harvest. Under matrilocal residence, men usually did not move very far from the family they were raised in, so they were available to help out there from time to time. Therefore, marriage usually did not involve compensation to the groom's family.

patrilocal residence   A pattern in which a married couple lives in the locality associated with the husband's father's relatives.

matrilocal residence   A pattern in which a married couple lives in the locality associated with the wife's relatives.

Ambilocal residence is especially well suited to situations where the economic cooperation of more people than are available in the nuclear family is needed but where resources are limited in some way. Because the couple can join either the bride's or the groom's family, family membership is flexible, and the two can live where the resources look best or where their labour is most needed. This was once the situation on the peninsulas and islands along the Maine coast, where extended family households were based on ambilocal residence. The same residential pattern was common among food-foraging peoples, such as the Mbuti of Africa's Ituri Forest. Traditionally, a

Mbuti married someone from another band, so one spouse had in-laws who lived elsewhere. Thus, if foraging was poor in their part of the forest, the couple had somewhere else to go where food might be more readily available. Ambilocality greatly enhanced their opportunity to find food. It also provided a place to go if a dispute broke out with someone where the couple lived. Consequently, Mbuti camps were constantly changing their composition as people split off to live with their in-laws, while others joined from other groups. For food foragers, who find their food in nature and who maintain an egalitarian social order, ambilocal residence can be a crucial factor in both survival and conflict resolution.

Under **neolocal residence**, a married couple forms a household in an independent location. This occurs where the independence of the nuclear family is emphasized. In industrial societies such as Canada, where most economic activity occurs outside rather than inside the family and where it is important for individuals to be able to move where jobs are found, neolocal residence is better suited than any of the other patterns.

Children growing up in same-sex families experience similar emotional, social, and sexual development as those in opposite-sex families.

> **ambilocal residence** A pattern in which a married couple may choose either matrilocal or patrilocal residence.
>
> **neolocal residence** A pattern in which a married couple establishes its household in a location apart from either the husband's or the wife's relatives.

Members of modern Maya extended families carry out various activities on the household plaza; here, for example, making tortillas.

This Trobriand Island chief, shown in front of his house, will be succeeded by his sister's son. Hence, men who will become chiefs live avunculocally.

Avunculocal residence, in which a married couple lives with the groom's mother's brother, is favoured by the same factors that promote patrilocal residence, but only in cultures where descent through women is deemed crucial for the transmission of important rights and property. Such was the case among the people of the Trobriand Islands in earlier times, where each individual was a member of a group of relatives who traced their descent through their mother, their mother's mother, and so on, to the one woman all others were descended from. Each of these descent groups held property, consisting of hamlet sites, bush and garden lands, and, in some cases, beachfronts to which members had access rights. These properties were controlled each generation by a male chief or other leader who had inherited these rights and obligations. But because descent was traced exclusively through women, a man could not inherit these from his father. Thus, succession to positions of leadership passed from a man to his sister's son. For this reason,

> **avunculocal residence**   A pattern in which a married couple lives with the husband's mother's brother.
>
> **sororal polygyny**   A man marries several women who are sisters.

a man who was in line to take control of his descent group's assets took his wife to live with the one he would succeed—his mother's brother. This enabled him to observe how the older man cared for his hamlet's affairs, as well as learn the oral traditions and magic he would need to be an effective leader.

Although Trobriand leaders and chiefs lived avunculocally, most married couples in this society lived patrilocally. This allowed sons to fulfill their obligations to their fathers, who helped build up and nurture them when they were small; in return, the sons inherited personal property such as clay pots and valuable stone axe blades from their fathers. This also gave men access to land that their father's descent groups controlled in addition to their own, enabling them to improve their own economic and political position in Trobriand society. In short, here, as in any human society, practical considerations played a central role in determining where people lived following marriage.

PROBLEMS OF FAMILY AND HOUSEHOLD ORGANIZATION

Effective though the family may be at organizing economic production, consumption, inheritance, and child-rearing, at the household level relationships within the family inevitably involve a certain amount of conflict and tension. This does not mean they may not also involve a great deal of warmth and affection. Nevertheless, at least the potential for conflict is always there and must be dealt with lest families become dysfunctional. Different forms of families are associated with different sorts of hierarchies and tensions; the means employed to manage these tensions differ accordingly.

Polygamous Families

Within polygamous families, there is serious potential for conflict between the multiple spouses of the individual they are married to. For example, under polygyny (the most common form of polygamy), the wives must be able to get along with a minimum of bickering and jealousy. One way to handle this is through **sororal polygyny**, or marriage to women who are sisters. Presumably, women who have grown up together can get along as co-wives of a man more easily than women who grew up in different households. Another mechanism is to provide each wife with a separate dwelling within a household compound and perhaps require the husband to adhere to a system of rotation for sleeping purposes. The latter at least prevents the husband from playing obvious favourites among his wives. In some polygynous groups, women enjoy considerable economic autonomy. In cultures where women's work is hard and boring, polygyny allows sharing of the workload and alleviates boredom through companionship with the co-wives.

Polygynous families also may solve economic problems. Among the Hawazama pastoralists of Sudan, one wife and her children live in the nomad camp and practise animal husbandry. A second wife and her children live in a settlement, where they raise crops. Thus each portion of the family is involved in either herding or farming, which enhances the chances of survival in a challenging environment.[15]

In polyandrous families, two distinctive structural characteristics may cause difficulty. One is that a woman's older husbands are apt to dominate the younger ones. The other is that, under conditions of **fraternal polyandry** (where, for example among the much studied Nayar of India, co-husbands are brothers), the youngest brothers are likely to be considerably younger than their wives, whose reproductive years are limited. This reduces a young husband's chances of reproducing successfully, relative to older husbands. Not surprisingly, when polyandrous families break up, it is usually the younger husbands who depart.[16]

Extended Families

Extended families, no matter how well they may work, have their own potential areas of stress. Decision making in such families usually rests with an older individual, and other family members must defer to the elder's decisions. In-marrying spouses must adjust their ways to conform to the expectations of the family they have come to live with. To combat these problems, people rely on various techniques to enforce harmony, including dependence training and the concept of "face" or "honour." Dependence training involves raising people who are more inclined to be compliant and accept their lot in life than are individuals raised to be independent. One of the many problems young people in North American society face, as they experiment with extended family living, is that they generally have been raised to be independent, making it hard to defer to others' wishes when they disagree.

The concept of "face" may constitute an especially potent check on the power of senior members of extended families. Among pastoralists of northern Africa, a young man can escape from ill treatment at the hands of a father or an older brother by leaving the patrilocal extended family to join the family of his maternal relatives, in-laws, or even an unrelated family willing to take him in.[17]

Mark van Manen/Vancouver Sun

Some North Americans have attempted to re-create the extended family in the formation of communes—for example, this commune in Langley, British Columbia. These attempts sometimes run into trouble as members cope with the stress associated with extended family organization they are unprepared for.

Because men lose face if their sons or brothers flee in this way, they are generally at pains to control their behaviour to prevent this from happening. Women, who are the in-marrying spouses, also may return to their family of birth if they are mistreated in their husband's family. A woman who does this exposes her husband and his family to scolding by her kin, again causing loss of face.

When all else fails to restore harmony, siblings may be forced to demand their share of family assets to set up separate households. In this way, new families emerge. Divorce, too, may be possible. In cultures that practise matrilocal residence, divorce rates tend to be high, reflecting how easily unsatisfactory marriages can be terminated. In some cultures with patrilocal residence, by contrast, divorce may be all but impossible, at least for women (the in-marrying spouses). This was the case in rural Taiwan, for example, where women were raised to be cast out of their families.[18] When they married, they exchanged their dependence on fathers and brothers for absolute dependence on husbands and, later in life, sons.

fraternal polyandry A woman marries several men who are brothers.

Without the option of divorce, to protect themselves against ill treatment, women went to great lengths to develop the strongest bond possible between themselves and their sons so that the latter would rise to their mother's defence when necessary. So single-minded were many women toward developing such relationships with their sons that they often made life miserable for their daughters-in-law, who were seen as competitors for their sons' affections.

Nuclear Families

Just as extended families have built into them particular sources of stress and tensions, so too do nuclear families, especially in modern industrial societies where the family has lost one of its chief reasons for being: its economic function as a basic unit of production. Rather than staying within the fold, working with and for each other, one or both adults in a marriage must seek work outside the family. Furthermore, their work may keep them away for prolonged periods. If both spouses are employed, the requirement for workers to go where their jobs take them may pull the husband and wife in different directions. Neolocal residence also tends to isolate husbands and wives from both sets of kin. Isolation from kin means that a young mother-to-be must face pregnancy and childbirth without the assistance and support of female kin. Instead, for regular advice and guidance, she must turn to physicians (who are more often men than women), books, and friends and neighbours, who themselves may be inexperienced. The problem continues through motherhood, in the absence of experienced women within the family as well as a clear model for childrearing.

The impermanence of the nuclear family itself may constitute a problem, in the form of anxieties over old age. Once the children are gone, who will care for the parents in their final years? In North American society, no requirement exists for children to do so. North American governments have established numerous agencies and facilities to care for the elderly. In cultures where adult children have traditionally cared for their elderly parents, changing demographics and government policies may threaten this practice. China's one-child policy, put in place in 1978, was designed to reduce out-of-control population growth. However, fewer children also meant few adult children to care for the elderly.

Female-Headed Families

In North America, as increasing numbers of adults have sought escape from dysfunctional nuclear families through divorce, and as young females have chosen to keep infants

Al Harvey, The Slide Farm, www.slidefarm.com

In Canada, single mothers who are heads of households are often placed in no-win situations: if they work to support the household, they are seen as unfit mothers; if they stay home with the children, they are labelled "deadbeats."

born outside of a marriage or common law relationship, a dramatic rise in single-parent families headed by women has occurred. In 2001, 1.3 million Canadian families (15.6 percent) were lone-parent families.[19] In the vast majority of cases (81.3 percent in Canada), the children remain with their mother, who then faces the problem of having to provide for them as well as for herself. In divorce cases, fathers are usually required to pay child support, but they are not always able or willing to do this, or the amount is often not sufficient to cover expenses.

As with working women who remain with their husbands, kin may not be available to look after the single mother's children, so outside help must be sought and (usually) paid for, making it even more difficult for the mother to support her family adequately. To compound the problem, women sometimes lack the skills necessary to secure more than menial and low-paying jobs, not having acquired such skills earlier as a result of raising children. Even when they do have skills, women are often not paid as much as men working at the same jobs.

The Anthropologist's World

Public Health Surveillance and First Nations Self-Government

John O'Neil

Medical anthropologists John O'Neil, Joseph Kaufert, Pat Kaufert, and Kue Young at the University of Manitoba have worked closely with epidemiologists and other public health practitioners to document deteriorating health conditions and health service problems in First Nations communities for the past several decades. While this research has identified important trends in health conditions and has contributed to the development of improved health services, First Nations communities often feel alienated from the research and stigmatized by the results. Increasingly, First Nations communities have expressed a feeling of having been "researched to death" and are resistant to participating in health-related research.

Building on insights provided by the work of French philosopher Michel Foucault, this group of anthropologists has initiated a program of research that is intended to support the First Nations objective of gaining control over the technologies of public health surveillance that are fundamental elements of self-government. From this theoretical perspective, "governing" requires the capacity to monitor the needs and actions of a population. For First Nations communities, these monitoring activities remain largely under the control of federal and provincial government agencies and institutions. As a result, progress toward First Nations self-government is undermined in subtle but insidious ways.

O'Neil and his colleagues are attempting to address this problem by working in partnership with First Nations authorities in Manitoba to develop First Nations public health surveillance capacity. Beginning in 1996 with the development of a longitudinal health survey and continuing with a variety of projects that examine health service data in the context of training workshops for First Nations health workers, this team opened the Manitoba First Nations Centre for Aboriginal Health Research, which provides an opportunity for First Nations authorities and university-based experts to develop health information systems that support the health policy and programming needs of First Nations and other Aboriginal communities.

SOURCES: J.D. O'Neil, J. Reading, and A. Leader, "Changing the Relations of Surveillance: The Development of a Discourse of Resistance in Aboriginal Epidemiology," Human Organization 57, no. 2 (1998): 230–37.

Not surprisingly, as the number of single-parent families has increased, so has the number of women (and, of course, their children) who live below the poverty line. In 2003 nearly half of all female-headed families in Canada were in a low-income situation.[20] Moreover, these women and children are the ones most severely affected by cutbacks made in social welfare programs since 1980. The good news, however, is that since 1996 female-headed family incomes have been rising, partly because of increased participation of women in the workforce.

Single-parent families are neither new nor restricted to industrialized societies such as Canada. They have been known and studied for a long time in the countries of the Caribbean basin, where men historically have been exploited as a cheap source of labour on plantations. Under such conditions, men have no power and few economic rewards; hence they are tenuously attached at best to any particular household. These are held together by women, who, as producers of subsistence foods, provide the means of economic survival for the family. Similar female-headed households are becoming increasingly common in other developing countries, too, as development projects increasingly restrict women's ability to earn a living wage.

Thus, women constitute the majority of the poor, the underprivileged, and the economically and socially disadvantaged in most of the world's societies. In developing countries, the situation has been made worse by "reforms" that the International Monetary Fund (IMF) requires of countries when foreign debt repayments are being negotiating. Cutbacks in government education, health, and social programs for debt service have their most direct (and negative) impact on women and children, while further development designed to increase foreign exchange (for debt repayment and the financing of more industrialization) also comes at women's and children's expense. Meanwhile, the prices people must pay for basic life necessities increase (to cut down on unfavourable trade balances).

At the start of this chapter we posed a number of questions relating to the effectiveness of the family, as it is known today in North America, in meeting human needs. From what we have just discussed, it is clear that neolocal nuclear families impose considerable anxiety and stress on the individuals in such families. Deprived of the security and multiplicity of emotional ties found in polygamous, extended, or consanguineal families, these nuclear families find that if something goes wrong, it is potentially more devastating to the individuals involved.

Yet it is also obvious that alternative forms of family and household organization come complete with their own distinctive stresses and strains. Whereas, for example, Hutterite communities may have more immediate access to close family members than a nuclear family, there are challenges in this type of socializing unit also. So, to the question of which alternative is preferable, we must answer that it depends on what problems need to be overcome and what price we are willing to pay.

In North America, it is clear that the problems inherent in the "traditional" nuclear family have led to a marked decline in the percentage of households such families occupy. Meanwhile, the conditions that gave rise to these families in the first place have changed. As well, same-sex couples with children are seeking legal and public recognition for their families. So far, no single family structure or ideology has arisen to supplant the nuclear family, nor can we predict which (if any) of the alternatives will gain pre-eminence in the future. The only certainty is that family and household arrangements, not just in North America but throughout the world, will continue to evolve, as they always have, as the conditions to which they are sensitive continue to change.

Chapter Summary

1.   What is the family?
The human family is a group composed of a married or common law couple with or without children, or a lone parent with dependent children. Dependence on group living for survival is a basic human characteristic. Nurturing children traditionally has been the adult female's job, although men also may play a role, and in some cultures men are even more involved with their children than are women. The family can take many forms, but the specific form that families take is related to particular social, historical, and ecological circumstances. There is a perception that the presence of adults of both sexes is advantageous, since gender-appropriate roles are learned from them. [21]

2.   What is the difference between family and household?
Households are task-oriented residential units. In the vast majority of cases, households are made of families, though some household members may not be relatives. In response to different historical and ecological circumstances, the family may take any of a number of forms. The smallest unit, consisting of mother, father, and their dependent children, is called the nuclear family. The nuclear family is widespread and is not limited to particular environments. In Canada, for example, it is found both in major Canadian cities and in the High Arctic.

3.   What are some of the problems of family and household organization?
In neolocal nuclear families, individuals may become isolated from the support of kin, so spouses must work out their own solutions to any problems associated with living together and raising children. On the other hand, families that contain several adults in a large household must find methods to control tensions that arise among members.

Questions for Critical Thought

1. In this chapter we have examined several definitions of family. Now it is your turn. How do you define a family? What do you think might be an ideal family form for modern, urban Canadians?

2. Identify childrearing practices in your own culture that serve to mould gender identity (e.g., dress.)

3. Single-parent families are becoming increasingly common in North America. What programs might help these families thrive?

4. Many people in North America have strong feelings about families in which the adult members are involved in a same-sex relationship. In Canada, many provinces have legalized same-sex marriage, and this has also legitimized same-sex families. Do you think that being raised in a same-sex family would harm a child? Why or why not? In what ways are same-sex families similar to opposite-sex families? In what ways are they different?

Internet Resources

Health Canada: Canada's Seniors
http://www.phac-aspc.gc.ca/seniors-aines/pubs/factoids/2001/toc_e.htm

Statistical snapshots of Canada's seniors. Also provides a list of related links.

Men, Reproductive Rights, and Gender Equality
http://www.unfpa.org/swp/2000/english/ch04.html

This UN site examines gender equality, men's roles and changing realities, violence, gender inequality, and cultural expectations, as well as men's support for sexual and reproductive health. An excellent resource for students of gender and the family.

Inuit Childrearing
http://www.tungasuvvingatinuit.ca/eng/children.htm

A brief discussion of Inuit childrearing, as well as new initiatives for children in Inuit communities.

Not Just Numbers: A Canadian Framework for Future Immigration

http://immigrationcanada.pro/2010/06/ the-future-of-canada-immigration/

An extensive discussion of immigration issues, including categories or classes for immigration qualifications. This site gives readers an idea of the challenges and problems faced by families and government officials with regard to immigration policies.

Mormon Church History—Polygyny

http://lds.org

The Mormon Church website, in which a detailed explanation of polygamy can be researched.

A Profile of Canadian Families

http://www.ccsd.ca/factsheets/family

A statistical profile of Canadian families, full of useful statistics and demographic information.

Suggested Readings

For a list of suggested readings, visit the textbook's website at **http://www.havilandcultural4e.nelson.com**.

Notes

1. D. Bell, "Defining Marriage and Legitimacy," *Current Anthropology* 38 (1997): 237–53.

2. B.B. Ingoldsby, "Family Origins and Universality," in *Families in Multicultural Perspective,* ed. B.B. Ingoldsby and S. Smith (New York: Guilford Press, 1995), 94.

3. Statistics Canada, "2006 Census: Families, Marital Status, Households, and Dwelling Characteristics," http://www.statcan.gc.ca/daily-quotidien/070912/dq070912a-eng.htm.

4. J. Goody, *The Development of the Family and Marriage in Europe* (Cambridge: Cambridge University Press, 1983), 44–46.

5. J. Collier, M.Z. Rosaldo, and S. Yanagisako, "Is There a Family? New Anthropological Views," in *Rethinking the Family: Some Feminist Questions,* ed. B. Thorne and M. Yalom (New York: Longman, 1982), 34–45.

6. Statistics Canada, "2001 Census: Marital Status, Common-Law Unions, and Families," *The Daily,* November 6, 2002, http://www12.statcan.ca/english/census01/products/analytic/companion/fam/canada.cfm, accessed September 12, 2003.

7. Statistics Canada, "2006 Census: Families, Marital Status, Households, and Dwelling Characteristics."

8. C.R. Ember and M. Ember, *Encyclopaedia of Sex and Gender.* (New York: Springer Verlag, 2003).

9. J.L. Briggs, "Inuit Morality Play: The Emotional Education of a Three-Year-Old," *Social and Economic Studies* 67 (1998).

10. K.A. Dettinger, "When to Wean," *Natural History* 49 (October 1997).

11. A.D. McMillan, *Native Peoples and Cultures of Canada: An Anthropological Overview* (Vancouver: Douglas and McIntyre, 1988).

12. Statistics Canada, "More Seniors Living with a Spouse, More Living Alone and Fewer Living in Health Care Institutions," 2001, http://www12.statcan.ca/english/census01/products/analytic/companion/fam/canada.cfm, accessed February 17, 2007.

13. O.P. Dickason and D.T. McNab, *Canada's First Nations: A History of Founding Peoples from Earliest Times* (Toronto: Oxford University Press, 2009).

14. P.I. Erera, *Family Diversity: Continuity and Change in the Contemporary Family* (Thousand Oaks: Sage, 2002).

15. B.J. Michael, "Patterns of Family Relations," in *Ethnographic Essays in Cultural Anthropology: A Problem-Based Approach,* ed. R.B. Morrison and C.R. Wilson (Itasca: F.E. Peacock, 2002).

16. N.E. Levine and J.B. Silk, "Why Polyandry Fails," *Current Anthropology* 38 (1997): 385–87.

17. L. Abu-Lughod, *Veiled Sentiments: Honor and Poetry in a Bedouin Society* (Berkeley: University of California Press, 1986), 99–103.

18. M. Wolf, *Women and the Family in Rural Taiwan* (Stanford: Stanford University Press, 1972), 32–35.

19. Canadian Council on Social Development, "Stats & Facts–Family: A Canadian Profile," 2007, http://www.ccsd.ca/factsheets/family, accessed February 17, 2007.

20. Statistics Canada, "Income and Earning Trends," http://www.statcan.ca/english/research/85-570-XIE/2006001/tables/tablea1-1.htm, 2006, accessed February 17, 2007.

21. For detailed discussion, see B.D. Miller, ed., *Sex and Gender Hierarchies* (Cambridge: Cambridge University Press, 1993).

9 Kinship and Descent

© Getty Images

Kinship relations are the fundamental building blocks of human society. Some form of family organization is almost universal in world cultures. Kinship and descent remain vital today, even though a number of the functions of kinship have been replaced by the institutions of citizenship, including educational, legal, and administrative bureaucracies.

KEY QUESTIONS

1. What Are Descent Groups?

Kin groups are made up of our relatives, both consanguineal (blood) and affinal (in-laws). We organize our kin along descent groupings. A descent group is a kind of kinship group whereby being a lineal descendant of a particular real or mythical ancestor is a criterion of membership. Descent may be reckoned exclusively through men, exclusively through women, or through both.

2. What Functions Do Descent Groups Serve?

Descent groups of various kinds—lineages, clans, and moieties—are convenient devices for solving a number of problems that human societies commonly confront: how to maintain the integrity of resources that cannot be divided without destruction; how to generate workforces for tasks that require a labour pool larger than a household can provide; and how to allow members of one sovereign local group to claim support and protection from members of another. Not all cultures have descent groups; in many foraging and industrial societies, some of these problems are handled by the kindred, a group of people with a living relative in common. The kindred, however, does not exist in perpetuity, as does the descent group, nor is its membership as clearly and explicitly defined. Hence, it is generally a weaker unit than the descent group.

3. How Do Descent Groups Form?

Descent groups arise from extended family organization, as long as problems of organization exist that such groups help solve. This is most apt to happen in food-producing groups. First to develop are localized lineages, followed by larger, dispersed groups such as clans. Over time, kinship terminology itself is affected by and adjusts to the kinds of descent or other kin groups important to a culture.

4. How Do Anthropologists Study Descent?

Throughout this chapter we will see how anthropologists employ a variety of techniques to understand not just who is descended from whom, but how descent systems function in societies. Through ethnographic methods, the descent systems of a multitude of the world's cultures have been understood. These disparate systems are given classifications. The representations of these descent systems are made using symbolic representations, in chart format. Other areas of research into descent are rather recent, such as the extraction of DNA from living, historic, and prehistoric samples.

Any human social life requires the establishment of a social structure consisting of a network of relations between individuals and groups of individuals. These relations all involve certain rights and duties which need to be defined in such a way that conflicts of rights can be resolved without destroying the structure.[1]

Kinship has long been one of the most important areas of anthropological study. Early anthropologists—including Radcliffe-Brown, Evans-Prichard, and Malinowski—all conducted important ethnographic studies of kinship. These early studies revealed that kinship was much more than a means of naming relations. Indeed, kinship carried with it deep cultural meanings and obligations and was deeply embedded in economic and ritual structures.

Every culture develops some sort of family or household structure as a means to address various needs, such as to foster economic cooperation between the sexes, to provide a setting conducive to childrearing, and to regulate sexual activity. Family and household organization can be an efficient and flexible means for rising to these challenges, but the fact remains that many cultures confront problems that are beyond the coping abilities of families and households.

For example, members of a sovereign local group often need some means of claiming support and protection from individuals in another group. This can be crucial for defence against natural or human disasters: if people have the right of entry into local groups other than their own, they can secure protection or critical resources their own group cannot provide. Another example: a group often needs to share rights to some means of production that cannot be divided without its destruction. This is witnessed in horticultural societies, where division of land becomes impractical beyond a certain point. The problem can be avoided if land ownership is vested in a corporate system that outlives its members. A final example: people often need some means to provide cooperative workforces for tasks that require more people than the household alone can provide.

kinship The people we are related to through blood (consanguineal) and marriage (affinal).

One way of dealing with these sorts of problems is by developing a formal political system, with personnel to make and enforce laws, keep the peace, allocate resources, and perform other regulatory and societal functions. A common practice in nonindustrial societies—especially horticultural and pastoral societies—is to develop kinship groups.

A **kinship** group is composed of the people we are related to—both our consanguineal (blood) relatives and our affinal (through marriage) relatives. Kinship plays an important role in the social life of every human group, however complex its culture. Kin may be divided into three groups: *nominal, effective,* and *intimate* or *core.*[2] We may have little or no contact with *nominal kin,* even though we are usually aware of their existence. We meet *effective kin* fairly regularly, at family functions such as weddings, funerals, and reunions. We maintain continuing, close relationships with our *intimate kin,* who usually include our extended family—parents, siblings, aunts and uncles, and grandparents, both affinal and consanguineal. In Canadian society, the size of our kin group is influenced by personal choice and, to a lesser extent, by proximity, gender, and class factors.[3]

In rural and preindustrial societies, kinship is the focal point of social organization: members live in close proximity and generally form economic bonds—in terms, for example, of land ownership or water use. In urban, industrial societies, modern "cults" of individualism and privacy, as well as the increased mobility and the nuclear family structure, have altered extended-family kinship systems to a degree. In addition, formal institutions such as day care centres, banks, and schools have usurped what were once family obligations.

WHY WE STUDY KINSHIP

Virtually everyone has kin, whether biological or adopted, and these "relatives" play an important role in our lives. We begin learning our kinship from birth. The way we classify our relatives seems natural and logical to us, in the same that other, very different kinship systems seem natural and logical to their own members.

Kinship involves not only how we classify our relatives but also how we organize our family, the support and assistance we can count on, whom we will marry, our residential patterns, and how we view our world and our future. Kinship defines our gender roles, how many children we will bear, what will happen to us when we grow old, and even what faith we will practise.

On this altar, King Yax-Pac of the ancient Maya city of Copan portrays himself and his predecessors, thereby tracing his descent back to the founder of the dynasty. In many human groups, such genealogical connections are used to define each individual's rights, privileges, and obligations.

Kinship is culturally diverse, and it is dynamic. When you strive to understand this diversity, remember that you are also seeking to understand aspects of you own behaviour and how this behaviour is influenced by kinship.

URBAN KINSHIP SYSTEMS IN CANADA

In the early part of the 20th century,[4] researchers assumed that urbanization and industrialization would reduce the significance of kinship in Canadian society—that the nuclear family would replace extended kin groups, and that non-kin ties (i.e., friends) would become more important in our lives than kin. Supposedly, an *isolated nuclear family* structure functions more efficiently in our urban environment than an unwieldy extended family.[5] However, recent studies have disputed this isolated nuclear family hypothesis. Extended kinship ties in Canada remain fundamental to the well-being of individuals and nuclear families. Kin groups establish patterns of mutual aid, especially among parents and adult children and their families. Such aid includes financial assistance, the provision of child care during vacations, and regular gift giving. This *modified extended family*[6] does not require residential proximity or restrictive rights and obligations; it maintains close emotional ties and a network of reciprocal support, and it is still common in 21st-century Canadian families.

Canada is a multicultural society that has been strongly influenced by Aboriginal cultures, immigration patterns, and ethnic, linguistic, and cultural complexities. Early immigrants to Canada, mainly of French, British, and Irish descent, were organized in a nuclear family structure but developed strong kin ties with other relatives in Canada. The nonmechanized farms of the past required human labour. Extended-family units in Canada commonly farmed collectively to supply the needed labour. Following mechanization, many of these collective farming enterprises dispersed as young people sought employment and educational opportunities in urban centres. More recent immigrants to Canada, such as Italian Canadians, tend to maintain close ties with kin in their country of origin, thanks to global transportation and communication systems, while also maintaining close ties with relatives already in Canada. Neolocal nuclear families are the basic kinship unit, although other members of the extended family usually live nearby. New immigrants often substitute friends, especially of the same ethnic origin, if they do not have any family in Canada; or, as with Italian Canadians, they include neighbours and friends in their kinship network. Known as **fictive kinship**, this practice is common among many Canadian people, not just recent immigrants.

fictive kinship Friends not biologically related but considered part of a kin group.

In Canada, then, kinship tends to be voluntary and selective, with no strong obligations, compared with, for example, a tribal horticultural kin group. Under normal circumstances, the nuclear family does not operate in isolation: a modified extended-family support system, involving frequent communication, visiting, and support, is available to each family. Given the vastness of Canada, the degree of contact is not determined by geographical proximity, but rather by closeness of the individuals, with parents and adult children enjoying the most interaction.

DESCENT GROUPS

In nonindustrial societies, a common way of organizing a society along kinship lines is by creating what anthropologists call descent groups. A **descent group** is any publicly recognized social entity requiring lineal descent from a real or mythical ancestor for membership. Members of a descent group trace their connections back to a common ancestor through parent–child links. This feature may explain why descent groups are found in so many cultures. They appear to stem from the parent–child bond, which is built upon as the basis for a structured social group.

Descent groups define membership clearly; in their absence, membership overlaps and it is not always clear where an individual's primary loyalty belongs. Membership can be restricted in a number of ways. The most common way is by tracing membership through one sex. In this way, each individual is automatically assigned from birth to the mother's or father's group and to that group only.

Unilineal Descent

Unilineal descent (sometimes called *unilateral descent*) establishes descent group membership through the male or the female line. In non-Western cultures, unilineal

descent groups are quite common, especially in "middle-level" societies—the large variety of horticultural and pastoral societies, which are neither hunting-gathering nor industrial. At birth, an individual is assigned membership in a specific descent group, which may be traced either by **matrilineal descent**, through the female line, or by **patrilineal descent**, through the male line.

There seems to be a close relationship between the descent system and a culture's economy. Generally, patrilineal descent predominates where the man is the breadwinner, as among pastoralists and intensive agriculturalists, where male labour is a primary factor. Matrilineal descent is important mainly among horticulturists, where women are the breadwinners. Many matrilineal cultures are found in South Asia, one of the cradles of food production in the Old World. These include cultures in India, Sri Lanka, Indonesia, Sumatra, Tibet, and South China, and on many Indonesian islands. Matrilineal systems also were prominent in some North American Aboriginal groups, such as the Huron and Iroquois, and still occur in many parts of Africa, including among the Bemba of Zambia.

In all cultures, the kin of both mother and father are important components of the social structure. That descent is reckoned patrilineally, for example, does not necessarily mean that maternal relatives are unimportant. It simply means that, for purposes of *group membership*, the mother's relatives are excluded. Similarly, under matrilineal descent, the father's relatives are excluded for purposes of group membership. For example, we saw in early chapters how important paternal relatives are among the matrilineal Trobriand Islanders. Although children belong to their mothers' descent groups, fathers play an important role in nurturing them and building them up. Upon marriage, the bride's and groom's paternal relatives contribute gifts, and throughout life, a man may expect his paternal kin to help him improve his economic and political position in society. Eventually, sons may expect to inherit personal property from their fathers.

Patrilineal Descent and Organization

Patrilineal descent (sometimes called *agnatic* or *male descent*) is the more widespread of the two unilineal descent systems. The male members of a patrilineal descent group trace their descent through other males from a common ancestor (see Figure 9.1). Brothers and sisters belong to the descent group of their father's father, their father, their father's siblings, and their father's brother's children. A man's son and daughter also trace their descent through the male line to their common ancestor. In a typical patrilineal group, the responsibility for training the children rests with the father or his elder brother. A woman belongs to the same descent group as

descent group Any publicly recognized social entity requiring lineal descent from a particular real or mythical ancestor for membership.

unilineal descent Descent that establishes group membership exclusively through either the mother's or the father's line.

matrilineal descent Descent traced exclusively through one's mother's grandmother's line, etc., to establish group membership.

patrilineal descent Descent traced exclusively through one's father's grandfather's line, etc., to establish group membership.

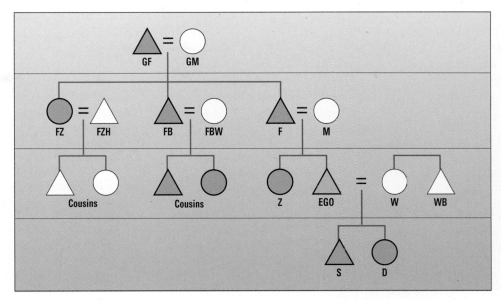

Figure 9.1

How patrilineal descent is traced. Only the individuals symbolized by a filled-in circle or triangle are in the same descent group as ego. *F* stands for father, *B* for brother, *H* for husband, *S* for son, *M* for mother, *Z* for sister, *D* for daughter, and *W* for wife.

In patrilineal and other cultures that promote the dominance of men over women, this practice sometimes goes to the extreme of inflicting physical, as well as social, disabilities on women. In earlier times, North American women often wore tight corsets, and today women wear high-heeled shoes. The result in these cases is actual physical impairment.

her father and his brothers, but her children cannot trace their descent through them. A woman's paternal aunt's children, for example, trace their descent through the patrilineal group of the woman's husband.

A patrilineal culture is very much a man's world; no matter how valued women may be, they inevitably find themselves in a difficult position. Far from resigning themselves to a subordinate position, however, they actively manipulate the system to their own advantage as best they can.

Matrilineal Descent and Organization

In one respect, matrilineal descent is the opposite of patrilineal: it is reckoned through the female line (see Figure 9.2). The matrilineal pattern differs from the patrilineal, however, in that descent does not automatically confer authority. Thus, although patrilineal societies are patriarchal, matrilineal cultures are not necessarily matriarchal. Although descent passes through the female line and women may have considerable power, women do not hold exclusive authority in the descent group: they share it with men. These are the brothers, rather than the husbands, of the women through whom descent is reckoned. The adaptive purpose of the matrilineal system is to provide continuous female solidarity within the female labour pool. Matrilineal systems are usually found in farming communities where women undertake much of the productive work.

In the matrilineal system, brothers and sisters belong to the descent group of the mother's mother, the mother, the mother's siblings, and the mother's sister's children. Males belong to the same descent group as their mother and sister, but their children cannot trace their descent through them. For example, the children of a man's maternal uncle are considered members of the uncle's

Original Study

The Domus: Households Through the Ages

Liam Kilmurray

Architecture embodies and expresses certain principles of order and classification. As a constructed cultural space it is a defined context where people undertake particular activities at particular times. Hence, meaning is realized through social practices. (Parker-Pearson and Richards 1994, 40)

The myriad rules of kinship and descent that this chapter addresses are reflected in residential patterns. Matrilineal cultures possess compounds, longhouses, or individual huts, which contain married daughters and their families. Patrilineal cultures have households reflecting male membership, and other cultures have households associated with avuncular or other descent systems. Regardless of the actual descent system in operation, all groups reside in a household of some form. When did the idea of the "household" emerge? What were the first houses like, and what can we learn from the evolution of the household?

The household, however its residents are designated, is more than mere bricks and mortar, or wattle and daub. The household occupies a crucial position in the evolution of human society and kinship patterns. It also reflects symbolic orders—an area that has spawned much research in recent years. Hodder (1990), for example, associates the idea of the *domus* (Latin for "house") with the "concept and practice of nurturing and caring. . . . It obtains its dramatic force from the exclusion, control and domination of the wild, the outside" (1990, 45). Whether through archaeological or ethnographic studies, the house, or household, reveals much about the culture that occupies it. The Dogon of Mali build their houses so that they resemble a human body, at least conceptually, with the chief's house at the head

of the village and the longhouses of the lineages arranged so that they represent the limbs of the community (Lane 1994; cf. Wilson 1988, 67). The Mbuti pygmies orient their houses so that they face relatives or friends, and they will orient a house so that it does not face those they are in dispute with. Thus the house as a conceptual construct represents many aspects of social structure.

The earliest forms of "residence" that we can identify are the base camps of earlier hominids such as *Homo habilis*, who lived some two-and-a-half million years ago. These early bases were little more than a raised platform or a cave entrance, safe from predators. These camps are associated with the emergence of monogamous pair bonding in human groups—a major step forward in the emergence of what would become the family. The archaeological detection of the base camp is associated with evidence for the earliest family unit, comprising mother, father, and children. For the next two million years—a time when humans were mobile hunter-gatherers or foragers—there was little in the way of architectural development of the "house."

A startling discovery was made in France in 1958 at a site called Terra Amata. A series of huts dated to some 380,000 years ago revealed one of the first housing "complexes." On the Mediterranean coast, close to what is now the city of Nice, a series of shallow dwellings ranging from 8 to 15 metres long and 4 to 6 metres wide were constructed. Toward the centre of each hut was a fireplace, with ashes indicating the use of fire. The houses consisted of small poles supported by rocks for walls, with larger poles in the centre to support a roof. These structures would have held some twenty to forty people. Evidence from Terra Amata suggests that as human groups became more complex, among the more important tasks undertaken was the construction of households built to a fairly standardized pattern. Little can be said regarding the kinship structures of those who

occupied Terra Amata, but we can certainly appreciate the choice of location, along the French Riviera. Here, ancient hominids constructed what were likely the world's first beachfront properties.

In what is now the Czech Republic, we catch a further glimpse of the development of human housing. About 27,000 years ago, at a site today called Dolni Vestonice, huts were constructed of mammoth bone and animal skins. The tusks and their imprints remain, allowing anthropologists to reconstruct the actual living quarters of these Upper Paleolithic peoples. These were semisubterranean houses, built into the ground to escape the harsh winter temperatures. They were substantial dwellings, with the largest hut measuring some 15 metres long by 6 metres wide. There were also five shallow hearths dug into the floor. Elsewhere on the site, a separate hut had a kiln—one of the first ever built. In total, the buildings housed around 100 people, making this a substantial settlement for the time. Of interest at Dolni Vestoniche is evidence of the human ability to utilize the local environment. Instead of wood, the houses were made from the broad, strong bones of mainly woolly mammoth. Covered in hides and interlaced branches, the house would have been the centre of the world for these people—places where early social relations would have been forged and kinship systems would have played an important role.

Some 20,000 years later, around 7000 BC, the development of the household took a huge leap forward with the construction of the first large-scale settlements in the world. True towns emerged in the Middle East, where agriculture had been adopted and complex settlements developed. Two examples are Jericho, where perhaps the world's oldest "real" houses are found, and Çatal Hüyük, where the deep symbolism of the house first becomes apparent. Çatal Hüyük, on the Konya Plain in Turkey, was excavated in 1958 by James Mellaart and would prove to be one of the most enigmatic settlements ever constructed.

Çatal Hüyük is a unique settlement, one that allows us a glimpse into the earliest towns and their households. It held some 6,000 people and would have been the largest such settlement in existence at the time. Of interest to many anthropologists is that the town was comprised of numerous small houses attached together. Each house appears to have had its own ritual shrine, which housed both images of wild animals and their actual remains. These animals were mostly auroch, the ancestor of cattle, and their presence has been interpreted as a representation of the external world tamed and brought into the *domus* (Hodder 1990; cf. Hodder 1998). The people of Çatal Hüyük had literally domesticated the wild, bringing the remains of animals into the interior of their houses. The houses had plastered walls, separate areas for cooking, and hearths for providing heat. Human remains have been found in pits beneath the floors—a practice found in many places, one that links the dead, the living, and the household in one continuous immortal system, akin to a kinship structure. It is noteworthy that at Çatal Hüyük, there were no obvious public buildings and no houses with distinctive features. This has been interpreted as signifying an absence of social classes and that each household was a self-sufficient unit, not just economically but also in terms of spiritual practices.

As agriculture spread westward, the longhouse became the most common form of household. A culture known as the Linear Band Keramic (LBK), named after their ceramic style, built longhouses over wide parts of northern, western, and central Europe. The rectangular outlines of these LBK longhouses, which were built between 5500 and 4800 BC, have been detected from post holes in the soil. They commonly measured some 7.5 to 45 metres long and 5 to 7 metres wide, and they were the largest buildings in the world at that time (Fagan 1996, 85). They consisted of massive timber posts, most often in five rows, two for the external walls and three inside for roof support. Along the external sides were dug trenches, from which daub came for the walls and into which rubbish often went, and

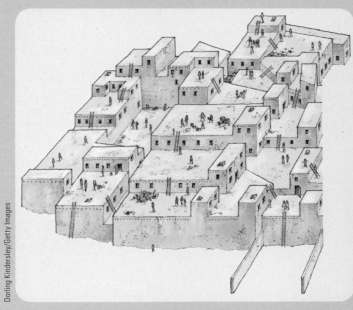

At the Neolithic settlement of Jericho, the houses were attached to one another, with entrance gained through the roof. This would have cut down on construction needs, kept rodents out, and perhaps aided in defence.

occasionally burials. These longhouses were multipurpose structures, and many in northwest Europe contained distinctive Y-shaped postmarks at the centre, or front, which may have supported a raised storage area (Hachem 2000). By this time, the longhouse had taken on deep symbolic meaning. In LBK houses, some of the dead were buried beneath the floorboards. Whittle thinks that the "link between graves and houses suggests that the longhouse served in part as a metaphor for the continuity of human life" (1996a, 181; cf. Whittle 1996b). These structures were more than just households; they helped maintain a sense of order, orienting people's daily lives, and no doubt played a large role in reflecting and determining kinship structures.

The LBK longhouse form is found in other places as well. In Canada, the Iroquoian peoples built them as residences, as did the Aboriginal fishing communities in what is now British Columbia. The villages of the LBK had a very similar "dispersal" and orientation to their longhouses, and usually a large majority were oriented in the same direction. Remarkably, the Huron and other Iroquoian peoples in Canada not only built very similar longhouses but also oriented their houses in a particular order. This was done to catch as much sunlight as possible. Also, the entrances were thereby faced away from the prevailing winds.

Like all Iroquoian peoples, the Huron lived in extended family longhouses. Each was a bark-covered structure supported by vertical wooden posts. Openings were located at each end, but there were no windows. They ranged in length from 10 to 75 metres (Trigger 1985). Most were 7.5 metres wide. A tall protective palisade constructed of large posts surrounded some longhouse villages.

Inside, the typical longhouse was lined by sleeping platforms on both sides of a central passageway. These platforms were some 1 to 1.5 metres off the ground and some 3 metres away from the central passage. The spaces under the platforms were used to store mainly wood, which was also sometimes stored in the vestibules at the end of the longhouse. The central passage contained the hearths, each 2 to 3 metres long, which were used for heat. Smaller fires were spaced around at random and used for cooking. A centrally placed opening in the roof allowed smoke to escape.

The Huron residence pattern appears to have been matrilocal. This is reflected in the household structure. The basic unit among the Huron people was the extended family. Because the Huron

CONTINUED

Dorling Kindersley/Getty Images

CONTINUED

were a matrilineal society, the extended family normally comprised a woman and her daughters or a group of sisters, with their husbands and children, all of whom normally lived in one longhouse (Trigger 1987, 46–47).

In terms of understanding the solid construction of the longhouses, and their continuing symbolic importance, note that they were not built for one person, or one family, but for generations. Neolithic houses represented a "continuation of the lineage, immortalised in wood and stone" (Hodder 1990). So too did the longhouses of the Iroquois and other groups such as the Hazda and the Fijians, whose dwellings continue to play an important role in social life. In many cases, the house form is linked to gender roles, and the physical divisions of the house are used to reinforce social categories. There are distinct areas of the house associated with women, often at the rear of the house, and entrances are often linked with men. Instead of merely reflecting kinship patterns through the ages, "the house, in all its structural ramifications, is equally likely to be a sociological precursor and foundation of social

systems founded on such abstractions as descent, lineage, and clan" (Wilson 1988, 75).

There is still much to learn about the household. Ethnographic research among peoples such as the Dogon and the Mbuti reveals the centrality of the household not just as a physical locale but as a conceptual space, one in which social and kinship networks are mapped and decided and where the cosmology of these groups is anchored. Both the physical nature of the house and the idea of the household have changed through time. The house, whatever material it is built of, houses not just people but ideas and concepts. It reflects and creates lasting kinship ties. The longhouse survives in many parts of the world, often alongside nuclear family houses that are powered by solar power. Whichever form the house takes, it is still an essential signifier of the household, and the family unit.

SOURCES: A. Whittle, Europe in the Neolithic *(Cambridge: Cambridge University Press, 1996a); Whittle, "Houses in Context: Buildings as Process," in* Neolithic Houses in Northwest Europe and Beyond, *ed. T. Darvill and J. Thomas (Oxford: Oxbow Books, 1996b), 13–26;*

B.M. Fagan, Eyewitness to Discovery *(New York: Oxford University Press, 1996); P. Wilson,* The Domestication of the Human Species *(New Haven: Yale University Press, 1998); I. Hodder, "The Domus: Some Problems Reconsidered," in* Understanding the Neolithic of North-Western Europe, *ed. M. Edmonds and C. Richards (Glasgow: Cruithne Press, 1998), 84–101; B. Trigger,* Natives and Newcomers: Canada's "Heroic Age" Reconsidered *(Montreal and Kingston: McGill–Queen's University Press, 1985); I. Hodder,* The Domestication of Europe *(Oxford: Blackwell, 1990); P.J. Lane, "The Temporal Structuring of Settlement," in* Parker-Pearson and Richards, Architecture and Order, *196–216; L. Hachem, "New Observations on the Bandkeramic House and Social Organization,"* Antiquity *74 (2000): 308–12; M. Parker-Pearson and C. Richards, "Architecture and Order: Spatial Representation and Archaeology," in* Architecture and Order: Approaches to Social Space, *ed. M. Parker-Pearson and C. Richards (London: Routledge, 1994), 38–72; Trigger,* The Children of Ataentsic: A History of the Huron People to 1660 *(Montreal and Kingston: McGill-Queen's University Press, 1987). See also the New York State Museum website, http://www.nysm. nysed.gov/IroquoisVillage/constructionone. html, which describes the structure, functions, and materials associated with an Iroquois longhouse.*

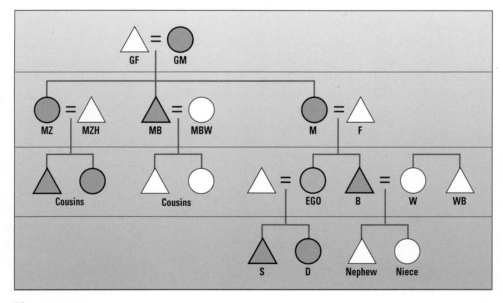

Figure 9.2

How matrilineal descent is traced. This diagram, which traces descent matrilineally, can be compared with that in Figure 9.1 (page 197), showing patrilineal descent. The two patterns are virtually mirror images. Note that a man cannot transmit descent to his own children.

Gender Perspectives

The Kinkeepers

In most extended families, one special person takes on the responsibility of maintaining formal and informal ties with other extended-family members, keeping the lines of communication open and offering support and comfort when needed. Typically, this kinkeeper is a female, often an older woman, who values the extended family and aims to promote solidarity among family members. She is in charge of telephoning Aunt Mary, or more likely today, e-mailing her to catch up on the news. She sends cards and gifts to all the nieces and nephews on their birthdays, and acknowledges special occasions, such as weddings, anniversaries, and graduations. She regularly visits family members, especially shut-ins and young couples with a new baby, and organizes holiday gatherings to bring the kin together under one roof. Kinkeepers are responsible for offering emotional support to kin in crisis—for example, by taking care of sick children—and almost always become the primary caregiver for elderly parents.

The kinkeeper reminds other family members to fulfill their familial responsibilities, such as sending birthday cards; failing that, she often takes over the responsibility rather than see a family member neglected. But kinkeepers also make decisions about whether to maintain close ties with certain kin. Thus, by the very nature of their work, kinkeepers possess a certain power within their family; without their ministrations, kin ties tend to break down.

Kinkeepers are found in every society and in every social class. In modern Western society, however, under the pressure of neoliberal economics to dismantle the social safety net, kinkeepers are being increasingly called up to provide many "community services" previously relegated to government agencies. As these government services continue to be cut back, kinkeepers are expected to pick up the slack by volunteering their unpaid labour. Women, then, are faced with competing types of work: housework, child care, labour market work, elder care, and kinship work.

SOURCES: M. diLeonardo, "The Female World of Cards and Holidays: Women, Families, and the Work of Kinship," in Gender in Cross-Cultural Perspective, *ed. C.B. Brettel and C.F. Sargent (Upper Saddle River: Prentice Hall, 1997); E.D. Nelson and B.W. Robinson,* Gender in Canada *(Toronto: Prentice-Hall Canada, 1999), 380; G.N. Ramu, "Kinship Networks," in* Courtship, Marriage, and the Family in Canada, *ed. G.N. Ramu (Toronto: Gage, 1980), 157.*

wife's matrilineal descent group. Similarly, a man's children belong to his wife's, but not his, descent group.

Although not true of all of them, a common feature of matrilineal systems is the weak link between husband and wife. The wife's brother, and not the husband/father, distributes goods, organizes work, settles disputes, administers inheritance and succession rules, and supervises rituals. The husband has legal authority not in his own household but in that of his sister. Furthermore, his property and status are inherited by his sister's son rather than by his son. Thus, brothers and sisters maintain lifelong ties with one another, whereas marital ties can easily be severed. In matrilineal groups, unsatisfactory marriages are more easily ended than in patrilineal groups, at least until children are born of the union.

Matrilineal clans formed the basis of Iroquoian kinship. Each clan owned a longhouse, in which the members of their clan lived.[7] Matrilocality was preferred; typically, a longhouse consisted of an elder woman, her husband, their daughters and families, and any unmarried sons. Senior women of matrilineages, known as "clan mothers," were held in great esteem. They were responsible for overseeing domestic tasks in the households and for allocating farmland to the women of the clan. If these senior women were opposed to the men heading off to war, they could withhold supplies; the men usually complied with their wives' and mothers' wishes. Clan mothers also played an important role in selecting or demoting chiefs and advisers. In one regard, the political power of clan mothers can be likened to that of a senate or president, in that they wielded a veto power over certain political decisions. The great respect shown to these clan mothers, their control over resources, and their obvious political power led early European observers to identify this culture as a matriarchy. This belief, however, proved inaccurate. Iroquois culture was egalitarian: neither men nor women dominated the culture.[8]

Double Descent

Double descent, also called double unilineal descent, whereby descent is reckoned both patrilineally and matrilineally at the same time, is very rare. In this system, descent is matrilineal for some purposes and patrilineal for others. Generally, where double descent is reckoned, the matrilineal and patrilineal groups take action in different spheres of society.

double descent A system tracing descent matrilineally for some purposes and patrilineally for others.

For example, among the Yakö of eastern Nigeria, property is divided into both patrilineal line possessions and matrilineal line possessions.[9] The patrilineage owns perpetual productive resources, such as land, whereas the matrilineage owns consumable property, such as livestock. In an effort to achieve balance, the legally weaker matrilineal line is somewhat more important in religious matters than the patrilineal line. Through double descent, a Yakö might inherit grazing lands from the father's patrilineal group and certain ritual privileges from the mother's matrilineal line.

Ambilineal Descent

Unilineal descent provides a convenient way of restricting descent group membership to avoid problems of divided loyalty and the like. A number of cultures, many of them in the Pacific and in Southeast Asia, accomplish the same task in other ways. The resultant descent groups are known as *ambilineal, nonunilineal,* or *cognatic.* **Ambilineal descent** provides a measure of flexibility not normally found under unilineal descent; each individual has the option of affiliating with either the mother's or the father's descent group.

In many of these cultures, an individual is allowed to belong to only one group at a time, regardless of how many groups he or she may be eligible to join. Thus, the group may be divided into the same sorts of discrete and separate groups of kin as in a patrilineal or matrilineal culture. Other cognatic societies, however, such as the Samoans of the South Pacific or the Bella Coola and the southern branch of the Kwakwaka'wakw of the Pacific coast of North America, allow overlapping membership in a number of descent groups.

FORMS AND FUNCTIONS OF DESCENT GROUPS

Descent groups with restricted membership are usually more than mere groups of relatives providing warmth and a sense of belonging. In societies that lack civil institutions, or where the liberal-democratic model is followed, descent groups take on a more corporate function. In what are mainly nonindustrialised societies, they are tightly organized working units providing security and services in what can be a difficult,

uncertain life. Besides acting as economic units providing mutual aid to their members, they may support the aged and infirm and help with marriages and deaths. Often, they play a role in determining who an individual may or may not marry. The descent group also may act as a repository of religious traditions, such as ancestor worship.

The Lineage

A **lineage** is a corporate descent group composed of consanguineal kin who trace descent through known links back to a common ancestor. The term is usually employed where a form of unilineal descent is the rule, but some ambilineal groups are similar. The word "corporate" here means acting as a single "body."

The lineage is ancestor-oriented; membership in the group is recognized only if relationship to a common ancestor can be traced and proved. An individual may have no legal or political status except as a lineage member. Since "citizenship" is derived from lineage membership and legal status depends on it, political and religious power is derived from it as well. Important religious and magical powers, such as those associated with the cults of gods and ancestors, also may be bound to the lineage.

Because the corporate lineage endures after the deaths of members with new members continually born into it, it has a perpetual existence that enables it to take corporate actions, such as owning property, organizing productive activities, distributing goods and labour power, assigning status, and regulating relations with other groups. The lineage is a strong, effective base of social organization. But here the resemblance ends to the Western meaning of "corporate"; the latter refers to a *corporation,* where membership is based on business principles and whose goal is profitability.

A common feature of lineages is their exogamy. That is, lineage members must find their marriage partners in other lineages. One advantage of lineage exogamy is that potential sexual competition within the group is curbed, promoting the group's solidarity. Lineage exogamy also means that each marriage is more than an arrangement between two individuals; it amounts as well to a new alliance between lineages. Finally, lineage exogamy supports open communication within a culture by promoting the diffusion of knowledge from one lineage to another.

The Clan

A Huron trader from the village of Ihonatiria, exhausted and hungry, stumbled into the distant village of Contarea. Although tensions had existed between the two

ambilineal descent Descent in which the individual may affiliate with either the mother's or the father's descent group.

lineage A corporate descent group whose members trace their genealogical links to a common ancestor.

Anthropologist Peggy Reeves Sanday with members of a matrilineal clan among the Minangkabau of Sumatra gathered for a house-raising ceremony. The one adult male is the brother of the senior female leader (the woman on Sanday's left); he is the clan's male leader. Absence of other men reflects the predominance of women in this society.

Peggy Sanday A.F.E.

villages for some time, the lone Huron trader was immediately welcomed into the longhouse of the Turtle clan. He was fed, clothed, and entertained, at no cost to himself. He was given this welcome because the Huron Confederacy was based on clan lines, which cut across local village and kinship loyalties and which involved various clans from different villages in a symbiotic relationship. Whether it was the Huron or the Scottish Highland clans, the clan provided an external support system that criss-crossed different villages and that went above and beyond immediate local family obligations.

As generation succeeds generation and new members are born into a lineage, its membership may become unmanageably large or too much for the lineage's resources to support. When this happens, **fission** occurs; that is, the lineage splits into new, smaller lineages. When fission occurs, usually the members of the new lineages continue to recognize their ultimate relationship to one another. The result of this process is the appearance of a second kind of descent group, the *clan*. The term **clan** and its close relative, the *sib*, have been used differently by various anthropologists, and a certain amount of confusion exists about their meaning. The clan (or sib) is defined as a noncorporate descent group whose members assume descent from a common ancestor (who may be real or fictive) but who are often unable to trace the actual genealogical links back to that ancestor. This stems from the great genealogical depth of the clan, whose founding ancestor lived so far in the past that the links must be assumed rather than known in detail. A clan differs from a lineage in another respect: it lacks the residential unity generally—although not

invariably—characteristic of a lineage's core members. As with the lineage, descent may be patrilineal, matrilineal, or ambilineal.

Because clan membership is dispersed rather than localized, it usually does not hold tangible property corporately. Instead, it tends to be more a unit for ceremonial matters and for external aid in times of great need. Only on special occasions will the members gather for specific purposes. Like lineages, clans may regulate marriage through exogamy. Because their membership is dispersed, they give individuals entry rights into local groups other than their own.

Clans often depend on symbols—of animals, plants, natural forces, and objects—to provide members with solidarity and a ready means of identification. These symbols, called *totems*, are often associated with the clan's mythical, or real, origin and reinforce an awareness of their common descent with what the totems represent. **Totemism** was defined by British anthropologist A.R. Radcliffe-Brown as a set of "customs and beliefs by which there is set up a special system of relations between the society and the plants, animals, and other natural objects

fission The splitting of a descent group into two or more new descent groups.

clan A noncorporate descent group whose members claim descent from a common ancestor without actually knowing the genealogical links to that ancestor.

totemism The belief that people are related to particular animals, plants, or natural objects by virtue of descent from common ancestral spirits.

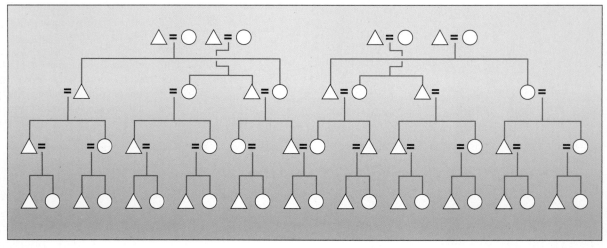

Figure 9.3

The kinship pattern of the kindred. These people are related not to a common ancestor but, rather, to a living relative, here the sister and brother shown at the centre of the bottom row.

that are important in the social life."[10] Among the Haida on Canada's west coast, important families were divided into totemic groups with such names as Bear, Killer Whale, Cannibal Spirit, Salmon, and Beaver.[11]

Moieties

One other kind of descent group is the moiety. When the entire culture is divided into only two major descent groups, whether they are equivalent to clans or involve an even more all-inclusive level, each group is called a **moiety** (after the French word for "half"). Moiety members also believe they share a common ancestor but cannot prove it through definite genealogical links. As a rule, the feelings of kinship among members of lineages and clans are stronger than those among members of moieties. This may be due to the larger size and more diffuse nature of the latter groups. Moiety exogamy is the general rule in these societies.

Like clans and lineages, moieties are often exogamous and thus are bound together by marriages between their members. And like clans, they provide members rights of access to other communities. Even if a community does

not include any clan members, an individual's moiety members will still be there to turn to for hospitality. Finally, moieties may perform reciprocal services for each other, as among the Mohawks and other Iroquoian nations of southern Ontario and New York State. Among them, individuals turned to members of the opposite moiety for the necessary rituals when a member of their own moiety died. Such interdependence between moieties, again, served to maintain the integrity of the entire society.

Bilateral Descent and the Kindred

Important though descent groups are in many cultures, they are not found in all cultures, nor are they the only kinds of nonfamilial kinship groups found. *Bilateral descent*, a characteristic of Western society as well as a number of foraging groups, affiliates a person with close relatives through both sexes; in other words, the individual traces descent through both parents, all four grandparents, and so forth, recognizing multiple ancestors. Theoretically, a person is associated equally with all consanguineal relatives on both the mother's side of the family and the father's. Thus, this principle relates an individual lineally to all eight great-grandparents and laterally to all third and fourth cousins. Since such a group is too large to be socially practical, it is usually reduced to a smaller circle of paternal and maternal relatives, called the kindred. The **kindred** may be defined as a group of people closely related to one living individual through both parents (see Figure 9.3).

moiety Each group that results from a division of a society into two halves on the basis of descent.

kindred A group of consanguineal kin linked by their relationship to one living individual; includes both maternal and paternal kin.

North Americans are familiar with the kindred; those who belong are simply called relatives. It includes the relatives on both sides of the family who are seen on important occasions, such as family reunions and funerals. Excepting Aboriginals, who often trace their kindred back a very long time, most people in Canada can identify the members of their kindred up to grandparents and first, if not always second, cousins. The limits of the kindred, however, are variable and indefinite; no one can be absolutely certain which relatives to invite to important functions and which to exclude. Inevitably, situations arise that require some debate about whether to invite particular, usually distant, relatives. Kindreds are thus not clearly bounded and lack the discreteness of unilineal or ambilineal descent groups.

Because of its bilateral structure, a kindred is never the same for any two persons except siblings (brothers and sisters). Thus, no two people (except siblings) belong to the same kindred. As for the kindreds of ego's parents, these range from grandparents lineally to cousins too distant laterally for ego to know, and the same is true of ego's aunts and uncles. Thus, the kindred is composed not of people with an ancestor in common but rather of people with a living relative—ego—in common. Furthermore, as ego goes through life, the kindreds he or she is affiliated with will change. When young, individuals belong to the kindreds of their parents; ultimately, they belong to the kindreds of their sons and daughters as well as their nieces and nephews.

The ego-centred kindred, with its vague boundaries, temporary nature, and changing composition, is the form of kinship that most Canadians experience in their daily lives. Unlike descent groups, kindred are not self-perpetuating—they ceases with ego's death. A kindred has no constant leader, nor can it easily hold, administer, or pass on property. With the expansion of the capitalist market economy, it is the form of kinship that much of the world's cultures are coming to experience. But this is not to imply that the kindred is without important functions. It is the unit that supplies support—both emotional and financial—in times of need. It also acts as a ceremonial group for rites of passage: around birth, initiation ceremonies, marriages, funerals, and the like.

Kindreds are often found in industrial societies such as Canada, where mobility weakens contact with relatives. Individuality is emphasized in such societies, and strong kinship organization is usually not as important as it is among non-Western peoples. Bilateral kindred groups also may be found in societies where kinship ties are important; sometimes they even occur alongside descent groups.

The Descent Group

Just as various types of families occur in different societies, so do various kinds of nonfamilial kin groups. Descent groups, for example, are *not* a common feature of foraging societies, where marriage acts as the social mechanism for integrating individuals within communities. The absence of descent groups is a feature that foragers share with urbanized, industrial societies around the world. It is in horticultural, pastoral, and many intensive agricultural cultures, sometimes known as the "middle-range societies," that the descent group usually provides the structural framework upon which the fabric of the social organization rests.

Lineages arise from extended-family organization, as long as organizational problems exist that such groups help solve. All that is required, really, is that as members of existing extended families find it necessary to split off and establish new households elsewhere, they not move too far away; that the core members of such related families (men in patrilocal, women in matrilocal, and members of both sexes in ambilocal extended families) explicitly acknowledge their descent from a common ancestor; and that they continue to participate in common activities in an organized way.

Another way clans may arise is through legal fictions to integrate otherwise autonomous units. For example, the five Iroquoian nations of what now is New York State—the Mohawk, Oneida, Onandaga, Cayuga, and Seneca—developed clans simply by behaving as if lineages of the same name in different villages were related. Thus, their members became fictitious brothers and sisters. By this device, members of, say, a "Turtle" lineage in a Seneca village could travel to a Mohawk village and be welcomed in and hosted by members of another "Turtle" lineage. In this way, the Five Nations, also known as the League of the Iroquois, achieved a wider unity than had previously existed. The larger Iroquoian community, now known as the Six Nations (near Brantford, Ontario), was formed when the Tuscarora Indians joined the League in the 18th century.

Under conditions of rapid social and economic change, and through the penetration of the market economy, extended families and lineages may undergo change. For example, new economic opportunities in towns and the availability of alternative occupations for individuals may conflict with the residential unity of extended families and (usually) lineages. Or lineages may lose their economic bases if developing bureaucratic institutions like the Canadian Aboriginal Affairs and Northern Development take control of resources. In such circumstances, lineages would be expected to disappear as important organizational units. Clans, however,

Genetic Anthropology and the Descent of the Cheddar Man

Liam Kilmurray

It has often been said that the family of the Chinese philosopher Confucius, known as the Kongs, has the longest recorded living pedigree in the world. The Kong family tree is now in its 83rd generation since the death of Confucius and claims 2 million or more known descendants. The Japanese emperor's line of descent goes back to at least 660 BC. The British Royal family, the House of Windsor, can claim descent back to Alfred the Great in the early ninth century. In recent years, the ability to extract and map DNA has led to the growth of genealogical studies in anthropology. Using these new techniques, the longest lineage in human history, a "descent" line of some 9,000 years, was uncovered in 1997. A British schoolteacher and two children were linked to the 9,000-year-old Cheddar Man. The discovery of Britain's oldest traceable relative is a fascinating tale not just of heritage and descent, but also of archaeological detection using DNA.

Genetic anthropology has made great progress over the past few decades, often leaving those who are not geneticists at a loss regarding their findings. The scientific means available to anthropologists studying DNA are remarkable (Pálsson 2007). New pronouncements are made almost every month. Some years ago, the separation of chimpanzees and humans was found to be much more recent than had long been thought, dating not from 15 million but from only 6 million years ago. Recently, the Neanderthals were determined to have been too genetically

© Kevin Wheal/Alamy

distant to have interbred with humans. These data, however, are questioned by some anthropologists, and the case cannot be considered closed. Perhaps most controversially, genetic data have been used to argue that all modern humans are descended from a group of hominids living in southern Africa some 150,000 to 200,000 years ago. This is known as the Eve hypothesis, or the Out of Africa hypothesis, and is at odds with the existing understanding that modern humans derived from earlier *Homo erectus* populations (for a discussion of the implications of the Eve hypothesis, see Stringer and McKie 1996). The extraction and analysis of DNA is an exhilarating field, one that is literally mapping the movements of peoples since prehistoric times. In British prehistoric studies there has long been a debate over whether the current population stems from original hunter-gatherers of the Palaeolithic period, or from more recent Neolithic agriculturalists who would have arrived some 6,000 or 7,000 years ago. The case of Cheddar Man has had a large impact on this debate.

Originally excavated in 1903 at Gough's Cave in Cheddar Gorge, Somerset, England, the remains of Cheddar Man stayed under wraps until 1997. Britain's oldest complete human skeleton was then analyzed using mitochondrial DNA (mtDNA), which traces DNA links through the maternal line (Richards and

Macaulay 2001). He appears to have died violently at approximately 23 years of age; the cause was probably a hole in his skull. Whether this hole resulted from a ritual practice or a violent act is unknown. Using data gathered from Cheddar Man's DNA, Dr. Brian Sykes, a professor of human genetics at Oxford University, attempted to locate living descendants from the local Cheddar region who might have DNA connections with Cheddar Man.

Dr. Sykes had also worked on that other remarkable descendant from prehistory, 5,000-year-old Otzi the Ice Man, found in the Tyrolean Alps in 1991 (Sykes 2006; cf. Spindler 1994). In the case of Cheddar Man, Sykes tested DNA from his 9,000-year-old tooth and from a 12,000-year-old tooth taken from another specimen found at the same cave. After months of research, he then examined the cells of 15 pupils from the Kings of Wessex School, as well as five adults from local Cheddar families. The tests revealed two exact matches and one match with a single mutation. The two exact matches were schoolchildren, whose names were not released. The revelation of the close match appeared on television, and as the camera focused on the schoolchildren it was announced that the close match was actually their history teacher, Adrian Targett. He was found to be carrying what is called the genetic haplo group U5, which indicated that he shared a common ancestor with Cheddar Man through his maternal line.

For British prehistorians, this was a remarkable success story. Not only had they bridged some 90 centuries and 300 generations, but they had also made a very strong case that the British people, in this region at least, had not strayed very far from home and were in fact descendants of the pre-agricultural peoples of the island, not of incoming agriculturalists. The exact genetic makeup of Britain's peoples, like that of most of the world's, is in fact a mélange of many different groups. However, recent research has demonstrated the continuance of some ancient "genetic" groups.

Anthropology and genetic research is a growing domain, one that is not limited to archaeology. Linguistic anthropologists utilize the findings of DNA studies in order to better map the movements and changes of the world's languages. For example, a correlation has been made between people of the west of Ireland with Gaelic names and a limited genetic variance. In a groundbreaking study, researchers at Trinity College Dublin analyzed the DNA of Irish men with Gaelic surnames (*Inside Ireland* 2000). They discovered that an ancient gene, carried by most men in western Europe over 10,000 years ago, was present in large numbers of Irish men. In the province of Connaught, on the extreme west of Europe, almost all men (98.3 percent) carry this particular gene. Such studies contribute to the anthropological understanding of the movement of people in prehistory, and of descent and marriage systems.

Elsewhere, medical anthropologists are deeply involved in genetic research as they attempt to unravel past metabolic diseases or the contemporary genetic basis of human physiological issues. Genetic anthropology is a fast-growing field with tremendous implications for both prehistoric and contemporary anthropology studies. As for the modern descendant of the Cheddar Man, "I am overwhelmed, a bit surprised," said Mr. Targett, the 42-year-old history teacher. "I've been in the cave a few times, but I never realized it was home. . . . We all have 9,000-year-old ancestors," he said, "I just happen to know who mine was."

SOURCES: B. Sykes, Blood of the Isles: Exploring the Genetic Roots of Our Tribal History *(New York: Bantam Books, 2006);* K. Spindler, The Man in the Ice *(Guernsey: Guernsey Press, 1994);* Inside Ireland *88 (2000).* C. Stringer and R. McKie, African Exodus: The Origins of Modern Humanity *(New York: Henry Holt, 1996);* M. Richards and V. Macaulay, "The Mitochondrial Gene Tree Comes of Age," American Journal of Human Genetics *68 (2001): 1315–20;* G. Pálsson, Anthropology and the New Genetics *(Cambridge: Cambridge University Press, 2007)*

NAC-092418/National Archives of Canada

Iroquoian clans were a legal fiction that allowed people to travel back and forth between villages of the "Five Nations" in what is now New York State. This portrait, done in 1710, shows a member of the Mohawk Nation. Behind him stands a bear, which represents his clan.

might survive, if they continue to provide an important integrative function. This helps explain a clan's continued strength and vitality among First Nations North Americans today: They perform an integrative function among kin who are geographically dispersed as well as socially diverse but in a way that does not conflict with the mobility that is characteristic of North American society. The same socially adaptive functions of clan organization may account for why clans remain significant in Chinese Canadian and other immigrant communities.

In cultures where the small domestic units—nuclear families or single-parent households—are of primary importance, bilateral descent and kindred organization are almost inevitable. This can be seen in modern industrial societies, in newly emerging societies in the developing world, and in many foraging cultures throughout the world.

KINSHIP TERMINOLOGY AND KINSHIP GROUPS

Any system of organizing people who are relatives into different kinds of groups, whether descent-based or ego-oriented, is bound to have an important effect on the ways relatives are labelled. Because of the importance of kinship in organizing the lives of people in nonindustrial societies, the study of kinship terminology was once at the very centre of anthropological study. As the central importance of kinship in social life has declined, so has anthropology's interest in its study. Nevertheless, the ways in which people classify their relatives offer many

Dynamic Anthropology

Resolving a Native American Tribal Membership Dispute

Harald E.L. Prins

In autumn 1998, I received a call from the tribal chief of the Aroostook band of Micmacs in northern Maine asking for help in resolving a bitter tribal membership dispute. The conflict centred on the fact that several hundred individuals had become tribal members without proper certification of their Micmac kinship status. Traditionalists in the community argued that their tribe's organization was being taken over by "non-Indians." With the formal status of so many members in question, the tribal administration could not properly determine who was entitled to benefit from the available health, housing, and education programs. After some hostile confrontations between the factions, tribal elders requested a formal inquiry into the membership controversy, and I was called in as a neutral party with a long history of working with the band.

My involvement as an advocacy anthropologist began in 1981, when these Micmacs (also spelled Mi'kmaq) first employed me, along with Bunny McBride, to help them achieve U.S. government recognition of their Indian status. At the time, the Micmacs formed a poor and landless community not yet officially recognized as a tribe. During that decade, we helped the band define its political strategies, which included petitioning for federal recognition of their Indian status; claiming their traditional rights to hunt, trap, and fish; and even demanding return of lost ancestral lands.

To generate popular support for the effort, I co-produced a film about the community (*Our Lives in Our Hands*, 1986). Most important, we gathered oral histories and detailed archival documentation to address kinship issues and other government criteria for tribal recognition. The latter included important genealogical records showing that most Micmac adults in the region were at least "half-blood" (having two of their grandparents officially recorded as Indians).

Based on this evidence, we effectively argued that Aroostook Micmacs could claim Aboriginal title to lands in the region. Also, we were able to convince politicians in Washington, DC, to introduce a special bill to acknowledge their tribal status and settle their land claims. When formal hearings were held in 1990, I testified to the U.S. Senate as an expert witness for the Micmacs. The following year, the *Aroostook Band of Micmacs Settlement Act* became federal law. This made the band eligible for the financial assistance (health, housing, education, and child welfare) and economic development loans that are available to all federally recognized tribes in the United States. Moreover, the law provided the band with funding to buy a 5,000-acre territorial base in Maine.

Flush with federal funding and rapidly expanding its activities, the 500-member band became overwhelmed by complex bureaucratic regulations now governing their existence. Without formally established ground rules determining who could apply for tribal membership, and overlooking federally imposed regulations, hundreds of new names were rather casually added to its tribal rolls.

By 1997, the Aroostook band population had ballooned to almost 1,200 members, and Micmac traditionalists were questioning the legitimacy of many whose names had been added to the band roster. With mounting tension threatening to destroy the band, the tribal chief invited me to evaluate critically the membership claims of more than half the tribe. In early 1999, I reviewed the kinship records submitted by hundreds of individuals whose membership on the tribal rolls was in question. Several months later, I offered my final report to the Micmac community.

After traditional prayers, sweetgrass burning, drumming, and a traditional meal of salmon and moose, I formally presented my findings. Based on the official criteria, about 100 lineal descendants of the original members and just over 150 newcomers met the minimum required qualifications for membership; several hundred others would have to be removed from the tribal roster. After singing, drumming, and closing prayers, the Micmac gathering dispersed.

Today, the band numbers about 850 members and is doing well. It has purchased several tracts of land (collectively over 600 acres), including a small residential reservation near Presque Isle, now home to about 200 Micmacs. Also located here are new tribal administration offices, a health clinic, and a cultural centre.

important clues to the inner workings of their lives. The fact is that the terminology system in common use in Canada—known as the Eskimo system—is just one of six different systems for classifying kin.

In classifying a relative, there are a limited number of distinctions that can be made. Common distinctions include whether the relative is male or female, which generation he or she belongs to, and whether that person is from the father's or the mother's side of the family. In the various systems of kinship terminology, any one of these factors may be emphasized at the expense of others. But regardless of the factors emphasized, all kinship terminologies accomplish two important tasks. First, they classify similar kinds of persons into specific categories; second, they separate different kinds of persons into distinct categories. Generally, two or more kin are merged under the same term when the individuals share similar status, which then emphasizes these similarities.

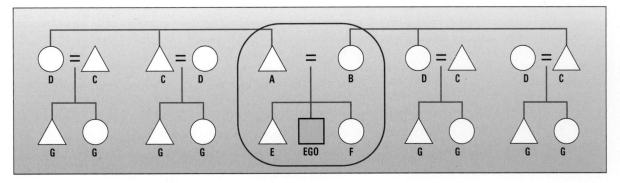

Figure 9.4

The Eskimo system of kinship terminology emphasizes the nuclear family (surrounded by the red line). Symbols with the same letters are referred to in the same way by ego.

The six different systems of kinship are the Eskimo, Hawaiian, Iroquois, Crow, Omaha, and Sudanese or descriptive systems, each identified according to the way cousins are classified. The names of these systems are not limited to the cultural group they are named after. For instance, the Eskimo system is also practised among Europeans. The names simply derive from the vagaries of anthropological terminological classification.

Eskimo System

The **Eskimo system** of kinship terminology, comparatively rare among all the world's systems, is the one used by Euro-Canadians and Anglo-Americans, as well as by a number of North American foraging peoples, including the Inuit, and other hunter-gatherer people, such as the Ju/'hoansi. The Eskimo or lineal system emphasizes the nuclear family by specifically identifying the mother, father, brother, and sister, while lumping together all other relatives into a few general categories (see Figure 9.4). For example, the father is distinguished from the father's brother (*uncle*), but the father's brother is not distinguished from the mother's brother (both are called *uncle*). The mother's sister and father's sister are treated similarly, both called *aunt*. In addition, all the sons and daughters of aunts and uncles are called *cousin*, thereby making a generational distinction but without indicating the side of the family they belong to or even their sex.

Unlike other terminologies, the Eskimo system provides separate and distinct terms for each nuclear family member. This is probably because the Eskimo system generally is found in societies where the dominant kin group is the bilateral kindred, in which only immediate family members are important in day-to-day affairs. This is especially true of modern North American society, where the family is independent, living apart from, and not directly involved with, other kin except on ceremonial occasions. Thus, people in Canada distinguish

between their closest kin (parents, siblings, and children) but lump together (as aunts, uncles, cousins, nieces and nephews) other kin on both sides of the family.

Hawaiian System

Canadians visiting Hawaii often comment on the frequency with which Hawaiians use the terms "aunt" and "cousin," calling very many people by the same term. The result is not just one of formality, but seems to have an endearing quality, making Hawaiian social interactions appear warm and genuinely affectionate. The **Hawaiian system** of kinship terminology, common (as its name implies) in Hawaii and other Malayo–Polynesian-speaking areas but also found among the Coast Salish First Nations of southwestern British Columbia and among other cultures as well, is the least complex system, in that it uses the fewest terms. In the Hawaiian system all relatives from the mother's and father's sides of the family, and of the same generation and sex, are referred to by the same term (see Figure 9.5). For example, mother, mother's sister, and father's sister are referred to by the same kinship term. In ego's generation, male and female kin (different sex) are distinguished by terminology, but terms for brothers and sisters are the same as for cousins.

The Hawaiian system reflects the absence of strong unilineal descent and is usually associated with ambilineal

Eskimo system A system of kinship terminology, also called the lineal system, that emphasizes the nuclear family by specifically distinguishing mother, father, brother, and sister, while lumping together all other relatives into broad categories such as uncle, aunt, and cousin.

Hawaiian system Kinship reckoning in which all relatives of the same sex and generation are referred to by the same term.

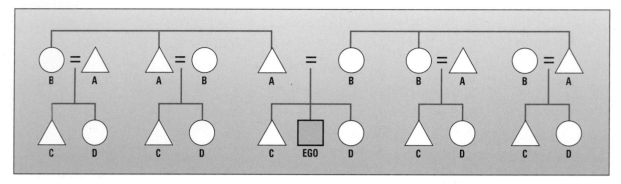

Figure 9.5
The Hawaiian kinship system.

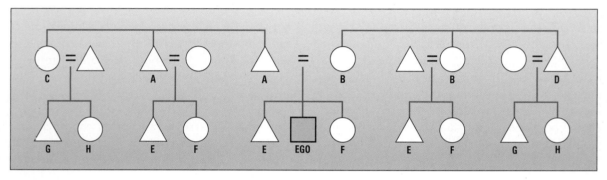

Figure 9.6
The Iroquois system of kinship terminology.

descent. Because ambilineal rules allow individuals the option of tracing their ancestry back through either side of the family, and members on both the father's and the mother's side are viewed as more or less equal, a certain degree of similarity is created among the father's and the mother's siblings. Thus, they are all simultaneously recognized as being similar relations and are merged under a single term appropriate for their sex. In like manner, the children of the mother's and father's siblings are related to ego in the same way brothers and sisters are, ruling them out as potential marriage partners.

Iroquois System

In the early 16th century, members of Jacques Cartier's expedition up the St. Lawrence River would have been confused by the translations of Iroquois kinship

Iroquois system   Kinship terminology wherein a father and father's brother are given a single term, as are a mother and mother's sister, but a father's sister and mother's brother are given separate terms. Parallel cousins are classified with brothers and sisters, while cross–cousins are classified separately but (unlike in Crow and Omaha kinship) are not equated with relatives of some other generation.

terminology. They would have heard Iroquoians use the words "uncle" and "cousin" for a wide variety of relatives. In the **Iroquois system** of kinship terminology (and the Crow and Omaha to follow), there exists an important distinction between *parallel* and *cross* cousins. The offspring of two sisters or of two brothers are related to one another as parallel cousins, while the offspring of brother and sister are cross cousins. In the Iroquois system, the father and father's brother are referred to by a single term, as are the mother and mother's sister; however, the father's sister and mother's brother are given separate terms (see Figure 9.6). In an individual's own generation, brothers and male parallel cousins are referred to by the same term, as are one's sisters and female parallel cousins. Cross cousins (offspring of parental siblings of opposite sex; that is, mother's brother's children or father's sister's children) are distinguished by terms that set them apart from all other kin. In fact, in hundreds of nonindustrial societies, cross cousins are often preferred as spouses, for marriage to them reaffirms alliances between related lineages.

Iroquois terminology, named for the Iroquois of northeastern North America, is widespread in matrilineal or double descent and emphasizes unilineal descent

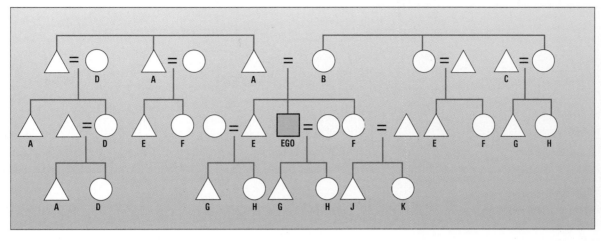

Figure 9.7
The Crow system is the obverse of the Omaha system, shown in Figure 9.8.

In matrilineal societies with Crow kinship, sisters remain close to one another throughout their lives. Such a people are the Hopi, in whose traditional housing sisters lived in adjacent rooms. Under these circumstances, very little differentiates a mother and her sister, or siblings and the children of the mother's sister. The mother's brother and his children, however, live elsewhere.

groups. It was, for example, the terminology in use until recently in rural Chinese society.

Crow System

The Crow Indians of Omaha and the Hopi of Arizona focus their kinship terminology on the mother's side. Many social practices are oriented on the maternal line, which explains the importance of the female members of one's lineage. In the preceding systems of terminology, some relatives were grouped under common terms, while others of the same generation were separated and given different labels or terms. In the Crow system, another variable enters the picture: The system ignores the distinction between generations among certain kin.

The **Crow system** (named for the Crow of Montana) is found in many parts of the world. This complex system is associated with strong matrilineal descent organization, and it groups differently the relations on the father's side and the mother's side (see Figure 9.7). Cross cousins

Crow system Kinship classification usually associated with matrilineal descent in which a father's sister and father's sister's daughter are called by the same term, a mother and mother's sister are merged under another, and a father and father's brother are given a third. Parallel cousins are equated with brothers and sisters.

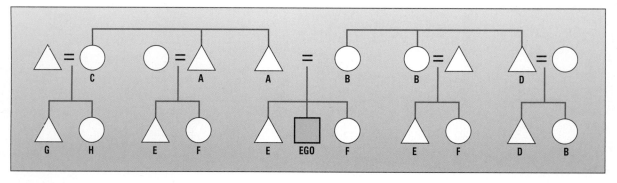

Figure 9.8
The Omaha kinship system.

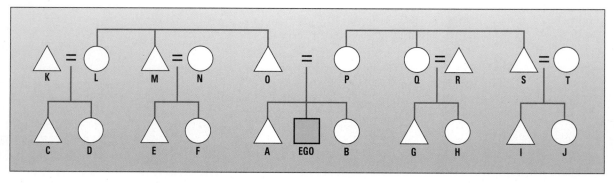

Figure 9.9
The Sudanese kinship system.

on the father's side are equated with relatives of the parental generation, while those on the mother's side are equated with ego's children's generation. Otherwise, the system is much like Iroquois terminology.

Omaha System

The **Omaha system** (named for the Omaha of Nebraska) is the patrilineal equivalent of the matrilineal Crow system. Thus, a mother and her sister are designated by a single term, the father and his brother are merged under another, and parallel cousins are merged with brothers and sisters (see Figure 9.8). Cross–cousins are referred to by separate terms. A man will refer to his brother's children using the

Omaha system The patrilineal equivalent of the Crow system; the mother's patrilineal kin are equated across generations.

Sudanese or descriptive system The system of kinship terminology whereby a father, father's brother, and mother's brother are distinguished from one another, as are a mother, mother's sister, and father's sister; cross and parallel cousins are distinguished from one another as well as from siblings.

same terms as his own children, but he will refer to his sister's children using different terms. Generational merging on the mother's side is a feature of this system. For example, ego's mother's patrilineage is called "mother's brother"; age and generation do not matter. Interestingly, generational merging does not happen on the father's side, even though fathers and brothers are called by the same terms.

Sudanese or Descriptive System

The **Sudanese or descriptive system** is found among the peoples of southern Sudan in Africa. Otherwise, it is found among few of the world's societies, although it has come to replace Iroquois terminology among rural Chinese. In this system, each and every relative in the kindred is potentially called by a separate kin term. The mother's brother is distinguished from the father's brother, who is distinguished from the father; the mother's sister is distinguished from the mother as well as from the father's sister (see Figure 9.9). Each cousin is distinguished from all others as well as from siblings. It is therefore more precise than any of the other systems (including that used by Anglo-Canadians), which may be one reason why it is so rare. In few societies are all aunts, uncles, cousins, and siblings treated differently from one another.

Chapter Summary

1. What are descent groups?

A common form of kinship is the descent group, in which membership is traced from a common ancestor through a series of parent–child links. Unilineal descent establishes kin group membership exclusively through the male or female line. Matrilineal descent is traced through the female line; patrilineal, through the male. The descent system is closely tied to a society's economic base. Patrilineal descent is commonly found where men are the main breadwinners, matrilineal descent where females form the core of social life, but not necessarily are they the main breadwinners. The male members of a patrilineage trace their descent from a common male ancestor. In the matrilineal pattern, descent is traced through the female line. Unlike the patrilineal pattern, which confers authority on men, matrilineal descent does not necessarily confer authority on women, although women usually have more of a say in decision making than they do in patrilineal cultures. The matrilineal system is common in cultures where women perform much of the productive work.

2. What functions do descent groups serve?

Descent groups are often highly structured economic units that provide aid and security to their members. They also may be repositories of religious tradition, with group solidarity enhanced by worship of a common ancestor. In whatever descent system is in operation, marriages between members of different groups represent alliances between the two groups. Descent systems outlive their members, providing ontological security for the clan or lineage.

3. How do descent groups form?

Descent groups develop from extended family groups, usually in response to organizational needs. They emerge usually in food-producing groups, beginning as smaller lineages and often developing into larger groups such as clans. In any culture, rules dictate how kinship relationships are defined. Factors such as sex and generational or genealogical differences help distinguish one kin from another. The Hawaiian system is the simplest system of kinship terminology. All relatives of the same generation and sex are referred to by the same term. The Eskimo system, used by Euro-Canadians and Anglo-Americans, stresses the nuclear family and merges all other relatives in a given generation into a few large, generally undifferentiated categories. In the Iroquois system, a single term is used for a father and his brother and another term for a mother and her sister. Parallel cousins are equated with brothers and sisters but distinguished from cross cousins. The same is true in the Omaha and Crow systems, except they equate cross cousins with relatives of other generations. The relatively rare Sudanese or descriptive system assigns a different kin term for each aunt, uncle, cousin, and sibling.

4. How do anthropologists study descent?

Anthropologists use different methods to calculate peoples' relationship structures and to understand the role a descent system plays in society. By conducting archaeological excavations, ethnographic research, and cross-cultural analyses, anthropologists have compiled an extensive list of the world's different descent systems. These systems are given different classifications and are depicted in descent charts and tables. Recent research has used the extraction of DNA to trace the descent of ancient individuals and groups.

Questions for Critical Thought

1. How do you identify your relatives? Are you closer to some cousins than to others? Do you have fictive kin who are like family? Do you feel closer to your mother's or your father's side of the family, or both equally? How important to you are your extended kin? How many generations of your kin can you trace?

2. When in your life has the ability to trace your descent been the most important or obvious? When are you made aware of your kin group? In your family are names at birth assigned in reference to ancestors or other kin?

3. How are changes in North American families altering how North Americans view descent? How do these changes contrast with those occurring in other cultures?

4. Do you think that urbanization has affected your kinship networks? If so, in what ways?

5. Identify your kinkeeper. What roles does he or she perform? What would happen to the cohesion of your extended family if you lost this kinkeeper?

6. As an exercise, draw your own kinship chart, using yourself as "ego" at the centre of the chart. How many relatives can you identify?

Internet Resources

The Nature of Kinship

http://www.as.ua.edu/ant/Faculty/murphy/436/kinship.htm

This site offers extensive coverage of terms and concepts in the study of kinship. The site was developed from a course by M.D. Murphy at the University of Alabama.

Systems of Kinship

http://www.umanitoba.ca/faculties/art/anthropology/tutor/index.html

An excellent site on kinship. It explains descent kinship terminology, marriage systems, and residence rules, with many ethnographic examples. This site provides brief explanations of a vast number of kinship terms and concepts.

Kinship Chart

http://home.honolulu.hawaii.edu/~rob/ANTH200/e-kin.html

Have some fun and create your own kinship chart using this site.

Kinship, Descent Groups, and
Family Organization

http://anthro.palomar.edu/kinship/default.htm

Developed by Dr. Dennis O'Neil at Palomar College, California, this website offers a comprehensive survey of every aspect of kinship studies.

Suggested Readings

For a list of suggested readings, visit the textbook's website at **http://www.havilandcultural4e.nelson.com**.

Notes

1. A. Radcliffe-Brown, *Structure and Function in Primitive Society* (New York: Free Press, 1957), 43–44.

2. R. Firth, *Two Studies of Kinship in London* (London: Athlone Press, 1956), 103.

3. G.N. Ramu, "Kinship Networks," in *Courtship, Marriage, and the Family in Canada*, ed. G.N. Ramu (Toronto: Gage, 1979), 96–114.

4. The following discussion is taken from Ramu, "Kinship networks."

5. T. Parsons, "The Kinship System of Contemporary United States," *American Anthropologist* 45 (1943).

6. E. Litwak, "Occupational Mobility and Extended Family Cohesion," *American Sociological Review* 29 (1960).

7. R. Bruce Morrison and C. Roderick Wilson, eds., *Native Peoples: The Canadian Experience* (Toronto: Oxford University Press, 2004).

8. N. Bonvillain, "Women and Men," in *Cultural Constructs of Gender*, 2nd ed. (Upper Saddle River: Prentice Hall, 1998).

9. C.D. Forde, "Double Descent Among the Yakö," in *Kinship and Social Organization,* ed. P. Bohannan and J. Middleton (Garden City: Natural History Press, 1968), 179–91.

10. A.R. Radcliffe-Brown, "Social Organization of Australian Tribes," *Oceania Monographs* 1, no. 29 (Melbourne: Macmillan, 1933).

11. J.W. Friesen, *Rediscovering the First Nations of Canada* (Calgary: Detselig, 1997).

10 Social Stratification and Groupings

Common-interest groups congregate for economic, social, religious, and political reasons. In this picture, anti-G8 activists protest in London, England.

KEY QUESTIONS

1. What Principles Besides Kinship and Marriage Do People Use to Organize Societies?

People group themselves by gender, age, common interest, and position to deal with problems not conveniently handled by marriage, the family, or descent groups. In addition, certain groups within a culture may use stratification to enjoy preferential treatment for themselves at the expense of other groups.

2. What Are Common-Interest Associations?

Common-interest associations are formed to deal with specific problems and range from fully voluntary to compulsory. They have been a feature of human societies since the advent of the first farming villages several thousand years ago, but they have become especially prominent in modern industrial or industrializing societies.

3. What Is Social Stratification?

Stratification is the division of society into two or more groups of people that do not share equally in wealth, power, or prestige. Groups may be stratified based on age, gender, class, ethnicity, or race.

4. What Is the Validity of Race as a Social Category?

The issue of race has a complex history in anthropological studies. The concept of race has often been employed as a stratification agent. What is the current standing of race in anthropology? To what degree can we still discuss the idea of races? In this chapter we examine the history of race in anthropological studies and examine the physiological basis for categorizing people along racial lines.

Social organization based on kinship and marriage has received an extraordinary amount of attention from anthropologists. Kinship and marriage operate as organizing principles in all cultures. In the small-scale cultures that anthropologists so often study, they are usually the most important organizational principles. There is a certain fascination in the almost mathematical way in which kinship systems appear to function. To the unwary, all this attention to kinship and marriage may convey the impression that these are the only principles of social organization that really count. Yet other principles of social organization not only exist but are also quite important. In this chapter we consider grouping by gender, class, age, race, and common-interest associations, and the principles of social, ethnic, and gender stratification.

GROUPING BY GENDER

Although we differentiate between gender and sex, the two concepts are linked: women bear children, and men place great importance on their sexual prowess. These biological functions are strongly influenced by cultural attitudes and values.

A discussion of gender grouping inevitably turns to gender roles. Some division of labour along gender lines is characteristic of all human groups. In some cultures, men and women may share tasks, and people may perform work normally assigned to the opposite sex; in others, men and women are rigidly segregated in what they do. Among 17th-century Iroquoian peoples, such as the Huron of southern Ontario, society was divided into two parts consisting of sedentary women, who resided in their community year-round, and nomadic men, who were seasonally absent. The women living in villages were "blood" relatives of one another, and their job was to grow the corn, kidney beans, and squash the Huron relied on for subsistence. Although the men built houses and palisades that protected the villages and helped women clear the fields, their hunting, fishing, trading, warring, and diplomacy were all pursued at some distance from the villages. As a consequence, men were transients in the villages, likely present for only brief periods.

Although masculine activities were considered more prestigious than women's work, women were explicitly acknowledged as the sustainers of life. Moreover, women headed the longhouses (dwellings that matrilocal extended families occupied), descent and inheritance passed through women, and ceremonial life was centred on women's activities. Men held leadership positions outside their households, on the councils of the villages, tribes, and the League of Five Nations; but the women of their lineages nominated them for these positions and held veto power over them. In this way, male leadership was balanced by female authority. Overall, the term "separate but equal" accurately describes relations between the sexes in traditional Iroquoian society; neither sex was dominant over or submissive to the other. Outside observers in the 19th century commented widely on the apparent absence of rape in Iroquoian communities. Even in warfare, sexual violation of female captives was virtually unknown.

Groupings by gender are even more evident among the Mundurucu of the Amazon. Here men not only worked apart from women but ate and slept separately as well. All men over 13 lived in a large house of their own; women with their young children occupied two or three houses grouped around that of the men. Men associated with men, women with women. The relationship between the sexes was one of opposition. The Mundurucu believed that sex roles had once been reversed, with women ruling over men and controlling the sacred trumpets that are the symbols of power and that represent the generative capacities of women. But because women could not hunt, they could not supply the meat demanded by the ancient spirits contained within the trumpets. This enabled men to take the trumpets from the women and establish their dominance. Ever since, the trumpets had been kept carefully guarded and hidden in the men's house, and no woman could see them under penalty of gang rape. Thus, Mundurucu men expressed fear and envy toward women, whom they sought to control by force. For their part, the women neither liked nor accepted a submissive status, and even though men occupied all formal positions of political and religious leadership, women were autonomous in the economic realm.

Although important differences exist, there are nonetheless interesting similarities between Mundurucu beliefs and those of traditional European (including Euro-Canadian) cultures. The idea of rule by men replacing an earlier state of matriarchy (rule by women), for example, was held by many 19th-century intellectuals, who believed that older Palaeolithic cultures had been matriarchical. Moreover, the idea that men may use force to control women is deeply embedded in Islamic, Judaic, and Christian traditions; even today, in spite of changing attitudes, a Canadian woman is sexually assaulted every six minutes and one out of four is sexually assaulted at some time in her life.[1] A major difference between Mundurucu and traditional European society is that, in the latter, women have not had control of their economic activities. Although this is now changing, women in Canada and other Western countries still have a

Harassment or Intimidation Will Not Be Tolerated In This Workplace.

Please report any incidents or concerns to:

_____.

In industrial nations like Canada and the United States, women have been expected to tolerate unwanted sexual advances in the workplace. In recent years, laws against harassment have achieved a more egalitarian workplace.

considerable distance to go before they achieve economic equality with men.

AGE GROUPING

Age grouping is so familiar that it and gender sometimes have been called the only universal factors for determining a person's position in society. In North America today, children's first friends generally are children their own age, especially schoolmates. At specified ages, North Americans are allowed to do things reserved for adults, such as driving a car, voting, and drinking alcoholic beverages. As North Americans age, they are labelled "pre-teens", "teenagers," "middle-aged," and then "senior citizens" based solely on their age.

Age classification plays a significant role in non-Western societies as well. Many cultural groups distinguish between immature, mature, and elderly people. Among the Ju/'hoansi, chronological age has little meaning, but old age is divided into three categories: *n!a*, who are elders; *m da !ki*, who are very old; and *m da kum kum*, meaning old to the point of helplessness.[2]

Age grading in modern North American society is exemplified by the education system, which specifies that at six years of age all children must enter the first grade.

An organized class of people with membership based on age is known as an **age grade**. Entry into and transfer out of age grades may be accomplished individually, either because of biological changes, such as puberty, or changing social status, such as marriage or childbirth. Among male Maasai, passing from the warrior **age-set** into the elder age-set is marked by great ritual and ceremony as well as by many new privileges, such as the right to get married.

Advanced age brings with it more respect (for women it may even mean social equality with men). This is the case with elderly Yanomami women, who possess a higher status as elders than when they were of child-bearing age. An elderly woman's responsibilities toward her husband diminish at this time, and she may move her hammock closer to her grown children if her husband takes a second, younger wife. Elderly Yanomami women are sometimes used as messengers between enemy villages for they will not be harmed. Elders can serve as valuable enculturation forces. In most indigenous cultures, the elders are considered repositories of accumulated wisdom; they are the "living libraries" for their people. Elderhood is the time when individuals gain freedom from many subsistence activities and when they begin playing a major role in passing the values, beliefs, and social and behavioural norms of their culture on to their grandchildren.

age grade An organized category of people based on age; every individual passes through a series of such categories during a lifetime.

age-set A group of people born in the same time period. Age-sets may hold political, religious, military, or economic power as a group.

Dynamic Anthropology

Gender, Racialization, Labour, and Language in Multicultural Toronto

Bonnie McElhinny,
Kori Allan,
Lalaie Ameeriar

Bonnie McElhinny (PhD, 1993, Stanford University) is an associate professor in anthropology and women and gender studies who works on issues linked to gender, the Philippines, and the Filipino diaspora. Her SSHRC-funded research focuses on historical and contemporary investigations of North American interventions into Filipino health care and child care practices, and reactions and resistance to these. Her current work includes an investigation into early-20th-century attempts to address high infant mortality rates in the Philippines.

Anthropologist Lalaie Ameeriar met Farah during a workshop at a settlement services agency in downtown Toronto mandated to assist with the integration of highly skilled immigrant workers from a range of countries. Farah was a foreign-trained nurse who had migrated to Toronto six years before their interview, who had worked as a nurse in Pakistan for sixteen years, and who was currently working at Coffee Time donuts. She had been called to the front of the class to help the workshop coordinator demonstrate appropriate bodily comportment during a job interview. As Farah shifted uncomfortably in her seat, trying to sit "appropriately," the instructor, Anne, began calling out various instructions in the style of a drill sergeant. "Never put your bag on the table because it's not your table—put it on the floor, it's a sign of respect; it's all right to put your arm on the table, but don't lean on it; there is no right or wrong, but just don't be too forward; you can cross your legs, but don't switch crossing them too often, and don't tap your feet; be on time; your language, do

not translate in your head; use simple sentences; change your name if it's hard to pronounce; be aware of nonverbal behavior; don't wear bright colours and keep your traditional dress at home."

A major contemporary problem in Canada involves the unemployment of highly skilled foreign workers (e.g., doctors, engineers, lawyers), which is known in Canada as "the foreign-trained professionals" problem. In 2007, fewer than 25 percent of foreign-trained professionals were working in their professions, which is particularly significant in Canada, which has the highest immigration rate in the world and relies on immigration for the net growth of the labour force. The foreign-trained professionals problem is described almost exclusively through the stereotype of a taxicab driver who was a doctor in his home country, so women's experiences of unemployment are often overlooked in Canadian understandings of the problem. Yet immigrant women ages 25 to 54 (considered "core working age") have much higher unemployment rates than both immigrant men and Canadian-born women, regardless of how long they have been in Canada. Despite higher levels of education, immigrant women occupy lower wage work, such as clerical, sales, and service, and the unemployment rate for recently arrived immigrant women is almost three times that of Canadian-born women. Therefore, while there are high levels of skilled-worker immigration to Canada, and the Canadian economy relies on such labour migrations for growth, paradoxically this does not translate into the employment of such workers into Canadian labour markets. How does this happen?

It is often written off as a bureaucratic problem in which the federal government manages immigration and the provincial government manages labour, thus leaving a gap in government understandings of immigrant labour needs. Furthermore, much of the blame is put on the role of regulatory bodies that control who can work in different

professions. However, anthropological work in government-funded settlement agencies has demonstrated that often the immigrants themselves are blamed. That is, these agencies teach immigrant workers that their failure to acclimatize, or integrate into Canadian society, has led to their unemployment. This aligns with theories of the modern neoliberal state, and the decline of the welfare system in Canada, in which responsibility for success or integration lies with the individual. So, immigrants are taught in government-funded agencies that the reason they cannot find work is because they have names that are "too foreign" or they wear "traditional dress." The problem of unemployment becomes gendered when immigrant women are instructed not to wear traditional dress, or makeup that is too bright, or to bring their children to interviews (falsely assuming that as women they all have children). In fact, instructions in many of these workshops teach these women that the way they manage their bodies keeps them from finding work, which demonstrates the intersection of multiculturalism and gender.

Theorists of multiculturalism and gender (e.g., Mohanty 1991; Povinelli 2002; Ticktin 2008; Razack 1998) have demonstrated the complicated ways that women are subjected to disciplining by the state. Feminist theorist Chandra Mohanty (1991) has argued that the gender and racial regimes of contemporary liberal states function through the "unmarked" categories of belonging—that is, gendered male and racialized as "white." In fact, women's bodies become a crucial site to witness the larger politics of gender and nationalism in contemporary North America. In the context of settlement services agencies, women are shown videos and given lessons on how to behave "Canadian," which explicitly addresses the ways they talk, dress, and move their bodies.

Anthropologist Kori Allan investigates the ways that settlement counsellors and policy makers have often argued that language is a key barrier to immigrant integration into the Canadian labour market. For instance, Naeem "Nick" Noorani exhorts that "English is key," making it number one in his "7 Secrets of Success for Canadian Immigrants," which he outlined in his keynote address for the annual TESL conference in Toronto (in 2008). This focus on language competency is another way in which the foreign-trained professionals integration problem is constructed as resulting from immigrants' individual deficiencies. To help new immigrants gain professional employment commensurate with their qualifications, Citizenship and Immigration Canada has introduced the Enhanced Language Training Initiative (ELT). The ELT classes that Kori participated in focused on teaching "good" communication skills to prepare job-seeking immigrants for interviews, networking, and meeting with recruiters. These lessons were not neutral; rather, instructors prescribed particular ways of speaking that were meant to convey and foster actions and attitudes valued by employers in the knowledge-based economy—flexibility, entrepreneurialism, and self-discipline. These lessons thus focused on constructing ideal workers and citizens who embodied particular values—that is, how they conducted their bodies and talked were seen as reflecting appropriate ways of being "Canadian" and a "good" worker.

ELT instructors recognized that talk is evaluated in job interviews as inseparable from the candidate's personality and fit with corporate values. Most employers conduct behavioural-based interviews that try to assess one's attitude toward work by asking general questions like "What is your greatest weakness?" Here communication skills, or how one answers questions, are meant to demonstrate that one "genuinely" has the right attitude and values desired by the employer (i.e., for teamwork). Such "fit" candidates are valued because they can monitor themselves and thus decrease training and management costs.

To help ELT students answer interview questions, instructors tried to make explicit the implicit cultural background knowledge they needed to know in order to answer appropriately. They also evaluated students' performances in role-playing activities in line with (imagined) employer values. In doing so, instructors encouraged students to reflect upon their abilities and characteristics by conceptualizing them as skills that workers can acquire to increase their economic value (Heller 2005; Urciuoli 2008). Additionally, students were asked to think of themselves as projects in need of improvement. Ideal answers to interview questions accordingly involved constructing narratives around the reflexive recognition of a "problem" and then one's capacity and willingness to fix it. This ideology of lifelong learning constitutes workers as subjects who should continually acquire new skills to improve themselves (Olssen 2008). Through the prescription of these ideal values, ELT instructors encouraged new immigrants to accept responsibility for their professional development rather than locate responsibility in the state or the market, or in other systemic barriers that new immigrants faced, such as professional-accreditation bodies.

Such behavioural-based modes of employee selection also open up a space for covert discrimination, as personal attributes and attitudes are difficult to evaluate and, in practice, are often based on proxies that take race and gender into account, even though such grounds for discrimination are illegal (Grugulis and Vincent 2009). So when employers say that candidates lack language or communication skills, they often are using the term as a gloss for perceived culturalized/racialized/ethnicized deficiencies. For example, an ELT teacher, Tony, noted that if Vik is an evil engineer "he won't get a job, he will end up working at [a corner store]" (June 16, 2008). Tony also made a joke about employers wanting "to make sure you're not a 'terrorist'" through behavioural-based interview questions. Such comments play on culturalizing and racializing stereotypes of the "Other" and conflate the varied experiences of newcomers (cf. Thobani 2007). These stereotypes are also implicit in advice given to ELT students. For example, a pamphlet that lists a series of tips on how to adapt to "Canadian workplace culture" included the following: "In Canada a person's authority is related to their position and responsibility. Women hold the same kinds of positions as men and have the same level of authority." Here, the imagined figure of the patriarchal male immigrant is reproduced. The reader is assumed to be a male who would have a problem with gender equality in the workplace. Paradoxically, it assumes male immigrants are likely to discriminate against women, instead of addressing the discrimination they may face as foreign or racially marked bodies. Furthermore, the advice demonstrates a gendered bias, as it does not address professional immigrant women. When teachers and counsellors tried to manage and teach sociocultural difference, they thus made stereotypical assumptions about new immigrants' cultural background knowledge as well as generalizations about what constitutes Canadian workplace culture. These well-meaning instructors thus ended up constructing homogenizing cultural stereotypes in problematic ways.

Not only was interpersonal discrimination typically unacknowledged in ELT classes, but talk about systemic discrimination was also silenced. Students largely did not focus on language as their greatest barrier to integration, for they recognized that regardless of how they sell themselves in interviews, their work experience is devalued in local labour markets that value Canadian experience. ELT students thus often expressed their frustration after hearing the same tired advice on communication skills and on improving the self, rather than receiving concrete employer connections through ELT. Although the ELT programs Kori examined were largely unsuccessful at helping their clients find professional work, counsellors evaluated such criticisms not as a reflection of the quality of their services or as an opportunity to challenge dominant discourses and practices, but rather as characteristic of attitudes in need of adjustment (Dunk 1996). These programs thereby contributed to the reproduction of "deskilled" labour forces—that is, the reproduction of professional immigrants working at Coffee Time—as well as the reproduction of the active unemployed—those who take

CONTINUED

CONTINUED

responsibility for improving themselves in "appropriate" ways in order to get a job. The integration problem thereby gets blamed on individuals rather than on broader and systematic discriminatory practices and institutions. Talk and language training are thereby key means of reproducing inequality and constructing difference rather than mere "secrets to success[ful]" integration.

Canadian immigration policy leads to other forms of underemployment for immigrants as well. Social and economic shifts in North America in the past 30 years, including the Baby Boomers' own baby boom and the rising labour force participation of mothers with children under six, have created an acute need for child care for families of all classes. Although in much of its social policy Canada has a more universal, publicly funded approach than the United States, in the realm of child care Canada is more similar to the United States than to European Union countries: unlike many European countries, neither Canada nor the United States has a national child care policy. In North America, child care is provided in informal (in-home care) and formal (licensed family child care homes and child care centres) settings. The recent revival in the use of domestic workers as caregivers in many families with dual-career professional couples reflects this privatized approach to child care. Anthropologist Shellee Colen develops the theoretical notion of *stratified reproduction* to describe the forms of child care that result. Stratified reproduction means that "physical and social reproductive tasks are accomplished differentially according to inequalities that are based on hierarchies of class, race, ethnicity, gender, place in a global economy, and migration status and that are structured by social, economic and political forces" (1995, 78).

During the 1980s, many Filipinas entered Canada through the Foreign Domestic Movement (FDM), a program in which domestic workers were eligible to apply for landed immigrant status after two years of live-in service with a designated employer. Programs earlier in the 20th century had recruited European domestics, but these domestics were given landed immigrant status

upon arrival. As recruitment turned to the Caribbean in the mid-1950s and the Philippines in the 1980s, access to citizenship rights was more sharply curtailed. In 1992, the FDM was replaced by the Live-in Caregiver Program (LCP), a program in which eligibility criteria for entry to Canada became more restrictive than in the FDM, partly in the name of improving the quality of child care (often for white children) in Canada (Bakan and Stasiulis 1997a; Arat-Koç 1999). All applicants must have university education but are not allowed to undertake additional education while working in the FDM. Close to 12 percent of all Philippine-born arrivals came under the LCP category between 1980 and 2001, and Filipina/os overwhelmingly accounted for those recruited (25,846 out of 32,474, or 79.6 percent of arrivals). Filipina/o migration to Canada has thus taken on a distinctive gendered skew, with almost 60 percent of immigrants from the Philippines during this period being women (Kelly 2006, 11). Many professionals—nurses, midwives, graduate students in linguistics, office workers—now come to Canada through the LCP, hoping to find work in their own careers afterward, though these hopes are often dashed. In 2006, 57.5 percent of all Filipina/os in Canada were women (Statistics Canada 2006). Much work has been conducted on the LCP. Research on and by Filipina/o live-in caregivers describes the horrific working conditions: frequent incidents of overtime without pay, sexual harassment, the constraints of the live-in requirement, and the *de facto* lack of legal protections (Arat-Koç 2001; Bakan and Stasiulis 1997; Elvir 1997; England and Stiell 1997; Macklin 1994; Pratt 1999; Stasiulis and Bakan 2005; Velasco 1997). Similarly, many scholars have critiqued the policy contexts that enable the entry of live-in caregivers in Canada. Scholars like Pratt (1999, 2004), for example, have critiqued the racialization of gendered care work in Canada, as well as the Philippine state's labour export policy and the Canadian state's prioritization of this form of social reproduction. In so doing, these scholars have made more visible the injustices perpetrated by such labour migration policies. Hence, for the Filipina/o community, immigra-

tion and migration inevitably bring to the fore gender concerns, specifically those of women. Gender concerns are linked to the forms that youth concerns take as well. Many youth, once reunified with their mothers after a long separation, experience problems. Several rich documentary films exist on these topics: *When Strangers Reunite* (Bautista and Boti 1999); *Modern Heroes, Modern Slaves* (Boti 1997); *Brown Women, Blonde Babies* (Boti and Bautista 1992). In sum, a series of government policies and regulatory decisions, while creating a more multicultural country, have also resulted in stratification based on presumed attributes of gender, race/ethnicity, and language.

Sources: S. Arat-Koç, *Caregivers Break the Silence: A Participatory Action Research on the Abuse and Violence, Including the Impact of Family Separation, Experienced by Women in the Live-In Caregiver Program* (Toronto: Intercede, 2001); Arat-Koç, "'Good Enough to Work But Not Good Enough to Stay?' Foreign Domestic Workers and the Law, in *Locating Law: Race/Gender/Class Connections*, ed. Elizabeth Comack (Halifax: Fernwood, 1999), 129–52; A. Bakan and D. Stasiulis, "Foreign Domestic Worker Policy in Canada and the Social Boundaries of Modern Citizenship," in *Not One of the Family: Foreign Domestic Workers in Canada*, ed. A. Bakan and D. Stasiulis (Toronto: University of Toronto Press, 1997), 29–52; F. Bautista and M. Boti, *When Strangers Reunite*, Productions Multi-Monde, 1999, 55m; M. Boti (dir.), *Modern Heroes, Modern Slaves*, Diffusion Multi-Monde, 1997, 44m; M. Boti and F. Bautista (prods.), *Brown Women, Blonde Babies*, Diffusion Multi-Monde, 1992, 30m; S. Colen, "'Like a Mother to Them': Stratified Reproduction and West Indian Childcare Workers and Employers in New York," in *Conceiving the New World Order: The Global Politics of Reproduction*, ed. Faye Finsburg and Rayna Rapp (Berkeley: University of California Press, 1995), 78–102; T. Dunk, "Culture, Skill, Masculinity, and Whiteness: Training and the Politics of Identity," in *The Training Trap: Ideology, Training, and the Labour Market*, ed. T. Dunk, S. McBride, and R.W. Nelson (Winnipeg: Fernwood Publishing, 1996), 101–23; M. Elvir, "The Work at Home Is Not Recognized: Organizing Domestic Workers in Montreal," in *Not One of the Family*, 147–56; K. England and B. Stiell, "They Think You're as Stupid as Your English Is': Constructing Foreign Domestic Workers in Toronto," *Environment and Planning* A 29 (1997): 195–215;

I. Grugulis and S. Vincent, "Whose Skill Is It Anyway?: 'Soft' Skills and Polarization," *Work, Employment, and Society* 23, no. 4 (2009): 597–615; M. Heller, "Globalization, the New Economy, and the Commodification of Language and Identity," *Journal of Sociolinguistics* 7, no. 4 (2003): 473–92; P. Kelly, "Filipina/os in Canada: Economic Dimensions of Immigration and Settlement," *Joint Center of Excellence for Research on Immigration and Settlement—Toronto* 48 (2006): 1–37; A. Macklin, "On the Inside Looking In: Foreign Domestic Workers in Canada," in *Maid in the Market: Women's Paid Domestic Labour*, ed. W. Giles and S. Arat-Koç (Halifax: Fernwood Publishing, 1994), 13–39; C. Mohanty, "Introduction," in *Third World Women and the Politics of Feminism*, ed. C. Mohanty,

A. Russo, and L. Torres (Bloomington: Indiana University Press, 1991); M. Olssen, "Understanding the Mechanisms of Neoliberal Control: Lifelong Learning, Flexibility, and Knowledge Capitalism," in *Foucault and Lifelong Learning: Governing the Subject*, ed. A. Feges and K. Nicoll, (London and New York: Routledge, 2008), 34–47; E. Povinelli, *The Cunning of Recognition: Indigenous Alterities and the Making of Australian Multiculturalism* (Durham: Duke University Press, 2002); G. Pratt, "From Registered Nurse to Registered Nanny: Discursive Geographies of Filipina Domestic Workers in Vancouver, B.C.," *Economic Geography* 75 (1999): 215–36; S. Razack, *Looking White People in the Eye: Gender, Race, and Culture in Courtrooms and Classrooms* (Toronto: University of

Toronto Press, 1998); D. Stasiulis and A. Bakan, *Negotiating Citizenship: Migrant Women in Canada and the Global System* (Toronto: University of Toronto Press, 2005); S. Thobani, *Exalted Subjects: Studies in the Making of Race and Nation in Canada* (Toronto: University of Toronto Press, 2007); M. Ticktin, "Sexual Violence as the Language of Border Control: Where French Feminist and Anti-Immigrant Rhetoric Meet," *Signs* 33, no. 4 (2008); B. Urciuoli, "Skills and Selves in the New Workplace," *American Ethnologist* 35, no. 2 (2008): 211–28; P. Velasco, "'We Can Still Fight Back': Organizing Domestic Workers in Toronto," in *Not One of the Family*, 157–64.

In many cultures it is common for children of the same age to play, eat, and learn together, such as these Maasai boys, who are gathering for the first time to receive instruction for their initiation into an age grade.

Animals Animals/Earth Sciences/MaXx Images

In North America, people rely on the written word, rather than on their elders, for long-term memory. Moreover, some people have become so accustomed to rapid change that they tend to assume that the experiences of their grandparents and others of the oldest generation are hardly relevant in today's world. North Americans retire from their jobs at a specified age, usually around 65. Some of them live their final years in "retirement communities," segregated from the rest of society. Indeed, retirement from the workforce implies that an individual has nothing further to offer society and should stay out of the way of those who are younger. The status of the elderly is even more problematic because they now constitute so large (and growing) a part of the overall population in the West. By 2026, one in every five people in Canada will be a senior, making up 21 percent of the population, compared with 13 percent in 2000.[3] Reaching old age seems less of an accomplishment than it once did and so commands less respect. Yet the stereotype of elderly people sitting on the periphery of society with nothing to offer is slowly giving way to an image of vibrant seniors enjoying active lifestyles, such as anthropologists Counts and Counts found among "RVers" (recreational vehicle enthusiasts). Senior RVers are modern-day nomads—some two or three million strong—who enjoy freedom, independence, and adventure as they take to North American highways. Seniors credit RVing with giving them a zest for life, and a strong sense of community prevails among RVers in RV parks. Some of their sociocultural features are very similar to those of other nomadic peoples. For example, they practise reciprocal aid and food sharing (potlucks), and they congregate and disperse seasonally.[4]

Anthropologists have studied aging from several perspectives: the status and treatment of the aged; the cultural knowledge they possess; and recently, the life experiences of elderly people. They have asked such questions as these: Do elderly people live a good life? How do they define a good life? How has modernization affected their lives? How do elders perceive their advancing age, and what coping strategies do they employ? Are elders held in high esteem and valued by other age-sets in their culture? And, how are they cared for as they grow older?[5]

COMMON-INTEREST ASSOCIATIONS

The proliferation of **common-interest associations** is a theme intimately associated with world urbanization and its attendant social upheavals. This fondness for joining common-interest associations no doubt reflects the reality that individuals, especially in North America, often are separated by physical distance from their brothers, sisters, and age mates. As a result, they have to search out like-minded companions for support and friendship.

Common-interest associations have often been referred to in the anthropological literature as voluntary associations, but that term is misleading. The act of joining may range from a fully voluntary act to one required by law. For example, it is not really compulsory to join a labour union, but unless potential employees do, they cannot work in a unionized organization. The term "voluntary association" really refers to associations that are not based on sex, age, kinship, marriage, or territory but that result from the act of joining. Therefore, the act often may be voluntary, but it does not have to be.

common-interest associations Associations not based on age, kinship, marriage, or territory but that result from the act of joining.

Kinds of Common-Interest Associations

The diversity of common-interest associations is astonishing. In Canada, they include women's groups like the Status of Women, business and professional women's associations, and MADD (Mothers Against Drunk Drivers); men's groups, such as the Kiwanis and Kinsmen; parent, teacher, and alumni associations; religious organizations; political parties; support groups like Alcoholics Anonymous; chambers of commerce; labour unions—the list could go on and on. Their goals may include recreation, friendship, and the promotion of certain values, as well as the pursuit of power and economic well-being. Associations such as the Tribal Unions of West Africa preserve traditional songs, history, language, and moral beliefs among various ethnic minorities. Similar organizations have kept traditions alive among Canadian First Nations. Another significant force in the formation of associations may be a supernatural experience common to all members. Well-known examples include the Crow Indian Tobacco Society; the Kachina cults of the Hopi; and the secret associations of the Kwakwaka'wakw (Kwakiutl) of British Columbia, whose cycles of rituals are known only to initiates. Other traditional forms of association are military, occupational, political, and entertainment groups, and university or college clubs, not to mention sports groups and co-ops of every kind.

Men's and Women's Associations

For many years, scholars dismissed women's contributions to common-interest associations as less important than those of men. However, scholars have shown this kind of thinking to be culture bound. In some cultures, women have not formed associations to the same extent men have because the demands of raising a family and their daily activities have not permitted it and because men, and society, have not always encouraged them to do so. Earlier in Canada's history, when rural women were limited to the home, in relative isolation, they had little chance to participate in common-interest associations. However, this also held true for men. Very quickly, as settlers moved into new regions, social clubs cropped up to organize picnics, dances, and sliding parties as a means of alleviating the loneliness of frontier living. The same holds true for contemporary immigrants to Canada. Support groups can ease their transition to Canadian life by providing social networks for both men and women.

As cross-cultural research indicates, women do play important roles in associations of their own and even in those in which men predominate. Among the Crow, women participated in the secret Tobacco Society,

Nongovernmental organizations such as Amnesty International are common-interest associations that promote the rights of people around the world. Shown here is a press conference for Amnesty International.

as well as in their own exclusive groups. In Canada's Northwest Territories, the Native Women's Association provides training and education as well as counselling services to Native women of the Western Arctic. The NWA has been incorporated since 1978 and continues to provide a forum for women's issues in the Far North.[6] Women's rights organizations, consciousness-raising groups, nurses' organizations, and other professional organizations for women are examples of associations arising directly or indirectly out of today's social climate. Similar associations are also often found in societies that are socially stratified. We turn now to social stratification as a major principle of social organization.

SOCIAL STRATIFICATION

Globalization and instant worldwide communications have made social stratification a crucial topic for modern theorists. **Social stratification** is a system whereby some members of a society are ranked higher or lower relative to other members. It is a common and powerful phenomenon found in most of the world's cultures, past and present. Members of lower ranked social strata tend to be denied the same privileges as those in higher strata, including equal access to basic resources. The way people are ranked varies, but stratification is commonly based on age, gender, class, ethnicity, or race.

Anthropologists measure the degree of stratification in a given group according to an individual's access to wealth, power, and prestige. **Wealth** may include financial resources, material possessions, wives and children, and the potential for future earnings. **Power** relates to the ability to overcome obstacles to reach personal, financial, and professional goals, and **prestige** is the social esteem others hold for an individual. Anthropologists disagree over which of these dimensions of stratification is the most important, and it is essential to recognize that the ways in which power, wealth, and prestige are perceived differ greatly cross-culturally. In Canada, individuals gain wealth, prestige, and power from their professions. Among the Maasai, a man gains wealth and prestige from the size of his family (the number of wives and children) and the size of his family's cattle herd.

Social stratification is most common in **stratified societies**, where ranking and inequality among members vary, thus creating different levels of social position and quality of life. Stratified societies first arose when state-level societies, and the ensuing specialization of occupations, began some 5,000 to 6,000 years ago. Since then, as states have become more complex and specialized,

social stratification Institutionalized inequality resulting in some groups receiving differential access to power, wealth, and prestige.

wealth Accumulation of financial resources, material possessions, wives and children, and the potential for future earnings.

power The ability to reach personal, financial, and professional goals regardless of obstacles.

prestige The social esteem others hold for an individual.

stratified societies Societies in which ranking and inequality among members vary.

stratification has intensified. In contrast, members of **egalitarian cultures** depend mainly on their abilities for social positions. A poor hunter may become a wealthier hunter if he (occasionally she) has the ability; he is not excluded from a prestigious social position because he comes from a group of poor hunters. Poor hunters do not constitute a social stratum. Furthermore, they have as much right to a group's resources as any other members. In an egalitarian system, no one can deny a poor hunter his fair share of food, the right to be heard when important decisions are made, or anything else a man is entitled to. This situation differs markedly from the inequalities and restrictions found in stratified societies.

Theories of Stratification

Fundamental to the study of social stratification is this question: Why is inequality so prevalent?[7] The **functionalist theory of stratification** suggests that inequality is necessary for the maintenance or *functioning* of complex societies. Such societies require a wide variety of professions of varying degrees of specialization. For example, Canadian society includes maintenance workers, teachers, and physicians—all of them needed, yet each possessing a different status. According to this functionalist theory, to entice the best people into difficult professions that require a great deal of time (education and training) and sacrifice (personal and financial), there must be incentives at the end of the long road. Fewer people would train for years to become a surgeon if they could attain the same level of wealth, power, and prestige by working as a janitor.

The functionalist theory certainly has some strengths, but it also has several weaknesses. First, in complex societies we do not always reward the professions that are most involved in *maintaining* society. In North America, for example, nonfunctional entertainment has a high value placed on it. Thus, Sidney Crosby makes a salary of around $8.7 million a year as a hockey player, while a nurse makes around $60,000 a year—1/145th his salary. The wealth, power, and prestige attached to these two professions differ dramatically. Second, functionalists do not account for the barriers to entering the high-prestige professions; ethnic minorities, women, and those from lower socioeconomic strata often do not have the same opportunities for education and thus high-paying employment. Third, this theory assumes that everyone is motivated to seek the highest paying, highest status jobs, when other factors such as a desire for meaningful work and to help others may take precedence. Focusing solely on money reduces humans to what has been termed *"Homo economicus."*

Countering the functionalist theory, the **conflict theory of stratification** emphasizes conflict between those in the upper levels of society, who attempt to maintain the status quo, and those in the lower levels, who struggle for a more equitable division of wealth, power, and prestige. Conflict theorists contend that people in the upper levels use their influence within governments, industry, and educational and religious institutions to keep others satisfied with their lower status. The conflict theory takes its cue from the 19th-century writings of Karl Marx, who viewed the world as a constant struggle between the bourgeoisie (those who own the resources) and the proletariat (the working class).[8] Marx believed that the bourgeoisie, with all their power, had convinced the proletariat that if they failed to reach the highest echelons of society, it was their own fault—they had not tried hard enough. But the conflict theory tends to ignore other contributing factors, such as personal choice, ability, and effort.

Social stratification is a general term used to describe the different social positions that groups occupy and to highlight the inequalities experienced by various groups around the world. Within this broad category are several forms of stratification, but before we look at these, it is worth our while to examine the concept of **race**.

Racial Stratification

Any examination of social stratification would be incomplete without considering the inequalities surrounding the interrelated concepts of race and ethnicity. Often the differences between human groups, whether seen as racial or ethnic, can lead to social inequality, discrimination, and what has commonly become known as racism. **Racism** is the belief that one race is superior to another owing to biological and cultural features. Although this attitude sounds remarkably like ethnocentrism, behind racism lies exploitation. Instances of horrific racial discrimination in the 20th century are numerous, including the Holocaust of the Second World War, South Africa's

egalitarian cultures Groups in which members enjoy equal access to resources and positions.

functionalist theory of stratification A theory suggesting that inequality is necessary to maintain complex societies.

conflict theory of stratification A theory suggesting that a power struggle takes place between the upper and lower levels of society.

race Group of people who are categorized based on biological and behavioural traits.

racism The perception that some groups are biologically and culturally inferior to other groups.

⚬ *Original Study* ⚬

Race and Anthropology: Skin Deep

Liam Kilmurray

Among his own people the color of the Ethiopian is not notable, and among the Germans red hair gathered into a knot is not unseemly for a man. You are to count nothing odd or disgraceful for an individual which is a general characteristic of his nation. (Lucius Seneca, 4 BC–AD 65)

In anthropological studies, people are often categorized—for example, through the inclusive and exclusive terminology of kinship; through membership in households and social groups; and through a variety of cultural and ethnic designations. Humans are also categorized based on "race."* This designation rests on a variety of physical traits, most notably skin colour, which Langdon refers to as that "troubling aspect of human anatomy" (2005, 186). Other traits are also used to categorize the "races," such as body shape (height and breadth) and the shape or dimensions of cheeks, eyes, nose, and lips.

Attempts to classify the human "races" are hardly a modern endeavour. There are records relating to the classification of peoples going as far back as the Egyptians. In 1350 BC the Egyptians had a classification system in which they used red for themselves, black for the Africans to the south, and white for Europeans and North Africans. The Egyptians were not aware of the Americas or Australia. They had black pharaohs, and the slaves they kept were differentiated by ethnicity rather than colour. During the eight and ninth centuries, the Arabs of North Africa

controlled a slave trade in which they took people from many regions, but mainly Slavs from eastern Europe—thus, the word "slaves." Europeans, mainly English and French, would construct their own infamous slave trade during the 17th century, taking slaves primarily from western Africa.

The Spanish and Portuguese, as they conquered Central and South America, debated whether the peoples of the newly discovered lands had souls. In 1512, after much deliberation, Pope Julius II decreed that the Indians of the Americas were in fact descendants of

© The Art Archive/Alamy

Head measurements, testing for Aryan qualities, late 1930s.

Adam and Eve and were in possession of souls; therefore they could not have their liberty or lives taken without good reason. But these papal announcements were not obeyed, and the peoples of the New World were enslaved and murdered on a large scale—an indication of the underlying racism that prevailed among European nations. During the 17th century, peoples from outside Europe, from what was called the New World, were often paraded at Royal Courts as curiosities. In 1677 the philosopher and economist William Petty even suggested that these "savages" were the "missing link" between Caucasians and other humans. During this period of

European dominance and colonialism, it became necessary to see "the other" as nonhuman. As people were judged according to their skin colour and other physical features, the word "race" became a popular term. To summarize, the conquest of new and vast colonies resulted in the "racialization of the world" (Satzewich and Liodakis 2010, 11).

Early writers loosely associated with the emergent science of anthropology resorted to ethnographic data on the customs of "primitive" peoples supplied by field anthropologists in order to disparage the level of civilization of these peoples. European scholars, such as Carl Linnaeus, began to write about the human "races." In 1758, in the tenth edition of his *General System of Nature,* he established four basic colour types in descending order of the possession of civilized traits: white Europeans, red Americans, yellow Asians, and black Africans. In 1775, Johann Friedrich Blumenbach, in his *De generis humani varietate nativa* (On the Natural Varieties of Mankind), classified the "races" into five distinct branches: Caucasian, Mongolian, Ethiopian, American, and Malay. In 1842, as Europeans continued to seek justifications for colonialism, a Swedish anatomist named Anders Retzius gave us the "cephalic index." This was a dangerous tool (one that would also be used by physical anthropologists) that measured people's skulls in order to classify them into one of the "races." It was also used to analyze fossil specimens and to classify people as "indeterminate" in terms of their "race" (i.e., they were of mixed ancestry). The cephalic index was arrived at by dividing the maximum head breadth by the maximum head length and multiplying the result by 100. This provided people with an index for their

CONTINUED

CONTINUED

type of brain, and they could thereafter be slotted into one of the predetermined racial categories.

The English scholar Francis Galton (1822–1911) was another influential figure in the classification of the "races" (he was also a cousin of Charles Darwin). He was viewed as an early anthropologist, but he was also a eugenicist who studied psychometrics, the measurement of the skull, which was linked to the aforementioned cephalic index.

Eugenicism is the philosophy of "race" improvement through forced sterilization or increased reproduction of the "desired" "races." The work of eugenicists was to have a profound impact on racial classification and stereotyping. Around the same time, some anthropologists imported the ideas of Darwin and Wallace on natural selection and applied them to entire societies, arguing that the fittest society would survive and flourish. The fittest society, in this school of thought referred to as Social Darwinism, was, of course, Victorian Britain. Other, non-European cultures were deemed inferior, as were their populations.

While most academics in the 20th century rejected racial stereotyping, racism gained strength socially. Racist thinking was prominent in various realms. For example, in the United States, the American Breeders Association published influential documents that mixed short, readable articles and reviews on a variety of topics, including plant and animal breeding, with calls for sterilization of delinquents and for racist immigration laws. In 1924, largely because of the association's lobbying, American immigration laws were changed to restrict the entry of all but northern European or Nordic immigrants. Even southern Europeans were not considered racially pure enough for the "white man's country." A small minority of scholars were overt racists. Some, such as Galton, were loosely associated with anthropology; others, such as Kossina, were more steeped in the anthropological and archaeological literature.

In 1912, Gustav Kossinna published *Die deutsche Vorgeschichte* (German Prehistory), which raised the idea of *Rassenkampf* ("race" struggle) which, within a few years, would influence the Nazi thinking and lead to the Holocaust against Jewish people and other minority groups. Kossinna equated the Aryans with the early German people, arguing that they were superior and destined to rule Europe. The Nazis gloried in the idea of a genetically pure Aryan "race." That this was absurd was evident to more insightful scholars, including Franz Boas, who noted that the first Aryan had been a speaker of an Indo-European tongue, whose genetic combinations, while not really important, certainly had not resulted in a tall, blond, and blue-eyed "race."

Boas, like most academic anthropologists of the era, argued passionately against such racist views and was opposed to racial designations, especially when these were associated with moral or mental pronouncements. Boas and his supporters contended that misguided theories and constructs—including eugenics and the cephalic index—were promoting biological determinism, that is, the notion that various attributes are governed by biological (genetic) factors. At a 1934 meeting of the International Congress of Anthropological and Ethnological Sciences, Boas, along with Alfred Haddon and Earnest Hooton, decided to replace the term "race" with the term "ethnicity." Boas in particular rejected the concept of "race," arguing that "the existence of any pure race with special endowments is a myth, as is the belief that there are races all of whose members are foredoomed to eternal inferiority" (1945, 20). Furthermore, he drew up a list of statements to the effect that "(1) a race is not an objective or demonstrable descent group; (2) there is as much physical variation within a race as between races; (3) there are no clear-cut geographical and biological lines between the races; and (4) there is no correlation between race on the one hand and either mental or cultural characteristics on the other." In 1942, Ashley Montagu published "Man's Most Dangerous Myth: The Fallacy of 'Race,'" in which he attacked the stereotyping of "races" and the use of skin colour as a method of classification. Its immediate impact was limited.

Despite anthropologists' efforts to block the rise of racial stereotyping, which was based to some degree on earlier "fringe" anthropological writings, not until the late 20th century did anthropologists finally shake off the stain of racial classifications. It is quite fitting that the physical sciences dispelled this myth of the "races," for it was after all from many of the early physical sciences that the supposedly empirical evidence for racial inequality had sprung. The physical sciences within anthropology had played a key role in influencing scholars, and the data from the physical sciences had been misused by racist thinkers to justify slavery and all sorts of discrimination.

Physical anthropology has made up for its earlier role in promoting racial categorization, with all the problems it generated. With advances in the field, and with a newer, postwar cohort of anthropologists, the idea of the "races" was approached from a biological perspective. It was now argued that there had always been gene flow and that there could be no such thing as a genetically homogenous population. Therefore, the term "pure race" was an absurdity. Indeed, genetic inbreeding is *harmful*, and lack of outside input on a genetic level can have negative effects on populations and individuals. Also, a limited gene pool makes it harder for natural selection to operate.

Anthropologists also directly addressed the question of skin colour and the other physical features that were believed to be characteristic of certain groups of people. To this end, the skills of paleoanthropologists were put to work and an explanation that went back millions of years was constructed:

The black skin of Africans, Australian Aborigines, and all peoples who live in sun-drenched lands was found to be due to the long exposure to sun and to natural selection killing off those who could not procreate sufficiently due to an inability to acclimatize. In the tropics, natural selection favours darker skin because such skin protects against overexposure to the sun and the skin cancer that results from this exposure. When humans migrated to sun-poorer regions in the north, dark skin was no longer needed to fend of solar radiation, but low vitamin D3 levels became a problem and light skin colour evolved (Harris 2004). Having dark skin in northern climes where the sun is weak can lead to a vitamin D deficiency, and this leads in turn to calcium deficiency and weak bones. Light skin lets more sunlight through, which leads to increased production of vitamin D3, which is necessary for calcium absorption and bone growth.** This prevents bone degeneration and the onset of rickets. Thus a person's skin colour is a reflection of the amount of time his or her ancestors spent in or outside of the tropics.

How does this happen genetically? Skin colour is influenced by hemoglobin, carotene, and melanin. Melanin comes in two types: phaeomelanin (red to yellow) and eumelanin (dark brown to black). Melanin is produced from the amino acid tyrosine; albinos lack the enzyme that generates that reaction. The colour of your skin is simply a matter of genetic ancestry, time, and environment. There is as much—usually *more*—variation between two people of the same "race" as there is between two people from completely different "races." An English person may share more genetic traits with a Hazda from Africa than with someone from Germany or Italy, depending on what genetically based characteristics (other than skin colour) are considered (Farley 2005, 6). The number of genes that code for the phenotypic expressions of lip, hair, and skin colour and so on are remarkably few.

They are simply not important, and they are a result of past exposure to specific environments and to the actions of natural selection and drift. Environment plus isolation, plus natural selection and time, led to the "races"—it is as simple as that: "Race is indeed a pre-eminently socio-historical concept. Racial categories and the meaning of race are given concrete expression by the specific social relations and historical context in which they are embedded" (Omi and Winant 2004, 11).

It has been said that beauty is skin deep, and to that, anthropologists can add that the essence of humanity, our "beauty," does not reside on the surface of our skins, which merely reflect past environments and genetic expressions. Many differences exist among peoples in the world today, and sometimes skin colour is conflated with other issues such as ethnicity, social class, politics, and culture (Eller 1999). While the use of racial thinking and classification remains a social practice, we can dismiss the idea that one's skin colour reflects anything substantial in relation to our mental abilities or any behavioural traits. Anthropology did have an early association with racial categorization, but it has strived to shake this off and to focus on what unites people, even while cataloguing their differences. Today, anthropologists recognize that the concept of "race" is culturally constructed according to economic, political, and social agendas, rather than biological realities. Finally, because human populations have been interbreeding for many thousands of years, there are no separate "races": we are all of one "race"—the human "race."

* The word "race" comes from the Old French *rasse*, from Italian *razza*, and from the Latin *generatio*, meaning "to beget." "Race" was historically defined in a myriad of ways by different scholars, who sometimes stressed different aspects of physiology. The approach followed here is taken from Satzewich and Liodakis (2010, 10) who state, "We use quotations around the term 'race' to denote that the term is a socially constructed category for classifying humans, with no real biological referent and . . . with little analytical, *sui generis*, value in the social sciences. In the past, the physical characteristics of humans that have been used to classify groups have included skin colour, eye colour, hair type, nose shape, lip shape, body hair, and cheek bone structure."

** Other factors are important in the evolution of skin colour, such as the amount of cloud cover and the diet of the people in question.

SOURCES: F. Boas, *Race and Democratic Society* (New York: J.J. Augustin, 1945); J.D. Eller, *From Culture to Ethnicity to Conflict: An Anthropological Perspective on International Ethnic Conflict* (Ann Arbor: University of Michigan Press, 1999); J. Farley, *Majority–Minority Relations* (Upper Saddle River: Pearson Prentice Hall, 2005); M. Harris, "How Our Skins Got Their Colour," in *Rethinking the Colour Line*, 7–9; J.H. Langdon, *The Human Strategy* (Oxford: Oxford University Press, 2005); M. Omi and H. Winant, "Racial Formations," in *Rethinking the Colour Line*, 7–9; V. Satzewich and N. Liodakis, *"Race" and Ethnicity in Canada* (Toronto: Oxford University Press, 2010); Seneca, *Moral Essays*, trans. John W. Basore, 3 vols. (Cambridge, MA: Harvard University Press, 1975). See also J. Huxley and A.C. Haddon, "The Racial Question—Theory and Fact," *Antiquity* 9 (1935): 261–76.

apartheid regime, and the genocide in Rwanda. It is important to point out that since racial categories have no validity, what we are really examining is ethnic discrimination and conflict. Still, the term "racism" is used to define these acts.

Canada has its own history of racial discrimination, such as the reservation system forced on First Nations peoples, the internment of the Japanese during the Second World War, the relocation of Blacks from Africville, the enactment of exclusionary laws against the Chinese, and, more recently, the backlash against immigrants from Muslim countries. The sad fact is that Canada suffers from institutionalized racism, or what has been called "democratic racism,"[9] and that it permeates virtually every aspect of Canadian life.

First Nations peoples were stripped of their land, and their traditional subsistence patterns were disrupted, which affected their ability to support themselves and led to poverty, loss of identity, and severe social problems. In a concerted effort to assimilate First Nations peoples into mainstream society, children were taken from their parents to live at residential schools, where they were forced

Tom Jackson is representative of First Nations people who are overcoming social, economic, and political barriers to achieve recognition and success in their chosen careers.

to learn the white man's ways. It has taken decades for First Nations peoples to overcome these obstacles, and only recently have they begun to acquire the resources—such as higher education—necessary to improve their economic and political situation. An increasing percentage, albeit still quite small, of First Nations young people are completing high school, attending university, and assuming professional careers in law, medicine, and business. A vibrant First Nations artistic and entertainment community has taken shape in Canada. However, as with African Americans in the United States, First Nations people are still disproportionately represented in the lower ranks of society. Says Phil Fontaine, the former National Chief of the Assembly of First Nations, "As far

environmental racism Racial discrimination in environmental policy making and the enforcement of regulations that lead to, for example, the targeting of specific communities for waste disposal, power stations, or toxic dumps.

as Aboriginal people are concerned, racism in Canadian society continues to invade our lives institutionally, systematically and individually."[10]

Only recently has Canada faced up to many of the racist acts of its past. In 2009, Prime Minister Stephen Harper offered an official apology to Aboriginal people regarding the residential schools, which had such a negative impact on Canada's indigenous people. The residential school system was not, however, an isolated case. An equally distressing episode of racial discrimination in Canada took place in 1964, when the people of Africville, Nova Scotia, were forcefully relocated and their homes were razed. Africville had been founded in 1838 on the northern edge of Halifax by the descendants of American slaves. The 400 residents lived in abysmal conditions—they were victims of what Denise Allen calls "**environmental racism**."[11] Basic necessities, such as running water, electricity, sewers, paved streets, and playgrounds for children were denied to Africville citizens. Halifax city officials repeatedly refused the people's petitions for these services, even though they collected taxes from the residents. Halifax citizens considered Africville an embarrassment and shunned the area. Over the years, several industries, unwanted in white neighbourhoods, were built near Africville, among them a dump, toxic waste disposal pits, a stone and coal crushing plant, a slaughterhouse, and a prison.

In 1947, Africville was rezoned for industrial and harbour development, and calls for the relocation of the residents intensified. The Baptist Church, the centre of the community, was destroyed even before the relocation began. In 1964, officials began the relocation in earnest. The people were forced from their homes and given $500 for relocation. Their belongings were transported away in garbage trucks, and the community was bulldozed in the middle of the night.

City officials claimed they were relocating the residents for humanitarian reasons—Africville was a slum, and the residents would enjoy opportunities for employment and education in their new location, as well as improved living conditions and racial integration. In reality, the agenda of these officials was mired in racism, and they destroyed the community for economic advantage and without consulting the people of Africville. Few of the promises they made were kept: Former residents of Africville continued to suffer socioeconomic disadvantage and lived in crowded public housing. Many were reduced to accepting social welfare. Young people had difficulty adjusting and became embroiled in criminal activity and alcohol and drug abuse. Pamela Brown calls the act of removing the people from Africville "urban removal,"[12] while others have labelled it communal ethnic cleansing.[13]

The people of Africville, Nova Scotia, lived in abysmal conditions brought on by systemic racism against African Canadians. The 1964 forced relocation of the citizens is a blight on Canadian history.

CP PHOTO / Halifax Chronicle Herald

The people of Africville had little education and low incomes and were chronically underemployed. Yet despite all their problems and the lack of services, their community was close-knit and they wanted to continue living in Africville. Removing them without considering either their wishes or the ramifications of doing so was an act of racism. Activist Denise Allen calls the urban removal "an unholy alliance by Government and the businesses it serves, to deliberately slaughter our community to death. . . . The destruction of Africville was part of an agenda that placed the accumulation of capital before people. The hopes and needs of Black citizens were apparently insignificant to government officials."[14]

When the people of Africville were forced out of their homes, they lost their community identity. Yet to this day, their memories of Africville continue to give them a sense of self and roots. Former residents hold summer gatherings at the park established by the federal government in 2002 to reaffirm their community identity. In recent years, calls for an apology and compensation for the residents of Africville have grown louder. As a further step in this process of recognition, in 2010 the mayor of Halifax apologized for the city's role in the demolishing of Africville.

Aboriginal people and African Canadians have both experienced terrible discrimination down through the years. In this they are joined by Chinese Canadians. In the 19th and 20th centuries, anti-Chinese sentiments ran high in British Columbia, and although over time this attitude has been tempered by growing social maturity among Canadian citizens, intolerance is evident to this day.[15]

One of the early problems was the perception that the Chinese were not permanent immigrants; instead, they were viewed as a short-term labour pool (sojourners)

and were expected to return to their homeland once the need for their labour disappeared. Racism against the Chinese began in the early period of immigration, between 1858 and 1923, in large part because of difficult economic times in British Columbia and the irrational fear that the Chinese were competitors for resources. Those Chinese working on railway construction were considered a necessary evil and were seen as little more than human horses or living pieces of machinery. The first anti-Chinese bill was passed in 1885 (soon after the CPR was finished), mostly to appease British Columbians, who considered the Chinese "a public menace." The civil rights of those Chinese already in Canada were curtailed between 1875 and 1923, culminating in the 1923 Chinese Immigration Act, which excluded Chinese from immigrating to Canada and legalized the inferior status of Chinese Canadians.

Besides being subjected to legal restrictions, Chinese immigrants faced violent racial hostility, as evidenced by the 1887 and 1907 anti-Chinese riots in Vancouver. Crowds of hooligans vandalized Chinese homes and tried to intimidate the Chinese into leaving. During the 1907 riot, slogans on banners read "A White Canada and No Cheap Asiatic Labor" and "White Canada— Patronize Your Own Race and Canada." In the minds of these rioters, patriotism meant defending a white Canada. Even children were not safe from the racists: calls for segregating Chinese children in a separate school were heard, and in 1922 Chinese children in the Victoria school system were segregated in one school, setting off a year-long boycott by Chinese parents that ended with the children returning to their regular schools.

Racism and discrimination against the Chinese was firmly entrenched in Canadian society by the time the Chinese Immigration Act was passed in 1923. Although this exclusionary period resulted in many social and familial hardships for Chinese immigrants, one of the most far-reaching consequences was that it jeopardized their ability to earn a decent living. Even when they were hired, they had to settle for lower wages than whites, and they were excluded from many occupations. The end result was that many Chinese set up their own businesses, mostly in the service sector.

There is no question that discrimination against the Chinese was based on race and that exclusionary laws were aimed at the Chinese as a racial group, whether they were citizens or not. Measures such as the $50 head tax—imposed on Chinese in 1885, and rising to $500 by 1903—were intended to control the number of Chinese immigrating to Canada. These measures prevented Chinese men from bringing their families to Canada. This sort of systematic discrimination is known as legally sanctioned or **institutionalized racism**. The underlying reason for institutionalized racism is to maintain a group of people on the margins of society, with little collective power, in order to maintain a ready supply of cheap labour.

Following the Second World War, many of the discriminatory laws against Chinese Canadians were rescinded. They were allowed to vote, and the Chinese Immigration Act was repealed in 1947, partly because China had been an ally during the war and it had become an embarrassment to discriminate against them, and partly because anti-Asian sentiments had shifted toward Japanese Canadians. Even so, Chinese immigrants were still considered second-class citizens and continued to experience social, economic, and residential segregation. Their response to the hostility and harassment was to retreat into their own ethnic enclaves and build isolated Chinese communities.

In 1962 the Canadian government changed the requirements for immigration, thereby opening the borders to Chinese and other immigrants. Soon after, further adjustments to immigration policies placed all immigrants on the same level, regardless of ethnic background. Many Chinese who came to Canada after 1962 were urbanites from Hong Kong and Taiwan, whose backgrounds were very different than those of earlier immigrants from rural mainland China.

Today, Chinese Canadians enjoy access to higher education and professional and technical occupations, which has led to upward mobility. But it would be naive to assume that race no longer creates barriers for Chinese

Canadians. Most of their upward mobility is owing to the changing socioeconomic situation in Canada, and periodic instances of discrimination remind Chinese Canadians that despite their accomplishments, they are still seen as foreigners by other Canadians. For example, a 1979 *W5* broadcast suggested that foreign students in Canada were taking away university openings that should have gone to qualified Canadian students. The program showed scenes of classrooms full of Chinese students, implying that the Chinese students were still foreigners, even though the students had been born in Canada, and indeed, many were fifth-generation Canadians. Protests from Canadian-born Chinese and the universities they attended later forced the network to issue an apology for the distorted statistics and stereotyping of all Chinese as foreigners.

The treatment of the Chinese is impossible for us to justify in the 21st century. Yet it is explainable (though not understandable) in part. The Chinese were visibly different from Euro-Canadians, they lived on the margins of Canadian society, and they exhibited some traditional behaviour that led mainstream Canadians to believe that the Chinese were culturally inferior. This perception allowed most Canadians to accept the injustices imposed on the Chinese. In other words, because the Chinese were so different, Canadians felt no affinity or empathy for their lot; it was as easy to ignore them as it was to ignore the plight of Canada's Aboriginal people.

Today, Muslim Canadians are dealing with similar hostility, suspicions, and restrictions on their personal freedoms as a backlash against Muslims following the 9/11 terrorist attacks. Several hate crimes, such as the June 12, 2006, attack on a Muslim cleric in Montreal by a knife-wielding man asking if he wanted to "die a martyr,"[16] and the vandalism of an Islamic school in Mississauga, Ontario, on June 7, 2006,[17] are evidence of increasing distrust and hostility toward Muslim Canadians. Notwithstanding the seriousness of individual attacks, the pervasive mistrust of the Muslim community may do even more to damage the sense of well-being and belonging that Muslims enjoyed in Canada before 9/11. The fear of backlash against Canadian Muslims increased dramatically when several would-be terrorists were arrested in Toronto in June 2006 for allegedly plotting to bomb Canadian petroleum facilities. Some Muslims now say they live in fear because of the way others link their religious beliefs to terrorism.

institutionalized racism Legally sanctioned restrictions based on the ideology that whites are biologically and socially superior to nonwhites.

social class A category of individuals who enjoy equal or nearly equal prestige according to the evaluation system.

Class and Caste

A **social class** may be defined as a category of individuals of equal or nearly equal prestige according to the system of evaluation. The qualification "nearly equal"

iStockphoto

Homeless people are a common feature of stratified societies; Canada and the United States, for example, have in recent years seen the growth of a caste-like underclass.

is important, for a certain amount of inequality may arise even within a given class. Canada is a class society, with labels such as upper, middle, and lower class generally tied to income levels. The class that people belong to is earned through endeavour or **achieved status**. Canadians experience unequal access to education and employment opportunities based on gender, ethnicity, and age, which often determine wealth and ensuing status.

A **caste** is a particular kind of social class—one with a fairly fixed or impermeable membership. Castes are strongly endogamous, so that offspring are automatically members of their parents' caste. This is known as **ascribed status**. The classic case is the caste system of India. Coupled with strict endogamy and membership by descent in Hindu castes is an association of particular castes with specific occupations and customs. Such customs include food habits and styles of dress, along with rituals involving notions of purity and impurity. The literally thousands of castes are organized into a hierarchy of four named categories, at the top of which are the priests, or *Brahmins*, the bearers of universal order and values and of highest ritual purity. Below them are the powerful—although less pure—warriors. Dominant at the local level, besides fulfilling warrior functions, they control all village lands. Furnishing services to the landowners, and owning the tools of their trades, are two lower ranking, landless caste groups: artisans and labourers. At the bottom of the system, owning neither land nor the tools of their trade, are the outcasts, or "untouchables." In India, these people are considered the most impure of all, although they constitute a large labour pool at the beck

and call of those who control economic and political affairs—the landholding warrior caste.

Although some argue that the term "caste" should be restricted to the Indian situation, others find this usage much too narrow, since caste-like situations are known elsewhere in the world. In South Africa, for example, although the situation is now changing, blacks traditionally were relegated to a low-ranking stratum in society; until recently, they were barred by law from marrying nonblacks and could not hold property except to a limited degree in specified "black homelands." Most blacks still perform menial jobs for whites, but even the small cadre of middle-class blacks that exist were until recently prohibited from living where whites do, or even swimming in the same water or holding the hand of someone who was white. These restrictions resemble the concept of purity and impurity found in the Hindu caste system; in South Africa, whites feared pollution of their purity through improper contact with blacks.

Social classes also are manifested through **patterns of association**: not just who interacts with whom but also how and in what context. In Western society, informal, friendly relations take place mostly within our own class. Relations with members of other classes tend to be less informal and occur in the context of specific situations. For example, a corporate executive and a janitor normally are members of different social classes. They may have frequent contact with each other, but it occurs in the setting of the corporate office and usually requires certain stereotyped behavioural patterns.

Another way that social classes are manifested is through **symbolic indicators**. Included here are activities and possessions indicative of class. For example, in North American society, symbolic indicators include occupation (a garbage collector has different class status than a physician); wealth (rich people generally are in a higher social class than poor people); dress (designer or discount); form of recreation (upper-class people are expected to play golf rather than shoot pool down at the pool hall—though they can shoot pool at home or

achieved status Status an individual earns.

caste A special form of social class in which membership is determined by birth and remains fixed for life.

ascribed status Status people are born into.

patterns of association Whom we associate with and in what context, reflecting social class.

symbolic indicators In a stratified society, activities and possessions indicative of social class.

∞ *The Anthropologist's World* ∞

Respecting the Elders

Liam Kilmurray

A new Israeli political party led by a 79-year-old retired spy is shaking up the balance of power after winning seven seats in the country's parliament. The Pensioners' Party's surprisingly strong showing could make them a player in forming the centrist Kadima party's ruling coalition. (Westervelt, NPR radio)

That dramatic announcement, made on Israeli radio on April 2, 2006, set the scene for what was to become a major pensioners' movement that erupted in Israel and that has since gained a foothold in parts of eastern Europe. Leading individuals, often with storied lives, are gathering pensioners around political issues and uniting them into a political force. Such a thing is a rare event in contemporary times. In many parts of the world, the elders, those aged and sometimes infirm members of society, are often presumed to reside in retirement homes and are socially "excommunicated," as noted by Hiam Hazan (1990). Depending on their income and that of their family network, they can live out their lives either in relative comfort or in abject poverty.

Gerontology (the study of elders) is a vibrant subfield in anthropology. It encompasses research ranging from Neolithic ancestral tombs to the health of 21st-century pensioners. There is evidence that in prehistory, elders were treated with special attention, at least in death. The burial rites of the rare individual who lived past 40 are often different from those of any other burial. Such was the case with the "old man of Skateholm"—who some 6,000 years ago lived to the ripe age of 60. This would have been exceptionally rare for those times, and in recognition of this fact his burial rites contrasted with those of everyone else: cremation rather than inhumation (Tilley 1996, 35). Indeed, ancestor cults likely extend much deeper into the past, perhaps as far back as Palaeolithic times in Europe, some 40,000 years ago.

Much of the world in recent times has experienced the aging of the workforce. This, combined with reductions in social services and market swings, has left many of the world's elderly in a perilous state. The issue has become a political talking point. Old people have traditionally participated in elections much more than younger people and are more inclined to join political organizations (Healey 2010). The contemporary Western world seems fixated on youth, evidenced through ceaseless media depictions of young actors, models, and musicians of all genders. Contrasted with this is the "position of the old person as a defenceless potential victim" (Hazan 1990, 79).

The recent appearance of "grey-interest" parties across Europe has raised eyebrows in many academic quarters (Walker 1998). Such parties have traditionally focused on single social issues and have generally not been political. Old people across the world usually vote for a variety of political parties based on issues that go beyond age. Recently, however, these elders have not simply voted along traditional political lines, but have organized their own political parties. In Israel, the subject of the elderly, including their depiction in the media, has been an area of inquiry for some time (Hazan 1990). It is in Israel, as noted earlier, that a broad-focused political party of pensioners has emerged. This new political entity, known as Gil, stood in the crucial and charged 2006 elections for the Israeli Knesset. The results were startling: while Kadima won the 2006 elections, taking 22 percent of the vote and 29 Knesset seats, the mighty Likud Party was reduced to 9 percent and 12 seats. However, Gil, the "pensioners' party," took 7 seats with 6 percent of the vote. Given the complex nature of Israeli politics, the Gil bloc has the opportunity to be highly influential.

Developments like these may mark a change in the way we view old people, specifically in Western nations. While it has long been known that elders are treated with great respect in Aboriginal cultures the world over, this is not usually the case in what we consider modern or developed nations. Far from burying one's dead beneath ancient floorboards, as some prehistoric Europeans or people at Çatal Hüyük did, North Americans have distanced death, taken it away from the house, and isolated it in marked-off hospices and cemeteries. In this manner, the elderly become just one step away from such isolation.

At the end of October 2011, the world population hovers around the 7 billion mark, and of this number, some 516 million are over 65. That is just 7.6 percent of the world's population (UN), but that percentage is growing rapidly as the world's birthrate falls. Although a minority, old people are politically more active than other population segments. The grey-interest parties should perhaps be taken seriously, researchers argue. The success of Gil in Israel may be a warning that the future might just belong to the old, who will drive the political agenda for years to come.

This is witnessed also with the emergence of other elder organizations, such as The Elders, who include eminent political and cultural figures such as Desmond Tutu, Nelson Mandela, Jimmy Carter, and Kofi Annan (http://www.theelders.org). Organizations such as The Elders and Gil may force the issues of elderly people onto the political agenda, bringing the ancestors back into the light. Anthropological examination of the old, whether in contemporary or ancient times, is a valuable contribution to our understanding of human societies. It teaches us that our lives span generations and that the elders are an essential part of society.

SOURCES: Eric Westervelt, Nation Public Radio, April 2, 2006, http://www.npr.org/templates/story/story.php?storyId=5318404; S. Hanley, "The Emergence of Pensioners' Parties in Contemporary Europe," in *Young Generation Under Pressure? The Financial Situation and the "Rush Hour" of the Cohorts 1970–1985 in a Generational Comparison*, ed. Joerg Chet Tremmel (Berlin: Springer Verlag, 2010), 225–44; H. Hazan, "Victim into Sacrifice: The Construction of the Old as a Symbolic Type," *Journal of Cross-Cultural Gerontology* 5 (1990): 77–84; C. Tilley, *An Ethnography of the Neolithic* (Cambridge: Cambridge University Press, 1996); A. Walker, "Speaking for Themselves: The New Politics of Old Age in Europe," *Education and Ageing* 13, no. 1 (1998): 13–36; United Nations, Population Division, "World Population Ageing 1950–2050," http://www.un.org/esa/population/publications/worldageing19502050/pdf/90chapteriv.pdf; http://www.theelders.org.

Symbolic indicators of class or caste include factors of lifestyle, such as the kind of housing we live in.

in a club); residential location (large houses in upscale neighbourhoods or smaller houses in older neighbourhoods); material possessions (car model); and so on. The fact is that all sorts of status symbols indicate class position, including such measures as the number of bathrooms in an individual's house. At the same time, symbolic indicators may be cruder reflections of class position than verbal indicators or patterns of association. One reason is that access to wealth may not be entirely restricted to upper classes, so that individuals can buy symbols suggestive of upper-class status whether or not this really is their status. To take an extreme example, the head of an organized crime ring may display more of the symbols of high-class status than members of old, established upper-class families. For that matter, someone from an upper class may choose a simpler lifestyle than is customary. Instead of driving a Mercedes, he or she may drive a beat-up Volkswagen.

While cultural anthropologists catalogue the ways in which the differences between social classes are manifested and represented, another branch of anthropology—ecological anthropology—speculates on emerging genetic differences between classes. This is not in any way a revival of eugenic thought; rather, it is a warning that the growing disparities in wealth between the social classes may end up having an evolutionary impact. Life is apt to be less hard for members of an upper class as opposed to a lower class. This shows up in a tendency toward lower infant mortality and longer life expectancy for the upper class. Another tendency is for greater physical stature and robustness among upper-class people, the result of better diet and protection from serious illness in their juvenile years. Charles L. Harper contends that in "industrialized cultures, selection processes operate

more on socioeconomic factors, and these factors influence the genetic makeup of populations."[18] This is a provocative statement, meant to highlight the emerging differences in health care and diet between the classes. But it serves as a signal that the growing chasm between social classes may not be limited to patterns of association or symbolic indicators.

Mobility

All stratified societies offer at least some **mobility**, and this helps ease the strains in any system of inequality. Even the Hindu caste system, with its tight restrictions, has a surprising amount of flexibility and mobility, not all of it associated with the recent changes that "modernization" has brought to India. As a rather dramatic case in point, in the state of Rajasthan, those who own and control most of the land and who are wealthy and politically powerful are not of the warrior caste, but of the lowest caste. Their tenants and labourers, by contrast, are Brahmins. Thus, the group ritually superior to all others finds itself in the same social position as untouchables, whereas the landowners who are the Brahmins' ritual inferiors are superior in all other ways. Meanwhile, a group of leather workers in the untouchable category have gained political power in India's new democracy and are trying to better their position by claiming that they are Brahmins who were tricked in the past into doing defiling work. Although individuals cannot move up or down the caste hierarchy, whole groups can do so depending on claims they can make for higher status and on how well they can manipulate others into

mobility The ability to change one's class position.

acknowledging their claims. Interestingly, the people at the bottom of India's caste system traditionally have not questioned the validity of the system itself so much as their particular position within it. They are, however, increasingly organizing into caste-based political parties to pursue political and economic improvements, often with violent results.

With their limited mobility, caste-structured groups exemplify **closed-class systems**. Those that permit a great deal of mobility are referred to as **open-class systems**. Even here, however, mobility is apt to be fairly limited. In North America, in spite of the "rags to riches" ideology, most mobility involves a move up or down only a notch, although if this continues in a family for several generations, it may add up to major changes.

Gender Stratification

Gender stereotypes are preconceived ideas or guidelines regarding what behaviours and roles are considered feminine or masculine. It is our culture's gender stereotypes, not biological differences, that channel us into our various gender roles. Thus, gender stratification is culturally defined. Accordingly, the status of women varies from one culture to another. Status inequality between men and women is known as **gender stratification**. Like social stratification, gender stratification includes unequal access to wealth, power, and prestige.

Inequality between genders manifests itself in many ways. Anthropologists measure the status of women within cultural groups according to the kinds of social and political positions they hold, the economic importance and cultural value attached to their work, and the control they have over their own bodies (e.g., the right to practise birth control). Yet such measurements do not tell the whole story, because religious, political, economic, and social factors often come into play.

Social scientists have grappled with the question of why virtually all groups practise some degree of gender inequality. Two factors are generally focused on: economics

In Canada, the ability to move up in the system of stratification is increasingly dependent on access to higher education.

and warfare. The control of production strategies and resources may be a primary factor in gender inequality. In cultures where men monopolize production, they tend to be the dominant gender, even if women contribute significantly to the family's economic well-being. The key is *control*. The gender that controls production and distribution of material goods will dominate a group. Even in relatively egalitarian cultures, such as food-foraging groups, men control the distribution of highly prized meat and as a result have more power and a higher status. In other cultures where women have some control over the distribution of resources, they tend to enjoy more status. This explanation raises a question: Why is it men rather than women who so often control production and distribution of a group's resources? The answer appears to lie in the division of labour: Women tend to spend most of their time inside the home completing domestic and child care duties, while men spend most of their time outside the home, hunting (providing

closed-class systems Stratified societies that severely restrict social mobility.

open-class systems Stratified societies that permit a great deal of social mobility.

gender stratification Unequal access to wealth, power, and prestige, which results in a disadvantaged, subordinate position for women.

The hijab worn by these Muslim women is seen as a symbol of female oppression by outsiders, but as an expression of faith and ethnic identity by those who wear them.

meat), clearing fields (distributing land), or working as wage earners (providing income). Although this explanation may fit with earlier times in Western society when women routinely remained in the home, it hardly fits with a hunter-gatherer lifestyle, where the women gather food outside the home as much as or more than men and rely on older children or aged parents to care for small children. Indeed, women in foraging cultures usually enjoy nearly equal status with the men. In contemporary Western society, women have the opportunity to work outside the domestic sphere, and this has increased their status significantly, although in many cases they still do not receive the same rewards as men in the form of higher status positions and monetary compensation. For example, in 2003, Canadian women who worked full-time earned 71 cents for every dollar their male counterparts earned.[19]

A second explanation suggests that men who are regularly involved in warfare, as is witnessed among the Yanomami, bring their aggression home, where women consequently tend to defer to them. A higher value is placed on sons (future warriors), and women are viewed merely as bearers of sons or as a bargaining chip with other groups. Yet in groups where the men spent extended periods of time outside the village at war, such as the 18th-century Iroquois, the women appeared to have experienced a higher status.

The discussion of *purdah* in the following Gender Perspectives box illustrates the difficulty of measuring and interpreting gender stratification from another's perspective.

Ethnic Stratification

Whereas the concept of race is based on fallacious reasoning, ethnicity is a reliable concept. As we saw in Chapter 2, ethnicity is derived from a sense of shared

Gender Perspectives

Purdah

Hidden beneath voluminous folds of black cloth, women silently move through Muslim society, an enigmatic mystery to most Westerners. These women are observing the ancient custom of *purdah,* or female seclusion, which requires women past the age of puberty to wear concealing clothing outside the home. Interpretation of the Quran's exhortation for modest dress varies considerably. Some Muslim women believe they need only dress conservatively; others believe they must conceal their entire bodies, even to gloved hands and veiled faces. Geraldine Brooks offers firsthand observations of this diversity as she saw it in the Cairo airport:

> *Women from Pakistan, on their way to jobs in the Gulf, floated by in their deliciously comfortable* salwar kameez—*silky tunics drifting low over billowing pants with long shawls of matching fabric tossed loosely over their heads. Saudi women trod carefully behind their husbands, peering from behind gauzy face veils and 360-degree black cloaks that made them look, as Guy de Maupassant once wrote, "like death out for a walk." Afghani women also wore 360-degree coverings, called* chadris—*colorful crinkly shrouds with an oblong of embroidered lattice work over the eyes. Women from Dubai wore stiff, birdlike masks of black and gold that beaked over the nose but left their luminous, treacle-colored eyes exposed.*

Some Palestinians and Egyptians wore dull-colored, floor-length button-through coats and white headscarves; others wore bright calf-length skirts with matching scarves held in place by headbands of seed pearls.

Seclusion goes beyond wearing concealing garments, headscarves, and veils; under the rules of *purdah* women must be kept isolated from males to preserve their modesty. Among the Pakhtun of Swat, Pakistan, women seldom leave their homes. If they do, they are always in the company of other women or a male relative. They avoid contact with unknown men for fear others will think the meeting sexual. In earlier times, if a woman broke *purdah* she risked mutilation, such as having her nose cut off, or being killed by her husband to restore his honour. In some urban centres, such as Cairo, *purdah* is not as strictly enforced; many educated women choose modest Western clothing and a simple head covering, and most have the freedom to visit friends, shop, and generally enjoy their independence. However, a recent resurgence of *purdah* has been noted among these women as a way to reaffirm their Muslim beliefs and traditions.

Westerners tend to view *purdah* as a symbol of Middle Eastern patriarchy, female oppression, and the male supremacy ideology central to Middle Eastern male identity. This is not entirely accurate; many Muslim women wish to wear their traditional garb, even after immigrating to North America. *Purdah* is seen as a protection from the outside world, from prying eyes, and from unwanted sexual advances. Katherine

Bullock found that many Muslim women view their traditional dress code as a sign of "'purity,' 'modesty,' a 'woman's Islamic identity,' and . . . 'submission to God and a testament that you're Muslim.' Halima, a convert to Islam, adds that Hijab symbolizes 'the woman's power to take back her own dignity and her own sexuality.'"

In Canada, a Muslim woman's right to wear traditional garb has been repeatedly challenged. In 1995, several students were expelled from a Quebec high school when they refused to remove their headscarves. Young Muslim women have reported hostile encounters with Canadians who have protested their dress, angrily accusing them of setting back the women's movement with such traditions. Muslim women appear confused by these actions, as the following statement attests: "If Canada boasts you can practice your religious freedom of thought and beliefs, if a woman believes she should wear her Hijab why shouldn't she? She's not hurting anybody, I mean if people can go down Yonge Street [Toronto] almost naked, why should her putting a scarf on her head bother people, even for that matter wearing a veil on [her] face, why should that upset somebody?" (Bullock, p. 7)

SOURCES: G. Brooks, *Nine Parts of Desire: The Hidden World of Islamic Women* (New York: Anchor Books, 1994), 21–22; K. Bullock, "You Don't Have to Wear That in Canada," 2001, http://www.themodernreligion.com/women/hijab-canada.htm, accessed March 13, 2001; C. Lindholm and C. Lindholm, "Life Behind the Veil," in *The Gender Reader,* 2nd ed., ed. E. Ashton-Jones, G.A. Olson, and M.G. Perry (Needham Heights: Allyn and Bacon, 2000); S. Smith, "The World of Women," in *Families in Multicultural Perspective,* ed. B.B. Ingoldsby and S. Smith (New York: The Guilford Press, 1995).

identity and common cultural features. Outsiders readily identify members of an ethnic group by their language, dress, cuisine, and religious practices. Yet ethnicity is not fixed; it is constantly changing in reaction to new circumstances (e.g., immigration to a new country like Canada), and no ethnic group is entirely homogeneous.

Canada is a pluralistic society, with members coming from virtually every corner of the world. Ideally, when people immigrate to Canada they are free to retain their own culture while enjoying the benefits of becoming members of Canadian society. In reality, though, new Canadians are somewhat expected to conform to or assimilate into the dominant culture, through language, behaviour, clothing, and so on. An individual or group who fails to do so may run the risk of being considered an outsider. A second difficulty pertains to visible minorities, who constituted 16.2 percent of the Canadian population in 2006 and who represent between 30 to 50 percent of the population in cities such as Toronto, Vancouver, and Montreal. However, because they are and always will be physically different, they always will be considered separate from white Canadians, however much they adapt their behaviour. Linked to these considerations is the concept of multiculturalism, Canada's official policy since 1971, which recognizes no dominant official culture but regards all cultures as equal.[20] As of yet, multicultural policies in Canada have failed to eliminate racial and ethnic inequality, instead creating only superficial harmony. Nor do most ethnic groups have the power and resources to promote their cultural heritage. For example, even though language schools are common in Canada, with very few exceptions the language of instruction in regular schools is either French or English.[21]

The history of Canadian immigration is rife with discrimination and ethnic intolerance. Initially, two ethnic groups moved to Canada—the French and the English. Later waves of immigration brought people from Ireland, Scotland, and eastern and southern European countries, Asia, and, more recently, the Caribbean and Latin America. Most of these groups have, to varying degrees, experienced discrimination, exploitation, and unequal access to opportunities within Canada. When Ukrainians began immigrating to Canada more than a century ago, many Canadians greeted them less than enthusiastically, some even demanding that Slavic peoples be excluded from Canada. An article that appeared in the May 13, 1901, *Winnipeg Telegram* illustrates the prevailing attitude toward Ukrainians at that time:

> That there are few people who will affirm that Slavonic immigrants are desirable settlers, or that they are welcomed by the white people of Western Canada. . . . Those whose ignorance is impenetrable, whose customs are repulsive, whose civilization is primitive, and whose character and morals are justly condemned, are surely not the class of immigrants which the country's paid immigration agents should seek

> to attract. Better by far to keep our land for the children, children's children, of Canadians than to fill up the country with the scum of Europe.[22]

Ukrainians, like other immigrants, were paid lower wages than other workers, and they worked in wretched and often dangerous conditions. During the First World War, Ukrainians, as well as Bulgarians, Poles, Serbians, Germans, Croatians, Italians, and Jews, were declared "enemy aliens."[23] Nearly 6,000 Ukrainians were interned in one of two dozen internment camps throughout Canada between 1914 and 1920. Thousands of others had to report to the police and carry identity papers with them. Foreign language use was banned. Many lost their right to vote in the 1917 federal election, were not allowed to join the Canadian Armed Forces, and faced public persecution and discrimination. By 1918, French and English Canadians were clamouring for the deportation of all these "foreigners." The internees were used as forced labourers to develop Banff National Park and work in the mines of British Columbia, the steel mills of Ontario and Nova Scotia, and the lumber camps of northern Ontario and Quebec. The program so benefited Canadian corporations and the government that the internment continued on for two years after the end of the First World War. Why were such drastic measures taken? Was it wartime xenophobia, bigotry against a new immigrant population, or the economic benefits of a forced-labour system? Likely a combination of these factors contributed to the internment of Ukrainians—setting a precedent for the 1941 internment of Japanese Canadians.[24] The fact that much of the foregoing is not very well known among a younger generation of Canadians illustrates the hidden yet pervasive nature of systemic racism.

Anthropologists do not shirk from such data or from criticizing the past or present practices of their own governments. It is generally recognized that Canada is a liberal nation that is open to many immigrants and that is usually, despite some problems, committed to equality and multiculturalism. Yet gaining acceptance in Canada has been a long struggle for many different groups. Today these diverse groups, such as African Canadians and Chinese and Japanese, have become respected, successful citizens of Canada. They have achieved this through hard work and through the processes of both adapting to Canadian customs and maintaining their cultural and ethnic legacies. They contribute to the Canada of today—and to its social stratification.

Chapter Summary

1.   What principles besides kinship and marriage do people use to organize societies?

People group themselves by gender, age, common interest, and position to address problems that are not dealt with through marriage, the family, or descent groups. Also, some groups within a culture may employ stratification to gain preferential treatment for themselves and their followers at the expense of other groups. All cultures categorize people according to gender, the division of labour, or age grouping. Age grades exist in some parts of the world. These are usually groups of people organized by gender and age.

2.   What are common-interest associations?

Common-interest associations have emerged to deal with particular problems in stratified societies. They have existed since the beginning of farming several thousand years ago. They are found in areas where rapid social change and urbanization have occurred. These associations have replaced social organization based on kinship or age groups. Membership in such groups can be voluntary or compulsory.

3.   What is social stratification?

Stratification is the division of society into two or more groups of people who do not have equal access to wealth, power, or prestige. Groups may be stratified along the lines of age, gender, class, ethnicity, or race. Social stratification ranks people relative to one another. The lower ranks normally have limited wealth, power, and prestige. The members of stratified society therefore possess different degrees of inequality. This differs from egalitarian cultures, where equality in wealth, power, and status are the norm. Two theories attempt to explain the presence of stratification: the functionalist theory and the conflict theory. Functionalists argue that inequalities are necessary to maintain the functioning of complex societies, whereas conflict theorists believe there is a constant struggle between lower and upper classes.

4.   What is the validity of race as a social category?

The issue of race has a long and complex history in anthropology. In past and present societies, it has often been used as a basis for racism or racial stratification. Generally, racism is the belief that some races are inferior to others. In contemporary anthropology, race is no longer used to categorize people; rather, it is recognized as a social construct. Race is often associated with other categories, such as caste and ethnicity, as the basis for grouping people into different categories.

Questions for Critical Thought

1. Are you a part of an age group as described in this chapter? If so, how does it define itself, and what are its functions?

2. Have you had an experience that made you aware of certain behaviours stemming from social stratification? Where did this occur? What was your role in the encounter? How aware of it were you at the time? Did it seem out of place, or was it an appropriate interaction?

3. Gender stratification still exists in Canada. Provide some examples of gender stratification that you have witnessed or experienced in Canadian society.

4. Research an ethnic group (preferably your own) and determine what, if any, discrimination members have experienced since immigrating to Canada. How did these immigrants overcome the limitations that discrimination placed on their lives?

5. Since 9/11, Muslims have experienced increasing discrimination. Why is it that humans tend to stereotype an entire group of people based on the actions of a few? Have your attitudes toward ordinary Muslim Canadians changed since 9/11? Explain your feelings.

Internet Resources

Women's Issues in the Third World

http://www.globalissues.org/HumanRights/ WomensRights.asp

A large website with many useful links to topics such as child marriages, honour killings, the feminization of poverty, and human rights. Also has links to specific regions and countries of the world where issues of women's rights are considered.

You Don't Have to Wear That in Canada

http://www.themodernreligion.com/women/ hijab-canada.htm

A thoughtful piece on the issues faced by female Muslim immigrants to Canada regarding restrictions and discrimination they face in Canada because they choose to wear the hijab. Of particular importance is the discussion of why Muslim women wear the hijab.

Ukrainians Want Acknowledgement of Injustice

http://www.infoukes.com/history/internment/ booklet02/doc-040.html

This article appeared in the University of Western Ontario's *Gazette*. It addresses the internment in Canada of Ukrainians during the First World War and suggests that Canada should make redress.

Women: Still Something to Shout About

http://www.newint.org/issue270/270keynote.html

This site presents the view that widening gaps between the rich and the poor are a ruthless killer, especially of women and children. An interesting summary of the rampant poverty and inequality in the world today.

The Hindu Caste System

http://www.hindubooks.org/sudheer_birodkar/hindu_history/castevedic.html

This site provides a comprehensive, historical look at the caste system in India. Also provides links to other sites on Hinduism, Christianity, and Islam.

http://www.idsn.org

Home page of the International Dalit Solidarity Network (IDSN). IDSN works on a global level for the elimination of caste discrimination and similar forms of discrimination based on work and descent.

Suggested Readings

For a list of suggested readings, visit the textbook's website at **http://www.havilandcultural4e.nelson.com**.

Notes

1. National Advisory Council on the Status of Women.

2. R.B. Lee, *The Dobe Ju/'hoansi*, 3rd ed. (Toronto: Nelson Thomson Learning, 2003).

3. J. Johnson, "Saskatchewan Population Sinking," *The Star Phoenix* (Saskatoon), Marxh 14, 2001.

4. D.A. Counts and D.R. Counts, *Over the Next Hill: An Ethnography of RVing Seniors in North America* (Peterborough: Broadview Press, 1998).

5. S. Fedorak, *Anthropology Matters!* (Peterborough: Broadview Press, 2007).

6. http://www.nativewomens.com

7. The following discussion is adapted from K. Davis and W.E. Moore, "Some Principles of Stratification," in *Social Stratification: Class, Race, and Gender in Sociological Perspective,* ed. D.B. Grusky (Boulder: Westview Press, 2001), 55–64.

8. D. McLellan, *Karl Marx: Selected Writings* (Oxford: Oxford University Press, 2000).

9. F. Henry and C. Tator, *The Colour of Democracy: Racism in Canadian Society* (Toronto: Nelson, 2006), 22.

10. P. Fontaine, "Modern Racism in Canada," Donald Gow Lecture, School of Policy Studies, Queen's University, Kingston, 1998, http://www.queensu.ca/sps/events/lectures/donald_gow/98lecture.pdf.

11. D. Allen, "Lessons from Africville," *Shunpiking,* September 6, 2001, http://www.shunpiking.com/bhs/Lessons%20from%20Africville.htm.

12. P. Brown, "Africville: Urban Removal in Canada," 1996, http://www.hartford-hwp.com/archives/44/170.html, accessed February 20, 2007.

13. K. Petersen, "The Ethnic Cleansing of Africville: Identity Politics in Canada," 2004, http://www.dissidentvoice.org/Mar04/Petersen0329.htm, accessed February 20, 2007.

14. Allen, "Lessons from Africville."

15. The following examination of racial discrimination against Chinese Canadians is taken from P.S. Li, *The Chinese in Canada* (Toronto: Oxford University Press, 1988).

16. CBC News, "Toronto Man Attacked in Hate Crime in Canada," June 12, 2006, http://pluralism.org/news/view/13488, accessed February 25, 2007.

17. *Mississauga News,* "Islamic School Vandalized in Mississauga (Canada)," June 7, 2006, http://pluralism.org/news/view/13480, accessed February 25, 2007.

18. C.L. Harper, *Environment and Society* (Toronto: Pearson/Prentice Hall, 2008).

19. Statistics Canada, "Women in Canada," *The Daily,* March 7, 2006, http://www.statcan.ca/Daily/English/060307/d060307a.htm, accessed February 18, 2007.

20. A. Fleras and J.L. Elliot, *Engaging Diversity: Multiculturalism in Canada* (Toronto: Nelson Thomson, 2002), 16.

21. Li, *The Chinese in Canada.*

22. B. Cherney, "Ukrainian Immigration," October 28, 2000, http://www.mbnet.mb.ca/~rfmorris/featuring/immigration/ukrainian.immigration.html, accessed March 13, 2001.

23. C. Gruske, "Ukrainians Want Acknowledgement of Injustice," *The Gazette,* February 3, 1989, http://www.infoukes.com/history/internment/booklet02/doc-040.html, accessed March 13, 2001.

24. G.W. Kakodyniak, "Internment of Ukrainians in Canada 1914–1920," 1998, http://www.infoukes.com/history/internment, accessed October 19, 2003.

11 Political Organization and the Maintenance of Order

AFP/Getty Images

Dakar, Senegal: A Canadian soldier adjusts the national flag on an armoured vehicle shortly after his arrival at Dakar airport, Senegal, July 29, 2005. Canadian soldiers travel to Sudan to restore peace in the war torn Darfur region. According to UN estimates, between 180,000 and 300,000 people died in the region after early 2003, as rebels and government forces, along with proxy militias, stepped up their offensives. More than two million people have been displaced.

KEY QUESTIONS

1. What Is Political Organization?

In anthropology, political organization refers to the means a culture uses to maintain order internally and manage its affairs with other cultures externally. Such organization may be relatively uncentralized and informal, as in bands and tribes, or centralized and formal, as in chiefdoms and states.

2. How Is Order Maintained Within a Culture?

Social controls may be internalized—"built into" individuals—or externalized in the form of sanctions. Built-in controls rely on deterrents such as personal shame and fear of supernatural punishment. Positive sanctions encourage approved behaviour, while negative sanctions discourage disapproved behaviour. Negative sanctions formalized and enforced by an authorized political body are called laws. Similarly, cultures do not maintain order through law alone.

3. How Is Order Maintained Between Cultures?

Just as the threatened or actual use of force may maintain order within a culture, it also may manage affairs among bands, lineages, clans, or other autonomous political units. Not all cultures rely on force, because some do not practise warfare as we know it. Such cultures have views of themselves and their place in the world quite different from those characteristic of centrally organized states.

4. How Do Political Systems Obtain People's Allegiance?

A political organization cannot function without the loyalty of those it governs. To a greater or lesser extent, political organizations use religion to legitimize their power. In uncentralized systems people give loyalty and cooperation because everyone participates in making decisions. Centralized systems rely in part on force and coercion, although these may lessen the system's effectiveness. Legitimacy, achieved through consent, is always the most cost-effective form of rule.

"I am the state." With this sweeping statement, Louis XIV declared absolute rule over France, becoming not just its king but its lawmaker, its court, its judge, its jailer, and its executioner—in short, the seat of all political power in France. Pierre Trudeau said "Just watch me" before introducing martial law in Quebec in 1970. In a sense, both these leaders saw themselves as above the law.

Louis XIV took a great deal of responsibility on his royal shoulders; had he actually performed each of these functions, he would have been doing the work of thousands of people, the number required to keep the machinery of a large political organization such as a state running. As a political organization, the 17th-century French state was not much different from those that exist in modern times. All large states require elaborate centralized structures, with hierarchies of executives, legislators, and judges who initiate, pass, and enforce laws that affect large numbers of people.

Complex centralized political structures are a product of mainly the 17th and 18th centuries. In 1500, Europe was home to around 500 political entities. By 1900 that number had been reduced to 30 or so. The map of the world changed again dramatically between 1990 and 2010. Outside the developed world, some cultural groups depend on far less formal organization. In cultures such as the Hadzabe, flexible and informal kinship systems prevail, with leaders who lack coercive power. Among groups such as the Mbuti, problems such as homicide and theft are perceived as serious "family quarrels" rather than as affairs affecting the entire community. Between these two polarities of political organization lies a world of variety, including cultures with chiefs, Big Men, and charismatic leaders, as well as segmented tribes with multicentric authority systems. Such diversity prompts this question: What is political organization?

The term "political organization" refers to the way power is distributed and embedded in a cultural group, whether it involves organizing a net hunt or passing legislation. In other words, political organization is linked to the way power is used to coordinate and regulate behaviour so that order is maintained. Political organization is an important component of

band A small group of related households occupying a particular region who gather periodically but do not yield their sovereignty to the larger collective.

human behaviour. But we should resist the temptation to restrict our examination to military or police structures—this is neither the only aspect of political organization nor even its most important one. Some form of political organization exists in all human groups.

KINDS OF POLITICAL SYSTEMS

Political organization is the means a human group uses to maintain social order and reduce social disorder. It assumes a variety of forms among the peoples of the world, but scholars have simplified this complex subject by identifying four basic kinds of political systems: uncentralized bands and tribes, and centralized chiefdoms and states. The following discussion is in no way meant to suggest an evolutionary "progress" from primitive to advanced political organization. Rather, each of these systems is designed to meet the needs of a population living within a specific setting.

Uncentralized Political Systems

In many non-Western cultural groups, marriage and kinship form the principal means of social organization. The economies of these groups are of a subsistence type, and populations are typically quite small. Leaders do not have the power to force compliance with the society's customs or laws, but if individual members do not conform, they may become the target of scorn and gossip or even be ostracized. Important decisions are usually made in a democratic manner by a consensus of adults, often including women as well as men; dissenting members may decide to act with the majority, or they may choose to adopt some other course of action, if they are willing to risk the social consequences. This form of political organization provides great flexibility, which in many situations confers an adaptive advantage.

Band Organization

The **band** is a small group of politically independent though related families and is the least complex form of political organization. Bands are found among foragers, hunters, and other nomadic groups. They organize themselves into politically autonomous extended-family groups. They will camp together, although they often split into smaller groups for periods to forage for food or visit other relatives. Bands are kin groups, composed of men and/or women who are related (or assumed to be)

Documentary Educational Resources

Toma, a Ju/'hoan leader or *kxau* of the /Gausha band, is known to many North Americans through the documentary film *The Hunters*.

as well as their spouses and unmarried children. Bands may be characterized as associations of related families who occupy a common (often vaguely defined) territory and who live there together for as long as environmental and subsistence circumstances are favourable. The band is the oldest form of political organization, since all humans once were hunters and gathers.

In small, egalitarian groups where everyone is related and where almost everyone values getting along, the potential for conflicts to develop is much reduced. Many disputes are settled informally through gossip, ridicule, direct negotiation, or mediation—for example, among most Aboriginal peoples of Canada. For conflict resolution, the emphasis is placed on community healing rather than punishment. When all else fails, unhappy individuals have the option of joining another band where they have relatives.

Decisions affecting a band are made with the participation of all adult members, with an emphasis on achieving **consensus** rather than a simple majority. Leadership is based on ability, and leaders maintain their position only as long as they retain the community's confidence. They have neither a guaranteed hold on their position nor the power to force people to abide by their decisions. A leader who exceeds what people are willing to accept quickly loses followers.

An example of informal band leadership is found among the Ju/'hoansi of the Kalahari Desert. Each Ju/'hoan band is composed of a group of families who live together, linked through kinship to one another and to the leader, who is usually male but sometimes female. Each band has rights to the territory it occupies and to the resources within it, but two or more bands' territories

may overlap. The leader, called the *kxau*, or "owner," is the focal point for the band's theoretical ownership of the territory. That leader, male or female, symbolically personifies the rights of band members to ownership. These rights are acknowledged by others.

The leader is responsible for planning when and where the group will move when local food resources are no longer adequate. When the move begins, his or her position is symbolically at the head of the line. He or she chooses the site for a new settlement and has the first choice of a spot for his or her own fire. The leader may also play a role in organizing hunting parties, trading expeditions, and gift-giving and marriage arrangements. That said, individual families have a great deal of autonomy in decision making. The leader is not a judge and does not punish other band members. Wrongdoers are judged and regulated by public opinion, which is usually expressed by gossip among band members. An important technique for resolving disputes—or avoiding them in the first place—is mobility. Those who are unable to get along with others of their group simply "vote with their feet" and move to another group where kinship ties give them entry rights.

A similar pattern is found among North American First Nations peoples, such as the Slavey of northern Canada. Traditionally, leaders were chosen from the most successful hunters, while senior women controlled kinship (marriage and group composition). Elders held important positions in the band: they chose the leaders and served as teachers, historians, and political advisers. Individuals with special powers provided healing and ritual services and maintained social control over the group. The band members settled their own disputes; for the most serious offences, the culprit might be banished from the band. As with the Ju/'hoansi, decision making was based on consensus, and anyone unhappy with a decision was free to vote with their feet.[1]

Following the 1899 and 1921 treaties (numbers 8 and 11), chiefs and band councils were established, although not to everyone's satisfaction. These early Slavey chiefs were chosen from among the traditional leaders, and the councillors were leaders of local bands. More recently, leaders have been elected by majority vote, which is at odds with the principles of Slavey

consensus A general agreement among adult members of a group.

THE CANADIAN PRESS/Jeff McIntosh

Current Chief of the Assembly of First Nations, Shawn Atleo, addresses an audience.

political and social organization. In the 1960s, when their territories were threatened by megaprojects such as the Mackenzie Valley Pipeline, the Slaveys allied themselves with other Dene peoples to form the Dene Nation. The Dene Nation sought political autonomy and greater control over their traditional lands. Also, Slavey communities in the Northwest Territories formed a regional Slavey organization—the Deh Cho First Nation Council. In the 1990s the Dene challenged the federal government's claim of jurisdiction over their lands.[2]

Tribal Organization

Another type of uncentralized authority system is the **tribe**, a word that, among the general public, is commonly applied to *any* group that is not organized into a state. Sometimes the term is applied even to non-Western peoples who in fact had strongly centralized states—for example, the Aztecs. This practice is no more warranted than calling the Chinese people a tribe. Europeans coined the term tribe to label people they regarded as inferior to supposedly civilized Europeans.

Anthropologists, however, would say that a tribal system is one that involves separate bands or villages integrated by factors such as kinship and clans. People

are united into communities or age grades or associations that crosscut kinship or territorial boundaries. People who belong to tribes sacrifice a degree of household autonomy to a larger-order group in return for greater security against enemy attacks or starvation. Typically, a tribe has an economy based on some form of farming or herding. Since these production methods usually yield more food than those of a foraging band, tribal membership is usually larger than band membership. Bands' population densities are usually less than one person per square kilometre; by contrast, tribal population densities always exceed one person per square kilometre and may be as high as 250 per square kilometre.

Each tribe consists of two or more small, autonomous local communities, which may form alliances with one another for various purposes. As with bands, tribal political organization is informal and temporary. Whenever a situation requiring political integration of all or several groups within the tribe arises—perhaps for defence, or to pool resources in times of scarcity—they join in a cooperative manner. When the issue is resolved, each group returns to its autonomous state.

Leadership among tribes is informal. The Blackfoot, for example, did not think of government as something fixed and all-powerful, and leadership was not vested in a central authority. A local leader was a man respected for his wisdom and hunting prowess. His advice therefore was sought frequently, but he had no formal means of control and could not force any decision on those who asked for his help. Group decisions were made by

tribe A group of nominally independent communities occupying a specific region and sharing a common language and culture integrated by some unifying factor.

public consensus, although the leaders would attempt to persuade others through their oratory. Among the social mechanisms that induced members to abide by group decisions were gossip, criticism, withdrawal of cooperation, and the belief that antisocial actions caused disease.

Another example of tribal leadership is the Melanesian Big Man. Such men are leaders of localized descent groups or of a territorial group. The Big Man combines a small amount of interest in his tribe's welfare with a great deal of self-interested cunning and calculation for his own gain. His authority is personal; he does not come to office in any formal sense, nor is he elected. His status is the result of acts that raise him above most other tribe members and that attract to him a band of loyal followers.

Typical of this form of political organization are the Kapauku and the Chimbu of Papua New Guinea. Among the Kapauku, the Big Man is called the *tonowi,* or "rich one." To achieve this status, one must be male, wealthy, generous, and eloquent; physical bravery and skill in dealing with the supernatural are two other frequent characteristics of a *tonowi,* but these are not essential. The *tonowi* functions as the headman of the village unit.

Kapauku culture places a high value on wealth, so it is not surprising that a wealthy man is viewed as successful and admirable. Yet the possession of wealth must be coupled with the trait of generosity, which in this culture means not gift giving but a willingness to make loans. Wealthy men who refuse to lend money to other villagers may be ostracized, ridiculed, and in extreme cases actually executed by a group of warriors. This social pressure ensures that economic wealth is rarely hoarded but instead is distributed throughout the group.

Through the loans he makes, the *tonowi* acquires his political power. Other villagers comply with his requests because they are in his debt (often without paying interest) and do not want to have to repay their loans. Those who have not yet borrowed from the *tonowi* may wish to do so in the future, so they, too, want to keep his goodwill.

The Clan

In many tribal groups the organizing unit and seat of political authority is the *clan*—that is, an association of people who believe themselves to share a common ancestry. Within the clan, elders or headmen regulate members' affairs and represent their clan in relations with other clans. The elders of all the clans may form a council that acts *within* the community, or *for* the community in dealings with outsiders. Because clan members usually do not all live together in one community, clan organization facilitates joint action with members of other communities when necessary.

Another form of tribal kinship bond that provides political organization is the **segmentary lineage system**. This system is similar in operation to the clan, but it is less extensive and is relatively rare. The best-known examples are East African cultures such as the Somali and the Dinka or Nuer of the Sudan. These people are pastoral nomads who are highly mobile and widely scattered over large territories. Unlike other East African pastoralists (such as the Maasai), they lack the age-grading organization that cuts across descent group membership. Political organization among segmentary lineages is usually informal, although older tribal members may exercise some personal authority.

The ethnographic study of Nuer political organization was undertaken before the severe disruptions caused by 30 years of civil war in southern Sudan, which recently achieved independence from northern Sudan after voting in favour of it during a referendum. Among the Nuer of southern Sudan, who number some 200,000 people (with another 500,000 or so in other parts of Sudan and a smaller population in Ethiopia), at least 20 clans exist. Each is patrilineal and is segmented into maximal lineages; each of these is in turn segmented into major lineages, which are segmented into minor lineages, which in turn are segmented into minimal lineages. The minimal lineage is a group descended from one great-grandfather or great-great-grandfather.

segmentary lineage system A form of political organization in which a large group is broken up into clans, which are further divided into lineages.

Local shamans help maintain social order in bands and tribes. Shown here is Shaman Vargas of Indi Community, Pastaza, Ecuador.

Gonzalo Zumendi/agefotostock/Firstlight

The lineage segments among the Nuer are all equal, and no leadership or political organization exists above the level of the autonomous minimal or primary segments.[3] The lineage's superstructure is merely an alliance and becomes active only during conflicts between any of the minimal segments. In serious disputes between members of different minimal lineage segments, members of all other segments take the side of the contestant they are most closely related to; the issue is then addressed between the higher order lineages involved. This system of political organization is known in anthropology as *complementary* or *balanced opposition*.

Disputes among the Nuer are frequent, as they are among other groups with similar organization, and under the segmentary lineage system, they can lead to widespread feuds. Any resulting social disruption is minimized by the actions of the "leopard-skin chief," who is not really a chief, but rather a holder of a ritual conciliation office. The leopard-skin chief has no political power and is viewed as standing outside the lineage network. All he can do is try to persuade feuding lineages to accept payment in "blood cattle" instead of taking another life. His mediation gives each side the chance to back down gracefully before people are killed. If the participants are for some reason unwilling to compromise, the leopard-skin chief has no authority to enforce a settlement.

Age-Grade Organization

Age-grade systems provide a tribe with a means of political integration beyond the kin group. Under this system, youths are initiated into an age grade and pass from one age grade to another at appropriate ages. Age grades and sets cut across territorial and kin groupings and thus may

be important means of political organization. Among the Tiriki of East Africa, the warrior age grade guards the country, while judicial elders resolve disputes. Between these two age grades are elder warriors, who are in a sense understudies to the judicial elders. The oldest age grade, the ritual elders, advise on matters involving the well-being of all the Tiriki people. Thus, the tribe's political affairs are in the hands of the elders age grades and their officers, while the military affairs are usually controlled by younger men. Among East African pastoralists, those (like the Tiriki) with crosscutting age-grade organization generally experience less feuding than those with segmentary lineage organization. This is thought to be generally due to the collective authority invested in the elders.

Voluntary Association Organization

Common-interest associations that function as politically integrative systems within tribes are found in many parts of the world, including Africa, Melanesia, and India. A good example of association organization existed during the 19th century among the Plains peoples of Canada. The basic Cree territorial and political unit was the band, but the men were organized into military societies, or warriors' clubs. Among the Cree—and indeed, the ancient Aztec as well—a young man might be invited to join one of these societies when he performed a brave deed, whereupon he became familiar with the society's particular insignia, songs, and rituals. In addition to military functions, such as keeping order in the camp and on the hunt and guarding against enemy attack, these warrior societies performed rituals that strengthened group solidarity. Such groups are still found today—for example, the Mohawk Warrior Society.

Centralized Political Systems

In bands and tribes, authority is uncentralized and each group is economically and politically autonomous. Political organization is vested in kinship, age, and common-interest groups. Populations are small and relatively homogeneous, with people engaged mostly in the same sorts of activities throughout their lives. As populations increase, as technology becomes more complex, and as trade networks and labour specialization produce surpluses of goods, the opportunity for some individuals or groups to exercise control increases. In such groups, political authority and power are concentrated in a single individual—the chief—or in a body of individuals—the state. The state is found in societies where each individual must interact on a regular basis with large numbers of people whose interests are diverse and who are neither kin nor close acquaintances.

Chiefdoms

A **chiefdom** is a regional polity in which two or more local groups are organized under a single ruling individual—the chief—who is at the head of a ranked hierarchy of people. The world-famous monument of Stonehenge is thought to have been built by a chiefdom-level society. An individual's status in such a polity is determined by his or her closeness of relationship to the chief. Those closest receive deferential treatment relative to those in lower ranks.

The office of the chief is usually hereditary, passing from a man to his own or his sister's son, depending on whether descent is reckoned patrilineally or matrilineally. Unlike the leaders of bands or lineages, the chief is generally a true authority figure, and his authority unites his people in all affairs and at all times. For example, a chief can distribute land among his community members and recruit people into his military service. Chiefdoms, such as those found among the historic Sioux Indians, have a recognized hierarchy consisting of major and minor authorities who control major and minor subdivisions. Such an arrangement is, in effect, a chain of command, one that links leaders at every level. This chain binds tribal groups to the chief's headquarters, be it a mud-and-dung hut or a marble palace. Although chiefs inherit their offices, in practice they maintain power through personal abilities and as exemplars of what is almost always seen as a semisacred position.

The chief controls the economic activities of his people. Typically, chiefdoms are redistributive systems: the chief has control over surplus goods and perhaps even over the community labour force. Thus, he may demand a quota of rice from farmers, which he will redistribute to the entire community. Similarly, he may recruit labourers to build irrigation works, a palace, or a temple.

The chief also may amass a great amount of personal wealth and pass it on to his heirs. Land, cattle, and luxury goods produced by specialists may be collected by the chief and become part of his power base. High-ranking families of the chiefdom may engage in the same practice and use their possessions as evidence of status.

An example of people using this form of political organization is the Kpelle of Liberia in West Africa.[4] Among them is a class of paramount chiefs, each of whom presides over one of the Kpelle chiefdoms (each of which is now a district of the Liberian state). The paramount chiefs' traditional tasks include hearing disputes, preserving order, seeing to the upkeep of trails, and maintaining "medicines." They are also salaried officials of the Liberian government, mediating between it and their people. Other rewards a paramount chief receives include a commission on taxes collected within his chiefdom, a commission for labourers furnished for the rubber plantations, a portion of court fees collected, a stipulated amount of rice from each household, and gifts from people who come to request favours and intercessions. In keeping with his exalted station, a paramount chief has at his disposal uniformed messengers, a literate clerk, and the symbols of wealth: many wives, embroidered robes, and freedom from manual labour.

chiefdom A regional polity in which two or more local groups are organized under a single chief, who is at the head of a ranked hierarchy of people.

A Kpelle town chief settles a dispute.

Beneath each Kpelle paramount chief are several lesser chiefs: one for each district, one for each town, and one for each quarter of all but the smallest towns. Each acts as a kind of lieutenant for his minor chief and also serves as a liaison between him and those of lower rank. Unlike paramount or district chiefs, who are comparatively remote, town and quarter chiefs are readily accessible to people at the local level.

The Kpelle political system may be stable today, but chiefdoms in all parts of the world have long been highly unstable. This instability is the result of lesser chiefs attempting to wrest power from higher ranking chiefs or of paramount chiefs vying with one another for supreme power.

state In anthropology, a centralized political system with the power to coerce.

nation Communities of people who see themselves as "one people" on the basis of common ancestry, history, society, institutions, ideology, language, territory, and (often) religion.

State Systems

The **state** is the most formal of political organizations. In the state, political power is centralized in a government, which may legitimately use force to regulate the affairs of its citizens as well as relations with other states.

Increased food production results in increased population. Together, these lead to landscape modifications, such as irrigation and terracing. They also lead to carefully managed rotation cycles, intense competition for clearly demarcated lands, and rural populations large enough to support market systems and a specialized urban sector. As overcrowding develops and resources become scarcer, corporate groups that stress exclusive membership proliferate, ethnic differentiation and ethnocentrism become more pronounced, and the potential for social conflict rises dramatically. An increase in hierarchical authority and a loss of individual freedom and autonomy is the price that humanity has paid for the ability to live together in far greater concentrations. State institutions—bureaucracies, a military, a police force, an official religion, and so on—have provided the necessary institutions for living together at high densities.

Although their guiding ideology purports that they are permanent and stable, states encompass a host of contradictory forces. The fact is that since their first appearance some 5,000 to 6,000 years ago in the Middle East, states have been anything but permanent; over the long term, they show a clear tendency toward instability and collapse. Nowhere have states even begun to show the staying power exhibited by more uncentralized political systems, which are still the longest-lasting social forms invented by humans.

An important distinction to make at this point is that between **nation** and state. Today, there are roughly 192 states in the world recognized by the UN, and most of them did not exist before the Second World War. By contrast, probably about 5,000 *nations* exist in the world today. "What makes each a nation is that its people share a language, culture, territorial base, and political organization and a common history."[5] Today, states commonly have living within their boundaries people of more than one nation—for example, the First Nations of Canada. Rarely do state and nation coincide, although we do have some examples, such as Iceland and Japan. By contrast, some 73 percent of the world's states are multinational.[6]

Canada was a region of nations long before Europeans "discovered" this land. First Nations and Inuit peoples covered the vast expanse of this country, albeit sparsely; each nation spoke a distinctive language, and each possessed vibrant, diverse cultural traditions. Each nation occupied a loosely defined territory, with a long-standing history of occupation and adaptation to its

Peter Arnold, Inc

particular environment. But the newly arrived French and English colonists refused to recognize the First Nations and Inuit peoples as true nations, regarding these groups as small nomadic bands with informal leaders, who simply did not meet the criteria for "real" nations.[7] Early colonialists applied the construct of *"terra nullius,"* which posited that lands deemed empty of "civilization" were open for conquest. Today, First Nations, Inuit, and Métis peoples are seeking recognition of their nationhood and their inherent right to self-determination. They want to regain control of their affairs and to make their own decisions regarding the preservation and development of their distinct cultures. Self-government would enable Aboriginal people more control over affairs within their communities as well as the power to deliver programs and services— such as education, child welfare, and health care—in ways that fit with their Aboriginal values.[8]

Under Section 35 of the Constitution Act (1982), the Canadian government recognized Aboriginal peoples' right to determine matters related to their culture, identity, traditions, and language; but because each nation is unique, negotiations have to be conducted on a nation-by-nation basis. Self-government arrangements have already been settled with the Sechelt Indian Band in British Columbia, the Cree-Naskapi of Quebec, and the Yukon First Nations.[9] Métis groups also seek the power to direct and influence decisions that affect their lives, but so far with little success since they are not formally recognized as a nation. Inuit groups have taken a slightly different approach, preferring to remain within the sphere of public government. After decades of negotiations, the eastern portion of the Northwest Territories separated in 1999 to form a new territory, Nunavut, for the Inuit people of the Canadian Arctic.

Western forms of political organization are state governments. Another example of a state is that of the Swazi, a Bantu-speaking people who live in Swaziland in southern Africa.[10] They are primarily farmers, but they value cattle raising more highly than farming: The wealth, power, and rituals of their authority system are all intricately linked with cattle. In addition to farming and cattle raising, certain people have become specialists in rituals, smithing, wood carving, and pottery. They trade their goods and services, although the Swazi do not have elaborate markets.

The Swazi authority system is characterized by a highly developed dual monarchy, a hereditary aristocracy, and elaborate kinship rituals. The king—currently Mswati III, who has reigned since 1986—and his mother are by tradition the central figures of all national activity, linking all the people of the Swazi state. They preside over higher courts, summon national gatherings, control age classes, allocate land, disburse national wealth, take precedence in ritual, and help organize important social events.

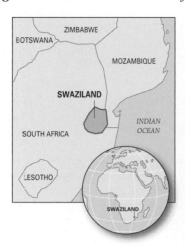

Advising the Swazi king are the senior princes, usually his uncles and half-brothers. Between the king and the princes are two specially created *tinsila,* or "blood brothers," who are chosen from certain commoner clans. These men are the king's shields; they protect him from evildoers and serve him in intimate personal situations. In addition, the king is guided by two *tindvuna,* or councillors, one civil and one military. The people of the state make their opinions known through two councils: the *liqoqo,* or Privy Council, composed of senior princes, and the *libanda,* or Council of State, composed of chiefs and headmen and open to all adult males of the state. The *liqoqo* may advise the king, make decisions, and carry them out. For example, they may rule on questions about land, education, traditional ritual, court procedure, and transport.

Swazi government extends from the smallest local unit—the homestead—upward to the central administration. The head of a homestead has legal and administrative powers; he is responsible for the crimes of those under him, controls their property, and speaks for them before his superiors. On the district level, political organization is similar to that of the central government. The relationship between a district chief, however, and his subjects is personal and familiar; he knows all the families in his district. The main check on any autocratic tendencies he may exhibit rests in his subjects' ability to transfer their allegiance to a more responsive chief. Swazi officials hold their positions for life and are dismissed only for treason or witchcraft. Many of these structures of governance have survived into the 21st century.

Political Leadership and Gender

There is a common belief that women rarely hold positions of political leadership. Actually, anthropologists and other researchers have found a number of examples of women exercising political power. First, a number of

Gender Perspectives

Minority Women in Canadian Politics

For the most part, a narrow class of people has monopolized the political arena in Canada—typically white, affluent males—while new social groups, such as minority women, have been under-represented. Canada's past Prime Minister Kim Campbell is an exception to this male-only domination, and she herself ruled for a very short period of time. Minority women are defined as belonging to ethno-racial groups outside the two "charter" groups, the French and the English. Canada's Minister of Health, Leona Aglukkaq, is a rare exception, the first Inuk in Canadian history to be appointed to the Cabinet of Canada. The Inuit, however, do not consider themselves a minority group. These women face a double jeopardy: they are women and they belong to a minority group, which means they do not receive the same advantages and privileges as majority groups, in much the same way as gender-based social forces have historically kept women subordinate to men. Minority women, however, are subordinated on two fronts—as

women and as minorities—and thus they face more barriers than either majority women or minority men, meaning they must deal with the limitations placed on them as a result of both gender and ethnic origin. Because of these barriers, minority women are relatively few in Canadian politics, especially at the federal level, but they are becoming a presence to reckon with.

Two models have been presented to analyze inequality within the Canadian political system. The first, known as the similarity model, proposes that women seeking political office in Canada must possess the same social and political resources (e.g., high educational and occupation experience) as men do. If they meet these requirements, then the disparities should diminish. Thus, those minority women who are successful in achieving political stations will have the same qualifications as majority women and men and will have the same opportunities.

The second model suggests that minority women must surpass the standards set for majority women and men. Known as the compensation model, this approach recognizes the restrictive and

biased nature of recruitment into the political arena, and submits that to overcome the disadvantage of being both a woman and a member of a minority group, these women must have exceptional credentials, far exceeding those of the social groups they are competing with, to overcome negative stereotypes and serious barriers.

Black's (2000) study found that minority women do have greater accomplishments relative to majority women and minority men. In addition, women, regardless of ethnic origin, tend to have greater accomplishments than men. Black found that the hurdles for women are generally higher than for men, and minority women have the added disadvantage of ethnicity, thus forcing them to achieve even greater heights in order to accomplish their goals.

SOURCE: J.H. Black, "Entering the Political Elite in Canada: The Case of Minority Women as Parliamentary Candidates and MPs," *Canadian Review of Sociology and Anthropology* 37, no. 2 (2000). Reprinted with permission of the Canadian Sociological Association / La Société Canadienne de Sociologie.

female politicians presently head or have recently headed governments. Among them: Corazon Aquino (Philippines), Benazir Bhutto (Pakistan), Gro Harlem Brundtland (Norway), Indira Gandhi (India), Margaret Thatcher (Great Britain), and Angela Merkel (Germany). In the summer of 2010, Julia Gillard became Australia's first ever female prime minister; and in early 2011, Dilma Rousseff became the first female president of Brazil. The last monarch of Hawaii was a woman. Powerful queens such as Elizabeth I of England and Catherine the Great of Russia are other examples.

There are a number of societies in which women enjoy as much political power as men. In band societies, it is common for women to have as much say in public affairs as men, even though the latter more often than not are the nominal leaders of their groups. Among the Iroquoian nations of southern Ontario and New York State, leadership positions above the household level were filled by men. But those men were beholden to women for the political power they held; only the latter could appoint men to high office. Moreover, women actively lobbied

the men on the councils and could remove someone from office whenever it suited them.[11]

As these cases make clear, the low visibility of women in politics does not necessarily mean they have been excluded from politics, nor does it mean that men have more power in political affairs. Sometimes, though, women play more visible roles, as in the dual-sex systems of West Africa. The Igbo of Nigeria, who so fascinated 19th-century anthropologists (partly because parents would kill twins as an abomination), possessed separate political institutions for men and women that provided each sex with its own autonomous sphere of authority, as well as areas of shared responsibility.[12] At the centre of these respective spheres of authority were a male *obi*, considered the head of government though in fact he presided over the male community, and a female *omu*, the acknowledged mother of the whole community but in practice concerned with the female section. Unlike a queen (although both she and the *obi* were crowned), the *omu* was neither the *obi*'s wife nor the previous *obi*'s daughter.

Joseph Brant, George Romney, oil on canvas, National Gallery of Canada

Shown here is the Iroquois chief Joseph Brant (1742–1807). Although Iroquoian chiefs were always men, they served strictly at the pleasure of women, whose position in society was equal to that of men.

The *obi* had a council of dignitaries to advise him and to act as a check against any arbitrary exercise of power; in the same way, the *omu* was served by a council of women in equal number to the *obi*'s male counsellors. The *omu* and her councillors established rules and regulations for the community market (marketing was a women's activity) and heard cases involving women brought to her from throughout the town or village. If such cases also involved men, then she and her council would cooperate with the *obi* and his council. Widows also went to the *omu* for the final rites required to end their period of mourning

for a dead husband. Since the *omu* represented all women, she had to be responsive to her constituency and would seek their approval and cooperation in all major decisions.

In addition to the *omu* and her council, the Igbo women's government included a representative body of women chosen from each quarter or section of the village or town on the basis of their ability to think logically and speak well. At the village or lineage level were political pressure groups of women who acted to stop quarrels and prevent wars.

In the Igbo system, then, women managed their own affairs, and their interests were represented at all levels of government. Moreover, they had the right to enforce their decisions and rules by applying sanctions similar to those men employed. These included strikes, boycotts, and "sitting on a man" or woman. Political scientist Judith Van Allen describes the latter:

> To "sit on" or "make war on" a man involved gathering at his compound, sometimes late at night, dancing, singing scurrilous songs which detailed the women's grievances against him and often called his manhood into question, banging on his hut with the pestles women used for pounding yams, and perhaps demolishing his hut or plastering it with mud and roughing him up a bit. A man might be sanctioned in this way for mistreating his wife, for violating the women's market rules, or for letting his cows eat the women's crops. The women would stay at his hut throughout the day, and late into the night if necessary, until he repented and promised to mend his ways. ... Although this could hardly have been a pleasant experience for the offending man, it was considered legitimate and no man would consider intervening.[13]

Given the high visibility of women in the Igbo political system, it is surprising that when the British imposed colonial rule on these people, they failed to recognize the autonomy and power these women possessed. The British had been blinded by their Victorian values. In their mistaken view, a woman's mind was not strong enough for such "masculine" subjects as science, business, and politics; her place was clearly in the home. So it was inconceivable to them that women might play an important role in politics. As a consequence, the British introduced "reforms" that destroyed women's traditional autonomy and power without providing alternative forms. In this case, far from enhancing women's status (as Western people like to think their influence does), the British robbed Igbo women of their equality and made them subordinate to men.

And the Igbo situation is not unusual in this regard. Historically, in state-organized societies, women usually have been subordinate to men. As Eleanor Leacock points out in her book *Myths of Male Dominance*, when states impose their control on societies where the sexes are relatively equal to each other, the situation almost invariably changes so that women become subordinate to men.[14]

POLITICAL ORGANIZATION AND THE MAINTENANCE OF ORDER

Whatever form political organization may take, and whatever else it may do, it is always involved in one way or another with maintaining social order. Always it seeks to ensure that people behave in acceptable ways, and always it defines the proper action to take when they do not. In chiefdoms and states, there is some sort of authority that has the power to regulate the affairs of society. In bands and tribes, however, people behave generally as they are expected to, without the direct intervention of any centralized political authority. To a large degree, gossip, criticism, fear of supernatural forces, and the like serve as effective deterrents to antisocial behaviour.

As an example of how such seemingly informal considerations serve to keep people in line, we may look at the Wape people of Papua New Guinea, who believe that the ghosts of dead ancestors roam lineage lands, protecting them from trespassers and helping their hunting descendants by driving game their way.[15] These ghosts also punish those who have wronged them or their descendants by preventing hunters from finding game or by causing them to miss their shots, thereby depriving people of much-needed meat. Nowadays, the Wape hunt with shotguns, which the community purchases for the use of one man, whose job it is to hunt for all the others. The cartridges used in the hunt, however, are invariably supplied by individual community members. Not always is the gunman successful; if he shoots and misses, it is because the owner of the fired shell, or some close relative, has quarrelled or wronged another person, whose ghost relative is securing revenge by causing the hunter to miss. Or, if the gunman cannot even find game, it is because vengeful ghosts have chased the animals away. As a proxy hunter for the villagers, the gunman is potentially subject to ghostly sanctions in response to collective wrongs by those he hunts for.

For the Wape, then, successful hunting depends on avoiding quarrels and maintaining tranquillity within

the community so as not to antagonize anybody's ghost ancestor. Unfortunately, complete peace and tranquillity are impossible to achieve in any human community, and the Wape are no exception. Thus, when hunting is poor, the gunman must discover what quarrels and wrongs have occurred within his village in order to identify the proper ancestral ghosts to appeal to for renewed success. Usually, this is done at a special meeting, where confessions of wrongdoing may be forthcoming. If they are not, questioning accusations are bandied about until resolution occurs. But even with no resolution, the meeting must end amicably in order to prevent new antagonisms. In this way, the behaviour of all comes under public scrutiny, reminding everyone of what is expected of them and encouraging everyone to avoid acts that will cast them in an unfavourable light.

Internalized Controls

The Wape concern about ancestral ghosts is a good example of internalized, or cultural, controls—beliefs so thoroughly ingrained that each person becomes personally responsible for his or her own conduct. **Cultural control** may be thought of as control by the mind, in contrast to **social control**, which involves blatant coercion. Examples of cultural control also can be found in North American society; for instance, people refrain from committing incest not so much from fear of legal punishment as from a sense of deep disgust at the thought of the act and from the shame they would feel in performing it. Obviously, not all members of North American society feel this disgust, or such a high incidence of incest would not occur, especially between fathers and daughters; but then no deterrent to misbehaviour is ever 100 percent effective. Cultural controls are built in, or internalized, and rely on deterrents such as fear of supernatural punishment—ancestral ghosts sabotaging the hunting, for example—and magical retaliation. Like the devout Christian who avoids sinning for fear of hell, the individual expects some sort of punishment, even though no one in the community may be aware of the wrongdoing.

Externalized Controls

Because internalized controls are not wholly sufficient even in bands and tribes, every society develops customs or **sanctions** designed to encourage conformity to social norms. Sanctions are externalized controls and involve varying mixes of cultural and social control. According to Radcliffe-Brown, "a sanction is a reaction on the part of a society or of a considerable number of its members to a mode of behaviour which is thereby approved (positive sanctions) or disapproved (negative sanctions)."[16]

cultural control Control through beliefs and values deeply internalized in the minds of individuals.

social control Control over groups through coercion and sanctions.

sanctions Externalized social controls designed to encourage conformity to social norms.

Rigoberta Menchu won the 1992 Nobel Peace Prize for her work on behalf of indigenous peoples. Awards such as the Nobel Prize are examples of positive sanctions, by which societies promote approved behaviour.

Sanctions operate within social groups of all sizes. Moreover, they need not be enacted into law to play a significant role in regulating peoples' behaviour: "They include not only the organized sanctions of the law but also the gossip of neighbors or the customs regulating norms of production that are spontaneously generated among workers on the factory floor. In small scale communities … informal sanctions may become more drastic than the penalties provided for in the legal code."[17] If, however, a sanction is to be effective, it cannot be arbitrary. Sanctions must be consistently applied, and the culture's members must know generally of their existence.

Social sanctions can be positive or negative. Positive sanctions consist of incentives to conformity, such as awards, titles, and recognition by one's neighbours. Negative sanctions consist of threats, such as imprisonment, corporal punishment, or ostracism from the community for violation of social norms. One example of a negative sanction discussed earlier is the Igbo practice of "sitting on a man." If some individuals are not convinced of the advantages of social conformity, they are still more likely to obey their culture's rules than to accept the consequences of not doing so.

Also, sanctions can also be formal or informal, depending on whether a legal statute is involved. In North America, the man who wears tennis shorts to a church service may be subject to a variety of informal sanctions, ranging from disapproving glances from the clergy to the chuckling of other parishioners. If, however, he were to show up without any pants on, he would be subject to the formal negative sanction of arrest for indecent exposure. Only in the second instance would he have been guilty of breaking the **law**.

Formal sanctions, such as laws, are always organized. They are attempts to precisely and explicitly regulate people's behaviour. Other examples of organized sanctions include, on the positive side, awards of merit, such as the Order of Canada, Citizen of the Year, and recognition for heroic deeds. On the negative side are loss of face, exclusion from social life and its privileges, seizure of property, imprisonment, and even bodily mutilation or death.

Informal sanctions emphasize cultural control and are diffuse in nature, involving spontaneous expressions of approval or disapproval by members of the community. They are, nonetheless, highly effective in enforcing a large number of seemingly unimportant customs. Because most people want to be accepted, they are willing to acquiesce to the rules that govern dress, eating, and conversation, even in the absence of actual laws.

To understand how informal sanctions work in the context of power relationships, read "Limits on Power in Bedouin Society" on the CourseMate site. This especially interesting example shows how sanctions act not only to control people's behaviour but also to keep individuals in their place in a hierarchical society.

Another agent of control in human groups, whether they possess a centralized political system or not, may be witchcraft. An individual will hesitate to offend a neighbour when that neighbour can retaliate by resorting to black magic. Similarly, individuals who do not wish to be accused of witchcraft will behave with greater circumspection. In a classic anthropological study, E.E. Evans-Pritchard reported that among the Azande of the Sudan, people who think they have been bewitched may consult an oracle, who, after performing the appropriate mystical rites, may then establish or confirm the identity of the offending witch.[18]

Confronted with this evidence, the accused witch usually will agree to cooperate in order to avoid any additional trouble. Should the victim die, the relatives of the deceased may choose to make magic against

law Formal negative sanctions.

NEL

⚭ *Original Study* ⚭

Social Movements

Liam Kilmurray

Social anthropologists, sociologists, and indeed, most social scientists study political organizations in some form or other. Among the areas of interest to these researchers are the maintenance of law and order, the kinds of political systems in operation in human societies, and areas such as power, legitimacy, rights, and dispute resolution. One subfield that embraces most of these areas, at least in opposition, is known as social movement studies. This is a vibrant topic that involves observing the activities of a variety of social protest movements.

Social movement studies examine groups as diverse as the early suffragettes, Aboriginal protest groups, and radical environmental social movements. This includes examining the overarching political structures within which social movements operate and protests take place. This dual nature of the field makes it a fascinating area of study. Anthropologists encounter democratic social movements protesting in pseudo-fascist nations, as well as fascist social movements rioting in democratic or even in communist nations. The world of social movements is exciting and has been the subject of intense anthropological debate. It has also garnered much media attention. In recent years, social movements have become powerful agents of change—they have forced revolutions and stopped clearcutting of tropical forests—but they have also often failed.

For anthropologists, the first question is "What is a social movement?" Social movements, according to Blumer (1969, 99), are a "collective enterprise seeking to establish a new order of life ... and derive their motive power on the one hand from dissatisfaction with the current form of life, and on the other hand, from wishes and hopes for a new system of living." There are many other definitions—so many, in fact, that the renowned social movement theorist Alberto Melucci claimed that "everything that moves is a social movement" (1996). Such is the broad remit of this area of analysis! Staggenborg's recent definition outlines those exact areas of anthropological interest: She describes social movements as "consist[ing] of networks of individuals, cultural groups, alternative institutions, and institutional supporters as well as political movement organizations" (2008, 7).

Anthropological involvement with the world of social movements requires a holistic examination of the phenomenon, of its structure, function, and component parts, and of what makes social movements work. Importantly, social movements are collective efforts, and therefore social and cultural products, and thus can be analyzed as collective representations.

Analysis of social movements also requires understanding their tactics (and those of their opposition), the challenges they face, and the various strategic resources they deploy. Most anthropologists would then attempt to link social movements to the broader social setting within which they operate. Which forms of protest work best in Taiwan, or in Toronto? What impact do social movements have in different cultures? How and why do they succeed or fail? Why do certain social movements generate opposition? Why do social movements persist or decline?

Analyses of a variety of older and more recent social movements, such as the Animal Liberation Front and Greenpeace, have shown that the strongest social movements emerge from contentious political issues. Organizations such as Earth First—and its earlier manifestation, Deep Ecology—are good examples. These social movements draw their support from people who are concerned about the environment—usually about local areas whose development destiny is caught up in commercial interests and government regulations (or the absence thereof). Discontent about the absence of regulation or about the violation of environmental standards has led to many sustained and effective environmental social movements and to prolonged and often successful programs. Examples include the Greenpeace movement to protect whales and the Earth First opposition to clearcut logging.

Environmental social movements usually court media coverage as part of their strategy to raise awareness and gather recruits. Thus it is not uncommon to encounter dramatic images of Greenpeace activists unfurling protest banners from the world's buildings, or Earth First members chaining themselves to giant Douglas firs in the forests of British Columbia. Hundreds of thousands of marchers take to the world's cities in support of Earth Day each year, and indigenous peoples and environmentalists are imprisoned for blockading indigenous lands and preventing development.

What quickly becomes evident from studying social movements is that they generally exist outside the main political spectrum. (The entrance of the Green Parties into mainstream politics implies that they are not, therefore, social movements but rather political movements.) Because social movements exist outside mainstream politics, anthropological research focuses on the tactics they employ. Some social movements are born from violence, or at least they gain traction from resisting violent suppression of formerly peaceful tactics. Such was the case with the Gay Rights movements in the United States, which are now most prominently represented by the lesbian, gay, bisexual, and transgender (LGBT) social movements. In the repressive social atmosphere of 1969 (at least as far as homosexuality was concerned), homosexuals would meet in a bar in New York City known as the Stonewall Inn. One night those inside, many of them homosexual, became upset by what they perceived as the heavy-handed tactics of police, and over the next few days riots erupted on the streets outside. In this episode, peaceful demonstrations were also a major protest tactic, but much of the media coverage focused on the violence, from both protesters and police forces.

In recent years, Canada and other parts of the world have witnessed a new form of convergence among various social movements. One such example is the alignment between Aboriginal peoples and environmentalists. In a variety of cases, what were formerly quite distinct movements begin to move toward one another in terms of the goals they seek. This alignment has been witnessed at many sites across Canada, such as the tar sands in Alberta and the Frontenac Ventures uranium mines near Bancroft, Ontario. Aboriginal chiefs, whether Dene, Inuit, or Algonquin, are finding common cause with environmentalists in their efforts to protect sacred ground. This ground can be part of ancestral traplines or complex land claims; it can be of interest to non-Native people for an endangered variety of tree or to Native people as the site of sacred burials. What is common is the desire to mobilize people to protest and to campaign to save the land or resource; this is the essence of social movements.

The manner in which a social movement operates, its tactics, has a great bearing on the course it will take. Media coverage of violent protest will initially spike, broadcasting rioters and by extension their issues and platforms. However, it has been demonstrated that violent tactics sometimes reap only temporary rewards; initial publicity may give way to fatigue or even a reaction against the issues because of the violence involved. That is what happened with some of the protests in Clayoquot Sound, where some protesters, to preserve ancient forests, had hammered spikes into the trees to damage logging equipment. As the prospect of injuries to local workers mounted, many people turned away from the protesters' issues, and not just their tactics. It should be noted that Greenpeace itself disavowed the practice of spiking trees. This is an important issue for social movements, as often some protesters act of their own volition and do not represent the movement's aims.

Anthropologists have studied protest movements in order to understand the tactics, mobilization efforts, and general cultural structure of these (typically) grassroots movements. They have mapped the rise and fall of certain social movements and have attempted to predict the tactics best suited to specific political structures.

Getty Images 98300438

Activists from the Indonesian action group Pro Fauna hang from trees holding placards during an anti-deforestation protest in a protected forest area in Mojokerto, East Java, on April 7, 2010. They are claiming that classifying palm oil plantations as forests will reduce the amount of natural preserves for wildlife. Unchecked deforestation, often to make way for palm oil plantations, has made Indonesia the world's third largest greenhouse gas emitter, according to most estimates.

Social ethnographic projects have been undertaken in which anthropologists immerse themselves within the social movement in order to fully understand the mechanisms at play in their daily functioning (Edelman 2001, 310). What emerges from many such studies is that civil society—that is, organizations outside the mainstream political structures—is a vibrant part of social life. These groups incorporate many walks of life, and their membership can span all facets of the social stratum. Moreover, the manner in which protesters are accommodated or suppressed by the authorities reveals a great deal about the legitimacy of the state or governing structure. As the world's population increases, if scarce resources dwindle further and pollution continues, the world will most likely witness an upsurge in social movements. Anthropologists are at the front lines of many such movements, documenting the protests and observing the reactions from authorities. They also examine the internal politics of the social movements, their demographic structures, and their policies, aims, and tactics.

Studies of current social movements have involved anthropologists in areas such as Native studies, cultural studies, and policing tactics. The field of social movements is "hot" not only in anthropological studies—it is quickly becoming a common form of ethnography, one in which the anthropologist takes on important academic and social responsibilities. A grounded knowledge of social movements will contribute significantly to the anthropological understanding of culture and culture change.

SOURCES: H. Blumer, *Symbolic Interactionism* (Englewood Cliffs: Transition, 1969); N. Crosley, *Making Sense of Social Movements* (Buckingham: Open University Press, 2002); M. Edelman, "Social Movements: Changing Paradigms and Forms of Politics," *Annual Review of Anthropology* 30 (2001): 285–317; Y. Ibrahim, "Between Revolution and Defeat: Student Protest Cycles and Networks," *Sociology Compass* 4, no. 7 (2010): 495–504; A. Melucci, *Challenging Codes: Collective Action in the Information Age* (Cambridge: Cambridge University Press, 1996); S. Staggenborg, *Social Movements* (Toronto: Oxford University Press, 2008).

the witch, ultimately accepting the death of some villager as evidence both of guilt and of the efficacy of their magic. For the Azande, witchcraft provides not only a sanction against antisocial behaviour but also a means of dealing with natural hostilities and death. No one wishes to be thought of as a witch, and surely no one wishes to be victimized by one. By institutionalizing their emotional responses, the Azande successfully maintain social order. (For more on witchcraft, see Chapter 12.)

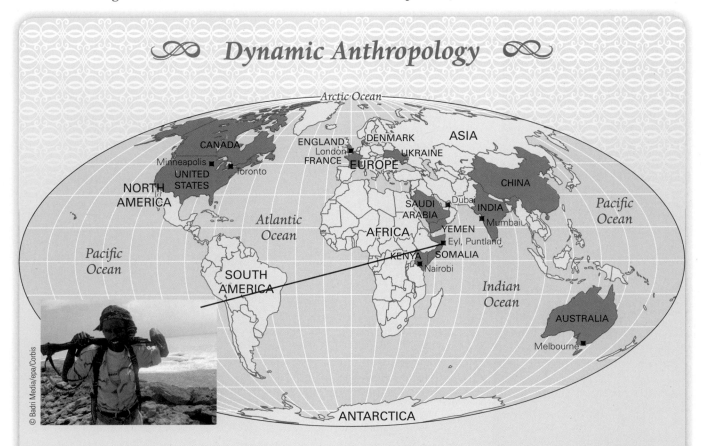

Dynamic Anthropology

Pirate Pursuits in Puntland?

Abshir Boya, a towering Somali pirate, is active in coastal waters off the Horn of Africa, which juts deep into the Arabian Sea. He lives in the old fishing port of Eyl in Puntland, an autonomous territory in Somalia. By 2009, Eyl had become a pirate haven, holding a dozen hijacked foreign ships and their multinational crews.

Most of the few hundred other pirates based in Puntland are, like Boyah, Darod clansmen who have been pushed out of their traditional fisheries by foreign commercial fleets polluting their coasts and depleting their fish stocks. Since 1991, Somalia has been splintered by rebellions, clan rivalries, and foreign armed interventions. It no longer has a centralized power system maintaining

law and order for its citizens, who survive on an average annual income of $600. With a national economy in tatters, Boyah and his clansmen spied the wealth passing through the Arabian Sea and decided to grab a share.

Bankrolled by emigrated Somali investors living in cities such as Melbourne, Dubai, Nairobi, London, Toronto, and Minneapolis, pirate gangs are equipped with radios, cell phones, and GPS, as well as semiautomatic pistols, assault rifles, and rocket-propelled grenade launchers bought in Yemen. Speeding across the open sea in skiffs, they chase cargo ships, oil tankers, and cruise ships from around the world, including the United States, Canada, Denmark, France, Saudi Arabia, India, and China.

Some pirate captains have banked their success, including Boyah, who claims to have led more than

25 hijackings. Shipowners pay huge ransoms, often topping $1 million per ship. Somali sea bandits—about a thousand in total—collectively net between $80 and $150 million annually. They are obliged to pay their backers and to share their earnings with many poor relatives in their large clans. Far bigger profits go to Lloyd's of London, which earns an extra $400 million a year on piracy insurance for ships plying these dangerous waters.

The UN has called on nations with vessels in the area to repress piracy with military force. Today, a dozen navies patrol one million square miles of sea. Many Somali pirates have been killed or captured. Criminal prosecution of piracy in international waters is a big problem, owing to questions over jurisdiction, but many are now in jail in half a dozen foreign countries.

SOCIAL CONTROL THROUGH LAW

As we have noted, not all disputes are resolved through formalities of the legal system. Among the Inuit of northern Canada, all offences are considered to involve disputes between individuals; thus, they must be settled between the disputants themselves. One way they may do so is through a song duel, in which they heap insults on each other in songs specially composed for the occasion. The people's interests are represented by spectators, whose applause determines the outcome. If, however, social harmony cannot be restored—and that, rather than to assign blame and to punish, is the goal—one or the other disputant may move to another band. Among the Inuit, the alternative to peaceful settlement is to leave the group. Ultimately, no binding legal authority exists.

In Western society, by contrast, someone who commits an offence against another person is subject to a series of complex legal proceedings. In criminal cases the primary concern is to assign blame and punish, rather than to help the victim. The offender will be arrested by the police; will be tried before a judge and, perhaps, a jury; and, if the crime is serious enough, will be fined, imprisoned, or even executed. Rarely does the victim receive restitution or compensation. Throughout this chain of events, the accused party is dealt with by (presumably) disinterested police, judges, jurors, and jailers, who may have no personal acquaintance whatsoever with the plaintiff or the defendant. How strange this complicated system must seem from the standpoint of traditional Aboriginal cultures. Clearly, the two systems operate under distinctly different assumptions.

Recognition of the disparities between these two systems, coupled with the disproportionate number of Aboriginal people in Canadian prisons, has led government officials and First Nations leaders to consider alternative justice systems, such as sentencing circles. In sentencing circles the accused is brought before representatives of the Aboriginal community, who decide how the conflict should be resolved. This practice is growing, especially in the Canadian North and on the Prairies.[19] Opponents of sentencing circles fear that the system is not structured enough and that the community will "let the criminal off too easy" or fail to meticulously enforce any punishments mandated.

Definition of Law

Once two Inuit settle a dispute by engaging in a song contest, the affair is considered closed; no further action is expected. Would we choose to describe the outcome of such a contest as a legal decision? How are we to distinguish between social sanctions in general and those to which we apply the label of law?

The definition of "law" was a lively point of contention among anthropologists in the 20th century. In 1926, Malinowski argued that the rules of law are distinguished from the rules of custom in that "they are regarded as the obligation of one person and the rightful claim of another, sanctioned not by mere psychological motive, but by a definite social machinery of binding force based … upon mutual dependence."[20] In other words, laws exemplify social control because they employ overt coercion. An example of one rule of custom in contemporary North American society might be the dictate that guests at a dinner party should repay the person who gave the party with entertainment in the future. A host or hostess who does not receive a return invitation may feel cheated of something thought to be owed but has no legal claim against the ungrateful guest for the $22.67 spent on food. If, however, an individual was cheated of the same sum by the grocer when shopping, the law could be invoked. Although Malinowski's definition introduced several important elements of law, his failure to distinguish adequately between legal and nonlegal sanctions left the problem of formulating a workable definition of law in the hands of later anthropologists.

An important pioneer in the anthropological study of law was E. Adamson Hoebel, according to whom "a social norm is legal if its neglect or infraction is regularly met, in threat or in fact, by the application of physical force by an individual or group possessing the socially recognized privilege of so acting."[21] In stressing the legitimate use of physical coercion, Hoebel de-emphasized the traditional association of law with a centralized court system. Although judge and jury are fundamental features of Western jurisprudence, they are not the universal backbone of human law. Some anthropologists have proposed that a precise definition of law is impossible—and perhaps even undesirable. When we speak of "the law," are we not inclined to fall back on our familiar Western

The Okimaw Ohci Healing Lodge in Maple Creek, Saskatchewan, is a prison for Aboriginal women that incorporates traditional spiritual healing.

A protester walks through riot police in Toronto at the G20 summit of 2010. Heavily armed police have sanction to use force against any protesters.

conception of rules enacted by an authorized legislative body and enforced by the judicial mechanisms of the state? Can any concept of law be applied to the Nuer or the Inuit, for whom the notion of a centralized judiciary is virtually meaningless? How shall we categorize duels, song contests, and other socially condoned forms of self-help that seem to meet some but not all the criteria of law? Ultimately, it is always of greatest value to consider each case in its own cultural context. Nonetheless, a working definition of law is useful for purposes of discussion and cross-cultural comparison, and for this, law is adequately characterized as a system of formal negative sanctions.

Functions of Law

In *The Law of Primitive Man* (1954), Hoebel writes of a time when the notion that property should be generously shared was a fundamental precept of Cheyenne life. Subsequently, though, some men assumed the privilege of borrowing other men's horses without bothering to obtain permission. When Wolf Lies Down complained of such unauthorized borrowing to the members of the Elk Soldier Society, the Elk Soldiers not only had his horse returned to him but also secured an award for damages from the offender. The Elk Soldiers then announced that, to avoid such difficulties in the future, horses no longer could be borrowed without permission. Furthermore, they declared their intention to retrieve any such property and to administer a whipping to anyone who resisted their efforts to return improperly borrowed goods. The case of Wolf Lies Down and the Elk Soldier Society clearly illustrates three basic functions of law. First, it

defines relationships among members of a culture, determining proper behaviour under specified circumstances. Knowledge of the law permits each person to know his or her rights and duties in respect to every other person. Second, law allocates the authority to employ coercion in the enforcement of sanctions. In societies with centralized political systems, such authority is generally vested in the government and its judicial system. In cultures that lack centralized political control, the authority to employ force may be allocated by the chief, the elder, or some other leader directly to the injured party. Third, law functions to redefine social relations and to ensure social flexibility. As new situations arise, law must determine whether old rules and assumptions retain their validity and the extent to which they must be altered. Law, if it is to operate efficiently, must allow room for change.

In practice, law is rarely the smooth and well-integrated system described here. In any given culture, various legal sanctions may apply at various levels. Because the people are usually members of numerous subgroups, they are subject to the dictates of these diverse groups. For example, each Kapauku of New Guinea, studied by Pospisil, is simultaneously a member of a family, a household, a sublineage, and a confederacy and is subject to all their laws. In some cases it may be impossible for an individual to submit to contradictory legal indications: "In one of the confederacy's lineages, incestuous relations between members of the same clan were punished by execution of the culprits, and in another by severe beating, in the third constituent lineage such a relationship was not punishable and … was not regarded as incest at all. In one of the sub-lineages, it became even a preferred type of marriage."[22]

Furthermore, the power to employ sanctions may vary from level to level within a given group. The head of a Kapauku household may punish a household member by slapping or beating, but the authority to confiscate property is vested exclusively in the headman of the lineage. Analogous distinctions exist in Canada among municipal, provincial, and federal jurisdictions. The complexity of legal jurisdiction makes generalizations about law difficult.

Crime

Nation-states with centralized governments make a clear distinction between offences against the state and offences against individuals, usually glossed under the headings of criminal versus civil offences. *Black's Law Dictionary* tells us that "the distinction between a crime and a tort or civil injury is that the former is a breach and violation of the public right and of duties due to the whole community considered as such, and in its social and aggregate capacity; whereas the latter is an infringement or privation of the civil rights of individuals merely."[23] Thus, a reckless driver who crashes into another car may be guilty of a crime by endangering public safety. The same driver also may be guilty of a tort by causing damages to the other car and personal injury, and the other driver may sue for his or her costs.

As we have observed, an important function of sanctions, legal or otherwise, is to discourage the breach of social norms. A person contemplating theft is aware of the possibility of being caught and punished. Yet even in the face of severe sanctions, individuals sometimes violate the norms and subject themselves to the consequences of their behaviour. What is the nature of crime in non-Western cultures?

In cultures without centralized governance, all offences are viewed as against members, and, importantly, against the community, rather than against the state, rendering the distinction between crime and tort irrelevant. Indeed, a dispute between individuals may seriously disrupt the social order, especially in small groups where the number of disputants, though small in absolute numbers, may be a large percentage of the total population. Although in the past the Inuit had no effective domestic or economic unit beyond the family, a dispute between two people would interfere with the ability of members of separate families to come to one another's aid when necessary and was consequently a matter of wider social concern. The goal of judicial proceedings in most non-criminal cases is to restore social harmony rather than to punish an offender. When distinguishing between offences of concern to the community as a whole and

One means of psychological evaluation is the Western polygraph ("lie detector").

those of concern to only a few individuals, we may refer to offences as public or private, rather than distinguishing between the more Western ethnocentric concepts of criminal and civil offences. In this way we avoid imposing our own values and assumptions, which would unnecessarily limit broader cross-cultural understandings of law.

Basically, disputes are settled in one of two ways. First, disputing parties may, via argument and compromise, voluntarily arrive at a mutually satisfactory agreement. This form of settlement is referred to as **negotiation** or, if it involves an unbiased third party's assistance, **mediation**. In bands and tribes a third-party mediator has no coercive power and thus cannot force disputants to abide by such a decision, but as a person who commands great personal respect, the mediator often may bring about a settlement.

Second, in chiefdoms and states, an authorized third party may issue a binding decision that the disputing parties will be compelled to respect. This process is referred to as **adjudication**. The difference between mediation and adjudication is essentially a difference in authorization. In a dispute settled by adjudication, the disputing parties present their positions as convincingly as they can, but they do not participate in the ultimate decision making.

The adjudication process is not universal; but every culture employs some form of negotiation to settle disputes. Negotiation often acts as a prerequisite or an alternative to adjudication. For example, in the resolution of

negotiation The use of direct argument and compromise by the parties to a dispute to arrive voluntarily at a mutually satisfactory agreement.
mediation Settlement of a dispute through negotiation assisted by an unbiased third party.
adjudication Mediation with an unbiased third party making the ultimate decision.

The Anthropologist's World

Dispute Resolution: The Anthropologist in the Middle

Rodney Nelson

For an anthropologist, the concept of dispute resolution is becoming more familiar as indigenous populations around the world are seeking restitution, reconciliation, consultation, and even partnerships in development. Anthropologists need to understand these differences as they may find themselves in the position of mediating disputes between two or more parties. Often these conflicts are based on cultural misunderstandings or a lack of understanding of cultural traditions. Cultural anthropologist Rodney Nelson unexpectedly found himself in such a position between the Coast Tsimshian First Nations (Metlakatla and Lax Kw'alaams), the Prince Rupert Port Authority, and the federal government.

The Prince Rupert Port Authority, along with several large Canadian corporations, has a vested interest in the $160 million dollar Fairview Container Terminal facility located on British Columbia's coast. The facility is part of the Canadian government's billion-dollar Pacific Gateway Strategy to increase economic development in the area and to create a primary passageway for shipping goods between Asia and the North American heartland. During this development, disputes arose, for the facility was being built on traditional Tsimshian territory. The site was being built on the site of an old village, and archaeological materials had already been removed. The next phase would consume two more traditional village sites, and their archaeological importance would be lost forever. The main concerns of the local bands (Metlakatla and Lax Kw'alaams) related to damage to archaeological sites and their traditional fishing grounds. The bands also voiced concerns over increased sea traffic, lack of up-to-date governmental environment regulations, and increasing pollution, which would damage local fish stocks. Damage to the salmon

populations would have a direct impact on Tsimshian livelihoods.

Metlakatla Chief Harold Leighton stated that their concerns would have to be addressed before Phase One of the construction project could begin. Port Authority CEO Don Krusel proposed a compensation package that would include economic development for the Tsimshian people and that would address their concerns about land use. Both the chief and the Port Authority wanted to find an equitable solution, but negotiations were producing little success.

In 2007, Rodney Nelson was Chair of the Council on Corporate Aboriginal Relations. The council planned a meeting in Prince Rupert to discuss the "duty to consult" (a legal doctrine in Canada that binds corporations to discuss and accommodate Aboriginal people's concerns when such corporations will have an impact on Aboriginal rights or treaty rights). Many of the meeting's attendees were seeking to develop or maintain partnerships with Aboriginal communities across Canada. This meeting also provided an opportunity for First Nations and corporations to discuss how to accommodate Aboriginal communities in large industrial projects. The council consisted of Aboriginal community representatives and corporate representatives. It was recognized that the corporate sector is morally, legally, and economically bound to consult with First Nations on projects that have an impact on their lives. Both First Nations and corporations have been requesting that the federal government provide clear regulations and procedures to define a "meaningful consultation." This request has gone unanswered to this day.

Several days before the Council on Corporate Aboriginal Relations meeting, there was an emergency call from then Minister of International Trade, David Emerson, to resume negotiations. This meant that the elected chiefs were not available to meet with the council, as they were needed in the negotiations. Left at the council meeting were the heads of large Canadian corporations, some whom had vested interests in the port, as well as some of the traditional

chiefs of the Tsimshian people. The council meeting quickly turned into a negotiation to understand Tsimshian governance structures. It wasn't long before a call was made to the lawyers telling them to stop the negotiation with the bands until the traditional chiefs could be included. From an anthropological perspective, Tsimshian approaches to governance and politics were crucial information that had not been given to the Port Authority. This information would greatly affect the negotiation's outcome.

The Tsimshian have a governance structure that recognizes both elected and traditional chiefs. The elected chiefs run the day-to-day operations and administer band business. The traditional chiefs are the holders of stories and of wisdom and are responsible for the land. The Tsimshian people recognize both types of chiefs as legitimate authorities. During the negotiations, issues of who had the right to speak on behalf of the community or culture became increasingly difficult as the political and governance structure was not fully understood. It was the anthropologist's task to recognize the traditional governance structures and persuade the parties involved to allow the traditional chiefs into the negotiations. The traditional chiefs were frustrated that they had never been consulted by the Port Authority. Bringing this new party to the table resulted in a new understanding of traditional Tsimshian governance structures and allowed for increased community engagement and negotiations. Several major stakeholders continue to work with the traditional chiefs to foster a new understanding and to forge new partnerships.

It is important to understand that indigenous experience, culture, and attitudes to process and law will vary with the individual, community, and culture. Consultation and negotiations should take place early in any project and include the opinions and expectations of the communities involved. Negotiations should always remain highly flexible and open to accommodate the needs and expectations of the community when possible. All too often, negotiations fail owing to a simple need of the community that is not being addressed, such as the need for a road, a school, or even a well for fresh water. While this may seem insignificant to a large corporation or a government, it is very important to the daily lives of the people in the community.

One role of an anthropologist engaging in conflict resolution is to understand the needs and culture of organizations or governments that are part of negotiations. While impartiality is vital to conflict resolution, anthropologists are often biased for the protection of the community and culture. It is important to recognize this bias and work toward understanding all sides of the argument. Organizations and governments have their own values and expectations. They are often under tight timelines and can lose millions of dollars in project delays. These values often conflict with community values. So differences must be acknowledged and dealt with early in any negotiation.

Also, cultures interpret and manage conflict differently. In the case of the Tsimshian, historical conflicts with surrounding communities and nations are not unheard of, but there are rules and restrictions on these conflicts–for example, the communities in conflict are expected to seek a balanced approach that engages the elders, chiefs, and community members. Traditional Tsimshian conflict resolution employs the concepts of fairness and compensation and is seen as a negotiation of equals between communities and nations.

Understanding the values of both a culture and an organization can aid in conflict resolution. The anthropologist tries to create a safe space for negotiation between the parties. Creating an understanding through education is the first step in negotiations and will sometimes alleviate the issues. When this understanding has been attained, the anthropologist can then change role from educator to facilitator and begin to discuss the wants and needs of both sides.

In the case of the Tsimshian and the Port Authority, the two main points of dispute were the protection and handling of traditional archaeological materials and the protection of the environment. The community's hidden wishes included recognition and partnerships for economic growth. The idea of partnerships and agreements was on the table right away from the Port Authority; however, in Tsimshian culture it is important to recognize tradition, history, and leadership before discussing such a possibility. Once this was understood and agreements for the protection of the environment and material culture were discussed, the talks of partnership and benefits could begin.

Today the tensions are still high between the Coast Tsimshian and the Port Authority; yet they are talking. Phase Two of the port project is currently deep in consultation over environmental assessments and economic partnerships with the bands. In 2010 the Prince Rupert Port Authority announced a joint venture between the Metlakatla Development Cooperation, the Prince Rupert Port Authority, and the Lax Kw'alaams band to purchase Watson Island, a sawmill and pulp-and-paper facility, along with harvesting rights from the city of Prince Rupert.

Also, Lax Kw'alaams has entered into a trade agreement with China to provide logs from the Prince Rupert area using the Port Authority as its shipping partner. The Coast Tsimshian have a forest licence to harvest 550,000 cubic metres of timber a year, but there is no sawmill in the region to process the logs. This tripartite partnership and the purchase of the island facilities will help meet the demands of the agreement with China. However, the Gitxaala Nation to the south of Prince Rupert has asserted a claim and injunction against this purchase, stating they have a claim to this traditional territory and were never consulted. Mediation is inevitable. An anthropologist's work is never done.

SOURCES: Fairview Container Port Project, Prince Rupert Port Authority, News Release, August 2007; "Rupert Port Dispute Gets Help," *Vancouver Sun*, June 2007; Prince Rupert Port Authority, News Release, August 2007; Council on Corporate Aboriginal Relations, Conference Board of Canada, 2007; Indigenous Dispute and Conflict Management, National Alternative Dispute Resolution Advisory Council, Australia, 2006; R. Golbert, "An Anthropologist's Approach to Mediation," *Cardozo Journal of Conflict Resolution* 11, no. 1 (2008).

North American labour disputes, striking workers may first negotiate with management, often with the mediation of a third party. If the state decides the strike constitutes a threat to the public welfare, the disputing parties may be forced to submit to adjudication. In this case, the responsibility for resolving the dispute is transferred to a presumably impartial judge, who may, for example, find in favour of the workers or order back-to-work legislation.

In many politically centralized cultures, incorruptible supernatural (or at least nonhuman) powers are thought to make judgments through trial by ordeal. Among the Kpelle of Liberia, for example, when guilt is in doubt, an ordeal operator licensed by the government may apply a hot knife to a suspect's leg. If the leg is burned, the suspect is guilty; if not, innocence is assumed. But the operator does not merely heat the knife and apply it. After massaging the suspect's legs and determining that the knife is hot enough, the operator then strokes his own leg with it without being burned, demonstrating that the innocent will escape injury. The knife is then applied to the suspect. Up to this point—consciously or unconsciously—the operator has read the suspect's nonverbal cues: gestures, the degree of muscular tension, amount of perspiration, and so forth. From this the operator can judge whether or not the accused is showing enough anxiety to indicate probable guilt; in effect, a psychological stress evaluation has been made. As the knife is applied, it is manipulated to either burn or not burn the suspect, once this judgment has been made. The operator easily does this manipulation by controlling how long the knife is in the fire, as well as the pressure and angle at which it is pressed against the leg.[24]

Similar to this practice is the use of the lie detector (polygraph). An incorruptible nonhuman agency is thought to establish who is lying and who is not, whereas in reality the polygraph operator cannot just "read" the needles of the machine. He or she must judge whether or not they are registering a high level of anxiety brought on by the testing situation, as opposed to the stress of guilt. Thus, the polygraph operator has much in common with the Kpelle ordeal operator.

POLITICAL ORGANIZATION AND EXTERNAL AFFAIRS

Although the regulation of internal affairs is an important function of any political system, it is by no means the sole function. Another is the management of external or international affairs—relations not just between states but also between different bands, lineages, clans, or whatever the largest autonomous political unit may be. Although intergroup relations over the centuries have generally been characterized by peaceful contacts, mediated by mutually beneficial trade and diplomacy, these peaceful modes of interaction may sometimes fail and hostilities leading to deadly conflict may erupt.

War

Groups have gone to war for thousands of years. Is the need to wage war an instinctive feature of the human personality? What are the alternatives to violence as a means of settling disputes between groups?

It is important to point out that war is not a universal phenomenon. The Ju/'hoansi of southern Africa, the Arapesh of New Guinea, the Hopi of North America, and others, may engage in interpersonal violence, but they do not practise warfare as we know it.

We have ample reason to suppose that war has become a problem only in the past 10 000 years, since the development of food-production techniques and (even more recently) with the emergence of centralized states. Although history offers many examples of serious warfare from Greek, Roman, and medieval times—often with horrendous casualties—it can be argued that warfare has reached crisis proportions only in the past 150 years. This is due in part to the invention of modern war-fighting techniques and weaponry, such as the machine gun,

world views The conceptions, explicit and implicit, an individual or a group has of the limits and workings of its world.

motorized warfare, aerial bombardment, mass production of weapons, and the international arms trade. Increasingly, violence is being directed against civilian populations. In contemporary warfare, we have reached the point where civilian casualties outnumber those of soldiers. Thus, war is less an age-old problem than a relatively recent one.

Among foragers, with their uncentralized political systems, warfare is all but unknown, although violence sometimes occurs. Because territorial boundaries and membership in foraging bands are fluid and loosely defined, a man who hunts with one band today may hunt with a neighbouring band tomorrow. Also, warfare among foragers is rendered somewhat impractical by the systematic interchange of marriage partners among foraging groups—it is likely that someone in each band will have a sister, a brother, or a cousin in a neighbouring band. Moreover, the absence of a food surplus does not permit prolonged combat. Where populations are small, food surpluses absent, property ownership minimal, and state organization nonexistent, the likelihood of organized violence by one group against another is minimal.[25]

Despite the view of the farmer as a gentle tiller of the soil, it is among such people, along with pastoralists, that warfare becomes prominent. One reason may be that food-producing peoples are far more prone to the pressures of population growth than are foragers, whose numbers generally are maintained well below carrying capacity. This population growth, if unchecked, can lead to resource depletion. One solution may be the seizure of some other group's resources. In addition, the commitment to a fixed piece of land inherent in farming makes such groups somewhat less fluid in their membership than foragers. In rigidly matrilocal or patrilocal societies, each new generation is bound to the same territory, no matter how small it may be or how large the group trying to live within it.

The availability of virgin land may not serve as a sufficient deterrent to the outbreak of war. Among slash-and-burn horticulturists, for example, competition for land previously cleared of virgin forest often leads to hostility and armed conflict. The centralization of political control and the possession of valuable property among farming peoples provide many more stimuli for warfare. When such groups are organized into states, the violence of warfare is most apt to result in indiscriminate killing. This development has reached its peak in modern states. Indeed, much (but not all) of the warfare observed in stateless societies (so-called tribal warfare) has been induced by states, as a reaction to their colonial expansion.[26]

Another difference between food-gathering and food-producing populations lies in their different **world views**. As a general rule, foragers tend to conceive of themselves as a part of the natural world and in some sort of balance with it. Western Abenaki hunters thought

In Mexico, as in many countries of the world, armed conflict has become commonplace as governments dominated by one ethnic group impose their rule through coercion and brute force in order to control the labour and resources of subaltern groups. Shown here are police of the Mexican state of Chiapas, with local Maya and (in the bags) the bodies of sympathizers of the Zapatista rebel movement. The Zapatista movement was launched in 1992 to mark 500 years of exploitation by Spanish colonialism and its modern successors in Mexico.

that animals, like humans, were composed of both a body and a personal spirit. Thus, when beaver, muskrat, or waterfowl were killed, the hunters could not just toss their bones into the nearest garbage pit. Proper respect required that their bones be returned to the water, with a request that the species be continued. Such attitudes may be referred to as part of a **naturalistic world view**.

The Abenakis' respect for nature contrasts sharply with the kind of world view prevalent among farmers and pastoralists, who do not find their food *in* nature but impose their dominance *on* nature to produce food for themselves. The attitude that nature exists only for human use may be referred to as an **exploitative world view**. With such an outlook, it is a small step from dominating the rest of nature to dominating other human groups for the benefit of one's own. The exploitative world view, prevalent among food-producing peoples, is an important contributor to intersocietal warfare.

A comparison between the Western Abenakis and their Iroquoian neighbours to the west is instructive. Among the Abenakis, warfare was essentially a defensive activity. These foragers, with their naturalistic world view, believed they could not operate in someone else's territory, since they did not control the necessary supernatural powers. Furthermore, operating far below carrying capacity, they had no need to prey upon the resources of others. The Iroquois, by contrast, were slash-and-burn horticulturists who engaged in predatory warfare. Evidence indicates significant environmental degradation around their settlements, suggesting overutilization of resources such as wood, beaver, and deer. Although the Iroquois went to war to replace men lost in previous battles, the main motive was to achieve dominance by making their victims acknowledge Iroquoian superiority. This changed in the 1650s as their main aim became to

dispel the Huron Confederacy and take over their role as middlemen in the emergent fur trade with the French.[27] Many members of vanquished tribes were adopted into Iroquoian clans. The payment of tribute purchased "protection" from the Iroquois, which no doubt helped offset the depletion of resources near the village of the would-be protectors. The price of protection went further than this, though; it included constant and public ceremonial deference to the Iroquois, free passage for their war parties through the subjugated group's country, and the contribution of young men to Iroquoian war parties.

A comparison between the Iroquois and Europeans is also instructive. Sometime in the 16th century, Iroquoian nations determined to end warfare among themselves by directing their predatory activities against outsiders rather than one another. The famous Deganawida, known to the Iroquois as The Peacemaker, brought the Great Law of Peace to the Iroquois. He preached unity and peace and symbolically buried a hatchet under a tree, giving rise to this same expression.[28] Under the Great Law of Peace, the famous League of the Iroquois came into being. The Iroquois successfully held European expansion at bay until the end of the 18th century, and some admirers, including Benjamin Franklin, used their example as inspiration for the new union of the 13 American colonies in 1776 that resulted in the founding of the United States. The descendants of the League of the Iroquois still holding to their ancient traditions are today known as the Six Nations of Oshweken, Ontario.

naturalistic world view The belief that humans are merely one part of the natural world.

exploitative world view The belief that nature exists for humans to dominate and exploit.

CP PHOTO/D. Morel/AP

Canadian peacekeepers are a reflection of Canada's fundamental belief in peace not war, dialogue not bullets.

Canada's Role in International Peacekeeping

As noted earlier, external affairs refers to much more than warfare; diplomatic offices, trade relations, and international aid are all examples of enduring external affairs. In Canada, international peacekeeping is an important component of foreign policy. In 1957, Prime Minister Lester B. Pearson received the Nobel Peace Prize for his establishment of an international peacekeeping force within the UN Security Council. Since then, Canada has participated in numerous military peacekeeping missions, sending more than 100,000 men and women on more than 40 missions. Former UN Secretary-General Boutros Boutros-Ghali stated, "Peacekeeping is a technique that expands the possibilities for both the prevention of conflict and the making of peace."[29]

The peacekeepers' roles have evolved over the years. Besides going on military missions to supervise ceasefires and the withdrawal of forces, Canada has involved itself through the RCMP, Elections Canada, and the Canadian Red Cross. During the Cambodia mission in 1991–93, UN peacekeepers disarmed warring factions, repatriated refugees, upheld human rights, and organized provisional elections. In Somalia in 1992 and 1993, peacekeepers ensured the equitable distribution of relief supplies. In 2003, Canadian soldiers went to Afghanistan to help the people rebuild their country.

Peacekeepers are also peace *builders*—they work to re-establish normal life in war-torn countries. In Rwanda, for

structural violence The widespread practice in many societies of inflicting harm on subordinate sectors of society by indirect means—such as poorer housing, schooling, or health care—rather than through the direct exercise of force and coercion.

example, Canadian troops opened airports and restored communications systems; in Haiti, the RCMP has trained a local police force; and in Afghanistan, peacekeepers are working to restore vital services (e.g., digging wells in the rural areas for clean, safe water). The primary goal of peacekeeping is to establish conditions in troubled societies that will enable the people to resolve their differences and build a better future. By convincing people to lay down their weapons and settle their grievances without violence, peacekeepers seek to accomplish what the UN was established to do.[30] All of this comes at a cost, however; the current mission to Afghanistan has resulted in the deaths of more than 150 Canadian soldiers. At stake for both peacekeepers and the Afghanis is what political system will prevail and whether that system will be legitimate.

POLITICAL SYSTEMS AND THE QUESTION OF LEGITIMACY

Whatever form a culture's political system may take and however the people may go about their business, it must find some way to obtain the people's allegiance. In uncentralized systems, where every adult participates in all decision making, loyalty and cooperation are freely given, since each person is considered a part of the political system. As the group grows larger, however, and the organization becomes more formal, the problems of obtaining and keeping public support become greater.

This problem becomes especially acute in complex societies in which the population has become divided into social classes. In class-based societies, social classes are social segments that have differential access to wealth and power. Upper classes—elites—dominate ownership of the means of production and access to higher political office. Middle classes may control their own labour and modest amounts of wealth and property, while lower classes may control little or none of their own labour power, being forced to till the soil as peasants on land owned by others. Under capitalism, the lower classes occupy the bottom rungs of the occupational ladder, earning low or minimum wages and living at or below the poverty line.

Given this social inequality, centralized political systems increasing rely on coercion as a means of social control. Coercion may be expressed *overtly* by legal sanctions for breaches of law, such as nonpayment of rent or tribute, or *covertly*, by rules that force people to accept poorer housing, lower wages, and/or inadequate access to health care, education, and opportunities for upward mobility. This latter form of coercion is often referred to as **structural violence**—in other words, violence that people experience by their position in society and not by actual physical punishment. The greater vulnerability of the poor to infectious disease is a primary example of structural violence, as documented by medical anthropologist Paul Farmer.[31]

The reliance on force, however, is a two-edged sword. Coercion tends to lessen the effectiveness of a political system and raise the costs of ruling for the elite. For example, the personnel needed to apply force must be large and may itself grow to be a political power. The emphasis on force certainly creates resentment among those it is applied to, which lessens cooperation. Police states are generally short-lived, and most elites choose less-extreme forms of social control.

Basic to this political process is the concept of legitimacy, or the right of political leaders to rule. Like force, legitimacy is a form of support for a political system; unlike force, legitimacy is based on the values a particular culture believes most important. For example, among the Kapauku the legitimacy of the *tonowi's* power comes from his wealth; the kings of Hawaii and of England and France were thought to have a divine right to rule; and the head of the Dahomey state in western Africa acquired legitimacy through his age, as he was always the oldest living male.

Legitimacy grants the right to hold, use, and allocate power. Power based on legitimacy may be distinguished from power based on force alone: obedience to the former results from the belief obedience is "right"; compliance to power based on force results from fear of the deprivation of liberty, physical well-being, life, and material property. Thus, power based on legitimacy is symbolic and depends not on any intrinsic value but rather on the positive expectations of those who recognize and accede to it.

In recent decades, anthropologists and other social scientists have been highly influenced by the ideas of Antonio Gramsci, the Italian communist and philosopher, whose concept of *hegemony* is relevant here. In class societies, ruling elites attempt to frame their ideas in a form that is acceptable to the society as a whole. Hegemony equals legitimacy when the ideas of the ruling class are identified not as the narrow interests of the dominant elite, but rather as expressing the "natural" order of things and simple "common sense." The acceptance of such arguable concepts as the inevitability of the market, the natural superiority of men, and the necessity of the "war on terror" are examples of the successful application of hegemonic ideology in contemporary society.

RELIGION AND POLITICS

Historically, religious belief has been one of the most effective means for elites to ensure legitimacy of their rule. The anthropologist and museum director Stephen de Borheyghi famously noted that the invention of heaven and hell has had a more profound effect on cultural evolution than the invention of the wheel. Religious belief is far more cost-effective than marshalling armies and police to ensure compliance.

Religion is intricately connected with politics. Religious beliefs may influence laws: Acts that people believe to be sinful, such as incest, are often illegal as well. Often it is religion that legitimizes the political order, whether among the historic Aztec or the Europeans. In both industrial and nonindustrial societies, belief in the supernatural is reflected in the political organization. The effect of religion on politics was perhaps best exemplified in medieval Europe. Holy wars were fought over the smallest matter; labour was mobilized to build immense cathedrals in honour of the Virgin Mary and other saints; and kings and queens ruled by "divine right," pledged allegiance to the pope, and asked his blessing in all important ventures, be they marital or martial. In the pre-Columbian Americas, the Aztec state was a religious state, or theocracy, one that thrived in spite of more or less constant warfare carried out to procure captives for human sacrifices to appease the Aztec's bloodthirsty gods. In Peru, the Inca emperor proclaimed absolute authority based on the proposition he was descended from the Sun God.

Despite the trend toward states based on more secular ideologies—democracy, socialism, and capitalism—examples of states based on religion still exist. Modern Iran in 1979 was proclaimed an "Islamic republic," and its first head of state, the Ayatollah, was the most holy of all Shiite Muslim holy men. Religious fundamentalism is also a significant political force in modern states as diverse as Egypt, Israel, India, Pakistan, and the United States.

In many regions of the world, religion and politics are inextricably bound up in hostilities between opposing groups. Such is the case with Israelis and Palestinians in their long-standing struggle.

Chapter Summary

1. What is political organization?

Political organization is the manner in which a culture maintains order and manages its internal and external affairs. Political organization and control are the ways power is distributed and embedded in cultures. Through political organization, cultures maintain social order, reduce disorder, manage public affairs, and regulate relations with outsiders.

2. How is order maintained within a culture?

Social controls may be internalized—"built into" individuals—or externalized in the form of sanctions. Built-in controls rely on deterrents such as personal shame and fear of supernatural punishment. Positive sanctions encourage approved behaviour, while negative sanctions discourage disapproved behaviour. Negative sanctions formalized and enforced by an authorized political body are called laws. Yet cultures do not maintain order through law alone.

For example, in band-level societies, band leaders are usually older men, or sometimes women, with personal authority. Bands tend toward more egalitarian relations between men and women, when compared to other forms of organization. The tribe is composed of separate bands or other social units tied together by such unifying factors as descent groups, age grading, or common interest. As in the band, political organization is transitory, and leaders have no formal means of maintaining authority. In chiefdoms, power is concentrated in a single chief whose acknowledged authority is accepted as legitimate and serves to unite his community in all matters. The most centralized of political organizations is the state. It has a central power that can use force to administer an often rigid code of laws to maintain order, even sometimes beyond its borders. The hallmarks of the state are a large bureaucracy and a stratified society where economic functions and wealth are distributed unequally.

3. How is order maintained between cultures?

Two kinds of cultural control exist: internalized and externalized. Internalized controls are self-imposed by individuals. These rely on such deterrents as personal shame, fear of divine punishment, and magical retaliation. Every culture develops externalized controls, called sanctions, which mix cultural and social control. Positive sanctions, in the form of rewards or recognition, involve the position a culture or a number of its members take toward approved behaviour; negative sanctions, such as threat of imprisonment, corporal punishment, or "loss of face," reflect societal reactions to disapproved behaviour. Law defines relationships among a group's members, thus dictating proper behaviour under various circumstances. Legal systems also allocate authority to employ coercion to enforce sanctions. In centralized political systems, this authority rests with the government and court system. In uncentralized systems, this authority is given, by convention and tradition, directly to the injured party.

4. How do political systems obtain people's allegiance?

The threat of violence, not necessarily the actual use of violence, is important in maintaining allegiance (and order). However, other components of society are used to obtain allegiance. Religion is intricately woven into the life of the people in both industrial and nonindustrial countries. In the past, its presence was inevitably felt in the political sphere. Today, more secular ideologies predominate, where ethics, laws, and self-interest are paramount, although religion is still a significant force for individuals and families. However, for a number of governments, religious fundamentalism provides the main source of hegemonic political power and legitimacy.

Questions for Critical Thought

1. In this chapter we read about the use of informal sanctions (as opposed to formalized, codified laws) to control individual behaviour in a group. What are examples of such sanctions? How do they operate in large societies that do have more codified laws? Are the two necessarily in total accord?

2. In many countries the press has taken on the role of watching and reporting on the behaviour of powerful individuals. How can this serve as a sanction? What are the potential benefits of such publications and broadcastings? What are the potential drawbacks?

3. Do informal sanctions operate in Canadian society? If so, how effective are they at various levels of our political organization?

4. "Canada has generally maintained a 'peace not war' ideology, as evidenced by its role in international peacekeeping forces." Do you agree or disagree with this statement? Provide reasons for your answer.

5. Our Canadian legal system is increasingly criticized for failing to solve the crime problem in Canada. Is this criticism justified? In what ways? How might the system be changed to provide more of a deterrent to criminal activity?

6. Religious fundamentalism as a source of political hegemony is a recent phenomenon that counters the long-term trend toward more secular political systems. Give an example or examples of a fundamentalist regime and of a more secular one. What do you think are the underlying reasons for the rise of fundamentalism?

Internet Resources

Aboriginal Self-Government

http://www.afn.ca/uploads/files/aga/pursuing_self-determination_aga_2011_eng%5B1%5D.pdf

This comprehensive site highlights the concept of self-government, policy frameworks, negotiations, mechanisms for implementation, existing treaties and land claim agreements, and the various approaches to self-government.

http://ainc-inac.gc.ca/eng/1100100016293 and http://www.ualberta.ca/~walld/NUNSEPT2.html

A comprehensive site discussing many aspects of Aboriginal self-government, including approaches, evolution, arrangements, and chronology.

Canada and Peacekeeping

http://peacekeeper.ca

Created by a former peacekeeper, this site examines the history, current status, and future prospects of Canadian peacekeeping forces.

Assembly of First Nations

http://www.afn.ca

A huge site with extensive links to related pages. Includes links to programs, press releases, and current events.

Ending Violence Against Women and Girls

http://www.unfpa.org/swp/2000/english/ch03.html

A UN site addressing the issues of gender-based violence in cultures around the world. Boxes include "Women's Attackers Seldom Punished in Pakistan" and "Killings in Sweden Spark Debate About Domestic Violence." Other topics include "Trafficking in Women and Girls," "'Honour' Killings," and "Impacts on Reproductive Health."

Nation, State, and Economy

http://www.mises.org/nsande.asp

An extensive site reviewing the essence of nationalism, with links to Prussia and Austria.

Political Anthropology

http://www.openanthropology.org/ANTH423

The basic concepts and current research in political anthropology are set out in this course taught by Maximilian Forte at Montreal's Concordia University.

Suggested Readings

For a list of suggested readings, visit the textbook's website at **http://www.havilandcultural4e.nelson.com**.

Notes

1. M. Asch, as cited in *The Cambridge Encyclopedia of Hunters and Gatherers*, ed. R.B. Lee and R. Daly (Cambridge: Cambridge University Press, 1981), 342–43.

2. M. Asch and S. Smith, "Slavey Dene," in ibid., 48–49.

3. E.E. Evans-Prichard, *The Nuer: A Description of the Modes of Livelihood and Political Institutions of a Nilotic People* (Oxford: Oxford University Press, 1969).

4. J.L. Gibbs, Jr., "The Kpelle of Liberia," in *Peoples of Africa*, ed. J.L. Gibbs, Jr. (New York: Holt, Rinehart and Winston, 1965), 216–18.

5. J.W. Clay, "What's a Nation?," in *Talking About People*, ed. W.A. Haviland and R.J. Gordon, 2nd ed. (Mountain View: Mayfield, 1996), 188.

6. P.L. Van Den Berghe, "The Modern State: Nation Builder or Nation Killer?" *International Journal of Group Tensions* 22, no. 3 (1992): 193.

7. J.W. Friesen, *Rediscovering the First Nations of Canada* (Calgary: Detselig, 1997).

8. Indian and Northern Affairs Canada, "Federal Policy Guide— Aboriginal Self-Government," July 21, 2000, http://www.ainc-inac.gc.ca/al/ldc/ccl/sgb-eng.asp, accessed March 21, 2001.

9. Ibid.

10. H. Kuper, "The Swazi of Swaziland," in *Peoples of Africa*, ed. J.L. Gibbs, Jr. (New York: Holt, Rinehart and Winston, 1965), 475–512.

11. E. Leacock, *Myths of Male Dominance* (New York: Monthly Review Press, 1982).

12. K. Okonjo, "The Dual Sex Political System in Operation: Igbo Women and Community Politics in Midwestern Nigeria," in *Women in Africa*, ed. N. Hafkin and E. Bay (Stanford: Stanford University Press, 1976), 45–58.

13. J. Van Allen, "Sitting on a Man: Colonialism and the Lost Political Institutions of Igbo Women," in *Women in Society*, ed. S. Tiffany (St. Albans: Eden Press, 1979), 169.

14. Leacock, *Myths of Male Dominance*.

15. W.E. Mitchell, "A New Weapon Stirs Up Old Ghosts," *Natural History Magazine*, December 1973, 77–84.

16. A.R. Radcliffe-Brown, *Structure and Function in Primitive Society* (New York: Free Press, 1952), 205.

17. A.L. Epstein, "Sanctions," in *International Encyclopedia of Social Sciences*, vol. 14 (New York: Macmillan, 1968), 3.

18. E.E. Evans-Pritchard, *Witchcraft, Oracles, and Magic Among the Azande* (London: Oxford University Press, 1937).

19. T. Mandamin, "Harmony in the Community: Aboriginal Justice Sentencing Initiatives," *Law Now* 21, no. 1 (1996): 17–20.

20. B. Malinowski, *Crime and Custom in Savage Society* (London: Routledge, 1951), 55.

21. E.A. Hoebel, *The Law of Primitive Man: A Study in Comparative Legal Dynamics* (Cambridge, MA: Harvard University Press, 1954), 28.

22. L. Pospisil, *Anthropology of Law: A Comparative Theory* (New York: Harper and Row, 1971), 36.

23. H.C. Black, *Black's Law Dictionary* (St. Paul: West, 1968).

24. J.L. Gibbs, Jr. [interview], *Faces of Culture: Program 18* (Fountain Valley: Coast Telecourses, 1983).

25. B. Knauft, "Violence and Sociality in Human Evolution," *Current Anthropology* 32 (1991): 391–409.

26. N.L. Whitehead and R.B. Ferguson, "Deceptive Stereotypes About Tribal Warfare," *Chronicle of Higher Education*, November 10, 1993, A48.

27. D.K. Richter, "War and Culture: The Iroquois Experience," *William and Mary Quarterly*, 3rd series, 40, no. 4 (1983): 528–59.

28. D.R. Snow, *Archaeology of Native North America* (New York: Prentice Hall, 2008).

29. Department of Foreign Affairs and International Trade, "Backgrounder: Canada and Peacekeeping," 2001, http://www.unac.org/peacekeeping/en/un-peacekeeping/fact-sheets/una-canada-backgrounder-for-journalists, accessed March 20, 2001.

30. Ibid., 6.

31. P. Farmer, *Pathologies of Power: Health, Human Rights, and the New War on the Poor* (Berkeley: University of California Press, 2003).

12 Religion and the Supernatural

Liam Kilmurray

Religion and art are intertwined practices. In this image, the feast dishes and bentwood chests of the Kwakwaka'wakw are shown. These were ceremonial objects, used in spiritual ceremonies. Museum of Anthropology Vancouver.

KEY QUESTIONS

1. What Is Religion?

To define religion in a satisfactory way presents an insurmountable challenge, as anthropologists have discovered. Definitions range from the practice (ritual) of religion to the ideas and beliefs of religion. Regardless of the definition used, the goal of anthropologists is to understand the role that religion plays in culture, not to discern the "truth" of religious beliefs.

2. What Are Religion's Identifying Features?

Religion involves various rituals—prayers, songs, dances, offerings, and sacrifices—that people use in the hope of gaining assistance from supernatural beings and powers. These beings and powers may consist of gods and goddesses, ancestral and other spirits, and impersonal powers. In all human groups certain individuals are skilled at dealing with the supernatural and help other members in their ritual activities. A body of myths rationalizes or explains a religious system in a manner consistent with people's experience of the world in which they live.

3. Why Is Religion a Cultural Universal?

Whether or not a particular religion accomplishes what people believe it does, all religions serve a number of important psychological and social purposes. They reduce anxiety by explaining the unknown and making it understandable, and they teach oral traditions and behavioural codes to the next generation. Religious beliefs may provide comfort and the hope of assistance in times of crisis. Religion offers a form of social control by providing notions of right and wrong, setting precedents for acceptable behaviour, and transferring the burden of decision making from individuals to supernatural powers. Finally, religion plays an important role in maintaining social solidarity.

According to the Iroquois origin myth, the earth was once covered with water and shrouded in darkness; only water animals lived there. Then the Great Spirit commanded his pregnant daughter, Sky Woman, to bring light to the world below. He wrapped her in light and dropped her through a hole in the sky. Waterfowl rose to cushion Sky Woman's descent, and muskrat brought dirt from the seabed to make dry land for Sky Woman. Turtle rose to hold the land in place as it spread and grew larger, until the land became the size it is today. Sky Woman gave birth to a daughter; in time this daughter met a man, who placed two arrows within her. The daughter bore twins; the good twin was called Sapling. The evil twin, called Flint, killed his mother during his birth. In grief, Sapling created the sun from his mother's face; Flint made darkness to drive the sun west. Sapling brought the moon and stars from his mother's breast, and created mountains and rivers; Flint jumbled the mountains and made the rivers crooked. Sapling planted forests and fruit trees; Flint sent storms to tear at the land. Sapling then made humans, and planted maize and tobacco; Flint made monsters, weeds, and vermin. Sapling defeated Flint and banished him to an underground cave, though Flint still sends out wicked spirits, ensuring that good and evil are in all things.

There are more than 40 versions of this Iroquois origin myth, but regardless of the account, this myth conveys several interwoven themes of central importance to the Iroquois. The myth portrays the constant struggle between good and evil—the Iroquois world is composed of good but always tainted with evil. The main character of this myth is a woman, exemplifying the importance of women in Iroquois communities—women are the source of all life and sustenance. The myth also describes the interdependence of all things in nature—waterfowl, muskrat, and turtle all helped save Sky Woman, the mother of humankind. The twins are a reflection of the duality in Iroquois social organization; the twins lived in the same lodge for a while, facing each other across a fire, similar to traditional Iroquois living arrangements, and the Iroquois village is divided into two halves of a moiety.[1]

To members of other religions, such beliefs may seem irrational and arbitrary, but in fact they are neither. The Iroquois religion of traditional times was not only logical but also the very model of Iroquois social organization. Iroquois cultures were divided into two independent moieties, each with its own economy, rituals, and authority. An individual was introduced into one of these moieties (which were *not* based on kinship), and his or her membership was regularly reinforced through a series of ceremonies that reaffirmed the balance and reciprocity

The Birth of the Earth by Arnold Jacobs/Arnold Jacobs

Origin or creation myths often exemplify the interdependence of all things in nature. Shown here is Sky Woman's descent to earth, helped by Turtle and Geese.

between men and women and between moieties. The rites of birth and death were shared by the whole community; a deceased individual's moiety immediately began to grieve, while the other moiety offered condolences and organized the burial.

The Iroquois religion entered into virtually every aspect of Iroquois life and culture. It was the basis of the simultaneously dualistic and unified world view of individual Iroquois. It provided numerous points of mediation so that the two moieties could continue to exist together as a single community. It sanctified the community by linking its origin with the realm of the supernatural, and it offered divine sanction to *rites of passage* that softened life's major transitions. By providing an afterworld that was the mirror image of Iroquois society at the best of times, it answered the question of death in a manner that reinforced social structure. In short, Iroquois religion provided a solid foundation for the stability and continuity of Iroquoian culture and individual existence.

All religions fulfill numerous social and psychological needs. Some of these—the need to confront and explain death, for example—appear to be universal; indeed, we know of no group of people anywhere who have been without religion for any extended period. Whether it is manifested in Aztec gods or Apache rain dances, religion is unbound by time. Religion gives meaning to individual and group life, drawing power from "the time of the gods in the Beginning," and it offers continuity of existence beyond death. The social aspects of religion are no less important than the psychological ones. A religion may reinforce group norms, provide moral sanctions for individual conduct, and furnish the substratum of common purpose and values upon which the equilibrium of the community depends.

In the 19th century, the European intellectual community suggested that science ultimately would destroy religion by showing people the irrationality of their myths and rituals. The emergence of scientific socialism and a host of Communist states in the world also placed religion under some stress. Indeed, many still believe that as scientific explanations replace those of religion, the latter will wither on the vine. This has not happened. Science, far from destroying religion, may have contributed to the creation of a veritable religious boom by removing traditional psychological props while creating, in its technological applications, a host of new problems: threat of nuclear catastrophe; epidemic health scares; unease about the consequences of new developments in biotechnology, such as the cloning of animals, the production of new strains of genetically engineered organisms, and the ability to store human sperm and eggs for future fertilization; economic insecurity as machines replace workers; and fear of loneliness in a society that isolates us from our kin and places impediments in the way of establishing deep and lasting friendships. In the face of these new anxieties, religion offers social and psychological support. Religion, then, reduces anxiety and keeps confidence high, which serves to keep people in some sort of shape to cope with reality. It is this that gives religion its survival value.

New developments in biotechnology, such as cloning, which produced the sheep Dolly, have been a source of new anxieties. Answers to these anxieties are often sought in religion.

Not only do traditional mainstream religions (Christianity, Judaism, and Islam) continue to exist, but fundamentalist forms of these religions are experiencing a dramatic increase in popularity. Islamic fundamentalism in countries such as Algeria and Iran, Jewish fundamentalism in Israel, and Hindu fundamentalism in India all continue to grow in strength. In North America and elsewhere, Christian fundamentalist denominations are growing at phenomenal rates—conservative estimates are that there are 30 million Christian fundamentalists in the United States alone.[2] Their churches are also heavily engaged in proselytizing in Africa and South and Central America.

Many ask why so many people in every corner of the world turn to religious fundamentalism. On a very basic level, fundamentalism (or revivalism, as it is sometimes called) means returning to the fundamentals of a religion. By and large, the phenomenon began in the early 20th century. Fundamentalism is a reaction to modernism and to religion's loss of influence in society. A misconception concerning fundamentalism is that all fundamentalists are radicals—or worse still, terrorists. Although there certainly are radical elements within many of the fundamentalist sects, radicalism is not why fundamentalism appeals to so many people.

Because fundamentalism crosses so many religious denominations, it is hard to generalize about. But there are some basic tenets found in virtually all fundamentalist religions. Many people believe that fundamentalists adhere to a literal translation of their sacred texts, and this is true to some extent; for most fundamentalists, however, the inerrancy of these texts (scripturalism) and the supreme authority of these writings are far more important.[3] Fundamentalists see themselves as guardians of the truth and see their sacred scriptures as sources of inspiration, comfort, and rules for living. They resist change brought on by modernism and maintain that traditional beliefs and doctrine, moral codes, and patterns of behaviour still have a place in their present. They also believe that religion should be integrated into all aspects of culture: family, schools, courts, the economy, politics, and so on. Many fundamentalist families and communities tend to be patriarchal; males hold authority within the family, the community, and the church, and women take a secondary place in society. This subordination of women has caused considerable strife and controversy within many fundamentalist groups.

Fundamentalists do not totally reject science and technology; they do, however, protest the way that science and technology have led to a secular ideology. If science conflicts with their beliefs, they reject the science.[4] Fundamentalism also contains an element of activism—adherents have a strong desire to convert

Far from causing the death of religion, the growth of scientific knowledge, by producing new anxieties and raising new questions about human existence, may have contributed to the continuing practice of religion in modern life. North Americans continue to participate in traditional religions, such as Judaism (top), Islam (middle), and Christianity (bottom).

religion A set of rituals, rationalized by myth, that mobilizes supernatural powers to achieve or prevent transformations of state in people and nature.

others to their beliefs and to change the world to fit their concept of how it should be. Returning to our original question, fundamentalism offers followers a clear-cut, logical world in which there is no allowance for deviation. This guidance enables followers to cope with and reshape their changing world. In the following Original Study, "Understanding Islam," you will learn more about fundamentalist elements in Islam.

Despite the surge in fundamentalism and the apparent health of most **religions**, religious affiliation has decreased sharply in many parts of Europe, where people presumably face similar dilemmas, and we would be remiss to ignore this fact. Similarly, the Canadian census demonstrates a dramatic decline in church attendance over the past 50 years, especially in Quebec.[5] Some parts of the country have become quite polarized in religious attitudes. For example, British Columbia has the largest concentration of people with no religious affiliation; and countrywide, the number of Canadians over 15 reporting no religious affiliation has risen to 19 percent, or just around 5 million people.

THE ANTHROPOLOGICAL APPROACH TO RELIGION

Defining religion is a fascinating challenge for anthropologists. Indeed, owing to its importance and multiple understandings, some anthropologists, such as Max Weber, refuse to define it at all. Anthropologist Anthony F.C. Wallace defined religion as "a set of rituals, rationalized by myth, which mobilizes supernatural powers for the purpose of achieving or preventing transformations of state in man and nature."[6] Underlying this definition is a recognition that people, when they cannot fix serious problems that cause them anxiety, turn to supernatural beings and powers for assistance. To do so requires ritual, which Wallace sees as the primary phenomenon of religion, or "religion in action." One of the most often cited—and controversial—definitions was framed by anthropologist Clifford Geertz. He contended that religion is (1) a system of symbols that acts to (2) establish powerful, pervasive, and long-lasting moods and motivations in people by (3) formulating conceptions of a general order of existence and (4) clothing these conceptions with such an aura of factuality that (5) the moods and motivations seem uniquely realistic.[7]

Thus, we have a variety of conflicting definitions, none of which satisfy all schools of thought. Although religion is difficult to define, given that its meanings can vary from one group to another, it is reasonable to suggest that religion is a survival mechanism that gives people the strength to cope with their reality along with some sense

Original Study

Understanding Islam

Islam is the fastest-growing faith community in the world. Some scholars speculate that by 2050 Islam will surpass Christianity as the largest faith community in the world.

The Prophet Muhammad (570–632) was a minor clansman of the ruling tribe in his home city of Mecca in western Saudi Arabia. A merchant-trader by profession, he travelled throughout the Middle East and was thus exposed to Jewish and Christian communities. In the process, he became fascinated with the heritage and theology of both religions.

While still a young man, Muhammad came to believe that there was only one god and started to practise private meditation. In 610, at the age of 40, during one of his many private retreats, he heard a voice that he later discerned to be that of the Angel Gabriel. The voice told Muhammad that he was ordained to be the prophet and messenger of God. Further revelations followed over the next 23 years. Recorded and compiled by the prophet's followers, these revelations became the Quran, Islam's sacred book.

The central revelation to the Prophet Muhammad was that "there is no god but Allah." The Prophet Muhammad did not claim that this was a new revelation. Quite to the contrary, it was the same message that Allah had revealed to Adam and that Allah had repeated through subsequent prophets and messengers. Chief among these prophets and messengers were Noah, Abraham, Moses, and Jesus. The truth that God had revealed to the Jewish people through Moses and Jesus, the Prophet Muhammad now offered to the Arab people in their own language. The Prophet Muhammad claimed that Allah was none other than the God of Jews and Christians.

Muhammad began to enthusiastically preach the revelations of Allah, first in Mecca and then in other parts of Saudi Arabia. At first he encountered much opposition, some of it violent. Not only did his monotheism (the worship of only one god) call into question the prevalent polytheism (the worship of many gods) of 7th-century Arabia, but his message also contained a profound challenge to the lifestyles of the rich and their oppression of the poor. Eventually he emerged as a powerful political leader, a social reformer, and a spiritual guide. By the time of his death, virtually all of Arabia was Muslim.

Unlike Christianity, which was the persecuted religion of a minority for the first 300 years of its history, Islam quickly became powerful. One hundred years after the prophet's death, the Islamic empire stretched from Spain to Iran, an empire greater than Rome at its zenith. The new religion was spread by way of commerce, human contact, conquest, and the works of Islamic scholars and mystics.

The People of the Book

Muslims refer to themselves, to Jews, and to Christians as "the People of the Book." But they believe that the Hebrew scriptures and the Christian scriptures contain errors. To correct these errors, Muslims believe, God has revealed the Quran through the Prophet Muhammad. Muslims believe that God dictated each word of the Quran—directly and infallibly—to the Prophet. Contained in its 114 chapters is God's full, final, and definitive revelation.

The basic statements of the Quran can be summarized as follows:

1. Allah has created the world.
2. A person is absolutely subject to the will of Allah in all matters.
3. A person must carry out the tasks which Allah assigns to her/him.
4. After this life, Allah will reward or punish each person in the measure in which he/she has lived according to the will of Allah.

This sacred book enjoys a position of unrivalled esteem in the Muslim community. To understand and appreciate the sacredness of the Quran in the larger context of Islamic life, let us employ an analogy: The Quran is to Muslims what Jesus is to Christians, what the Torah is to Jews, and what the natural environment is to Native peoples.

The Five Pillars of Islam

The life of the faithful Muslim is based on the Five Pillars of Islam:

1. The Shahada (Profession of Faith): Several times a day Muslims repeat, "There is no god but Allah and Muhammad is his messenger."
2. Salat (Prayer): Muslims pray five times a day—at sunrise, at noon, in the afternoon, at sunset, and after dark. Muslims pray facing Mecca. They may pray anywhere, but on Fridays they are encouraged to join other Muslims in prayer at the mosque.
3. Sawm (Fasting): During the month of Ramadan, Muslims abstain from food and drink between sunrise and sunset. Fasting is meant to develop self-discipline and compassion for those who do not have enough to eat or to drink.
4. Zakat (Almsgiving): Muslims donate 2.5 percent of their earnings to charity. Almsgiving is meant to restore the economic balance in society.
5. Hajj (Pilgrimage): Health and wealth permitting, each Muslim makes a pilgrimage to Mecca at least once in his or her lifetime. The focus of this pilgrimage is the Ka'ba, a large, cube-shaped structure, the original of which Abraham is believed to have built.

In addition to observing the Five Pillars of Islam, the faithful Muslim practises jihad (struggle). The "big jihad" is the struggle against the evil within oneself. The "little jihad" is the struggle to establish God's will on earth and, if necessary, to defend the Islamic community against aggression.

CONTINUED

CONTINUED

"God Is One"

The heart of Islam is its declaration of the oneness of God. The power and grace of God encompass the whole of creation. Every page of the Quran exclaims with passionate intensity: "Your God is One God; there is no God but the Living, the Eternal." And this One God is the creator. He is immaterial, all-powerful, all-pervading, all-just, compassionate, merciful, and benevolent.

Muslims claim that Christians have compromised monotheism by worshiping Jesus as God. They cannot accept the Christian doctrine of the Incarnation because they do not believe that God can assume a human form. Furthermore, the Christian doctrine of the Trinity is simply not reconcilable with the Islamic emphasis on the oneness of God.

Jesus is known in the Quran as Isa. The Quran refers to Jesus as a prophet and a messenger of God. He was sent by God to proclaim to the Jewish people that there is no god but Allah. The Quran refers to Jesus as a "word" of God but denies that Jesus is divine. The Quran claims that Jesus is only a "servant" of God.

Muslims honour Mary as the mother of Jesus but not as the Mother of God. She is mentioned no less than 34 times in the Quran. Muslims believe that Mary conceived Jesus by God's spirit.

Muslims do not believe that the Prophet Muhammad was divine, nor do they worship him. He is perceived rather as a messenger of God—albeit as the final messenger of God—as the founder and legislator of Islam, and as the perfect moral model for all who adhere to the Islamic faith.

Muslims believe in free will, in the resurrection of the dead, in the final judgment, and in heaven and hell. The followers of Islam are forbidden to eat pork, drink alcohol, gamble, or charge interest on money.

Unlike Christians, Muslims do not believe in original sin. There is no priesthood in Islam and, strictly speaking, any Muslim in good standing can lead others in prayer. Each Muslim has direct and personal access to God.

Shi'ites and Sunnites

Most Muslims are either Sunni or Shi'ite. Sunnites give supremacy to the divinely revealed Shari'a (Islamic Law), which is based on the Quran and the sayings of the Prophet. Shi'ites, on the other hand, give supremacy to the divinely inspired leader who interprets the Shari'a. For Shi'ites, the Light of the Prophet Muhammad is passed on to his descendants, and only a descendant of the Prophet Muhammad can be the leader of the Islamic community. For the Sunnites, on the other hand, the leader of the Islamic community is the one whom the community recognizes as its leader and who unifies the community.

Ninety percent of Muslims are Sunni. But most Muslims in Yemen and in Iran are Shi'ite. The Shi'ite legal scholars are known as mullahs. The chief interpreter of the Shari'a for Shi'ites in Iran is the Ayatollah.

Islamic Revivalism and Islamicization

Over the past 30 years, Islamic revivalism and Muslim fundamentalism have touched most Muslim communities around the globe. This phenomenon is partly attributable to the political independence that many Arab and Muslim countries achieved after the Second World War. But to get a more profound grasp of this significant development within the Islamic world, one must examine Islam with a view to some of its unique qualities as a religion.

Islam plays a very determining role in the lives of its followers. There is a definiteness and a certainty to this religion. The Quran, for example, in addition to being a manual of spiritual discipline, contains an immense body of moral, social, and legal ordinances. An entire way of life is spelled out for the believer. Yet Islam is not a religion geared primarily to the individual or to individual salvation. It is, in fact, one of the most communal of the world's major faiths. Communal solidarity is its very cornerstone. The individual is anchored in the community of believers.

The Muslim faith calls its adherents to establish a social order that does not separate the sacred from the secular, religion from society, or faith from politics. This order is established and governed by Islamic law, which expresses the will of Allah.

Four themes characterize Islamic revivalism:

1. A rejection of Western moral and social values.
2. A search for identity and authenticity and a desire to root society in Muslim rather than in Western values.
3. Economic and political discontent within Muslim countries.
4. The reassertion of Islam as an ideology that will bring about political, cultural, and religious liberation as well as social justice.

Islamic revivalists maintain that modern Muslim societies have failed because they have strayed from Islam. To remedy this situation, many Muslims worldwide are committing themselves to Islamicization—a process of renewal and reform that is meant to create a more moral and just society wherever Muslims find themselves. Islamicization is the reassertion of Islam in personal and social life.

Muslim revivalists claim that Islamicization will restore human dignity and a sense of identity. They argue from the life of the Prophet, from the experience of the early Muslim community, and from the Qur'an itself that today's Islamic community should be a religio-political entity ruled by God's will as expressed in Islamic law. In this vision of things, the chief function of government is to enable the individual to live a good Muslim life in the context of community. The First and Second Gulf Wars (in 1991 and 2003) have reinforced the trend toward Islamicization and Islamic revivalism. Muslims in various parts of the world are inclined to be sympathetic to Iraq and opposed to the Western powers.

Muslim–Christian Relations

Due to immigration, there is a growing Muslim population in the West. At the time of the latest census (2001) there were over half a million Muslims in Canada. In the countries of Western Europe, the number of Muslims is also growing. Some observers see the growing size of the Muslim communities as a threat to Western values or to Christianity. They point to the lack of religious liberty for Christians and other non-Muslims in some Islamic countries.

Dialogue between Christians and Muslims is still in the initial phases but is growing on an international scale. Both parties are making an effort to understand each other's positions and to overcome the negative stereotypes that they have about each other.

The Roman Catholic Church has committed itself to dialogue with Islam. In its Declaration on the Relationship of the Church to Non-Christian Religions, the Second Vatican Council spoke of the affinities between Christianity and Islam and called for a new era in Christian–Muslim relations:

Upon the Moslems, too, the Church looks with esteem. They adore one God, living and enduring, merciful and all-powerful, Maker of heaven and earth and Speaker to men. They strive to submit wholeheartedly even to His inscrutable decrees, just as did Abraham, with whom the Islamic faith is pleased to associate itself. Though they do not acknowledge Jesus as God, they revere Him as a prophet. They also honor Mary, His virgin mother; at times they call on her, too, with devotion. In addition they await the day of judgment when God will give each man his due after raising him up. Consequently, they prize the moral life, and give worship to God especially through prayer, almsgiving, and fasting.

Although in the course of the centuries many quarrels and hostilities have arisen between Christians and Moslems, this most sacred Synod urges all to forget the past and to strive sincerely for mutual understanding. On behalf of all mankind, let them make common cause of safeguarding and fostering social justice, moral values, peace, and freedom.

SOURCES: P. McKenna, "Understanding Islam," ed. K. VanLoon, *Scarboro Missions Magazine*, 1991. Reprinted with permission of *Scarboro Missions Magazine*.

---

of control over their lives. Regardless of the definition, it has not been the place of anthropologists to determine the "truth" of any particular religion; rather, they have endeavoured to understand a religion as it is understood by the people of the culture they are studying.

One difficulty with defining religion arises from the considerable variability in types of religions. Food-foraging peoples, whose technology for manipulating their environment is limited and who tend to see themselves more as part of nature, rather than its masters, hold a naturalistic world view. Among food foragers, religion is usually inseparable from the rest of daily life. It also mirrors and confirms the egalitarian nature of social relations in their cultures, in that individuals do not pray to high-ranking deities or ask for their aid the way members of stratified societies do. By contrast, in Western societies, which have an ideological commitment to overcoming problems through technology and organization, religion is less a part of daily activities and is restricted to specific occasions. Moreover, a Western society's hierarchy of supernatural beings—for instance, God, the angels, and the saints of some Christian groups—reflects and confirms the stratified nature of that society.

Many religions do not fit these two extremes, instead falling somewhere in between. The Doukhobors are a faction of the Russian Orthodox Church that split off in the 1650s because of the increasing emphasis the original Church placed on ritual rather than equality, and on the glorification of war rather than peace. After enduring many years of persecution under the tsars, the Doukhobors finally immigrated to Canada in 1899. *Dukho-borets* means "spirit wrestlers"—that is, people who wrestle with the spirit of truth.[8] Traditional Doukhobors are Christians, but they also believe that the goodness of God is found in the hearts and minds of ordinary people, not in institutionalized churches, scriptures, or religious leaders. To the Doukhobors, God is not a supernatural being but the spirit, wisdom, and love found in every person. As you can see, it is difficult to place Doukhoborism within a naturalistic or institutionalized religious world view.

Religious activity may be less prominent in the lives of social elites, who see themselves as more in control of their own destinies, than it is in the lives of peasants or the lower classes. Among the latter, religion may afford some compensation for their subordinate position in society. Yet religion is still important to the elite in that it rationalizes the system in such a way that people are not as likely to question the existing social order as they might otherwise. After all, people who can hope for a better existence after death may be more willing to put up with a disadvantaged position in life. In this way, religious beliefs serve to influence and perpetuate conceptions, if not actual relations, between different classes of people. This returns us to the definition developed by Geertz, who viewed religion as a functional motivator.

THE PRACTICE OF RELIGION

Much of religion's value flows from the activities its practice calls for. Religion is performative and is acted out through ritual, ceremony, and observances. Participation in religious ceremonies may bring a sense of personal transcendence—a wave of reassurance, security, and even ecstasy—or a feeling of closeness to fellow participants. Although religious rituals and practices vary considerably, all of them serve the same basic social and psychological purposes.

Supernatural Beings and Powers

One of the hallmarks of religion is a belief in supernatural beings and forces. Although some religions—such as Doukhoborism—do not believe in divine beings, others hold that belief in the divine implies belief in both good and bad supernatural beings. When attempting to control by religious means what cannot be controlled in other ways, humans turn to prayer, sacrifice, and other religious rituals. This presupposes a world of supernatural beings who have an interest in human affairs and to whom people may turn for aid. We divide these beings into three categories: major deities (gods and goddesses), ancestral spirits, and other spirit beings.

Gods and Goddesses

Gods and goddesses are the most powerful and remote of supernatural beings. They are seen as controlling the universe. If several are recognized (**polytheism**), each has charge of a particular part of the universe. Such was the case with the pantheon of gods in ancient Greece: Zeus was lord of the sky, Poseidon was ruler of the sea, and Hades was lord of the underworld and the dead. In addition to these three brothers were a host of other deities, female as well as male, each similarly concerned with specific aspects of life and the universe.

Pantheons, or collections of gods and goddesses such as those of the Greeks, are common in non-Western states. Since states usually have grown through conquest, their pantheons often develop as local deities of conquered peoples are incorporated into the official state pantheon. Another frequent feature of pantheons is the presence of a supreme deity, who may be all but totally out of reach to humans. The Aztecs of Mexico, for instance, recognized a supreme pair to whom they paid little attention. These were Huitzilopochtli and Tezcatlipoca, who, together with a variety of other gods, headed the Aztec pantheon. Because their existence was so remote, they were unlikely to be interested in human affairs. The sensible practice, then, was to focus attention on deities who were more directly concerned with human matters.

Whether or not a people recognize gods, goddesses, or both has to do with how men and women relate to each other in everyday life. Generally speaking, cultures that subordinate women to men define the godhead in exclusively masculine terms. For example, in the Greek pantheon, the goddess Hera is usually identified as consort to Zeus; she is portrayed as a jealous, petty wife. Similarly, Aphrodite, the goddess of love, exists to bring pleasure to men. Male godheads are found among groups whose economies are based on the herding of animals or on intensive agriculture carried out by men. In such groups, fathers are distant and controlling figures to their children.

Goddesses, by contrast, are likely to be most prominent in groups where women make a major contribution to the economy and enjoy relative equality with men, and where men are more involved in their families, as in farming communities. As an illustration, the early Hebrews, like other pastoral nomadic tribes of the Middle East, described their god in masculine, authoritarian terms. By contrast, goddesses played central roles in religious ritual and the popular consciousness of the region's agricultural peoples. Associated with these goddesses were concepts of light, love, fertility, and procreation. Around 1300 BC the Hebrew tribes entered the land of Canaan and began to practise agriculture; this required them to establish a new kind of relationship with the soil. As they came to depend on rainfall and the rotation of the seasons, they became more concerned about fertility, and as a result they adopted many of the Canaanite goddess cults. Belief in the Canaanite goddesses was diametrically opposed to the original Hebrew cult, but it catered to the human desire for security, which here meant seeking to control the forces of fertility.

When the Israelite tribes sought national unity in the face of a military threat from the Philistines, and when they strengthened their identity as a "chosen people," the goddess cults lost out to followers of the old masculine tribal god. The gods, then, can be changed, and their decrees can be altered to suit current social circumstances. The ancient masculine-authoritarian concept of god has been perpetuated through time, not just in the Judaic tradition but also among Christians and Muslims, whose religions stem from the old Hebrew religion. As a consequence, this masculine-authoritarian model has played an important role in perpetuating a relationship between men and women in which the latter traditionally have been expected to submit to the "rule" of men at every level of Jewish, Christian, and Islamic society.

polytheism Belief in several gods and/or goddesses (as contrasted with monotheism—belief in one god).

pantheon A collection of gods and goddesses.

Ancestral Spirits

A belief in ancestral spirits is consistent with the widespread notion that human beings are comprised of two parts: a body and some kind of vital spirit. For example, the Penobscot maintained that each person had a personal spirit that could detach itself and travel about apart from the body. Given such a concept, the idea of the spirit being freed from the body by death and having a continued existence seems quite logical.

Where a belief in ancestral spirits exists, these beings often are seen as retaining an active interest and even membership in society. Much like living persons, ancestral spirits may be benevolent or malevolent, and no one is ever quite sure what their behaviour will be. The same feeling of uncertainty—"How will they react to what I have done?"—may be displayed toward ancestral spirits as tends to be displayed toward people of a senior generation who hold authority over individuals. Thus, spirits may reflect and reinforce social control.

A belief in ancestral spirits is found in many parts of the world, especially among people with unilineal descent systems. In several such African cultures, the concept is especially elaborate. Ancestral spirits often behave like humans. They are able to feel hot, cold, and pain, and they may be capable of dying a second death by drowning or burning. They even may participate in family and lineage affairs, and seats will be provided for them, even though the spirits are invisible. If annoyed, they may send sickness or even death. Eventually, they are reborn as new members of their lineage, and in groups that hold such beliefs, adults need to observe infants closely to determine just who has been reborn.

Deceased ancestors were important in the patrilineal society of traditional China. For the gift of life, a boy was forever indebted to his parents, owing them obedience, deference, and a comfortable old age. Even after their death, he provided for them in the spirit world, offering food, money, and incense on the anniversaries of their births and deaths. People collectively worshipped all lineage ancestors periodically throughout the year. The birth of sons was considered an obligation to the ancestors, for this ensured that the latter's needs would continue to be attended to even after their own sons died. These beliefs provided a strong sense of continuity linking the past, present, and future.

Animism

One of the most widespread beliefs about supernatural beings is **animism**—the belief that nature is animated by all sorts of spirits. Animals and plants, like humans, all may have their individual spirits, but so too may springs, mountains, stones, weapons, ornaments, and so on. In addition, the woods may be full of a variety of unattached or free-ranging spirits. Generally speaking, though, such spirits are less remote from people than gods and goddesses and are more involved in daily affairs. They may be benevolent, malevolent, or neutral. They may be awesome, terrifying, lovable, or even mischievous. Since they may be pleased or irritated by human actions, people are obliged to be concerned about them.

Animistic beliefs are found everywhere: from Southern Sudan, to Japan (Shinto practices), to the American Plains (some elements of Siouan belief). It is even found among New Age and Wiccan groups. Animism is typical of those who see themselves as a part of nature rather than superior to it. This takes in most food foragers, as well as those food-producing peoples who recognize little difference between a human life and that of any growing thing. Among such societies, gods and goddesses are relatively unimportant but the woods are full of all sorts of spirits, and it is these spirits that individuals turn to for curing, that help or hinder the shaman, and that the ordinary hunter may meet when off in the woods.

Animatism

It is often thought that supernatural beings automatically are vested with supernatural powers. Often, but not always. Some Melanesians, for example, think of mana as a force inherent in all objects. It is not in itself physical, but it can reveal itself physically. A warrior's success in fighting is not attributed to his own strength but to the mana contained in an amulet that hangs around his neck. Similarly, a farmer may know a great deal about horticulture, soil conditioning, and the correct time for sowing and harvesting but nevertheless depends on mana for a successful crop. Far from being a personalized force, mana is abstract in the extreme, a power lying always just beyond reach of the senses. As R.H. Codrington described it, "Virtue, prestige, authority, good fortune, influence, sanctity, luck are all words which, under certain conditions, give something near the meaning. ... Mana sometimes means a more than natural virtue or power attaching to some person or thing."[9] This concept of impersonal power was widespread among North American First Nations. The Iroquois called it *orenda;* to the Sioux it was *wakonda;* to the Algonquians it was *manitu.*

In the early 20th century, anthropologist R.R. Marett of Oxford University called this concept of impersonal power animatism. The two concepts, **animatism** and

animism A belief in spirit beings thought to animate nature.

animatism A belief that the world is animated by impersonal supernatural powers.

© Annemiek Veldman/Kipa/Corbis

The French anthropologist Claude Lévi-Strauss spent much of his career researching world myths. He maintained that many myths contain the same functional message and can be analyzed by anthropologists to reveal certain underlying structural truths about society.

animism, are not mutually exclusive. They often are found in the same culture, as in Melanesia and among North American First Nations groups.

Myths

The distinction that history is true and myth is false is quite arbitrary.[10]

The role of mythology in maintaining beliefs should not be overlooked. **Myths** are explanatory narratives that rationalize religious beliefs and practices. Myths invariably focus on human existence: where we and everything in our world came from, why we are here, and where we are going. They are symbolic expressions of meaning. Myths depict and describe an orderly universe and set the stage for orderly behaviour.[11] To Westerners, the word "myth" immediately brings to mind a story about imaginary events, but the people who have developed a particular myth do not see it that way. To them, myths are true stories, analogous to historical documents in modern North American culture. In an Inuit myth, when the sea goddess Sedna's angry bird husband brought on a violent storm, Sedna's desperate father threw her from their boat. She clung to the side of the boat, but her father cut off her fingers, joint by joint, and she sank to the bottom of the sea, where she remains today. Sedna's fingers, however, became the sea animals that Inuit now hunt.[12] In anthropology, research into mythology is exemplified by the work of Claude Lévi-Strauss, who argued that all myths transmit information and that their underlying structures can be teased out

myth A sacred narrative explaining how the world came to be in its present form.

priest or **priestess** A full-time religious specialist.

by deep analysis, thus revealing the concerns, strictures, and beliefs of prehistoric and contemporary people. His anthropological research on mythology led to a flurry of comparative mythology. He is remembered today as one of the fathers of anthropology.[13]

All societies have myths, whether they are transmitted through social memory and oral traditions or written down on parchment or laptops. In literate cultures, this mythology is written, such as in the Judaeo-Christian account of Creation in the Old Testament's Book of Genesis. As you have already seen, holy books are perceived as the absolute truth by religious fundamentalists. In nonliterate cultures, myths are maintained through oral histories or storytelling. Myths invariably recount the doings of various supernatural beings and thus serve to reinforce belief in them.

Studying mythology in nonliterate cultures presents its own challenges. Mathias Guenther, Professor of Sociology and Anthropology at Wilfrid Laurier University, has studied the trickster in Ju/'hoansi mythology, yet he readily admits this is a difficult task because of the ambiguity of these beliefs. The Ju/'hoansi trickster is a mythological and spiritual being that changes his identity and appearance from lewd prankster to divine creator, goblin to god, human to jackal, and that goes by many names. Yet for all his ambiguity, the trickster creates understanding and order within the Ju/'hoansi world:

> As creator, as well as culture hero, he may bring into the world beings, things, and conditions of importance to nature and humankind, as well as structure and order. Thanks to his creative acts or antics there is now fire and cooking, the rivers and water holes of the Kalahari, the vocal sounds and body patterns of some animals, healing medicine and trance arrows, rain magic, and the knowledge of procreation (as well as death).[14]

Such storytelling is shared widely among the world's cultures, especially among hunter-gatherers, and these stories are normally the domain of religious specialists.

Religious Specialists

Priests and Priestesses

In all cultures, certain individuals are responsible for guiding and supplementing the religious practices of others. They are skilled at influencing supernatural beings and forces. They have undergone special training, and they may display certain personality traits that make them especially suited for their job. A full-time specialist is known as a **priest** or **priestess**. He or she is a socially initiated, ceremonially inducted member of a recognized religious organization. Such was the case

∞ *The Anthropologist's World* ∞

Dane–zaa Spirituality and Ecology

Robin Ridington

Robin Ridington is Professor Emeritus in Anthropology at the University of British Columbia, having taught there from 1967 to 1975. He received his PhD in Anthropology from Harvard University. Dr. Ridington has worked with the Dane-zaa people of northeastern BC since 1964 and is also a renowned audio and video documentarian.

The Beaver Indians call themselves Dane-zaa in their Athapaskan language. The name means "real people" or "our people." They have lived for thousands of years in the lands north of the upper Peace River in what is now Alberta and British Columbia. They refer to their territory as Dane-zaa nunne, "the people's land." Archaeologists tell us that the area near Charlie Lake, BC, has been continuously occupied for at least 10,500 years. Dane-zaa spiritual practices are integral to their way of living on the land.

The Dane-zaa and their ancestors have always lived by hunting and fishing, supplemented in season by berries, cambium from poplar trees, and the roots and stalks of other edible plants. Dane-zaa nunne is what ecologists call an edge zone habitat. Rich prairie country adjacent to the Peace River supported a large population of bison. Mountains to the west were home to mountain sheep, goats, and whistlers (marmots). Muskeg country to the east continues to support moose, caribou, deer, beaver, and other fur-bearing animals. Lakes and rivers supplied whitefish, grayling and trout.

The Dane-zaa have always had an intimate knowledge of their land and its resources. They moved with the seasons from one area to another, following the advice of their leaders, who often used dreams to understand relationships between people and game. For the Dane-zaa, animals are non human persons endowed with the ability to choose whether or not to give themselves away to human hunters. Individual hunters use dreams to visualize the place where the hunter's trail and that of an animal would come together. Dane-zaa elders teach that an animal must know that a hunter will be generous with the meat before it will give itself to him. Both boys and girls received training in bush skills by being sent out to obtain power from an animal or natural feature of the land. They called this vision quest, *shin kaa*, "to seek a song."

Stories passed on from generation to generation were an important means of teaching about the land and its resources and preparing young people for *shin kaa*.* Doig River elder Billy Attachie told

Robin Ridington, 1996

The "last Dane-zaa Dreamer," Charlie Yahey, holding a Dreamer's Drum.

anthropologists Robin and Jillian Ridington, "Those stories I remember, that's what I live by now." The "wise stories" that Billy referred to are part of Dane-zaa narrative technology. Northern hunters like the Dane-zaa have traditionally found it far more useful to carry plans and information in their minds, rather than to be burdened with carrying material artifacts. Billy went on to tell how he learned to hunt, "just by the story":

> I remember where we practise tracking moose, me and Tommy Dominic, just by the story, by wind. We track with. The moose come from the west, the west wind. Just follow the wind. Just by the story we found this moose.

Aboriginal people of the North American subarctic have evolved adaptive strategies that place great emphasis on the authority of individual intelligence, yet acknowledge the social responsibility required of a system in which animals and humans alike are interdependent members of a single community. They recognize that success in hunting and other activities depends more on the possession of knowledge and on reciprocities with other persons, both human and non-human, than on the possession of particular material goods. They rely on narrative knowledge that is in the possession of individuals, rather than on knowledge that is mediated through supra-individual institutions. Unlike more sedentary people who can accumulate wealth in the form of material possessions, subarctic people recognize knowledge as a form of wealth. Physical objects may be lost, but knowledge stays with a person throughout his or her life. Knowledge can be communicated and shared through narrative. Drawing upon narrated knowledge, a person can use environmental resources to make material objects as they are needed at a particular site.

Before Europeans came to Dane-zaa nunne and introduced firearms in the 18th century, hunts were often organized by people know as *Naachin*, "Dreamers," who used their dreams to visualize how people could cooperate in surrounding or driving animals. During the fur trade period, individuals or small groups of hunters using guns were able to provide meat for their families and for the traders, who were dependent on the Dane-zaa for their food supplies. Dreamers took on the role of helping their people adapt to the changes brought about by European contact. When the Dane-zaa were introduced to Christianity in the 1860s, their Dreamers interpreted it in a way that was distinctively their own. They were able to follow *yagatunne*, the trail to heaven, in their dreams. Their guide to the trail was a song sent down by the people who

CONTINUED

CONTINUED

had gone before them. In this way, they adapted their traditional role as leaders in the hunt to new conditions. Dane-zaa storytellers say that one of their first Dreamers, Makenunatane, predicted the coming of Europeans. He began his life as a hunt chief and ended it as a prophet who foretold the changes that would come to his people and their land. The last Dreamer was Charlie Yahey, who died in 1976. Robin Ridington was

fortunate in being able to record his songs, stories, and oratory. In one of the recordings he says that because of them, "the world will listen to my voice."

When a Dreamer returned from his dream journey, he woke up singing the song he had been following. Dane-zaa singers know these songs and the stories behind them. The Dreamers' dance is still an important part of Dane-zaa life. When people dance together around

a common fire, they remove bad feelings that may have developed between individuals and recognize their common heritage. Whenever a person dies, the Dane-zaa singers come together and sing for the person's spirit to begin its journey along *yagatunne*.

* For an analysis of Dane-zaa oral history, see R. Ridington and J. Ridington, Where Happiness Dwells *(Vancouver: UBC Press, in press).*

Werner Forman/Art Resource, NY

Cave paintings depicting the myths of the Dogon people, including the creation myth and representations of Amma Serou falling from heaven.

with Tenskwatawa, the Shawnee prophet and brother of the famous Tecumseh, who as medicine man for the Shawnee Nation led a revitalization movement that galvanized a pan-Indian movement and struck fear into settlers and the U.S. Army. Tenskwatawa established Prophetstown, where he urged Native people to abandon European ways and prophesied a great military victory for Tecumseh's American Indian Confederation. Tenskwatawa's leadership skills and oratory aided the warrior Tecumseh, and there were indeed victories for the Shawnee, though ultimately they were defeated at the Battle of Tippecanoe.

The priest is a familiar figure in Western societies. Such a person is often called by other names, such as minister,

pastor, rector, rabbi, or whatever the title may be in a given organized religion. Considering that the Judaic, Christian, and Islamic god is defined in masculine-authoritarian terms, it is not surprising that traditionally men have filled the most important positions in these religions. Only in cultures where women make a major contribution to the economy and in which both gods and goddesses are recognized are female religious specialists found. In the past, however, there were many priestesses, such as the Minoan and Hindu priestesses, who were quite powerful.

Shamans

Shamans are part-time religious specialists who acquire religious power individually, usually during times of solitude and isolation, at which point the Great Spirit, the Power, the Great Mystery, is revealed to them. These people become the recipients of special gifts, such as healing or divination, and when they return to their community, they often are given the religious role of **shaman** or **medicine person**.[15]

Typically, a person becomes a shaman by undergoing an apprenticeship, which consists of difficult stages commonly outlined in myths. These stages are often thought to involve torture and violence, such as dismemberment of the body or a period spent in the land of the dead, during which the shaman is taught by the souls of dead shamans and other spirit beings. Among North American Plains peoples such as the Sioux and the Blackfoot, any man could become a shaman, since no ecclesiastical organization provided rules and regulations to guide religious consciousness. The search for shamanistic visions was pursued by many adult Plains Aboriginal males, who would engage in bodily deprivation, even self-torture, to induce visions. Not all seekers were granted a vision, but failure carried no social stigma; the sincerity of the seeker carried the essential truth of the experience.[16]

The antiquity of shamanistic healing practices is suggested by cave paintings of ancient shamans dated to 30,000 years ago in the Chauvet Cave in France. A

shaman/medicine person A part-time religious specialist who has unique power acquired through his or her initiative; such individuals are thought to possess exceptional abilities for dealing with supernatural beings and powers.

In this picture, a Mexico City shaman, or medicine person, performs an ancient rite of blessing.

Neanderthal grave at Shanidar in Iraq had seven species of plants buried around the corpses. In Monte Verde in southern Chile (the earliest known habitation in South America), archaeologists have found gardens of medicinal plants. These species of plants are still used in healing practices; for example, the *boldo* plant is used as a diuretic, a laxative, and a treatment for liver problems by local indigenous peoples. On further research, *boldo* has been approved in Western countries such as Germany as a treatment for stomach and intestinal cramps as well as dyspepsia. Plotkin places this knowledge in a spiritual context by suggesting the shamans could never have learned everything they know about the medicinal properties of some plants, given the millions of plants and other organisms in a tropical forest, without supernatural assistance—in this case, a shaman's dreams.

The importance of shamanism should not be underestimated. For individuals, shamanistic practices release tension and promote feelings of ecstasy. They provide psychological assurance that health will be recovered or an attack turned back. In fact, a frequent reason for a shamanistic performance is to cure illness. The treatment itself may not be medically effective, but the improved state of mind that shamanism induces in the patient may be critical to his or her recovery.

Shamans may acquire so much power that they can do evil as well as good and thus be potentially dangerous. Moreover, the shaman may help maintain social control through the ability to detect and punish evildoers.

Rituals and Ceremonies

Although not all rituals are religious (graduation ceremonies, for example), those that *are* religious play a crucial role in religious activity. Religious ritual is the means through which individuals relate to the sacred;

it is religion in action. The activities associated with ritual vary and can include prayers, songs, sweatbaths, offerings, and sacrifices. Rituals are a means for reinforcing a group's social bonds and for relieving tensions; they are also a way to celebrate important events, and they render crises, such as death, less socially disruptive and less difficult for individuals to bear. Anthropologists, whether examining Papua New Guinean ceremonies or Zulu traditions, have classified rituals in various ways—for example, as **rites of passage** or **rites of intensification.**

Rites of Passage

Anthropologists Arnold Van Gennep and Victor Turner have analyzed the rites of passage that help individuals through the crucial stages of their lives, such as birth, puberty, marriage, parenthood, advancement to a higher class, occupational specialization, and death.[17] Gennep found it useful to divide ceremonies for all of these life events into three stages: **separation, transition,** and **incorporation.** The individual is ritually removed from the culture as a whole, then isolated for a period, and finally incorporated back into the group in his or her new status. In North America, one of the most widely distributed ritual practices is the vision quest. In Canada, this is practised by a number of Aboriginal nations, including the Ojibwa (or Anishenabe). Young boys, usually at around 10 years of age, are separated in the woods or hills until they receive their vision. This separation is key, and is what Turner referred to as a state of "liminality," where the seeker is "betwixt and between."[18] During this heightened emotional state, brought on by fasting and sleep deprivation, the seeker receives his vision. This vision has profound significance for the Ojibwa, for it provides a personal guardian spirit for the individual through life.[19]

Van Gennep described the male initiation rites of Australian Aborigines in traditional times. When the elders decided it was time for the initiation, the boys

rites of passage Rituals, often religious in nature, marking important stages in the lives of individuals, such as birth, marriage, and death.

rites of intensification Religious rituals enacted during a group's real or potential crisis.

separation In rites of passage, the ritual removal of the individual from society.

transition In rites of passage, a stage where the individual is isolated following separation and prior to incorporation into society.

incorporation In rites of passage, reincorporation of the individual into society in his or her new status.

Dynamic Anthropology

Reconciling Modern Medicine with Traditional Beliefs in Swaziland

Edward C. Green

Edward C. Green is a medical anthropologist. He was a senior research scientist at the Harvard School of Public Health and served as director of the AIDS Prevention Research Project at the Harvard Center for Population and Development Studies. He was appointed to serve as a member of the Presidential Advisory Council on HIV/AIDS (2003–2007). He has worked for over 30 years in international development.

Although the biomedical germ theory is generally known and accepted in Western societies today, this is not the case in many other societies around the world. In southern Africa's Swaziland, for example, many illnesses are generally thought to be caused by sorcery or by loss of ancestral protection. (Sexually transmitted diseases—STDs—and other contagious diseases are exceptions to these beliefs.)

Even where the effectiveness of Western medicine is recognized, the ultimate question remains: Why did a disease come to a particular person in the first place? Thus, for the treatment of disease, the Swazi have traditionally relied upon herbalists, diviner mediums through whom ancestor spirits are thought to work, and (more recently) Christian faith healers. Unfortunately, such individuals have usually been regarded as quacks and charlatans by the medical establishment. Yet the herbal medicines used by traditional healers are effective in several ways, and the reassurance provided patient and family alike through rituals that reduce stress and anxiety plays an important role in the patient's recovery. In a country where there is one traditional healer for every 110 people, but only one physician for every 10,000, the potential benefit of cooperation between physicians and healers seems self-evident. Nevertheless, it was largely unrecognized until proposed by anthropologists D.M. Warren (in Ghana) and later, me.

It was in 1981, when I was a Washington-based independent consultant, that I first went to Swaziland as a researcher for the Rural Water-Borne Disease Control Project, funded by the United States Agency for International Development. Assigned the task of finding out about knowledge, attitudes, and practices related to water and sanitation, and aware of the serious deficiencies of conventional surveys that rely on precoded questionnaires, I used instead the traditional anthropological techniques of open-ended interviews with key informants, along with participant observation. The key informants were traditional healers, their patients, and rural health motivators (women chosen by communities to receive eight weeks of training in preventive health care in regional clinics). Without such anthropological research, it would have been impossible to design and interpret a reliable survey instrument, but the added payoff was that I learned a great deal about Swazi theories of illness and its treatment.

Disposed at the outset to recognize the positive value of many traditional practices, I could also see how cooperation with physicians might be achieved. For example, traditional healers already recognized the utility of Western medicines for treatment of diseases considered not indigenous to Africa, and traditional preventive medicines were routinely given to children through inhalation, something like childhood vaccinations. Thus, nontraditional medicines and vaccinations might be accepted, if presented in ways that resembled traditional medicine.

Realizing the suspicion existing on both sides, I and my Swazi associate Lydia Makhubu (a chemist who had studied the properties of indigenous medicines) recommended to the Minister of Health a cooperative project focusing on a problem of concern to both health professionals and native healers: infant diarrheal diseases. These had recently become a health problem of high concern to the general public; healers wanted a means to prevent such diseases, and a means of treatment existed—oral rehydration therapy—that was compatible with traditional treatments for diarrhea (herbal preparations taken orally over a period of time). Packets of oral rehydration salts, along with instructions, were provided to healers in a pilot project, with positive results. This helped convince health professionals of the benefits of cooperation, while the healers saw the distribution of packets to them as a gesture of trust and cooperation on the part of their government.

Since then, further steps toward cooperation have been taken, such as work in prevention of AIDS, STDs, and TB. All of this demonstrates the importance of finding how to work in ways compatible with existing belief systems. Directly challenging traditional beliefs, as all too often happens, does little more than create stress, confusion, and resentment among people.

Adapted from E.C. Green, "The Planning of Health Education Strategies in Swaziland," and "The Integration of Modern and Traditional Health Sectors in Swaziland," in *Anthropological Praxis: Translating Knowledge into Action*, ed. R.M. Wulff and S.J. Fiske (Boulder: Westview Press, 1987), 15–25 and 87–97.

were taken from the village (separation), while the women cried and made a ritual show of resistance. At a place distant from the camp, groups of men from many villages gathered. The elders sang and danced while the initiates acted as though they were dead. The climax of this part of the ritual was a bodily operation, such as circumcision or the knocking out of a tooth. Anthropologist A.P. Elkin wrote, "This is partly a continuation of the drama of death. The tooth-knocking, circumcision or other symbolical act 'killed' the novice; after this he does not return to the general camp and normally may not be seen by any woman. He is dead to the ordinary life of the tribe."[20]

In this transitional stage, the novice might have been shown secret ceremonies, but the most significant element was his complete removal from the community. In the course of these Australian puberty rites, the initiate learned the lore that all adult men were expected to know. The trauma of the occasion was a pedagogical technique that ensured he learned and remembered everything; in a nonliterate culture, the perpetuation of traditions requires no less, so effective teaching methods are necessary.

On his return to the culture (incorporation), the novice was welcomed with ceremonies, as if he had returned from the dead, and acquired a new status and obligations. The individual's new rights and duties were thus clearly defined. He was spared, in this way, the problems that North American teenagers encounter as they are growing up, when they are neither adult nor child but a person of ill-defined status.

In the Australian case just cited, boys were prepared not just for adulthood but also for *manhood*. Fortitude is considered an important masculine virtue, and the pain of tooth knocking or circumcision helps instill this trait in initiates. In a similar way, traditional female initiation rites helped prepare Mende girls in West Africa for womanhood. After they began to menstruate, the girls

were secluded for weeks, or even months. They discarded the clothes of childhood, smeared their bodies with white clay, and dressed in brief skirts and many strands of beads. Shortly after entering this transitional stage, they underwent circumcision. Until their incorporation back into the community, they were trained in the moral and practical responsibilities of potential childbearers by experienced women in the Sande association. This training was accompanied by singing, dancing, and storytelling, and the initiates were very well fed. Thus they acquired both a positive image of womanhood and a strong sense of sisterhood.

Mende women emerged from their initiation as women in control of their sexuality, eligible for marriage and childbearing. The pain and danger of the circumcision, endured in the context of intense social support from other women, served as a metaphor for childbirth, which often took place in the same place of seclusion, again with the support of Sande women.

The Plains Sun Dance (sometimes called the Thirsting Dance) was also a rite of passage. In traditional times, Plains Aboriginal groups held this religious ceremony during the summer solstice, when all the bands assembled. Although each cultural group developed its own customs, some commonalities can be discerned. An individual had to sponsor the ceremony; among the Blackfoot and the Sarcee, a virtuous woman might vow to sponsor a ceremony if she had suffered a personal crisis such as illness in the family; among the Plains Cree and Ojibwa, a man promised to hold a Sun Dance if he returned safely from a battle; for the Assiniboine, the Sun Dance was an act of worship.[21]

The ritual began with the building of a ceremonial lodge. While the sponsor fasted, the warriors cut down a suitable tree for the sacred centre pole. They then constructed a circular lodge made of leafy branches around the pole. Plains Cree and Ojibwa built a "thunderbird nest" of branches at the top of the pole and hung offerings from it. Once the lodge was finished, the dancing began. The dancers danced to the rhythm of chanted prayers, blowing on eagle-bone whistles and never taking their eyes from the centre pole. They danced for days, going without food, water, or sleep. Sometimes—and this has been much misrepresented in some of the literature as barbaric—young men, in fulfillment of special vows to the Creator, had the muscles on their chests pierced and wooden skewers pushed through the wounds. Ropes, tied to the centre pole, were attached to the skewers. The men danced, and leaned back from the ropes until they tore free. The scars from this ordeal were proudly borne for the rest of their lives. The Sun Dance was also a time for people to strengthen their shared faith, visit friends,

Gender Perspectives

Standardizing the Body: The Question of Choice

Laura Nader

Laura Nader (born 1930) is an American anthropologist. She has been a professor of anthropology at the University of California, Berkeley, since 1960. (She was the first woman to receive a tenure-track position in the department.) Nader's current work focuses on how central dogmas are made and how they work in law, energy, science, and anthropology.

The question of choice is central to the story of how medicine and business generate controlling processes in the shaping of women's bodies. Images of the body appear natural within their specific cultural milieus. For example, breast implants are not seen as odd within the cultural milieu of the United States, and female circumcision and infibulation (also known as female genital mutilation or FGM) are not considered odd among people from the Sudan and several other African countries. However, many feminist writers differentiate FGM from breast implantation by arguing that North American women choose to have breast implants whereas in Africa women are presumably subject to indoctrination since they experience circumcision as young girls.

One of the most heated debates arising from the public health concern over breast implants is whether the recipients are freely situated—that is, whether their decision is voluntary or whether control is disguised as free will.

An informed response to the free choice argument requires knowing how the beauty-industrial complex works. Toward this end, corporate accountability researcher Linda Coco carried out field-work in multiple sites, gaining insights into the inner workings of a multibillion-dollar industry that segments the female body and manufactures commodities of and for the body.

Coco's research shows how some women get caught in the official beauty ideology, and in the case of silicone-gel breast implants some hundreds of thousands of women have been ensnared.

PROCEDURE	NUMBER DONE 2008	PERCENT DONE FOR WOMEN
Facial resurfacing and fillers (chemical peel, laser, collagen, etc.)	4,260,000	91%
Brow lift	42,000	89%
Eyelid surgery	221,000	86%
Nose reshaping	279,000	73%
Botox injection	5,000,000	94%
Face lift	113,000	91%
Upper arm lift	14,000	98%
Breast enlargement	307,000	100%
Tummy tuck	122,000	96%
Liposuction	245,000	89%
Leg veins/laser	222,000	88%

Selected cosmetic surgical and nonsurgical procedures in the United States (2008) and the percentage carried out for women. In total 1.7 million cosmetic surgeries were done and 10.4 million nonsurgical procedures (chemical peels, laser treatments, Botox injections, and so on), at a total cost of about $10.3 billion. Overall, the number of procedures is up 882 percent since 1992, and 63 percent since 2000.

But who gets caught and when are important to an understanding of the ecology of power. The average age of a woman having breast implantation is 36 years, and she has an average of two children. She is the beauty industry's insecure consumer recast as a patient with an illness the industry defines as hypertrophy (small breasts).

Coco quotes a past president of the American Society of Plastic and Reconstructive Surgery (ASPRS):

There is substantial and enlarging medical knowledge to the effect that these deformities [small breasts] are really a disease which result in the patient's feelings of inadequacies, lack of self-confidence, distortion of body image, and a total lack of well-being due to a lack of self-perceived femininity. ... Enlargement ... is therefore ... necessary to ensure the quality of life for the patient.

In other words, cosmetic surgery is necessary to the patient's psychological health.

The plastic surgeon regards the construction of the official breast as art, the aim being to reform the female body according to the ideals of classic Western art. One surgeon pioneering procedures for correcting deformity took as his ideal female figure that of ancient Greek statues, which he carefully measured, noticing the exact size and shape of the breasts, their vertical location between the third and seventh ribs, the horizontal between the line of the sternal (breast bone) border and the anterior axillary line, and so forth. In Coco's analysis the exercise of the plastic surgeon's technoart re-creates a particular static, official breast shape and applies this creation ostensibly to relieve women's mental suffering. The surgeon becomes a psychological healer as well as an artist.

Along with art and psychology, there is, of course, the business of organized plastic surgery, which responds to the demands and opportunities of market economics [see figure]. By the late 1970s and early 1980s there was a glut of plastic surgeons. The ASPRS began to operate like a commercial enterprise instead of a medical society, saturating the media with ads and even providing low-cost financing. The discourse became a sales pitch. Women "seek" breast implants to keep their husbands or their jobs, to attract men, or to become socially acceptable. Coco calls this "patriarchal capitalism" and questions whether this is free choice or "mind colonization."

Understanding "choice" led Coco to an examination of the power both in the doctor–patient relationship and in the control of information. She found that women "were told by the media, plastic surgeons, women's magazines, other women, and the business world that they could enhance their lives by enhancing their bust lines. ... [T]he social imperative for appearance was personalized, psychologized, and normalized." Social surveys indicate that, to the extent that women internalize the social imperative, they feel they are making the decision on their own.

Not surprisingly, women whose surgery resulted in medical complications often came to recognize the external processes of coercive persuasion that had led them to seek implants. In some ways, they resembled former cult members who had been deprogrammed: Their disillusionment caused them to question the system that had encouraged them to make the decision in the first place. The result was a gradual building of protest against the industry, expressed in networks, newsletters, support groups, workshops, and seminars. As have some former cult members, women have brought suit, testified before lawmakers, and challenged in other ways some of the largest corporations and insurance companies in the land.

The choice of implants, they learn, is part of a matrix of controlling processes in which women are subjects. Given the right circumstances it could happen to anyone. In the Sudan, the young girl is told that FGM procedures are done for her and not to her. In the United States the mutilation of natural breasts is also done for the recreation of femininity. Although power is exercised differently in these two cases, Coco notes the similarity: "The operation on the female breast in [North] America holds much of the same social symbolism and expression of cultural mandate as does FGM in Sudan. Thus, the question of why women choose breast augmentation becomes moot."

Breast implantation is now spreading elsewhere, most notably to China. Will it become a functional equivalent to foot-binding in China as part of the competition between patriarchies East and West? Whatever the answer, many social thinkers agree that people are always more vulnerable to intense persuasion during periods of historical dislocation—a break with structures and symbols familiar to the life cycle—in which the media can bring us images and ideas originating in past, contemporary, or even imaginary worlds.

Feminist researchers have sought to crack controlling paradigms such as those that define women's capacities and those that construct a standardized body shape and determine what is beautiful in women. Some of their writings are attempts to free the mind from the beauty constructions of cosmetic industries and fashion magazines. Others relay how the one model of Western beauty is affecting members of ethnic groups who aspire to look the way advertisements say they should. Choice is an illusion, since the restructuring of taste is inextricably linked to shifts in the organization of consumption.

Adapted from L. Nader, "Controlling Processes: Tracing the Dynamics of Power," *Current Anthropology* 38 (1997): 715–17.

---

find spouses, gamble, and race horses.[22] Amendments to the 1876 Indian Act banned the Sun Dance in order to suppress Aboriginal culture and hurry along assimilation policies. In 1951 that act was amended to reverse the ban on ceremonies like the Sun Dance. Today, the Sun Dance is still practised by some Aboriginal peoples, such as the Crow, and is one of several expressions of traditional Crow culture.[23]

Rites of Intensification

Rites of intensification are rituals that mark occasions of crisis in the life of the *group* rather than an individual. Whatever the precise nature of the crisis—be it a drought that threatens crops in the fields, the sudden appearance of an enemy war party, or the onset of an epidemic— mass ceremonies are performed to allay the danger to the group. This unites people in a common effort so that fear and confusion yield to collective action and a degree of optimism.

While death might be regarded as the ultimate crisis in an individual's life, it is, as well, a crisis for the entire group, especially if the group is small. A member of the group has been lost, and the group's equilibrium has been upset. The survivors, therefore, must restore balance. They also need to reconcile themselves to the loss of someone to whom they were emotionally tied. Funerary ceremonies, then, can be regarded as rites of intensification that permit the living to express their grief over the death while providing for social readjustment. Among some Melanesians, one part of the funerary rite was the eating of the dead person's flesh. This ritual cannibalism, witnessed by anthropologist

Shown here is a traditional Sun Dance lodge of the Blood First Nations.

Bronislaw Malinowski, was performed with "extreme repugnance and dread and usually followed by a violent vomiting fit. At the same time it is felt to be a supreme act of reverence, love and devotion."[24] This custom and the emotions accompanying it make plain an ambiguous attitude toward death: On the one hand, the survivors desire to maintain ties to the dead person, while on the other, they feel disgust and fear at the transformation wrought by death.

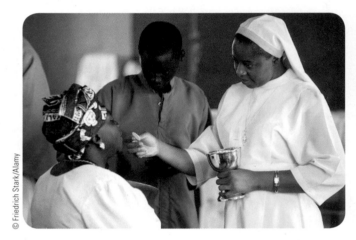

In this picture, a young Nigerian woman receives the Christian Eucharist.

RELIGION, MAGIC, AND WITCHCRAFT

Among the most fascinating aspects of ritual practices is the belief that supernatural powers can be compelled to act in certain ways for good or evil purposes. This is the classic anthropological notion of magic. Many cultures have magical rituals to ensure good crops, the replenishment of game, the fertility of domestic animals, and the avoidance or cure of illness in humans.

Westerners have tried to suppress these fantastic notions in their own consciousness, yet we continue to be fascinated by them. Books and films about witchcraft and demonic possession are avidly devoured and discussed, and sales of Ouija boards and other occult paraphernalia such as Tarot cards have increased dramatically in recent years. Thirty years ago, few newspapers

imitative magic Magic based on the principle that like produces like. For example, early cave art depicting animals with arrows in them has been interpreted as imitative magic, in that by drawing such images they would come true.

carried horoscope columns, but today almost all Canadian daily newspapers carry them regularly. Non-Western and peasant peoples tend to endow their world quite freely with magical properties, but so do many highly educated Western people. We will return to this topic later.

For the early ethnographers, the study and "explanation" of magic and witchcraft amounted to an acid test. As Western researchers came into contact with witchcraft practices, many of them found it difficult to maintain their scientific objectivity. Such issues are addressed in the classic studies by E.E. Evans-Pritchard, who worked among the Azande and Nuer peoples of Africa.[25] Anthropologists no longer distinguish between magic and religion. Far from being separate, magical practices often are part of religious rituals, and both magic and religion deal directly with the supernatural.

Sir James George Frazer, author of the classic *The Golden Bough*, made a useful distinction between two fundamental principles of magic. The first principle, that "like produces like," he called **imitative magic**. In Burma, for example, a rejected lover might engage a sorcerer to make an image of his would-be love. If this image were tossed into water, to the accompaniment of certain charms, the hapless girl would go mad. Thus, the girl would suffer a fate similar to that of her image.[26]

Frazer's second principle was **contagious magic**—the concept that things or persons once in contact can later influence each other. The most common example of contagious magic is the permanent relationship between an individual and any part of his or her body, such as hair or teeth. Frazer cites the Basutos of Lesotho, in southern Africa, who were careful to conceal their extracted teeth, lest these fall into the hands of certain mythical beings who could harm the owners of the teeth by working magic on them. Related to this is the custom, in Western societies, of treasuring objects that have been touched by special people.

Magic ritual is hardly unique to small-scale cultures such as the Trobrianders. Sports figures in the West are famous for turning to rituals, taboos, and fetishes for good luck. Baseball players practise various rituals, such as eating the same food before each game, wearing the same clothes (e.g., unwashed socks) while on a winning streak, and taking the same route to the ballpark to ensure a positive outcome in the game.[27] Fans have all witnessed their favourite players engaging in preparatory rituals, such as tugging their hats or tapping the bat on the plate before batting. These rituals provide comfort and a sense of control.

Conversely, many baseball players observe certain **taboos**, such as never stepping on the white foul lines or shaving before a game. Breaking these taboos would lead to bad luck. Players may also avoid activities that might sap their strength or cause a distraction, such as having sex the night before a game. Fetishes or charms (e.g., coins, chains, or crucifixes) believed to have supernatural powers are often used by players to aid or protect them. A new player may request a number previously worn by a successful player, hoping that it will bring him similar luck—a form of imitative magic. Baseball magic, rituals, fetishes, and taboos do not make a player perform well, but they do provide the player with a sense of control, which may ultimately mean the player does succeed.

Witchcraft

In Salem, Massachusetts, 200 suspected witches were arrested in 1692; of these, 19 were hanged, four died

in prison awaiting "trial," and one unfortunate man was pressed to death with stones for refusing to enter a plea. Despite the awarding of damages to descendants of some of the victims 19 years later, not until 1957 were the last of the Salem witches exonerated by the Massachusetts legislature. **Witchcraft** is an explanation of events based on the belief that certain individuals possess an innate psychic power capable of causing harm, including sickness and death. As you will see in the following examples, belief in witchcraft and fear of its practice have by no means disappeared in contemporary cultures. For example, as the Ibibio of Nigeria have become increasingly exposed to modern education and scientific training, their reliance on witchcraft as an explanation for misfortune has increased.[28] Furthermore, it is often the younger, more educated members of the Ibibio culture who accuse others of bewitching them. Often the accused are the older, more traditional members; thus we have an expression of the intergenerational hostility that often exists in fast-changing traditional cultures.

People turn to witchcraft to deal with everyday crises, especially sickness. Like religion, witchcraft provides an explanation for many happenings for which no cause can be discovered. Even if we could convince a person that his or her illness was due to natural causes, the victim would still ask, as the Ibibio do, "Why me? Why now?" Such a view leaves no room for pure chance; everything must be assigned a cause or meaning. Witchcraft provides the explanation and, in so doing, also provides both the basis and the means for taking counteraction. Witchcraft also serves as a form of social control; people suppress inappropriate behaviour, lest they be accused of being a witch.

Ibibio Witchcraft

Among the Ibibio, as among most peoples of sub-Saharan Africa, witchcraft beliefs are highly developed and long-standing. If a young and enterprising man cannot get a job or fails an exam, he has been bewitched; if a person becomes sick or is bitten

contagious magic Magic based on the principle that beings once in contact can influence one another after separation.

taboo A socially restricted behaviour.

witchcraft An explanation of events based on the belief that certain individuals possess an innate psychic power capable of causing harm, including sickness and death. Also includes beliefs and practices of benevolent magic.

by a snake, the reason is always the same—witchcraft. Indeed, almost all misfortune, including illness and death, is attributed to the malevolent activities of witches. The Ibibio's modern knowledge of the role that microorganisms play in disease has little impact; after all, it says nothing about *why* these were sent to the afflicted individual. If evil befalls a person, witchcraft is a far more satisfying explanation than something such as filial disobedience or violation of some taboo.

Ibibio witches are males or females who possess a special substance acquired from another established witch. This substance is made up of red, white, and black threads, needles, and other ingredients that a person acquires by swallowing it. From it comes a special power that causes harm, irrespective of whether its possessor intends to cause harm or not. The power is purely psychic, and Ibibio witches do not perform rites or make use of "bad medicine." This gives them the ability to change into animals and to travel any distance to get at their victims, whom they may torture or kill by transferring the victim's soul into an animal, which is then eaten.

To identify a witch, an Ibibio looks for behaviour out of the ordinary, such as not being fond of greeting people; living alone in a place apart from others; committing incest or adultery; not showing sufficient grief upon the death of a relative; and hardheartedness. Witches are apt to be socially disruptive people in the sense that their behaviour exceeds the range of variance considered acceptable.

Neither the Ibibio in particular nor Africans in general are alone in attributing most malevolent hap-

penings to witchcraft. Similar beliefs can be found in any human group, including North American cultures. As among the Ibibio, the powers (however they may be gained) are generally considered innate and uncontrollable; they result in activities that are the antithesis of proper behaviour, and persons displaying undesirable personality characteristics (however these may be defined) are generally the ones accused of being witches.

The Ibibio distinguish between "black witches," whose acts are especially diabolical and destructive, and "white witches," whose witchcraft is relatively benign, even though their powers are thought to be greater than those of their black counterparts. This exemplifies a common distinction between what Lucy Mair, a British anthropologist, has dubbed "nightmare witches" and "everyday witches."[29] The nightmare witch is the very embodiment of a culture's conception of evil—a being that flouts the rules of sexual behaviour and disregards every standard of decency. Nightmare witches, being almost literally the product of dreams and repressed fantasies, have much in common wherever they appear; the modern Navajo and the ancient Romans, like the Ibibio, conceived of witches who could turn themselves into animals and gather to feast on their victims. Everyday witches are often the community's nonconformists; they are morose, eat alone, are arrogant and unfriendly, but otherwise cause little trouble. Such witches may be dangerous when offended and retaliate by causing sickness, death, crop failure, cattle disease, or any number of lesser ills; hence people thought to be witches are treated cautiously and courteously, and one makes way for them if crossing their path.

NEO-PAGAN RELIGIONS

Anthropologists view renewed interest in paganism as a widespread cultural response to the decline in mainstream religions as well as to a rising fear of pending ecological crises. Paganism is an alternative expression of spirituality that traces its roots to pre-Christian times. Modern pagan religions are referred to collectively as **neo-paganism**. Yet neo-pagan religions exhibit a great deal of variety; each possesses its own beliefs, rituals, and standards.

One of the better-known and more recently revived neo-pagan religions is **Wicca**. Wicca, derived from the Anglo-Saxon word for witch, is the name given by its practitioners to the practice of witchcraft. The beliefs of most Wiccans involve elements of polytheism (worship of more than one supernatural being)

neo-paganism Modern pagan religions.

Wicca A neo-pagan belief system involving magic.

and animism (recognition of the spirit values of everything in nature).[30]

Founded by Gerald Gardner in 1951, Wicca is a modern version of an ancient magical religion, although, importantly, Wiccans believe their power comes from the inner self rather than the supernatural.[31] This belief contrasts with those of most major religions; it is also a source of suspicion, leading to the perception that Wiccans practise a form of dark magic. Gardner claimed to have been initiated into the New Forest Coven in 1939, in which rituals and practices had been passed down from pre-Christian times, but he likely assembled ideas and practices from several old religions such as Druidism to create modern Wicca, which in turn has been revised to generate various Wiccan traditions. Wiccans are organized into covens (groups), typically led by a high priestess, although men also can lead and belong to covens. Each coven can trace its lineage, or line of teaching passed down by initiated priests and priestesses, to Gardner. Gardner recorded Wiccan beliefs, rituals, invocations, and charms in the *Book of Shadows*, to be shared only with those initiated into Wicca, but much of the history and practice of Wicca is passed down through oral traditions. A coven in Canada owns the original *Book of Shadows*.

Although traditional witchcraft, as discussed earlier, appears to be a negative force, Wicca is not concerned with doing evil or causing harm. Wicca is a "mystery" religion, one that requires secret initiation rites to enter the coven, and coven members are ranked based on their level of training and skills in the craft. Wiccans believe in a balance between males and females and worship two deities, Goddess and God. These deities appear in different forms, depending on the season; for example, there is a Corn God as well as a Great Mother Goddess. The covens live by three fundamental beliefs or laws. The first law, known as the Wiccan Rede, states, "An ye harm none, do what ye will." In other words, this is an injunction to harm no one, similar to what is found in many other religions. The second law, known as the Threefold Law, states that a person's deeds (good or bad) will return to the doer three times over. The third law concerns reincarnation, although there is some disagreement over the way reincarnation works. Some covens hold that a soul may continuously be reborn, others that once a soul learns all of life's lessons, it earns eternal rest in Summerlands.

Ritual is an important component of Wicca. Wiccans do not, however, have holy buildings; any place in contact with the earth, such as a grove of trees or copse, will do for worship. Important symbols of Wicca are the broom, used for purifying an area before casting a circle, and the wand, cup, pentacle, and athame (a black-handled dagger), which represent the four elements: fire, water, earth, and air, respectively. Circle-casting begins with a Wiccan drawing a circle in the ground and purifying it. An altar is set up in the centre of the circle, where members perform magical and sacred rites by invoking the names of the Goddess and God and the powers of nature to create a Cone of Power. The rituals celebrate the processes of nature: conception, birth, mating, parenthood, maturation, and death.

A common misconception regarding Wicca, partly because Wiccans are referred to as witches, is that they worship Satan. Nothing could be further from the truth; Wiccans hold dear the values of truth, honesty, and integrity. They place a great deal of value on maintaining harmony with nature and are no more likely to commit evil than any other person. Wiccans in the old religion form were persecuted for centuries, particularly during the "Burning Times" in the 15th century, when the Christian Church in Europe spread misinformation about the Wiccan tradition and accused female practitioners of being Satanists. Thousands of accused witches were murdered even into the 18th century. Present-day Wiccans continue to be misunderstood, feared, and persecuted, owing in large part to ignorance about the religion. Anthropologist Lauren Kendall notes, "Many witches, wizards, druids, Cabalists, and shamans ... practice modern magic in contemporary England and the United States, where their ranks are comfortably reckoned in the tens of thousands.... The usual magician is ordinary, generally middle class, and often highly intelligent—a noticeable number of them have something to do with computers."[32] In Canada and the United States, Wiccan covens are campaigning for their practitioners to be recognized as legitimate clergy.

Wicca is not the only form of neo-paganism gaining popularity; **reconstructionist religions** are modern-day revivals of ancient pagan religions.[33] These religions are usually polytheistic—members believe in several gods and goddesses. They also emphasize the importance of scholarship, relying on classical texts such as the Nordic Eddas to keep in touch with their cultural history. Magic tends to play a lesser role in reconstructionist religions than in Wicca. There are numerous forms of reconstructionist religions: çsatrœ (Nordic, Norse); Baltic; Celtic; Druidism; Hellenismos (Greek); Kemetism (Egyptian); and Slavic.

reconstructionist religions Modern-day revivals of ancient pagan religions.

Modern Druidism is a reconstruction of the wisdom, lore, and ritual of ancient Druids. Druids are polytheistic and follow a calendar based on the stages of the sun, earth, and moon. They are particularly attracted to Neolithic monuments that have astronomical significance, such as Newgrange in Ireland and Stonehenge in England. Druid lore was passed down through the ages by means of closely guarded oral history, but little is known of the ancient rites. Although neo-Druids can be either male or female (as with Wicca), members are ranked based on years of training and acquired knowledge and expertise: Bards are the composers of verses and keepers of the lore; Ovates are the guardians and interpreters of the mysteries, as well as diviners. The highest-ranking members are the Druids, who are advisers and authorities on worship, law, and ceremony.

Neo-pagan religions belong to an intricate system of nature religions that are finding an increasing audience among educated, successful urbanites worldwide. The reason for this acceptance of what in the past would have been considered corrupt reasoning is manifold, just as with the reasons for accepting other religions. As people search for answers to the "big" questions, such as the meaning of life, but also question the realities of their daily lives, neo-pagan religions are increasingly meeting their needs.

THE ROLES OF RELIGION

Just as a belief in witchcraft may serve a variety of psychological and social needs, so do religious beliefs and practices. One psychological role of religion is to provide an orderly model of the universe. Beyond this, by explaining the unknown and making it understandable, religion reduces individuals' fears and anxieties. Recent research also points to the positive effect of religion and spirituality on an individual's health. In a study to determine the relationship between physical health and spirituality and religious practices, researchers concluded that those who profess spiritual beliefs and attend religious services are more likely to report good health and fewer physical ailments than those who do not.[34] Such research is ongoing, and there remain many interesting questions to explore in this regard.

Religion also serves to sanction a wide range of conduct. In this context, religion plays a role in social control, which does not rely on law alone. Right actions earn the approval of whatever supernatural powers a particular culture recognizes. Wrong actions may cause retribution through supernatural agencies.

In short, by deliberately *raising* people's feelings of guilt and anxiety about their actions, religion helps keep them in line.

Religion also sets precedents for acceptable behaviour. We have noted the connection between myths and religion. Usually, myths portray supernatural beings in ways that illustrate the culture's ethical code in action. So it is that Napi (also known as Nanabush in other First Nations groups), the Blackfoot trickster, is portrayed in the Blackfoot myths as tricking and punishing youths who mock others, lie, are greedy, or go in for extremes of behaviour. Moreover, the specific situations serve to teach Blackfoot youth appropriate behaviour in similar circumstances. The Bible's Old and New Testaments are rich in the same sort of material. Through the models it presents and the morals it espouses, religion serves to justify and perpetuate a particular social order. Thus, in the Jewish, Christian, and Islamic traditions, a masculine-authoritarian godhead, along with a creation story that portrays a woman as responsible for a fall from grace, serves to justify a social order where men exercise control over women.

A society's moral code, since it is considered divinely fixed, lifts the burden of responsibility for conduct from the shoulders of an individual who believes in the divine. It can be a tremendous relief to people to believe that the responsibility for the way things are rests with the gods, rather than with themselves, and that the burden of decision making can be transferred onto the shoulders of the divine.

Religion helps maintain social solidarity within a group. Participation in rituals, coupled with a basic uniformity of beliefs, helps bind people together and reinforce their identification with their own group. Particularly effective may be their participation together in rituals, when the atmosphere is charged with emotion. Whether the rituals take place at Stonehenge, a Medicine Wheel, or Canterbury Cathedral, this atmosphere is coloured by ritual language, symbolism, and the performance of ceremony. The exalted feelings that arise in such settings serve as a positive reinforcement in that people feel good as a result. Here, once again, we find religion providing psychological assurance while providing for the needs of society.

One other area where religion serves a social function is education. In our discussion of rites of passage, we noted that Australian puberty rites served as a kind of cram course in tribal lore. By providing a memorable occasion, initiation rites can enhance learning and thus help ensure the perpetuation of a nonliterate culture's knowledge and history. Education also may be served by rites of intensification. Often, such rites involve dramas

Members of the same religion may engage in, as well as suffer, persecution. In the former Yugoslavia, Roman Catholic Croats and Eastern Orthodox Serbs fought each other, while both fought Islamic Bosnians. In the Middle East, at the same time that Jews are the victims of violence from Islamic fundamentalists, Israeli security forces have directed violence against Muslims.

that portray matters of cultural importance. For example, among a food-foraging people, dances may imitate the movement of game and techniques of hunting. Among farmers a fixed round of ceremonies may emphasize the steps necessary for good crops. These rites help preserve knowledge important to a people's material well-being. It should be noted, however, that religions may in fact impede education. The opposition from certain school boards in the United States of America to the teaching of evolution and the forbidding of women to attend schools in some nations for religious reasons are examples of such impediments.

RELIGION AND CULTURAL CHANGE

Although the subject of culture change is taken up later in this book (see Chapter 15), no anthropological consideration of religion would be complete without some mention of *revitalization movements* and missionism. For example, in 1931, at Buka in the Solomon Islands, a religious cult suddenly emerged, its prophets predicting that a deluge would soon engulf all whites. This would be followed by the arrival of a ship laden with European goods. The believers were to construct a storehouse for the goods and to prepare themselves to repulse the colonial police and eventually to end British rule. Because the ship would arrive only after the islanders had used up all their own supplies, they ceased working in the fields. Although the cult leaders were arrested, the movement continued for some years.

This was not an isolated instance. Such "cargo cults"—and many other movements promising the resurrection of the dead, the destruction or enslavement of Europeans, and the coming of utopian riches—have sporadically appeared throughout Melanesia for a hundred years or more. Since these cults are widely separated in space and time, their similarities are apparently the result of similar social conditions. When cold reality offers no respite from the daily frustrations of cultural deterioration and economic deprivation, religion offers the solution.

Revitalization Movements

From the 1890 Ghost Dance of many North American Aboriginals to the Mau Mau of Kenya, religious reactions to European domination are so common that anthropologists have sought to formulate their underlying causes and general characteristics. Yet **revitalization movements**, as they are now called, are by no means restricted to the colonial world; in North America alone, hundreds of such movements have sprung up. Among the more widely known are Mormonism, which began in the 19th century; the more recent Unification Church of the Reverend Sun Myung Moon; the Branch Davidians, whose "prophet" was

revitalization movements Social movements, often of a religious nature, with the purpose of totally reforming a society.

David Koresh; and the Heaven's Gate cult led by Marshall Herff Applewhite and Bonnie Lu Nettles. As these four examples suggest, revitalization movements show a great deal of diversity, and some have been much more successful than others.

A revitalization movement strives to construct a more satisfying life based on an idealized past. The movement is usually led by a visionary or messiah. The emphasis in this definition is on the reformation not just of the religious sphere of activity but also of the entire social system. Such a drastic solution is attempted when a group's anxiety and frustration have become so intense that the only way to reduce the stress is to overturn the entire social system and replace it with a new one.

Given the numerous sources of anxiety in North American society today, ranging from science and technology to what many regard as a breakdown of the family and morality, we may expect to see a propagation of various revitalization movements for the next few years.

Anthropologist Anthony Wallace has outlined a sequence common to all expressions of the revitalization process.[35] First is the normal state of society, in which stress is low and sufficient cultural means of satisfying needs exist. Under certain conditions, such as domination by a more powerful group or severe economic depression, stress and frustration are steadily amplified; this ushers in the second phase, or the period of increased individual stress. If there are no significant adaptive changes, a period of cultural distortion follows, in which stress becomes so chronic that socially approved methods of releasing tension begin to break down. This steady deterioration of the culture may be checked by a period of revitalization, during which a dynamic cult or religious movement grips a sizable proportion of the population. Often the movement will be so out of touch with reality that it is doomed to failure from the beginning. This was the case with the Heaven's Gate doomsday cult, in which 39 individuals committed suicide based on a conviction their spiritual essences would reunite with extraterrestrials in a spaceship that awaited them behind the tail of the Hale-Bopp comet to take them "home." This self-destruction was the case also with the Branch Davidians, when the suspicions of government authorities led to an assault on the cult's compound. In reaction, cult members committed mass suicide by deliberately immolating themselves in their headquarters.

More rarely, a movement may tap long-dormant adaptive forces underlying a culture, and an enduring religion may result. Such was the case with Mormonism. Although heavily persecuted at first and hounded from place to place, Mormons adapted to the point that their religion thrives in the United States today. Indeed, revitalization movements lie at the root of all known religions—Judaism, Christianity, and Islam included.

In the United States, Mormonism is an example of a revitalization movement that is enormously successful and gaining acceptance in the wider society. By contrast, the Branch Davidians so antagonized elements of mainstream society that a confrontation occurred, ending with the mass immolation of many cult members.

Missionism

From the days of the Recollet order in New France to the current Christian missions in Africa and Central America, missionaries have spread around the world, converting, or attempting to convert, indigenous peoples to institutionalized belief systems. This process, known as missionism, has caused dramatic changes in the world views and cultural systems of indigenous peoples. As such, we must consider missionism a powerful force of culture change.[36]

Religious conversion is a controversial subject. On the one hand, the destruction of traditional belief systems and the disruption of cultural systems can lead to serious social problems. On the other, missionaries believe that spreading their teachings is a righteous goal. Although anthropologists decry the destruction of any cultural group's traditional beliefs, they also recognize that many contemporary missionaries have moved beyond their colonial past as agents of cultural imperialism. Missions often provide much-needed services in the form of new schools and teachers, infrastructure (e.g., water and waste facilities), and assistance in dealing with repressive regimes. Missionaries sojourn to war-torn and disaster areas to lend much-needed support and medical aid. Nonetheless, the ethics of offering medical aid while attempting to convert desperate people—conversion for aid—has generated considerable debate.

Local responses to missionism have varied considerably from one culture to another. For example, the Mardu of the Western Desert in Australia possessed a powerful belief system known as the Dreaming.[37] To the Mardu, the Dreaming or Dreamtime was the time when mystical beings, such as Rainbow Snake and Cloud Beings, created the world and populated it with part-human, part-animal, and part-divine beings who became the founding ancestors of the Mardu. The Mardu obeyed the Law of the Dreaming beings, which controlled all aspects of their lives.

When Europeans arrived in the Western Desert, the Mardu lost their traditional subsistence strategies as Europeans encroached on their land, and many moved to a town called Jigalong. A Protestant mission was established in Jigalong in 1945, and Mardu children were placed in residential schools, where they were indoctrinated into Christianity and forced to give up the Dreaming Law. This has echoes of Canada's residential school system, in which Native children were also taken from their homes to be schooled in Christian ways and to prevent them from learning and practising their own language and culture. In Australia, Aborig- ines speak of a "lost generation" of children who were forced to attend residential schools. Despite the missionaries' efforts, the Mardu clung to their beliefs and continued to hold rituals to teach their children the Dreaming Law. Culture clash ensued, such as when Mardu men tried to claim 12-year-old girls as their brides, according to the Dreaming Law, and the missionaries resisted.

The Dreaming Law had tightly controlled the lives of the Mardu. Without it, sexual promiscuity and the number of unmarried mothers increased, and conflict, alcoholism, and gambling became rampant in Jigalong. Mardu elders blamed these problems on the loss of the Dreaming Law. A split in the community developed, with some people wishing to modernize and choose a new way of life, and others wanting to uphold the Dreaming Law.

Eventually, though, the missionaries admitted defeat and the mission closed in 1969. However, the community was changed forever and is still dealing with many problems resulting from colonialism and missionism. In the 1980s, some Mardu returned to the desert life and reaffirmed their Dreaming Law; others, though, are caught between two worlds.

Regardless of the response to missionism and whether the missionaries are successful, the impact of missionism on indigenous cultures has been dramatic, resulting in significant culture change. The Mardu experience with missionism is one that is, as we have noted, shared with other peoples around the world. This highlights the power of religion and spirituality in people's daily lives—a power that is visible in attempts to convert others to one's own religion and in peoples' resorting to spiritual beliefs to sustain them in the face of colonial onslaughts.

The Dreaming Law belief system of Australian Mardu organizes and gives meaning to their lives.

Chapter Summary

1. What is religion?

There are many definitions of religion, which can focus on its practice (ritual) or on the beliefs that comprise the religion. Religion is found in all cultures. It consists of beliefs and behaviour patterns by which people try to control areas of their world otherwise beyond their control. Religion is organised, social, and transformative. It may be defined as a nonempirical belief and faith in one or multiple gods. Adherents subscribe to articles of faith, such as commandments.

2. What are religion's identifying features?

Religion involves various rituals—prayers, songs, dances, myths, offerings, and sacrifices—that people use in the hope of gaining assistance from supernatural beings and powers. These beings and powers may consist of gods and goddesses, ancestral and other spirits, and impersonal powers. Religion can involve special liturgy and special language, such as Urdu or Latin. Most religions have specialists—priests and priestesses and/or shamans—to guide religious practices and to intervene with the supernatural world.

3. Why is religion a cultural universal?

Religion (including magic and witchcraft) is universal, as is the human need to understand life and death. Religion thus serves a number of important psychological and social purposes. First, it sanctions a wide range of conduct by providing notions of right and wrong. Second, it sets precedents for acceptable behaviour and helps perpetuate an existing social order. Third, religion serves to lift the burden of decision making from individuals and places responsibility with the gods. Fourth, religion plays a large role in maintaining social solidarity.

Questions for Critical Thought

1. Many have felt that with the advance of technology and Western scientific investigation, "irrational" religious beliefs gradually would fade away to be replaced by "logical knowledge." Has this been the case? Is it ever likely to occur? Why or why not?

2. What is the purpose of myths? What is their relationship to social organization? How do the functions of myths compare with those of "history" in various societies?

3. How do we in the West regard menstruation—as unclean, something to hide, "the curse," or as a natural symbol of womanhood? As a woman, do you feel comfortable discussing your menstrual cycle with men present? As a man, do you feel comfortable hearing about a woman's menstrual cycle?

4. How does spiritual revival among First Nations groups serve to strengthen their cultural identity?

5. Research a contemporary neo-pagan religion. What are the basic tenets of this religion? What purposes and needs does this religion fulfill? Why do you think neo-pagan religions are becoming increasingly popular in Western societies?

6. Do you think that trying to convert people to one's own religion is ethical? Why or why not? If culture is integrated, what impact will religious conversion have on the other systems of culture (e.g., economics, social organization, and so on)?

Internet Resources

Religions of the World

http://www.bbc.co.uk/religion/religions

This site contains descriptions of many religions, past and present, such as Christianity, Mormonism, Taoism, and Islam, as well as world views such as agnosticism and atheism.

The Ute Sun Dance

http://www.crystalinks.com/sundance.html

A description of the Sun Dance in Colorado.

Religion

http://anthro.palomar.edu/religion/default.htm

An introduction to the anthropology of religion, including discussions of common elements, trancing, and magic.

Salem Witch Trials

http://law2.umkc.edu/faculty/projects/ftrials/salem/SALEM.HTM

A riveting account of the trial of Sarah Good for witchcraft. Also provides a link to the Witch Trials Memorial, which reminds us that these women were real people.

Wicca

http://www.wicca.com/celtic/wicca/wicca.htm

An extensive site with historical, religious, and social information on Wicca and neo-paganism.

Suggested Readings

For a list of suggested readings, visit the textbook's website at **http://www.havilandcultural4e.nelson.com**.

Notes

1. D.R. Snow, *The Iroquois* (Cambridge, MA: Blackwell, 1994).

2. S. Jones, "Fundamentalism," *Religious Movements*, http://www.brown.edu/Departments/Anthropology/publications/FUNDMNTALISM.htm, 1998, accessed March 4, 2007.

3. R. Antoun, *Understanding Fundamentalism: Christian, Islamic, and Jewish Movements* (Walnut Creek: Alta Mira Press, 2001).

4. D. Ludden, "Book Review of *In the Beginning Was the Word* by R.W. Hood, Jr., P.C. Hill, and W.P. Williamson" (New York: Guilford Press, 2005), http://www.skeptic.com/eskeptic/06-07-07.

5. W. Clark and G. Schellenberg, *Who's Religious?* Statistics Canada Cat. no. 11–008.

6. A.F.C. Wallace, *Religion: An Anthropological View* (New York: Random House, 1966), 107.

7. C. Geertz, "Religion as a Cultural System," in *Anthropological Approaches to the Study of Religion*, ed. Michael Banton (London: Tavistock, 1999), 1–46; N.K. Frankenberry and H.H. Penner. "Clifford Geertz's Long Lasting Moods, Motivations, and Metaphysical Conceptions," *Journal of Religion* 79, no. 4 (1999): 617–40.

8. K.J. Tarasoff, *Spirit Wrestlers: Doukhobor Pioneers' Strategies for Living* (Ottawa: Legas, 2002).

9. Quoted by G. Leinhardt, "Religion," in *Man, Culture, and Society*, ed. H. Shapiro (London: Oxford University Press, 1960), 368.

10. E. Leach, *Claude Lévi-Strauss* (Chicago: University of Chicago Press, 1974).

11. For an inclusive anthology of world myths, consult C.S. Littleton, *Mythology* (London: Duncan Baird Publishers, 2002).

12. J. Blodgett, "Whale Bone," in *Inuit Art: An Anthology* (Winnipeg: Watson and Dwyer, 1988), 31.

13. C. Lévi-Strauss, *La Pensée Sauvage* (Paris: Plon, 1962); cf. "The Structural Study of Myth," *Journal of American Folklore* 68, no. 270 (1955): chapter 11.

14. M. Guenther, *Tricksters and Trancers* (Bloomington: Indiana University Press, 1999), 101.

15. For a discussion of shamanism, see E.J. Langdon, "Shamans and Shamanisms: Reflections on Anthropological Dilemmas of Modernity," *Vibrant* 4, no. 2 (2007): 27–28.

16. M.J. Plotkin, "Shamans," in *Medicine Quest* (New York: Viking Penguin, 2000), 178–202.

17. A. Van Gennep, *The Rites of Passage* (Chicago: University of Chicago Press, 1960).

18. V. Turner, *The Forest of Symbols: Aspects of Ndembu Ritual* (Ithaca: Cornell University Press, 1970).

19. D. Merkur, "The Ojibwa Vision Quest," *Journal of Applied Psychoanalytical Studies* 4, no. 2 (2002): 149–70.

20. A.P. Elkin, *The Australian Aborigines* (Garden City: Doubleday/Anchor Books, 1964).

21. J.W. Friesen, *First Nations of the Plains: Creative, Adaptable, Enduring* (Calgary: Detsilig, 1999).

22. A.D. McMillan, *Native Peoples and Cultures of Canada: An Anthropological Overview* (Vancouver: Douglas and McIntyre, 1988), 136–37.

23. W.H. Oswalt and S. Neely, *This Land Was Theirs: A Study of North American Indians*, 5th ed. (Mountain View: Mayfield, 1996).

24. B. Malinowski, *Magic, Science, and Religion, and Other Essays* (Garden City: Doubleday/Anchor Books, 1954), 50.

25. E.E. Evans-Prichard, *Witchcraft, Oracles, and Magic Among the Azande* (Oxford: Oxford University Press, 1937); and *Theories of Primitive Religion* (Oxford: Oxford University Press, 1965).

26. J.G. Frazer, "Magic and Religion," in *The Making of Man: An Outline of Anthropology*, ed. V.F. Calverton (New York: Modern Library, 1931), 693.

27. G. Gmelch, "Baseball Magic," in *Annual Editions: Anthropology 05–06*, ed. E. Angeloni (Dubuque: McGraw-Hill/Dushkin, 2000).

28. D. Offiong, "Witchcraft Among the Ibibio of Nigeria," in *Magic, Witchcraft, and Religion*, ed. A.C. Lehmann and J.E. Myers (Palo Alto: Mayfield, 1985), 152–65.

29. L. Mair, *Witchcraft* (New York: McGraw-Hill, 1969), 37.

30. V. Crowly, "Wicca as Nature Religion," In *Nature Religion Today: Paganism in the Modern World*, ed. J. Pearson, R.H. Roberts, and F. Samuel (Edinburgh: Edinburgh University Press, 1998).

31. The material on Wicca is predominantly taken from K. Junker and V. Vergara, "Wicca," *Religious Movements* home page, http://www.wicca.com/celtic/wicca/wicca.htm, 2001, accessed October 24, 2003.

32. L. Kendall, "In the Company of Witches," *Natural History*, October 1990.

33. The discussion of reconstructionist religions is taken from W. Walker, "Neo-Pagan, Heathen, and Reconstructionist Religions," **http://www.witchvox.com/basics/intro.html**, 2002, accessed October 23, 2003.

34. J.D. Campbell, D.P. Yoon, and B. Johnstone, "Determining Relationships Between Physical Health and Spiritual Experience, Religious Practices, and Congregational Support in a Heterogeneous Medical Sample," *Journal of Religion and Health* 49 (2010): 3–17.

35. A.F.C. Wallace, *Culture and Personality*, 2nd ed. (New York: Random House, 1970), 191–96.

36. S. Fedorak, *Anthropology Matters!* (Peterborough: Broadview Press, 2007).

37. R. Tonkinson, *The Mardu Aborigines: Living the Dream in Australia's Desert*, 2nd ed. (Toronto: Holt, Rinehart and Winston, 1991).

13 The Arts

Simon Brascoupé

No known culture is without some form of art, even though that art may be applied to purely utilitarian objects. Art can also reflect religious and spiritual beliefs, and it can transmit cultural teachings.

KEY QUESTIONS

1. What Is Art?

Although the idea of art serving nonuseful, nonpractical purposes seems firmly entrenched in the thinking of modern Western peoples, in other cultures art often serves what are regarded as important, practical purposes.

2. Why Do Anthropologists Study Art?

Anthropologists have found that art reflects a people's cultural values and concerns. This is especially true of the verbal arts—myths, legends, and tales. From these the anthropologist may learn how a people order their world and may discover much about the history of a culture. As well, art, no matter the medium, may provide insights into values, benefits, and world views and may suggest things about a people's history.

3. What Are the Functions of the Arts?

Aside from adding pleasure to everyday life, the various arts serve a number of functions. Myths, for example, set standards for orderly behaviour, and the verbal arts generally transmit and preserve a culture's customs and values. Songs, too, may do this within the restrictions that musical form imposes. The visual arts provide an avenue for interpreting historical events and preserving traditional crafts. Artistic expression promotes cultural identity and a sense of pride in one's cultural heritage; this is exemplified by body art in all its forms. For many indigenous groups, such as the Inuit, artwork provides significant economic value.

In North America, the arts are often seen as luxurious and incidental, as something to be engaged in for personal enjoyment or to provide pleasure for others. This attitude becomes apparent whenever public funds are in short supply; on the local level, during battles over school budgets, art programs are often the first to be cut. Unlike sports, which are usually supported more than the arts because they are perceived as providing skills thought to be essential to success in a competitive world and as promoting nationalism, the arts are deemed nonessential: pleasurable and worthwhile, but also expensive. On the national level, fiscal conservatives often push the government to cut arts funding, on the premise that such funding lacks the practical importance of defence or infrastructure programs. Indeed, artists and their supporters are often seen as something of an elite, subsidized at the expense of hard-working "practical" people. Yet calls to protect Canada's cultural heritage, especially in light of strong influences from U.S. media, are equally vociferous. Canada has a long tradition of public funding and support for the arts. Canadians take great pride in their visual, literary, and performing arts and hold artistic expression as one essence of a distinct Canadian culture.

The fact is that artistic behaviour is as basic to human expression as language. Just as speech is used to communicate feelings and make statements, art is also a form of expression. And just as free speech is considered a fundamental right of all Canadians, so too is artistic freedom. Moreover, art is not created only by a special category of persons called "artists"; folk or popular art is also a vital component of artistic expression. All humans adorn their bodies in certain ways and in doing so make symbolic statements about who they are, both as individuals and as members of social groups. Similarly, all people tell stories in which they express their values, their hopes, and their concerns and thereby reveal much about themselves and their view of the world. Artistic expression both reflects and shapes our social structure and cultural identity and often promotes a cultural group's uniqueness. In short, all people engage in artistic behaviour as they use their imagination to interpret, understand, and enjoy life. And they have been doing this for at least 40,000 years. Far from a luxury afforded or appreciated by a handful of aesthetes or escapists, art is a social behaviour that every human participates in to some degree and takes joy from.

The idea that art is nonuseful and nonpractical seems firmly entrenched in the thinking of modern Western peoples. For example, Iroquois false face

Perhaps the oldest means of artistic expression is body decoration. Shown here are Moroccan women with their hands dyed with henna to celebrate a royal wedding.

Christopher Pillitz/The Image Bank/Getty

masks were, and still are, used in ceremonies. These masks, carved from the living tree and then painted, were intrinsic to Iroquoian curing rituals. As such, they were treated with the utmost reverence. Today, they are often placed on display in museums, where they may be seen and admired as exquisite works of art. However, these masks are sometimes displayed adjacent to concession stands or popcorn machines; as sacred objects, they were never intended to go on general public display—a practice that the Iroquois find disrespectful.

Westerners distinguish between *high art*—art that is expensive, produced by formally trained artists, and difficult to acquire—and *pop* or *folk art*—art that is easy to acquire, produced by ordinary people, and is without high monetary value, though it may possess a great deal of intrinsic value. It has even been suggested that pop art may have a more profound effect on the public due to its accessibility; many more people will hear a country music band at a local bar than will attend an opera, and many more people will enjoy a stitchery display at a local fair than will visit an art gallery. Regardless of the type of art, like any aspect of culture, art is inextricably intertwined with everything else that people do, and it offers us glimpses into other aspects of our lives, including human values and world views. It is worth noting that sometimes what starts as folk art becomes so highly prized that it moves into the fine art category; also, sometimes fine artists are inspired by pop art—the primary example being Andy Warhol, whose pop art pieces are now worth millions each.

To people today, making exquisite objects of gold and precious stones to place in a tomb might seem wasteful. Yet something similar happens when a Navajo artist creates an intricate sand painting as part of a ritual act, only

Much of the world's art is created for functional rather than aesthetic purposes. Shown here, counterclockwise, are examples of art used in healing and blessing ceremonies (a Navajo sand painting), to express cultural identity (Caribana Festival), and for political purposes (graffiti from Katatura, Namibia).

to destroy it once the ritual is over. Johann Sebastian Bach did the very same thing when, almost 300 years ago, he composed his cantatas for church services. These compositions were "throwaway" music, meant to be discarded after the services they were written for. That many of them are still performed today is something of an accident, for Bach did not compose them for posterity. In many human societies, creating the art is often of greater importance than the final product itself. Take Valentine's Day decorations: Every Western schoolchild eagerly makes Valentine's decorations in anticipation of February 14, only to discard them the next day.

Whether a particular work of art is intended to be appreciated purely as such or to serve some practical purpose, it will in every case require the same special combination of symbolic representation of form and expression of feeling that constitutes creative imagination. Insofar as the creative use of the human ability to symbolize is universal and both expresses and is shaped by cultural values and concerns, it is an important subject for anthropological study.

As an activity or kind of behaviour that contributes to human well-being and that helps give shape and significance to life, art is related to yet different from religion. The dividing line between the two is often blurred; it is not easy to determine, for example, precisely where art stops and religion begins in an elaborate ceremony involving ornamentation, masks, costumes, songs, dances, myths, and effigies. Christmas and Ramadan are two excellent examples; both contain important religious symbolism, yet many of the symbols, such as lights and decorations, also have an element of popular art attached to them. And like magic, music, dance, and other arts may be used to "enchant"—to exploit the innate or psychological biases of another person or group so as to cause them to perceive social reality in a way that is favourable to the interests of the enchanter. It is in this same light that we might view the art on Upper Palaeolithic caves or the triple spirals on Neolithic monuments. Art is used to heighten the senses, and in specific ritual settings it contributes to the inculcation of beliefs, playing on emotion, fear, hope, and wonder in order to help "deliver" the ultimate message.

Defining art is a difficult task. In a very broad sense, art is a creative means for expressing symbolic thought, for using our human imagination to interpret, understand, and enjoy life. Art embraces many forms of symbolic expression, from the visual, performing, and literary arts as broad categories, to more specific artistic media, such as body or decorative art, painting, sculpture, folk music, square dancing, opera, oral histories, graffiti, and poetry. We will examine some of these media later in this chapter.

What constitutes art varies, depending on factors such as audience expectations, and what is considered art in one context may be considered not to be art in another. Negative reactions to forms of artistic expression often arise when the message is misunderstood. The exhibiting of Michelangelo's *David* caused a storm among some patrons, who did not perceive the naked statue as a wonderful piece of art celebrating the human form and the artist's ability to render it in stone, but rather as something lewd because of its nakedness. Another case in point is the 1990 video "We're Talking Vulva" by Lorri Milan and Shawna Dempsey of Winnipeg. This immensely popular video has been shown on rock video stations around the world. The video was screened at the Third International Istanbul Biennial, one of seven entries chosen to represent Canada.[1] And yet, when the same video was shown in 2001 to high school students specializing in art, parents protested.

THE ANTHROPOLOGICAL STUDY OF ART

When approaching art as a cultural phenomenon, be it the analysis of the decorative characteristics of Zulu shields or the ceramics of the Maya, anthropologists have the pleasant task of cataloguing, photographing, recording, and describing all possible forms of imaginative activity in any particular culture.

An enormous variety of forms and modes of artistic expression exist in the world. Because people everywhere continue to create and develop in new directions, no point of diminishing returns is foreseeable for the interesting process of collecting and describing the world's ornaments, body decorations, variations in clothing, blanket and rug designs, pottery and basket styles, architectural embellishments, monuments, ceremonial masks, legends, work songs, dances, and so on. The collecting process, however, eventually leads to analysis and generalizations about relationships between art and the rest of culture.

Anthropologists examine how people express their social structure and cultural patterns through art, and how these traditional artistic expressions change through time. Anthropologists studying art consider the artist who creates the art, the meaning or symbolism of the art, and its importance within a culture.[2] For example, the perception of status differences in Western art goes beyond the product, to the artist. Just as fine art holds a higher position in Western society than folk art, a financially successful painter or sculptor possesses more prestige than the rural woman who makes quilts and sells them at local country fairs. Yet each is an artist.

A good way to begin a study of the relationships between art and the rest of culture is to examine critically some of the generalizations already made about specific arts. Since it is impossible to cover all art forms in the space of a single chapter, we will concentrate on just a few: verbal arts, music, visual art, and body art.

Shaman by Markosee Karpik, 1974, whalebone/Art Gallery of Ontario, Gift of Samuel & Esther Sarick, 1988, © Markosee Karpik

Among the Inuit, the artist does not impose his or her will on the medium, but rather seeks to help what is already there to emerge from hiding. Shown here is a whalebone carving, titled *Shaman*, by Markosee Karpik of Pangnirtung, Nunavut, and acquired by the Art Gallery of Ontario in 1988.

The Anthropologist's World

Museums, Anthropology and the MOA (Museum of Anthropology)

Liam Kilmurray

Museums and anthropology have always been intimately linked. The first museums began as "curiosity cabinets": collections of exotic artifacts in the homes of the wealthy. Today, the world's great museums possess many different types of artifacts, ranging from Michelangelo's *David* to rare crystals from far beneath the earth. However, many museums are most concerned with anthropological areas of inquiry. The public, and academic, fascination with cultural artifacts has been a driving force behind the museum "industry." Some museums focus entirely on ethnography, such as the Quai Branly Museum in Paris; others focus on specific cultural groups, such as the Museum of the American Indian in Washington, DC. An ongoing public fascination with the ancient past supports many other institutions, such as the renowned Museum of Antiquities in Cairo and the Museum of Archaeology in Paris. The latter traces the history of the settlement of that city and is located under the streets of Paris itself (as is the Museum of Archaeology in Montreal).

There has always been a strong relationship between museums and anthropology, as both have the furtherance of human cultural understandings as a stated goal. Museums have employed many anthropologists over the centuries, either on excavations or in the exhibiting or preserving of artifacts. Museums are one important outlet for anthropologists to present to the public their understanding of the human species. Around the world, Inuit clothing or Celtic jewelry are displayed and interpreted in glass cases and exhibition halls. Other museums have become more interactive, constructing entire villages to replicate the past, such as at Jorvik in York, England, where visitors ride a small train through a re-creation of the region's Viking past, complete with sounds, smells, and artifacts. Jorvik is an example of the newer interpretive approach, which many museums are beginning to undertake as they attempt to stay relevant to visitors and to move away from the older museum world of "stuffy" rooms packed with artifacts.

Liam Kilmurray

Another example is the Museum of Anthropology (MOA) in Vancouver. Founded in 1949 in the basement of UBC's main library, it possesses one of the finest anthropological collections in the Americas. The MOA is set against the Point Grey cliffs on the UBC campus, adjacent to the Department of Anthropology. It holds some 36,000 ethnographic objects and 535,000 archaeological objects, many of these from BC's Northwest Coast. In the Audain Gallery, the museum's new, 5,800-square-foot temporary-exhibition hall, world-class travelling exhibits as well as those developed in-house are showcased. Because of its wonderful collections and innovative approach to exhibits, the museum has received accolades from around the world. Along with its general collections, the MOA is especially renowned for its stunning collection of West Coast Native art, including an exquisite display of Haida artist Bill Reid's works.

The MOA reflects the newer approaches that have emerged in the museum world. For example, outdoor space is used in such a way that visitors are able to walk through a re-created village, between the longhouses. Similarly, the totems in the Great Hall allow the visitor to walk among these tremendous creations and gain a sense of scale (in much the same way as at the Museum of Civilization in Gatineau-Hull).

In a further move away from the older "stand and stare" approach to artifacts, there is an emphasis on making more accessible the cultural objects the museum houses. Inside the MOA, many of the exhibits are set in metal and glass "boxes" that can be opened and closed by visitors and that contain many wonderful artifacts (see image). This simple approach, along with the use of indoor and outdoor interactive spaces, had made the MOA a unique Canadian museum, set in idyllic surroundings surrounded by water and trees. All of the exhibits are presented thoughtfully and interactively. It is a museum that not only entertains the curious but also educates and inspires.

VERBAL ARTS

The term **folklore** was coined in the 19th century to denote the unwritten stories, beliefs, and customs of European peasantry, as opposed to the traditions of the literate elite. The subsequent study of folklore, **folkloristics**, has become a discipline allied to but somewhat independent of anthropology, working on cross-cultural comparisons of themes, motifs, genres, and structures from a literary as well as ethnological point of view. Many linguists and anthropologists prefer to speak of a culture's oral traditions and verbal arts rather than its folklore and folktales, recognizing that creative verbal expression takes many forms and that the implied distinction between folk and "fine" art is a projection of the recent attitude of European (and European-derived) cultures onto others.

The verbal arts include narratives, dramas, poetry, incantations, duelling songs, proverbs, riddles, word games, and even naming procedures, compliments, and insults, when these take structured and special forms. Narratives seem to be one of the easiest kinds of verbal arts to record or collect. Perhaps because they also are the most publishable, with popular appeal in North American society, they have received the most study and attention. Generally, narratives have been divided into three basic and recurring categories: myth, legend, and tale.

Myths

The word "myth," in popular usage, refers to something that is widely believed to be true but probably is not. Actually, a myth provides a rationale for religious beliefs and practices. Myth making is an extremely important form of human creativity, and the study of the myth-making process provides valuable clues to the ways people perceive and think about their world. One of the most common types of myths is the origin or creation myth, which explains the beginnings of all things. Following is a typical origin myth traditional with the Western Abenaki of northwestern New England and southern Quebec:

> In the beginning, Tabaldak, "The Owner," created all living things but one—the spirit being who was to accomplish the final transformation of the earth. Man and woman Tabaldak made out of a piece of stone, but he didn't like the result,

folklore A 19th-century term first used to refer to the traditional oral stories and sayings of European peasants and later extended to traditions preserved orally in all societies.

folkloristics The study of folklore (as linguistics is the study of language).

their hearts being cold and hard. This being so, he broke them up, and their remains today can be seen in the many stones that litter the landscape of the Abenaki homeland. But Tabaldak tried again, this time using living wood, and from them came all later Abenakis. Like the trees from which the wood came, these people were rooted in the earth and (like trees when being blown by the wind) could dance gracefully.[3]

Such a myth, insofar as it is believed, accepted, and perpetuated in a culture, may be said to express a world view—that is, the unexpressed but implicit conceptions of people's place in nature and of the limits and workings of their world. Extrapolating from the details of the myth, we might conclude that the Abenaki recognize a kinship among all living things; after all, they were all part of the same creation, and humans even were made from living wood. Moreover, an attempt to make them of non-living stone was not satisfactory. This idea of a closeness among all living things led the Abenaki to show special respect to the animals they hunted; after killing a beaver, muskrat, or waterfowl, the hunter showed respect by returning the animal's bones to the water, with a request that it continue its kind. Failure to respect animals' rights would result in their unwillingness to continue sacrificing their lives so that people might live.

A characteristic of explanatory myths such as this one is that the unknown is simplified and explained in terms of the known. This myth accounts for the existence of rivers, mountains, lakes, and other features of the landscape, as well as of humans and all other living things. It also sanctions particular attitudes and behaviours. It is a product of past and present creative imagination, and it is a work of art as well as a potentially religious statement.

One aspect of mythology that has attracted a good deal of interest over the years is the similarity of certain themes in the stories of peoples living in separate parts of the world. One of these themes is the myth of matriarchy, or one-time rule by women. In a number of cultures, stories recount a time when women ruled over men. Eventually, so these stories go, men were forced to rise up and assert their dominance over women to combat their tyranny or incompetence (or both). In the 19th century a number of European scholars interpreted such myths as evidence of an early stage of matriarchy in the evolution of human culture. Although a number of societies are known where the two sexes related to each other as equals (Western Abenaki society was one), never have anthropologists found one where women ruled over or dominated men. The interesting thing about myths of matriarchy is that they generally are

Raven and the First Men, by Haida artist Bill Reid, represents a First Nations creation myth.

found in cultures where men have a much higher social status than women, but where the latter have considerable autonomy.[4] Under such conditions, male dominance is insecure, and a rationale is needed to justify it. Thus, myths of men overthrowing women and taking control mirror an existing paradoxical relationship between the two sexes.

Myth making is an extremely important kind of human creativity, and the study of myth making provides valuable clues to the ways in which people perceive and think about their world.

Legends

Legends are stories told as true and set in the postcreation world. Commonly, legends consist of pseudo-historical narratives, and it is this "historical" characteristic that distinguishes legends from myth. Legends usually account for the deeds of heroes, the movements of peoples, and the establishment of local customs, with a mixture of realism and the supernatural or extraordinary. As stories, they are not necessarily believed or disbelieved, but they usually serve to entertain, as well as to instruct and to inspire or bolster pride in family, community, and nation.

Legends are not confined to nonliterate, nonindustrialized societies. To a degree, in literate states, the function of legends has been taken over by written history. Yet much of what passes for history, to paraphrase one historian, consists of the legends we develop to make ourselves feel better about who we are.[5] The Riel Rebellion, involving military actions by the Métis in 1869 and 1885, is portrayed in Canadian history books as a treacherous uprising rather than a desperate bid for survival in the face of encroaching European settlement. Riel and his people were resisting dispossession, but to this day, thanks to history books, many Canadians still believe that Riel led a treasonous rebellion against the federal government. The former Soviet Union was especially well known for similar practices, such as Stalin's distortion of the past for political gain. Historians, when attempting to separate fact from fiction, often incur the wrath of people who will not willingly abandon what they wish to believe is true, whether or not it really is.

Legends may incorporate mythological details, especially when they make an appeal to the supernatural, and are therefore not always clearly distinct from myth. The Mwindo epic of the Nyanga people follows that being through the earth, the atmosphere, the underworld, and the remote sky, thus giving a complete picture of the Nyanga people's view of their world's organization and limits. Legends also may incorporate proverbs and incidental tales and thus may be related to other forms of verbal art. A recitation of the Kambili epic of the Mande, for example, has been said to include as many as 150 proverbs.

For anthropologists, a major significance of the secular and apparently realistic portions of legends relates to the clues they provide to a culture's approved or ideal ethical behaviour. The subject matter of legends is essentially problem solving, and the content is likely to include heroic deeds involving combat, warfare, confrontations, and physical and psychological trials of many kinds. Certain questions may be answered explicitly or implicitly. Do the people justify homicide? What kinds of behaviour are considered brave or cowardly? What is the etiquette of combat or warfare? Do the people honour or recognize a concept of altruism or self-sacrifice? Here again, however, pitfalls occur in the process of interpreting art in relation

legends Stories told as true and set in the postcreation world.

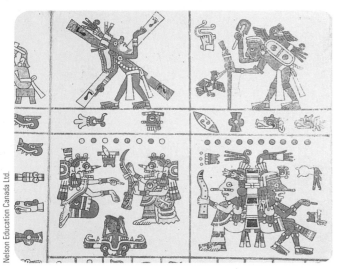

Part of an ancient Aztec manuscript. In the reign of King Itzcoatl, the Aztecs rewrote their history in a way to better glorify their past. In politically centralized states, such rewriting of history is a common practice.

to life. It is always possible that certain kinds of behaviour are acceptable or even admirable, with the distance or objectivity art affords, but are not at all approved for daily life in the present. In Western cultures, murderers, charlatans, and rakes sometimes have become popular heroes and the subjects of legends; however, North Americans do not approve of or want to emulate the morality of characters like Billy the Kid and the Mad Trapper. Yet the legendary deeds of heroes like Sam Steele and Buffalo Bill all epitomize our notions of heroism.

Tales

Tale is a nonspecific label for a third category of creative narratives: those which are purely secular, nonhistorical, and recognized as fiction for entertainment, although they may draw a moral or teach a practical lesson as well. Consider this brief summary of a tale from Ghana, known as "Father, Son, and Donkey":

> A father and his son farmed their corn, sold it, and spent part of the profit on a donkey. When the hot season came, they harvested their yams and prepared to take them to storage using their donkey. The father mounted the donkey, and they all three proceeded on their way until they met some people. "What? You lazy man!" the

tale A creative narrative recognized as fiction for entertainment.

motif A story situation in a folktale.

people said to the father. "You let your young son walk barefoot on this hot ground while you ride on a donkey? For shame!" The father yielded his place to the son, and they proceeded until they came to an old woman. "What? You useless boy!" said the old woman. "You ride on the donkey and let your poor father walk barefoot on this hot ground? For shame!" The son dismounted, and both father and son walked on the road, leading the donkey behind them until they came to an old man. "What? You foolish people!" said the old man. "You have a donkey and you walk barefoot on the hot ground instead of riding?" And so it goes. Listen: when you are doing something and other people come along, just keep on doing what you like.

This is precisely the kind of tale that interests scholars of traditional folklore. It is an internationally popular "numbskull" tale, and versions of it have been recorded in India, the Middle East, the Balkans, Italy, Spain, England, and North America, as well as in West Africa. It is classified or catalogued as exhibiting a basic **motif**, or story situation (in this case, father and son trying to please everyone), one of the many thousands found to recur in world folktales. Allowing for variations in detail, every version reflects the same basic sequence of events, sometimes called the "syntax" of the tale: a peasant father and son work together, a beast of burden is purchased, the three set out on a short excursion, the father rides and is criticized, the son rides and is criticized, both walk and are criticized, and a conclusion is drawn.

A surprising number of motifs in European and African tales can be traced to ancient sources in India. Is this good evidence of diffusion from a "cradle" of civilization, or is it an example of diffusion of tales in contiguous areas? Of course, purely local tales exist. In any particular culture, anthropologists likely could categorize local types of tales: animal, human experience, trickster, dilemma, ghost, moral, scatological, nonsense tales, and so on. In West Africa, for example, there is a remarkable prevalence of animal stories, with creatures such as the spider, the rabbit, and the hyena as the protagonists. Many were carried to the Americas; the Uncle Remus stories about Brer Rabbit, Brer Fox, and other animals may be survivors of this tradition.

The significance of tales for anthropologists rests partly in their distribution. Tales provide evidence of either cultural contacts or cultural isolation and of limits of influence and cultural cohesion. Debated for decades now, for example, has been the extent to which the culture of West Africa was transmitted to the southeastern United States. As far as folktales are concerned, one school of folklorists has always insisted on European origins; another school, somewhat more recently, points to African prototypes. Anthropologists are interested, however, in more than these questions of distribution. Like legends, tales often illustrate local solutions to universal human ethical problems, and in some sense they state a moral philosophy. Anthropologists see that whether the tale of the father, the son, and the donkey originated in West Africa or arrived there from Europe or the Middle East, the very fact that it is told in West Africa suggests that it states something valid for that culture. The tale's lesson that one must have at least some self-confidence in the face of arbitrary social criticism is therefore something that can be read into the culture's values and beliefs.

Popular fiction is a modern manifestation of the age-old art of storytelling that also follows certain motifs that promote a society's values. When J.K. Rowling's *Harry Potter and the Philosopher's Stone* (1997) was first published, the story captured our imagination because it contained many of the best elements of folktales. Harry was a brave hero fighting powerful villains, but he was also a social misfit. In a male version of the "Cinderella" motif, Harry was transported to a magical world where he was special and his life took on new meaning. The story of a fairly ordinary boy living a rather unpleasant life and then suddenly becoming powerful and important resonates with us all.[6]

Other Verbal Arts

Myths, legends, and tales, prominent as they are in anthropological studies, turn out to be no more important than the other verbal arts. For the Awlad 'Ali Bedouin of Egypt's Western Desert, for example, poetry is a lively and active verbal art, especially as a vehicle for personal expression and private communication. These people use two forms of poetry. One is the elaborately structured and heroic poems that men chant or recite only on ceremonial occasions and in specific public contexts. The other is the *ghinnáwa*, or "little songs," which punctuate everyday conversations. Simple in structure, these deal with personal matters and feelings that are more appropriate to informal social situations, and older men regard them as the unimportant productions of women and youths. Despite this official devaluation in the male-dominated society of the Bedouin, however, *ghinnáwa* play a vital part in daily life. In their "little songs," individuals are shielded from the consequences of making statements and expressing sentiments that contravene the moral system. Paradoxically, by sharing these "immoral"

sentiments only with intimates and veiling them in impersonal traditional formulas, people are allowed a sanctioned outlet for otherwise taboo thoughts or opinions. Disaster jokes serve the same function in contemporary North American society.

In all cultures, the words of songs constitute a kind of poetry. Poetry and stories recited with gestures, movement, and props become drama. Drama combined with dance, music, and spectacle becomes a public celebration. The more we look at the individual arts, the clearer it becomes that they often are interrelated and interdependent.

THE ART OF MUSIC

> Padded with power, here they come
> International loan sharks backed by the guns
> of market-hungry military profiteers
> whose word is a swamp and whose brow is
> smeared with the blood of the poor
>
> Bruce Cockburn 1985, "Call It Democracy"*

The study of music in specific cultural settings, beginning in the 19th century with the collection of folksongs, has developed into a specialized field called **ethnomusicology**. Like the study of folktales for their

ethnomusicology The study of a society's music in terms of its cultural setting.

*CALL IT DEMOCRACY WRITTEN BY BRUCE COCKBURN © 1985 GOLDEN MOUNTAIN MUSIC CORP. (SOCAN) USED BY PERMISSION

🙞 *Original Study* 🙜

A Perspective on Aboriginal Art

Simon Brascoupé

Simon Brascoupé, Anishinabeg/ Haudenosaunee is an adjunct professor at Carleton University and Trent University. Simon is a renowned artist whose works are displayed at the Smithsonian and the Museum of Civilisation in Gatineau. He is currently the Director of the First Nations Centre, National Aboriginal Health Organization.

There is no word for "art" in Aboriginal languages, and this has been misinterpreted to mean that First Nations, Inuit, and Métis are primitive and without culture. Yet Aboriginal peoples have produced beautiful, meaningful art reflecting their environment and cultures for thousands of years. Since the beginning of time, they have painted, carved, woven, sewn, and fired aesthetically beautiful art. These works reflect world views that see the world holistically and as sacred. Aboriginal art symbolizes teachings centred on creation, values, and ceremony. Art teaches about balance in the world through mirrored images in hair combs or contrasting colours in beadwork. Art signifies meaning in its design, such as the repeated sky domes in Haudenosaunee (Iroquois) beadwork to signify the creation. Beaded designs encode recipes for medicinal flowers and plants and remind us that these flora are our relatives. To Aboriginal peoples, art encapsulates all of their cultural experience; unlike the hierarchical classification system of art—fine art, craft, and so on—Aboriginal art is free of limiting dichotomies such as women versus men, art versus craft, and fine versus primitive. Aboriginal art

history incorporates the continuity from past to present; it reminds us of who we are and where we come from. Ancient rock art, for example, enables contemporary Aboriginal artists to commune directly with the vision of their ancient ancestors.

Contemporary artists such as Norval Morrisseau and others invented the Anishinabeg or Woodland style of art. Joseph Jacobs, along with Duffy Wilson and others, invented the Haudenosaunee (Iroquois) stone-carving style. While there is not a word for "art," art, invention, and creativity are found

Elk and Elk Spirit symbolizes an old creation teaching. The elk created the universe by simply calling out. My ancestors followed the elk into the Ottawa region following the receding of the glaciers. In a concrete way the elk created the conditions for my ancestors' survival by providing food, shelter, and spirit to live and survive in the region.

throughout Aboriginal cultural life. This is witnessed in the internationally known artists on the one hand, and on the other hand in elders such as my grandmother Sarah Patterson, who passed down her cultural knowledge through her own works.

It is informative to explore Aboriginal perspectives of art, which include all forms of cultural expression: beadwork, carving, painting, clothing, drum making, and so on. Bill Reid, the great

Haida artist, said that if there wasn't a word for "art" in Aboriginal languages, then "the people of the past had no appreciation of the 'formal' elements of their creations, that they had no aesthetic criteria by which to distinguish good works from bad, that they were not moved by excellence and beauty. Without a formal and critical public, the artists could never, in these societies as in any other, have produced the great works that they did" (Ames 1992, 70–71). He was arguing that Haida culture had a critical appreciation for art that enabled his ancestors to produce great and beautiful art. To prove his point, all we have to do is visit a museum to see all the wonderful art produced in the past! Bea Medicine gets at the heart of the discussion when she writes that "perhaps ... there is no word for 'art' in American-Indian languages, but it may simply be another dimension of the deficit models by 'Others' which have plagued American Indians/Alaska Native linguistic and philosophical systems for too long" (Medicine, n.d.). She argues that Aboriginal cultures are stereotyped because it serves others to label Aboriginal cultures as uncivilized and primitive. In cultures that see the world holistically, as connected and nonhierarchical, and in which commercialism does not exist, words like "art" or "health" do not exist. Robert Davidson said recently that "there is so much art, in fact, I don't even think there was a word for art, it was a way of life."

A knowledge of Aboriginal art history and an informed perspective are important toward understanding the origins, meaning, and purposes of Aboriginal art. Some say the first totem pole floated to shore from the ocean on the Northwest Coast. Some of the oldest Anishinabeg paintings are beautiful rock art paintings of rich red ochre on rock faces along the rivers and lakes. These paintings depict ancient migrations, teachings, and ceremonies. Gerald McMaster, Cree contemporary art curator at the Art Gallery of Ontario (AGO) in Toronto, has presented Aboriginal art history in a historical chronology exhibition of beautiful arrow and spear heads that go back thousands of years. The exhibit tells the history of climate, cultural, and technological change. It's also a story of cultural change in hunting societies, from large to smaller mammals, and of a shift from spear to bow and arrow. At the Rochester Museum and Science Center (RMSC) in Rochester, New York, one can view the Haudenosaunee hair comb collection. The artist Karen Hodge Russell says, "These hair combs meet all aesthetic elements and principles of art, while communicating the stories, values and beliefs of the person who wore them" (Brascoupé 2010). The hair comb exhibit is from a period in the 1700s when the Haudenosaunee (People of the Longhouse, or Iroquois) were encountering considerable stress and change. The images on these beautiful hair combs depict clan symbols, families, historical events, and teachings. Russell has been researching hair combs using an innovative method that analyzes them through a physical, emotional, mental, and spiritual lens. Similarly, the AGO and RMSC exhibits show how some Aboriginal art changed over time while retelling Aboriginal histories. So like the Venus of Willendorf in Austria or the Lascaux cave paintings in France, Aboriginal peoples have their own distinct art and their own art history.

Aboriginal peoples pass on knowledge orally and symbolically through their art. Anthropologists and Aboriginals alike have speculated on what meanings much of the art may have held. For example, what exactly was it that the Oiseau Rock Anishinabeg artists wanted to pass on to future generations? And what might have been the purpose of the petroglyphs found across Canada? This is the remarkable nature of art: An artist thousands of years ago can communicate through time to contemporary populations, including contemporary artists. The artist simply looks directly at the art to gain insight to its meaning and intention. Aboriginal art relies also on the use of symbols to signify meaning, such as the four cardinal points in the Medicine Wheel used in Anishinabeg teachings. The Medicine Wheel can signify the four sacred directions

Simon Brascoupé

Oiseau Rock: Graffiti, Fish, and Mermaid. In this photo we see the Oiseau Rock site on the Ottawa River. It is covered in graffiti and is the most defaced national treasure in Canada.

or the healing process that starts with talking and leads to the healing journey through listening, learning, healing, and becoming healed. Norval Morrisseau, the master Ojibway artist, created a whole symbolic language with roots into the Midewin teachings of his grandfather that are found in Midewin birchbark scrolls and rock paintings. He painted human beings, animals, fish, and plants as one, connected by spirit lines and sacred circles divided to show the balance of life. This Anishinabeg or Woodland style of art can be found everywhere in the Anishinabeg world on posters, books, prints, and buildings. Harold South-

wind's Woodland paintings feature prominently on the community centre in Sagamok First Nation, Ontario. This style is ubiquitous, as important to the Ojibwa as the triple spiral is to Celts or the *Mona Lisa* to Italians. Encoded in these images are cultural teachings, values, and history. For example, when you see a Woodland painting of a buffalo, it could symbolize the value "respect." The buffalo represents the true meaning of respect because of its ability to give and show respect to life and give of itself. Woodland Aboriginal art is part of the healing process necessitated by the historical trauma caused by colonization. Art reinforces Anishinabeg identity and brings meaning to contemporary life.

The cave art painted on the walls of Lascaux can be found in Western art history textbooks and is protected as a national and indeed international treasure. Yet the rock art found across Canada is not afforded the same protection or respect. For example, the Oiseau Rock site on the Ottawa River is covered in graffiti and is the most defaced national treasure in Canada. The destruction of these pictographs continues to this day; only in 2010 were signs erected warning the public not to destroy these paintings.

There are two types of rock art: Petroglyphs are carvings in rock, and pictographs are painted. On the east coast, Mi'kmaq painted animals, humans, and traditional symbols. More recently, they painted the arrival of Europeans, guns, churches, Christian symbols, and sailboats. A major site for Mi'kmaq art is Kejimkujik National Park in southwestern Nova Scotia. On the Canadian Shield from Quebec to northern Saskatchewan there are

CONTINUED

CONTINUED

more than 500 Anishinabeg (Algonquin, Cree, Ojibwa) rock art sites. Radiocarbon dating found one site to be 2,000 years old; another site is estimated to be 5,000 years old. The paintings of thunderbirds, animals, fish, and families in canoes teach us the secrets of survival and a sustainable life. The Peterborough petroglyph site contains hundreds of images of humans, birds, turtles, snakes, and canoes. Both pictographs and petroglyphs are found in British Columbia. Some petroglyphs can only be viewed when the tide is out, revealing images of fish. Rock art sites are also found in the Arctic, with images of humans, animals, and transformative figures. This national heritage is Canada's oldest and most common art and is part of a genre of art found everywhere in the world. If these paintings were defined in Canada as "art" with the same reverence as the cave paintings are in Spain and France, they would be better protected.

The most intriguing thing about Canada's rock art is that the knowledge and meaning it contains still exist in the oral teachings of Aboriginal peoples. We cannot ask the Upper Paleolithic hunter-artists of cave art in France what was on their minds 30,000 years ago, but we can listen to and learn from contemporary Aboriginal artists about what Aboriginal rock art can teach us. Hunting, fishing, and gathering societies have survived for thousands of years by living in harmony with nature. In contrast, the modern industrial world has been around for a few hundred years and is clearly unsustainable. In 1987, the UN report *Our Common Future* contended that the world could learn much about a sustainable way of life from indigenous peoples and the knowledge they possess. Elders inform us that healing is necessary to recover our sustainable past. The world needs to listen to Aboriginal peoples across Canada and the world to learn about living in harmony with nature and to make decisions for the seven generations to come (Brascoupé 1996).

In the 1960s, Aboriginal artists started putting their mark on the international art world. Artists like Norval Morrisseau and Tony Hunt, Sr., became international stars. Hunt travelled around the world carving Kwakiutl totem poles and performing; he had been taught by his grandfather Mongo Martin, and he set out to revitalize Northwest Coast art. He and other artists such as Bill Reid, Doreen Jensen, Frieda Diesing, and Robert Davidson started a cultural revolution on the Northwest Coast. Many of these artists were driven to bring their culture to life through the visual, sculptural, musical, and dance arts. In the 1960s, Inuit artists brought Inuit culture to an international audience. These Inuit artists, skilled in traditional arts, quickly mastered printmaking and carving. Artists like Kenojuak Ashevak created iconic prints like the *Enchanted Owl*. Norval Morrisseau revitalized Anishinabeg culture and promoted Aboriginal art as art, both in Canada and on the international stage. Métis artists like Bob Boyer and Edward Poitras provided leadership to have Aboriginal art recognized in Canada. Early on, artists began to organize, and Norval Morrisseau and others formed the Indian Group of Seven along with Jackson Beardy, Eddy Cobiness, Alex Janvier, Daphne Odjig, Carl Ray, and Joseph Sanchez. This was a period of cultural revitalization from the Northwest Coast, Prairies, Woodlands, East Coast, and Arctic.

At the same time, these artists were concerned about ending colonization and residential schools. They were trying to understand the suffering and dysfunction in their communities, now known as historical trauma. Aboriginal artists across Canada responded by creating images based on Aboriginal teachings, values, and ceremonies to revitalize their communities and to educate the outside world. However, outsiders were blinded by stereotypes and trapped in colonial language that could not accurately explain what was happening. Where Aboriginal people saw truth and teachings, outsiders saw myth and stories. Art critics, historians, and anthropologists were stuck with language constructs such as "primitive art" and made sharp distinctions between arts, crafts, and souvenirs. They would label Woodland art as "shamanic art," whereas Native communities saw Anishinabeg art as part of their culture and identity. Woodland art was seen as primitive and was sometimes referred to as "legend art" that visually told stories or myths. Aboriginal artists have resisted these characterizations by saying it is not myth or legend but "teachings" and "knowledge." While some viewed these ideas as naive and as stemming from a primitive past, artist and elders saw the art for its ability to heal communities. It is said that Canadians are patient and kind, and even though there was this great divide in understanding, there began a wonderful dialogue between Aboriginal peoples and Canadians that started moving in interesting directions in the 1980s and 1990s.

The debate as to whether Aboriginal art is "art" in the eyes of the art establishment began in earnest in the 1980s. In 1985 a group of Aboriginal artists formed SCANA (Society of Canadian Artists of Native Ancestry) with the goal of advocating for Aboriginal art exhibitions in the National Gallery of Canada. Their view was that they were artists first and wanted major exhibitions with an Aboriginal voice and with Aboriginal curators. Two groundbreaking exhibitions opened in 1992: "INDIGENA: Perspectives of Aboriginal Peoples on 500 years," Canadian Museum of Civilization; and "Land, Spirit, Power: First Nations" at the National Gallery of Canada. The irony that it took 500 years to recognize Aboriginal art in Canada was not lost. In 2008 another major shift happened at the Art Gallery of Ontario's new Canadian galleries, where Canadian and Aboriginal art were exhibited side by side. In hindsight, it seems natural and intuitive to exhibit art in this way. The exhibition's curator, Gerald McMaster (Cree), expanded the definition of art with this exhibit by including Inuit carvings, Anishinabeg beadwork, Haida masks, and works by Norval Morrisseau and Kent Monkman, alongside Canadian artists Paul Kane, Cornelius Krieghoff, and Emily Carr.

Over the past three decades, First Nations, Inuit, and Métis peoples have experienced a cultural revitalization known as the healing and wellness movement. The arts—visual, music, dance, literature, theatre, and new media—play a key role in community healing and decolonization. Canadian assimilation policies beginning in the 1850s, such as residential schools and the outlawing of traditional cultural practices, have had a *catastrophic* impact on Aboriginal identity and health. Children were forcefully removed from their families and placed in residential schools; many faced loneliness as well as psychological, physical, and sexual abuse. The historical trauma experienced by residential school survivors and their children is now recognized as post-traumatic stress, and much of the dysfunction in Aboriginal communities is attributed to such intergenerational trauma. Elders and community members went back to their traditions, teachings, and cultures to find ways such as healing circles and ceremonies to return individuals to their healing journey. The resurgence in the arts marked the revitalization in Aboriginal culture that has ushered in a new day for First Nations, Inuit, and Métis identities.

SOURCES: M.A. Ames, *Cannibal Tours and Glass Boxes: The Anthropology of Museums* (Vancouver: UBC Press, 1992); S. Brascoupé, interview with Karen Hodge Russell, December 6, 2010; Brascoupé, "Aboriginal Vision of the Future: Interweaving Traditional Knowledge and New Technologies," in *Visions of the Heart: Canadian Aboriginal Issues,* ed. D.A. Long and O.P. Dickason (Toronto: Harcourt Brace Canada, 1996), 355–75; B. Medicine, n.d. "Lakota Views of 'Art' and Artistic Expression," n.d., http://www.danaclaxton.com/assets/Bea_Medicine.pdf, accessed January 4, 2011.

own sake, ethnomusicology is both related to and somewhat independent of anthropology. Nevertheless, it is possible to sort out several concepts of interest to general anthropology from the field's various concerns.

To begin, we may ask these questions: How does music reflect a culture? What is considered important when distinguishing music from other modes of expression? What aspects of music are considered important in Western and non-Western cultures? Music is a form of communication that includes a nonverbal component; often, music transmits emotions rather than ideas. This nonverbal component of music makes it difficult to analyze. In fact, it is even difficult to agree on a definition of music, and ethnomusicologists often rely on a working definition to distinguish between "music" and that which is "musical."

Much of the early development of musicology was based on the study of Western European music and on the elements considered important in European music (rhythm, melody, tonality). But these elements may not reflect the spiritual significance of African, First Nations, East Indian, or Asian music.

Early investigators of non-European music were struck by the apparent simplicity of melody and by the endless repetition of phrases. A great deal of non-European music was dismissed as "primitive" and formless when in fact it was complex in structure and quite sophisticated. African music, which is based on simultaneous multiple rhythmic patterns (polyrhythms), demonstrates remarkable precision. These polyrhythms are integral to modern jazz, world music, and folk music. While much of European music employs melodic lines based on 12 equal steps, Arabic and East Indian music often uses melodic lines of 24 equal steps. Thus, the sounds may often sound "out of tune" or strange to the unaccustomed ear. However, these non-European songs evoke emotions and feelings as well as or better than European styles.

Although anthropologists do not necessarily need to untangle the complicated technical matters of music, they will want to know enough to be aware of the degree of skill involved in a performance. This allows a measure of the extent to which people in a culture have learned to practise and respond to this often-important creative activity. Moreover, the distribution of musical forms and instruments can reveal much about cultural contact or isolation.

Functions of Music

Even without concern for technical matters, anthropologists can profitably investigate the function of music in human groups. First, people have expressed themselves through music for a very long time. The earliest multi-note, playable musical instrument, the flute, is dated to 7000–6000 BC in China. Bone flutes and whistles as old as 40,000 years have been found by archaeologists. Historically known food-foraging peoples have their own form of music. In the Kalahari Desert, for example, a Ju/'hoansi hunter off by himself might play a tune on his bow simply to help while away the time. In northern New England, Abenaki shamans used cedar flutes to call game, lure enemies, and attract women. A drum with two rawhide strings stretched over it to produce a buzzing sound, thought to represent singing, gave the shaman the power to communicate with the spirit world.

Dynamic Anthropology

Picturing Anthropology

Liam Kilmurray

Photography is an important part of anthropology and is used widely in the discipline. Archaeologists use aerial photography to highlight ancient sites from the air, often after droughts reveal an underlying pattern in the ground. Within ethnographic studies, photographs are essential to communicating the daily lives, artifacts, and environments of the peoples being studied. Anthropologists from diverse backgrounds travel the world with camera equipment in tow in order to fully document the phenomena they are studying. But it is not just anthropologists who get "around the world"—so do anthropology students. As part of Anthropology Week, the Department of Sociology and Anthropology at the University of Ottawa recently launched an annual photo competition for students and staff. The entries for the past two years have included a variety of striking images from around the world. Two examples are selected here. This first was taken by an undergraduate student, Marika Galadza, on her travels to Japan. In her own words:

The festival is held in January in Sakiyama township, on the Goto Islands in Nagasaki Prefecture, Japan. The festival is considered one of the most unique experiences to behold for a foreigner. It involves men of all ages partaking in tests of strength such as a town-wide tug of war and children's sumo competitions.

The game in this photo is one of such skill testing and strength building exercises. The men insulate their bodies from the harsh cold by smearing themselves with mud, drinking sake, and staying active during the festival. One of the main attractions of the festival

Middle-school boys run for the prize at the Hetomato festival.

This photograph depicts a group of Shuar from Gualaquiza in the province of Zamora Chinchipe, Ecuador.

is a 300 kg straw sandal called a zorii which is used to capture un-married women in, and parade around the village to announce their marriageability. While women do not feature prominently in this festival, there is one event where

women married in the last year are dressed in kimonos, hoisted on barrels and dual each other in a small racket game resembling badminton.

The second image was taken by William Strachan, an honours undergraduate student specializing in conflict studies and human rights. In his own words:

This photograph depicts a group of Shuar from Gualaquiza in the province of Zamora Chinchipe, Ecuador. It was taken in August 2009 following a series of dances meant for welcoming guests, honouring nature, and revering life. The guests were a group of Canadian youths on a trade and development mission with Global Vision's Junior Team Canada. The Shuar were dressed and decorated in traditional attire and accompanied their dances to music performed in their native Quechua language.

The camera is an essential part of the tool kit in many different fields of anthropology, so anthropologists need to be skillful photographers. Photography competitions such as the one at the University of Ottawa are held at other institutions. They encourage students to document, and to think about, the places and the peoples they visit. Essential skills are learned, and often a small prize is offered—not least publication in an anthropology text!

Music is also a powerful cultural agent. Many marginalized groups have used music for purposes of self-identification, bringing the group together through their music, sometimes in an effort to counter a dominant culture's influence or to raise their voices in social and political commentary. The hippie movement of the 1960s used music to protest the consumer-oriented values of mainstream society. In North America, many examples exist of marginalized social and ethnic groups attempting to gain a larger audience and more compassion for their plight through song. This is the case with rap artists such as Shawn "Jay-Z" Carter and Kanye West, as well as with ethnic groups that sponsor musical festivals to bring people together. Familiar to Canadians are Bruce Cockburn, Buffy Sainte-Marie, Bob Dylan, and Joni Mitchell, who have supported civil and human rights causes in their music. Indeed, the celebrity status of these performers led to the broader dissemination of their social and political beliefs. Such celebrity status comes from skill in performing and communicating with the intended audience. Indeed, music can often convey political messages that may not be allowed in narrative. An example is Canadian musician Bruce Cockburn's biting depiction of the International Monetary Fund in his song "Call It Democracy":

> North South East West
> Kill the best and buy the rest
> It's just spend a buck to make a buck
> You don't really give a flying ....
> About the people in misery
>
> IMF dirty MF
> Takes away everything it can get
> Always making certain that there's one thing left
> Keep them on the hook with insupportable debt
>
> And they call it democracy

Using music as a medium for social and political commentary seems particularly important for young people. Indeed, "music is not just something young people like to do. It is in many respects the model for their involvement in culture."[7]

Canadians celebrate multiculturalism through music. Examples are Ukrainian Yevshen dancers, Jewish klezmer bands, and the Celtic folk music of the Atlantic provinces and Quebec. Potlatches and pow-wows demonstrate First Nations groups' affirmation and celebration of their ethnic identity. Music plays an important part at these events, thus becoming closely bound to the group identity, both from within and from outside the group. It should be understood, too, that these associations of music with groups are dependent not simply on words alone but also on tonal, rhythmic, and instrumental conventions. For example, Scottish gatherings would not be "Scottish" without the sound of bagpipes and the fiddle.

This power of music to shape identity has been recognized everywhere, with varying consequences. The English recognized the power of the bagpipes for creating an esprit de corps among the Highland regiments of the British army and encouraged it within certain bounds, even while suppressing piping in Scotland itself under the Disarming Act. Over time, the British military piping tradition was assimilated into the Scottish piping tradition, so the blend was accepted and spread by Scottish pipers. As a result, much of the supposedly Scottish piping we hear today consists of marches written within the conventions of the English musical tradition, although shaped to fit the physical constraints of the instrument.

The English adoption of the Highland bagpipe into Scottish regiments is an instance of those in authority employing music to further a political agenda. So too

A phenomenally popular music form in the Western world today, rap music originated as a street cultural movement among inner-city black youth.

Groups often express their cultural identity through music and dance. Shown here is a First Nations powwow at Chippawa Hill, Ontario.

in Spain, the dictator Francisco Franco (who ruled from 1939 to 1975) established community choruses in even the smallest towns to promote the singing of patriotic songs. Similarly, in Brittany and Galicia, music is playing an important role in attempts to revive the spirits of the indigenous Celtic cultures in these regions. Indeed, Celtic dancing has developed an international reputation. But, however played or for whatever reason, music (like all art) is an individual creative skill that each of us can cultivate and be proud of, whether from a sense of accomplishment or from the sheer pleasure of performing. It is a form of social behaviour that promotes a communication or sharing of feelings and life experience with other humans. Moreover, because individual creativity is constrained by the traditions of the particular group, each culture's art is distinctive and helps define its members' sense of identity.

The social function of music is perhaps most obvious in songs, since these contain verbal text. Songs serve many purposes, entertainment being only one of them. Work songs have served to coordinate heavy, dangerous, or boring labour, such as weighing anchor, felling trees, or shucking oysters. Songs also have been used to soothe babies to sleep, charm animals into giving more milk, keep witchcraft at bay, advertise goods, and much more. Songs also may serve social and political purposes, spreading particular ideas swiftly and effectively by giving them a special form involving poetic language and rhythm and by attaching a pleasing and appropriate tune, be it solemn or light.

In Australia, traditional Aboriginal songs have taken on a legal function, in that they are being introduced into court as evidence of early settlement patterns. This evidence has helped the Aborigines claim more extensive landownership, thus allowing them greater authority to use the land and to negotiate and profit from the sale of natural resources. This had been impossible before. The British, after annexing Australia, had declared the land ownerless (*terra nullius*). The Aborigines had preserved their records of ownership in song and story, but these were not admissible in the British courts. In the early 1970s, the Aborigines exposed the injustice of this and the Australian government began responding in a more favourable (albeit limited) fashion, granting claims of traditional ownership to groups in the Northern Territory. Proof of Aboriginal ownership included recordings of traditional songs indicating traditional settlement and travel patterns and land use.[8]

Music gives a concrete form, made memorable and attractive with melody and rhythm, to basic human ideas. Whether the song's content is didactic, satirical, inspirational, religious, political, or purely emotional, the important thing is that the formless has been given

form and that feelings difficult to express in words alone are communicated in a symbolic and memorable way that can be repeated and shared. The group is thereby united and has the sense that its shared experiences, whatever those may be, have shape and meaning. This, in turn, shapes and gives meaning to the community. This community of listeners may in fact be a smaller segment of the group itself; indeed, the music may be revolutionary music whose aim is to smash society and not bind it together. Even so, music functions as a way of giving voice to a group of people and uniting them.

VISUAL ART

To many Westerners, the first image that springs to mind in connection with the word "art" is some sort of visual art, be it a painting, a drawing, a sculpture, or a totem pole. And indeed, in many parts of the world, people have been expressing their artistic talents in one way or another for a very long time—etching designs in bone or wood, gourds or pots; engraving pictures in rock or painting them on cave walls, textiles, and animal hides; and carving shapes out of stone or wood, antler or bone, or even their own bodies. As with musical art, some form of visual art is a part of every historically known culture.

Much like verbal art and music, visual art can convey political, cultural, and social messages. A good example, albeit sometimes dangerous, is graffiti tagging. Graffiti is a form of artistic expression that has become prominent in urban settings. Urban youth scratch, paint, or spray their "tags" or nicknames on the sides of buildings and vehicles—even entire subway trains. Hip-hop graffiti originated in the subways of New York in the 1960s and 1970s and continues to flourish today in many large cities around the world. Subways provided a perfect milieu for graffiti writing—a way for writers to display their work to the riding public and especially to other graffiti writers. Although graffiti writing originally began with Puerto Rican youths, graffiti artists today come from all socio-economic backgrounds, are usually quite young, and are almost always males.

Earlier in this chapter we asked the question, "What is art?" Many people, especially government and city officials, refuse to recognize graffiti as a form of artistic expression, viewing it as vandalism rather than art. Anthropologists explore why youths write graffiti and what motivates them to continue doing so even in the face of public and government pressure and with the inherent dangers of climbing onto bridges, tall buildings,

Gender Perspectives

On Being a Man

"Real men don't cry." "Real men don't eat quiche." We have all heard these sentiments expressed, but have you ever stopped to wonder why males must "act like a man" or "be a man"? And do men everywhere seek to be "manly"? Is there a culture of manhood? These gender images or ideals for males are as significant as those for females.

Gender images vary from one culture to another, but beneath the superficial differences lie some interesting similarities. Cross-cultural comparisons suggest that regardless of lifestyle, geographical location, or standard of living, males are required to pass a test in order to be accepted as a man. For example, the Truk fishers of the South Pacific risk their lives to maintain a manly image, engaging in dangerous activities such as deep-sea fishing in shark-infested waters to prove their manhood. They are encouraged to think strong, manly thoughts, and their youths engage in brawls, heavy drinking, and sexual conquests, again to prove their manhood. Among East African cultural groups, such as the Maasai, adolescent boys must undergo ritual circumcision without flinching or crying out lest they be branded unworthy of man-

hood and bring shame on their lineage. Even among the peaceful Ju/'hoansi, young boys must earn their manhood by single-handedly tracking and killing an antelope. In the Balkans, a real man is a heavy drinker, spends money freely, fights bravely, and raises a large family, thus proving his sexual prowess.

North America has not escaped this pressured manhood; indeed, popular culture, especially Hollywood films, promotes whisky-swilling, gun-toting cowboys and Rambo-style heroes who would rather die in battle than risk being labelled unmanly. Even such innocuous institutions as the Boy Scouts aim to turn little boys into strong men. These ideals, though presented in technologically complex images, are eerily similar to the Truk, Maasai, and Ju/'hoansi male's quest for manhood.

Some say we socialize our boys to be tough; others suggest that socialization has little to do with it. From a young age, our little boys strive to be manly, play with boys' toys like guns, wrestle, and play rough. In high school, sports jocks rule—how is the young man who would rather play a flute than hockey or football labelled? What happens to the young man who cries in disappointment after losing a basketball game? Indeed, sports have often been

touted as the way to make boys into men; by succeeding at sports a young man can stake his claim to masculinity (Whitson 1990).

Social scientists have put forth countless explanations to explain the seemingly universal imagery of manhood. Feminists and Marxists see the concept of manhood as a mechanism for oppressing females. Biological arguments suggest that males had to develop masculine tendencies, such as aggression and male bonding, in order to survive as hunters. Psychoanalytic theories suggest that males must defend themselves against castration anxieties. Psychological and neo-Freudian theorists focus on a young man's need to create a separate identity from his mother and defend against eternal childhood by performing a great deed. Although each has its limitations, these theories attempt to explain why males risk everything to be manly, and why "real men don't cry."

SOURCES: D. Whitson, "Sport in the Social Construction of Masculinity," in Sport, Men, and the Gender Order: Critical Feminist Perspectives, *ed. M.A. Messner and D.F. Sabo (Champaign: Human Kinetics Books, 1990); also, adapted from D.D. Gilmore, "The Manhood Puzzle," in* Gender in Cross-Cultural Perspective, *ed. C.B. Brettell and C.F. Sargent, 2nd ed. (Upper Saddle River: Prentice Hall, 1997), 185–97.*

and trains. Most studies suggest that graffiti writers seek recognition, even fame. Graffiti was originally a means for members of the hip-hop subculture—usually disenfranchised, impoverished youths living in decaying neighbourhoods—to feel empowered and to visibly and artistically express their resistance to authority. This art form became the voice of disaffected youth from ghettos. In the 1990s graffiti moved beyond the subway systems into venues such as freight trains, rocks, signs, fences, and even legal walls like Phun Phactory and Halls of Fame in New York City. Graffiti has become a legitimate art form, one that is constantly changing but that still fulfills the need for expression. The social significance of graffiti has not escaped the attention of scholars such as Joseph Patton, recipient of a 2007 Watson Fellowship. Patton cross-culturally examines public markings,

including rock art, murals, and graffiti, from a historical and cultural context.[9]

As symbolic expression, visual art may be representational, by imitating nature, or abstract, drawing from natural forms but representing only their basic patterns and arrangements. Actually, the two categories are not mutually exclusive, for even the most naturalistic portrayal is partly abstract in that it generalizes from nature and abstracts patterns of ideal beauty, ugliness, or typical expressions of emotion. But between the most naturalistic and the most schematic or symbolic abstract art lies a continuum. In some of the First Nations artwork on Canada's Northwest Coast, for example, animal figures may be so highly stylized as to be difficult for an outsider to identify. Although the art is abstract,

Burke Museum of Natural History and Culture, University of Washington

This stylized painting on a ceremonial shirt represents a bear. Although the art of the Northwest Coast First Nations often portrays actual animals, they are not depicted in a naturalistic style. To identify them, we must be familiar with the conventions of this art.

the artist has drawn from nature, albeit exaggerating and deliberately transforming some of its shapes to express a particular feeling toward them. Because the artists carry out these exaggerations and transformations according to the canons of Northwest Coast First Nations culture, their meanings are understood not just by the artist but by other community members as well.

Canadian Visual Art

Torn between prehistory and modernity, Aboriginal art is captivating, both in the inventiveness of its forms and the richness of its repertoire. Yet these painters, now celebrated by the world's greatest museums, have remained faithful to their tradition, rituals, and cosmogony vibrant with poetry and invention.[10]

The visual arts have flourished in Canada for millennia. From the first petroglyphs, originating some 7,000 years ago, to the abstract paintings found in modern-day art galleries, Canadian art has provided artists and art lovers with a wide range of artistic expression. Each region, each cultural group, and each artist has brought a distinctive flavour to Canadian art. This diversity is also evident in the vast array of media for visual arts—from watercolours and oil paintings to prairie quilting, from Inuit sculpture to First Nations basket weaving and beading.

Although diversity characterizes contemporary Canadian art, trends over the past century reflect the manner in which Canadian cultures have influenced artistic styles. One of the earliest artists to make a lasting impression on Canadian art was Paul Kane. Fascinated with First Nations peoples, Kane travelled westward across Canada, sketching all he saw. His powerful watercolours and field sketches provide a valuable record of western Canadian life in the mid-1800s. When he returned to Toronto, Kane spent six years creating a series of 100 oil paintings and wrote his pivotal work, *Wanderings of an Artist Among the Indians of North America*, published in 1859.[11]

Early in the 20th century, some of Canada's most influential artists joined together to form the Group of Seven. Lawren Harris, J.E.H. MacDonald, Arthur Lismer, F.H. Varley, Franz Johnston, Franklin Carmichael, and A.Y. Jackson intended to showcase the natural beauty of Canada to all Canadians through their landscape paintings. They were consumed with the belief that art "must grow and flower in the land before the

Dr. William E. Haviland

Quilting is presently enjoying a revival on the Canadian Prairies and in the Maritime provinces. This ancient craft, traced back to Egyptian times, binds people together around the world. Quilts have been used to honour those who have died of AIDS, symbolizing hope for a cure, and to bring warmth and comfort to American soldiers far from home.

country be a real home for its people."[12] The Group of Seven's 1920 exhibition at the Art Gallery of Toronto was an important moment in the history of Canadian art, representing a growing sense of nationalism and the Group's desire to capture the spirit of Canada in their paintings.[13]

The Group of Seven's passion for Canadian scenery influenced other Canadian artists, such as Emily Carr, who spent much of her career painting fishing villages and First Nations totem poles north of Victoria, BC. Carr's paintings document a bygone era; as the Aboriginal world around her disintegrated, her work reflected those changes. Her paintings gained international attention when they were included in Marius Barbeau and Eric Brown's anthropological exhibition, "Canadian West Coast Art, Native and Modern," at the National Gallery in 1927.[14] Following her death in 1945, Carr's work continued to gain an international reputation; today she is considered one of Canada's foremost artists.

In the 1960s, at a time when Western society was experiencing political and social turmoil, the artistic community began questioning the very nature of art. This was a time of experimentation, alternative art forms, and increasing abstraction. By the 1970s, artists recognized that the ideas rooted in art and the process of creating art were more important than the art itself. "Conceptual art often pointed to issues or the power embedded in institutions or society, raising questions and offering multiple layers of meaning rather than presenting singular, fully developed points of view."[15] Today, we continue to witness diversity in art—sculpture, painting, video, and photography—each reflecting the multiplicity of media and artists in Canada.

By the middle of the 20th century, art connoisseurs recognized the vitality of Canadian Aboriginal art forms. In particular, Inuit sculpture captured the imagination of museums and art collectors the world over. Inuit art can be traced back at least 4,000 years. The first significant artifacts come from the Dorset culture (600 BC–AD 1000).[16] These people carved land and sea animals, human figures, masks, and face clusters out of bone, ivory, and wood. The Thule, believed to be the ancestors of today's Inuit, succeeded the Dorset peoples. Their art also included human and animal figures, but most of the artwork from this time featured graphic designs on objects such as combs, needle cases, harpoon toggles, and gaming pieces.[17]

Contemporary Inuit art, although still influenced by the past, is constantly evolving. In fact, the soapstone carvings so popular with contemporary art collectors around the world are a relatively recent innovation. Besides affording a sense of cultural identity and pride, Inuit artwork has become a major source of revenue for Inuit peoples, and in the process artists have earned international recognition and acclaim. Inuit artists use a variety of local materials: weathered and fossilized whalebone, walrus ivory, and caribou antler, as well as the famous soapstone. As with other Canadian art forms, Inuit art is also highly variable; each community produces its own distinctive style, although traditional themes of Arctic wildlife, Inuit hunting and family scenes, spirits, mythology, and shamanistic images remain most popular.

BODY ART

Humans are willing to endure pain and discomfort, waste precious time and resources, and risk chastisement from more conservative sectors of society in an attempt to enhance their physical appearance—to become more attractive, distinctive, or acceptable to other members of a group.[18]

Body art can take many forms—from something as innocuous as rubbing red ochre into the hair or wearing makeup and jewellery, to the serious business of cutting

Emily Carr's vibrant paintings brought the culture of the Northwest Coastal peoples alive.

Alan Marsh/Firstlight

Body art, such as the piercing and tattooing shown here, is a way for people to symbolically express their individuality, as well as their values, beliefs, and world view.

intricate patterns into the skin or piercing and tattooing various body parts. Yet this search for personal identity also creates a sense of community or group membership with like-minded people who participate in similar body modification. Body art is not a frivolous endeavour; patterns and designs created by painting, styling, tattooing, or piercing serve as a symbolic language, a way of expressing values, beliefs, and world views.

Because the norms of any given culture vary, forms of body modification also vary. Body art in traditional cultures tends to remain constant and unchanging for generations, but in the West, fashions and styles can change from one season to the next. Westerners also have a choice of which styles and practices they will adopt, and whether they will adhere to any of the so-called norms, whereas in traditional cultures, adopting the artistic norms of the culture may not be voluntary. Thus, human appearance is a cultural construct as well as a biological creation.

Body Painting

Many cultures create colourful, imaginative human bodies through body painting and makeup. The Romans referred to the ancient inhabitants of Scotland as *picti*, or the Picts, because of their practice of body tattooing and painting. In contemporary New Guinea, women paint their faces red, blue, and white, and the Tchikrin people of Brazil paint their limbs red and their torsos black. In the Sudan, Nuba men paint their bodies white on one side and black on the other, and the women paint their bodies either red or yellow. Although body paint is more common in traditional cultures, it is also found in the West. In North America, Japan, and Europe, punks display vividly multi-coloured bodies, while Goths paint themselves white, with huge, black, skull-like eyes and jet-black lips.

This body art plays far more than an aesthetic role; it also communicates ancient mythology, represents group values and religious beliefs, and sets each group apart as visually distinct. This is certainly true of Goths, who feel alienated from mainstream society and who express this separateness with their body art. Body painting also can mark the celebration of important events in a person's life. Among Nuba males, colours represent different age grades; only members of older age grades can wear deep yellow or jet black. The importance of body painting can differ based on gender. Nuba men spend hours applying makeup and creating intricate patterns, while the women simply apply the colour that represents their kinship group. This tradition exemplifies the tendency for males throughout the animal world to be more elaborately decorated than females—the so-called peacock syndrome. Conversely, women in the West are more decorative but use makeup for cosmetic rather than artistic purposes. However, there are examples of Western men decorating their bodies, such as the hippies of the 1970s, who applied psychedelic and flowery designs. An interesting trend is currently emerging among sports fans that can be likened to traditional body painting; football fans, for example, adorn their faces with brightly coloured designs to identify with their team. To summarize, people paint their bodies for many reasons—to enhance their appearance, to protest, to exhibit rank, to demonstrate personal or group identity, and to celebrate religious and other rituals.

Tattooing

Tattoos are created by injecting a pigment beneath the skin. Unlike body paint, which washes off, tattoos are a permanent and usually irreversible art form. Defining the role of tattooing can be difficult. Is tattooing a symbol of status or rebellion, a traditional marker, or a contemporary artistic expression? Is it a sign of individuality or of group identity? In fact, tattoo art is all of these and much more. In traditional cultures, tattoos often mark significant stages or rites of passage in a person's life, such as passing through puberty and into adulthood. A young Nuba girl may receive her first tattoo when her breasts grow.

As an art form, tattooing has flourished in many variations around the world. One of the most intricate forms is found among the New Zealand Maori, whose *moko*, facial swirls, are chiselled into the face as a sign of cultural pride. Tattoos traditionally afforded Maori men and women special privileges and rank. In Canada, Aboriginal groups such as the Cree and the Inuit also produced distinctive styles of tattooing to express links with spirit guardians. The Inuit used a sooty thread sewn through the skin with a needle to create permanent markings, while other early groups likely used bone or antler splinters dipped in berry juice.

The origins of tattooing remain unclear, although the fact that tattooing is so widely distributed suggests that the custom is ancient. The body of "Otzi the Iceman," the 5,000-year-old hunter discovered in an Alpine glacier, had 15 tattoos, including parallel stripes around the left wrist. Researchers at the University of Graz, in Austria, have speculated that instead of the tattoos being ornamental, they may in fact have been medicinal.[19] The plain styles used for Otzi's tattoos, and the fact that they were placed on what are now considered acupuncture points, gives them reason to think that he may have been given them as treatment for joint pains or some other ailment.

Two female Egyptian mummies dated to 4,000 years ago had dots and dashes tattooed on their bodies. Ancient Incas, Mayas, and Aztecs also had sophisticated tattooing styles, as did the Iberians, Gauls, Goths, Teutons, Picts, Scots, and Britons. Many consider Japanese tattooing of the Edo Period (1600–1868) to be the epitome of tattoo art. Most European groups, except for the Greeks and Romans, used tattooing to customize their bodies. Even early Christians and Crusaders were tattooed. However, this changed when Constantine declared Christianity the official religion of the Roman Empire and banned tattooing in 325, essentially shutting down the practice until British explorers reintroduced tattooing to the West from Polynesia in the 18th century. British sailors under the command of Captain James Cook were introduced to what local Polynesians called *ta-tau*, meaning "to mark or tap," and thus the word "tattoo" entered the English language. Later, tattooing became a symbol of working-class men in North America. By the mid-20th century,

bikers, convicts, and other marginalized groups had taken up the art.

Body Adornment

Adorning our bodies with flowers, shells, feathers, or metals is an ancient custom found in most cultural groups around the world. Such adornment may serve to make individuals, both male and female, more attractive; it may be seen as magical (e.g., a talisman) or of religious significance; it may symbolize wealth (e.g., a diamond necklace, a Kula shell necklace) and status (e.g., a wedding ring, a chief's feather headdress); or it may assert identity, such as scarification of the face that reveals clan membership.

One form of adornment is body piercing—that is, puncturing the skin with holes for decorative reasons. The most universal site for piercing is the earlobe, closely followed by the nose and lips. Once pierced, the holes are adorned with all manner of artwork. The Maasai stretched their pierced ears, inserting increasingly larger plugs and heavier jewellery. Leaders of the Amazon

Amazon Brazil Chief Raoni of the Megranoti Kayapo Nation with botoque lip plate and feather cocar headdress.

Kayapo stretched their bottom lip out by inserting plates the size of saucers; these are known as labrets, or lip plugs. These lip plugs symbolized status and manhood; among the Kayapo the labret embodied the value placed on oratory skills, just as nose piercing among some New Guinea groups denoted the importance of smell. The Inuit also had stretched labret piercings, both above and below their lips. During a blood-letting ritual, the Maya royals pierced their tongues with a stingray thorn to appease the gods and ancestors.[20]

Anthropologists have documented the historical pedigree of body piercing around the world, but it has now become the fastest-growing type of body decoration in the West. Westerners have adopted many expressions of this art; multiple ear piercings (a way for the less adventurous to express their unique identity), and nostril, septum, lip, eyebrow, navel, nipple, and genital piercings have all become common. Although some no doubt view these extreme piercings as barbaric, in fact they are a way for individuals to take control of their own bodies.

Painting, tattooing, and piercing are by no means the limit of our attempts to modify our bodies. Hair and nails are also expressions of beauty, power, and identity. Humans cut, braid, knot, dye, backcomb, and adorn their hair with all manner of decorative pieces, including ribbons, shells, flowers, and bones. Hairstyling is an ancient custom, one that is a universal practice in contemporary groups and that can be quite intricate. For example, Maasai warriors smear their long hair with red ochre, fat, and clay, then twist it into 400 or so strands, which are then grouped as three braids and bound around long, pliant sticks.

This design signals group identity and marks individual status in the group. Western examples include skinheads, who shave their heads; punks, who wear "Mohawks"; and rappers, who sport razor designs. Hairstyles often communicate class; for example, the silver wigs that aristocrats wore in 17th-century England were a sign of power and status.

Body art is an ancient, dynamic custom that has served to beautify, customize, and display rank, status, ethnicity, group membership, and much more. In anthropology, body art is seen as a universal feature of traditional cultures and as an informative indicator of age, status, family position, and group affiliation.

From the masked dancers of the Iroquois, to the face painting of the Amazonians, to the lead guitar sounds of U2, art—that skillful creation of the human mind—has astounded and entertained us. The black and red bulls on the cave walls of Lascaux and the intricate patterns of artists such as Simon Brascoupé and Bill Reid have also taught us much about the culture within which the art is created. In their quest to discover and document culture, anthropologists have studied much of the world's corpus of art, both ancient and modern. They seek to understand not just the social conditions of the production of art, but the underlying structure, that is, the rules that govern the production and consumption of art. Art provides us with a window into the human mind; it gives us an intimate vision of the creative processes that go into the manufacture of artistic objects. We learn from art the fears, hopes, observations and joys of the artists and the cultures they hail from. For these reasons, anthropologists are, and will likely always be, drawn to art.

Chapter Summary

1.   What is art?

Art is the human practice of interpreting and depicting the world. This includes the human imagination, the human past and present, and how the artist envisions these worlds. Art stems from the uniquely human ability to use symbols to give shape and significance to the physical world for more than just a utilitarian purpose.

2.   Why do anthropologists study art?

Art, in all its diverse forms, reveals much about the individual and the culture that produces it. Anthropologists study art for a variety of reasons, chief among these for the information that art provides about the society within which it is produced. What is considered art, what is not, and which media are considered appropriate all reveal fundamental concerns about the culture at hand. The history of art and the types

of information carried through art, whether in song, in folk tales, or on canvas, all demonstrate the central role of creativity in society.

3.   What are the functions of the arts?

The arts serve a number of functions that range from entertainment to honouring the gods, from depicting knowledge of the environment to documenting modern life on film. In their diverse formats, the arts therefore have both aesthetic and functional aspects. For example, art such as myths and legends, beyond entertaining, can set standards for "proper" behaviour; verbal arts transmit a culture's customs, as do music and song. The visual arts both interpret history and preserve traditional crafts. Artifacts such as the Two Row Wampum serve as mnemonic devices for preserving traditions. For many indigenous groups, artwork has significant economic value. Finally, art and artists express and promote cultural identity—for example, in the form of body art.

Questions for Critical Thought

1. In this chapter the Navajo tradition of sand painting is used to illustrate how sometimes the "art" is the process of creation rather than what is produced. What other traditions stress the act over the product? Why would Western people think more in terms of the resulting object than the act of creation? What does this tell observers about Western values?

2. Why is art perceived as elitist and nonproductive in Western society? Is this a valid viewpoint? How does it differ from other cultures' opinions, and how might Western culture itself belie such a statement?

3. How does art participate in politics? Why are various art forms (music, visual and graphic arts, literature, etc.) so important to nationalist or ethnic groups existing under the influence of foreign dominant cultures?

4. How does music reflect a culture's beliefs, norms, and values? How does music evoke emotions from listeners?

5. Is censorship a necessary part of the arts? If yes, who should decide on censorship rules?

6. Should public monies be directed toward the arts in Canada? Why or why not? Is there a department of fine arts at your college or university? Does the institution have a policy on what students can exhibit?

7. Interview someone you know who has numerous body piercings or tattoos, who wears unique clothing, or who has an original hairstyle. Determine this person's reasons for choosing a particular form of body art, certain designs, particular body parts, and so on.

Internet Resources

Museums

http://www.quaibranly.fr/index.php?id=accueil&L=1

Official site of the Quai Branly Museum, in French, English, and Spanish. The museum specializes in ethnographic displays.

http://www.uwo.ca/museum

The site for the Museum of Ontario Archaeology, which focuses on the human occupation of southwestern Ontario over the past 11,000 years.

http://www.jorvik-viking-centre.co.uk

This interactive museum in York, England, focuses on the Vikings. The museum itself is built on top of a 1,000-year-old Viking village known as Jorvik.

Paul Kane's Great Nor-West

http://www.umanitoba.ca/cm/vol2/no26/kane.html

A comprehensive examination of Paul Kane's life and work, displaying some of his paintings.

The Group of Seven and Their Contemporaries

http://www.mcmichael.com/collection/seven/index.cfm

This site includes brief biographies of the Group of Seven artists and samples of their work.

Inuit Art

http://www.pem.org/ourland

A comprehensive site discussing Inuit art and its history. The site includes photographs of Inuit art.

Native Art

http://www.nativeamericanmuseumart.com/NAMA/newnama/index.html

A Tuscarora Iroquois art museum, the Native American Art Museum is dedicated to strengthening, preserving, and revitalizing Native American arts, languages, and cultures. The museum is part of an effort to rebuild the economy through tourism and education.

Music and Anthropology

http://www.umbc.edu/MA/index/ma_ind.htm

The *Journal of Musical Anthropology of the Mediterranean* presents several journal articles reflecting on music and culture.

Throat Singing

http://www.mustrad.org.uk/articles/inuit.htm

A study of throat singing among the Inuit, including an interview with a professional throat singer.

Urban Expression

http://www.graffiti.org

A comprehensive examination of graffiti. Provides a good historical overview.

Suggested Readings

For a list of suggested readings, visit the textbook's website at **http://www.havilandcultural4e.nelson.com**.

Notes

1. M. Medusa, "Shawna Dempsey and Lorri Milan," 1994, http://www.oboro.net/index_2_e.html, accessed July 4, 2001.

2. For a detailed discussion, see H. Morphy, "Art as a Mode of Action: Some Problems with Gell's *Art and Agency*," *Journal of Material Culture* 14, no. 1 (2009): 5–27; H. Morphy and M. Perkins, *The Anthropology of Art: A Reader* (Oxford: Blackwell, 2006); and A. Gell, *Art and Agency* (Oxford: Clarendon Press, 1998).

3. W.A. Haviland and M.W. Power, *The Original Vermonters: Native Inhabitants, Past and Present*, rev. and exp. ed. (Hanover: University Press of New England, 1994), 193.

4. P.R. Sanday, *Female Power and Male Dominance: On the Origins of Sexual Inequality* (Cambridge: Cambridge University Press, 1981), 181.

5. M. Stoler, "To Tell the Truth," *Vermont Visions* 82, no. 3 (1982):, 3.

6. J.K. Rowling, *Harry Potter and the Philosopher's Stone* (London: Bloomsbury Press, 1997).

7. S. Firth, "The Cultural Study of Popular Music," in *Cultural Studies,* ed. L. Grossberg, C. Nelson, and P. Treichler (New York: Routledge, 1992), 74–86.

8. G. Koch, "Songs, Land Rights, and Archives in Australia," *Cultural Survival Quarterly* 20, no. 4 (1997).

9. S. Nelson, "College Nominates Four for Watson Fellowship," *The Mac Weekly,* http://www.themacweekly.com/college-nominates-four-for-watson-fellowship-1.2532129, 2006, accessed December 1, 2006.

10. B. Geoffroy-Schneiter, *Primal Arts* (New York: Assouline, 2006), 371.

11. "Who Was Paul Kane? 2001, "Our Heritage," http://ourheritage.net/who/kanewho.html, accessed April 4, 2001.

12. *Canadian Art at the McMichael (1996–2000),* "The Group of Seven and Their Contemporaries," http://www.mcmichael.com/collection/seven/index.cfm, accessed March 29, 2001.

13. Ibid.

14. Department of Fine Arts, Okanagan University College (1999), "Important Moments in the History of Canadian Visual Culture: R.J. Belton," http://www.ouc.bc.ca/fiar/1918_45.html, accessed March 13, 2001.

15. *Modern and Contemporary Art at the McMichael. (1996–2001).* Retrieved March 27, 2001, from http://www.mcmichael.com/modern.htm.

16. Museum of Inuit Art, "Inuit Art Background," 2001, http://www.harrisinuitgallery.com/artinfo.htm, accessed April 3, 2001.

17. Ibid.

18. The following discussion is predominantly taken from T. Polhemus and H. Randall, *The Customized Body* (London and New York: Serpent's Tail, 2000).

19. L. Dorfer, M. Moser, F. Bahr, K. Spindler, E. Egarter-Vigl, S. Giullén, G. Dohr, and T. Kenner, "A Medical Report from the Stone Age?" *The Lancet,* September 18, 1999.

20 American Museum of Natural History, "Body Art: Marks of Identity," n.d., http://www.amnh.org/exhibitions/bodyart, accessed October 7, 2011.

14 Anthropology at Work

Applied anthropologists work all over the world in many different fields. Here, Simbu dancers of Papua New Guinea are painted as skeletons.

KEY QUESTIONS

1. What Is Applied Anthropology?

The areas in which the applied anthropologist is "put to work" are wildly diverse. Anthropologists work in human resources departments for corporations; they are employed in marketing, the military, the government, and in health and education.

2. How Did Applied Anthropology Develop?

Applied anthropology developed from a variety of sources in the United Kingdom, Canada, and the United States. Central to this emergence was the need for anthropologists to work outside academe and to apply their skills to private and government issues such as land claims and the needs of the corporate world. The Second World War was a major impetus to the establishment of applied anthropology.

3. What Are Some of the Challenges Facing the Applied Anthropologist?

Many of the challenges facing applied anthropologists relate to the differences between applying research in the academic and the nonacademic worlds. Applied anthropologists also face the issue of bias. Yet another issue is the peril of having their work co-opted by government agencies or private firms. Other challenges relate to the question of who, ultimately, controls the data they produce, and what use might be made of it.

4. What Does the Future Hold for Applied Anthropology?

The future of applied anthropology is quite bright in terms of employment prospects, with more and more graduates in anthropology finding employment outside the academic realm. However, the use to which anthropological data are put causes some anthropologists to voice concerns, specifically in terms of the growth of applied anthropology in the military arena.

WHAT IS APPLIED ANTHROPOLOGY?

The question "What is applied anthropology?" is a complex one. One approach is to view it as consulting work undertaken by anthropologists relating to practical problems. An applied anthropologist uses a holistic knowledge of culture, behaviour, social relations, and social structures to address practical concerns. An applied anthropologist, then, is someone employed by an agency or company to generate data that are relevant to solving some practical issue. Essentially, an applied anthropologist applies the skills, training, and knowledge of anthropology to venues outside the academic setting. This covers a wide area, such as nongovernmental organizations (NGOs), international bodies, museums, band councils, and a variety of research institutes, some of which we will discuss below.

Many applied anthropologists are also academic anthropologists; that is, they sometimes work as applied anthropologists while remaining academics. Being an applied anthropologist does not therefore rule out an academic career. Indeed, experience in applied anthropology can be quite beneficial to a later academic or research career.

The diverse realms of applied and academic anthropology are always tethered to the anthropological perspective; it could not be otherwise. But as practices, applied and academic anthropology are quite distinct from each other, in terms of both practice and expectations. For example, applied anthropology entails more interdisciplinary work. Also, different expectations arise when it comes to publishing findings: Within academe the anthropologist usually publishes under his or her own name; on the applied side, by contrast, publications typically appear under the company or employer name. Also, most applied anthropology is not aimed at an academic audience and is published in internal reports rather than, say, as journal articles. Another important difference between academic and applied anthropology relates to how the data gleaned from the anthropological perspective are put to use—which can be problematical (see below).

This chapter aims to provide a solid understanding of what applied anthropology is and where it is practised and to highlight some of the challenges and successes associated with it. We will begin with a history of the field. We will then examine some of its various branches, such as health, business, and the military.

applied anthropology Consulting work undertaken by anthropologists relating to practical problems.

THE HISTORY OF APPLIED ANTHROPOLOGY

I think that in the very combination of practical and theoretical interests lies the proper task of the Institute. There is a gap between the theoretical concerns of the anthropology of the schools on the one hand, and practical interests on the other. This gap must be bridged over, and in doing this the Institute can make itself very useful.[1]

Not until Bronislaw Malinowski published *Practical Anthropology* in 1929 did a clearly defined applied anthropology began to emerge. This is not to suggest that he invented it. The term "practical anthropology" had been coined much earlier, in the 1860s, by James Hunt, the founder of the Anthropological Society of London. In fact, anthropological data had been used throughout the 19th century in a variety of contexts. For example, the Canadian and American governments employed physical anthropologists to classify immigrant populations based on their skull and facial characteristics. Also, linguistic anthropologists had a long albeit stormy history of employment during treaty negotiations in both Canada and the United States. For this reason, many Aboriginal peoples continue to look askance at anthropologists, viewing them mainly as ethnographers with forms to fill out, or as linguists with charts and graphs to document their communities. Much of the present-day distrust stems from the roles that early anthropologists played in treaty making, which invariably resulted in the loss of land and culture for many Aboriginal peoples. Anthropologists are still trying to move beyond this legacy; many people, especially indigenous people, remain wary of them.

In the middle of the 19th century, the Ethnological Society was founded in London, England, as were similar organizations. This marked the beginnings of applied anthropology. Initially, applied anthropologists were attached to the foreign offices and the military units of various countries. These early anthropologists set out to study and document the life ways of "exotic" cultures. However, anthropology did not fare well during colonial times, for its practitioners had competing goals. On the one hand, they wanted to apply their skills to gathering information about the peoples and places they were encountering; on the other, the colonial authorities were more interested in statistics pertaining to military and government projects. This created problems that would reverberate down through the years, for anthropologists became associated with foreign domination, despite their lofty goal of helping "emancipate" humanity.

In the early 19th century the U.S. Congress asked Henry Schoolcraft to compile a report on the status of

American Indians. The resulting report,[2] which detailed conditions on American Indian reservations, was among the first North American projects of applied anthropology. However, in his capacity as Indian agent, Schoolcraft also negotiated the Treaty of Washington (1836). That treaty deprived the Ottawa and Chippewa peoples of enormous tracts of land—some 55,997 square kilometres—and for that, Schoolcraft was partly responsible. In his defence, he was genuinely concerned (though paternalistic) about the well-being of the Native people who were being affected—indeed, for the welfare of *all* Native American Indians. Even so, he was a product of the times, in that he supported government schools and mission schools, believing that they were necessary in order to educate and "Christianize" Native Americans. He also urged that the Native people be taught agriculture to compensate for the loss of their hunting grounds and he took a firm stand against the distribution of alcohol among American Indians.

Another notable applied anthropologist was Philleo Nash, an American who began his academic career as a prehistoric archaeologist at the University of Toronto. But he is mainly remembered as "an anthropologist in the White House," to which he served as an adviser on race relations as well as on military affairs. For many years he was also commissioner of the U.S. Bureau of Indian Affairs.

Despite these early developments, the promise of an applied anthropology soon faltered. This was partly because administrators and governments wanted immediate data on Aboriginal peoples that included clear judgments on, for example, the suitability of certain Aboriginal populations for farming, conversion, and "civilizing." Simply put, the goals and approaches of anthropologists were at odds with the needs and goals of government agencies.

Then, during the Great Depression of the 1930s, a distinct field of applied anthropology began to emerge. Much of its work involved social analyses of poverty

The renowned anthropologist Bronislaw Malinowski was among the first to recognize the need for an applied anthropology separate from academic anthropology.

and government aid policies. As a further important development, the Society for Applied Anthropology was founded in 1941. Its first president was Eliot Chapple, and among its founding members were luminaries such as Margaret Mead and Fred Richardson. The SfAA was a professional organization devoted to addressing a host of issues outside of the academic domain, including social and political ones. At that time, anthropology as a discipline was just over a century old, but during that century it had compiled a vast store of ethnographic and other cultural knowledge relating to kinship systems, social structures, and so on. It had forged an impressive and sophisticated set of theories and concepts for describing, explaining, and interpreting human cultures. This knowledge, which coalesced with the founding of the SfAA, would be put to use on the battlefields of Europe and Asia during the Second World War.

Second World War

The Second World War was a sad opening for applied anthropology. Just as with many other fields (technology, for example), the needs of the war spurred developments in both practice and theory. In 1942, as the war entered its third year, the *Journal of Applied Anthropology* was launched (renamed *Human Organization* in 1949). Among the early contributors were Margaret Mead, Ruth Benedict, Clyde Kluckhohn, and Gregory Bateson—people who would set the agenda for much of American anthropology over the following decades.

In Britain, too, anthropologists were heavily involved in the war effort, and in much the same way as in North America (see below). Between the 1930s and the 1960s, British anthropologists wrote a great deal about the social problems and challenges facing the various peoples who were under British colonial rule. The North American and European organizations devoted to applied anthropology shared a similar broad goal: to construct a platform for applying anthropological skills to social arenas such as employment, immigration, indigenous peoples, land claims, and so forth. However, the war effort soaked up much of the energy and time of early applied anthropology.

When the Second World War began—in 1939 for Canada and most of Europe, in 1941 for the United States—anthropologists were actively sought by government departments and especially by the military. They were expected to do their civic duty as loyal citizens and their professional duty as anthropologists. Applied anthropologists contributed to the war effort in a number of ways. Many worked as translators of Japanese, German, and a host of other languages. Many others worked as "cultural translators," providing information, insights, and analyses as well as predictions of the enemy's behaviour. They helped familiarize their country's forces with the social and cultural practices of other peoples, whether enemy or allied. It was hoped that by explaining the cultural bases of certain practices, anthropologists might help mitigate misunderstandings and contextualize "exotic" practices and beliefs.

Anthropologists also worked on the home front throughout the war, helping gauge the mood of the population and working to predict shortages and needs that might arise from the massive reorganization of the labour force. Internationally, anthropologists applied their learning to help ease the many issues arising from, for example, the stationing of millions of North American soldiers in European countries. Essentially, anthropologists like Margret Mead and Clyde Kluckhohn were providing an understanding of culturally grounded behavioural patterns. Anthropologists with specific skills were matched to specific military needs. For example, experts on Russia liaised with intelligence personnel dealing with Russia, while anthropologists with knowledge of Japanese customs worked with the U.S. forces when they were sent to the Pacific arena. The book *The Chrysanthemum and the Sword* is an example of the type of literature that anthropologists produced during this period.[3] Ruth Benedict, the author, undertook ethnological research of the Japanese and German cultures in order to provide cultural information to the American government and army, for both military and diplomatic purposes.

After the war, applied anthropologists continued to work for the Allies as they established new modes of governance in the defeated nations. The collapse of Imperial Japan and Nazi Germany, and the large-scale movement of peoples during and after the war, led to the founding of, literally, new nations. In many ways the war was a crucible for applied anthropology, one in which these experts excelled, thereby proving not only that anthropology had a practical side but also that anthropological knowledge of the world and its cultures was essential. The Second World War had provided applied anthropologists with a window of opportunity to demonstrate their particular skills in a large number of areas.

After the war, most anthropologists returned to their academic pursuits. Some had become disillusioned with the use that had been made of their training on the killing fields of Europe and the Pacific. In their view, the "science of humanity" had been recruited to the cause of killing, and the mere presence of anthropologists in a war sat uneasily with them. This unease was exemplified, perhaps, by Project Camelot, a controversial social science project designed to study national conflicts and social breakdowns, using Chile as an example. Concern

from both government and anthropologists that this project was too close to military goals and covert operations led to its cancellation by Congress in 1965.[4]

Over the next few decades, applied anthropologists were still engaged with practical issues, such as the conditions on American Indian reservations and Canadian Indian reserves. As Western nations and companies extended their political and economic reach after the war, anthropologists were called on occasionally to provide pertinent information in many areas, such as ethnic relations and social housing. Generally, though, anthropologists returned to their quiet academic pursuits in the 1950s and 1960s. Today, applied anthropology is a vast field, one that draws from both professional applied anthropologists and academic ones. Organizations abound, especially in North America and Europe. In the United States there are a multitude of large umbrella organizations, including the Consortium of Practical and Applied Anthropology (COPPA), which links American departments of anthropology with applied components and acts as a repository of journals, news, and information on applied anthropology.

Applied Anthropology in Canada

Applied anthropology was practised in Canada in the late 19th century. The work of George Mercer Dawson of the Geological Survey of Canada serves as an example. While not strictly what we might term applied anthropology today, the ethnographic work of Dawson and others certainly drew from their anthropological training. They were employed as part of the major survey of Canada's West Coast, and they made recommendations to the federal government relating to the conditions and treatment of several First Nation peoples, including the Haida and the Kwakwaka'wakw.

The staff of the Geological Survey of Canada, 1888.

In the early 20th century, famed ethnographer Diamond Jenness worked with Inuit peoples in the North and, controversially, was involved in discussions about relocating several Inuit bands. In his later years, Jenness opposed the relocation of Inuit bands, calling the practice a "form of apartheid."[5] Jenness was responsible for some of the earliest ethnographic research among the Inuit. He also provided the earliest known sound recordings of any Inuit group, whose voices, songs, stories, and mythologies were all captured by this intrepid anthropologist.

In Canada, applied anthropology was not as affected by the war as it was other places. Not until after the war was practical anthropology carried out on any great scale. The Hawthorne-Tremblay Report is the best example of anthropology being applied to social issues during the postwar years. This report, commissioned by the **Department of Indian Affairs**, beginning in 1948 employed around 50 researchers, most of whom were anthropologists.[6] The goal of this report was to compile a databank of information on Canada's Aboriginal population, for the purposes of a policy review relating to the Indian Act. The Hawthorne-Tremblay Report made more than 150 recommendations, many of which were never acted on; even so, it had a strong influence, for it showed that large, cooperative teams employed to compile practical anthropological data could succeed. Also, the report, although later governments left it to languish, did raise public awareness of the successes of Aboriginal peoples with regard to their survival in harsh environments and their technological mastery. The same report highlighted some of the awful conditions and intrusive legislation that bedeviled many communities.

Applied anthropologists in Canada, like their counterparts in the United States, put their cultural training to work for various government bodies, for which they addressed issues such as immigration and Aboriginal peoples. But despite large projects such as the Hawthorne-Tremblay Report, applied anthropology in Canada was limited in both scope and employment opportunities until the late 1960s. In fact, anthropology itself was just beginning to gather steam in Canada as an important social science. In 1960 there were only two Canadian departments of anthropology; by 1969 there were more than 20, with 13 augmented departments, most of which were attached to sociology.

Beginning in the 1970s, Canadian applied anthropologists engaged in research involving Aboriginal peoples, and such projects accounted for most applied research.[7] Another main area of employment was immigration studies, given that each year throughout that decade more than 200,000 new immigrants entered Canada. In this regard, anthropologists studied and compiled reports on resettlement, multiculturalism, ethnic relations, and a host of other areas. Alongside work on Aboriginal issues and immigration, applied anthropologists involved themselves more and more in the corporate world—for example, in marketing, advertising, human relations, and various other areas that together are often referred to as the "anthropology of business." A crucial part of business anthropology sets out to provide employers with information on consumer behaviour.

Applied anthropology in Canada is today a prominent field. In 1992 the Society for Applied Anthropology in Canada established the Weaver-Tremblay Award, which is presented to the anthropologist who best reflects the ideal of social and political engagement in anthropology.[8] In the following sections we discuss some of the domains of applied anthropological research.

DOMAINS OF APPLIED ANTHROPOLOGY

Applied anthropologists today work in a wide variety of settings ranging from the identification of human remains using forensic anthropological skills, to the design of ergonomic chairs for students, to analyses of market trends for large corporations. Applied anthropology has a fascinating history within the broader discipline of anthropology, ranging from the battlefields of the Second World War to the advocacy of human rights in today's conflict zones. By examining the world of applied anthropology, we can learn about the practical aspects of anthropological expertise and how anthropologists have an impact in many different areas.

As we have seen throughout this text, anthropology is an eclectic field of diverse research interests united by the "anthropological perspective." That perspective incorporates a holistic approach to cultural phenomena, one in which all aspects of society, and all components of individual and group life, are examined through the anthropological lens. Because of this diversity and anthropology's staggered origins in fields such as botany, natural history, ethnography, and geology, anthropology lends itself strongly to practical applications. Next we discuss only some of the domains of applied anthropology.

Department of Indian Affairs A department of the Government of Canada with responsibility for policies relating to Aboriginal peoples in Canada.

TABLE 14.1	APPLIED ANTHROPOLOGY FIELDS AND ASSOCIATED ANTHROPOLOGICAL STUDY AREAS
Domain	**Possible Anthropology Study Focus**
Housing	Architecture, health
Health/disability studies	Medical/physical anthropology
Corporate	Anthropology of business, economic anthropology
Indigenous issues	Cultural anthropology, archaeology, Aboriginal studies
Cultural resource management	Archaeology
Military	Linguistic/medical/cultural anthropology
Ethnography	Cultural anthropology, ethnographic studies
Museum	Cultural anthropology, archaeology
Environmental/ecological	Physical/ecological/palynology, etc.
Environmental impact assessment	Cultural ecology, environmental anthropology
Social impact studies	Environmental/biological/ecological anthropology
The 'mega' project	Variety of anthropology skills

AP Photo/Hidajet Delic

Srebrenica Massacre site.

Forensic Anthropology: Grave Evidence

Forensic anthropology applied to human rights cases raises different kinds of questions in relation to how anthropologists might engage social and political worlds and what kind of "products" might emerge from this engagement. The goals of our work, and the methods, techniques, and engagements used to achieve them, are often quite different from the concerns of anthropologists based in academic institutions.[9]

forensic anthropology The examination of human skeletal remains. Part of physical anthropology, this field often works with law enforcement agencies to determine the identity of unidentified bones.

forensic archaeologist An archaeologist who controls a site, recording the position of all relevant finds and recovering any clues associated with the remains.

The skulls were slowly uncovered, the dust and soil of recent years brushed off carefully. Other human bones emerged as the forensic anthropologist worked diligently, focused on his craft and on the hard task ahead. As the excavation continued, the members of the forensic team were surrounded by the media, mourning families, and security forces. Forensic anthropologists had done this type of work before, in Rwanda, Kosovo, Guatemala, and even British Columbia.

Their archaeological and forensic expertise takes applied anthropologists to many disaster sites around the world. They use their skills to find, excavate, clean, and classify ancient hominids or—in the applied area—victims of mass murder, plane crashes, genocide, and natural disasters.

Forensic anthropology is the analysis of skeletal remains for legal purposes. Law enforcement authorities call on forensic anthropologists to identify human remains and to determine, if possible, the cause of death. Forensic anthropologists specializing in skeletal remains commonly work closely with **forensic archaeologists**. The relationship between the two is rather like the one between a forensic pathologist, who examines a corpse to establish time and manner of death, and a crime scene investigator, who searches the site for clues. The forensic anthropologist deals with human remains—often only bones and teeth; the forensic archaeologist controls the site, recording the position of all relevant finds and recovering any clues associated with the remains. From skeletal remains, the forensic anthropologist can determine the age, sex, race, and stature of the deceased, as well as physical abnormalities or trauma (e.g., broken bones). Even some details of an individual's health and nutritional history can be determined from the bones. Thus several kinds of anthropologists analyze human remains for a variety of purposes, contributing to the documentation and correction of violence committed by humans past and present.

One of the best-known forensic anthropologists in North America is Clyde C. Snow. He has been practising in this field for more than 40 years—first for the U.S. Federal Aviation Administration and more recently as a freelance consultant. Besides the usual police work, Snow has studied the remains of General George Armstrong Custer and his men from the 1876 battle at Little Big Horn. In 1985 he went to Brazil, where he identified the remains of the notorious Nazi war criminal Josef Mengele.

Dr. Snow was instrumental in establishing the first forensic team devoted to documenting cases of human rights abuses around the world. This began in 1984 when he went to Argentina at the request of a newly elected civilian government to help identify the remains of *desaparecidos*, or "disappeared ones"—the 9,000 or more people who were eliminated by death squads during seven years of military rule. A year later, he returned to give expert testimony at the trial of nine junta members and to teach Argentineans how to recover, clean, repair, preserve, photograph, X-ray, and analyze bones. Besides providing factual accounts of the fate of victims to their surviving kin and refuting the assertions of revisionists that the massacres never happened, Snow and his Argentinean associates provided crucial evidence to convict several military officers of kidnapping, torture, and murder. Since Snow's pioneering work, forensic anthropologists have become increasingly involved in investigations of human rights abuses in all parts of the world, from Chile to Guatemala, Haiti, the Philippines, Rwanda, Iraq, Bosnia, and Kosovo. Meanwhile, they continue to do important work for more typical clients. In the United States these clients include the FBI and city, state, and county medical examiners' offices.

Forensic anthropologist Dr. Owen Beattie teaches biological and forensic anthropology at the University of Alberta in Edmonton and serves as consultant in physical anthropology for the Office of the Chief Medical Examiner in Alberta. Beattie has conducted forensic investigations for coroners, police departments, and medical examiners across Canada and has helped investigate human rights violations around the world. In the mid-1990s, he served as part of a UN team that exhumed and analyzed victims of the 1994 Rwandan massacres.

Beattie has used his considerable forensic expertise to help solve some of the most fascinating mysteries of the Canadian Arctic. He is most famous for his work on the remains of members of the doomed 1845–48 Franklin Expedition to find the Northwest Passage. This work, published as *Frozen in Time: The Fate of the Franklin Expedition,*[10] was an international bestseller. Beattie's forensic examination suggests that the men died in 1846 of lead poisoning stemming from faulty soldering of the seals of their canned goods.

Frozen in Time: The Fate of The Franklin Expedition by Owen Beattie and John Geiger. Bloomsbury Publishers, 2004.

The frozen remains of Franklin crewmember John Torrington, who died shortly after the expedition's ships, the *Erebus* and *Terror*, became trapped in ice.

AP Photo/Rodrigo Abd

The excavation of mass graves by the Guatemalan Foundation for Forensic Anthropology (Fernando Moscoso Moller, Director) documents the human rights abuses committed during Guatemala's bloody civil war, a conflict that left 200,000 people dead and another 40,000 missing. In 2009, in a mass grave in the Quiche region, Diego Lux Tzunux uses his cell phone to photograph the skeletal remains believed to belong to his brother Manuel, who disappeared in 1980. Genetic analyses allow forensic anthropologists to confirm the identity of individuals so that family members can know the fate of their loved ones. The analysis of skeletal remains provides evidence of the torture and massacre sustained by these individuals.

❧ *Original Study 1* ❧

Forensic Anthropology and the Pickton Farm Murders

Tracy Rogers

Tracy Rogers is a forensic anthropologist, the director of the Forensic Science Program at the University of Toronto Mississauga, and an associate professor in the Department of Anthropology.

Forensic anthropology is the application of anthropological skills and knowledge to assist the police, coroners, medical examiners, and pathologists in their investigations. In North America, forensic anthropology usually involves applying bioanthropological and archaeological expertise, while in Britain these specialties are divided between forensic anthropologists (in the lab) and forensic archaeologists (on the scene). In practical terms, North American forensic anthropologists attend a crime scene to determine whether the bone is human, to clarify the nature of the remains (archaeological, historic, forensic, etc.), and to help locate clandestine graves, human remains, and related evidence. They help the police with the proper documentation and recovery of the body and exhibits at the scene. This includes mapping the grave and excavating the body and related evidence to help reconstruct the events that took place at the crime scene. Once the body has been taken to the morgue, the forensic anthropologist provides a biological profile (age, sex, ancestry, stature, unique characteristics) of the skeletal remains to help police identify the deceased. Forensic anthropologists also examine the bones for evidence of injury or damage that could be useful to the pathologist in determining the cause of death or anything that happened to the body after death (e.g., dismemberment).

In 2002, the RCMP and the Vancouver Police Department undertook the largest serial killer crime scene investigation in Canadian history. Over approximately 20 years, more than 60 women had disappeared from Vancouver's Downtown East Side. The police investigation progressed sporadically over the years, but it was not until the spring of 2002 that the Pickton property in Port Coquitlam could be concretely linked to the disappearances. The 16-acre crime scene was a small-scale pig farm. It was not clear how many of the missing women might be associated with this scene, nor where their bodies or related evidence might be concealed. Investigators decided to be as thorough as possible. Besides examining the 53 vehicles and 16 buildings on the farm, they ordered a full excavation of the property in an effort to locate buried remains and/or evidence. Civilians with specialized knowledge in operating heavy equipment were hired to excavate materials and take them to the screening and sorting area, where a team of anthropology graduates from across Canada searched the dirt for anything not natural to the soil. The property was divided into 20 by 20 metre squares and systematically excavated and documented. Undergraduate and graduate students with training in forensic anthropology, bioarchaeology, and archaeology worked in shifts to examine the excavated soil by hand as it moved along a conveyor belt. Nonbiological objects were removed for evaluation by an identification police officer, and Tracy Rogers, a forensic anthropologist, was hired to examine bone and biological material recovered from the scene in order to determine whether it was human, provide a biological profile and/or identifying features, and assess trauma/damage. Two additional forensic anthropologists, Richard Lazenby and Owen Beattie, helped in this process over the course of the 18-month investigation.

As a result of the investigation, more than 16,000 exhibits were seized, more than 130,000 scene photos were taken, 542 fingerprints were lifted, thousands of animal bones were examined and eliminated from the case, human remains were discovered both above and below ground, and Robert Pickton was charged with 27 counts of first degree murder. Due to the complexity of the case and associated evidence, six of the counts were severed and the trial proceeded on those six. In December 2009, Robert Pickton was convicted of 6 counts of second degree murder; he was ultimately sentenced to 25 years without parole, the maximum penalty for such a crime in Canada.

Forensic anthropologists are valuable members of the investigative team at outdoor, fire, and unusual crime scenes. Their knowledge of body dumpsite characteristics, search indicators, and animal activity helps investigators narrow potential search sites for clandestine graves and scattered bones/body parts. Their training in scene documentation, mapping, and excavation ensures that the context and relationships of objects and landmarks at a scene are recorded, allowing the investigative team to reconstruct the events that occurred at the scene leading up to and following the death and/or deposition of the body. At the Pickton property, for example, the forensic anthropology search team was responsible for recovering most of the buried exhibits, and the forensic anthropologist, Tracy Rogers, made recommendations about the search protocol that led to the recovery of human remains in their proper context. Forensic anthropologists also analyze human skeletons, provide information to help identify the deceased, and in some cases help the pathologist determine the sequence of events that led to the death. Most American states and Canadian provinces have at least one forensic anthropologist on staff or working on a contract basis, and those with large populations and high crime rates may employ several forensic anthropologists. To become a forensic anthropologist, one must earn a PhD in anthropology, preferably with a specialization in forensic anthropology. During this process, graduate students usually gain practical experience by working on forensic cases with their supervisors.

SOURCES: Owen Beattie, Young Alberta Book Society, 1998, http://www.culturenet.ucalgary .ca/yabs/beattieo.html, accessed October 16, 2000; Owen Beattie, 8th Annual Young Scientist Conference, n.d., http://ftp.ei.educ.ab.ca/dept/ ins/beattie/html, accessed October 16, 2000.

In 1999, Beattie supervised removal of the frozen remains of a 15th-century hunter discovered in a remote glacier in Tatshenshini-Alsek National Wilderness Park, British Columbia. The ancient hunter and the artifacts associated with his body have generated strong interest among the scientific and First Nations communities. Beattie has also conducted archaeological and forensic investigations into the 1719 disappearance of Captain James Knight's ships, the *Albany* and *Discovery*, on their way to explore Hudson Bay. Beattie's 1989–91 excavations raise doubts about the theory that the explorer and his men died of starvation. These conclusions are found in *Dead Silence: The Greatest Mystery in Arctic Discovery*.[11]

The field of forensic anthropology has grown significantly over the past few decades and has become popularized in many television shows that depict crime-fighting detectives using the skills of forensic and physical anthropologists. Whether forensic anthropologists are excavating the remains of a recent massacre or uncovering enigmatic prehistoric individual human remains, their work is an important subfield of modern applied anthropology. This importance is illustrated by the contribution that anthropologists and graduate students made in the sad case of the Pickton murders in BC.

Ethnography

Ethnography, as we discussed in Chapter 1, is the controlled participant observation of a given cultural field. It is one of the subfields of cultural anthropology, but it is also a large part of applied anthropology. A vital component of ethnography—indeed, of all anthropology—has always been ethics.[12] The Society for Applied Anthropology developed its *Code of Ethics* in 1949, based on a diligent set of rules pertaining to the treatment of participants and the information they reveal or that is gathered

Ethnography is an important part of applied anthropology. Here, Canadian anthropologist Richard Lee learns from Ju/'hoansi elders.

from studying them. Notwithstanding its problematic links with colonialism in its very early days, the history of ethnographic inquiry has long reflected that the purpose of most ethnography has been purely academic and that ethnographers are held to a very high ethical standard. Most ethnographic research is undertaken from within academe and for purely academic reasons, such as to teach students or advance knowledge. Increasingly, however, anthropologists are being hired by the private sector, and this development has raised specific challenges. The place of ethnographic research in applied anthropology is quite complex and can raise troublesome issues of ethics and questions about the use of the data that are gathered by ethnographers. Even when applying their expertise for practical purposes, ethnographers must still adhere to the ethics codes of the various anthropological associations (the American Anthropological Association, the Canadian Anthropological Association, and so on).

In modern applied ethnography, the purpose of the research and the use of the resulting data can raise some very troubling questions. For example, a large mining corporation may employ a team of anthropologists to conduct ethnographic or archaeological research into indigenous peoples who use and/or reside near the land sought by the company. What would be the purpose of such research? It is likely not knowledge for the sake of enlightenment; it is not to fill in the blank spaces of prehistory and to contribute to our understanding of these peoples. The employer—here, the mining company—may be seeking to gain leverage over the indigenous people, to be forewarned of possible complications resulting from their mining ventures, and to be informed enough to present their case to the public or in the courts should a debate arise about the safe or ethical use of lands and resources. This places the traditional standards of ethnography under severe stress. The researcher's data may in the end cause harm to the indigenous people nearby, or harm to their environment. There is no easy answer to these troubling questions for applied anthropology. The simple fact that one is "selling" one's anthropological skills outside the academic setting can result in the loss of control over the resulting data and the purposes to which it is put.

Other examples of applied ethnography can be found in the corporate world. A case in point: A corporation may hire an ethnographer to study how the members of a large, possibly multicultural workforce interact with one another and with management. Corporate anthropology is addressed in this chapter's Original Study 2.

Whether applied ethnographic research is undertaken in Cree towns or in the offices of major corporations, the same anthropological skills are needed. These anthropologists must also practise very similar techniques, such as interviews and the use of assistants from the local community (formerly referred to as "informants," a term now out of favour owing to

Irven DeVore/Anthro-Photo File

negative connotations of "informing" on one's community). Similar ethnographic research skills are thus seen in both academic and applied ethnography: Immersion within, and a thorough knowledge of, the community, is required. This is true whether the ethnography takes place among Llongot headhunters or in a major industrial plant.

However, there are differences between academic and applied ethnography. For instance, where once the ethnographer could choose which community to work with, now the actual "community" is chosen by the stakeholders, those who "pay the bills." Also, the standard ethnographic time frame of around a year spent living and working with any given community is no longer really feasible in many cases, as the stakeholders usually require data in a hurry. This situation often results in the skills of the applied ethnographer falling under the laws and rules of the "market"—a development that surely would have horrified the founders of ethnographic research.

Corporate Anthropology

Applied anthropology has many facets, and we have examined just a few of these so far. We turn our attention now to the fast-growing field of corporate or business anthropology. This is not the same as the "anthropology of business," which is the anthropological analysis of business, and not an applied field. Applied business/corporate anthropology itself includes marketing, systems analysis, cross-cultural understanding in the business world, advertising, and human resource studies for large corporations. What corporate managers want from anthropologists is detailed information on how their company and workforce actually function, as opposed to their own internally generated organization charts and graphs. The corporate anthropologist is required to explain how the company's operations might be improved, streamlined, and made more effective. What the anthropologist is really doing is an ethnography of the business environment. Indeed, some see ethnography as "an excellent approach to understanding products within a consumer landscape."[13] As the late business anthropologist Brian Burkhalter added, "In brief, in any business or public situation requiring extensive knowledge about how a local community, culture, group, or group of businessmen think, feel, believe, or act, there is an opportunity for applied anthropology to make policy suggestions based on ethnographic research."[14] In the following Original Study, Anishinaabeg applied anthropologist Rodney Nelson discusses not only the corporate world and applied anthropology, but also how these can intersect with indigenous cultures and traditional knowledge.

Applied Anthropology and the Military

We have already seen how applied anthropology played an important role in the military during colonial days and the Second World War. We will therefore confine our discussion of the military to just a few current observations. Some anthropologists today are hired by military organizations in a variety of areas. In the United States, the *New York Times* reported recently on a semi-secret project known as the Human Terrain System, an experimental program run by the Pentagon, which assigns anthropologists (among other social scientists) to U.S. army combat units fighting in Afghanistan and Iraq. In October 2007, U.S. Defense Secretary Robert Gates "authorized a $40 million expansion of the program, which will assign teams of anthropologists and social scientists to each of the 26 American combat brigades in Iraq and Afghanistan."[15] Their mission is to liaise with local people, and to translate and understand the specific characteristics and cultural practices such as local customs and taboos, so as to smooth the path for military–civilian cooperation. "Since early September, five new teams have been deployed in the Baghdad area, bringing the total to six."[16]

Some anthropologists are uncomfortable with the role that anthropology is being called on to play in war zones. Dr. Patricia Omidian, an associate professor and the head of social sciences for the Aga Khan University's Faculty of Arts and Sciences in Karachi, Pakistan, claims that "militarized anthropology subverts our work and puts us on an ethical slippery slope."[17] In response, Col. Martin Schweitzer, commander of the 82nd Airborne Division unit working with the anthropologists in Afghanistan, reports that the unit's combat operations were reduced by 60 percent after the anthropologists and other scientists arrived, and that this allowed the soldiers to concentrate more on improving security, health care, and education for the local population. Whether other sociopolitical factors contributed to such a decline in combat operations is not stated, but it is suggested that the presence of anthropologists in the field reduced the need for combat operations.

Even so, most anthropologists are extremely wary of becoming involved in military projects. In late 2008 the Association of American Anthropologists amended its *Code of Ethics* specifically in response to this militarization, stating that "in accordance with the Association's general position on clandestine and secret research, no reports should be provided to sponsors that are not also available to the general public."[18] This, along with other amendments, is geared toward ensuring that anthropologists do not conduct covert operations and become embroiled in military operations.

✽ *Original Study 2* ✽

A Tale of Two First Nations: Traditional Knowledge in Today's Business World

Rodney Nelson

I often get asked what I do for a living. I usually respond saying that I am an anthropologist and then wait for the typical responses: "I always liked dinosaurs! It must be fun to dig up all those bones," or, "Wow! I love ancient cultures like Egypt and Greece." I always smile and prepare my typical response: "I am a corporate anthropologist. I work mainly with First Nations helping to set up businesses and promote economic development." I usually get a confused look and some people even admit that they don't think they know what an anthropologist does. In reality, anthropologists are working in many fields and disciplines. We are involved in every aspect of human society and culture, including business.

Today there are more than 200 First Nations communities across Canada (Statistics Canada 2006). Many of these communities are facing ongoing social and economic hardships such as low employment, high suicide rates, and increasing diabetes and other health issues. Many communities do not have safe drinking water or access to the medical treatments that others in Canada enjoy. To help alleviate these issues, many First Nations leaders and elders are looking toward economic development as a way to create wealth and prosperity in their communities. As Northwest Coast Tsimshian businessman Calvin Helin says, "First Nations have been doing business for thousands of years so being in business is not new or a colonial process" (CCCR 2010). Several elders and leaders such as Chief Sophie Pierre of the Ktunaxan/Kinbasket Nation, Chief Clarence Louie of the Osoyoos, and Chiefs Sam Bull and George Halfe of Whitefish Lake First Nation see

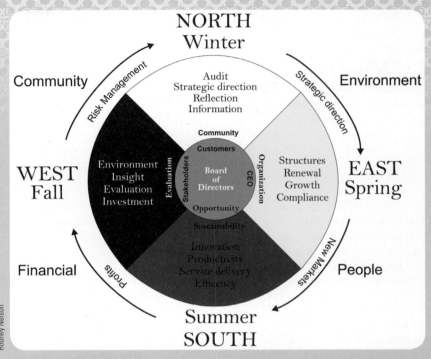

Rodney Nelson

Using the best of both worlds this image depicts the concept of incorporating both traditional and corporate governance to create an Aboriginal governance framework for business.

economic development as a way for First Nations to attain self-governance and sustainable, healthy communities. Economic development is the process by which people build organizations and partnerships that connect profitable business with other interests and values of the community (Helin 2009). As an anthropologist, I am working with these leaders, elders, and communities to help them realize this goal.

Traditional Teachings

Discussions of traditional knowledge for First Nations often generate images of saving the rainforests or protecting fishing areas. But traditional knowledge is more than an understanding of the land and the environment. It is the knowledge of those who have walked before us (our ancestors) that has been passed on through generations to define and govern the way we think and act today and in the future. It grounds

who we are and forges our identity and decision making. Traditional knowledge extends into every aspect of our lives (Nelson 2010).

Many elders have told me that we all have a responsibility to one another and to the earth we walk on. These beliefs are reflected in many First Nations traditional teachings, such as the Seven Generations Teachings, the Grandfather Teachings, and the Teachings of the Medicine Wheel. These traditional teachings or ways of knowing are passed on through stories, traditions, ceremonies, medicines, dances, and other forms of knowledge sharing (Crowshaw 2005). Elders are often the traditional knowledge holders of the community, but everyone can hold, follow, and share in traditional knowledge (Johnston 2005).

The Seven Generation Teachings emphasize that decisions made today will have an effect on seven generations into the future. So this future outcome must be considered when decisions are being

CONTINUED

CONTINUED

made (Seven Generations Education Institute 2010). Seven generations in the future is our children's children's child. It is a generation we will never meet, but looking out for them is looking out for your family. Therefore, we all must consider future outcomes when making life decisions.

The Seven Grandfather Teachings come from many stories passed on from generation to generation and reflect the concept of *mino bimaadiziwin*, or how to live "the good life". The Ojibway story of the Grandfather Teachings tells of how the Creator gave seven grandfathers the responsibility to watch over the people. To do this they sent a helper to share the teachings of how to live in harmony with the world. The boy helper was visited seven times and was given the teachings to spread to the four directions (Benton-Banai 1979). The teachings of the seven grandfathers are *zaagidwin* (love), *dbaadendiziwin* (humility), *gwekwaadiziwin* (honesty), *aakwade'ewin* (bravery), *nbwaakaawin* (wisdom), *debwewin* (truth), and *mnaadendimowin* (respect) (Albert 2010). This philosophy provides guidance on how we are to govern our actions and behaviours.

The Teachings of the Medicine Wheel are another set of teachings that represent the four directions, east, south, west, and north:

- The east signifies the eagle and represents birth, renewal, vision, the mental, wisdom, and spring.
- The south signifies the wolf and represents youth, community, engagement, enlightenment, the spiritual, and summer.
- The west signifies the buffalo and represents reflection, emotions, objectivity, and fall.
- The north signifies the bear and represents the elders, reflection, insight, the physical, and winter.

Today, the challenge facing First Nations is to keep these traditional teachings alive and to incorporate them into everyday life. These traditional teachings are guides for how we are to act and make decisions. This can also apply to the corporate world when businesses incorporate traditional teachings into their governance structures.

Traditional Knowledge and Business

I have been fortunate to be able to work closely with several Mohawk and Anishinabeg (Odawa, Ojibwa, Nipissing, and Algonquin) leaders and elders, helping them incorporate traditional teachings into their businesses. Many First Nations businesses are different from non–First Nations businesses because they have the added responsibilities to their communities and the goal of overall betterment of their culture. Success is measured not only in profits but also in social contributions to the community. In some cases, profits are sacrificed for the betterment of community. This philosophy runs counter to the typical business model of making profit for a few shareholders.

Traditional teachings can guide business in making important decisions such as whether to invest in communities, expand the business, or support environmental policies. Traditional knowledge can also provide a foundation for the values of an organization. The Grandfather Teachings provide the foundations of supporting the nation, community, and family along with notions of honesty, integrity, peace, and wisdom. These values can be incorporated into corporate value systems, thus guiding the organization in how it does business. Traditional teachings such as the Seven Generations Teachings can help a business create a strategic direction. This strategy will sustain the organization for many generations to come, and not just be geared towards immediate profitability.

Traditional Knowledge and the Environment

Traditional teachings can offer insights into understanding First Nations businesses. One of the most common forms of incorporating traditional knowledge into business practices is in the area of environmental protection. Many businesses today have adopted "green practices" that protect the environment while maintaining profits. The Seven Generations Teachings are part of this philosophy. When a business considers how its decisions will affect seven generations from now, their environmental policies will reflect these decisions. Many businesses call this corporate social responsibility (CSR) and are slowly adding environmental policies to their business practices. For First Nations, CSR is more than environmental policies; it is a way of life and is ingrained in traditions and teachings.

Seven Generations Teachings and Goodfish Lake Development Corporation

The Goodfish Lake Development Corporation (GFLDC) is one First Nation business that has embraced traditional knowledge and applied it to its environmental policies (Nelson 2007). It is owned and operated by the Whitefish Lake First Nation, which is home to more than 2,300 Cree, in Alberta 200 kilometres north of Edmonton. In the 1970s, the band faced high unemployment and many people were leaving the community to find work in the nearby oil sands. The band needed a sustainable business that would keep its members in the community and employed. Chief Sam Bull had a vision to create an industrial dry-cleaning and garment-sewing business that could service the nearby oil sands. This led to the creation of the GFLDC. The company is now one of the largest dry-cleaning companies in Canada. GFLDC has taken the Seven Generations Teachings into its own boardroom and, on the advice of its elders and community representatives, has developed strict environmental guidelines to protect the land for generations to come. These traditional teachings have been directly integrated into its business philosophy and policies. The company views protection of the environment for future generations as a corporate priority and has attained the International Organization for Standardization's ISO 14001-2004 standardization for environmental management systems.

Success in Traditions—St. Eugene Mission Resort

Many First Nations have succeeded in business and are seeing their communities begin to prosper. But many more are struggling to find solutions to their problems. Many First Nations do not have the location or land base to support large-scale economic development. Some bands look to business development off-reserve in order to find success. Others have become innovative, using their land and history to create economic opportunities. The St. Eugene Mission Resort is one business that has taken a tragic history and turned it into a success story.

The St. Eugene Mission Resort is a five-star resort with a golf course and casino. It provides revenue and jobs to the community and is a source of pride for its members. But it is also part of a dark time in Canadian history. The resort started off as a mission school in 1912 and was one of the first industrial and residential schools in Canada. Many residential survivors tell of the hardships and devastating emotional and physical abuse they experienced in the years when St. Eugene was a school. One of its own survivors, Sophie Pierre, became chief of the St. Mary's band and has been instrumental in making the change from the school building being a source of pain and a reminder of darker days to it being a source of pride and success for her community.

Chief Pierre is the past chief of St. Mary's First Nation in Cranbrook, BC, and is the administrator of the Ktunaxa-Kinbasket Tribal Council, which represents more than 1,500 Ktunaxan/Kinbasket people. Chief Pierre is also one of the great First Nations leaders of today and has worked for her community for more than 30 years. She is a strong supporter of economic development that maintains traditional knowledge and world views. When the time came for the community to decide what to do with the old residential school, the debate was heated and ongoing. Chief Pierre describes the time as one of anger, frustration, and pain over what many had experienced at the school (Pierre 2007). At one meeting, an elder stood up and spoke the words that would lead the community to where it is today. The elder said that the mission represented too much pain and has been a bad thing for their com-

munity for so long. He suggested that there needed to be a way to turn it into an opportunity for the community to begin a healing process. That was the birth of the $40 million St. Eugene Mission Resort, a world-class hotel, golf course, and casino.

The resort was a result of the community trying to heal from a tragic situation. The concept of healing is a principal teaching of the Medicine Wheel. It maintains that, while life is forever interrelated by the four directions, we all have freedom of choice in everything we do. The St. Eugene Mission Resort offered a chance of rebirth and hope for the community. This hope represents the eastern direction of the wheel. The south represents the mental healing the survivors need. The west reflects letting go and emotional healing, while the north represents the link to spiritual healing, as well as reflection on the historical past of the mission and the impact it had on the community.

Conclusion

As a corporate anthropologist, I help businesses and communities merge their traditional teachings with their business practices. Many businesses that take this path are accepted and respected by the communities because they are still using traditional values. I often find myself in the middle of a disagreement between the band office that runs the development corporation and the community, which has its own expectations of the organization. My background in anthropology allows me to negotiate an understanding based on the traditional values of the culture and the expectations of business.

Today, many First Nations still do not have the means to create economic development in their communities. Barriers such as lack of funding, ongoing social issues, politics at every level, and the restrictions of the Indian Act make it difficult to promote economic development. Many First Nations are becoming more creative and looking internationally for opportunities that may help their communities. Some still fight to get water they can drink, as well as access to the health care and social services

that many take for granted. Economic development may be an answer to these issues by creating opportunities and wealth in communities. Wealth brings infrastructure such as housing, health facilities, roads, hydro, and water and sewage mains. It increases social services such as education, suicide prevention, social assistance, and day care. It creates employment and opens opportunities to promote cultural activities and pass on traditions. It helps restore the wellness and pride of a community and nation. It might even reduce the ongoing issues of substance abuse and reduce the high suicide rate of First Nations youth—a rate that is five times the national average. Until this happens, many First Nations will continue to live in Third World conditions in one of the wealthiest countries in the world. Today, First Nations are taking control of their own destiny and working towards economic sustainability through economic development. They are doing it on their own terms, and one of their strategies of success has been to incorporate traditional knowledge into business practices.

SOURCES: B. Johnston, Ojibway Heritage *(Toronto: McClelland & Stewart, 2005); C. Crowshaw,* Sacred Ways of Life: Traditional Knowledge *(Ottawa: National Aboriginal Health Organization, 2005); C. Helin,* Dances with Dependancy *(Woodland Hill: Raven Crest Publishing, 2009); R. Nelson, "Traditional Knowledge in the Board Room: A Quest for a New Model of Corporate Governance,"* Journal of Aboriginal Management *(2010): 28–35; Statistics Canada, "Aboriginal Identity Population" (Ottawa: Statistics Canada, 2006); CCCR (Canadian Centre for Community Renewal), "Community Economic Development," 2010, http://www.cedworks.com/CEDdefinition.html; Seven Generations Education Institute, "Anishinaabe Mino Bimaadizwin: Principles for Anishinaabe Education," 2010, http://www.7generations.org; E. Benton-Banai,* The Mishomis Book: Voices of the Ojibway *(Minneapolis: University Of Minnesota Press, 1979); J. Albert, Elder [interview by Rodney Nelson], in* Conversations with an Elder, *2010; R. Nelson,* From Vision to Venture *(Ottawa: Conference Board of Canada, 2007); S. Pierre interviewed by Rodney Nelson, 2007.*

In Canada, scholars of the military speak of the emergence of an "embedded anthropology," where the contribution is geared more toward understanding the intricacies of military life. For example, anthropologist Anne Irwin of the University of Calgary studied the behavioural patterns of Canadian soldiers on deployment to Afghanistan. Irwin's study is more a social anthropological analysis of military life than research for the purposes of military intelligence. She examined how soldiers bolster their identities by sharing their battlefield experiences through storytelling with their peers.[19] While the Canadian military does not have anthropologists on Human Terrain teams, soldiers are provided with cultural awareness training, and it may be argued that a militarization of applied anthropology is developing. Others might argue that there is an "anthropologicalizing" of the military under way. Anthropologists in the military possess the capacity to aid the soldiers who employ them and to do good work on the ground. However, many in academe are opposed to the use of anthropologists for military purposes. As applied anthropology becomes, once again, linked with military endeavours, and analyses of the military demonstrate the growing role of women, questions surrounding sex, gender, and violence become increasingly germane, and are addressed in the Gender Perspectives feature box below.

Medical Anthropology

One area in applied anthropology that has seen prolific growth in recent years is medical anthropology. **Medical anthropology** is the subfield of cultural anthropology that analyses how cultures and societies are organized around health and related issues. It has been suggested that *all* medical anthropology is applied anthropology, and indeed that is mostly true. Much of the growth in applied medical anthropology has involved a multitude of large projects that have been undertaken over the past few decades. An applied medical anthropologist, much like a forensic anthropologist, may work as part of a UN project in the developing world, or for a private charity such as *Médicins Sans Frontières,* or for organizations such as Oxfam. Much like a forensic anthropologist, a medical anthropologist must deal with a host of political and social challenges that in many cases impede their research. Applied medical anthropologists—or more accurately of late, medical anthropological teams—must overcome these challenges in order to deliver their services. These

medical anthropology The subfield of cultural anthropology that analyses how cultures and societies are organized around issues of health and related issues.

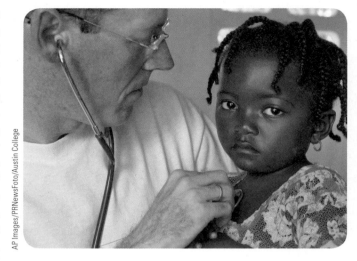

Medical anthropologists often work in developing countries. Here, a child is medically examined.

AP Images/PRNewsFoto/Austin College

include working in war zones or in famine areas and dealing with often hostile environments. Such issues are not normally encountered in academic anthropology, and this makes medical applied anthropological research a very special subfield. Whether in the academic or the applied domain, almost all medical anthropology has practical applications.

Environmental Health and Justice

Our contribution could be most effective, we decided, in broadening the definition of victims of environmental rights abuse and in illustrating the processes and mechanisms which initiate, structure, legitimize, and reproduce victimization. As anthropologists, we could provide the descriptive rationale for human environmental rights.[20]

Jerry Kobalenko/Firstlight

The physical, social, and spiritual health of a northern Cree community in an era of rapid change is the subject of Naomi Adelson's insightful monograph *Being Alive Well.*

Gender Perspectives

Sex, Gender, and Human Violence

At the start of the 21st century, war and violence are no longer the strictly male domains that they were in many societies in the past. War has become embedded in civilian life in many parts of the world, and it impacts the daily lives of women and children. Moreover, women now serve in the military forces of several states, although their participation in combat is often limited. Some female soldiers in the United States argue that gender should not limit their participation in combat; they consider themselves as strong, capable, and well trained as their male counterparts. Others believe that biologically based sex differences make war a particularly male domain.

Scientists have long argued that males are more suited to combat because natural selection has made them on average larger and stronger than females. This idea, known as sexual selection, was first put forward by Charles Darwin in the 19th century. Darwin contended that the physical specializations of males in animal species—such as horns, vibrant plumage, and, in the case of humans, intelligence and tool use—demonstrate selection acting upon males to aid in the competition for mates. In these scenarios, male reproductive success is thought to be optimized through a strategy of "spreading seed"—in other words, through sexual activity with as many females as possible.

Females, on the other hand, are gatekeepers who optimize their reproductive success through caring for individual offspring. According to this theory of sexual selection, in species where male–male competition is high, males will be considerably larger than females and aggression will serve males well. In monogamous species, males and females will be of similar sizes.

Primatologist Richard Wrangham has taken the idea of sexual selection even further. In his book *Demonic Males*, he explores the idea that both patriarchy and male aggression have an evolutionary basis. He writes that humans, like our close cousins the chimpanzees, are "party gang" species characterized by strong bonds among groups of males who have dominion over an expandable territory. These features "suffice to account for natural selection's ugly legacy, the tendency to look for killing opportunities when hostile neighbors meet" (Wrangham and Peterson 1996, 168). Violence in turn generates a male-dominated social order: "Patriarchy comes from biology in the sense that it emerges from men's temperaments out of their evolutionarily derived efforts to control women and at the same time have solidarity with fellow males in competition against outsiders" (ibid., 125). Wrangham allows that evolutionary forces have shaped women as well, but he suggests that females' evolutionary interests cannot be met without cooperation with males.

Feminist scholars have pointed out that these scientific models are "gendered" in that they incorporate the norms derived from the scientists' culture. Darwin's original model of sexual selection incorporated the Victorian gender norms of the passive female and active male. The Canadian primatologist Linda Fedigan (1986) suggests that in Darwinian models, women evolved in positive directions only by a "coat tails" process whereby females were "pulled along" toward improved biological states by virtue of the progress of the genes they shared with males. Wrangham's more recent *Demonic Males* theory has been similarly shaped by culture; that is, it incorporates the dominant world order (military states) and the gender norms (aggressive males) it values. In both cases, the putatively scientific theory has created a natural basis for a series of social conventions.

This does not mean that biological differences between the sexes cannot be studied in the natural world. Instead, scientists studying sex differences must be especially sensitive to how they may be projecting cultural beliefs onto nature. Meanwhile, the attitudes of some women soldiers continue to challenge generalizations regarding "military specialization" by gender.

SOURCES: L.M. Fedigan, "The Changing Role of Women in Models of Human Evolution," Annual Review of Anthropology 15 (1986): 25–66; R. Wrangham and D. Peterson, Demonic Males (Boston: Houghton Mifflin, 1996).

Much of the work of applied medical anthropologists involves environmental health and justice. Throughout the 19th and 20th centuries, as the industrial system of production grew, so did the production of pollutants. Thousands of new chemical compounds were released into the atmosphere, water, and soil and found their way into the food chain and into our bodies. For decades the industrial world celebrated its triumph over nature and the wealth of new products created. But gradually the unpaid bills for unbridled growth began to come due. Mounting levels of cancer, asthma, and birth defects led to a search for causes. Today, increasingly conclusive evidence links many of these conditions to the expansion and intensification of the industrial system.

One outcome has been the environmental movement, made up of citizen activists who are determined to defend their families and communities. Closely linked to medical anthropology, the **environmental justice** movement has emerged to explore environmental pollution

environmental justice A social movement in which citizen activists organize to defend against environmental threats to community health and well-being.

and health. Medical anthropologist Harriet Rosenberg of York University has researched one of the best-known cases of toxic pollution and citizen response—the infamous Love Canal.[21]

Although it is quite an old example, the case of Love Canal demonstrates the need for impact assessments and applied anthropologists. Medical anthropologists, had they been involved from the start, might have galvanized the academic community to act on behalf of the Love Canal residents. As it transpired, they were on their own initially. Love Canal is just upriver from Niagara Falls on the southeastern edge of the city of Niagara Falls, New York. Dug at the turn of the 20th century, the actual canal never carried barge traffic, but from 1920 to 1945 it served as a dumpsite for toxic wastes from the nearby Hooker Chemical plant, a division of Occidental Petroleum. After the dumpsite was filled to capacity, it was closed, buried under a clay cap, and covered with soil. The city government then took over the land, and during the postwar housing boom built a primary school directly on top of the former dump. By the 1970s, developers had built a subdivision there of more than 700 homes.

The families of Love Canal, in the course of raising their children, began to notice ominous signs. Children jumping in rain puddles in the schoolyard found the soles of their sneakers melting away, and mothers as well as doctors were alarmed by the number of newborns with birth defects and by the appearance of rare cancers in older children. Asthma, allergies, skin disorders, and chronic respiratory ailments also appeared in disturbingly high numbers.

Families were demanding answers, and under the leadership of the Love Canal Homeowners Association (LCHA), they began to lobby municipal and state health authorities to address the multiplying health problems. The government's response followed a pattern that has become familiar to all environmental justice activists. There was nothing unusual about the high level of ailments, officials insisted—this was just the usual variation around statistical norms. When the mothers in the community pressed the officials, they found their concerns dismissed as the fears of "hysterical housewives." Nevertheless, news reports spread word of the health problems, and real estate values plummeted. The largely working-class families had sunk their life savings into their homes and simply couldn't afford to abandon them and live elsewhere.

Their situation seemed hopeless until a few academics at local universities accepted the concerns of the homeowners at face value and began to conduct independent environmental studies. These studies confirmed the LCHA's worst fears: unacceptably high levels of a list of toxins had been found in the schoolyard and the soil of backyards, and was even oozing from the walls in the basements of homes. Most prominent among these was dioxin, the most toxic chemical ever created, dangerous at a few parts per billion.

A young mother named Lois Gibbs took the leadership of the LCHA, and the Love Canal community rose to statewide and then national prominence as a toxic disaster area. Finally, the cumbersome government bureaucracy acknowledged the serious health dangers facing the residents of Love Canal, and in 1979 President Jimmy Carter authorized the relocation of residents as well as compensation for the lost equity in their homes.[22]

The Love Canal story became a prototype for communities all over North America that faced health threats from unacknowledged sources of toxic waste, smokestack industries, and the release of pollutants into the water and air. Lois Gibbs became an internationally prominent environmental crusader and founded what is now the Center for Health, Environment, and Justice in Falls Church, Virginia. For its part, the U.S. government set aside a budgetary allocation, known as the Superfund, for the massive clean-up required to remove toxic wastes and restore sites to human use. Anthropologists, spurred on by concern for the environment and for those suffering from environmental injustice, launched and participated in forums and debates about Love Canal. Anthropological publications on environmental justice increased in number, and applied anthropologists contributed a nonpartisan (or so they argued) voice to the debate, helping at least to air out the issue of environmental health.

Similar examples of communities affected by toxic pollution in Canada include the tar ponds in Sydney, Nova Scotia; the tar sands in Alberta, which affect neighbouring First Nations groups; and the tainted-water tragedy in Walkerton, Ontario, in May 2000, when runoff from a local livestock farm infected the water supply with *E. coli,* which cost seven people their lives and injured many others.[23] While environmental scientists conduct research in such cases to determine the level of toxic risk to humans and animals, medical anthropologists chronicle the social movements that spring up to fight the polluters and, at times, governments that are slow to acknowledge the legitimacy of their concerns. These are just some of the issues facing applied medical anthropology; there are many more, which we have not the space to address. Medical anthropology is one of the largest fields of applied anthropology. As long as there exist issues such as poverty, starvation, and environmental injustice, there will be a need for medical anthropologists to work in these areas.

Disability Studies

Other applied anthropologists bring medical and ethnographic expertise to disability studies. In what is sometimes called the "disabled community," anthropologists' training is put to much use. The disabled community is broad and diverse; it is found in hospitals, retirement homes, universities, the workplace—everywhere disabled people are found. It can thus be a subject of ethnographic analysis as much as the Bedouin or the Hazdabe, with the caveat that the community being studied will have different needs than other communities. For those who work with the disabled community, there are of course other challenges besides, which require a wide knowledge of fields such as physiology and psychology, and also compassion. The applied anthropologist in the disabled community may be employed by a hospital to study the delivery of medical services to cultural minorities or any identifiable group with disabilities or health issues.

The student of medical anthropology may end up being employed as a disability specialist working with a major national organization such as the Canadian National Institute for the Blind or War Amps of Canada. Cultural anthropologist Pamela Block is an associate professor in the Occupational Therapy Program of the School of Health Technology and Management at Stony Brook University in New York State. She describes disability studies as "in direct contrast to medical and rehabilitation models of disability, which focus on the physiological aspects of disability, the 'fixing' of atypical, 'broken' physiology."[24] Her anthropological training has brought a different approach to disability studies, where "disability is seen as part of the continuity of the human condition, as part of an identity reliant as much on socio-economic factors as on physiological factors."[25] For an applied anthropologist, the disability community is one that must be studied just like any other cultural grouping. Along with medical treatments, the dynamic of the group and both its collective identity and the identities of its individual members must be understood in order for analysis to succeed.

Elsewhere in the realm of disability studies, others with anthropological training may be hired to conduct research on disabled student communities. Such was the case with the National Educational Association of Disabled Students (NEADS), based in

Ottawa. In 2003, NEADS conducted a major national research program that aimed to understand the range and quality of academic materials in alternative formats for students with disabilities in Canada's postsecondary schools. Two detailed surveys were created, one directed at students, the other for service providers such as librarians. This project highlighted the need for improved access to technologies such as Kurzweil 3000, tactile graphics, and other alternative technologies.[26] An anthropologist was hired to construct these surveys and to quantify the responses. The skills of the anthropologist were needed for a variety of reasons. The anthropologist was required to construct pertinent questions for surveys of both the student body and the service providers, to understand the specific pedagogical challenges facing the disabled student body, and to collate the data using SPSS (the Statistical Package for the Social Sciences). The result was a comprehensive analysis of the current conditions of access to academic materials in alternative formats at many of Canada's postsecondary institutions, from both the student and the service provider perspectives. The project identified the strengths and weaknesses of current systems and reported on the needs and expectations of the disabled student population.[27] Applied anthropology therefore can also be directed toward educational institutions—in this case, the large disability community within the broader academic community.

SALVAGE ARCHAEOLOGY

The domain of applied anthropology that incorporates archaeological skills is known, generally, as **salvage archaeology**. However, this type of archaeology also falls within the broader field of **cultural resource management (CRM)**. CRM deals with more than archaeology; it includes the management or mitigation of historical landscapes, historical records, old buildings, heritage sites, and so forth. Here we will focus on the archaeological side of CRM in Canada. Some countries, including the United States, Britain, and Australia, have

salvage archaeology The collection of archaeological data and materials from any given site deemed to be in danger of destruction, as from new construction or weather damage.

cultural resource management (CRM) The practice of managing cultural resources, such as arts and heritage. It incorporates cultural heritage management, which is concerned with traditional and historic culture and the material culture of archaeology.

∞ *Dynamic Anthropology 1* ∞

The Baby Formula Controversy

Liam Kilmurray

The provocative headlines that reverberated in the media in 1974 included "Baby Killer!", "Third World Action Group Guilty of Libel," and "Anthropologist Takes on a Major International Company Called Nestlé." Such headlines highlighted the fact that anthropologists working in developing countries normally can be relied on to stick up for peoples who are sometimes oppressed, while avoiding the condescension sometimes associated with colonial or development projects. The notoriety of what became known as the "baby formula controversy" brought much attention to applied anthropology and to attempts by anthropologists to make a difference. The baby formula controversy really began with the charity organization War on Want, who reproached Nestlé for its advertising campaign for the sale of baby formula in developing nations. Many people were incensed by what they perceived to be the overbearing and underhanded approach of Nestlé's marketing campaign, and concerned about the damage that might result should its marketing succeed, and a boycott of Nestlé was launched. Penny Van Esterik, a Canadian anthropologist, documented and participated in this campaign, which aimed to convince mothers in (mainly) developing countries to abandon the ancient human method of nurturing infants, known as breast-feeding, in favour of bottled formula. Most of the target audience for Nestlé's advertising and sales campaign were impoverished, uneducated, and often illiterate.

The Nestlé Corporation used its substantial economic might to promote its powdered milk formula. It did so through a major advertising campaign, which suggested that mothers who continued to breast-feed were endangering the health of their children, and by co-opting local doctors to support the promotion of the bottle formula. The campaign promoted the bottle formula as providing physical and psychological advantages over breast milk. The formula was advertised as safe, modern, progressive, and beneficial to both mother and newborn baby. On the other hand, breast-feeding was cast as backward and associated with disease, danger, and poverty.

In this light, Penny Van Esterik was involved in the campaign, along with UNICEF and the WHO, to bring to light the pressures that Nestlé was placing on women in developing nations. The campaign had its highs and lows, and Nestlé had some successes, including proving that its product was safe. But Van Esterik was able to demonstrate the associated needs that came with the bottle formula, which were substantial yet had been overlooked by many. For example, the baby bottle formula required regular, daily access to clean-flowing water, and little heed was given to the fact that fresh running water was very often simply not available in these areas.

The flaw in Nestlé's plan had not been an oversight, and Van Esterik argued that it simply wanted to start mothers on the bottle (after which there could be little going back) so that they would be obliged to keep purchasing Nestlé products. The media campaign and the coalition of major charitable bodies along with the determination and anthropological training of Van Esterik eventually resulted in a victory for natural breast-feeding, in the lifting of the breast-feeding stigma, and in the demise of formula sales in the developing world. All of this illustrates the importance of applied anthropology and the life-or-death scenarios that applied anthropologists are sometimes involved in.

SOURCE: M. Muller, "The Baby Killer: A War on Want Investigation into the Promotion and Sale of Powdered Baby Milks in the Third World" (London: War on Want, 1974).

Here, Liam Kilmurray surveys a line of test squares that will be excavated in order to outline proto-Huron longhouses at this 15th-century village site at Jarrett-Lahmer.

laws to protect their archaeological heritage. In this regard, Canada "has been a pioneer, with an early, computerized national archaeological survey."[28] CRM exists in Canada because developments on Crown or private property may require that the builder obtain a clearance certificate from the relevant ministry (usually the Ministry of Heritage). In the United States, developments on federally owned lands, or on private lands using federal funds, require similar clearance from archaeological firms, which are contracted to excavate or mitigate sites.

Broken projectile point, Ontario.

✺ *Dynamic Anthropology 2* ✺

Development Anthropology and Dams

Over a 35-year career in scholarly and applied work, Michael M. Horowitz, president and executive director of the Institute for Development Anthropology (IDA) and distinguished professor of anthropology at SUNY–Binghamton, has made pioneering contributions to applied anthropology. His work has focused on equitable economic growth, environmental sustainability, conflict resolution, and participatory government in the former colonial world.

Since co-founding IDA in 1976, Horowitz has been its principal leader. He has played a key role in bringing anthropology forward as an applied science in international development organizations such as the World Bank, the UN Fund for Women, and the U.S. Agency for International Development (USAID), as well as NGOs such as Oxfam and the International Union for the Conservation of Nature. He has mentored several generations of young scholars and professionals—paying particular attention to those from developing countries—encouraging the application of anthropology's comparative and holistic methodologies and theories to empower low-income majorities in the so-called underdeveloped world.

Horowitz's work with pastoralists and floodplain dwellers has had substantial positive impact on the well-being of small producers and landholders in developing countries. A clear example of this is the impact of his work on the lives and livelihoods of people living downstream of a hydroelectric dam in West Africa. Beginning in the 1980s, he and his IDA team carried out rigorous anthropological research along the Senegal River, which flows through Mali, Senegal, and Mauritania. Their study showed that traditional, pre-dam,

© Earth Observatory—NASA

Visible from space, China's Three Gorges hydroelectric dam is the world's biggest and most powerful hydroelectric dam. About 2,300 metres long and 185 metres high, it controls the Yangtze, the world's third largest river. After fifteen years of construction with a price tag of US$22 billion, it became operational in 2009. The dam was built to provide a clean energy alternative to coal and to control flooding along the Yangtze River. However, it has been controversial since its inception, flooding ancient archaeological and cultural sites, displacing more than 1.4 million people, and causing significant ecological changes, including risks of landslides that threaten some 4 million people. Not one social scientist was consulted in the planning and assessment phase of the Three Gorges Dam.

flood-recession farming yielded better results than irrigated agriculture and was better for the environment.

This finding influenced decisions made by these countries and affiliated NGOs to manage the system with a controlled release from the Manatali Dam in Mali in order to reproduce as nearly as possible the pre-dam flow system. Horowitz's long-term field research demonstrated that seasonal flooding would provide economic, environmental, and sociocultural benefits for nearly one million small producers.

Recognized by national governments, NGOs, and development funding agencies, the work of Horowitz and his IDA colleagues on

the Senegal River Basin Monitoring Activity (SRBMA) was a breakthrough in the concepts of resettlement and river management, and it continues to influence development policy. Prior to the IDA's work in West Africa, no hydroelectric dam had ever been managed with a controlled flood. Since then, the IDA has been asked to help apply the SRMBA model to other parts of the world, including the lower Zambezi River in Mozambique and the Mekong River in Laos, Cambodia, and Vietnam.

Adapted from W. Young, ed., "Kimball Award Winner," Anthropology News 41, no. 8 (2000): 29, with update based on personal communication with IDA, November 2003.

The Anthropologist's World

Sustainable Archaeology: What Is the Future for Our Past?

Neil Ferris and Rhonda Nelson

The primary directive of archaeology is to make interpretations about the past based on the material culture that is recovered from excavation. Have you ever wondered what happens to all those artifacts and raw data after they've been excavated?

In 1975 the Ontario Heritage Act legislated that any alteration or removal of archaeological evidence from its original context would require an individual to hold a licence issued by the Minister of Tourism and Culture. This legislation, in association with initiatives introduced in the 1990s to the Planning Act and the Environmental Assessment Act, motivated a surge in commercial archaeology in Ontario. As this kind of development-motivated archaeology expanded in the decades that followed, so too did the material culture that was collected. Museums and universities, already reaching their storage capacity for archaeological collections derived from excavations conducted throughout the 20th century, had no excess space available to house or keep up with the pace of incoming collections. As licensees under the Ontario Heritage Act were respon-

sible for the curation and stewardship of artifacts and data that resulted from their excavations, collections tended to be stored in disparate locations under a variety of different conditions. Data collection methods were not standardized and varied widely. The result has been a wealth of accumulated archaeological

A reconstructed ceramic cooking vessel from the Dunsmore site (mid-to-late 15th century) located in southern Ontario.

material and knowledge, but a limited capacity for researchers, First Nations communities, and the interested public to access and interpret it.

In 2009 the Canadian Foundation for Innovation and the Ontario Ministry of Research and Innovation awarded

to Dr. Neal Ferris at the University of Western Ontario and Dr. Aubrey Cannon at McMaster University a multimillion-dollar grant to amend this inaccessibility issue in southern Ontario. These partnered institutions are renovating and constructing new space for the curation of archaeological collections and developing innovative, state-of-the-art laboratories for materials analysis. The guiding premise of the project is to facilitate communication and the dissemination of research among researchers and commercial archaeologists, First Nations, and others with an interest in this archaeological record. The artifact repositories will be connected and interoperable via standardized data collection protocols and a shared relational database management system. This will allow digital data of the entire compiled record of thousands of archaeological excavations across Ontario to be instantly accessible anywhere. The ultimate aim is to shift practice toward a sustainable archaeology that constantly reuses existing data and that integrates archaeological and non-archaeological interests in the record. Digital archiving, relational database design, and interoperability are the future of archaeological collections management—and accessible research—in Canada, as we join the ranks of similar initiatives already underway in the Britain, the United States, and Europe.

Private archaeological firms bid on these contracts. These contracts range from the "clearance" of just one field to the clearance of an entire stretch of land intended for a highway or other large project. Thus, salvage archaeological excavations can be vast and prolonged, or tiny and achieved in one afternoon, with a single arrowhead the sole discovery.

The CRM industry employs almost 70 percent of North American archaeologists. Most of the projects undertaken by CRM archaeologists are small-scale clearance or salvage digs. Usually, small parcels of recently ploughed land are "walked," and any surface finds, whether fragments of pottery, tools, or bones, are marked with small flags. If concentrations of artifacts or specific features are revealed, these may require further investigation. If so, test pits may be dug to determine the presence or absence of substantial archaeological material. Should this phase reveal features or artifact spreads indicating substantial archaeological material, the archaeological team may excavate a trench. If there is further evidence, a full scale excavation may be ordered.

The contributions of salvage archaeologists working in the private sphere are many. First, the developers of a specific site receive (usually) clearance to go ahead and undertake their work with the assurance that they will not be destroying a valuable part of the area's heritage. Second, the general public is served, because rare or important archaeological sites are preserved or fully excavated, thus contributing to our knowledge of the past. Third, students often gain valuable experience (which is hard to come by) working as field hands and gaining expertise, as well as employment skills suited to archaeological work. Practical, or salvage, archaeology is therefore an important component of the applied anthropological world.

Other Domains of Applied Anthropology

There is a vast and often bewildering variety of domains in which anthropologists can apply their skills. These domains are too many to adequately address here. There are anthropologists working in pure statistical analysis, in gerontology studies, in land claims involving Aboriginal peoples—the list is almost endless. Note also that there are many areas in which different *types* of anthropologists work together. Many projects employ more than one type of anthropologist at a given time. We examine some of these areas next.

Development Anthropology and Megaprojects

Some applied anthropologists work on megaprojects. These include large undertakings, such as the construction of highways, dams, industrial refineries, or power stations, which can require many applied anthropologists. Usually, such projects require anthropologists from multiple subfields as well as input from other specialists such as geographers, geologists, and sociologists. For instance, the construction of a highway can impact a broad area containing many different cultures, landscapes, rivers, flora, and fauna. Therefore, specialists in all of these areas may be employed to undertake impact assessment studies.

A department of natural resources or a First Nation band council may hire anthropologists to undertake an impact assessment study. In this capacity, anthropological teams may advise on resource use and land management. This may involve expertise in woodlands, watersheds, and the cultural interactions between humans and these resources. Many of the skills required for such a broad knowledge base are taught in cultural ecology, which is the subfield of anthropology that studies interactions between humans and their environments. For the anthropologist, knowledge of past environmental conditions is often helpful in understanding current use of resources, as well as in predicting possible future scenarios. Anthropology is well suited to this form of prediction and analysis, given its focus on areas as diverse as past human adaptive strategies and in-depth understandings of soil morphology. In this way, knowledge about the collapse of the classic Maya or of the annual floods of the Nile in ancient Egypt can actually be of practical modern use. Such was the case some time ago with the Mackenzie Valley Pipeline and with the James Bay Agreement; both these projects stand as testament to the input that anthropologists can have on megaprojects, through their involvement with policy makers and Aboriginal peoples.[29]

Museum Anthropology

One of the oldest types of applied anthropology is museum anthropology. Many anthropology departments (especially in Europe) offer graduate degrees in museum curation (or "museology"). The links between museums and anthropology are many, for a deep knowledge of cultures and their pasts is essential to the museum world. Students enrolled in museology programs are taught the techniques of preserving, displaying, maintaining, and understanding the provenance of ancient and contemporary artifacts. One recent development is worth noting. In British Columbia, Michael Ames, curator of the Museum of Anthropology (MOA) has launched a project to "deschool" museums.[30] This is considered a form of "advocacy anthropology," and involves doing away with the stuffy academic aura associated with museums and offering instead an interactive and participatory approach (see MOA box in Chapter 13).

In summary, some applied anthropological domains are oriented toward a singular skill, such as museum studies or linguistics; others are the domain of multiple anthropologists oriented toward many different types of anthropological expertise. Some applied realms, such as museology and ethnography, have been part of anthropology since the very beginning; others, such as cultural ecology and corporate anthropology, are quite new to anthropology and the applied domain.

THE FUTURE OF APPLIED ANTHROPOLOGY

Many anthropologists—and anthropological texts—discuss the future with a mix of trepidation and excitement. Some are pessimistic about and fearful of the growing homogeneity fostered by increasing globalization. Others argue that cultures have always been "altered," but nevertheless adapt and survive. They see the future with much more enthusiasm, contending that despite increased globalization, people and cultures interpret and use the idioms of the globalizing world in their own distinctive ways. Thus, as we have seen in this text, the way a bottle of pop is perceived in one culture may not be how it is perceived in another. Similarly, that technology is used and "situated" in a particular way in one culture does not necessarily mean it will be so used or situated in another.

The role of the applied anthropologist in the future—in this brave new world of increased technological capacity and instantaneous communication—is destined be an important one and is likely to witness

Anthropologist Marjorie Shostak in the field, Kalahari Desert, Botswana.

much growth. This growth will likely be the result of continued poverty, disasters, and other conditions that require the presence of many different anthropologists, among them environmental specialists, impact assessment teams, and health care workers. Medical anthropologists continue to find work in government-sponsored projects of inoculation and other major health drives. Also, applied anthropologists with expertise in health will continue to participate in large- and small-scale NGO-sponsored projects. The field of development anthropology is also quite likely to witness sustained growth, as major projects such as oilfields, nuclear power plants, highways, and hydroelectric projects are increasingly undertaken in the developed and the developing worlds.

One crucial issue for both academic and applied anthropology is the future of anthropological education. Many argue that there is a need for institutions to tailor anthropological education more toward practical issues. Advocates of practical anthropology point to the often paltry number of courses that are geared specifically toward applied issues. Health is one such example; there is a need for more courses that deal with the medical side of anthropology *and* with the social aspects of health issues. Another area of future expansion in applied anthropology will surely be related to the needs of indigenous peoples around the world. Canada needs more Aboriginal people trained in the methods of applied anthropology, more Aboriginal museum curators and archaeologists, and more courses that relate to cultural sensitivity in Aboriginal health issues. Some progress has been made in this regard, with heritage sites such as Head-Smashed-In Buffalo Jump in Alberta and Wanuskewin Heritage Park in Saskatchewan both being managed by Native Canadians. In this vein, Eldon Yellowhorn, an archaeology professor at Simon Fraser University, has become president of the Canadian Archaeological Association. Overall, it appears that anthropology will undergo a profound shift in the coming decades, with more applied courses and more and more anthropology students entering the professional world, using anthropology's training in a practical manner. Meanwhile, the number of academic anthropologists hired full-time by universities is likely to keep diminishing as anthropology becomes more and more an applied skill.

CONCLUSION

Applied anthropology as a discipline has carved out a place for itself as a relevant, much needed component in public policy, program development, program evaluation, interventions, and a number of other areas critical to the health of the public sphere. Still, in order to establish themselves as an important voice in such issues, anthropologists must compete with professionals from a number of other disciplines. Students of applied anthropology, then, must be keenly cognizant of the shifting functions and possibilities of their field and must be readily able to articulate the many services it has to offer a changing world.[31]

> The student of anthropology has many possible future worlds awaiting her. There exist a vast array of exciting fields in which to work and conduct research. The scale of employment in applied anthropology has both broadened and increased, offering many career chances both inside and outside academe. Graduates with advanced anthropology degrees can enter, and have entered, careers that focus on applying anthropological knowledge. Anthropology students can be found in a variety of industries, ranging from corporate business and marketing to medical organizations, hydro projects, and cultural resource management. Within these areas and many others, anthropologists can make a difference, bringing their analytical and problem-solving skills to bear on issues such as human rights, dispute settlement, and environmental justice.

Our discussion of the history of applied anthropology revealed that it is not a new field of inquiry; it has, in fact, been present in one form or another since the founding days of anthropology. In this chapter we have focused on some of the ways that anthropologists can apply their training to nontraditional fields. We have seen that this path can lead to some rather startling outcomes. An applied anthropologist can take on a major international corporate company, and eventually win. The work of an applied anthropologist can take him to the White House, or take her to the killing fields of the world, working as a forensic anthropologist or archaeologist. Applied anthropology can enrich our understanding of the world's cultural diversity, or warn us of the threatened extinction of peoples, languages, and species. It can also lead to abuses, to the misappropriation and misuse of anthropological data, and to violations of anthropological principles. (These problems also exist in academic anthropology.) Generally, though, applied anthropology offers students a way to learn about cultures and provides them with careers in diverse fields. Applied anthropology offers students and professional anthropologists opportunities to put their specialized learning to good use and to become anthropologists at work.

Chapter Summary

1. What is applied anthropology?
Applied anthropology is the putting into practice, outside of the academic setting, of anthropological skills and resources. Applied anthropology has always been a part of anthropology, but has become much more prevalent over the past few decades. As disease and poverty increase and as more and more major development projects are undertaken (mainly in the developing world) the need for applied anthropologists has grown.

2. How did applied anthropology develop?
The domains of applied anthropology are myriad. Anthropologists of all types are employed in a very diverse set of employment areas. Some of these areas, such as medical anthropology or forensic anthropology, involve the anthropologist in political and social situations that can be contentious. Some areas of applied anthropology draw upon specific skill sets, such as the employment of archaeologists in CRM projects and linguists in translation areas. Other areas require diverse anthropological skills and team work. University courses in anthropology can be linked to a variety of future careers in applied anthropology. All of these areas require a thorough understanding and grounding in the basic theories, terms, and constructs of anthropology.

3. What are some of the challenges facing the applied anthropologist?
Applied anthropologists have been engaged with important social issues during the past few decades. The work of an applied anthropologist can result in conflict with major corporations or with local communities. The decisions that they make and the work that they do can have a profound impact on the peoples and societies in which they work. Whether in teams or as individuals, applied anthropologists can make a difference, and their research and findings can have important ramifications for individuals and groups alike.

4. What does the future hold for applied anthropology?
The future of applied anthropology is rather bright. There is a growing recognition that many large projects and developments do require anthropological expertise. Some have questioned whether this will place stress on the original goals of anthropology; others argue that the world is rapidly changing and that anthropologists, and the institutions that teach anthropology, must adapt to current circumstances and embrace the idea that more and more anthropologists will be employed in the practical realm.

Questions For Critical Thought

1. What are some of the differences between applied and academic anthropology?

2. What are some of the problems that face an applied anthropologist?

3. What will an anthropology student need to focus on to become an applied anthropologist? What career choices are open to students of anthropology?

4. Does the application of anthropological skills to practical areas clash with the historical goals of anthropology?

5. What areas of applied anthropology will likely grow in the near future, and why?

Internet Resources

Society for Applied Anthropology

http://www.sfaa.net

The home page for the Society for Applied Anthropology provides access to publications of the society, meeting reports, and general news on applied anthropology.

COPAA (Consortium of Practicing and Applied Anthropology Programs)

http://www.copaa.info

An American consortium of university departments and programs designed to advance the practice of applied anthropology.

American Anthropological Association

http://www.aaanet.org

Home page of the American Anthropological Association.

Notes

1. B. Malinowski, "Practical Anthropology," *Africa: Journal of the International African Institute* 2, no. 1 (January 1929): 22–38 at 22.

2. H. Schoolcraft and S. Eastman, *Historical and Statistical Information Respecting the History, Condition, and Prospects of the Indian Tribes of the United States* (Philadelphia: Lippincott, Grambo, 1851).

3. Ruth Benedict, *The Chrysanthemum and the Sword: Patterns of Japaense Culture* (New York: Mariner, 1989).

4. G.E. Lowe, "The Camelot Affair," *Bulletin of Atomic Scientists* 22, no. 5 (1966).

5. D. Jenness, "Eskimo Administration II: Canada," Technical Paper no. 14 (Montreal: Arctic Institute of North America, 1964), 58.

6. A.M. Ervin and L. Holyoak, "Applied Anthropology in Canada: Historical Foundations, Contemporary Practice, and Policy Potentials," *NAPA Bulletin* 25, no. 1 (2006): 134–55.

7. E.J. Hedican, *Applied Anthropology in Canada: Understanding Aboriginal Issues* (Toronto: University of Toronto Press, 2008).

8. Canadian Anthropology Society (CASCA), "Prix Weaver-Tremblay Award 2008," *Newsletter* 2, no. 2 (Fall 2008).

9. M. Doretti and J. Burrell, "Gray Spaces and Endless Negotiations: Forensic Anthropology and Human Rights," in *Anthropology Put to Work*, ed. L. Field and R.G. Fox (Oxford: Berg, 2007), 45–64 at 46.

10. O. Beattie and J. Geiger, *Frozen in Time: The Fate of the Franklin Expedition* (London: Bloomsbury Publishing, 1987).

11. O. Beattie and J. Geiger, *Dead Silence: The Greatest Mystery in Arctic Discovery* (Toronto: Penguin, 1993).

12. Kingsolver, "Thinking and Acting Ethically in Anthropology," in *Thinking Anthropologically*, ed. P.K. Salzman and P.C. Rice (Upper Saddle River: Pearson-Prentice Hall, 2008), 68–75.

13. G. Graffam, "Design Anthropology Meets Marketing," *Anthropologica* 52 (2010): 155–64.

14. B. Burkhalter, "If Only They Would Listen: The Anthropology of Business and the Business of Anthropology," in *Classics of Practicing Anthropology, 1978–1998*, ed. P.J. Higgins and J.A. Paredes (Oklahoma City: Society for Applied Anthropology, 2000), 77–86.

15. D. Rohde, "Army Enlists Anthropology in War Zones," *New York Times*, October 5, 2007, http://www.nytimes.com/2007/10/05/world/asia/05afghan.html?_r=2&pagewanted=alL, accessed August 11, 2011.

16. Ibid.

17. P.A. Omidian, "Living and Working in a War Zone: An Applied Anthropologist in Afghanistan," *Practicing Anthropology* 31 (2009): 4–11.

18. http://aaanewsinfo.blogspot.com.

19. A. Chung, "U.S. Army Recruiting Anthropologists," *Toronto Star*, November 25, 2007, http://www.thestar.com/News/article/279646, accessed August 11, 2011.

20. B. Johnson, 2000. "Human Rights and the Environment," in *Classics of Practicing Anthropology, 1978–1998*, ed. P.J. Higgins and J.A. Paredes (Oklahoma City: Society for Applied Anthropology, 2000), 223–30 at 225–26.

21. H. Rosenberg, "From Trash to Treasure," in *Articulating Hidden Histories*, ed. J. Schneider and R. Rapp (Berkeley: University of California Press, 1997), 190–204.

22. L. Gibbs, *Dying from Dioxin: A Citizen's Guide to Reclaiming Our Health and Rebuilding Democracy* (Boston: South End Press, 1995); L.M. Gibbs, *Love Canal: The Story Continues* (Gabriola Island: New Society, 1998).

23. M. Barlow and E. May, *Frederick Street: Life and Death on Canada's Love Canal* (Toronto: HarperCollins, 2000); C. Perkel, *Well of Lies: The Walkerton Water Tragedy* (Toronto: McClelland and Stewart, 2002).

24. P. Block, "Doing Cultural Anthropology and Disability Studies in Rehabilitation Training and Research Contexts," in *Anthropology Put to Work*, ed. L. Field and R.G. Fox (Oxford: Berg, 2007), 85–101 at 87.

25. Ibid.

26. L. Kilmurray and N. Faba, *Access to Academic Materials for Post-Secondary Students with Print Disabilities* (Ottawa: National Educational Association of Disabled Students, 2005), 234.

27. Ibid.

28. C. Renfrew and P. Bahn, *Archaeology: Theories, Methods, and Practice* (London: Thames and Hudson, 1996), 524.

29. N. Dyck and J.B. Waldram, eds., *Anthropology, Public Policy, and Native Peoples in Canada* (Montreal and Kingston: McGill–Queen's University Press, 1993).

30. Ervin and Holyoak, "Applied Anthropology in Canada."

31. S. Keida, "Recent Changes and Trends in the Practice of Applied Anthropology," *NAPA Bulletin* 29 (2008): 14–28 at 26.

15 Cultural Change and the Future of Humanity

Marilyn Angel Wynn/Getty

The ability to change has always been important to human cultures. Probably at no time has the pace of change equalled that of today, as traditional peoples all over the world are pressured to "change their ways" or be "run over" by "progress." But Aboriginal peoples are fighting back and gaining the world's attention. The picture here shows the Saxman Native village totem pole and longhouse, similar to those still used by the Tlingit, Haida, and Tsimshian tribes of British Columbia.

KEY QUESTIONS

1. How Do Cultures Change?

The mechanisms of change are innovation, diffusion, cultural loss, and acculturation. Innovation occurs when someone within a culture discovers something new that is then accepted by other members. Diffusion is the borrowing of something from another group, and cultural loss is the abandonment of an existing practice or trait, with or without replacement. Acculturation is the massive change that comes about with the sort of intensive firsthand contact that has occurred under colonialism.

2. What Is Modernization?

Modernization is an ethnocentric term referring to a global process of change by which traditional, nonindustrial cultures seek to acquire characteristics of industrially "advanced" societies. Although modernization generally has been assumed to be a good thing, and some successes have occurred, it often has led to greater social inequality as well as structural violence. Sometimes it leads to the destruction of cherished customs and values that people had no desire to abandon.

3. What Problems Will Have To Be Solved If Humanity Is to Have a Future?

If humanity is to have a future, human cultures will have to find solutions to problems posed by the increasing global disparity of wealth and power, exhaustion of fossil fuel supplies, pollution and global warming, and a growing culture of discontent. One difficulty is that, up to now, people have tended to see these problems as if they were discrete and unrelated. Thus, attempts to deal with one problem, such as food and fuel shortages, are often at cross-purposes with other problems, such as an inequitable global system for distributing basic resources. Unless humanity gains a more realistic understanding of the "global society" than presently exists, it will not be able to solve the problems whose solutions are crucial for its future.

As we have seen throughout this text, culture is the medium through which the human species solves the problems of existence. Various cultural institutions, such as kinship and marriage, political and economic organization, and religion, interconnect to form an integrated cultural system. Because systems generally work to maintain stability, cultures are often fairly stable and remain so unless either the conditions they are adapted to or human perceptions of those conditions change dramatically. Archaeological studies have revealed how elements of a culture may persist for long periods. In Chapter 5, for example, we saw how the culture of the Aboriginal inhabitants of the Maritimes and southern Quebec remained relatively stable for thousands of years.

Although stability may be a striking feature of many cultures, none are ever changeless, as the cultures of foragers, subsistence farmers, and pastoralists are all too often assumed to be. In a stable culture, change may occur gradually without altering in any fundamental way the culture's underlying logic. Sometimes, though, the pace of change may increase dramatically, causing a radical cultural alteration in a relatively short period. The modern world is full of examples as diverse as the breakup of the Soviet Union and what is currently happening in the Middle East in what has been termed the "Arab Spring." We must recognize that when anthropologists refer to culture change, they are not implying "progress," which is predominantly a nation-state concept, just as they are not suggesting that all change is adaptive. As you will see in this chapter, the so-called modernization of cultural groups has generally caused more problems than it has solved.

MECHANISMS OF CHANGE

Innovation

The early 21st century is a period of rapid and dramatic social, political, and economic change in many parts of the world. The ultimate source of all change is innovation, which can be defined as any new practice, tool, or principle that gains widespread acceptance within a group. Those that involve the chance discovery of a new principle we refer to as **primary innovations** or inven-

primary innovation The chance discovery or invention of a new principle.

secondary innovation Something new that results from the deliberate application of known principles.

tions; those that result from the deliberate applications of known principles are **secondary innovations**. The latter correspond most closely to the West's model of change as predictable and determined; the former involve an accidental discovery of one sort or another.

An example of a primary innovation is the discovery that the firing of clay makes it permanently hard. Presumably, accidental firing of clay occurred often in ancient cooking fires. An accidental discovery is of no account, however, unless someone perceives an application for it. This specific perception first took place about 25,000 years ago, when people began making figurines of fired clay. Pottery vessels were not made, however, nor did the practice of making objects of fired clay reach southwestern Asia until sometime between 7000 and 6500 BC, when people recognized a significant application of fired clay—that being, to make cheap, durable, and easy-to-produce containers and cooking vessels.

A culture's internal dynamics may encourage certain innovative tendencies, but they may also discourage others, and remain neutral with respect to yet others. Darwin's formulation of the principle of natural selection, Copernicus's discovery that the planets revolve around the sun, and Mendel's discovery of the basic laws of heredity are all instances of genuine creative insights out of step with the established needs, values, and goals of their time and place. In fact, Mendel's work remained obscure until 1900, 16 years after his death, when three scientists working independently rediscovered, all in that very same year, the laws of heredity. In the case of Copernicus, new discoveries caused a fury of opposition from forces unwilling to give up cherished beliefs, however erroneous they turned out to be. The implication of Darwin's theory of evolution through natural selection— that humans descended from the great apes—appalled Victorian Britain so greatly that his work was completely derided and denied. Galileo was threatened with torture if he did not renounce his finding that the earth revolved around the sun. History shows us that innovations are often hard won.

Although an innovation must be reasonably consistent with a society's needs, values, and goals if it is to be accepted, this in itself is not enough to assure its acceptance. Force of habit tends to be an obstacle to acceptance; people tend to stick with what they are used to, rather than adopt something new that will require some adjustment on their part. An example of this tendency is the continued use of the QWERTY keyboard (named from the starting arrangement of letters). Devised in 1874, the arrangement minimized jamming of type bars. Combined with other desirable mechanical features, it contributed to the first commercially successful typewriter. Yet the QWERTY keyboard has a number of serious

A Hopi woman firing pottery vessels. The discovery that firing clay vessels makes them indestructible (unless they are dropped or otherwise smashed) probably came about when clay-lined basins next to cooking fires in the Middle East were accidentally fired.

Stephen Trimble

drawbacks. The more typing we do in the "home row" (second from the bottom) of keys, the faster we can type, with the fewest errors and the least strain on the fingers. But with QWERTY, only 32 percent of the strokes are made on the home row, versus 52 percent on the upper row and 16 percent on the (hardest) bottom row. What's more, QWERTY requires overuse of the weaker (left) hand (for the right-handed majority) and the weakest (fifth) finger.

In 1932, after extensive study, August Dvorak developed a keyboard that avoids the defects of QWERTY (see Figure 15.1). Tests consistently show that the Dvorak keyboard can be learned in one-third the time; once

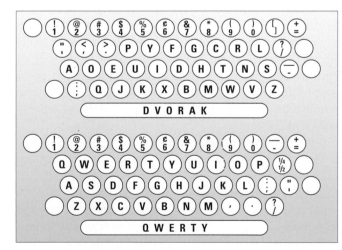

Figure 15.1

Dvorak and QWERTY keyboards, compared. Although superior to the latter in virtually every way, Dvorak has not been adopted owing to the head start enjoyed by QWERTY.

learned, typists increase their accuracy by 68 percent and their speed by 74 percent while experiencing significantly less fatigue. So why hasn't Dvorak replaced QWERTY? The answer is *commitment*. Because QWERTY had a head start, by the time Dvorak came along, manufacturers, typists, teachers, salespeople, and office managers were committed to the old keyboard; it was what they were used to.[1]

Such examples of the force of habit resisting innovation can be contrasted with another aspect of innovation: The functional utility of a technology changes monthly, as seems to be the case with cell phones and handheld electronic devices. Often the slightest of innovations— a different-shaped screen, perhaps—causes a new bout of consumption and further emulation and innovation. This form of innovation can be linked to the notion of planned obsolescence, where version 10.8 of the newest "gizmo" is still being sold even while version 11 is already in production. As the Marxist scholar Theodore Adorno once famously stated, "The people clamour for what they are going to get anyhow."

Diffusion

When the first colonists established permanent settlements in eastern Canada, many died during the harsh winters. Many more would have frozen to death had the nearby First Nations not provided them with warm moccasins and leather clothing and told them how to protect their homes from the fierce winter winds. And the settlers would have starved if the First Nations peoples had

Once our reflexes become adjusted to doing something one way, it becomes difficult to do it differently. Thus, when a North American or European goes to Great Britain, learning to drive on the "wrong" side of the road is difficult.

In the face of the AIDS epidemic sweeping southern Africa, the beliefs of several million Christian Zionists, such as the one being baptized here, are highly adaptive in that they militate against the kinds of sexual practices that spread the disease. That these beliefs are adaptive, however, is a consequence of, rather than a reason for, their origin.

not told them which plants were suitable for food and medicines. The borrowing of cultural elements from one culture by members of another is known as **diffusion**, and the donor group is, for all intents and purposes, the "inventor" of that element. So common is borrowing that the late Ralph Linton, an American anthropologist, suggested that borrowing accounts for as much as 90 percent of any culture's content. People are creative about their borrowing, however, picking and choosing practices, beliefs, and technologies from multiple possibilities and sources and then adapting them to fit pre-existing cultural norms. Usually their selections are limited to those compatible with the existing culture. Returning to our previous example, while the European colonists readily adopted First Nations' material culture to help them survive in a harsh climate, they had no interest in adopting their customs or religious beliefs; just the opposite, in fact—missionaries quickly followed the fur traders and fishermen to the shores of eastern Canada, bent on converting the First Nations to Christianity.

The tendency toward borrowing is so strong that it led Robert Lowie to comment. "Culture is a thing of shreds and patches." Yet these borrowed traits usually undergo sufficient modifications to make this wry comment more colourful than critically accurate. Moreover, existing cultural traits may be modified to accommodate borrowed ones. An awareness of the extent of borrowing can be eye-opening. Take, for example, the numerous things that early European North Americans borrowed from Aboriginal peoples. Domestic plants like tobacco,

diffusion The spread of customs or practices from one culture to another.

potatoes, avocados, beans, squash, tomatoes, peanuts, manioc, chili peppers, chocolate, and sweet potatoes, and especially corn, to name a few, furnish a major portion of the world's food supply. In fact, North American Aboriginal peoples remain the developers of the world's largest array of nutritious foods and the primary contributors to the world's varied cuisine.[2] Among drugs and stimulants, tobacco is the best known, but others include coca (in cocaine), ephedra (in ephedrine), datura (in pain relievers), and cascara (in laxatives). Early on, European physicians recognized that North America's Aboriginal peoples had the world's most sophisticated pharmacy, made from plants native to the Americas. Through diffusion, many of these local plants are now worldwide staples. More than 200 plants and herbs used by Aboriginal people for medicinal purposes have at one time or another been included in the *Pharmacopeia of the United States* or in the *National Formulary*. Varieties of cotton developed by North American Aboriginal peoples supply much of the world's clothing needs, while the woollen poncho, the parka, and moccasins are universally familiar items.

Perhaps the most powerful instruments of diffusion in the contemporary world are the media—television, radio, and print—specifically, the American media. In Canada, efforts to maintain a distinct cultural identity separate from that of the United States have proved incredibly difficult owing to the pervasiveness of American media. Many Canadians listen to American music, watch American television programs, and read American magazines. Protective legislation to limit the influence of American media has done little to slow the diffusion of American culture into Canada, and some fear that

Canadian culture will soon become merely a reflection of that of the United States. A similar situation exists in other parts of the world. Members of cultural groups geographically distant from the United States are constantly exposed to American media, again despite the efforts of their governments to maintain their distinct cultures. Hip-hop music, a product of the black American experience, skillfully marketed (usually by whites), has become a worldwide cultural phenomenon.

Cultural Loss

Most often people tend to think of change as an accumulation of innovations: adding new things to those already in existence. A little reflection, however, leads to the realization that often the acceptance of a new innovation leads to the loss of an older one. This sort of replacement is not just a feature of Western civilization. For example, in biblical times, chariots and carts were in widespread use in the Middle East, but by the sixth century, wheeled vehicles had virtually disappeared from Morocco to Afghanistan. They had been replaced by camels, not because of some reversion to the past by the region's inhabitants but because camels, used as pack animals, worked better. By the sixth century, Rome's roads, like her empire, had deteriorated, but camels, as long as they were not used to pull vehicles, were not bound to roads. The camel's longevity, endurance, and ability to ford rivers and traverse rough ground without people having to build roads in the first place made pack camels admirably suited to the region. Finally, they were labour-saving: a wagon required a man for every two draft animals, whereas a single person could manage from three to six pack camels.

FORCIBLE CHANGE

Innovation, diffusion, and cultural loss all may occur among people who are free to decide what changes they will accept. Not always, however, are people free to make their own choices; often, changes they would not willingly make themselves have been forced on them by some other group, usually in the context of conquest, colonialism, or globalization. In many cases, a direct outcome of this is a phenomenon that anthropologists call acculturation.

Acculturation

Acculturation occurs when groups with different cultural practices come into intensive contact, with subsequent profound changes in the original cultural patterns

DDB Stock Photography

Although the wheel has become a symbol of progress in Western cultures, wheeled transport is not always superior to other forms. Such was the case in pre-Columbian Mexico, where wheels were used on toys but not for transport. The existence of adequate alternatives made wheeled vehicles unnecessary.

of one or both groups. It always involves an element of force, which can be direct or indirect. An important variable is the disparity in wealth and power, who is dominant and who is subordinate. It should be emphasized that acculturation and diffusion are not equivalent terms; one culture can borrow from another without being in the least acculturated.

In the course of acculturation, any one of a number of things may happen. Merger or fusion occurs when two or more cultures shed their separate identities and form a single culture, as expressed by the "melting pot" ideology of Anglo-American culture in the United States, although in reality, despite the rhetoric of the ruling elite, the United States is no more a melting pot than any other Western country. Sometimes, though, one of the cultures loses its autonomy but retains its identity as a subculture in the form of a caste, class, or ethnic group; this is typical of conquest situations. This is certainly evident in Canada, where Aboriginal peoples have endured repeated attempts to assimilate them into Euro-Canadian

acculturation Major cultural changes people are forced to make owing to intensive firsthand contact between societies.

From 1900 to 1960, the Canadian government separated thousands of Aboriginal children from their parents and communities and sent them to be educated under the strict discipline of the residential school system. The violent disruption this policy effected on Aboriginal cultures has been implicated in many of the current problems facing Aboriginal peoples in Canada.

Once a thriving indigenous community, the Yanomami of Brazil have suffered catastrophic decline at the hands of ranchers, miners, and ruthless land developers.

cultures. Canada's history of attempting to assimilate Aboriginal groups is somewhat different from that of the United States—Canada used less violence and relied on more insidious methods, such as placing young children in residential schools in order to Europeanize them, over the protests of their parents. These children were not allowed to speak their traditional languages; they had to dress like Europeans, eat unfamiliar foods, and learn Euro-Canadian ways. As a result, many of the children who went through the residential school system lost their traditional culture, although they never fully accepted or were accepted by Euro-Canadian mainstream society. Despite the efforts of clergy, government officials, and other "well-meaning" citizens, these assimilation plans largely failed; in fact, they did far more harm than good. Many of the social ills plaguing Aboriginal communities today can be traced to the residential school experience that was forced upon a generation. On the plus side, Aboriginal groups still retain their distinctive culture, and significantly, this part of the country's heritage is now celebrated by all Canadians.

Extinction is the phenomenon whereby so many carriers of a culture die that those who survive often become refugees living among other cultures. Examples of this may be seen in many parts of the world today, such as in Brazil's Amazon basin. One particularly well-documented case occurred in 1968, when hired killers employed by ruthless land developers tried to wipe out several Aboriginal groups, including the Cinta-Larga, using arsenic, dynamite, and machine guns from light planes, and even attacking a village when an important religious ceremony was taking place. In northern Brazil, as a conservative estimate, at least 1,500 Yanomami

died in the 1980s, often victims of deliberate massacres, as cattle ranchers and miners poured into their homelands. By 1990, 70 percent of Yanomami lands in Brazil had been unconstitutionally expropriated. At the same time, their fish supplies had been poisoned by mercury contamination of rivers; and malaria, venereal disease, and tuberculosis were running rampant. The Yanomami were dying at an alarming rate of 10 percent per year, and their fertility had dropped to almost zero. Many villages were left without children or old people, and the survivors awaited their fate with a profound terror of extinction.[3]

The prevailing Brazilian attitude of the time is illustrated by the government's reaction when two Kayapó and an anthropologist travelled to the United States, where they spoke with members of several congressional committees, as well as officials of the Department of State, the Treasury, and the World Bank, about the destruction of their land and way of life caused by internationally financed development projects.[4] All three were charged with violating Brazil's Foreign Sedition Act. Fortunately, international expressions of outrage at these and other atrocities have brought positive changes from Brazilian authorities, and a more enlightened government is now in power in Brazil.

In Canada, the deliberate extinction of the Beothuk tells a similar tragic story. For many centuries the Beothuk lived in what is now Newfoundland. Along with the Mi'kmaq, they were probably the first inhabitants to meet European explorers and fishermen, for the bountiful cod fishing grounds were in Beothuk territory. Despite early friendly relations, an unfortunate incident, in which a fishing boat fired on a group of Beothuk, caused them to distrust the Europeans. As 18th-century European settlements grew more numerous, they pushed the Beothuk

As recent examples like the Rwandan tragedy demonstrate, genocide continues to occur in the world today, claiming more lives than war.

from their traditional lands. The Beothuk fought back, raiding settlers' fishnets for food, but this only made the settlers more determined to eliminate the Beothuk. Oral tradition in Newfoundland recounts a time in 1800 when several hundred Beothuk were driven out to their favourite sealing site and shot down like animals.[5] A reduction in their food supplies, coupled with diseases like tuberculosis, eventually decimated the Beothuk. The last survivors of the Beothuk were two women, Demasduwit and Shananditti, who lived with kindly settlers for the last years of their lives. We owe much of our knowledge about the Beothuk to their accounts. Shananditti, the last of the Beothuk people, died of consumption in 1829.[6]

Genocide

The Yanomami and Beothuk cases raise the issue of **genocide**—the extermination of one group of people by another.

The most widely known act of genocide in recent history was Nazi Germany's attempt to wipe out European Jews and Roma (gypsies) in the name of racial superiority. Unfortunately, the common practice of referring to this as *"the* Holocaust"—as if it were something unique or at least exceptional—tends to blind us to the fact that this thoroughly monstrous act was simply one more example of an all too common phenomenon. Between 1945 and 1987, a minimum of 6.8 million, but perhaps as many as 16.3 million, people were victims of internal (within-state) genocide, compared to the 3.34 million people who died in wars between countries from 1945 to 1980.[7] Sadly, genocide continues to occur today in places such as Iraq, where in 1988 the government began to use poison gas against Kurdish villagers. From 1992 to 1995, ethnic cleansing—mainly by Serb extremists, but also by

Croatians and by Albanian terrorists in Kosovo—resulted in 200,000 deaths in the wars following the breakup of Yugoslavia. In 1994, 500,000 to 800,000 Tutsis were hacked to death by Hutus in Rwanda.[8] More recently, in the Darfur region of Sudan, up to 300,000 people may have been the victims of genocide.[9] If such ugly practices are ever to be ended, we must gain a better understanding of them than currently exists. Anthropologists are actively engaged in pursuit of this knowledge, carrying out cross-cultural as well as individual case studies. One finding to emerge is the regularity with which religious, economic, and political interests are allied in cases of genocide and forcible culture change.

One example (out of many) of attempted genocide in the 20th century: Hitler's Germany against Jews and Roma (gypsies) during the 1930s and the 1940s.

A common agent of change in many nonindustrial societies is the religious missionary. Although these people see themselves as bringing enlightenment to indigenous peoples, many such missionaries seek to subvert the beliefs that lie at the heart of such cultures and that make life within them meaningful. In this picture we see a Sunday morning service at the grass hut church in the village of Mombala (Mambala) in Malawi, Africa.

genocide The extermination of one people by another, often in the name of "progress," either as a deliberate act or as the accidental outcome of one people's activities done with little regard for their impact on others.

Revitalization Movements

Revitalization is a common reaction to forcible change. It is a process touched on in Chapter 12. Revitalization may be viewed as a deliberate attempt by some members of a society to construct a more satisfactory culture by rapidly accepting multiple innovations but then shaping them according to their own world view. Once primary ties of culture, social relationships, and activities are broken and meaningless activity is imposed by force, individuals and groups characteristically react in ways that strike observers as fantasy, withdrawal, and escape.

REBELLION AND REVOLUTION

When the scale of discontent within a society reaches a certain level, the possibilities are high for rebellion and **revolution**, the toppling of a government by force. A clear and recent example is the regime changes and conflicts that have been part of the Arab Spring.

Questions such as why revolutions erupt and why they often fail to live up to the expectations of the people who launched them are problematic. It is clear, however, that the colonial policies of countries such as England, France, Spain, Portugal, and the United States during the 19th and 20th centuries have created

revolution The overthrow of a government by force.

a worldwide situation in which revolution is nearly inevitable. Despite the political independence that most colonies have achieved since the Second World War, more powerful countries—or in many cases, large corporations—continue to exploit them for their natural resources and cheap labour. This has led to deep resentment of rulers who are beholden to foreign powers and of the poverty and inequality that persist. Further discontent has been generated by the governing elites of newly independent states, when they attempt to assert their control over fellow citizens of sharply different ethnicities or religious beliefs. Thus, in many former colonies such as Algeria and Libya, people have taken up arms to resist annexation and absorption by imposed state regimes run by people regarded as outsiders. In their efforts to turn their states into nations, the governing elites of one nationality endeavour to strip the peoples of other nations within their states of their lands, resources, and sense of identity as a people. The phenomenon is so common as to lead anthropologist Pierre Van Den Berghe to label what modern states refer to as "nation building" as, in fact, "nation killing."[10] One of the most important facts of our time is that the vast majority of the distinct peoples of the world have never consented to be ruled by the governments of the states they find themselves living within.[11] Instead, they find themselves living within artificially constructed borders that often cut them off from fellow distinct peoples and sometimes force them to live within the boundaries of historic enemies. In many newly emerged countries, such groups feel they have no other option than to fight.

A leading cause of rebellion and revolution in the world today is the refusal of governing elites to recognize the cultural, economic, and political rights of people of other nationalities over whom the state has unilaterally asserted its authority. The Zapatista uprising in the state of Chiapas, Mexico, recently observed the 13th anniversary of its struggle.

Gender Perspectives

Reproductive Rights in Canada

Culture change often grows out of conflict and in contemporary democracies may be addressed by grassroots social movements. One of the most contentious issues in Canadian society has been the question of a woman's right to terminate a pregnancy. Access to safe, legal abortion has been the subject of continuous debate and has even led to violence. In the 1950s and 1960s, termination of pregnancy was extremely difficult to obtain. A woman had to go before a hospital committee, which had the discretion to determine whether the procedure would be performed under a narrow range of circumstances, such as the pregnancy being a threat to the life of the pregnant woman. The alternative, if a woman was desperate enough, was to seek an illegal "back-street" abortion, which often resulted in serious complications and compromised health for the woman.

With the rise of the feminist movement in the 1960s, and the publication of such important works as *Our Bodies Ourselves* by the Boston Women's Health Collective (3rd ed., 1998), women grew determined to "take control of their own bodies." Active political engagement on the issue of abortion, by such groups as the Canadian Abortion Rights Action League (CARAL), led to campaigns for clinics to provide safe abortions. Several of these opened in various provinces in the 1970s, the most famous of which were Dr. Henry Morgentaler's clinics. Opposition was vigorous; often led by religious organizations, many anti-abortion groups sprang up and began daily pickets in front of abortion clinics, so that people entering and leaving had to run a gauntlet of abuse. The anti-abortion forces recruited many people whose sincerity and integrity were not in doubt, but it also drew extremists who expressed their views by fire-bombing clinics and even assassinating doctors who performed abortions. These violent acts helped turn public opinion toward sympathy for the cause of abortion advocates. Polls in the 1970s and 1980s consistently showed that a strong majority of Canadians supported a woman's "right to choose." After years of court battles, which ended in Dr. Morgentaler's favour, the laws regarding abortion finally were repealed by Parliament. Women in Canada today have largely won the right to abortion on demand, although the circumstances do vary from province to province.

SOURCE: With permission of Canadian Abortion Rights Action League (CARAL).

The 1950s Algerian struggle for independence from France and the long struggle of the Vietnamese people, first against French colonialism and then against the United States (1945–1975), are typical examples. Of the 120 or so armed conflicts in the world today, 98 percent are in the economically poor countries of Africa, Asia, and Central and South America, almost all of which were at one time under European colonial domination. Of these wars, 75 percent are between the state and one or more cultures within the state's borders that are seeking to maintain or regain control of their persons, communities, lands, and resources in the face of what they regard as subjugation by a foreign power.[12]

Revolutions do not always succeed in accomplishing what they set out to do. Vladimir Lenin, for example, proposed far-reaching reforms to the social status of women in postrevolutionary Russia, only to see these repealed by Joseph Stalin. One of the stated goals of the Chinese Revolution was to liberate women from the oppression of a strongly patriarchal society where a woman owed lifelong obedience to some man or another—first her father, later her husband, and, after his death, her sons. Although some progress has been made, the effort overall has been frustrated by an entrenched tradition of extreme patriarchy extending back at least 22 centuries. With China's rapid industrialization after the death of Mao Zedong in 1975, more women began to work outside the house, but this is generally at jobs with low pay, low status, and no benefits. Indeed, the 1990s saw a major outbreak of the abduction and sale of women from rural areas as brides and workers. Women's no-wage domestic labour or low-wage labour outside the household has been essential to China's economic expansion, which relies on the allocation of labour by the heads of patrilineal households.[13] Whatever autonomy women may achieve for a while, they become totally dependent in their old age on their sons. This situation shows that the subversion of revolutionary goals, if it occurs, is not necessarily by political opponents. Rather, it may be a consequence of the revolutionaries' own cultural background.

Revolution is a relatively recent phenomenon, one that has occurred only during the past 5,000 years or so. Political rebellion requires a centralized political authority (chiefdom or state) to rebel against, and states (if not chiefdoms) have existed for only 5,000 years. In societies typified by tribes and bands and in nonindustrial societies lacking central authority, rebellion or political revolution could not have occurred.

MODERNIZATION

A common term for describing social and cultural changes as they are occurring today is **modernization**. This is often defined as an all-encompassing global process of cultural and socioeconomic change, whereby developing countries seek to acquire some of the characteristics common to industrial countries. Looking closely at this definitions reveals that "becoming modern" really means "becoming like us" ("us" being Canada and other industrial, capitalist societies), with the clear implication that to be not like us is to be antiquated and obsolete.

Theorists who do employ the term see modernization as consisting of four subprocesses. *Technological development* involves the replacement of traditional knowledge and techniques with the application of scientific knowledge. With *agricultural development* comes a shift from subsistence farming to commercial farming, raising cash crops for sale rather than for home consumption, with greater reliance on markets for selling farm products and purchasing goods. *Industrialization* entails machine production driven by fossil fuels replacing hand production in the home. Finally, *urbanization* is marked by population movements from rural settlements into cities, evidenced by the fact that in 2009, 51 percent of humans lived in urban settings. Although these four subprocesses are interrelated, they follow no fixed order of appearance.

Modernization brings other changes to the political realm. Political parties and some form of electoral machinery often appear, in tandem with the development of a bureaucracy. In education, the school system expands (at least for those who can afford it), literacy increases, and an indigenous educated elite develops. Religion may become less important as traditional beliefs

Whereas most items for daily use were once made at home, almost everything we use today is the product of specialized production—for example, the milk we buy in the food store.

and practices are undermined, although many countries, especially in the Islamic world, are attempting to combine modernization with intensified religion, with mixed results. A key impact is on the traditional rights and duties connected with kinship. The strength of the extended family may be weakened as more individualistic, market-driven forces foster the nuclear family form. Finally, where stratification is a factor, mobility increases as who you are (ascribed status) becomes less important than what you become (achieved status).

Two further features of modernization are linked with those already noted. The first, **structural differentiation**, is the division of single traditional roles, which embrace two or more functions (such as political, economic, and religious functions), into two or more separate roles, each with a single specialized function. This represents a kind of fragmentation of society, which must be counteracted by new **integrative mechanisms** if the society is not to disintegrate into a number of discrete units. These new mechanisms take such forms as formal governmental structures, official state ideologies, political parties, legal codes, and labour and trade unions as well as other common-interest associations. All of these crosscut other societal divisions and thus serve to develop what political scientists have come to call *civil society*, an important concept developed particularly in the well-known theories of Italian Marxist Antonio Gramsci (1890–1937). As noted in Chapter 11, Gramsci also developed the concept of **hegemony**, in referring to the ability of ruling elites to present their class interests in such terms that members of other classes accept their world view as so many self-evident truths. Examples include the American view that anyone can grow up to be president or become wealthy, or the Soviet view that only Communism would lead to contentment for the

modernization The process of cultural and socioeconomic change, whereby developing societies acquire some of the characteristics of Western industrialized societies.

hegemony Authority or control; control or dominating influence by one person or group, especially by one political group, over society or by one nation over others.

structural differentiation The division of single traditional roles, which embrace two or more functions (e.g., political, economic, and religious), into two or more roles, each with a single specialized function.

integrative mechanisms Cultural mechanisms that oppose a society's differentiation forces; in modernizing societies, they include formal governmental structures, official state ideologies, political parties, legal codes, and labour and trade unions and other common-interest associations.

masses. Hegemony was purveyed through institutions like the educational system and the media to provide the integrative mechanism, or ideological glue, binding highly differentiated societies.

An examination of two traditional cultures that have felt the impact of modernization will help pinpoint some of the problems such cultures have faced. The cultures are the Skolt Lapps, a division of the Saami people whose homeland straddles the Arctic Circle in Norway, Sweden, Finland, and Russia, and the Shuar of Ecuador.

Skolt Lapps and the Snowmobile Revolution

The Skolt Lapps, whose homeland is in northern Finland, traditionally supported themselves by fishing and herding reindeer.[14] Although they depended on the outside world for certain material goods, the resources crucial for their system were found locally. No one was denied access to critical resources, and little social and economic differentiation existed among the people. Theirs was basically an egalitarian culture.

Of particular importance to the Skolt Lapps was reindeer herding. Indeed, herd management is central to their definition of themselves as a people. These animals were a source of meat for home consumption or for sale to procure outside goods. They were also a source of hides for shoes and clothing, sinews for sewing, and antlers and bones for making certain objects. Finally, reindeer were used to pull sleds in the winter and as pack animals when no snow was on the ground. Understandably, the animals were the objects of much attention. The herds were not large, and without a great deal of attention, productivity suffered. Hence, most winter activities centred on reindeer.

In the early 1960s these reindeer herders speedily adopted snowmobiles (a Canadian invention) on the premise that the new machines would make herding physically easier and economically more advantageous. As early as 1967, most people had gotten rid of draft animals, and only four families were still using reindeer sleds for winter travel. Those who had not converted to snowmobiles felt disadvantaged compared with the rest.

The consequences of this mechanization were extraordinary and in part unexpected. The high cost of snowmobiles, spare parts, and fuel created a dependency on the outside world unlike anything that had previously existed. As snowmobile technology replaced traditional skills, the ability of the Lapps to determine their own survival without dependence on outsiders was lost. Accordingly, a sharp rise in the need for cash occurred. To get this, men had to regularly leave the Lapp community for wage work, or else rely on government pensions and welfare.

Was the resulting dependency on cash and outside help a price worth paying? In truth, snowmobiles made reindeer herding worse, not better. By 1971, average herd size had declined from 50 to 12, a number too small to be economically viable. The old close, prolonged, and largely peaceful relationship between herdsman and beast has changed to a noisy, traumatic relationship. Now, when men appear, they come speeding out of the woods on snarling, smelly machines that invariably chase the animals, often for long distances. Instead of aiding the reindeer in their winter food quest, helping females with their calves, and protecting them from predators, men appear either to slaughter or castrate them. Naturally enough, the reindeer have become suspicious. The result has been actual de-domestication, with reindeer scattering and running off to more inaccessible areas, given the slightest chance. Moreover, there are indications that snowmobile harassment has adversely affected reindeer birth rates. This is a classic illustration of the fact that change is not always adaptive.

This is more than just an economic problem, for in the traditional culture of this people, being a herder of reindeer is the very essence of manhood. Hence, today's nonherders not only are poor in a way they could not have been in previous times, but also are in a sense inadequate as "men." Another consequence has been the development of a stratified society out of the older egalitarian one. Reindeer herding now has much higher start-up costs and requires skills and knowledge that were not a part of traditional culture. Those who lack the cash and skills are dependent on others if they are to participate. Once again, it falls to anthropologists to document and try to explain the demise of traditional practices.

Paul A. Souders/Corbis Canada

A Saami man slaughtering his reindeer for their meat and hides.

The Shuar Solution

Although the Skolt Lapps have not escaped many negative aspects of modernization, the choice to modernize was essentially theirs. The Shuar (sometimes called Jivaro), by contrast, deliberately avoided modernization until they felt they had no other option if they were to fend off the same outside forces that elsewhere in the Amazon basin have destroyed whole societies. Threatened with the loss of their land base as more and more Ecuadorian colonists intruded on their territory, the Shuar in 1964 founded a fully independent corporate body, the Shuar Federation, to take control of their own future. Recognized by Ecuador's government, albeit grudgingly, the federation is officially dedicated to promoting the social, economic, and moral advancement of its members and to coordinating development with official governmental agencies.

Since its founding, the federation has secured title to more than 96,000 hectares of communal land; has established a cattle herd of more than 15,000 head as the people's primary source of income; has taken control of their education, using their language and mostly Shuar teachers; and has established their own bilingual broadcasting station and a bilingual newspaper. Obviously, all of this has required enormous changes by the Shuar, but they have been able to maintain a variety of distinctive cultural markers, including their language, communal land tenure, cooperative production and distribution, a basically egalitarian economy, and kin-based communities that retain maximum autonomy. Thus, for all the changes, they feel they are still Shuar and quite distinct from other Ecuadorians.[15]

The Shuar case shows that Amazonian nations are capable of taking control of their own destinies even in the face of intense outside pressure, if allowed to do so. Unfortunately, until recently, few have had that option. Prior to European invasions of the Amazon, more than 700 distinct groups inhabited the region. By 1900 in Brazil, the number was down to 270, and today approximately 180 remain.[16] Many of these survivors find themselves in situations not unlike that of the Yanomami, described earlier in this chapter. Nevertheless, many of these peoples are showing a new resourcefulness in standing up to the forces of destruction arrayed against them.

Modernization and the Developing World

In the previous examples, we have seen how modernization has affected indigenous peoples in otherwise "modern" states. Elsewhere in the developing world, whole countries are in the throes of modernization. Throughout Africa, Asia, and South and Central America we are witnessing the widespread removal of economic activities—or at least their control—from the family/community setting. Changes from an economy based on the family to one based on surplus and export include these: the altered structure of the family in the face of the changing labour market; the increased reliance of young children on parents alone for affection, instead of on the extended family; the decline of general parental authority; schools replacing the family as the primary educational unit; and the generation gap. The difficulty is that all of this is thrust upon traditional societies so quickly that they cannot adapt gradually. Changes that took generations to accomplish in Europe and North America are attempted within the span of a single generation in developing countries. In the process, the people affected often face the erosion of a number of dearly held values they had no intention of giving up.

Commonly, the burden of modernization falls most heavily on women. For example, the mechanization and commercialization of agriculture often involves land reforms that overlook or ignore women's traditional land rights, reducing their control of and access to resources. As a consequence, they are confined more and more to traditional domestic tasks, which, as cash cropping becomes people's dominant concern, are increasingly downgraded in value. To top it all off, the domestic workload tends to increase, because men are less available to help out, while tasks such as fuel gathering and water collection are made more difficult as common land and resources become privately owned and as woodlands are reserved for commercial exploitation. In short, with modernization, women often find themselves in an increasingly marginal position. While their workload increases, the value assigned to the work they do declines, as does their relative and absolute health and their nutritional and educational status.

Modernization: Must It Always Be Painful?

Although most anthropologists view the changes affecting traditional non-Western peoples critically, the more widespread public opinion has been that it has been beneficial—however disagreeable the "medicine" may be, it is worth it for the people to become just like "us" (i.e., the people of Europe and North America). This view of modernization, unfortunately, is based more on Western hopes and expectations than on reality. It is based more on a national economic balance of payments than on any consideration of specific peoples. No doubt, Western peoples would like to see the non-Western world attain the "high" levels of development seen in Europe and North America, as many Japanese, South Koreans, Taiwanese, and other Asians, in fact, have done since the end of the Second World War. Overlooked is the stark fact that the standard of living in

An urban slum near Juarez, Mexico. All over the world, people are fleeing to the cities for a "better life," only to experience disease and poverty in such slums.

Paul Conklin/PhotoEdit

the Western world is based on a rate of consumption of non-renewable resources, in which the wealthiest 20 percent of the world's population, mostly Westerners, consumes 80 percent of the goods and services produced.[17] Can most of the world's peoples realistically achieve such a standard of living without seriously compromising what is left of the planet's resources and environment? Perhaps yes, but if, and only if, the countries of the West drastically reduce their own overconsumption of resources. So far, they have shown no willingness to do this; in fact, they are moving in the opposite direction, despite assertions to the contrary. More non-Western people than ever, quite understandably, aspire to the standard of living that Western countries now enjoy, even though the gap between the rich and the poor people of the world is widening rather than narrowing. No longer satisfied with traditional values, people all over the world are migrating to the cities to find a "better life," all too often to live out their days in poor, congested, and disease-infested slums in an attempt to achieve what is usually beyond their reach. Unfortunately, despite all sorts of rosy predictions about a better future, the basic reality of poverty and loss of culture remains.

THE CULTURAL FUTURE OF HUMANITY

Whatever the biological future of the human species may be, culture remains the mechanism by which people solve the challenges of daily existence. Many anthropologists have noted with concern that the problems of human existence seem to be spinning out of control, outstripping

any culture's ability to find solutions to maintaining social and environmental harmony. To paraphrase anthropologist Jules Henry, although cultures are "for" people, they are also "against" them.[18] This dilemma is posing serious new problems for human beings. What can anthropologists tell us about the future of cultures?

One of the major problems with the enormous body of future-oriented literature that claims to address the many problems facing humanity is that it views the present social order in the developed world as the best of all worlds. The goal of development, then, becomes transferring all the "benefits" of modernity uncritically to the rest of the planet. The danger inherent in this tendency is neatly captured in anthropologist George Cowgill's comment: "It is worth recalling the story of the person who leaped from a very tall building and on being asked how things were going as he passed the 20th floor replied 'Fine, so far.'"[19] Another issue is a tendency to overlook local cultural and environmental contexts such as creating farms in areas that do not receive sufficient rainfall or where local customs do not accept a cash-based economy.

Against this background, anthropology's contribution to our view of the future is clear. With their holistic perspective, anthropologists are specialists at seeing how parts fit together into a larger whole. With their evolutionary perspective, they can see short-term trends in longer-term perspective. With more than 100 years of cross-cultural research behind them, anthropologists can recognize culture-bound assertions when they encounter them, and they are familiar with alternative ways to deal with a wide variety of problems.

One-World Culture?

In a famous treatise, *Jihad vs. McWorld* (1995),[20] social analyst Benjamin Barber contrasts the social, political, and economic forces pushing toward the development of a homogeneous world culture with the persistent and powerful regional social forces that resist the idea of homogenization. The idea that a "one-world culture" is emerging is based largely on the observation that developments in communication, transportation, and trade so closely link the peoples of the world that they are increasingly wearing the same kinds of clothes, eating the same kinds of food, reading the same kinds of newspapers, watching the same kinds of television programs, and communicating directly with one another via the Internet. The continuation of such trends, so this thinking goes, should lead North Americans who travel in the year 2100 to Patagonia, Mongolia, or New Guinea to find the inhabitants living in a manner identical or similar to them. But is this so, and would it be a good thing?

Certainly striking is the extent to which such items as Western-style clothing, iPods, Coca-Cola, and McDonald's hamburgers have spread to virtually all parts of the world. Indeed, many countries—Japan, for example—have moved a long way toward becoming "Westernized," outstripping the West in many aspects of modernity. Moreover, looking back over the past 5,000 years of human history, we can see a clear trend for political units to become larger and more all-encompassing while becoming fewer in number. Sociologist Charles Tilley has noted that in the year 1500, there were some 500 sovereign jurisdictions on the continent of Europe.[21] With the rise of the modern nation-state, by 1900 this number had been consolidated into fewer than 30. This trend continues with the formation of the European Union and the adoption of a common currency, the euro, by most member countries.

Could all world cultures merge into a single world political entity? One problem with such a prediction is that it ignores the one thing that all large states, past and present, irrespective of other differences between them, share: a tendency (eventually) to come apart. Not only have the great empires of the past, without exception, broken up into smaller independent states, but countries in virtually all parts of the world today are showing a tendency to fragment. The most dramatic illustrations of this in recent years have been the breakup of the Soviet Union into a dozen smaller independent states and the fragmentation of Yugoslavia into five battered but independent republics. It also can be seen in Basque and Catalonian nationalism in Europe; Scottish, Irish, and Welsh nationalism in Britain; Tibetan nationalism in China; Kurdish nationalism in Turkey, Iran, and Iraq; Sikh separatism in India; Tamil separatism in Sri Lanka;

Eritrean and Tigrean secession movements in Ethiopia; Puerto Rican nationalism in the United States; and so on—this list is far from exhaustive. Nor is Canada immune, as can be seen in First Nations' accelerating attempts to secure greater political and cultural self-determination, and in French-speaking Quebec's separatist movement. Canada has survived two Quebec sovereignty votes, one in 1980 and one more recently in 1995.

Many struggles for independence have been going on for years, such as the Karen resistance to the Burmese invasion of their territory in 1948; the takeover of Kurdistan by Iraq, Iran, and Turkey in 1925; and the numerous Russian takeovers of Chechnya. Even in relatively nonviolent cases, the stresses and strains are obviously there. In Canada, with its massive geographical size and regional differences, there is a perceived east–west schism, in particular a western sense of alienation from the federal government, which is located in eastern Canada. Similar stresses and strains may develop even in the absence of ethnic differences when regional interests within a large country increasingly compete.

Nunavut

On a more positive note, in 1993 the eastern half of the Canadian Northwest Territories separated to create the autonomous territory of Nunavut. Nunavut means "our land" in Inuktitut, the language of Inuit peoples. Of the 25,000 people who inhabit the 1.9 million square kilometres of eastern Arctic land, 85 percent are Inuit. The Nunavut Land Claims Agreement and the Nunavut Act, which created the territory, were signed in 1993. The agreement represents the largest Aboriginal land claims settlement in Canadian history and marks the beginning of new relations between Aboriginal Canadians and the rest of Canada.[22]

On April 1, 1999, the Canadian government handed over political control of Nunavut to the Nunavut Tungavik. Key features of this agreement include title to 350,000 square kilometres, including 35,000 square kilometres with mineral rights; equal Inuit representation on wildlife, resource, and environmental management boards; the right to harvest wildlife on lands and waters throughout the Nunavut settlement area; a share of federal government royalties from oil, gas, and mineral development on Crown lands; the right to negotiate with industry for economic and social benefits from nonrenewable resource development; the right to refuse sport or commercial development; and the right to establish self-government for the Nunavut Inuit.[23]

Nunavut is governed by a territorial assembly consisting of 19 elected representatives, who may or may not be Inuit. In fact, the Inuit are not constitutionally guaranteed control of the assembly. The government is

The Anthropologist's World

Aboriginal Rights in Canada

Edward J. Hedican

Edward J. Hedican is a social anthropologist with graduate degrees from McMaster Univerity (MA) and McGill University (PhD). His long-term ethnographic interests have been with Canadian Aboriginal peoples, especially concerning the Ojibwa or Anishenabe peoples living north of Lake Superior.

The discipline of anthropology has had a long history of involvement in Aboriginal issues in Canada. In 1884, a special committee of the British Association for the Advancement of Science was appointed to investigate the desperate plight of British Columbia's Aboriginal peoples. The committee secured the services of Franz Boas four years later and, with the aid of the new Ethnographic Bureau of Canada, laid the foundation for Boas's work on the Kwakwaka'wakw (Kwakiutl) (1897) and Bella Coola (1898). Much of Boas's scholarly reputation and the subsequent professionalization of anthropology in North America can be attributed to his Northwest Coast ethnographic work.

The National Museum in Ottawa subsequently served as the focus for the development of anthropology in Canada. Diamond Jenness, who earned an international reputation for his ethnographic studies of the Maori in New Zealand and the northern Inuit, Carrier, and Salish, was appointed its director in 1926.

Jenness's fieldwork helped him understand the problems of Aboriginal peoples. He and his staff at the museum became early advocates for Aboriginal rights, and were especially critical of government practices that denied Aboriginal peoples consultation on policy issues. Anthropologists played an even greater role in policy initiatives during the mid-1960s. British Columbia anthropologist Harry Hawthorn and his colleagues stated that "Indians should be regarded as 'Citizens Plus'"—that is, Aboriginal people should be regarded as equal citizens and enjoy the rights attached to their special status as founding First Nations.

The 1970s were dominated by resource and northern development issues such as the James Bay hydroelectric project in Quebec and the Mackenzie Valley Pipeline Inquiry in the Northwest Territories. Anthropologists played key roles in both these initiatives. In this context, the James Bay Agreement of 1975 can be seen as a laboratory for applied anthropology and its effectiveness in bringing forth the results of basic research in a legal context.

Over the following decades, new organizations emerged. The Society for Applied Anthropology in Canada (SAAC, founded in 1981) and the Canadian Association for Medical Anthropology (CAMA, founded in 1982) emphasized the practical aspects of anthropological research. These associations—now largely merged under the umbrella of the Canadian Anthropology Society/ Société canadienne d'anthropologie

(CASCA)—introduced a new generation of applied anthropologists to expanded research opportunities in such areas as mental health, cross-cultural studies in education, and gender issues.

One of the most significant of these research endeavours has involved a long-term study of diabetes among Aboriginal peoples in the Northwest Territories, headed by biological anthropologist Emoke Szathmary, currently the president of the University of Manitoba. The focus here is on the health consequences for Aboriginal peoples of resource development that destroys the forests on which they depend for their hunting and fishing livelihoods.

Today, anthropologists are forging ahead into an uncharted future. Research has begun on such topics as AIDS, genetically modified foods, and same-sex identity issues. In the 21st century, it is time for anthropologists to critically review their research as it pertains to Aboriginal issues in Canada. This review should be more than just a summary of specific field reports and journal articles. It should draw upon the commonalities of the anthropological experience, thereby clarifying common goals and achievements while identifying areas where new research is needed. Anthropologists should also seek greater Aboriginal involvement in defining the objectives and directions of applied research. A move in this direction would encourage continued growth in the applied sector of anthropology and demonstrate further anthropology's continued vitality and adaptability in the modern world.

made up of specialized departments—for example, the Department of Sustainable Development, which oversees the important issue of wildlife harvesting.[24] Of equal importance is the Department of Culture, Language, Elders, and Youth, which has been given the task of promoting cultural survival, including encouraging the use of Inuktitut in the workplace.

The creation of Nunavut came about from splintering the Northwest Territories, but rather than the fragmentation of a political entity, it heralded the beginning of self-determination and self-government for Aboriginal

peoples in Canada and may provide a model for future self-determination endeavours around the world.

The Rise of the Multinational Corporations

The Cold War between the Western nations, led by the United States, and the Soviet Bloc, led by Russia, extended from the end of the Second World War in 1945 to 1990. It ended with the dismantling of the Soviet Union, but while the Cold War continued, the bipolar world lent a degree of stability to international relations. Each superpower was constrained in its imperial designs by the presence of the other. In today's world, with only one remaining superpower—the United States (though China is quickly "catching up")—these restraints have been removed. The United States' claims to global hegemony, as illustrated by its recent invasion and occupation of Iraq and its presence in Afghanistan, put it at odds with many of its closest allies, including France, Germany, and a large segment of the Canadian public. What are some of the forces driving this unilateralism, and what can it tell us about the future of humanity?

The world's resistance to political integration seems to be offset, at least in part, by the rise of multinational corporations. These giant enterprises, many larger in scale than most of the UN's member-nations, are the subject of intense debate. Because the reach of corporations extends across state boundaries, some see them as a force for global unity despite the political differences that divide people. Others argue that their power and reach—including the ability to set international trade agendas—and the domination of international agencies such as the World Bank and the International Monetary Fund are the major obstacles to real grassroots democracy and bottom-up development for poorer nations.[25]

Multinational corporations are not new (the Hudson's Bay Company in Canada was chartered in 1670), but they were not common until the 1950s. Since then they have become a major force in the world. In a sense they are products of the technological revolution, for without sophisticated data-processing equipment, the multinationals could not keep adequate track of their worldwide operations. Though typically thought of as responding impersonally to outside market forces, large corporations are in fact controlled by powerful economic elites who benefit directly from their operations. Yet the world's largest individual stockholders and most powerful directors, unlike political leaders, are unelected and are known to few people. For that matter, most people cannot even name the five largest multinational corporations.[26]

The power of corporations extends far beyond governments and members of a society. Their control of television and other media, not to mention the advertising industry, gives them enormous power over the lives of millions of "ordinary" people in ways they little suspect. Canadian author and social critic Naomi Klein has documented this influence in her groundbreaking books *No Logo* and *The Shock Doctrine*, which address the history of the rise of the corporate culture of "branding" and the all-important marketing of images and products to consumers, especially youth.[27]

Peter Arnold, Inc.

Brazil's Grand Carajas iron ore mine is an example of the kind of project that states favour in their drive to develop. Not only does this introduce ecologically unsound technologies, but it also commonly has devastating effects on the people whose land is seized.

If one end of the corporate branding culture is in the suburban malls of the developed world, the other end of a product's journey lies in the sweatshops of Asia and Latin America. In their never-ending search for cheap labour, multinational corporations more than ever have come to favour women for low-skilled assembly jobs. With the mechanization of agriculture women are less able to contribute to their families' farming. This places pressure on them to seek jobs outside the household to contribute to its support. Without education or job skills, these women find that only low-paying jobs are open to them. Corporate officials, for their part, favour young and single female workers who can be paid low wages and laid off when they marry, and this has contributed to the emergence of a gender-segregated labour force. Higher paying jobs, or at least those that require special skills, are generally held by men, whose workday may be shorter since they do not have additional domestic tasks to perform. Men who lack special skills—and many do—are often doomed to lives of unemployment.

In developing countries, women have become a source of cheap labour for large corporations, as subsistence farming has given way to mechanized agriculture. Unable to contribute to their families' well-being in any other way, they have no choice but to take on menial jobs for low wages.

In sum, multinational corporations have become a major force in the world today, drawing people more firmly than ever into a truly global system of relationships. Although this brings with it potential benefits, it is also clear it poses serious new problems that now must be addressed.

Ethnic Resurgence

Despite the worldwide adoption of such items as cell phones, Coca-Cola, and the Big Mac, and despite pressure for traditional cultures to disappear, it is clear that cultural diversity is still very much with us in the world today. In fact, a tendency for peoples around the world to resist modernization, or to use it on their own terms, is strengthening. We have already alluded to the worldwide separatist movements, the success so far of the Shuar in retaining their own ethnic and cultural identity in Ecuador, and the increasing political activism of indigenous peoples around the world, including the recent success of Inuit peoples in Nunavut in the Canadian Arctic.

During the 1970s the world's indigenous peoples began to organize self-determination movements, culminating in the formation of the World Council of Indigenous Peoples in 1975. This council now has official status as a UN nongovernmental organization, with a secretariat based in Canada, and represents over 60,000,000 indigenous people globally, which allows it to present the cases of Aboriginal people before the world community. Leaders of this movement see their own societies as community-based, egalitarian, and close to nature and are intent on maintaining them that way. Further credibility to their cause came when 1993–2004 was declared the Decade of Indigenous Peoples.

Increasingly, Aboriginal peoples around the world are organizing to defend their own interests. Here, the Kayapo in Brazil protest against planned hydroelectric dams.

North Americans often have difficulty adjusting to the fact that not everyone wants to be just like they are. Children in Canada and the United States are taught to believe that "the North American way of life" is one that all other peoples aspire to, but it isn't only people such as the Shuar who resist becoming "just like us." In the world today, entire countries, having strived to emulate Western ways, have become disenchanted with those ways and suddenly backed off. The most striking recent cases of such a retreat from the West's vision of modernity is Iran, or Turkey's re-embracing of hard nationalism and its turn away from EU membership (although Turkey would argue that *Europe* has turned *them* away). In Iran, with the overthrow of the Shah in 1979, a policy of deliberate Westernization was abandoned in favour of a return to an Islamic republic out of a past "golden age," mythical though the latter may have been. However, Iranians have been unwilling to give up all the trappings of "modernity." On the streets of Tehran, women wear the latest fashions out of Paris or Milan, even while they cover their heads with the traditional women's *chador*. Iran today is a complex mixture of both Jihad and McWorld forces.

Sometimes, resistance to modernization takes the form of a fundamentalist reaction, as in this example of young Islamic women wearing the *hijab* or *chador*.

Cultural Pluralism

Many regard the prospect of a homogenized world culture with alarm, believing instead in the concept of **cultural pluralism**, in which more than one culture exists in a given society, as a more durable and functional model for human society.[28] Cultural pluralism is the social and political interaction of people with different ways of living and thinking within the same society or multinational state. Ideally, it implies a rejection of bigotry, bias, and racism in favour of respect for the cultural traditions of other peoples. In reality, it has rarely worked out quite that way, and this point is underscored by Britain and France both wavering in their support

cultural pluralism Social and political interaction of people with different ways of living and thinking within the same society.

for multiculturalism. Today, many countries are pluralistic, or multiethnic, which makes the issues of ethnic identity and ethnic conflict of practical importance. This also underscores the importance of an anthropological understanding of cultures and ethnicities.

As discussed in Chapter 2, Canada is one of the most culturally pluralist countries in the world; witness the vibrant diversity of cities such as Vancouver, Calgary, Toronto, and Montreal. For example, Chinese in Metropolitan Toronto, with their distinctive cultural traditions and values, exist side by side with other Torontonians. Besides tending to live in certain neighbourhoods, the Chinese maintain their own language, music, religion, and restaurants. The Chinese are not alone in maintaining their own way of life. An astonishing diversity of cultural groups within Canada, including Latin Americans, Middle Easterners, South and Southeast Asians, West Indians, Africans, Irish, Koreans, and Japanese, as well as Québécois and First Nations peoples, wish to keep their distinct cultural identities. In response to this ethnic and cultural diversity, the Canadian government under Pierre Trudeau proposed a Multiculturalism Act in 1971, which was eventually passed in 1988, making Canada the first country in the world to adopt multiculturalism as official policy. Unless some dramatic change in fundamental ideology occurs, Canada will remain a pluralistic country in the future.

Other familiar examples of cultural pluralism may be seen in Switzerland, where Italian, German, and French cultures exist side by side, and in Belgium, where the francophone Walloons and the Germanic-speaking Flemish have different cultural and linguistic heritages, but manage to coexist, if at times in a volatile manner. Switzerland is one of the few countries where pluralism has worked out to the satisfaction of all parties in the arrangement, perhaps because, despite linguistic differences, German, French, Italian, and Romansch-speaking Swiss are all heirs to a common European cultural tradition. In Northern Ireland, by contrast, the existence of groups who share a common tradition did not prevent decades of Protestant–Catholic violence and bloodshed in the streets of Belfast. It is clear that no single formula can be proposed to guarantee the peaceful coexistence of cultures within countries.

Ethnocentrism

The major barrier to the acceptance and spread of cultural pluralism is ethnocentrism, a concept introduced in Chapter 2. To a degree, pride in one's culture is a positive attribute. Some believe that to function effectively, a culture must instill the idea that its ways are "best," or at least preferable to those of other cultures. This provides

Ethnic neighbourhoods, such as Chinatown in Vancouver, are evident in most major Canadian cities.

Egyptian protestors demand the ouster of President Hosni Mubarak after four decades in power.

individuals with a sense of loyalty to their traditions, which in turn provide them with psychological support and bind them firmly to their particular group. The problem with ethnocentrism is that it all too easily can be taken as a charter for manipulating other cultures for the benefit of one's own, even though—as we saw in Chapter 11—this does not have to be the choice. When it is, however, unrest, hostility, and violence commonly result.

Global Apartheid

Ethnocentrism is the ideology behind the doctrine of apartheid, which was until the mid-1990s the official government policy of South Africa. Racial segregation[29] served to perpetuate the dominance of a white minority over a nonwhite majority through the social, economic, political, military, and cultural constitutions of society. With the coming to power in 1994 of the African National Congress led by Nelson Mandela, South Africa finally threw off the political yoke of apartheid. However, the economic effects of this racialized division of society persist.

The 1990 confrontation between the Mohawk Nation (including the Warrior Society) and the police and later the army, in Oka, Quebec, was symptomatic of First Nations' frustration with slow progress toward self-government and the right to determine their political and economic destiny. The Quebec and South African situations both reveal the willingness of governments to use their armies against people of other nationalities within their borders to promote the state's interests.

The whole world recognized the evils of apartheid. What is disturbing is that today's global society is structurally very similar—almost a mirror image of South Africa's society, even though no conscious policy of global

apartheid is practised. Today, about three-quarters of the world's people live in poverty and one-quarter in relative affluence, the latter concentrated in Europe, North America, and Japan. In the world today, the poorest 75 percent of the population make do with 30 percent of the world's energy, 25 percent of its metals, 15 percent of its wood, and 40 percent of its food. Life expectancy, as in South Africa, is lowest among nonwhites. Most of the world's weapons of mass destruction are owned by the United States, Russia, France, and Britain. As in South Africa, death and suffering from war and violence are distributed unequally; the world's poorest 70 percent of the population suffer more than 90 percent of violent deaths in all categories.

PROBLEMS OF STRUCTURAL VIOLENCE

One of the consequences of a system of apartheid, whether official or unofficial or on the state or global level, is the phenomenon of **structural violence**: violence exerted not by weapons and blows, but by situations, institutions, and social, political, and economic structures. A classic instance of structural violence is the economic collapse of the Greek and Irish economies in 2010. To survive, these countries had to make drastic cuts in social services, while industry downsizing and failures caused untold numbers of people to lose their jobs. As far as the victims of this economic calamity are concerned,

structural violence Violence exerted by situations, institutions, and social, political, and economic structures.

the effect is violent, even though the cause was not the hostile act of a specific individual. The source of the violence was an anonymous structure (the economy, specifically the banking sector), and this is what structural violence is all about.

There is not enough space in the rest of this chapter to cover all aspects of structural violence, but we can address some aspects that are of particular concern to anthropologists. While other scholars also consider the issue, anthropologists are less likely than other specialists to see these aspects of structural violence as discrete and unrelated. Thus, as synthesizers of the "bigger picture," they have a key contribution to make to the understanding of persistent modern-day crises such as hunger and overpopulation, environmental pollution, and widespread discontent in the world.

World Hunger

As often dramatized by events in various parts of Africa, a major source of structural violence in the world today is humanity's failure to provide food for all its people. Not only is Africa declining in its capacity to feed itself, but 52 countries worldwide by 1980 were producing less food per capita than they were 10 years previously, and in 42 countries available food supplies were not adequate to provide the caloric requirements of their populations.[30] In recent years North Korea has experienced repeated famines. One factor contributing to this food crisis is a dramatic growth in the world's population.

Population growth is more than a simple addition of people. If it were just that, the addition of 20 people a year to a population of 1,000 would double that population in 50 years; but because the added people beget more people, the doubling time is actually much less than 50 years. Hence, it took the whole of human history and prehistory for the world's population to reach 1 billion people, achieved in 1750. By 1950, world population had reached almost 2.5 billion, representing an annual growth rate of about 0.8 percent. And shortly after the turn of the millennium in 2000, it had reached 6 billion (see Figure 15.2). By the end of 2011, it was 7 billion.

The obvious question arising from the growing world population is this: Can we produce enough food to feed all those people? The majority opinion among agriculturalists is that we can do so, but how far into the future we can do it is open to question. In the 1960s a major effort was launched to expand food production in the poor countries of the world by introducing new high-yield strains of grains. Yet despite some dramatic gains from this "Green Revolution"—India, for example, doubled its wheat crop in six years and was on the verge of grain self-sufficiency by 1970—and despite the impressive output of North American agriculture, hundreds of millions continue to face malnutrition and starvation. In Canada, meanwhile, *edible* food worth millions of dollars is thrown out every day (far more food than is sent out for famine relief), and farms are going out of business in record numbers.

The immediate cause of world hunger has less to do with food *production* than with food *distribution*.

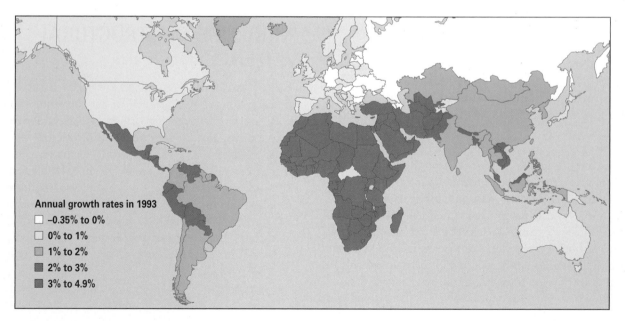

Figure 15.2

Population growth rates around the world.

For example, millions of acres in Africa, Asia, and Latin America once devoted to subsistence farming have been given over to the raising of cash crops for export to satisfy appetites in the world's "developed" countries for products such as coffee, tea, chocolate, bananas, and beef. Those who used to farm the land for their own food needs have been forced to relocate to the cities, to sprawling urban shantytowns where unemployment is rife, or to other areas ecologically unsuited for farming. In Africa such lands often are occupied by pastoral nomads; as farmers encroach on these, insufficient pasturage is left for livestock. The resultant overgrazing, coupled with the clearing of the land for farming, leads to increased loss of both soil and water, with disastrous consequences to nomad and farmer alike. In Brazil, which is highly dependent on outside sources of fossil fuels for its energy needs, millions of acres in the northeast were taken over for sugar production for making alcohol to fuel the vehicles in Rio. The people displaced by sugar production were given small holdings in the Amazon, where they now are being uprooted to make way for huge ranches for raising export beef.

One strategy urged upon developing countries, especially by Canadian and U.S. government officials and development advisers, is to adopt the practices that have made North American agriculture so incredibly productive. On the face of it, this seems like a good idea, but it overlooks the fact that it requires investment in expensive seeds, chemicals, and mechanization that neither small farmers nor poor countries can afford. Intensive agriculture on the Canadian model requires, in addition, enormous amounts of fossil fuels to run all the mechanized equipment. A well-known study of American agriculture by the agronomist David Pimentel estimated that for every single calorie of food output produced, the equivalent of eight calories of renewable fossil fuel were required to produce and distribute it.[31] By contrast, an Asian wet rice farmer using traditional methods produces up to 300 calories for each one expended. North American agriculture is wasteful of other resources as well: about 30 kilograms of fertile topsoil are ruined for every kilogram of food produced.[32] In the American Midwest, about 50 percent of the topsoil has been lost over the past 100 years. Meanwhile, toxic substances from chemical nutrients and pesticides pile up in unexpected places, poisoning ground and surface waters; killing fish, birds, and other useful forms of life; upsetting natural ecological cycles; and causing major public health problems. Despite its spectacular short-term success, serious questions arise as to whether such a profligate food production system can be sustained over the long run, even in North America.

AP/Wide World Photos

Hunger affects much of the world as a result of a world food system geared to satisfy an affluent minority in the world's developed nations.

Angelo Cavalli/agefotostock/Firstlight

In South America, where these tobacco crops are grown, agricultural development has caused increased malnutrition levels. As in many developing countries, modernization of agriculture has meant the conversion of land from subsistence farming to raising crops for export, making it increasingly difficult for people to satisfy their basic nutritional needs.

Pollution

It is ironic that a life-sustaining activity such as food production should constitute a health hazard, but that is precisely what it becomes when agricultural chemicals poison soils and waters, and when food additives (more than 2,500 are or have been in use) expose people to substances that all too often turn out to be harmful. And this is but part of a larger problem of environmental pollution. Industrial activities are producing highly toxic wastes at unprecedented rates and factory emissions are poisoning the air. For example, smokestack gases are clearly implicated in acid rain, which is causing damage to lakes and forests all over northeastern North America. Air containing water vapour with a high acid content is, of course, harmful to the lungs, but the health hazard is greater than this. As surface water and groundwater become more acidic, the solubility of lead, cadmium, mercury, and aluminum increases sharply. The increase of dissolved aluminum, in particular, is becoming truly massive, and aluminum consumption has been associated with senile dementia as well as Alzheimer's and Parkinson's diseases. Today, these rank as major health problems in Canada and the United States.

Added to this is the global warming problem—the greenhouse effect—caused by the burning of fossil fuels. Although much is unknown about the extent of global warming, climate scientists agree that it is real and that its long-term effects will be harmful. Unfortunately, the response from industry and energy interests has been similar to the campaign that tobacco companies carried out for so long to convince the public that smoking was not hazardous. These interests have launched a massive public relations campaign to persuade the public that global warming is not real; as a consequence, it has become very difficult to do anything about it. While the George W. Bush administration rejected the Kyoto Protocol to limit atmospheric emissions outright, Canada ratified it in December 2002. However, the Province of Alberta, whose wealth is closely tied to energy revenues, has threatened to block or veto the protocol.

As with world hunger, the structural violence from pollution tends to be greatest in the poorest countries of the world, where chemicals banned in countries such as Canada are still widely used. Moreover, industrial countries have taken advantage of the lax environmental regulations of developing states to get rid of hazardous wastes. In the United States, both government and industry have tried to persuade Aboriginal people on reservations experiencing severe economic depression that the solution to their problems lies in allowing disposal of nuclear and other hazardous waste on their lands. In Canada, too, First Nations and government officials examined the possibility of storing radioactive wastes on reservations in the north; however, the idea was discarded.

Meanwhile, as much manufacturing shifts from the developed to the developing countries of the world—a trend also encouraged by fewer safety and environmental regulations—lethal accidents such as the one in 1986 at Chernobyl may be expected to increase. In that incident, human error at a faulty nuclear reactor released radiation, causing numerous deaths, the relocation of 126,000 people, increased thyroid cancer, and damaged immune systems. Even more than 25 years later, increased birth defects and economic privation have plagued people living as far away as the Arctic, where Saami reindeer herds were contaminated by radioactive fallout. The radioactive leakage caused by an earthquake and tsunami near the Fukushima Daiichi nuclear plant in Japan in 2011 promises to be even more severe than the Chernobyl example. Indeed, development itself seems to be a health hazard; it is well known that indigenous peoples in Canada, Africa, the Pacific Islands, South America, and elsewhere were relatively free from diabetes, obesity, hypertension, and a variety of circulatory diseases until they adopted the ways of developed countries.

Population Control

Although the problems we have discussed so far may not be caused by population growth, they are certainly made worse by it. For one thing, it increases the scale of problems—for example, the waste that a small population generates is far easier to deal with than what a large one generates. For another example, it often nullifies efforts people make to solve the problems, such as when increased food production is offset by increased numbers of people needing to be fed. Although solving the population growth problem does not by itself make the other problems go away, it is unlikely those problems can be solved unless population growth is arrested.

As our earlier example of population demonstrated, the world's population has grown enormously since the beginning of the Industrial Age. Except in Europe and North America, where birth rates are significantly lower than death rates, the world saw no sign of a significant decline in birth rates prior to 1976. Impoverished people tend to have many children for the simple reason that children are their main resource. They provide the labour needed to work farms, and they are often the only source of security for the elderly; hence, having many offspring makes sense (especially where infant mortality rates are high). Historically, people were apt to limit their family size only when they became wealthy enough that money replaced children as their main support; at that point, children actually cost them money or other resources.

Given this, we can see why birth rates have for so long remained high in the world's poorest countries. Those who live in poverty see children as their only hope.

Nevertheless, since 1976 there have been some encouraging signs, such as China's steep decline in birth rates. China is one of 19 developing countries where birth rates actually have dropped *below* replacement levels (Chinese birth rates balance out at about 2.1 children per woman). This has led to recent discussions in China about whether to relax the one-child policy. In much of South Asia and Central and South America (again, some of the world's poorest countries), birthrates also have declined, but far less dramatically. Examples include Bangladesh, where the rate of births per woman has fallen from 6.2 to 3.4 (in just 10 years); Tunisia, where the rate has fallen from 7.2 to 2.9; and Mexico, which has moved 80 percent of the way to replacement level. The tragic appearance of the AIDS epidemic in many developing countries, especially sub-Saharan Africa, has slowed and even reversed rapid population growth, but this has been achieved at a terrible cost in human suffering.

The problem of who will care for elders in their old age is an issue for any society whose birth rates are below replacement level. The inevitable consequence is that the number of old people "explodes" relative to the number of productive people of younger age. Already countries such as Canada are beginning to worry about this. Canada has an aging population, one requiring comprehensive health care services, pension plans, and so on, and this will place an unfair burden on relatively few young, tax-paying adults.

Persistent Inequalities

Despite the difficulties, stabilization of the world's population appears to be a necessary step if the future's problems are ever to be solved. Without such steps, whatever else is done, the world's inability to provide enough food and distribute it equally seems inevitable. Up until about 1950, growth in the world's food supply came almost entirely from expanding the amount of cultivated land. Since then, it has come increasingly from the high-energy inputs of chemical fertilizers that new high-yield varieties of crops depend on, of pesticides and herbicides, and of fuel to run tractors and other mechanical equipment, including irrigation pumps. The source of almost all this energy is oil; yet, although the demand for food is projected to rise until at least the middle of the 21st century, oil supplies are diminishing and will surely decline over this same period. Many energy analysts are speaking of the approaching turning point of "peak oil," when fossil fuel will enter a permanently downward spiral. Unless a new energy source, such as hydrogen fuel cells, replaces oil, humanity faces an looming energy crisis of unimaginable proportions.

Dick Hemingway Editorial Photographs

With declining global birthrates, the proportion of elderly people is rapidly rising, with an associated increase in health care costs.

Insufficient or too costly food supplies are bound to result in increased structural violence in the form of higher death rates in the world's developing countries. This will have an impact on developed countries, with their relatively stable populations and high living standards. It is hard to imagine how such countries could exist peacefully side by side with others experiencing high death rates and abysmally low living standards. Already, the combination of overpopulation and poverty is causing a rising tide of migration from the impoverished countries to the more affluent ones of Europe and North America, with a consequent rise in intolerance, anti-foreign sentiments, and general social unrest. Recent uprisings in the Middle East have resulted in a massive increase in migrants fleeing countries such as Tunisia, Egypt, and Libya, most of them heading to Italy, where they are not necessarily welcome. Witness the public outcry (both anti-foreign and pro-compassion) when 600 desperate Chinese refugees tried to reach Canada's west coast in 1999. These refugees endured squalid conditions aboard decrepit cargo ships in the hopes of a better life in Canada, only to be met with hostility. As of 2001 only a few had been granted refugee status, hundreds had been deported back to China, and others were still in detention. A country as rich in resources and opportunities as Canada will continue to be a destination of choice for economic, social, and political refugees. The government and the people of Canada must decide how to deal with this issue in a compassionate and responsible manner.

replacement reproduction When birthrates and death rates are in equilibrium; people produce only enough offspring to replace themselves when they die.

Necessary though birth control may be for solving the future's problems, we have no reason to suppose that it will be sufficient by itself. The result would be only to stabilize situations as they are. The problem is twofold. For the past several years, the world's poor countries have been sold on the idea they should enjoy a living standard comparable to that of the rich countries. Yet the resources necessary to maintain such a standard of living, even at moderate levels, are running out. As we saw earlier in the chapter, this situation has led to entrenched injustices and the resultant culture of resentment and protest. The problem is not just of population growth outstripping food supplies, but also of unequal access to decent jobs, housing, sanitation, health care, and adequate police and fire protection. And it is one of steady deterioration and destruction of the natural environment as a result of increasing industrialization and overuse of the land. Displacement is one of the consequences; people on the margins often redirect their legitimate anger and grievances into nihilism, excessive drinking, substance abuse, petty crime, and domestic violence.

Some dramatic changes in cultural values and motivations, as well as in social institutions, are required. The emphasis on individual self-interest, materialism, and conspicuous production, acquisition, and consumption, characteristic of the world's richest countries, needs to be abandoned in favour of a more humane social ethic. The sources for these values can still be found in many of the world's non-Western cultures. Such values include a world view that sees humanity as part of the natural world rather than superior to it. Included, too, is a sense of social responsibility that recognizes that no individual, people, or state has the right to expropriate resources at the expense of others. Finally, an awareness is needed of how important supportive ties are for individuals, as is seen in kinship and other associations in the world's traditional societies. Is humanity up to the challenge? The answer is uncertain, but it appears that significant changes are bound to come, one way or another.

HUMANITY'S FUTURE

The preceding discussion may lead some readers to conclude that humanity's future is dismal indeed, that the road ahead is uphill and full of potholes. It is true that we have many problems to solve, and solve them we must. But humans have always been incredibly tenacious, overcoming seemingly insurmountable obstacles to survive. From our first tentative prehistoric steps out onto the savannas, to the roar of a space shuttle taking yet another payload to the international space station, we have overcome many hurdles, and we will continue to do so.

The key to our continued survival lies in our ability and willingness to see the earth as a benevolent host rather than a resource to exploit, and our fellow humans as partners rather than competitors. As partners we can find equitable solutions to our problems—solutions that do not favour any one people or political regime. We are at a crossroads in human history—what we do in the next 50 years will determine the kind of existence that future generations of humanity will inherit.

The greatest danger we face is apathy—a human tendency to pretend that nothing is wrong, that someone else will fix it, or, even worse, that there is nothing we can do. Whether we focus on environmental issues, human rights, or fair distribution of economic resources, each of us can make a difference. In the wise words of anthropologist Margaret Mead, "Never doubt that a small group of thoughtful, committed citizens can change the world. Indeed, it's the only thing that ever has."[33]

Chapter Summary

1. How do cultures change?
Although cultures may appear to be quite stable, culture change is characteristic of all cultures to a greater or lesser degree. The mechanisms of change are innovation, diffusion, cultural loss, and acculturation. Change may be accidental, intentional, or forced upon a people, and it may or may not be beneficial. Changes forced on many indigenous peoples have forced them to retreat to inaccessible places in the hope of being left alone; others have lapsed into apathy. In other cases, revitalization movements may appear and attempt to speed up the acculturation process to seek more of its economic benefits. Elsewhere, revolutionary movements try to transform the culture from within, while rebellions aim to replace one set of officeholders with another.

2. What is modernization?
Modernization refers to the global process of change in which traditional cultures begin to acquire the characteristics of industrially "advanced" societies. This process has often led to social inequality and structural violence. The process consists of four subprocesses: technological development, agricultural development, industrialization, and urbanization. Other changes follow in the areas of political organization, education, religion, and social organization.

3. What problems will have to be solved if humanity is to have a future?
Since future forms of culture will be shaped by decisions that humans have yet to make, they cannot be predicted with any accuracy. Thus, instead of trying to foretell the future,

a number of anthropologists are attempting to gain a better understanding of the existing world situation so that decisions may be made intelligently. Anthropologists are especially well suited for this, owing to their experience with seeing things in context, their long-term evolutionary perspective, their ability to recognize culture-bound biases, and their familiarity with cultural alternatives.

However humanity changes biologically, culture remains the chief means by which humans try to solve their problems of existence. Some anthropologists are concerned that there is a trend for the problems to outstrip any culture's ability to find solutions. Some believe that rapid developments in communication, transportation, and world trade will link people together to the point that a single more harmonious world culture will result. An alternative pathway is for humanity to move in the direction of cultural pluralism, where two or more cultures exist with respect for one another's differences. Some anthropologists maintain that pluralistic arrangements are the only feasible means of achieving global equilibrium and peace. An obstacle to the success of multiculturalism is entrenched ethnocentrism, one that must be countered by anthropological knowledge, among other things.

Solving the many problems of the global society, such as pollution, war, and inequality, depends also on lessening the gap between the living standards of impoverished and wealthy countries. This calls for dramatic changes in the values of Western societies, with their materialistic consumer orientation, as well as development of an ethic of social responsibility that recognizes that no people has a right to expropriate important resources at the expense of others. The surprising strength of recent worldwide anti-war and anti-globalization protest movements is a hopeful sign of change.

Questions for Critical Thought

1. Is tradition susceptible to change? What is the role of tradition in conjunction with the concept of cultural change discussed in this chapter? How important are tradition and change to a culture's health?

2. Do the benefits of modernization or globalization outweigh the harmful effects? For example, has North American free trade benefited or harmed Canada? Explain.

3. In your opinion, will continued modernization bring humanity, in the end, into a single homogeneous world culture? Does modernization mean absolute assimilation? How might tradition play a part in this process?

4. Powerful states often feel they have a responsibility to intervene in foreign affairs to speed the development of other countries or to calm political and social distress. Is this necessarily a wise idea? Even when the intentions are good, is the outcome always positive? Explain your answer.

5. Is Canada's multiculturalism beneficial or harmful to its national identity?

6. How can you and your community reduce consumption of food resources and nonrenewable resources? If every community took these measures, would it make a difference in global resources?

Internet Resources

Global Genocide

http://www.stanleyfoundation.org/publications/pab/BellamyPAB22011.pdf

A detailed source of statistics on the history of global genocide.

Yanomami Genocide

http://www.monitor.net/monitor/10-30-95/amazongenocide.html

Gives good background information and highlights events that are devastating the Yanomami culture.

Environmental Justice Movement

http://www.chej.org

The Center for Health, Environment, and Justice in Falls Church, Virginia, is a pioneering clearinghouse for grassroots activism in the environmental movement. It was founded by Lois Gibbs, the leader of the Love Canal Homeowners Association, whose families were being poisoned by a toxic waste site in Niagara Falls, New York.

Critiques of Contemporary Capitalism

http://www.naomiklein.org/main

Canadian journalist and filmmaker Naomi Klein has authored some of the most telling critiques of the excesses of runaway capitalism. Her classic study of branding in *No Logo* (2000) was followed by her critically acclaimed *The Shock Doctrine: The Rise of Disaster Capitalism*.

Nunavut

http://www.polarnet.ca/polarnet/nunavut.htm

Introduces students to the territory of Nunavut, and presents some background information on the political, economic, and social factors that went into creating this new land.

Living the Legacy: The Women's Rights Movement 1848–1998

http://www.legacy98.org/move-hist.html

A comprehensive historical, political, and social account of the women's movement from 1848 to 1998. Highly recommended for students wishing to update their knowledge of what the women's movement really stands for.

Quebec Sovereignty and Canadian National Unity

http://polisci.nelson.com/quebec.html

The 1998 Supreme Court of Canada decision on the ground rules for Quebec secession.

Women's Rights Are Human Rights

http://www.un.org/womenwatch

A UN site that examines international human rights treaties and conference agreements to provide women's rights. "Human Rights Treaties" and "International Conference Consensus Agreements."

Careers in Anthropology

http://www.canadian-universities.net/Universities/Programs/Anthropology-Careers.html

This site outlines what students can do with a degree in anthropology and provides links to several related pages. A valuable resource for students who are thinking about majoring in anthropology or who are about to graduate with an anthropology degree.

Anthropology in Canada

http://www.cas-sca.ca

The Canadian Anthropology Society/Societe canadienne d'anthropologie (CASCA) is Canada's national organization for social and cultural anthropology. Founded in 1983, CASCA's membership is national; constitutionally the leadership alternates between anglophone and francophone presidents. The society's journal *Anthropologica* is a forum for exciting new research.

Suggested Readings

For a list of suggested readings, visit the textbook's website at **www.havilandcultural4e.nelson.com**.

Notes

1 J. Diamond, "The Curse of QWERTY," *Discover* 18, no. 4 (1997): 34–42.

2. J. Weatherford, *Native Roots: How the Indians Enriched America* (New York: Ballantine, 1992).

3 T. Turner, "Major Shift in Brazilian Yanomami Policy," *Anthropology Newsletter* 32, no. 5 (1991): 46.

4. E. Dewar, *Cloak of Green* (Toronto: Lorimer, 1995).

5. P. Such, "Vanished People: The Archau Dorset and Beothuk People of Newfoundland," in *Rediscovering the First Nations of Canada,* ed. J.W. Friesen (Calgary: Detselig, 1997), 53.

6. Friesen, *Rediscovering the First Nations of Canada.*

7. P.L. Van Den Berghe, "The Modern State: Nation Builder or Nation Killer?" *International Journal of Group Tensions* 22, no. 3 (1992): 191–207 at 198.

8. OutThere News, n.d., "Bosnia: The Psychology of Genocide—What Makes People Mass Murderers?" http://www.ppu.org.uk/genocide/g_bosnia.html, accessed April 1, 2001.

9. J. Hagan and W. Rymond-Richmond, *Darfur and the Crime of Genocide* (Cambridge: Cambridge University Press, 2009).

10. Van Den Berghe, "The Modern State."

11. B. Nietschmann, "The Third World War," *Cultural Survival Quarterly* 11, no. 3 (1987).

12. Ibid., 7.

13. G. Hershatter, *Women in China's Long Twentieth Century* (Berkeley: University of California Press, 2007).

14. P.J. Pelto, *The Snowmobile Revolution: Technology and Social Change in the Arctic* (Menlo Park: Cummings, 1973).

15. J.H. Bodley, *Victims of Progress,* 3rd ed. (Mountain View: Mayfield, 1990), 160–62.

16. *Cultural Survival Quarterly* 15, no. 4 (1991): 3.

17. WorldWatch Institute, "Annual Reoport: 2009–2010," http://www.worldwatch.org/system/files/Annual%20Report%202009-2010.pdf, accessed August 11, 2011.

18. J. Henry, *Culture Against Man* (New York: Vintage Books, 1965), 12.

19. G.L. Cowgill, letter, *Science* 210, no. 4476 (1980): 1305.

20. B.R. Barber, *Jihad Versus McWorld* (New York: Times Books, 1995).

21. C. Tilley, ed., *The Formation of National States in Western Europe* (Princeton: Princeton University Press, 1975).

22. Nunavut Planning Commission, "Land Claim Review," n.d., http://www.arctic.ca/LUS/Nunavut.html, accessed April 7, 2001.

23. Q. Duffy, *The Road to Nunavut: The Progress of the Eastern Arctic Inuit Since the Second World War* (Montreal and Kingston: McGill–Queen's University Press, 2003).

24. S. Erwin, *Canadian Perspectives in Cultural Anthropology* (Toronto: Nelson Thomson, 2001).

25. R. Barnet and J. Cavanaugh, *Global Dreams: Imperial Corporations and the New World Order* (New York: Simon and Schuster, 1994).

26. J.H. Bodley, "Comment," *Current Anthropology* 38 (1997): 725.

27. Naomi Klein, *No Logo* (London: Picador, 2009); Klein, *The Shock Doctrine* (New York: Metropolitan Books, 2007).

28. D. Campbell and M. Schoolman, eds., *The New Pluralism: William Connolly and the Contemporary Global Condition* (Durham: Duke University Press, 2008).

29. Material on global apartheid is drawn from L. Kohler, "Global Apartheid," reprinted in *Talking About People: Readings in Contemporary Cultural Anthropology,* 2nd ed. W.A. Haviland and R.J. Gordon (Mountain View: Mayfield, 1996), 262–68.

30. B.H. Chasin and R.W. Franke, "U.S. Farming: A World Model?" *Global Reporter* 1, no. 2 (1983): 10.

31. W.S. Broecker, "Global Warming on Trial," *Natural History*, April 1992, 14.

32. Ibid.

33. E. Eisenber and M. Ruthsdotter, *Living the Legacy: The Women's Rights Movement, 1848–1998.* http://www.legacy98.org/move-hist.html, accessed November 25, 2000.

Glossary

acculturation: Major cultural changes people are forced to make owing to intensive firsthand contact between societies. (p. 355)

Acheulian tradition: A tool tradition associated with *Homo erectus* in Africa and Europe characterized by teardrop-shaped axes and flake tools. Named after the site where it was first defined, St. Acheul, France, it lasted from 1.5 million to about 150 000 years ago. (p. 59)

achieved status: Status an individual earns. (p. 233)

adjudication: Mediation with an unbiased third party making the ultimate decision. (p. 261)

affinal kin: Relatives by marriage. (p. 155)

age grade: An organized category of people based on age; every individual passes through a series of such categories during a lifetime. (p. 219)

age-set: A group of people born in the same time period. Age-sets may hold political, religious, military, or economic power as a group. (p. 219)

ambilineal descent: Descent in which the individual may affiliate with either the mother's or the father's descent group. (p. 202)

ambilocal residence: A pattern in which a married couple may choose either matrilocal or patrilocal residence. (p. 185)

androcentrism: Male-centeredness. (p. 21)

animatism: A belief that the world is animated by impersonal supernatural powers. (p. 279)

animism: A belief in spirit beings thought to animate nature. (p. 279)

anthropogenesis: The process whereby ecosystems are influenced or altered by humans. Examples include human impact on the environment through pollution, farming, or construction. (p. 99)

anthropology: The study of humankind in all times and places. (p. 4)

applied anthropology: The use of anthropological knowledge and techniques for solving practical problems, often for a specific client (p. 358); also, Consulting work undertaken by anthropologists relating to practical problems. (p. 326)

archaeology: The study of material remains, usually from the past, to describe and explain human behaviour. (p. 10)

ascribed status: Status people are born into. (p. 233)

Australopithecus: The earliest well-known hominin, who lived between 1 million and 4.2 million years ago and includes several species. (p. 54)

avunculocal residence: A pattern in which a married couple lives with the husband's mother's brother. (p. 186)

balanced reciprocity: A mode of exchange whereby the giving and the receiving are specific in terms of the value of the goods and the time of their delivery. (p. 132)

band: A small group of related households occupying a particular region who gather periodically but do not yield their sovereignty to the larger collective. (p. 244)

biological anthropology: The systematic study of humans as biological organisms. (p. 9)

bound morpheme: A morpheme that can occur in a language only in combination with other morphemes, as *–s* in English does to signify the plural. (p. 76)

bride-price: Compensation the groom or his family pays to the bride's family on marriage. (p. 168)

bride service: A designated period after marriage when the groom works for the bride's family. (p. 168)

carrying capacity: The number of people the available resources can support at a given technological level. (p. 104)

caste: A special form of social class in which membership is determined by birth and remains fixed for life. (p. 233)

chiefdom: A regional polity in which two or more local groups are organized under a single chief, who is at the head of a ranked hierarchy of people. (p. 249)

clan: A noncorporate descent group whose members claim descent from a common ancestor without actually knowing the genealogical links to that ancestor. (p. 203)

closed-class systems: Stratified societies that severely restrict social mobility. (p. 236)

code switching: The process of changing from one level of language to another. (p. 91)

colonialism: When one nation dominates another, through occupation (colonies), administration (military presence), and control of resources, thereby creating a dependency. (p. 5)

common-interest associations: Associations not based on age, kinship, marriage, or territory but that result from the act of joining. (p. 224)

conflict theory of stratification: A theory suggesting that a power struggle takes place between the upper and lower levels of society. (p. 226)

conjugal bond: The bond between a man and a woman who are married. (p. 155)

conjugal family: A family consisting of one (or more) man married to one (or more) woman and their offspring. The female may in fact be male, and the male may in fact be female. (p. 174)

consanguineal kin: Relatives by birth— that is, "blood" relatives. (p. 155)

consanguine family: A family unit consisting of a woman, her dependent offspring, and the woman's brothers. (p. 174)

consensus: A general agreement among adult members of a group. (p. 245)

conspicuous consumption: A term Thorstein Veblen coined to describe the display of wealth for social prestige. (p. 135)

consumption: The ingestion of food and the exploitation of available resources. (p. 139)

contagious magic: Magic based on the principle that beings once in contact can influence one another after separation. (p. 289)

conventional gestures: Body movements that have to be learned and can vary cross-culturally. (p. 77)

cooperation explanation: Forcing people outside their familial unit. (p. 159)

core vocabulary: In language, pronouns, lower numerals, and names for body parts, natural objects, and basic actions. (p. 81)

creole: A more complex pidgin language that has become the mother tongue of a significant population. (p. 91)

cross-cultural comparison: Comparing one particular aspect of a culture with the same aspect in others. (p. 18)

Crow system: Kinship classification usually associated with matrilineal descent in which a father's sister and father's sister's daughter are called by the same term, a mother and mother's sister are merged under another, and a father and father's brother are given a third. Parallel cousins are equated with brother and sisters. (p. 211)

cultural control: Control through beliefs and values deeply internalized in the minds of individuals. (p. 254)

cultural imperialism: Promoting one nation's values, beliefs, and behaviour as superior to all others. Often associated with the Western world inundating other cultural groups with technology, religion, and ways of living (most often via the media), but also through missionism (see Chapter 12), education, and economic control, thereby strongly influencing how people will live. (p. 5)

cultural pluralism: Social and political interaction of people with different ways of living and thinking within the same society. (p. 368)

cultural relativism: The thesis that one must suspend judgement on other people's practices to understand them in their own cultural terms. (p. 44)

cultural resource management (CRM): The practice of managing cultural resources, such as arts and heritage. It incorporates cultural heritage management, which is concerned with traditional and historic culture and the material culture of archaeology. (p. 341)

culture: The shared ideals, values, and beliefs that people use to interpret experience and generate behaviour and that are reflected by their behaviour. (p. 30)

culture bound: Theories about the world and reality based on the assumptions and values of one's own culture (p. 12); also, The interpretation of other practices and beliefs from the standpoint of one's own culture. A culture-bound interpretation can be biased and unwilling to accept the validity of alternative phenomena. (p. 174)

culture shock: The difficulty anthropologists have in adapting to a new culture that differs markedly from their own. (p. 13)

density of social relations: Roughly the number and intensity of interactions among the members of a camp or other residential unit. (p. 104)

Department of Indian Affairs: A department of the Government of Canada with responsibility for policies relating to Aboriginal peoples in Canada. (p. 329)

descent group: Any publicly recognized social entity requiring lineal descent

from a particular real or mythical ancestor for membership. (p. 196)

descriptive linguistics: The study of patterns and structure in language. (p. 11)

dialects: Varying forms of a language that reflect particular regions or social classes and that are similar enough to be mutually intelligible. (p. 88)

diffusion: The spread of customs or practices from one culture to another. (p. 354)

displacement: The ability to refer to objects and events removed in time and space. (p. 74)

double descent: A system of tracing descent matrilineally for some purposes and patrilineally for others. (p. 201)

dowry: Payment of a woman's inheritance at the time of her marriage, either to her or to her husband. (p. 168)

economic system: The production, distribution, and consumption of goods. (p. 122)

ecosystem: A system, or a functioning whole, composed of both the physical environment and the organisms living within it. (p. 99)

egalitarian cultures: Groups in which members enjoy equal access to resources and positions. (p. 226)

enculturation: The process that transmits a society's culture from one generation to the next. (p. 39)

endogamy: Marriage within a particular group or category of individuals. (p. 158)

environmental justice: A social movement in which citizen activists organize to defend against environmental threats to community health and well-being. (p. 339)

environmental racism: Racial discrimination in environmental policy making and the enforcement of regulations that lead to, for example, the targeting of specific communities for waste disposal, power stations or toxic dumps. (p. 230)

Eskimo system: A system of kinship terminology, also called the lineal system, that emphasizes the nuclear family by specifically distinguishing mother, father, brother, and sister, while lumping together all other relatives into broad categories such as uncle, aunt, and cousin. (p. 209)

ethnic boundary markers: Those indicators or characteristics, such as dress and language, that identify individuals as belonging to a particular ethnic group. (p. 36)

ethnicity: A group of people who take their identity from a common place of origin, history, and sense of belonging. (p. 36)

ethnocentrism: The practice of judging other cultures from the perspective of one's own culture. (p. 44)

ethnography: The collection of descriptive material on a culture. (p. 13)

ethnohistory: The study of cultures from the recent past using oral histories, archaeological sites, and written accounts left by explorers, missionaries, and traders. (p. 13)

ethnolinguistics: The study of the relation between language and culture. (p. 87)

ethnology: The comparative study of cultures to explain human behaviour. (p. 13)

ethnomusicology: The study of a society's music in terms of its cultural setting. (p. 307)

exogamy: Marriage outside the group. (p. 159)

exploitative world view: The belief that nature exists for humans to dominate and exploit. (p. 265)

extended family: A collection of nuclear families, related by ties of blood, that live together in one household. (p. 183)

family: A married or common-law couple with or without children, or a lone parent with dependent children. May sometimes include non-kin members. (p. 174)

female circumcision: The removal of all or part of a female's genitalia for religious, traditional, or socioeconomic reasons. (p. 157)

feminist anthropology: A subfield of anthropology that investigates gender and gender relations and that critically analyses gender roles, positions, and experiences. (p. 21)

fictive kinship: Friends not biologically related, but considered part of a kin group. (p. 195)

fission: The splitting of a descent group into two or more new descent groups. (p. 203)

folklore: A 19th-century term first used to refer to the traditional oral stories and sayings of European peasants and later extended to traditions preserved orally in all societies. (p. 304)

folkloristics: The study of folklore (as linguistics is the study of language). (p. 304)

forensic anthropology: A field of applied biological anthropology and archaeology that specializes in the identification of human skeletal remains for legal purposes (p. 10); also, The examination of human skeletal remains. Part of physical anthropology, this field often works with law enforcement agencies to determine the identity of unidentified bones. (p. 330)

forensic archaeologist: An archaeologist who controls a site, recording the position of all relevant finds and recovering any clues associated with the remains. (p. 330)

form classes: The parts of speech or categories of words that work the same way in a given sentence. (p. 76)

frame substitution: A method used to identify the syntactic units of language. For example, a category called nouns may be established as anything that will fit the substitution frame "I see a . . ." . (p. 76)

fraternal polyandry: A woman marries several men who are brothers. (p. 187)

free morphemes: Morphemes that can occur unattached in a language; for example, *dog* and *cat* are free morphemes in English. (p. 76)

functionalist theory of stratification: A theory suggesting that inequality is necessary to maintain complex societies. (p. 226)

gender: A set of standards and behaviours attached to individuals, usually, but not always, based on biological sex. (p. 21)

gender stratification: Unequal access to wealth, power, and prestige, which results in a disadvantaged, subordinate position for women. (p. 236)

generalized reciprocity: A mode of exchange in which the value of the gift is not calculated, nor is the time of repayment specified. (p. 132)

genetic explanation: Inbreeding is forbidden because cultural groups recognize the potential for impaired offspring. (p. 157)

genocide: The extermination of one people by another, often in the name of "progress," either as a deliberate act or as the accidental outcome of one people's activities done with little regard for their impact on others. (p. 357)

globalization: The process of opening up world markets using modern technology. (p. 141)

glottochronology: In linguistics, a method of dating divergence in branches of language families. (p. 81)

grammar: The entire formal structure of a language, consisting of all observations about the morphemes and syntax. (p. 76)

group marriage: Marriage in which several men and women have sexual access to one another. (p. 164)

Hawaiian system: Kinship reckoning in which all relatives of the same sex and generation are referred to by the same term. (p. 209)

hegemony: Authority or control; control or dominating influence by one person or group, especially by one political group, over society or by one nation over others. (p. 360)

historical linguistics: The study of language origins, language change, and the relationships between languages. (p. 11)

historic archaeology: The study of past cultures that possessed written records of their history. (p. 10)

holistic perspective: A fundamental principle of anthropology, that the various parts of culture must be viewed in the broadest possible context to understand their interconnections and interdependence. (p. 13)

hominid: Any member of a family (Hominidae) of two-legged primates including all forms of humans, extinct and living. (p. 54)

hominin: A tribe of hominoid primates, the hominini, to which all human species, including those that are extinct, are assigned. (p. 54)

Homo erectus: The species of *Homo* immediately postdating *Homo habilis*. The species generally refers to the Asian species, but some scholars contend that the African and European specimens are also this species. (p. 57)

Homo ergaster: An alternate (and the original) classification of the African species of *Homo* that is also called *H. erectus*. (p. 58)

Homo georgicus: A species of *Homo* dating to 1.8 million years ago in the Republic of Georgia. There is some question about whether it is actually *H. habilis* or *H. erectus*. (p. 58)

Homo habilis: The earliest species of the genus *Homo*. (p. 55)

Homo heidelbergensis: The species of *Homo* from about 500,000 or as much as 800,000 years ago to the appearance of Neanderthals. An alternate to the term "archaic *Homo sapiens*." (p. 60)

Homo sapiens: The modern human species. (p. 60)

homosexuality: Sexual attraction to (or sexual relations with) persons of the same sex. (p. 151)

horticulture: Normally small-scale cultivation of crops using hand tools such as digging sticks or hoes. (p. 98)

household: The basic residential unit where economic production, consumption, inheritance, childrearing, and shelter are organized and implemented; may or may not be synonymous with family. (p. 181)

human rights: A set of guidelines for the equal treatment of all people, regardless of gender, age, or ethnicity. (p. 45)

imitative magic: Magic based on the principle that like produces like. For example, early cave art depicting animals with arrows in them has been interpreted as imitative magic, in that by drawing such images they would come true. (p. 289)

incest taboo: The prohibition of sexual relations between specified individuals, usually parent–child and inter-sibling relations at a minimum. (p. 155)

incorporation: In rites of passage, reincorporation of the individual into society in his or her new status. (p. 283)

informal economy: The production of marketable commodities that for various reasons escape enumeration, regulation, or any other sort of public monitoring or auditing. (p. 137)

instinct explanation: Sometimes known as "familiarity breeds contempt," this explanation suggests that long-term association with family members discourages sexual interest. (p. 157)

institutionalized racism: Legally sanctioned restrictions based on the ideology that whites are biologically and socially superior to nonwhites. (p. 232)

integration: The tendency for all aspects of a culture to function as an interrelated whole. (p. 40)

integrative mechanisms: Cultural mechanisms that oppose a society's differentiation forces; in modernizing societies, they include formal governmental structures, official state ideologies, political parties, legal codes, and labour and trade unions and other common-interest associations. (p. 360)

intensive agriculture: Large-scale cultivators employing fertilizers, irrigation, equipment, and draft animals. (p. 110)

Iroquois system: Kinship terminology wherein a father and father's brother are given a single term, as are a mother and mother's sister, but a father's sister and mother's brother are given separate terms. Parallel cousins are classified with brothers and sisters, while cross cousins are classified separately but (unlike Crow and Omaha kinship) are not equated with relatives of some other generation. (p. 210)

key informants/respondents: Members of a culture who help the ethnographer interpret what she or he observes. The term "respondents" or "subjects" is lately preferred over "informants," since the latter has negative connotations associated with providing inside information to authorities. (p. 14)

kindred: A group of consanguineal kin linked by their relationship to one living individual; includes both maternal and paternal kin. (p. 204)

kinesics: A system of notating and analyzing postures, facial expressions, and body motions that convey messages. (p. 77)

kinship: The people we are related to through blood (consanguineal) and marriage (affinal). (p. 194)

language: A system of communication using sounds or gestures put together in meaningful ways according to a set of rules. (p. 74)

language family: A group of languages ultimately descended from a single ancestral language. (p. 80)

law: Formal negative sanctions. (p. 255)

legends: Stories told as true and set in the postcreation world. (p. 306)

levelling mechanism: A societal obligation compelling people to redistribute goods so that no one accumulates more wealth than anyone else. (p. 135)

levirate: The marriage custom whereby a widow marries a brother of her dead husband. (p. 164)

lineage: A corporate descent group whose members trace their genealogical links to a common ancestor. (p. 202)

linguistic anthropology: The study of how people use language to relate to each other and how they develop and transmit culture. (p. 11)

linguistic divergence: The development of different languages from a single ancestral language. (p. 80)

linguistic nationalism: The attempt by ethnic minorities, and even countries, to proclaim independence by purging their languages of foreign terms or reviving unused languages. (p. 83)

linguistics: The modern scientific study of all aspects of language. (p. 75)

marine transhumance: Seasonal migration of people from one marine resource to the next. (p. 131)

market exchange: The buying and selling of goods and services, with prices set by the powers of supply and demand. (p. 137)

marriage: The social institution under which a man and woman, or partners of the same gender, live as husband and wife by legal commitments and establish a claim to sexual access to each other. (p. 154)

matrilateral cross-cousin marriage: Marriage of a woman to her father's sister's son or of a man to his mother's brother's daughter (her cross-cousin on the paternal side, his cross-cousin on the maternal side). (p. 167)

matrilineal descent: Descent traced exclusively through one's mother's grandmother's line, etc., to establish group membership. (p. 196)

matrilocal residence: A pattern in which a married couple lives in the locality associated with the wife's relatives. (p. 184)

mechanized agriculture: Large-scale agriculture dependent on complex technology and biotechnology rather than human power to increase production. (p. 117)

mediation: Settlement of a dispute through negotiation assisted by an unbiased third party. (p. 261)

medical anthropology: The subfield of cultural anthropology that analyses how cultures and societies are organized around issues of health and related issues. (p. 338)

microculture: A group of people who share common interests and/or experiences, from which they take their identity. (p. 40)

mobility: The ability to change one's class position. (p. 235)

modernization: The process of cultural and socioeconomic change, whereby developing societies acquire some of the characteristics of Western industrialized societies. (p. 360)

moiety: Each group that results from a division of a society into two halves on the basis of descent. (p. 204)

money: Anything used to make payments for goods or labour as well as to measure their value; may be special-purpose or multipurpose. (p. 138)

monogamy: Marriage in which an individual has one spouse. (p. 161)

morphemes: In linguistics, the smallest units of sound that carry meaning. (p. 76)

motif: A story situation in a folktale. (p. 306)

Mousterian: A toolmaking tradition of the Neanderthals and their contemporaries of Europe, southwestern Asia, and North Africa. (p. 61)

multiculturalism: Describes a society, community, etc., made up of, involving, or relating to several distinct racial or religious cultures. Contrast with biculturalism or monoculturalism. (p. 31)

myth: A sacred narrative explaining how the world came to be in its present form. (p. 280)

nation: Communities of people who see themselves as "one people" on the basis of common ancestry, history, society, institutions, ideology, language, territory, and (often) religion. (p. 250)

naturalistic world view: The belief that humans are merely one part of the natural world. (p. 265)

natural selection: The evolutionary mechanism by which individuals with characteristics best suited to a particular environment survive and reproduce with greater frequency that those without them. (p. 50)

Neanderthal: *Homo neanderthalensis,* the representative group of the genus *Homo* living in Europe and the Middle East from about 125,000 years ago to about 30,000 years ago. (p. 61)

negative reciprocity: A form of exchange whereby the giver tries to get the better of the exchange. (p. 132)

negotiation: The use of direct argument and compromise by the parties to a dispute to arrive voluntarily at a mutually satisfactory agreement. (p. 261)

Neolithic Age: New Stone Age. In the Middle East, this period is dated between 8300 and 4500 BC. The Neolithic Age signalled the introduction of domesticated plants and animals, ceramics, and polished tone tools—all related to a change in the subsistence strategy from foraging to horticulture and agriculture. The name, derived from Greek, translates as "new stone age" (*neo* = "new," *lithos* = "stone"). (p. 109)

neolocal residence: A pattern in which a married couple establishes its household in a location apart from either the husband's or the wife's relatives. (p. 185)

neo-paganism: Modern pagan religions. (p. 290)

nuclear family: A married or common-law couple and their dependent children. (p. 174)

Oldowan tools: The earliest identifiable stone tools, which first appeared 2.5 million years ago. (p. 56)

Omaha system: The patrilineal equivalent of the Crow system; the mother's patrilineal kin are equated across generations. (p. 212)

open-class systems: Stratified societies that permit a great deal of social mobility. (p. 236)

paleoanthropology: The study of fossil remains with the goal of reconstructing human biological evolution. (p. 9); also, The study of extinct members of the genus *Homo sapiens*. (p. 53)

Paleolithic: The Old Stone Age, characterized by chipped stone tools. (p. 56)

pantheon: A collection of gods and goddesses. (p. 278)

paralanguage: The extralinguistic noises that accompany language, such as crying or laughing. (p. 78)

participant observation: A method of learning a people's culture through direct participation in their everyday life. (p. 13)

pastoralism: A subsistence strategy that relies on domesticated herd animals and usually requires seasonal movement to pastures. (p. 111)

patrilateral cross-cousin marriage: Marriage of a man to his father's sister's daughter. (p. 167)

patrilateral parallel-cousin marriage: Marriage of the children of two same-sex siblings. (p. 165)

patrilineal descent: Descent traced exclusively through one's father's grandfather's line to establish group membership. (p. 196)

patrilocal residence: A pattern in which a married couple lives in the locality associated with the husband's father's relatives. (p. 184)

patterns of association: Whom we associate with and in what context, reflecting social class. (p. 233)

patterns of subsistence: Food-procuring strategies. Sometimes called the subsistence round. (p. 98)

phonemes: In linguistics, the smallest classes of sound that make a difference in meaning. (p. 75)

phonetics: The study of the production, transmission, and reception of speech sounds. (p. 75)

pidgin: A language that combines and simplifies elements (vocabulary, syntax, and grammar) of two or more languages. (p. 91)

pluralistic societies: Societies that contain several distinct cultures and subcultures. (p. 36)

polyandrous family: A family consisting of a woman and her multiple husbands, along with their dependent children. (p. 175)

polyandry: The marriage of one woman to two or more men simultaneously. (p. 164)

polygynous family: A family consisting of a man and his multiple wives, along with their dependent children. (p. 174)

polygyny: The marriage custom in which a man has two or more wives simultaneously; a form of polygamy. (p. 161)

polytheism: Belief in several gods and/or goddesses (as contrasted with monotheism—belief in one god). (p. 278)

popular culture: The culture of our everyday lives—television, sports, fashion, arts and crafts, fiction, and music. (p. 16)

potlatch: A special celebration in which the people of a community come together to enjoy elaborate feasts, ceremonial dancing, and gift giving. The potlatch serves as an opportunity for chiefs to enhance their status with public displays of generosity. (p. 135)

power: The ability to reach personal, financial, and professional goals regardless of obstacles. (p. 225)

prehistoric/pre-contact archaeology: The study of ancient cultures that did not possess writing systems to record their history. (p. 10)

prestige: The social esteem others hold for an individual. (p. 225)

priest *or* **priestess:** A full-time religious specialist. (p. 280)

primary innovation: The chance discovery or invention of a new principle. (p. 352)

Primate Order: The group of mammals that include lemurs, lorises, tarsiers, monkeys, apes, and humans. (p. 50)

primatology: The study of nonhuman primates, their biology, adaptation, and social behaviour. (p. 9)

proxemics: The study of how people use physical space in interpersonal interaction and the role that cultural paradigms play in defining what is proximate and what is overproximate. (p. 78)

psychoanalytical explanation: Incest taboos are an attempt by offspring to repress their sexual feelings toward their parents of the opposite gender. (p. 157)

qualitative research: The gathering of data based on interviews, documents, and participant observation to understand human social behaviour. (p. 22)

quantitative research: The gathering of statistical and measurable data. (p. 22)

race: Groups of people who are categorized based on biological and behavioural traits. (p. 226)

racism: The perception that some groups are biologically and culturally inferior to other groups. (p. 226)

reciprocity: The exchange of goods and services of approximately equal value between two parties. (p. 131)

reconstructionist religions: Modern-day revivals of ancient pagan religions. (p. 291)

redistribution: A form of exchange in which goods flow into a central place where they are sorted, counted, and reallocated. (p. 135)

religion: A set of rituals, rationalized by myth, that mobilizes supernatural powers to achieve or prevent transformations of state in people and nature. (p. 274)

replacement reproduction: When birthrates and death rates are in equilibrium; people produce only enough offspring to replace themselves when they die. (p. 373)

revitalization movements: Social movements, often of a religious nature, with the purpose of totally reforming a society. (p. 293)

revolution: The overthrow of a government by force. (p. 358)

rites of intensification: Religious rituals enacted during a group's real or potential crisis. (p. 283)

rites of passage: Rituals, often religious in nature, marking important stages in the lives of individuals, such as birth, marriage, and death. (p. 283)

salvage archaeology: The collection of archaeological data and materials from any given site deemed to be in danger of destruction, as from new construction or weather damage. (p. 341)

sanctions: Externalized social controls designed to encourage conformity to social norms. (p. 254)

Sapir-Whorf hypothesis: The hypothesis, proposed by linguist B.L. Whorf, that states that language, by providing habitual grooves of expression, predisposes people to see the world in a certain way and thus guides their thinking and behaviour. (p. 87)

secondary innovation: Something new that results from the deliberate application of known principles. (p. 352)

segmentary lineage system: A form of political organization in which a large group is broken up into clans that are further divided into lineages. (p. 247)

separation: In rites of passage, the ritual removal of the individual from society. (p. 283)

serial monogamy: A marriage form in which a man or a woman marries or lives with a series of partners in succession. (p. 164)

sexual identity: The identity a person takes based on his or her sexual preference. (p. 151)

sexual orientation: The biological and psychological makeup of an individual. (p. 151)

shaman/medicine person: A part-time religious specialist who has unique power acquired through his or her initiative; such individuals are thought to possess exceptional abilities for dealing with supernatural beings and powers. (p. 282)

signal: A sound or gesture that has a natural or self-evident meaning. (p. 74)

silent trade: A form of barter with no verbal communication. (p. 134)

social class: A category of individuals who enjoy equal or nearly equal prestige according to the evaluation system. (p. 232)

social control: Control over groups through coercion and sanctions. (p. 254)

social explanation: Sometimes known as the "peace in the family" theory, this explanation suggests that competition over mates would interfere with normal family functions, such as acquiring adequate food resources. (p. 157)

social stratification: Institutionalized inequality resulting in some groups receiving differential access to power, wealth, and prestige. (p. 225)

social structure: The relationships of groups within a society that hold it together. (p. 31)

society: A group of people who live in the same region, speak the same language, and are interdependent. (p. 31)

sociocultural anthropology: The study of human behaviour in contemporary culture. (p. 12)

sociolinguistics: The study of the structure and use of language as it relates to its social setting. (p. 12)

sororal polygyny: A man marries several women who are sisters. (p. 186)

sororate: The marriage custom whereby a widower marries his dead wife's sister. (p. 164)

state: In anthropology, a centralized political system with the power to coerce. (p. 250)

stratified societies: Societies in which ranking and inequality among members vary. (p. 225)

structural differentiation: The division of single traditional roles, which embrace two or more functions (for example, political, economic, and religious), into two or more roles, each with a single specialized function. (p. 360)

structural violence: The widespread practice in many societies of inflicting harm on subordinate sectors of society by indirect means—such as poorer housing, schooling, or health care—rather than through the direct exercise of force and coercion (p. 267); also, Violence exerted by situations, institutions, and social, political, and economic structures. (p. 369)

subculture: A cultural subgroup differentiated by status, ethnic background, residence, religion, or other factors that functionally unify the group and act collectively on each member. (p. 34)

Sudanese or descriptive system: The system of kinship terminology whereby a father, father's brother, and mother's brother are distinguished from one another, as are a mother, mother's sister, and father's sister; cross and parallel cousins are distinguished from one another as well as from siblings. (p. 212)

swidden farming: An extensive form of horticulture in which the natural vegetation is cut, the slash is subsequently burned, and crops are planted among the ashes. (p. 110)

symbolic indicators: In a stratified society, activities and possessions indicative of social class. (p. 233)

symbols: Sounds or gestures that stand for meanings among a group of people. (p. 74)

syntax: In linguistics, the rules or principles of phrase and sentence making. (p. 76)

taboo: A socially restricted behaviour. (p. 289)

tale: A creative narrative recognized as fiction for entertainment. (p. 306)

technology: Tools and other material equipment, together with the knowledge of how to make and use them. (p. 130)

totemism: The belief that people are related to particular animals, plants, or natural objects by virtue of descent from common ancestral spirits. (p. 203)

touch: A form of body language involving physical contact. (p. 77)

transition: In rites of passage, a stage where the individual is isolated following separation and prior to incorporation into society. (p. 283)

tribe: A group of nominally independent communities occupying a specific region and sharing a common language and culture integrated by some unifying factor. (p. 246)

unilineal descent: Descent that establishes group membership exclusively through either the mother's or the father's line. (p. 196)

Upper Paleolithic peoples: The first people of modern appearance, who lived in the last part (Upper Paleolithic) of the Old Stone Age. (p. 62)

vocal characterizers: In paralanguage, sound productions such as laughing or crying that humans "speak" through. (p. 79)

vocalizations: Identifiable paralinguistic noises turned on and off at perceivable and relatively short intervals. (p. 79)

vocal qualifiers: In paralanguage, sound productions of brief duration that modify utterances in terms of intensity. (p. 79)

vocal segregates: In paralanguage, sound productions that are similar to the sounds of language but do not appear in sequences that can be properly called words. (p. 79)

voice qualities: In paralanguage, the background characteristics of a speaker's voice. (p. 79)

wealth: Accumulation of financial resources, material possessions, wives and children, and the potential for future earnings. (p. 225)

Wicca: A neo-pagan belief system involving magic. (p. 290)

witchcraft: An explanation of events based on the belief that certain individuals possess an innate psychic power capable of causing harm, including sickness and death. Also includes beliefs and practices of benevolent magic. (p. 289)

world views: The conceptions, explicit and implicit, an individual or a group has of the limits and workings of its world. (p. 264)

Bibliography

Abler, T.S. "In Memoriam. Sally M. Weaver (1940–1993)." *Anthropologica* 35 (1995).

Abu-Lughod, L. *Veiled Sentiments: Honor and Poetry in a Bedouin Society.* Berkeley: University of California Press, 1986.

———. *Writing Women's Worlds.* Berkeley: University of California Press, 1993.

Achterberg, J., B. Dossey, and L. Kolkmeier, L. *Rituals of Healing: Using Imagery for Health and Wellness.* New York: Bantam, 1994.

Adams, R.E.W. *Prehistoric MesoAmerica.* Norman: University of Oklahoma Press, 1991.

Adelson, N. *Being Alive Well: Health and Politics of Cree Well-Being.* Toronto: University of Toronto Press, 2000.

Ahmadu, F. "Rites and Wrongs: An Insider/Outsider Reflects on Power and Excision." In *Female "Circumcision" in Africa: Culture, Controversy, and Change.* Edited by B. Shell-Duncan and Y. Hernlund. London: Lynne Rienner, 2000. 283–312.

AIDS Monthly Surveillance Summary (through July 1997). San Francisco: Department of Public Health AIDS Office, 1997.

Albert, J. Interview by Rodney Nelson. Conversations with an Elder. 2010.

Allen, D. "Lessons from Africville." *Shunpiking.* September 5, 2001. http://www.shunpiking.com/bhs/Lessons%20from%20Africville.htm. Accessed February 20, 2007.

American Museum of Natural History. "A Body Arts Expo." http://www.coldsteel.co.uk/articles/BodyArtExpo.html. Accessed October 15, 2003.

Ames, M.M. *Cannibal Tours and Glass Boxes: The Anthropology of Museums.* Vancouver: UBC Press, 1992.

Amiran, R. "The Beginnings of Pottery-Making in the Near East." In *Ceramics and Man.* Edited by F.R. Matson. Viking Fund Publications in Anthropology no. 41 (1965). 240–47.

Antoun, R. *Understanding Fundamentalism: Christian, Islamic, and Jewish Movements.* Walnut Creek: AltaMira, 2001.

Arat-Koç, S. "'Good Enough to Work but Not Good Enough to Stay?' Foreign Domestic Workers and the Law." In *Locating Law: Race/Gender/Class Connections.* Edited by E. Comack, 129–52. Halifax: Fernwood, 1999.

———. *Caregivers Break the Silence: A Participatory Action Research on the Abuse and Violence, Including the Impact of Family Separation, Experienced by Women in the Live-In Caregiver Program.* Toronto: Intercede, 2001.

Appadurai, A., ed. *The Social Life of Things.* Cambridge: Cambridge University Press, 1986.

Armelagos, G. "Health and Disease in Prehistoric Populations in Transition." In *Understanding and Applying Medical Anthropology.* Edited by P. Brown. Mountain View: Mayfield, 1998. 59–69.

Armstrong, D.F., W.C. Stokoe, and S.E. Wilcox, "Signs of the Origin of Syntax." *Current Anthropology* 35 (1994): 349–68.

Arzt, D. "Terrorism and Terrorists." *Jurist: The Legal Education Network.* Pittsburgh: University of Pittsburgh School of Law, 2003.

Asch, M., and S. Smith. "Slavey Dene." In *The Cambridge Encyclopedia of Hunters and Gatherers.* Edited by R.B. Lee and R. Daly. Cambridge: Cambridge University Press, 1999. 46–50.

Ashton-Jones, E., G.A. Olson, and M.G. Perry, eds. *The Gender Reader.* 2nd ed. Needham Heights: Allyn and Bacon, 2000.

"Backgrounder: Canada and Peacekeeping." 2001. http://www.dfait-maeci.gc.ca/peacekeepinjg/back-e/asp. Accessed March 20, 2001.

Baer, H.A., M. Singer, and I. Susser. *Medical Anthropology and the World System: A Critical Perspective.* 2nd ed. Westport: Bergin and Garvey, 2004.

Bahuchet, Serge. "Spatial Mobility and Access to Resources Among the African Pygmies." 1991. HAL Archives: http://hal.archives-ouvertes.fr/hal-00261573/en.

Bakan, A., and D. Stasiulis. "Foreign Domestic Worker Policy in Canada and the Social Boundaries of Modern Citizenship." In *Not One of the Family: Foreign Domestic Workers in Canada.* Edited by A. Bakan and D. Stasiulis. Toronto: University of Toronto Press, 1997. 29–52.

Balikci, A. "Anthropology, Film, and the Arctic Peoples: The First Forman Lecture." *Anthropology Today* 5, no. 2 (1989): 4–10.

Barfield, T.J. "Introduction." *Cultural Survival Quarterly* 8, no. 2 (1984).

Barlett, P.F. "Industrial Agriculture." In *Economic Anthropology.* Edited by S. Plattner. Stanford: Stanford University Press, 1989. 253–91.

Barlow, M., and E. May. *Frederick Street: Life and Death on Canada's Love Canal.* Toronto: Harper and Row, 2000.

Barnett, H. Innovation: *The Basis of Cultural Change.* New York: McGraw-Hill, 1953.

Barnouw, V. *Culture and Personality.* 4th ed. Homewood,: Dorsey, 1985.

Baron, N. "Viewpoint: Instant Messaging and the Future of Language." *Communications of the ACM* 48, no. 7 (July 2005): 29–31.

Barr, R.G. "The Crying Game." *Natural History* 47 (October 1997).

Barth, F. *Nomadism in the Mountain and Plateau Areas of South West Asia: The Problems of the Arid Zone.* Paris: UNESCO, 1960. 341–55.

Basow, S.A. "The Motherhood Mandate." In *Gender in Canada.* Edited by E.D. Nelson and B.W. Robinson. Toronto: Prentice Hall Allyn & Bacon, 1992.

Bates, D.G., and F. Plog. *Human Adaptive Strategies.* New York: McGraw-Hill, 1991.

Bautista, F., and M. Boti. *When Strangers Reunite.* Productions Multi-Monde. Video, 55m, 1999.

Beattie, O., and J. Geiger. *Frozen in Time: The Fate of the Franklin Expedition.* London: Bloomsbury, 1987.

Bednarik, R.G. "Concept-Mediated Marking in the Lower Paleolithic. *Current Anthropology* 36 (1995): 606.

Bell, D. "Defining Marriage and Legitimacy." *Current Anthropology* 38 (1997): 241.

Benedict, R. *The Chrysanthemum and the Sword.* New York: Mariner Books, [1946]2005.

Benton-Banai, E. *The Mishomis Book: Voices of the Ojibway.* Minneapolis: University Of Minnesota Press, 1979.

Berdan, F.F. *The Aztecs of Central Mexico.* New York: Holt, Rinehart and Winston, 1982.

Bernardi, B. *Age Class Systems: Social Institutions and Policies Based on Age.* New York: Cambridge University Press, 1985.

Berry, E. (1963). "Foreword." In *Eating and Cooking Around the World: Fingers Before Forks.* New York: John Day, 1963.

Bezruchka, S. "Is Our Society Making You Sick?" *Newsweek*, February 26, 2001, 143.

Bibby, G. *The Testimony of the Spade.* London: Knopf, 1956. 241.

Bibeau, G. "World Health Organization in Encounter with African Traditional Medicine: Theoretical Conceptions and Practical Strategies." In *African Therapeutic Systems.* Edited by Z. Ademuwagun. Waltham: Crossroads Press, 1979.

"Biography of Richard B. Lee." December 2000. http://www.utoronto. ca/anthropology/Faculty/lee.htm. Accessed January 27, 2001.

Birdwhistell, R. *Kinesics and Context: Essays in Body Motion Communication.* Philadelphia: University of Pennsylvania Press, 1970.

Black, H.C. *Black's Law Dictionary.* St. Paul: West, 1968.

Black, J.H. (2000). "Entering the Political Elite in Canada: The Case of Minority Women as Parliamentary Candidates and MPs." *Canadian Review of Sociology and Anthropology 37,* no. 2 (2000).

Blackwood, E., and S.E. Wieringa. "Sapphic Shadows: Challenging the Silence in the Study of Sexuality." In *Female Desires: Same-Sex Relations and Transgender Practices Across Cultures.* Edited by E. Blackwood and S.E. Wieringa. New York: Columbia University Press, 1999.

Blench, R. *Pastoralists in the New Millennium.* London: Overseas Development Institute, 2001.

Blumer, H. *Symbolic Interactionism.* Englewod Cliffs: Transition, 1969.

Block, P. "Doing Cultural Anthropology and Disability Studies in Rehabilitation Training and Research Contexts." In *Anthropology Put to Work.* Edited by L Field and R.G. Fox. Oxford: Berg, 2007. 85–101.

Boas, F. *Race and Democratic Society.* New York: J.J. Augustin, 1945.

Boddy, J. *Wombs and Alien Spirits: Women, Men, and the Zar Cult in Northern Sudan.* Madison: University of Wisconsin Press, 1989.

Bodley, J.H. *Anthropology and Contemporary Human Problems.* 2nd ed. Palo Alto: Mayfield, 1985.

———. "Comment." *Current Anthropology* 38 (1997): 725.

———. *Victims of Progress.* 3rd ed. Mountain View: Mayfield, 1990.

Bonvillain, N. *Women and Men: Cultural Constructs of Gender.* 2nd ed. Upper Saddle River Prentice Hall, 1998.

———. *Language, Culture, and Communication: The Meaning of Messages.* 3rd ed. Upper Saddle River: Prentice Hall, 2000.

Boserup, E. *Women's Role in Economic Development.* New York: St. Martin's, 1970.

Bossen, L. *The Redivision of Labour: Women and Economic Choice in Four Guatemalan Communities.* Albany: SUNY Press, 1984.

———. *Chinese Women and Rural Development: Sixty Years of Change in Lu Village, Yunnan.* Lanham: Rowman and Littlefield, 2002.

Boston Women's Health Book Collective. *Our Bodies, Ourselves for the New Century: A Book by and for Women.* 3rd ed. New York: Simon and Schuster, 1998.

Boti, M., dir. *Modern Heroes, Modern Slaves.* Diffusion Multi-Monde. 44m, 1997.

Boti, M., and F. Bautista, prods. *Brown Women, Blonde Babies.* Diffusion Multi-Monde. 30m, 1992.

Bourgois, P. In *Search of Respect: Selling Crack in El Barrio.* 2nd ed. Cambridge and New York: Cambridge University Press, 2003.

Bradley, R. *The Significance of Monuments* London: Routledge, 1998.

Brascoupé, S. "Aboriginal Vision of the Future: Interweaving Traditional Knowledge and New Technologies." In *Visions of the Heart: Canadian Aboriginal Issues.* Edited by D.A. Long and O.P. Dickason. Toronto: Oxford University Press, 1996. 355–75.

Brettell, C.B., and C.F. Sargent, eds. *Gender in Cross-Cultural Perspective.* 2nd ed. Upper Saddle River: Prentice Hall, 1997.

Bridgman, R. *Safe Haven: The Story of a Woman's Shelter.* Toronto: University of Toronto Press, 2003.

Briggs, J.L. "Inuit Morality Play: The Emotional Education of a Three-Year-Old." *Social and Economic Studies 67* (1998). Institute of Social and Economic Research.

Broecker, W.S. "Global Warming on Trial." *Natural History* 14 (April 1992).

Brooks, G. *Nine Parts of Desire: The Hidden World of Islamic Women.* New York: Anchor Books, 1994.

Brown, P. "Africville: Urban Removal in Canada." 1996. http://www. hartford-hwp.com/archives/44/170. html. Accessed February 20, 2007.

Brown, P., ed. *Understanding and Applying Medical Anthropology.* Mountain View: Mayfield, 1998.

Buckley, T., and A. Gottlieb. "A Critical Appraisal of Theories of Menstrual Symbolism." In *Blood Magic: The Anthropology of Menstruation.* Edited by T. Buckley and A. Gottlieb. Berkeley: University of California Press, 1988. 1–53.

Bullock, K. "You Don't Have to Wear That in Canada." 2001. http://www. soundvision.com/news/hijab/hjb. canada1.shtml. Accessed March 13, 2001.

Burkhalter, B. "If Only They Would Listen: The Anthropology of Business and the Business of Anthropology." In *Classics of Practicing Anthropology, 1978–1998.* Edited by P.J. Higgins and J.A. Paredes. Oklahoma City: Society for Applied Anthropology, 2000. 77–86.

Cachel, S. "Dietary Shifts and the European Upper Paleolithic Transition." *Current Anthropology* 38 (1997): 590.

Campbell, J.D., D.P. Yoon, and B. Johnstone, 2010. "Determining Relationships Between Physical Health and Spiritual Experience, Religious Practices, and Congregational Support in a Heterogeneous Medical Sample." *Journal of Religion and Health* 49 (2010): 3–17.

Canada and the World. "Culture Shock: Immigrants Come to Canada with the Hope of Improving Life for Themselves and Future Generations but Fitting into an Entirely New Culture Isn't Easy." *Canada and the World Backgrounder* 63, no. 4 (January 1998).

Canadian Arctic Resources Committee. *Final Argument and Recommendations: The Mackenzie Valley Pipeline Inquiry.* Ottawa: Canadian Arctic Resources Committee, 1976.

Canadian Art at the McMichael. (1996–2000). "The Group of Seven and Their Contemporaries." http:// www.mcmichael.com/group.htm. Accessed March 29, 2001.

Canadian Federation of Agriculture. "The Canadian Farm." March 1998. http://www.cfa-fca/farms-e.htm. Accessed April 11, 2001.

Canadian Museum of Civilization. 1965 CBC interview with Marius Barbeau. http://www.civilization.ca/academ/barbeau/banaeng.html. Originally published in 1982 in the Oracle series, no. 44. of the National Museum of Man. Accessed August 11, 2003.

Caroulis, J. "Food for Thought." *Pennsylvania Gazette* 95, no. 3 (1996): 16.

Carson, R. *Silent Spring.* Boston: Houghton Mifflin, 1962.

Cashdan, E. "Hunters and Gatherers: Economic Behaviour in Bands." In *Economic Anthropology.* Edited by S. Plattner. Stanford, CA: Stanford University Press, 1989.

Cavallo, J.A. "Cat in the Human Cradle." *Natural History*, February 1990, 54–60.

CBC News. "Toronto Imam Attacked in Hate Crime in Canada." 12 June, 2006. http://www.pluralism.org/news/intl/index.php?xref=Anti-Muslim+Backlash+After+Canadian+Arrests&sort=DESC#headline12619. Accessed February 25, 2007.

———. "Grand Banks Cod Stocks Grow 69% Since 2007." September 16, 2010. http://www.cbc.ca/technology/story/2010/09/16/cod-grand-banks-wwf-nafo.html.

Census of Agriculture. "History of the Census of Agriculture." February 22, 2001. http://142.206.72.65/06_011_e.htm. Accessed April 11, 2001.

———. Centers for Disease Control Semi-Annual AIDS Report (through June 1996). Atlanta: 1997.

Chambers, J.K. "English: Canadian Varieties." In *Language in Canada.* Edited by J. Edwards. Cambridge: Cambridge University Press, 1998. 252–72.

Chambers, R. *Rural Development: Putting the Last First.* New York: Longman, 1983.

Chasin, B.H., and R.W. Franke. "U.S. Farming: A World Model?" *Global Reporter* 1, no. 2 (1983): 10.

Chee-Hong, B.C. "Habitat for Humanity in Slovakia: The Roma of Svinia—A Case Study." 2005. http://elearning.hfhu/documents/case/HFHU_Slovakia.pdf. Accessed February 25, 2007.

Cherney, B. "Ukrainian Immigration." October 28, 2000. http://www.mbnet.mb.ca/~rfmorris/Featuring/Immigration/Ukrainian.Immigration.html. Accessed March 13, 2001.

Chodorow, N. "Being and Doing: A Cross-Cultural Examination of the Socialization of Males and Females." In *Woman in Sexist Society.* Edited by V. Gornick and B.K. Moran. New York: Basic Books, 1971.

Clark, W.E.L. (1960). *The Antecedents of Man.* Chicago: Quadrangle Books, 1960.

———. *The Fossil Evidence for Human Evolution.* Chicago: University of Chicago Press, 1995.

Clay, J.W. "What's a Nation?" In *Talking About People.* 2nd ed. Edited by W.A. Haviland and R.J. Gordon, Mountain View: Mayfield, 1996.

Cohen, M.N. *Health and the Rise of Civilization.* New Haven: Yale University Press, 1989.

Cohen, M., and G. Armelagos. *Paleopathology and the Origins of Agriculture.* New Haven: Yale University Press, 1984.

Cohen, R., and J. Middleton, eds. *Comparative Political Systems.* Garden City: Natural History Press, 1967.

Colen, S. "'Like a Mother to Them': Stratified Reproduction and West Indian Childcare Workers and Employers in New York." In *Conceiving the New World Order: The Global Politics of Reproduction.* Edited by F. Finsburg and R. Rapp. Berkeley: University of California Press, 1995. 78–102.

Collier, J., M.Z.R., and S. Yanagisako. "Is There a Family? New Anthropological Views." In *Rethinking the Family: Some Feminist Questions.* Edited by B. Thorne and M. Yalom. New York: Longman, 1982. 25–39.

Combs, J. *Polpop: Politics and Popular Culture in America.* Bowling Green: Bowling Green University Popular Press, 1984.

Commission on the Future of Health Care in Canada. (2002). *The Romanov Report: Building on Values: The Future of Health Care in Canada.* Ottawa: Government Printers.

Conaty, G.T. "Economic Models and Blackfoot Ideology." *American Ethnologist* 22, no. 2 (May 1995): 403–9.

Connell, R.W. "Making Gendered People: Bodies, Identities, Sexualities." In *Revisioning Gender.* Edited by M.M. Ferree, J. Locker, and B. Hess. Thousand Oaks: Sage, 1999.

Coon, C.S. *A Reader in General Anthropology.* New York: Holt, Rinehart and Winston, 1948.

———. *The Story of Man.* New York: Knopf, 1954.

———. *Caravan: The Story of the Middle East.* 2nd ed. New York: Holt, Rinehart and Winston, 1958.

Cooper, A., H.N. Poinar, S. Pääbo, J. Radovcic, A, Debénath, M. Caparros, C. Barroso-Ruiz, J. Bertranpetit, C. Nielsen-March, C., R.E.M. Hedges, and B. Sykes. "Neanderthal Genetics" *Science* 277 (1997): 1021–24.

Corin, E. "Refiguring the Person: The Dynamics of Effects and Symbols in an African Spirit Possession Cult." In *Bodies and Persons: Comparative Perspectives from Africa and Melanesia.* Edited by M. Lambek and A. Strathearn. Cambridge: Cambridge University Press, 1998.

Counts, D.A. and D.R. Counts. *Over the Next Hill: An Ethnography of RVing Seniors in North America.* Peterborough: Broadview Press, 1998.

Cowgill, G.L. "Letter." *Science* 210 (1980): 1305.

Crane, L.B., E. Yeager, and R.L. Whitman. *An Introduction to Linguistics.* Boston: Little, Brown, 1981.

Crocker, W.H., and J. Crocker. *The Canela: Bonding Through Kinship, Ritual, and Sex.* Fort Worth: Harcourt Brace, 1994.

Crosby, A. *The Columbian Exchange: Biological and Cultural Consequences of 1492.* 30th anniversary ed. Westport: Praeger, [1972]2003.

Crosley, N. *Making Sense of Social Movements.* Buckingham: Open University Press, 2002.

Crowly, V. "Wicca as Nature Religion." In *Nature Religion Today: Paganism in the Modern World.* Edited by J. Pearson, R.H. Roberts, and F. Samuel. Edinburgh: Edinburgh University Press, 1998.

Crowshaw, C. *Sacred Ways of Life: Traditional Knowledge.* Ottawa: National Aboriginal Health Organization, 2005.

Cruikshank, J. "Changing Traditions in Northern Ethnography." n.d. http://arcticcircle.uconn.edu/Museum/Anthropology/NorthernReview/cruikshank.html. Accessed July 3, 2001.

———. "Oral Tradition and Material Culture: Multiplying Meanings of 'Words; and 'Things.'" 1992. http://sapir.ukc.ac.uk/PRM/prmroot/

musantob/thobrep1.html. Accessed July 5, 2001.

Cultural Survival Quarterly 15, no. 4 (1991): 38.

Dalton, G. *Traditional Tribal and Peasant Economics: An Introductory Survey of Economic Anthropology.* Reading: Addison-Wesley, 1971.

Daly, M. "African Genital Mutilation: The Unspeakable Atrocities." In *The Gender Reader.* Edited by E. Ashton-Jones, G.A. Olson, and M.G. Perry. Needham Heights: Allyn and Bacon, 2000. 462–85.

Damas, D. "Central Eskimo Systems of Food Sharing." *Ethnology* 11 (1972): 220–40.

Davis, K., and W.E. Moore. "Some Principles of Stratification." In *Social Stratification: Class, Race, and Gender in Sociological Perspectives.* Edited by D.B. Grusky. Boulder: Westview Press, 2001. 55–64.

Davies, J. "Turning the Tide: Enabling Sustainable Development for Africa's Mobile Pastoralists." *Natural Resources Forum* 32 (2008): 175–84.

Davis, S.H. *Victims of the Miracle.* Cambridge: Cambridge University Press, 1982.

Davis, W. *The Wayfinders* Toronto: Anansi Press, 2009.

Delaney, C., with D. Kaspin. *Investigating Culture.* Malden: Wiley-Blackwell, 2011.

Delisle, R.G. *Debating Humankind's Place in Nature: 1860–2000, the Nature of Paleoanthropology.* Upper Saddle River: Pearson-Prentice Hall, 2007.

DeVos, G.A. "Concepts of Ethnic Identity." In *Ethnic Identity, Creation, Conflict, and Accommodation.* Edited by L. Ramanucci-Ross and G.A. DeVos. 3rd ed. Walnut Creek: Altamira, 1995. 15–47.

de Waal, A. "Genocide in Rwanda." *Anthropology Today* 10, no. 3 (1994): 1–2.

de Waal, F. *Good-Natured: The Origins of Right and Wrong in Humans and Other Animals.* Cambridge, MA: Harvard University Press, 1996.

Demian. "Marriage Traditions in Various Times and Cultures." February 18, 2007. http://www.Buddybuddy.com/mar-trad.html. Accessed June 31, 2005.

DeMello, M. *Bodies of Inscription: A Cultural History of the Modern Tattoo Community.* Durham: Duke University Press, 2000.

Dennant, P. "Urban Expression ... Urban Assault ... Urban Wildstyle ... New York City graffiti." 1997. http://www.graffiti.org/faq/pamdennant.html. Accessed July 4, 2001.

Department of Anthropology, University of Toronto. "Janice Boddy." 2001. http://www.scar.utoronto.ca/acad/bios/data/boddy.html. Accessed June 26, 2001.

Department of Fine Arts, Okanagan University College. "Important Moments in the History of Canadian Visual Culture: R.J. Belton." 1999. http://www.ouc.bc.ca/fiar/1918_45.html. Accessed March 13, 2001.

Department of Sociology and Anthropology, Simon Fraser University. "Dr. Dara Culhane." October 2003. http://www.sfu.ca/sociology/01department/biographies/culhane.html. Accessed February 12, 2004.

Dettinger, K.A. "When to Wean." *Natural History* 49 (October 1997).

Dewar, E. *Cloak of Green.* Toronto: Lorimer, 1995.

Diamond, J. "The Curse of QWERTY." *Discover* 18, no. 4 (1997): 34–42.

Díaz del Castillo, B. [1519]. *The Conquest of New Spain.* Translated by J.M. Cohen. Harmondsworth: Penguin, 1973.

di Leonardo, M. "Introduction." *Gender at the Crossroads of Knowledge: Feminist Anthropology in the Postmodern Era.* Berkeley: University of California Press, 1991.

———. "The Female World of Cards and Holidays: Women, Families, and the Work of Kinship." In *Gender in Cross-Cultural Perspective.* Edited by C.B. Brettell and C.F. Sargent. Upper Saddle River: Prentice Hall, 1997. 340–350.

Dixon, E. James. "Peopling of the Americas." *Athena Review* 3, no. 2 (2002).

Doretti, M., and J. Burrell. "Gray Spaces and Endless Negotiations: Forensic Anthropology and Human Rights." In *Anthropology Put to Work.* Edited by L. Field and R.G. Fox. Oxford: Berg, 2007. 45–64.

Dorfer, L. M. Moser, F. Bahr, K. Spindler, E. Egarter-Vigl, S. Giullén, G. Dohr, and T. Kenner. "A Medical Report from the Stone Age?" *The Lancet* 354 (September 18, 1999).

Douglas, M. *Purity and Danger: An Analysis of the Concepts of Pollution and Taboo.* London: Routledge, [1966]1991.

Downe, P. "Unheard Voices at Risk: Women and AIDS." n.d. http://www.geocities.com/Wellesley/3321/win4c.htm. Accessed February 16, 2007.

Drapeau, L. "Aboriginal Languages: Current Status." In *Language in Canada.* Edited by J. Edwards. Cambridge: Cambridge University Press, 1998. 144–59.

Dubrow, S. "Book Review." *Canadian Journal of Native Studies* 11, no. 1 (1991). http://www.brandonu.ca/native/cjns. Accessed July 4, 2001.

Dundes, A. *Interpreting Folklore.* Bloomington, IN: Indiana University Press, 1980.

Dunk, T. "Culture, Skill, Masculinity, and Whiteness: Training and the Politics of Identity." In *The Training Trap: Ideology, Training, and the Labour Market.* Edited by T. Dunk, S. McBride, and R.W. Nelson. Halifax: Fernwood, 1996. 101–23.

duToit, B.M. *Human Sexuality: Cross-Cultural Readings.* New York: McGraw-Hill, 1991.

Dyck, N., and J.B. Waldram, eds. *Anthropology, Public Policy, and Native Peoples in Canada.* Montreal and Kingston: McGill-Queen's University Press, 1993.

Eastman, C.M. *Aspects of Language and Culture,* 2nd ed. Novato, CA: Chandler and Sharp, 1990.

Eaton, B., M. Shostak, and M. Konner. *The Paleolithic Prescription: A Program of Diet and Exercise and a Design for Living.* New York: Harper and Row, 1988.

Edelman, M. "Social Movements: Changing Paradigms and Forms of Politics." *Annual Review of Anthropology* 30 (2001): 285–317.

Ehrenreich, B., and D. English. *For Her Own Good: 150 Years of Experts' Advice to Women.* New York: Anchor Books, 1978.

Eighth Annual Young Scientist Conference. "Owen Beattie." n.d. http://ftp.ei.educ.ab.ca/dept/ins/beattie.html. Accessed October 16, 2000.

Elkin, A.P. *The Australian Aborigines.* Garden City: Doubleday/Anchor, 1964.

Eller, J.D. *From Culture to Ethnicity to Conflict: An Anthropological Perspective on International Ethnic Conflict.* Ann Arbor: University of Michigan Press, 1999.

Elvir, M. "The Work at Home Is Not Recognized: Organizing Domestic Workers in Montreal." In *Not One of* the Family: Foreign Domestic Workers in Canada. Edited by A. Bakan and D. Stasiulis. Toronto: University of Toronto Press, 1997. 147–56.

Ember, C.J., & M. Ember. *Cultural Anthropology*. 4th ed. Englewood Cliffs: Prentice-Hall, 1985.

———. "What Have We Learned from Cross-Cultural Research?" *General Anthropology* 2, no. 2 (1996): 5.

Endicott, K.L. "Gender Relations in Hunter-Gatherer Societies." In *The Cambridge Encyclopedia of Hunters and Gatherers*. Edited by R.B. Lee and R. Daly. Cambridge, UK: Cambridge University Press, 1999. 411–18.

England, K., and B. Stiell. "'They Think You're as Stupid as Your English Is': Constructing Foreign Domestic Workers in Toronto." *Environment and Planning A* 29 (1997): 195–215.

Epstein, A.L. "Sanctions." *International Encyclopedia of Social Sciences* 14. New York: Macmillan, 1968. 3.

Erera, P.I. *Family Diversity: Continuity and Change in the Contemporary Family*. Thousand Oaks: Sage, 2002.

Ervin, A.M. *Applied Anthropology: Tools and Perspectives for Contemporary Practice*. Toronto: Pearson, 2005.

Ervin, A.M., and L. Holyoak. "Applied Anthropology in Canada: Historical Foundations, Contemporary Practice, and Policy Potentials." *NAPA Bulletin* 25, no. 1 (2006): 134–55.

Erwin, A.M. *Canadian Perspectives in Cultural Anthropology*. Toronto: Nelson Thomson Learning, 2000.

Evans-Pritchard, E.E. *Witchcraft, Oracles and Magic among the Azande*. London: Oxford University Press, 1937.

———. *The Nuer: A Description of the Modes of Livelihood and Political Institutions of a Nilotic People*. Oxford: Oxford University Press, 1969.

Ewers, J.C. *The Horse in Blackfoot Indian Culture*. Washington, DC: Smithsonian Institute Press, 1985.

Fagan, B.M. *Eyewitness to Discovery*. New York: Oxford University Press, 1996.

Falk, D. "Ape-Like Endocast of 'Ape Man Taung.'" *American Journal of Physical Anthropology* 80 (1989): 335–39.

Farley, J. *Majority-Minority Relations*. Upper Saddle River: Pearson Prentice Hall, 2005.

Farmer, P. *AIDS and Accusation: Haiti and the Geography of Blame*.

Berkeley: University of California Press, 1992.

Fedigan, L.M. *Primate Paradigms: Sex Roles and Social Bonds*. Montreal: Eden Press, 1982.

———. "The Changing Role of Women in Models of Human Evolution." *Annual Review of Anthropology* 15 (1986): 25–66.

Fedorak, S. *Anthropology Matters!* Toronto: Broadview Press, 2007.

Ferraro, G. *Cultural Anthropology: An Applied Perspective*. Belmont: Thomson-Wadsworth, 2008.

Field Studies in Europe. "The Svinia Project." n.d. http://www.tru.ca/europe/svinia_porject.htm. Accessed February 25, 2007.

Firth, R. "Two Studies of Kinship in London." London: University of London, Athlone Press, 1956.

Fleising, U. "In Search of Genohype: A Content Analysis of Biotechnology Company Documents." *New Genetics and Society*, 20, no. 3 (2001):, 239–254.

Fleras, A., and J.L. Elliot. *Engaging Diversity: Multiculturalism in Canada*. Toronto: Nelson Thomson, 2002.

Fontaine, P. "Modern Racism in Canada." The 1998 Donald Gow Lecture, School of Policy Studies, Queen's University, Kingston, Ontario, 1998.

Forde, C.D. *Habitat, Economy, and Society*. New York: Dutton, 1950.

———. "Double Descent Among the Yakö." In *Kinship and Social Organization*. Edited by P. Bohannan and J. Middleton. Garden City: Natural History Press, 1968. 179–91.

Foucault, M. *The Birth of the Clinic: An Archaeology of Medical Perception*. New York: Vintage, 1975.

Fox, R. *Kinship and Marriage in an Anthropological Perspective*. Baltimore: Penguin, 1967.

———. *Encounter with Anthropology*. New York: Dell, 1968.

———. "Food and Eating: An Anthropological Perspective." n.d. http://www.sirc.org/publik/food_and_eating_3.html. Accessed August 27, 2003.

The Francophone Connection. "The Acadians of Nova Scotia." 2002. http://www.francophonie.gc.ca/communit/ne_shtml. Accessed August 13, 2003.

Frankenberry, N.K., and H.H. Penner. "Clifford Geertz's Long Lasting Moods, Motivations, and Metaphys-

ical Conceptions." *Journal of Religion* 79, no. 4 (1999): 617–40.

Frazer, J.G. "Magic and Religion." In *The Making of Man: An Outline of Anthropology*. Edited by V.F. Claverton. New York: Modern Library, 1931. 693–713.

Freccero, C. *Popular Culture: An Introduction*. New York: New York University Press, 1999.

Freeman, L.G. "Ambrona and Torralba: New Evidence and Interpretation." Paper presented at the 91st Annual Meeting of the American Anthropological Association, Chicago, 1992.

Fried, M. *The Evolution of Political Society: An Essay in Political Anthropology*. New York: Random House, 1967.

Friesen, J.W. *Rediscovering the First Nations of Canada*. Calgary: Detselig, 1997.

———. *First Nations of the Plains: Creative, Adaptable, Enduring*. Calgary: Detselig, 1999.

Frye, M. "Sexism." In *The Politics of Reality*. New York: Crossing Press, 1983. 17–40.

Gardner, R.A., Gardner, B.T., and Van Cantfort, T.E., eds. *Teaching Sign Language to Chimpanzees*. Albany: SUNY Press, 1989.

Gates, H. "Buying Brides in China—Again." *Anthropology Today* 12, no. 4 (1996): 10.

GCS Research Society. "Biruté Galdikas: Anthropologist." 1996. http://www.science.ca/scientists/Galdikas/galdikas.html. Accessed November 25, 2000.

Geertz, C. "Religion as a Cultural System." In *Anthropological Approaches to the Study of Religion*. Edited by M. Banton. London: Tavistock, 1999. 1–46.

Gell, A. "Technology and Magic." *Anthropology Today* 4, no. 2 (1988): 6–9.

Gell, A. *Art and Agency*. Oxford: Clarendon, 1998.

Genesee, F. Jr. Interview: "Faces of Culture: Program 18." Fountain Valley: Coast Telecourses, 1983.

———. "French Immersion in Canada." In *Language in Canada*. Edited by J. Edwards. Cambridge: Cambridge University Press, 1988. 305–26.

Geoffroy-Schneiter, B. *Primal Arts*. New York: Assouline, 2006.

Gibbs, J.L., Jr. "The Kpelle of Liberia." In *Peoples of Africa*. Edited by J.L. Gibbs, Jr. New York: Holt, Rinehart and Winston, 1965. 197–240.

Gibbs, L. *Dying from Dioxin: A Citizen's Guide to Reclaiming Our Health and Rebuilding Democracy.* Boston: South End Press, 1995.

———. *Love Canal: The Story Continues.* Gabriola Island,: New Society, 1998.

Giles, W. *Portuguese Women in Toronto: Gender, Immigration, and Nationalism.* Toronto: University of Toronto Press, 2002.

Gilmore, D.D. "The Manhood Puzzle." In *Gender in Cross-Cultural Perspective.* 2nd ed. Edited by C.B. Brettell and C.F. Sargent. Upper Saddle River: Prentice Hall, 1997. 185–97.

Girvan, S., ed. *Canadian Global Almanac 2003.* Toronto: John Wiley and Sons. 2002.

Gmelch, G. "Baseball Magic." In *Anthropology 05/06.* Edited by E. Angeloni. Dubuque: McGraw-Hill/Dushkin, 2000.

Goddard, V. "Child Labor in Naples." In *Talking About People.* Edited by W.A. Haviland and R.J. Gordon. Mountain View: Mayfield, 1993. 105–9.

Golbert, R. "An Anthropologist's Approach to Mediation." *Cardozo Journal of Conflict Resolution* 11, no. 1 (2008).

Goodall, J. *The Chimpanzees of Gombe: Patterns of Behavior.* Cambridge, MA: Belknap Press, 1986.

———. *Through a Window: My Thirty Years with the Chimpanzees of Gombe.* Boston: Houghton Mifflin, 1990.

Goodenough, W. (1970). *Description and Comparison in Cultural Anthropology.* Chicago: Aldine, 1970.

———. "Evolution of the Human Capacity for Beliefs." *American Anthropologist* 92 (1990): 597–612.

Goodman, A., and T. Leatherman, eds. *Building a New Biocultural Synthesis: Political-Economic Perspectives on Human Biology.* Ann Arbor: University of Michigan Press, 1998.

Goody, J. *The Development of the Family and Marriage in Europe.* Cambridge: Cambridge University Press, 1983.

Gordillo, G. "The Breath of the Devils: Memories and Places of an Experience of Terror." *American Ethnologist* 29, no. 1 (2002): 33–57.

Gordon, R. "Interview for Coast Telecourses." Los Angeles: 1981 (December).

Gordon, R.J., and M.J. Megitt. *Law and Order in the New Guinea Highlands.* Hanover: University Press of New England, 1985.

Gordon, R.J. *The Bushman Myth.* Oxford: Westview Press, 1992.

Gould, S.J. *Hens' Teeth and Horses' Toes.* New York: Norton, 1983.

———. *Full House: The Spread of Excellence from Plato to Darwin.* New York: Harmony Books, 1996.

Goulet, J.A. "The 'Berdache' / 'Two-Spirit': A Comparison of Anthropological and Native Constructions of Gendered Identities Among the Northern Athapaskans." *Journal of Royal Anthropological Institute* 2 (December 1996): 683–701.

Graffam, G. "Design Anthropology Meets Marketing." *Anthropolgica* 52 (2010): 155–64.

Green, E.C. "The Planning of Health Education Strategies in Swaziland" and "The Integration of Modern and Traditional Health Sectors in Swaziland." In *Anthropological Praxis: Translating Knowledge into Action.* Edited by R.M. Wulff and S.J. Fiske. Boulder, CO: Westview, 1987. 15–25, 87–97.

Greenhill, P. "Folkdrama in Anglo Canada and the Mock Wedding: Transactions, Performance, and Meaning." *Canadian Drama* 14 (1988): 172–73.

Grugulis, I., and S. Vincent. "'Whose Skill Is It Anyway?' 'Soft' Skills and Polarization." *Work, Employment, and Society* 23, no. 4 (2009): 597–615.

Guenther, M. *Tricksters and Trancers.* Bloomington: Indiana University Press, 1999.

Hachem, L. "New Observations on the Bandkeramic House and Social Organization." *Antiquity* 74 (2000): 308–12.

Haeri, N. "The Reproduction of Symbolic Capital: Language, State, and class in Egypt." *Current Anthropology* 38 (1997): 795–816.

Hagan, J., and W. Rymond-Richmond. *Darfur and the Crime of Genocide.* Cambridge: Cambridge University Press, 2009.

Hale, H. "The Tutelo Tribe and Language." *Proceedings of the American Philosophical Society* 21, no. 114 (1883).

Hall, E.T., and M.R. Hall. "The Sounds of Silence." In *Anthropology 86/87.* Edited by E. Angeloni. Guilford: Dushkin, 1986. 65–70.

Hanley, S. "The Emergence of Pensioners' Parties in Contemporary Europe." In *Young Generation Under Pressure? The Financial Situation and the "Rush Hour" of the Cohorts, 1970–1985 in a Generational Comparison.* Edited by J.C. Tremmel. Berlin: Springer Verlag, 2010. 225–44.

Hannah, J.L. *Dance, Sex, and Gender.* Chicago: University of Chicago Press, 1988.

Hansen, J., D. Dunn, R.B. Lee, P. Becker, and T. Jenkins. "Hunter-Gatherer to Pastoral Way of Life: Effects of the Transition on Health, Growth, and Nutritional Status." *South African Journal of Science* 89 (1994): 559–64.

Harper, C.L. *Environment and Society.* Toronto: Pearson/Prentice Hall, 2008.

Harries-Jones, P. "Canadian Anthropology in an International Context." *Canadian Review of Sociology and Anthropology* 34, no. 3 (1997): 249–58.

Harris, M. "How Our Skins Got Their Colour." In *Rethinking the Colour Line.* Edited by C.A. Gallagher. New York: McGraw-Hill, 2004. 7–9.

Harris Gallery. "Inuit Art Background." 2001. http://www.harrisinuitgallery.com/artinfo.htm. Accessed April 3, 2001.

Harrison, J., and R. Darnell. *Historicizing Canadian Anthropology.* Vancouver: UBC Press, 2007.

Hatch, E. *Culture and Morality: The Relativity of Values in Anthropology.* New York: Columbia University Press, 1983.

Hatcher, E.P. *Art as Culture: An Introduction to the Anthropology of Art.* New York: University Press of America, 1985.

Hauch, C. "Reciprocity on Skid Row." In *Peoples of the Past and Present: Readings in Anthropology.* Edited by J.L. Chodkiewicz. Toronto: Harcourt Brace, 1995.

Haviland, W.A., and M.W. Power. *The Original Vermonters: Native Inhabitants, Past and Present.* Rev. and exp. ed. Hanover: University Press of New England, 1994.

Hawkes, K., J.F. O'Connell, and N.G. Blurton Jones. (1997). "Hadza Women's Time Allocation, Offspring Provisioning, and the Evolution of Long Postmenopausal Life Spans." *Current Anthropology* 38 (1997): 551–77.

Hazan, H. "Victim into Sacrifice: The Construction of the Old as a Symbolic Type." *Journal of Cross-Cultural Gerontology* 5 (1990): 77–84.

Hedigan, E.J. *Applied Anthropology in Canada: Understanding Aboriginal*

Issues. Toronto: University of Toronto Press, 1995.

Heilbroner, R.L., and L.C. Thurow. *The Economic Problem.* 6th ed. Englewood Cliffs: Prentice-Hall, 1981.

Helin, Calvin. *Dances with Dependency.* Woodland Hill: Raven Crest, 2009.

Heller, M. "Globalization, the New Economy, and the Commodification of Language and Identity." *Journal of Sociolinguistics* 7, no. 4 (2003): 473–92.

Henry, F., and C. Tator. *The Colour of Democracy: Racism in Canadian Society.* Toronto: Nelson, 2006.

Henry, J. *"Culture Against Man.* New York: Vintage Books, 1965.

———. "A Theory for an Anthropological Analysis of American Culture." In *Anthropology and American Life.* Edited by J.G. Jorgensen and M. Truzzi. Englewood Cliffs: Prentice-Hall, 1974. 14.

Herdt, G. *The Sambia: Ritual, Sexuality, and Change in Papua New Guinea.* 2nd ed. Belmont CA: Thomson Wadsworth, 2006.

Hern, W. "Family Planning, Amazon Style." *Natural History* 101, no. 12 (December 1992).

Herskovits, M.J. *Economic Anthropology: A Study in Comparative Economics.* 2nd ed. New York: Knopf, 1952.

Hertzman, C. "Health and Human Society." *American Scientist* 89 (2001): 538–545.

Heshilwood, C., F. d'Errico, M. Vanhaeren, F. Niekerk, and Z. Jacobs. "Middle Stone Age Shell Beads from South Africa." *Science* 304, no. 5669: 404.

Hewlett, B.S. *Intimate Fathers.* Ann Arbor: University of Michigan Press, 1991.

Hewlett, B.S., and M.E. Lamb, eds. *Hunter-Gatherer Childhoods.* New Brunswick: Transaction, 2005.

Hickerson, N.P. *Linguistic Anthropology.* New York: Holt, Rinehart and Winston, 1980.

Higgins, P.J., and J.A. Paredes, eds. *Classics of Practicing Anthropology, 1978–1998.* Oklahoma City: Society for Applied Anthropology, 2000.

Hilts, P. *Smokescreen: The Truth Behind the Tobacco Industry Coverup.* New York: Addison-Wesley, 1996.

Hodder, I. *The Domestication of Europe.* Oxford: Blackwell, 1990.

———. The Domus: Some Problems Reconsidered'. In *Understanding the Neolithic of North-Western Europ.* Edited

by M. Edmonds and C. Richards. Glasgow: Cruithne, 1998. 84–101.

Hoe, B.S. *Beyond the Golden Mountain: Chinese Cultural Traditions in Canada.* Ottawa: Canadian Museum of Civilization, 1989.

Hoebel, E.A. *The Law of Primitive Man: A Study in Comparative Legal Dynamics.* Cambridge, MA: Harvard University Press, 1954.

———. *Anthropology: The Study of Man,* 4th ed. New York: McGraw-Hill, 1972.

Honigmann, J.J. "The Kaska Indians: An Ethnographic Reconstruction." *Publications in Anthropology* no. 51 (1954).

Hoodfar, H. *Between Marriage and the Market: Intimate Politics and Survival in Cairo.* Berkeley: University of California Press, 1997.

Howell, N. *Demography of the Dobe !Kung.* 2nd ed. Hawthorne: Aldine-DeGruyter, 2000.

Hultgren, A.K. 2011. "'Building Rapport' with Customers Across the World: The Global Diffusion of a Call Centre Speech Style." *Journal of Sociolinguistics* 15, no. 1 (2011): 36–64.

Hunter, D. "No 'Malice in Wonderland': Conservation and Change in the Three Halloweens of Ann Mesko." *Culture and Tradition* 7 (1983): 36–53.

Huntington, H. "How Table Manners Become Polite." 2002. http://search.csmonitor.com/durable/2000/11/28/p22s1.htm. Accessed August 27, 2003,

Huxley, J., and A.C. Haddon. "The Racial Question—Theory and Fact." *Antiquity* 9 (1935): 261–76.

Ibrahim, Y. 2010. "Between Revolution and Defeat: Student Protest Cycles and Networks." *Sociology Compass* 4, no. 7 (2010): 495–504.

Indian and Northern Affairs Canada. "Federal Policy Guide—Aboriginal Self-Government." July 21, 2000. http://www.ainc-inac.gc.ca/pr/pub/sg/plcy_e.html. Accessed March 21, 2001.

———. "Biographical data. Bernard Saladin d'Anglure: Northern Science Award Winner." 2003. http://www.ainc-inac.gc.ca/nr/prs/j-a2003/02293bbk-e.html. Accessed September 20, 2003.

Ingoldsby, B.B. "Family Origins and Universality." In *Families in Multicultural Perspective.* Edited by B.B. Ingoldsby and S. Smith. New York: The Guilford Press, 1995. 36–58.

"Islamic School Vandalized in Mississauga, Canada." *Mississauga News.*

June 7, 2006. http://www.pluralism.org/news/intl/index.php?xref=Anti-Muslim+Backlash+After+Canadian+Arrests&sort=DESC#headline12611. Accessed February 25, 2007.

"It's the Law: Child Labor Protection." *Peace and Justice News* 11 (November 1997).

Jacobs, M. "Living Together Replacing 'I Do' for Many." *Edmonton Sun.* July 17, 2002.

Jain, R.K. (1997). "Comment." *Current Anthropology* 38 (1997): 248.

Jefremovas, V. "Women Are Good with Money: The Impact of Cash Cropping on Class Relations and Gender Ideology in Northern Luzon, the Philippines." In *Women Farmers and Commercial Ventures: Increasing Food Security in Developing Countries.* Edited by A. Spring. Boulder: Lynne Rienner, 2000.

Jenness, D. Eskimo Administration II. Canada. Montreal: Arctic Institute of North America, Technical Paper no. 14, 1964.

Jiménez, N. "Immigrants Battle Chronic Low Income." CTVglobemedia Publishing. January 31, 2007. http://www.uofaweb.ualberta.ca/govrel/news.cfm?story=56029. Accessed January 31, 2007.

Johanson, D., and J. Shreeve. *Lucy's Child: The Discovery of a Human Ancestor.* New York: Avon, 1989.

Johnson, A.W., and T. Earle. *The Evolution of Human Societies, from Foraging Group to Agrarian State.* Stanford: Stanford University Press, 1987.

Johnson, B. "Human Rights and the Environment." In *Classics of Practicing Anthropology, 1978–1998.* Edited by P.J. Higgins and J.A. Paredes. Oklahoma City: Society for Applied Anthropology, 2000. 223–30.

Johnson, D. "Polygamists Emerge from Secrecy, Seeking Not Just Peace but Respect." In *Talking About People.* 2nd ed. Edited by W.A. Haviland and R.J. Gordon. Mountain View, CA: Mayfield. 129–31.

Johnson, J. "Saskatchewan Population Sinking." *Saskatoon Star Phoenix,* 14 March, 2001.

Johnson, L.M. "Indigenous Knowledge as a Basis for Living in Local Environments." In *Ethnographic Essays in Cultural Anthropology: A Problem-Based Approach.* Edited by R.B. Morrison and C.R. Wilson. Itasca: F.E. Peacock, 2002.

Johnston, B. *Ojibway Heritage.* Toronto: McClelland and Stewart, 2005.

Jolly, A. "Thinking like a Vervet." *Science,* 251 (1991): 574.

Jones, S. "Fundamentalism." 1998. http://religiousmovements.lib.virginia.edu/nrms/fund.html. Accessed March 4, 2007.

Joralemon, D. *Exploring Medical Anthropology.* Boston: Allyn and Bacon, 1999.

Joyce, C. *Witnesses from the Grave: The Stories Bones Tell.* Boston: Little, Brown, 1991.

Judd, E. *Gender and Power in Rural North China.* Stanford: Stanford University Press, 1994.

Junker, K., and V. Vergara. "Wicca." 2001. http://religiousmovements. lib.virginia.edu/nrms/wicca/html. Accessed October 24, 2003.

Kakodyniak, G.W. "Internment of Ukrainians in Canada 1914–1920." 1998. http://www.infoukes.com/history/internment. Accessed October 19, 2003.

Katz, R. *Boiling Energy: Community Healing Among the !Kung.* Cambridge: Harvard University Press, 1982.

Keida, S. "Recent Changes and Trends in the Practice of Applied Anthropology." *NAPA Bulletin* 29 (2008): 14–28.

Kedia, S., and J. van Willigen. *Applied Anthropology: Domains of Application.* London: Praeger, 2005.

Keenleyside, A., and R. Lazenby. *A Human Voyage: Exploring Biological Anthropology.* Toronto: Nelson Education, 2011.

Keesing, R.M. *Cultural Anthropology: A Contemporary Perspective.* New York: Holt, Rinehart and Winston, 1976.

Keith, L. "McGuinty Rejects Ontario's Use of Shariah Law and All Religious Arbitrations." Canadian Press. September 11, 2005. http://www.nosharia.com. Accessed October 21, 2006.

Kelley, J.H., and R.F. Williamson. "The Positioning of Archaeology Within Anthropology: A Canadian Historical Perspective." *American Antiquity* 61, no. 1 (January 1996): 5–20.

Kelly, P. "Filipina/os in Canada: Economic Dimensions of Immigration and Settlement." *Joint Center of Excellence for Research on Immigration and Settlement—Toronto,* no. 48 (2006): 1–37.

Kelly, R. "Witchcraft and Sexual Relations." In *Man and Woman in the New Guinea Highlands.* Edited by P. Brown and G. Buchbender, Special Publication no. 8. Washington: American Anthropological Association, 1976.

Kendall, L. "In the Company of Witches." *Natural History* 92 (October 1990).

Kenyatta, J. *Facing Mount Kenya.* New York: Vintage Books, 1965.

Khan, S., and J.C. Watson. "The Canadian Immigration Experiences of Pakistani Women: Dreams Confront Reality." *Counselling Psychology Quarterly* 18, no. 4 (2005): 307–317.

Khare, R.S., and M.S.A. Rao. "Introduction." In *Aspects in South Asian Food Systems: Food, Society, and Culture.* Edited by R.S. Khare and M.S.A. Rao. Durham: Carolina Academic Press, 1986.

Kidd, K.E. "Blackfoot Ethnography." *Archaeological Survey of Alberta* no. 8 ([1937]1986).

Kilmurray, L. "The Re-Generation of the Neolithic: Social Memory, Monuments, and Generations." *British Archaeological Reports,* August 2009.

Kilmurray, L., and N. Faba. "Access to Academic Materials for Post-Secondary Students with Print Disabilities." Ottawa: National Educational Association of Disabled Students, 2005.

Kingsolver, A. "Thinking and Acting Ethically in Anthropology." In *Thinking Anthropologically.* Edited by P.K. Salzman and P.C. Rice. Upper Saddle River: Pearson-Prentice Hall, 2008. 68–75.

Kirkpatrick, R.C. "The Evolution of Human Homosexual Behavior." *Current Anthropology* 41 (2000): 384.

Kirmayer, L.J., L. Boothroyd, A. Tanner, N. Adelson, E. Robinson, E., and C. Oblin. "Psychological Distress Among the Cree of James Bay." *Transcultural Psychiatry* 37 (2000): 35–56.

Kisliuk, M. *Seize the Dance! BaAka Musical Life and the Ethnography of Performance.* Oxford: Oxford University Press, 2000.

Kluckhohn, C. "Navajo Witchcraft." *Papers of the Peabody Museum of American Archaeology and Ethnology* 22, no. 2 (1944).

Knauft, B. "Violence and Sociality in Human Evolution." *Current Anthropology* 32 (1991): 391–409.

Koch, G. "Songs, Land Rights, and Archives in Australia." *Cultural Survival Quarterly* 20, no. 4 (1997).

Kohler, L. "Global Apartheid." Reprinted in *Talking About People: Readings in Contemporary Cultural Anthropology.* 2nd ed. Edited by W.A. Haviland & R.J. Gordon. Mountain View: Mayfield, 1996. 262–68.

"Korean Table Manners." http://www.esl-global.com/cultural_hints/manners.html. Accessed August 27, 2003,

Kottak, C.P. "The New Ecological Anthropology." *American Anthropologist,* new series, 101, no. 1 (March 1999): 23–35.

Kue Young, T. "Diabetes Mellitus Among Native Americans in Canada and the United States: An Epidemiological Review." *American Journal of Human Biology* 5, no. 4 (1993): 399–413.

Kuper, H. "The Swazi of Swaziland." In *Peoples of Africa.* Edited by J.L. Gibbs, Jr. New York: Holt, Rinehart and Winston, 1965. 475–512.

Kutsche, P. *Field Ethnography:. A Manual for Doing Anthropology.* Upper Saddle River: Prentice Hall, 1998.

Lacey, K., and K. Alderson. *Same-Sex Marriage: The Personal and the Political.* Toronto: Insomnia Press, 2004.

Lambek, M. *Knowledge and Practice in Mayotte: Local Discourses of Islam, Sorcery, and Spirit Possession.* Toronto: University of Toronto Press, 1993.

Lamphere, L., H. Ragone, and P. Zavella. *Situated Lives: Gender and Culture in Everyday Life.* New York: Routledge, 1997.

Lane, P.J. "The Temporal Structuring of Settlement." In *Architecture and Order: Approaches to Social Space.* Edited by M. Parker-Pearson and C. Richards. London: Routledge, 1994. 196–216.

Lang, S. "Lesbians, Men-Women, and Two-Spirits: Homosexuality and Gender in Native American Cultures." In *Female Desires: Same-Sex Relations and Transgender Practices Across Cultures.* Edited by E. Blackwood and S.E. Wieringa. New York: Columbia University Press, 1999.

Langdon, J.H. *The Human Strategy.* Oxford: Oxford University Press, 2005.

Lassiter, L.E. "Collaborative Ethnography and Public Anthropology." *Current Anthropology* 46, no. 11 (2005): 84–108.

Le Clair, E., and H.K. Schneider, eds. *Economic Anthropology: Readings in Theory and Analysis.* New York: Holt, Rinehart and Winston, 1968.

Leclerc-Madlala, S. "Bodies and Politics: Healing Rituals in the Democratic South Africa." In *Les cahiers de l'IFAS 2.* Edited by V. Faure. Johannesburg: French Institute, 2002.

Leach, E. *Claude Lévi-Strauss.* Chicago: University of Chicago Press, 1974.

———. *Social Anthropology.* Glasgow: Fontana, 1982.

Leavitt, G.C. "Sociobiological Explanations of Incest Avoidance: A Critical Review of Evidential Claims." *American Anthropologist* 92 (1990): 971–993.

Lee, R.B. *The Dobe Ju/'hoansi.* 2nd ed. Orlando: Harcourt Brace, 1993.

———. *The Dobe Ju/'hoansi.* 3rd ed. Toronto: Wadsworth/Thomson, 2003.

Lee, R.B., and R. Daly, eds. *The Cambridge Encyclopedia of Hunters and Gatherers.* Cambridge: Cambridge University Press, 1999. 1–19.

Lehmann, A.C., and J.E. Myers, eds. *Magic, Witchcraft, and Religion: An Anthropological Study of the Supernatural,* 3rd ed. Mountain View: Mayfield, 1993.

Leinhardt, G. "Religion." In *Man, Culture, and Society.* Edited by H. Shapiro. London: Oxford University Press, 1960. 382–401.

Lenski, G. *Power and Privilege: A Theory of Social Stratification.* New York: McGraw-Hill, 1966.

Leonard, L. "Adopting Female 'Circumcision' in Southern Chad: The Experience of Myab." In *Female "Circumcision" in Africa: Culture, Controversy, and Change.* Edited by B. Shell-Duncan and Y. Hernlund. London: Lynne Rienner Publishers, 2000. 167–92.

Leonard, W.R. "Food for Thought." *Scientific American* 13, no. 2 (2003): 62–71.

Leonard, W.R., and M. Hegman. "Evolution of P3 Morphology in *Australopithecus afarensis.*" *American Journal of Physical Anthropology* 73 (1989): 41–63.

Lerner, R.N. "Preserving Plants for Pomos." In *Anthropological Praxis: Translating Knowledge into Action.* Edited by R.M. Wulff and S.J. Fiske. Boulder: Westview, 1987. 212–222.

Lessem, D. "Interview with Biruté Galdikas." In *Physical Anthropology 95/96.* 4th ed. Edited by E. Angeloni, Guilford: Dushkin, 1995–96. 77–85.

Lett, J. *The Human Enterprise: A Critical Introduction to Anthropological Theory.* Boulder: Westview, 1987.

Levine, N.E., and J.B. Silk. "Why Polyandry Fails." *Current Anthropology* 38 (1997): 375–398.

Lévi-Strauss, C. 1955 "The Structural Study of Myth." *Journal of American Folklore* 68, no. 270, ch. 11.

———. *La pensée sauvage.* Paris: Plon, 1962.

———. "The Effectiveness of Symbols." In *Structural Anthropology,* vol. 1. New York: Basic Books, 1963.

———. "The Sorcerer and His Magic." In *Structural Anthropology,* vol. 1. New York: Basic Books, 1963.

Lewin, R. "Four Legs Bad, Two Legs Good." *Science* 235 (1987): 969.

———. "The Earliest 'Humans' Were More Like Apes." *Science* 236 (1987): 1062–63.

Lewis-Williams, J.D., T.A. Dowson, and J. Deacon. "Rock Art and Changing Perceptions of Southern Africa's Past: EzelJagdspoort Reviewed." *Antiquity* 67 (1993): 273–91.

Li, P.S. *The Chinese in Canada.* Toronto: Oxford University Press, 1988.

Lindholm, C., and C. Lindholm. "Life Behind the Veil." In The *Gender Reader.* 2nd ed. Edited by E. Ashton-Jones, G.A. Olson, and M.G. Perry. Needham Heights: Allyn and Bacon, 2000. 451–61.

Linton, R. *The Study of Man: An Introduction.* New York: Appleton, [1936]1964.

Littleton, C.S. *Mythology.* London: Duncan Baird, 2002.

Litwak, E. "Occupational Mobility and Extended Family Cohesion." *American Sociological Review* 29 (1960).

Livingstone, F. "Anthropological Implications of Sickle-Cell Gene Distribution in West Africa." *American Anthropologist* 58 (1958): 533–62.

Lock, M. *Encounters with Aging—Mythologies of Menopause in Japan and North America.* Berkeley: University of California Press, 1993.

Lowe, G.E. "The Camelot Affair." *Bulletin of Atomic Scientists* 22, no. 5 (1966).

Lowie, R.H. *Crow Indians.* New York: Holt, Rinehart and Winston, [1935]1966.

Lubbers, R.F.M. "The Globalization of Economy and Society." 1999. http://globus/lubpdfs/globaliz/thegloba/doc. Accessed August 20, 2003.

Ludden, D. "Book review of *In the Beginning Was the Word,* by R.W. Hood, Jr., P.C. Hill, and W.P. Williamson." *Skeptic,* 2006 (Winter).

Macklin, Ay. "On the Inside Looking In: Foreign Domestic Workers in Canada." In *Maid in the Market: Women's Paid Domestic Labour.* Edited by W. Giles and S. Arat-Koç. Halifax, NS: Fernwood, 1994. 13–39.

Mabulla, A.Z.P. "Hunting and Foraging in the Eyasi Basin, Northern Tanzania: Past, Present, and Future Prospects." *African Archaeological Review* 24 (2007): 15–33.

Mackie, M. *Gender Relations in Canada: Further Explorations.* Toronto: Harcourt Brace, 1991.

MacNiel, R. *The Right Place at the Right Time.* Boston: Little, Brown, 1982.

Madsen, A. "The Hadzabe of Tanzania: Land and Human Rights for a Hunter-Gatherer Community." Document no. 98. Copenhagen: IWGIA, 2000.

Magnarella, P.J. *Tradition and Change in a Turkish Town.* New York: Wiley, 1974.

Mair, L. *Witchcraft.* New York: McGraw-Hill, 1969.

Malinowski, B. "Practical Anthropology." *Africa: Journal of the International African Institute* 2, no. 1 (January 1929): 22–38.

———. *Crime and Custom in Savage Society.* London: Routledge, 1951.

———. *Magic, Science, and Religion, and Other Essays.* Garden City: Doubleday/Anchor Books, 1954.

Mandamin, T. "Harmony in the Community: Aboriginal Justice Sentencing Initiatives." *Law Now* 21, no. 1 (August–September 1996): 17–20.

Mandell, N., and A. Duffy. *Canadian Families: Diversity, Conflict, and Change.* Toronto: Harcourt Brace, 2000.

Manuel, G., and M. Posluns. *The Fourth World: An Indian Reality.* New York: Free Press, 1974.

Marlowe, F. "Why the Hadza Are Still Hunter-Gatherers." In *Ethnicity, Hunter Gatherers, and "Other": Association or Assimilation in Africa.* Edited by S. Kent. Washington: Smithsonian Institution Press, 2002. 247–75.

Martin, E. *The Woman in the Body: A Cultural Analysis of Reproduction.* Boston: Beacon Press, 1987.

———. Flexible Bodies: *Tracking Immunity in American Culture—from the Days of Polio to the Age of AIDS.* Boston: Beacon Press, 1994.

Mason, J.A. *The Ancient Civilizations of Peru.* Baltimore: Penguin Books, 1957.

Maybury-Lewis, D. "A New World Dilemma: The Indian Question in the Americas." *Symbols* (Fall 1993): 17–23.

McDougall, I., F.H. Brown, and C.J. Fleagle. "Stratigraphic Placement and Age of Modern Humans from Kibish, Ethiopia." *Nature* 433 (2005): 733–36.

McElroy, A., and P. Townsend. *Medical Anthropology in Ecological Perspective.* Boulder: Westview, 1996.

McGhee, R. *The Last Imaginary Place: A Human History of the Arctic World.* New York: Oxford University Press, 2005.

McGill University. "Social Studies of Medicine." 2004. http://www.mcgill.ca/ssom/#Lock. Accessed February 12, 2004.

McHenry, H.M. "Human Evolution." In *Evolution: The First Four Billion Years.* Edited by M. Ruse and J. Travis. Cambridge, MA: Belknap, 2009.

McKenna, J.J. "Bedtime Story." *Natural History* 50, October 1997.

McKenna, P. "Understanding Islam." *Scarboro Missions Magazine.* 1991. http://www.scarboromissions.com. Accessed February 27, 2007.

McLellan, D. *Karl Marx: Selected Writings.* Oxford: Oxford University Press, 2000.

McLellan, J. *Many Petals of the Lotus: Five Asian Buddhist Communities in Toronto.* Toronto: University of Toronto Press, 2002.

———. "Buddhism in the Multicultural Context of Toronto, Canada: Local Communities, Global Networks." 2003. http://alcor.concordia.ca/~csaa1/porter/lectures/JanetMcLellan.html. Accessed August 17, 2003.

McMillan, A.D. *Native Peoples and Cultures of Canada: An Anthropological Overview.* Vancouver: Douglas and McIntyre, 1988.

Mead, M. *Sex and Temperament in Three Primitive Societies.* New York: William Morrow and Co., 1935.

Medusa, M. "Shawna Dempsey and Lorri Milan." 1994. http://www.oboro.net/en/exhib9394/dempsey.htm. Accessed July 4, 2001.

Mellars, P. "Major Issues in the Emergence of Modern Humans." *Current Anthropology* 30 (1989): 349–85.

Melucci, A. *Challenging Codes: Collective Action in the Information Age.* Cambridge: Cambridge University Press, 1996.

Merkur, D. "The Ojibwa Vision Quest." *Journal of Applied Psychoanalytical Studies* 4, no. 2 (2002): 149–70.

Merriam, A.P. *The Anthropology of Music.* Chicago: Northwestern University Press, 1964.

Mesghinua, H.M. "Salt Mining in Enderta." *Journal of Ethiopian Studies* 4, no. 2 (1966).

Messer, E. "Anthropology and Human Rights." *Annual Review of Anthropology* 22 (1993): 221–49.

Michael, B.J. (2002). "Patterns of Family Relations." In *Ethnographic Essays in Cultural Anthropology: A Problem-Based Approach.* Edited by R.B. Morrison and C.R. Wilson. Itasca: F.E. Peacock.

Miles, H.L.W. "Language and the Orangutan: The O 'Person' of the Forest." In *The Great Ape Project.* Edited by P. Cavalieri and P. Singer. New York: St. Martin's Press, 1993. 42–57.

Miller, B.D., ed. *Sex and Gender Hierarchies.* Cambridge: Cambridge University Press, 1993.

Miller, C., and K. Swift. "One Small Step for Genkind." In *The Gender Reader.* 2nd ed. Edited by E. Ashton-Jones, G.A. Olson, and M.G. Perry. Needham Heights: Allyn and Bacon, 2000. 289–300.

Mitchell, L. *Baby's First Picture: Ultrasound and the Politics of Fetal Subjects.* Toronto: University of Toronto Press, 2001.

Mitchell, W.E. "A New Weapon Stirs Up Old Ghosts." *Natural History Magazine,* December 1973, 77–84.

Mithen, S. *The Singing Neanderthals: The Origins of Music, Language, Mind, and Body.* London: Weidenfeld and Nicholson, 2005.

"Modern and Contemporary Art at the McMichael." 1996–2001. http://www.mcmichael.com/modern.htm. Accessed March 27, 2001.

Mohanty, C. "Introduction." In *Third World Women and the Politics of Feminism.* Edited by C. Mohanty, A. Russo, and L. Torres. Bloomington: Indiana University Press, 1991.

Morrison, R.B., and C.R. Wilson. *Ethnographic Essays in Cultural Anthropology: A Problem-Based Approach.* Itasca: F.E. Peacock, 2002.

Morphy, H. "Art as a Mode of Action: Some Problems with Gell's Art and Agency." *Journal of Material Culture* 14, no. 1 (2009): 5–27.

Morphy, H., and M. Perkins. *The Anthropology of Art: A Reader.* Oxford: Blackwell, 2006.

Morrison, B.R., and R.C. Wilson, eds. *Native Peoples: The Canadian Experience.* Toronto: Oxford University Press, 2004.

Morsy, S.A. "Safeguarding Women's Bodies: The White Man's Burden Medicalized." *Medical Anthropology Quarterly* 5, no. 1 (1991): 19–23.

Mowat, F. *The Desperate People.* Boston: Little, Brown, 1959.

Muller, M. *The Baby Killer: A War on Want Investigation into the Promotion and Sale of Powdered Baby Milks in the Third World.* London: War on Want, 1974.

Multimania. "French Creole: A Language and a Culture." n.d. http://www.multimania.com/fdl/e-kreyol.html. Accessed June 21, 2001.

Murphy, R., J. Steward. "Tappers and Trappers: Parallel Processes in Acculturation." In *Theory in Anthropology.* Edited by R. Manners and D. Kaplan. New York: Aldine, 1968.

Mušinka, A. "Report on the Field Research into the Housing Situation of Roma in the Village of Svinia Slovakia." 2007. http://www.errc.org/cikk.php?cikk=1322. Accessed February 25, 2007.

Nader, L. "Controlling Processes: Tracing the Dynamic Components of Power." *Current Anthropology* 38 (1997): 714–715.

Nader, R., N. Milleron, and D. Conacher. *Canada Firsts.* Toronto: McClelland and Stewart, 1992.

Nanda, S. "Arranging a Marriage in India." In *The Naked Anthropologist.* Edited by P.R. DeVita. Belmont: Wadsworth, 1992. 139–43.

Nash, J. *We Eat the Mines and the Mines Eat Us: Dependency and Exploitation in Bolivian Tin Mines.* New York: Columbia University Press, 1979.

Nash, M. *Primitive and Peasant Economic Systems.* San Francisco: Chandler, 1966.

Neel, J.V. "Diabetes Mellitus: A 'Thrifty' Genotype Rendered Detrimental by 'Progress'?" *American Journal of Human Genetics* 14, no. 4 (1962): 353–62.

Nelson, E.D., and B.W. Robinson. *Gender in Canada.* Toronto: Prentice Hall Allyn and Bacon, 1999.

Nelson, Rodney. *From Vision to Venture.* Ottawa: Conference Board of Canada, 2007.

———. "Traditional Knowledge in the Board Room: A Quest for a New Model Of Corporate Governance." *Journal of Aboriginal Management* (2010): 28–35.

Newell, D., and R.E. Ommer. "Introduction: Traditions and Issues." In *Fishing Places, Fishing People: Traditions and Issues in Canadian Small-Scale Fisheries*. Edited by D. Newell and R.E. Ommer. Toronto: University of Toronto Press, 1999.

Ng, W.C. *The Chinese in Vancouver, 1945–80: The Pursuit of Identity and Power*. Vancouver: UBC Press, 1999.

Nietschmann, B. "The Third World War." *Cultural Survival Quarterly* 11, no. 3 (1987): 1–16.

Nilsen A.P. "Sexism in English: A 1990s Update." In *The Gender Reader*. 2nd ed. Edited by E. Ashton-Jones, G.A. Olson, and M.G. Perry. Needham Heights: Allyn and Bacon, 2000. 301–312.

Niven, J. *The Ice Master: The Doomed 1913 Voyage of the Karluk*. New York: Hyperion, 2000.

Nunavut Planning Commission. "Land Claim Review." n.d. http://www.arctic.ca/LUS/Nunavut.html. Accessed April 7, 2001.

Nurse, A. "But How Things Have Changed: Marius Barbeau and the Politics of Amerindian Identity." *Ethnohistory* 48, no. 3 (2001): 433–72.

O'Barr, W.M., and J.M. Conley. "When a Juror Watches a Lawyer." In *Talking About People*. 2nd ed. Edited by W.A. Haviland and R.J. Gordon. Mountain View: Mayfield, 1993. 42–45.

Obler, R.S. "Is the Female Husband a Man? Woman/Woman Marriage Among the Nandi of Kenya." *Ethnology* 19 (1980): 69–88.

Offiong, D. "Witchcraft Among the Ibibio of Nigeria." In *Magic, Witchcraft, and Religion*. Edited by A.C. Lehmann and J.E. Meyers. Palo Alto: Mayfield, 1985. 152–65.

Okonjo, K. "The Dual-Sex Political System in Operation: Igbo Women and Community Politics in Midwestern Nigeria." In *Women in Africa*. Edited by N. Hafkin and E. Bay. Stanford,: Stanford University Press, 1976. 49–58.

Olberg, K. "Culture Shock: Adjustments to New Cultural Environments." *Practicing Anthropology* 7 (1960): 177–82.

Olssen, M. "Understanding the Mechanisms of Neoliberal Control: Lifelong Learning, Flexibility and Knowledge Capitalism." In *Foucault and Lifelong Learning: Governing the Subject*. Edited by A. Feges and K. Nicoll. London and New York: Routledge, 2008. 34–47.

O'Mahoney, K. "The Salt Trade." *Journal of Ethiopian Studies*, 8, no. 2 (1970).

Omi, M., and H. Winant. "Racial Formations." In *Rethinking the Colour Line*. Edited by C.A. Gallagher. New York: McGraw-Hill, 2004. 7–9.

Omidian, P.A. "Living and Working in a War Zone: An Applied Anthropologist in Afghanistan." *Practicing Anthropology* 31 (2009): 4–11.

Ommer, R.E. "Rosie's Cove: Settlement Morphology, History, Economy, and Culture in a Newfoundland Outport." In *Fishing Places, Fishing People: Traditions and Issues in Canadian Small-Scale Fisheries*. Edited by D. Newell and R.E. Ommer. Toronto: University of Toronto Press, 1999.

O'Neil, J.D. "Cultural and Political Context of Patient Dissatisfaction in Cross-Cultural Clinical Encounters: A Canadian Inuit Study." *Medical Anthropology Quarterly* 3, no 4 (1989): 325–44.

O'Neil, J.D., J. Reading, and A. Leader. "Changing the Relations of Surveillance: The Development of a Discourse of Resistance in Aboriginal Epidemiology," *Human Organization* 57, no. 2 (1998): 230–37.

Oswalt, W.H. *Habitat and Technology*. New York: Holt, Rinehart and Winston, 1972.

Oswalt, W.H., and S. Neely. *This Land Was Theirs: A Study of North American Indians*. 5th ed. Mountain View: Mayfield, 1996.

Otten, C.M. *Anthropology and Art: Readings in Cross-Cultural Aesthetics*. Garden City: Natural History Press, 1971.

Our Heritage. "Who Was Paul Kane?" 2001. http://ourheritage.net/Who/KaneWho.html. Accessed April 4, 2001,

Overholt, C., M.B. Anderson, K. Cloud, and J.E. Austin, eds. "Women in Development: A Framework for Project Analysis. In *Gender Roles in Development Projects: A Case Book*. West Hartford: Kumarian Press, 1985. 3–16.

Pálsson, G. *Anthropology and the New Genetics*. Cambridge: Cambridge University Press, 2007.

Parades, J.A., and E.J. Purdum. "Bye, bye Ted …" *Anthropology Today* 6, no. 2 (1990): 9–11.

Parker, R. *Bodies, Pleasures, and Passions: Sexual Culture in Contemporary Brazil*. Boston: Beacon Press, 1990.

Parker-Pearson, M., and C. Richards. "Architecture and Order: Spatial Representation and Archaeology." In *Architecture and Order: Approaches to Social Space*. Edited by M. Parker-Pearson and C. Richards. London: Routledge, 1994. 38–72.

Parsons, T. "The Kinship System of the Contemporary United States." *American Anthropologist* 45 (1943).

Patterson, C.B. "In the Far Pacific at the Birth of Nations." *National Geographic* 170, no. 4 (1986): 460–99.

Peabody Museum of Archaeology and Ethnology. "Gifting and Feasting in the NWC Potlatch / What Is a Potlatch?" 1999. http://www.peabody.harvard.edu/potlatch/potlat2.html. Accessed June 25, 2001.

Peacock, J.L. *The Anthropological Lens: Harsh Light, Soft Focus*. New York: Cambridge University Press, 1986.

Pelto, P.J. *The Snowmobile Revolution: Technology and Social Change in the Arctic*. Menlo Park: Cummings, 1973.

Perkel, C. *Well of Lies: The Walkerton Water Tragedy*. Toronto: McClelland and Stewart, 2002.

Petersen, K. "The Ethnic Cleansing of Africville: Identity Politics in Canada." 2004. http://www.dissidentvoice.org/Mar04/Petersen0329.htm. Accessed February 20, 2007.

Plattner, S. "Markets and Market Places." In *Economic Anthropology*. Edited by S. Plattner. Stanford: Stanford University Press, 1989. 171–208.

Plotkin, M.J. "Shamans." In *Medicine Quest*. New York: Viking Penguin, 2000. 178–202.

Polanyi, K. "The Economy as Instituted Process." In *Economic Anthropology: Readings in Theory and Analysis*. Edited by E.E. LeClaire, Jr., and H.K. Schneider. New York: Holt, Rinehart and Winston, 1968. 122–67.

Polhemus, T., and H. Randall. *The Customized Body*. London and New York: Serpent's Tail, 2000.

Pope, G. "Bamboo and Human Evolution." *Natural History* 98 (October 1988): 56.

Pospisil, L.*The Kapauku Papuans of West New Guinea*. New York: Holt, Rinehart and Winston, 1963.

———. *Anthropology of Law: A Comparative Theory*. New York: Harper and Row, 1971.

Povinelli, E. *The Cunning of Recognition: Indigenous Alterities and the Making of Australian Multiculturalism*. Durham: Duke University Press, 2002.

Pratt, G. "From Registered Nurse to Registered Nanny: Discursive Geographies of Filipina Domestic Workers in Vancouver, B.C." *Economic Geography* 75 (1999): 215–36.

Price, T.D., and G.M. Feinman, eds. *Foundations of Social Inequality*. New York: Plenum, 1995.

Prins, H. *The Mi'kmaq: Resistance, Accommodation, and Cultural Survival*. Fort Worth: Harcourt Brace, 1996.

Progenix Corporation. "The History of Ginseng in the United States." 1998. http://progenixcorp.com/ushistory.html. Accessed March 12, 2001.

Radcliffe-Brown, A.R. "The Social Organization of Australian Tribes." Oceania Monographs 1, no. 29. Melbourne: Macmillan, 1931.

———. *Structure and Function in Primitive Society*. New York: Free Press, 1952.

Rains, P. "Pretty in Punk: Girls' Resistance in a Boys' Subculture [Review]." *Canadian Review of Sociology and Anthropology* 37, no. 2 (2000): 113.

Rajani, A. "FGM bibliography." 2001. http://www.scar.utoronto.ca/~97rajani/biblio.html. Accessed June 26, 2001,

Ramu, G.N. "Kinship Networks." In *Courtship, Marriage, and the Family in Canada*. Edited by G.N. Ramu. Toronto: Gage, 1979. 96–114.

Rapp, R. *Testing Women, Testing the Fetus: The Social Impact of Amniocentesis in America*. New York: Routledge, 1999.

Rappaport, R.A. "Ritual Regulation of Environmental Relations Among a New Guinea People." In *Environment and Cultural Behavior*. Edited by A.P Vayda. Garden City: Natural History Press, 1969. 181–201.

Rathgeber, E. "WID, WAD, GAD. Tendances de la recherche et de la pratique dans le champ du développement." In *Women, Feminism, and Development/Femmes, féminisme et développement*. Edited by H. Dagenais and D. Piché. Montreal and Kingston: McGill–Queen's University Press for the Canadian Research Institute for the Advancement of Women, 1994. 77–95.

Razack, S. *Looking White People in the Eye: Gender, Race, and Culture in Courtrooms and Classrooms*. Toronto: University of Toronto Press, 1998.

Reina, R. *The Law of the Saints*. Indianapolis: Bobbs-Merrill, 1966.

Remlinger, P.A. "Prof. and Grad Student Study Prostitution." *OnCampus News* 8, no. 8 (January 5, 2001). http://www.usask.ca/communications/ocn/jan5-01/feature4.shtml. Accessed January 5, 2007.

Renfrew, C., and P. Bahn. *Archaeology: Theories, Methods, and Practice*. London: Thames and Hudson, 1996.

Reynolds, V. "Primates in the Field, Primates in the Lab." *Anthropology Today* 10, no. 2 (1994): 3–5.

Rice, P.C. "Paleoanthropology 1996—Part II." *General Anthropology* 3, no. 2 (1997): 10.

Richard, G. "Debating Humankind's Place in Nature: 1860–2000." In *The Nature of Paleoanthropology*. Upper Saddle River: Pearson–Prentice Hall, 2007.

Richards, M., and V. Macaulay. "The Mitochondrial Gene Tree Comes of Age." *American Journal of Human Genetics* 68 (2001): 1315–20.

Richter, D.K. 1983. "War and Culture: The Iroquois Experience." *William and Mary Quarterly*, 3rd series, 40, no. 4 (1983): 528–59.

Ridington, R. *Trail to Heaven: Knowledge and Narrative in a Northern Native Community*. Vancouver: Douglas and McIntyre, 1988.

Ridington, R., and J. Ridington. *Where Happiness Dwells*. Vancouver: UBC Press, in press.

Roberts, C.A., and M. Cox. *Health and Disease in Britain: From Prehistory to the Present Day*. Stroud: Sutton, 2003.

Rohner, R.P., and E.C. Bettauer. *The Kwakiutl Indians of British Columbia*. Prospect Heights: Waveland Press, 1986.

Romano Kher. "Roma, Gypsies, Slovakia, Charity, Community Development." 2006. http://www.svinia.net. Accessed February 23, 2007.

Rosen, G. *A History of Public Health*. Baltimore: Johns Hopkins University Press, 1993.

Rosenberg, H. "From Trash to Treasure." In *Articulating Hidden Histories*. Edited by J. Schneider and R. Rapp. Berkeley: University of California Press, 1997. 190–204.

Rudolf, G. *Panama's Poor: Agents, Victims, and Historymakers*. Gainesville: University Press of Florida, 1999.

Ruhlen, M. *The Origin of Language: Tracing the Evolution of the Mother Tongue*. New York: John Wiley and Sons, 1994.

Sagoff, M. "Do We Consume Too Much?" *Atlantic Monthly* 279, no. 6 (January–June 1997): 80–96.

Sahlins, M. *Stone Age Economics*. Chicago: Aldine, 1972.

Salzman, P.C. "Political Organization Among Nomadic Peoples." *Proceedings of the American Philosophical Society* 3 (1967): 115–31.

Sampet, P. "Last words." *World Watch* 14, no. 3 (2001).

Sanday, P.R. *Female Power and Male Dominance: On the Origins of Sexual Inequality*. Cambridge: Cambridge University Press, 1981.

Sandford, S. *Management of Pastoral Development in the Third World*. London: John Wiley, 1983.

Satzewich, V., and N. Liodakis. *"Race" and Ethnicity in Canada*. Toronto: Oxford University Press, 2010.

Scarre, C. *The Human Past*. London: Thames and Hudson, 2005.

Scheffel, D. "Interview." *Ceskylid* 88, no. 1 (2001): 63–76.

———. *Svinia in Black and White: Slovak Roma and Their Neighbours*. Peterborough: Broadview Press, 2005.

———. "Slovakia's Roma." n.d. http://research.tru.ca/projects.php?section=single&id=377. Accessed February 6, 2007.

Scheper-Hughes, N. "The Global Traffic in Human Organs." *Current Anthropology* 41, no. 2 (2000): 191–224.

Schell, J. *The Fate of the Earth and The Abolition*. Stanford Nuclear Age Series. Stanford: Stanford University Press, 2000.

Scheper-Hughes, N., and M. Lock. "The Mindful Body: A Prolegomenon to Future Work in Medical Anthropology." *Medical Anthropology Quarterly* 1, no. 1 (1987).

Schoolcraft, H., and S. Eastman. *Historical and Statistical Information Respecting the History, Condition, and Prospects of the Indian Tribes of the United States*. Philadelphia: Lippincott, Grambo, 1851.

Schrire, C., ed. *Past and Present in Hunter-Gatherer Studies.* Orlando: Academic Press, 1984.

Schusky, E.L. *Variation in Kinship.* New York: Holt, Rinehart and Winston, 1975.

———. *Manual for Kinship Analysis.* 2nd ed. Lanham: University Press of America, 1983.

Seneca, Lucius Annasus. *Moral Essays.* Translated by J.W. Basore. 3 vols. Cambridge: Harvard University Press, 1975.

Seven Generations Education Institute. "Anishinaabe Mino Bimaadizwin: Principles for Anishinaabe Education." 2010. http://www.7generations.org.

Sheets, P. "Dawn of a New Stone Age in Eye Surgery." In *Archaeology: Discovering Our Past.* Edited by R.J. Sharer and W. Ashmore. Palo Alto: Mayfield, 1987. 230–31.

Shell-Duncan, B. and Y. Hernlund. "Female 'circumcision' in Africa: Dimensions of the Practice and Debates." In *Female "Circumcision" in Africa: Culture, Controversy, and Change.* Edited by B. Shell-Duncan and Y. Hernlund. London: Lynne Rienner, 2000. 1–40.

Shostak, M. Nisa: *The Life and Words of a !Kung Woman.* New York: Vintage, 1983.

Silverstein, K. "Millions for Viagra, Pennies for Diseases of the Poor." *The Nation,* 19 July, 1999, 13–18.

Sinclair, P.R., H. Squires, and L. Downton. "A Future Without Fish? Constructing Social Life on Newfoundland's Bonavista Peninsula After the Cod Moratorium." In *Fishing Places, Fishing People: Traditions and Issues in Canadian Small-Scale Fisheries.* Edited by D. Newell and R.E. Ommer. Toronto: University of Toronto Press, 1999.

Singer, M., F. Valentin, H. Baer, and Z. Jia. "Why Does Juan Garcia Have a Drinking Problem?" *Medical Anthropology,* 14, no. 1 (1992): 77–108.

Singh, G. (2004). "Immigrants Claim That Canada Conned Them." 2004. http://www.straight.com/content/cfm?id=15526. Accessed March 31, 2006.

Small, M.F. "Making Connections." *American Scientist* 85 (1997): 503.

———. "How Many Fathers Are Best for a Child?" April 2003. http://www.mnpoly.org/PolyArticles/how_many_fathers.htm. Accessed February 16, 2007.

Smith, S. "The World of Women." In *Families in Multicultural Perspective.* Edited by B.B. Ingoldsby and S. Smith. New York: The Guilford Press, 1995. 253–59.

Snow, D.R. *The Iroquois.* Cambridge, MA: Blackwell, 1994.

———. *Archaeology of Native North America.* New York: Prentice Hall, 2008.

Spindler, K. *The Man in the Ice.* Guernsey: Guernsey Press, 1994.

Spradley, J.P. *The Ethnographic Interview.* New York: Holt, Rinehart and Winston, 1979.

Spuhler, J.N. "Continuities and Discontinuities in Anthropoid-Hominid Behavioral Evolution: Bipedal Locomotion and Sexual Reception." In *Evolutionary Biology and Human Social Behavior.* Edited by N.A. Chagnon and W. Irons. North Scituate: Duxbury Press, 1979. 454–61.

Squires, S. "The Market Research and Product Industry Discovers Anthropology." *Anthropology Newsletter* 38, no. 4 (1997): 31.

Stacey, J. *Brave New Families.* New York: Basic Books, 1990.

Staggenborg, S. *Social Movements.* Toronto: Oxford University Press, 2008.

Star, M. "Asian Canada: The Economic and Cultural Energy That Asian Immigrants Are Bringing May Turn a Green and Promising Land into the Next California." *Transpacific* 68 (March 1997): 40.

Starrett, G. "Culture Never Dies: Anthropology at Abu Ghraib." In *Talking About People.* Edited by W.A. Haviland, R.J. Gordon, and L.A. Vivanco. Toronto: McGraw Hill, 2006. 24–26.

Stasiulis, D., and A. Bakan. *Negotiating Citizenship: Migrant Women in Canada and the Global System.* Toronto: University of Toronto Press, 2005.

Statistics Canada. "2001 Census: Marital Status, Common Law Unions. and Families." 2002. http://www12.statcan.ca/english/census01/products/analytic/companion/fam/canada.cfm. Accessed September 12, 2003.

———. "Canadian Families and Households: The Proportion of 'Traditional' Families Continues to Decline. 2003. http://www2.statcan.ca/english/census01/products/analytic/companion/fam/canada.cfm. Accessed September 18, 2003.

———. "Aboriginal Identity Population." Ottawa: Statistics Canada, 2006.

———. "Aboriginal Languages." http://www.statcan.ca/english/freepub/89-589-XIE/language.htm. 2004. Accessed January 16, 2007.

———. "Marriage." http://142.206.72.67/02/02d/02d_001a_e.htm. 2004. Accessed February 15, 2007.

———. "Income and Earning Trends." 2006. http://www.statcan.ca/english/research/85-570-XIE/2006001/tables/tablea1-1.htm. Accessed February 17, 2007

———. "More Seniors Living with a Spouse, More Living Alone, and Fewer Living in Health Care Institutions." 2001. http://www12.statcan.ca/english/census01/products/analytic/companion/fam/canada.cfm. Accessed February 17, 2007.

———. "Women in Canada." 2003. http://www.statcan.ca/Daily/English/060307/do60307a.htm. Accessed February 18, 2007.

——— . "Divorce." 2004. http://www.statcan.ca/Daily/English/040504/d040504a.htm. Accessed August 26, 2007.

———. "Farm Population by Province." 2001. http://www40.statcan.ca/101cst01/agric42a.htm. Accessed September 4, 2007.

———. "Family Portrait: Continuity and Change in Canadian Families and Households in 2006." 2006. http://www12.statcan.ca/english/census06/analysis/famhouse/cenfam1.cfm. Accessed September 12, 2007.

———. "Canada's Ethnocultural Portrait: The Changing Mosaic." 2001. http://www12.statcan.ca/english/census01/products/analytic/companion/etoimm/canada.cfm. Accessed September 14, 2007.

Stats and Facts. "Family: A Canadian Profile." Ottawa: Canadian Council on Social Development, 2007. http://www.ccsd.ca/factsheets/family. Accessed February 17, 2007.

Stebbins, K. "'Going Like Gangbusters': Transnational Tobacco Companies Making a Killing in South America." *Medical Anthropology Quarterly* 15 (2001): 147–70.

Steward, S. *On Longing: Narratives of the Miniature, the Gigantic, the Souvenir, the*

Collection. Baltimore: Johns Hopkins University Press, 1984. 117–25.

Stewart, D. "Expanding the Pie Before You Divvy It Up." *Smithsonian* 28 (1997): 82.

Stiles, D. "The Hunter-Gatherer 'Revisionist' Debate." *Anthropology Today* 8, no. 2 (1992): 13–17.

Stoler, M. "To Tell the Truth." *Vermont Visions* 82, no. 3 (1982): 3.

Storer, A. "Mobile Computing News: ConfucisIM and IMuttering: The New Language of IM." 2005. http://searchmobilecomputing.techtarget.com/originalContent/0,289142,sid40_gci1086276,00.html. Accessed February 8, 2007.

Straughan, B. "The Secrets of Ancient Tiwanaku Are Benefitting Today's Bolivia." In *Talking About People.* 2nd ed. Edited by W.A. Haviland & R.J. Gordon. Mountain View: Mayfield, 1996. 76–78.

Stringer, C., and R. McKie. *African Exodus: The Origins of Modern Humanity.* New York: Henry Holt, 1996.

Strum, S.C., and L. Fedigan. *Primate Encounters: Models of Science, Gender, and Society.* Chicago: University of Chicago Press, 2000.

Suárez-Orozoco, M.M., G. Spindler, and L. Spindler. *The Making of Psychological Anthropology II.* Fort Worth: Harcourt Brace, 1994.

Such, P. "Vanished People: The Archau Dorset and Beothuk People of Newfoundland [1978]." In *Rediscovering the First Nations of Canada.* Edited by J.W. Friesen. Calgary: Detselig, 1997. 53.

Susser, I. "Construction of Poverty and Homelessness in US Cities." *Annual Review of Anthropology* 25 (1996): 411–35.

Sutton, M.Q., and E.N. Anderson. *Introduction to Cultural Ecology.* Walnut Creek: Altamira, 2004.

Swisher, C.C., III, G.H. Curtis, T. Jacob, A.G. Getty, A. Suprijo, and Widiasmoro, "Age of the Earliest Known Hominids in Java, Indonesia." *Science* 263 (1994): 1118–21.

Sykes, B. *Blood of the Isles: Exploring the Genetic Roots of our Tribal History.* New York: Bantam, 2006.

Szathmáry, E.J. "Non-Insulin Dependent Diabetes Mellitus Among Aboriginal North Americans." *Annual Review of Anthropology* 23 (1994): 457–82.

Taft, M. *Discovering Saskatchewan Folklore: Three Case Studies.* Edmonton: NuWest Press, 1983. 73–78.

———. "Adult Halloween Celebrations on the Canadian Prairie." In *Halloween and Other Festivals of Death and Life.* Edited by J. Santino. Knoxville: University of Tennessee Press, 1994. 152–69.

———. "Men in Women's Clothes: Theatrical Transvestites on the Canadian Prairie." In *Undisciplined Women: Tradition and Culture in Canada.* Edited by P. Greenhill and D. Tye. Montreal and Kingston: McGill–Queen's University Press, 1997. 131–38.

Tarasoff, K.J. *Spirit Wrestlers: Doukhobor Pioneers' Strategies for Living.* Ottawa: Legas, 2002.

Taussig, M. *The Devil and Commodity Fetishism in South America.* Chapel Hill: University of North Carolina Press, 1986.

Thobani, S. *Exalted Subjects: Studies in the Making of Race and Nation in Canada.* Toronto: University of Toronto Press, 2007.

Thompson, R.H. *Toronto's Chinatown: The Changing Social Organization of an Ethnic Community.* New York: AMS Press, 1989.

Thorne, B., and M. Yalom, eds. *Rethinking the Family: Some Feminist Questions.* New York: Longman, 1982.

Thornhill, N. Quoted in *Talking About People.* Edited by W.A. Haviland and R.J. Gordon. Mountain View: Mayfield, 1993. 127.

Tian, G. *Chinese-Canadians, Canadian-Chinese Coping, and Adapting in North America.* Queenston: Edwin Mellen Press, 1999.

Ticktin, M. "Sexual Violence as the Language of Border Control: Where French Feminist and Anti-Immigrant Rhetoric Meet." *Signs* 33, no. 4 (2008).

Tilley, C. *An Ethnography of the Neolithic.* Cambridge: Cambridge University Press, 1996.

"Together They Stay a World Apart." *Smithsonian Magazine* 29, no. 8 (1998).

Tonkinson, R. *The Mardu Aborigines: Living the Dream in Australia's Desert.* 2nd ed. Toronto: Holt, Rinehart & Winston, 1991.

Trigger, Bruce. *Natives and Newcomers: Canada's "Heroic Age" Reconsidered.* Montreal and Kingston: McGill–Queen's University Press, 1985.

———. *The Children of Aataentsic: A History of the Huron People to 1660.* Montreal and Kingston: McGill–Queen's University Press, 1987.

———. *Understanding Early Civilizations: A Comparative Study.* Cambridge: Cambridge University Press, 2003.

———. *A Tribute to Richard F. Salisbury.* Royal Society of Canada, n.d.

Truswell, A.S., and J.D.L. Hansen, "Medical Research Among the !Kung." In *Kalahari Hunter-Gatherers: Studies of the !Kung San and Their Neighbors.* Edited by R.B. Lee and I. DeVore. Cambridge: Harvard University Press, 1976. 166–94.

Truswell, A.S., B.M Kennelly, J.D.L. Hansen, and R.B. Lee, "Blood Pressures of !Kung Bushmen in Northern Botswana." *American Heart Journal* 84 (1972): 5–12.

Turnbull, C. *The Forest People.* New York: Touchstone, 1962.

———. "The Mbuti Pygmies: An Ethnographic Survey." *Anthropological Papers of the American Museum of Natural History* 50, pt. 3. New York: 1963.

———. *The Human Cycle.* New York: Simon and Schuster, 1983.

———. *The Mbuti Pygmies: Change and Adaptation.* New York: Holt, Rinehart, and Winston, 1983.

Turner, T. "Major Shift in Brazilian Yanomami Policy." *Anthropology Newsletter* 32, no. 5 (1991): 1, 46.

UBC Press. "Do Glaciers Listen?" 2001. http://www.ubcpress.ca/search/title_book.asp?BookIC=4503. Accessed February 25, 2007.

UBC Reports. "Julie Cruikshank." 1991. http://www.publicaffairs.ubc.ca/ubcreports/1999/99mar18/auth-cruiksk.html. Accessed July 3, 2001.

University of Calgary. "Aboriginal Languages." 2003. http://www.fp.ucalgary.ca/howed/abor_lang.htm. Accessed January 16, 2007.

University of Manitoba. "Exogamy and Incest Prohibitions: Brian Schwimmer." November 1998. http://www.umanitoba.ca/anthropology/tutor/marriage/incest.html. Accessed April 12, 2001.

University of Toronto."A Brief History of Anthropology at the University of Toronto." 2001. http://www.chass.utoronto.ca/anthropology/history.htm. Accessed June 20, 2001.

———. "Barbeau, Marius. Barbeau Papers: Northwest Coast Files." 1988.

http://www.library.utoronto.ca/robarts/microtext/collection/pages/barbpaps.html. Accessed August 11, 2003.

University of Victoria Sexual Assault Centre. "Childhood Sexual Abuse Statistics." July 12, 1999. http://www.uvic.ca/~oursac/statistics.htm. Accessed March 15, 2001.

University of Western Ontario. "Meet Regna Darnell." 2001. http://publish.uwo.ca/~rdarnell/home.htm. Accessed January 13, 2001.

———. "Regna Darnell Curriculum Vitae." 2000. http://publish.uwo.ca/~rdarnell/CV-1.htm. Accessed January 13, 2001.

———. (1989, February 3). "Ukrainians Want Acknowledgement of Injustice: C. Gruske." *The Gazette*. http://www.infoukes.com/history/internment/booklet02/doc-040.html. Accessed March 13, 2001.

Urciuoli, B. "Skills and Selves in the New Workplace." *American Ethnologist* 35, no. 2 (2008): 211–28.

Van Allen, J. "Sitting on a Man: Colonialism and the Lost Political Institutions of Igbo Women." In *Women in Society*. Edited by S. Tiffany. St. Albans: Eden Press, 1979. 163–87.

van Baal, J., and A. van Beek. *Symbols for Communication: An Introduction to the Anthropological Study of Religion*. Assen: Van Gorcum, 1985.

Van Den Berghe, P.L. (1992). "The Modern State: Nation Builder or Nation Killer?" *International Journal of Group Tensions* 22, no. 3 (1992): 191–207.

Van Esterik, P. *Risks, Rights, and Regulation: Communicating About Risks and Infant Feeding*. Penang: World Alliance for Breastfeeding Action (WABA), 2002.

Van Gennep, A. *The Rites of Passage*. Chicago: University of Chicago Press, 1960.

Van Willigen, J. *Applied Anthropology: An Introduction*. Westport: Bergen and Garvey, 2002.

Vayda, A., ed. *Environment and Cultural Behavior: Ecological Studies in Cultural Anthropology*. Garden City: Natural History Press, 1969.

Veblen, T. *Theory of the Leisure Class: An Economic Study in the Evolution of Institutions*. New York: Macmillan, 1899.

Velasco, P. "'We Can Still Fight Back': Organizing Domestic Workers in Toronto." In *Not One of the Family: Foreign Domestic Workers in Canada*. Edited by A. Bakan and D. Stasiulis. Toronto: University of Toronto Press, 1997. 157–64.

Villagaria, M.G., R.L. Haedrich, and J. Fischer. "Groundfish Assemblages of Eastern Canada Examined over Two Decades." In *Fishing Places, Fishing People: Traditions and Issues in Canadian Small-Scale Fisheries*. Edited by D. Newell and R.E. Ommer. Toronto: University of Toronto Press, 1999.

Vitebsky, P. *The Shaman: Voyages of the Soul, Trance, Ecstasy, and Healing from Siberia to the Amazon*. Boston: Little, Brown, 1995.

Voget, F.W. *A History of Ethnology*. New York: Holt, Rinehart and Winston, 1975.

Vogt, E.Z. *The Zinacantecos of Mexico: A Modern Maya Way of Life*. 2nd ed. Fort Worth: Holt, Rinehart and Winston, 1990.

Waldram, J.B. *The Way of the Pipe: Aboriginal Spirituality and Symbolic Healing in Canadian Prisons*. Peterborough: Broadview Press, 1997.

Waldram, J.B., A. Herring, and T. Kue Young. *Aboriginal Health in Canada: Historical, Cultural, and Epidemiological Perspectives*. Toronto: University of Toronto Press, 1995.

Walker, A. "Speaking for Themselves: The New Politics of Old Age in Europe." *Education and Ageing* 13, no. 1 (1998): 13–36.

Walker, W. "Neo-Pagan, Heathen, and Reconstructionist Religions." 2002. http://www.witchvox.com/basics/intro.html. Accessed October 23, 2003.

Wallace, A.F.C. *Religion: An Anthropological View*. New York: Random House, 1966. 107.

———. *Culture and Personality*. 2nd ed. New York: Random House, 1970.

Ward, D. *The People: A Historical Guide to the First Nations of Alberta, Saskatchewan, and Manitoba*. Saskatoon: Fifth House, 1995.

Watkins, M., ed. *Dene Nation: The Colony Within*. Toronto: University of Toronto Press, 1977.

Wattenberg, B.J. "The Population Explosion Is Over." *New York Times Magazine*, November 23, 1997, 60.

Weatherford, J. *Indian Givers: How the Indians of the Americas Transformed the New World*. New York: Ballantine, 1988.

Weidman, H.H. "On Ambivalence and the Field." Hazel Hitson Weidman Papers, Harvard University, 1970.

Weiner, A.B. *The Trobrianders of Papua New Guinea*. New York: Holt, Rinehart and Winston, 1988.

Weitz, R. "What Price Independence? Social Relations to Lesbians, Spinsters, Widows, and Nuns." In *The Gender Reader*. Edited by E. Ashton-Jones, G.A. Olson, and M.G. Perry. Needham Heights: Allyn and Bacon, 2000.

Wekker, G. "What's Identity Got to Do with It? Rethinking Identity in Light of the Mati Work in Suriname." In *Female Desires: Same-Sex Relations and Transgender Practices Across Cultures*. Edited by E. Blackwood and S.E. Wieringa. New York: Columbia University Press, 1999.

"Welcome to Nunavut. (n.d.)." http://www.polarnet.ca/polarnet/nunavut.htm. Accessed April 7, 2001.

Werner, D. *Amazon Journey*. Englewood Cliffs: Prentice-Hall, 1990.

White, D.R. "Rethinking Polygyny: Co-wives, Codes and Cultural Systems." *Current Anthropology* 29 (1988): 529–72.

Whitehead, N., and R.B. Ferguson, eds. *War in the Tribal Zone*. Santa Fe: School of American Research Press, 1992.

———. "Deceptive Stereotypes About Tribal Warfare." *Chronicle of Higher Education*, November 10, 1993, A48.

Whitson, D. "Sport in the Social Construction of Masculinity." In *Sport, Men and the Gender Order: Critical Feminist Perspectives*. Edited by M.A. Messner and D.F. Sabo. Champaign: Human Kinetics Books, 1990.

Whittle, A. *Europe in the Neolithic*. Cambridge: Cambridge University Press, 1996.

———. "Houses in Context: Buildings as Process." In *Neolithic Houses in Northwest Europe and Beyond*. Edited by T. Darvill and and J. Thomas. Oxford: Oxbow Books, 1996. 13–26.

Wickwire, W. "Women in Ethnography: The Research of James A. Teit." *American Society for Ethnohistory* 40, no. 4 (1993): 539–67.

Wild, E.M., M. Teschler-Nicola, W. Kutschera, P. Steier, E. Trinkaus, and W. Wanek. "Direct Dating of Early Upper Palaeolithic Human Remains from Mladeč." *Nature* 435 (2005): 332–35.

Williams, A.M. "Sex, Drugs, and HIV: A Sociocultural Analysis of Two Groups of Gay and Bisexual Male Substance Users Who Practise Unprotected Sex." Unpublished manuscript, 1996.

Williamson, R.K. "The Blessed Curse: Spirituality and Sexual Difference as Viewed by Euro-American and Native American Cultures." *College News* 17, no. 4 (1995).

Wilson, P. *The Domestication of the Human Species.* New Haven: Yale University Press, 1998.

Winslow, D. "Rituals of First Menstruation in Sri Lanka." *Man* 15 (1980): 603–25.

Wolf, M. *Women and the Family in Rural Taiwan.* Stanford: Stanford University Press, 1972.

Wolpoff, M. "*Australopithecus*: A New Look at an Old Ancestor." *General Anthropology* 3, no. 1 (1996): 2.

Wrangham, R., and D. Peterson. *Demonic Males.* Boston: Houghton Mifflin, 1996. 168.

Wright, N. "IM Language Is Not Spoiling English Say Canadian Researchers." 2006. http://www.earthtimes.org/articles/show/7898.html. Accessed February 8, 2007.

Young Alberta Book Society. "Owen Beattie." 1998. http://www.culturenet.ucalgary.ca/yabs/beattieo.html. Accessed October 16, 2000.

Young, A. *Harmony of Illusions: Inventing Post-Traumatic Stress Disorder.* Princeton: Princeton University Press, 1995.

Young, W.C. *The Rashaayda Bedouin: Arab Pastoralists of Eastern Sudan.* Toronto: Harcourt Brace College, 1986.

Index

GFLDC (Goodfish Lake Development
        Corporation), 336
Ghana, 306
Ghinnáwa, 307
Gibbs, Lois, 340
Gil political party, 234
Giles, W., 38
Gillard, Julia, 252
Gitksan, 17
Gitxaala Nation, 263
Global apartheid, 369
Global economy, 141–142
Globalization, 141–142
Glottochronology, 81
Gods and goddesses, 278
The Gods Must Be Crazy, 176
The Golden Bough (Frazer), 289
Golden Orchid Association, 152
Goldschmidt, Walter, 45
Goodall, Jane, 10, 56
Goodfish Lake Development
        Corporation (GFLDC), 336
Gordon, Robert, 13–14
Goths, 318
Gough's Cave, 206
Gowdy, John, 122
Graffiti, 314–315
Grammar, 76
Gramsci, Antonio, 267, 360
Grand Carajas iron ore mine, 366
Grandfather Teachings, 335–336
Great Britain, 160
Great Law of Peace, 265
Great Plains. *See also* Northern Plains
    adaptation, 100–101
    horses and, 106, 108
    lifestyle of, 134
    migration to, 100
    religion and, 279, 282
    Sun Dance, 285, 287, 288
Greek gods and goddesses, 278
Green, Edward C., 284
Greenpeace, 256, 257
Green Revolution, 370
Grey-interest parties, 234
Grooming, 52
Group marriage, 164
Group membership, 82, 196, 313–314
Group of 20, 134
Group of Seven, 316–317
Groups, kinship, 207–212
Guan Yin, 152
Guatemala, 142, 182
Guatemalan Foundation for Forensic
        Anthropology, 331

Guenther, Mathias, 280
Guerrilla uprisings, 126
Guest labourers, 166
Gusii of Kenya, 169

H

Hadar Paleoanthropology Field
        School, 53
Haddon, Alfred, 228
Hadzabe, 65–66, 127, 244
Haida, 204, 308
Hair combs, 309
Haiti, 266
Hajj (pilgrimage), 275
Hale, Horatio, 12
Halfe, George, 335
Hall, Edward, 140–141
Hall, Mildred, 140–141
Harper, Charles L., 235
Harper, Stephen, 230
Harris, Lawren, 316
Harry Potter and the Philosopher's Stone
        (Rowling), 307
Haudenosaunee, 309
Haviland, William A., 103
Hawaiian system, 209–210
Hawazama pastoralists, 187
Hawthorn, Harry, 6, 14, 365
Hawthorne-Tremblay Report, 329
Hazan, Hiam, 234
Head measurements, 227–228
Health, of Ju/'hoansi, 15–16
Heaven's Gate cult, 294
Hebrews, 278
Hedican, Edward J., 365
Hegemony, 267, 360–361, 366
Helin, Calvin, 335
Heller, Monica, 83, 84–85
Henna, 300
Henry, Jules, 363
Herdt, Gilbert, 151–152
Heritage sites, 346
Herodotus, 4
Hetomato festival, 312
Hewlett, B. S., 176, 177–178
Hidatsa, 100
High art, 300
Higher education, 236
Hijab, 237, 368
Hindu, 233, 235–236, 273
Hip hop music, 355
Historical linguists, 11–12, 79–81
Historic archaeologists, 10
HIV/AIDS crisis, 127, 153–154, 354, 373
Hobbes, Thomas, 102

Hockey, 41
Hodder, I., 198
Hoebel, E. Adamson, 259, 260
Holistic perspective, 13–14
Holocaust, 357
Homeless people, 233
Hominid, 54
Hominins, 54–55
Hominin Sites and Paleolakes Drilling
        Project, 53
Homo, skull of, 58
Homo erectus, 57–60, 92
Homo ergaster, 57–60
Homo floresiensis, 67–68
Homogenization, 364
Homo georgicus, 57–60
Homo habilis, 55–57, 58
Homo heidelbergensis, 58, 60–61
Homo neanderthalensis, 60–62
Homo sapiens, 57, 60–62, 92
Homo sapiens idaltu, 62
Homosexuality, 151–152, 256. *See also*
        Sexual orientation
Honour-and-shame traditions,
        166–167
Honour killings, 166–167
Hoodfar, Homa, 142
Hooker Chemical, 340
Hooton, Earnest, 228
Hopi, 110, 169, 211, 264, 353
Horowitz, Michael M., 343
Horses, 100, 108
Horticulture, 98–99, 130
Household, 181. *See also* Family and
        household
Housing, 34, 183, 198–200, 235, 342, 350
Housing complexes, 198
HRAF (Human Relations Area Files), 19
Hudson's Bay Company, 366
Huitzilopochtli, 278
Human ancestors
    anatomically modern peoples, 62–64,
        66–68
    first hominins, 54–55
    homo erectus, 57–60, 92
    homo ergaster, 57–60
    homo georgicus, 57–60
    homo habilis, 55–57, 58
    homo sapiens, 57, 60–62, 92
Humanities, anthropology and, 21–22
Humanity, cultural future of,
        363–369
Human Organization, 327
Human Origins, 53
Human Relations Area Files (HRAF), 19